THE
GAGGING
OF GOD

THE GAGGING OF GOD

◆

Christianity Confronts Pluralism

◆

D. A. CARSON

APOLLOS

Leicester, England

The Gagging of God
Copyright © 1996 by D. A. Carson

Requests for information should be addressed to:

APOLLOS (an imprint of Inter-Varsity Press)
38 De Montfort Street, Leicester LEI 7GP, England

British Library Cataloging in Publication Data

A catalogue record for this book is available from the British Library.

ISBN: 0-85111-467-8

Edited by Elizabeth Yoder
Interior design by Joe Vriend

Printed in the United States of America

---

95 96 97 98 99 00 01 02 /❖ DH/ 10 9 8 7 6 5 4 3 2 1

This one is for Tiffany and Nicholas,
not because they can as yet understand much of it,
but because in a few years they will need it.

Contents

Preface

My interest in the subject of pluralism springs from several quite different kinds of experiences. The first is the ever present need to understand one's own culture. The need appears all the more pressing to those who move from culture to culture: their mobility exposes them to great diversity in outlook, eventually prompting them to wonder what makes their own world "tick." The need appears no less challenging to those who enjoy reading biographies and other historical studies: as we form opinions about past movements and periods, we begin to wonder what people will one day say about our own culture and period of history. Of course, hindsight is considerably overrated: it is not characterized by anything like the acuity that some people assign to it. Nevertheless, hindsight is far more accurate than prognostication about the future (that most disreputable fancy of horoscopes and social sciences); it is also more perceptive than most assessments of the present. Since we live in the present, however, the present is what we must try to understand, no matter how much we try to shed light from the past on the subject. And the one common theme of the great majority of commentators who seek to define Western culture at the end of the twentieth century is pluralism. Inevitably, then, I have been drawn into the vast literature on this subject, and find myself wrestling with it.

The second kind of experience that has pushed me to think about these matters arises from my vocation as a Christian teacher. For years I have taught courses in hermeneutics. I have watched hermeneutics change from the art and science of biblical interpretation to the "new hermeneutic" to deconstruction, with many stopping places along the journey and many interesting side roads. Everyone who has thought about these things has soon recognized that many forms of contemporary pluralism are tied to certain approaches to hermeneutics. A Christian teacher cannot think long about the former without reading more widely in the latter. As an antidote to the arrogant claims of positive knowledge common a century ago, the new hermeneutic is refreshingly restrained. Yet just when it might be expected to teach us humility, it has become the most imperious ideology of our day. It threatens us with a new ideological totalitarianism that is frankly alarming in its claims and prescriptions.

The third kind of experience that has nudged me to reflect on the characteristics of contemporary pluralism derives from my vocation as a Christian

9

preacher. For example, university missions must today deal with approaches and outlooks substantially different from anything I faced as an undergraduate thirty years ago. Many of these differences are nothing other than the outworking of one form or another of pluralism, both in the academic world and in the culture at large.

I am writing as a Christian. In my most somber moods I sometimes wonder if the ugly face of what I refer to as philosophical pluralism is the most dangerous threat to the gospel since the rise of the gnostic heresy in the second century, and for some of the same reasons. Part of the danger arises from the fact that the new hermeneutic and its assorted offspring are not entirely wrong: it would be easier to damn an ideology that was wholly and pervasively corrupt. But another part of the danger derives from the harsh reality that, as far as I can see, the new hermeneutic and its progeny are often profoundly wrong — and so popular that they are pernicious. In a happier frame, I suspect that giving voice to such suspicions will sound much too dour — and in any case, the truth is that I am ill equipped to make such a judgment. Besides, postmodernism is proving rather successful at undermining the extraordinary hubris of modernism, and no thoughtful Christian can be entirely sad about that. In any case, that the contemporary challenges are extraordinarily complex and painfully serious cannot reasonably be gainsaid.

The complexity of the subject leaves an author with a difficult choice. One may opt for a popular book that surveys a lot of material superficially, or one may opt for a profound probing of one small part of the subject. I have managed to err in both ways simultaneously: much of this book paints with a fairly broad brush, but here and there I worry away at particular aspects of the challenge, poking beneath the surface to grapple with a few questions that strike me as more urgent, or perhaps less well evaluated in the literature. If anything in the following pages equips some Christians to intelligent, culturally sensitive, and passionate fidelity to the gospel of Jesus Christ, or if it encourages some thoughtful unbelievers to examine the foundations again and so to find that Jesus is Lord, I shall be profoundly grateful.

Perhaps it will help some readers if I acknowledge that chapters 2 and 3 are the most theoretical. If they are initially too difficult, skip them. Although they lay a foundation for the rest of the book, the later chapters can be read with profit without them.

Some of the material in these pages has been grist for lectures delivered in Cambridge, England; Erskine Theological Seminary, South Carolina; the Graduate Student Fellowship in Wisconsin and in Michigan; and elsewhere. In particular, some of the material found here first saw the light of day in one of three essays: "Christian Witness in an Age of Pluralism," in *God and Culture*, Festschrift for Carl F. H. Henry, ed. D. A. Carson and John D.

Woodbridge (Grand Rapids: Eerdmans, 1993), 31–66; and two essays published in *Criswell Theological Journal*, "The Challenge of Pluralism to the Preaching of the Gospel," and "The Challenge from the Preaching of the Gospel to Pluralism." The appendix was first published (in Portuguese) in a slightly simpler form in the Festschrift for Russell Shedd, *Chamado Para Servir*, ed. Alan Pieratt (São Paulo: Edições Vida Nova, 1994), and (in English) in a form only slightly different, in the *Journal of the Evangelical Theological Society* 37 (1994), 381–94. I am grateful to the publishers for allowing me to incorporate that material here.

I should say something about the structure of the book. The first chapter introduces pluralism in its diverse forms, bringing up many points that are explored in detail later in the volume. Some overlap between chapter 1 and later chapters is thus inevitable, but the gain in having an overview was judged worth the price of minor repetition.

The title *The Gagging of God* was first used in a book by Gavin Reid. Its full title was *The Gagging of God: The Failure of the Church to Communicate in the Television Age* (London: Hodder & Stoughton, 1969). Its subtitle explains what Reid meant by the title. My use of the same words is twofold, as readers of this book will discover. They will also discover that, despite our best efforts to gag God, he is still there, and he is not silent (as Francis Schaeffer used to say).

My graduate assistant, Mr. Alan Hultberg, rendered careful assistance in tracking down sources that were sometimes difficult to find. Diane DeSmidt generously and competently prepared the indexes. Dr. Carl F. H. Henry, Dr. Kenneth S. Kantzer, Dr. Harold A. Netland, Dr. Kevin J. Vanhoozer, Mr. Kirk Allison, and Dr. John D. Woodbridge read parts of this work, and offered invaluable advice. I thank God for their generosity with their time, and for their wise counsel, and hope they will not be too disappointed by the few places where I have failed, rather foolishly, to follow their advice. Certainly this book would be far weaker than it is had they withheld their sage suggestions.

Soli Deo gloria.

D. A. Carson

Chapter 1

THE CHALLENGES OF CONTEMPORARY PLURALISM

A. Defining Pluralism

"Pluralism" is a surprisingly tricky word in modern discussion. For some, it has only positive connotations; for others, only negative. Some use it in combination with various spheres: cultural pluralism, ideological pluralism, intellectual pluralism, religious pluralism, and so forth. For our purposes it will be useful to consider not the spheres in which pluralism is found, but three kinds of phenomena to which the word commonly refers: empirical pluralism, cherished pluralism, and philosophical or hermeneutical pluralism.

1. Empirical Pluralism — use .

Empirical pluralism sums up the growing diversity in our culture. Observable and largely measurable, it is what David Tracy prefers to call "plurality." "Plurality," he writes, "is a fact."

"Pluralism is one of the many possible evaluations of that fact."[1] But although a few scholars have followed him in this usage, most still use "pluralism," in one of its uses, to refer to the sheer diversity of race, value systems, heritage, language, culture, and religion in many Western and some other nations. Paul Martinson prefers the rubric "factual pluralism";[2] in any case, the rubric is less important than the phenomenon.

---

1. "Christianity in the Wider Context: Demands and Transformations," in *Worldviews and Warrants: Plurality and Authority in Theology*, ed. William Schweiker and Per M. Anderson (New York: University Press of America, 1987), 2.
2. Paul V. Martinson, "Dynamic Pluralism," *Dialog* 28/1 (1989): 8.

Consider, for example, the remarkable ethnic diversity in America. The United States is the largest Jewish, Irish, and Swedish nation in the world; it is the second largest black nation, and soon it will become the third largest Hispanic nation. Moreover, these large proportions reveal nothing about the enormous diversity generated by countless smaller ethnic and racial communities. Compiling equally remarkable statistics in almost every other plane of American culture is an easy matter.

It is possible to overstate the novelty of this diversity. Jon Butler vigorously argues, for his own ideological purposes, that American life and culture were extraordinarily diverse in the eighteenth and nineteenth centuries, and correspondingly depreciates the degree of diversity reflected in the nation today.[3] Richard Pointer's recent study of colonial New York reinforces the trend among modern historians to find substantial pluralism in this country at its birth.[4] But although such work is a useful foil for those who picture colonial America as culturally monolithic, or who exaggerate modern empirical pluralism, it must be insisted that the range of contemporary diversity is, on any scale, vastly greater than has ever been experienced in the Republic before.

In the religious arena, the statistics are fascinating and sometimes differ from poll to poll.[5] Statistics for the larger denominations have floated a little, but not much. Protestants declined from about 67 percent to 57 percent between the years 1952 and 1987. Roman Catholicism is now increasing in numbers, owing in part to the influx of Hispanics, but the number of Roman Catholic clergy is declining disastrously, which at least suggests that both the *internal* strength of Catholicism in this country and its influence on the nation are on the wane. Most demographers insist that if present trends continue, WASPs (White, Anglo-Saxon Protestants) will be in a minority (about 47 percent) by the year A.D. 2000.[6]

---

3. Jon Butler, *Awash in a Sea of Faith: Christianizing the American People* (Cambridge: Harvard Univ. Press, 1990).

4. Richard W. Pointer, *Protestant Pluralism and the New York Experience: A Study of Eighteenth Century Diversity* (Bloomington: Indiana Univ. Press, 1988). That is also one of the leitmotifs of the recent textbook by Mark Noll, *A History of Christianity in the United States and Canada* (Grand Rapids: Eerdmans, 1992).

5. For example, the 1991 National Survey of Religious Identification, performed by two researchers from the City University of New York, found that 7.5 percent of their respondents indicated "no religion"; the Williamsburg Charter Survey on Religion and Public Life insists that while "religious nones" constituted only 5 percent of the population as recently as 1972, by 1988 they constituted 11 percent of the population. Whereas some polls put the percentage of Muslims in the U.S. at 0.5 percent (so the National Survey of Religious Identification [1991]), others say the percentage of Muslims now rivals the percentage of Jews (about 2 percent).

6. For some useful statistical data, cf. George Gallup, Jr., and Jim Castelli, *The People's Religion: American Faith in the 90s* (New York: Macmillan, 1989).

But such statistics do not tell the whole story. They have to be augmented by other observations. Frequently large-scale studies on what America believes focus little attention on the small but multiplying and growing movements on the fringes. There are substantial numbers of Hindus and Buddhists who have emigrated to the West, and who are now slowly winning converts. The familiar cults are holding their own; some of them, like the Mormons, are growing fairly rapidly. Numerous studies document the rise of New Age religions and the revitalization of various forms of neo-paganism. Not long ago witches' covens were virtually unknown; now they advertise in the newspapers. Current immigration patterns are bringing in more and more people with little heritage in the Judeo-Christian tradition, and this fact doubles the impact of the number of people within the country who for various reasons have lost or abandoned the tradition. None of this was foreseen by the Founding Fathers; little of it was foreseen forty years ago.

Even when the standard polls provide useful and interesting data,[7] a depth dimension is often missing. One of the best-known devices, the Princeton Religious Index, used by the Gallup organization, serves as a benchmark based on seven religious beliefs and practices: belief in God, religious preference, attendance at worship, confidence in the church, confidence in the clergy, the importance of religion, and religion's ability to answer current problems. In 1994, this index for the U.S. stands at 656 (on a scale with a maximum of 1000)—a little higher than the late 1980s, considerably lower than 1960. The percentage of those who say they attend worship services at least once a month has been remarkably stable for the last century. But such figures do not make sufficient allowance for several other factors. Some studies have suggested that the percentage of those who *say* they attend worship once a week or once a month may be double the percentage of those who do what they say. More importantly, the pressures of secularization ensure that formal religious observance may happily coexist with the marginalization of religion.

One hundred years ago, the *New York Times* had the sermons of Spurgeon telegraphed across the Atlantic so they could be printed in the Monday morning edition. Today the *New York Times* is more interested in chronicling the devices some neighborhoods are using to keep churches out or at least small—petitions, manipulated zoning laws, even litigation (March 24, 1994). Moreover, if the studies of Wuthnow are correct,[8] individualism and per-

---

7. One thinks, for instance, of George Gallup, Jr., and Sarah Jones, *100 Questions and Answers: Religion in America* (Princeton: Princeton Religion Research Center, 1989).

8. Robert Wuthnow, *The Restructuring of American Religion: Society and Faith Since World War II* (Princeton: Princeton Univ. Press, 1988); idem, *The Struggle for America's Soul: Evangelicals, Liberals, and Secularism* (Grand Rapids: Eerdmans, 1989).

sonal choice in religion have largely displaced loyalty to denominational structures and to inherited doctrinal bastions. This makes it easier for individuals to be syncretistic, or, worse, confusedly pluralistic—i.e., people without strong doctrinal commitments may take on highly diverse and even incompatible ideas and fuse them in some way (syncretism), or they may take on highly diverse and even contradictory ideas *without* fusing them, simply letting them stand, unaware that the elementary demands of consistency are being violated.

In short, the rise in empirical pluralism can scarcely be denied. Experts may debate the significance of this or that component,[9] but the trends are so unmistakable that they should not be ignored.[10]

Moreover, although most of the statistics just provided, along with many of the arguments in this book, have the United States in view, empirical pluralism is characteristic of most countries in the Western world. In Canada, regular attendance at public worship is only a fraction of what it is in the U.S., but the percentage of Canadians who *say* they hold religious, and specifically Christian, beliefs is not too far out of step with figures south of the 49th parallel: 67 percent of Canadians believe Jesus rose from the dead, 78 percent claim some sort of affiliation with a Christian denomination, 53 percent of adults reject the theory of evolution, 9 percent say God is "just an old superstition."[11] But again, the real advances in empirical pluralism in Canada are detected as much in other measurements as in the religion statistics: substantial immigration (from Haiti, the Indian subcontinent, the Pacific Rim, especially Hong Kong), changing levels of tolerance, rising biblical illiteracy, changing tolerances in the moral arena, the presence of minarets and Buddhist temples. Like Canadians, Australians score fairly high on personal belief in God, and very low in any ability to articulate the gospel or to become actively involved with a local church. It, too, has witnessed a flood of immigrants.

Many European countries are experiencing their own forms of empirical pluralism, forms that are sometimes much like those of their American counterparts, and sometimes very different (e.g., "guest workers" in France and Germany). A major study (nicely summarized in the *Christian Science Monitor* of November 22, 1991) demonstrates, not unexpectedly, the American bias

---

9. See, for example, the highly diverse essays in Mary Douglas and Steven M. Tipton, ed., *Religion in America: Spirituality in a Secular Age* (Boston: Beacon Press, 1983).

10. Of the various books that extrapolate present trends into the future, one of the sanest (and certainly one of the easiest to read) is Russell Chandler, *Racing Toward 2001: The Forces Shaping America's Religious Future* (Grand Rapids: Zondervan, 1992).

11. "God Is Alive," *Maclean's* 106/15 (April 12, 1993): 32–42.

both toward liberal individualism and toward some form of religious expression, over against a number of European countries.

In many countries, the growing empirical diversity of religions and ideologies is tied in part to fresh immigration patterns (often from their former colonies), and to a general decline in the hold of Judeo-Christian biases in outlook and values. As usual, the significance of almost every datum is disputed. For example, in his recent book Robin Gill argues that the perception in England that the churches are empty is not to be laid at the door of "secularization" and other cultural factors. The blame, rather, lies with church leaders who ignored the declining numbers at the turn of the century, and continued to build more buildings than were needed.[12] But even if he has uncovered some remarkable ecclesiastical bumbling, most observers think his analysis extraordinarily reductionistic, and his proposals for reversing the decline—essentially variations of good management techniques—extraordinarily optimistic. The pluralisms that now characterize England go far deeper than how many church buildings are empty, and turn on more than the mosque in Regents Park or the prevalence of Urdu in Leicester or the fact that the Cockney lilt is now less common in Metropolitan London than the West Indian lilt, though all of these realities are important indices. What is gaining is diversity; what is declining is *relative* cultural homogeneity. In short, in almost all Western nations (and some others), there is a marked rise in empirical pluralism.

This is neither intrinsically good nor intrinsically bad. Those who prefer that culture be variegated, racially mixed, religiously pluriform, and culturally diverse, will judge these developments good. The developments themselves may achieve some real good if they serve to break down cultural prejudice, racial arrogance, and religious bigotry. Christians may find the diversity an ideal setting for thoughtful articulation of the faith and for renewed evangelism. Alternatively, those who prefer the stability of recognized cultural norms may find the new pluralities not only discomfiting but vaguely threatening. And it would be naive to fail to acknowledge that these new realities may actually serve to fan the flames of hostility and tribalism. In order to maintain stability, governments may be tempted to arrogate more and more authority to themselves (since there are fewer and fewer shared values and norms). The end of this is hard to foresee, but it probably augurs little good. Christians may be tempted so to bemoan the dilution of centuries of Western culture that they perceive only threat and no opportunity.

But however the rise of empirical pluralism is perceived, the brute reality cannot seriously be doubted. This is empirical pluralism.

---

12. *The Myth of the Empty Church* (London: SPCK, 1993).

2. Cherished Pluralism

By "cherished pluralism" I mean to add an additional ingredient to empirical pluralism—approval. While some writers and thinkers (though certainly not all) on the New Right view empirical pluralism as a threat to stability, order, good government, and perhaps also to biblical Christianity, it is important to remember that many citizens want to retain the diversity. In other words, for them empirical pluralism is not only a raw datum, it is a good thing. In the words of Lesslie Newbigin, "It has become a commonplace to say that we live in a pluralist society—not merely a society which is in fact plural in the variety of cultures, religions and lifestyles which it embraces, but pluralist in the sense that this plurality is celebrated as things to be approved and cherished."[13]

> [This pluralism] holds that variety and diversity are a positive good, and the denial of variety and diversity is bad. In its extreme form, pluralism opposes syncretism, i.e., the combining of various traditions. Rather, it so affirms the integrity of a given approach to life that any attempt to change it is considered a moral violation.[14]

Os Guinness defines pluralization as "the process by which the number of options in the private sphere of modern society rapidly multiplies at all levels, especially at the level of world view, faiths, and ideologies."[15] This state of affairs can be so widely accepted as normal that it is saluted and approved. He comments:

> We have reached the stage in pluralization where choice is not just a state of affairs, it is a state of mind. Choice has become a value in itself, even a priority. To be modern is to be addicted to choice and change. Change becomes the very essence of life.[16]

In other words, the reality, empirical pluralism, has become "a value in itself, even a priority": it is cherished.

That this is not a universally held value is precisely what generates "culture wars," to use Hunter's expression.[17] Even if he sometimes exaggerates the differences that divide groups in our culture, and too easily deploys pur-

---

13. *The Gospel in a Pluralist Society* (Grand Rapids: Eerdmans, 1989), 1.

14. Ted Peters, "The Lutheran Distinctiveness in Mission to a Pluralistic World," *Dialog* 22 (1983): 296.

15. *The Gravedigger File* (Downers Grove: InterVarsity Press, 1983), 92.

16. Ibid., 96.

17. James Davison Hunter, *Culture Wars: The Struggle to Define America* (New York: Basic Books, 1992).

ple prose,[18] Hunter is right to point out that in the face of ⟨ versity some groups circle the wagons and fight off every other group. The battles are not just religious, of course. Yet Hunter rightly says that the culture wars are profoundly religious: they concern fundamentally opposing conceptions of authority, morality, truth, the good, revelation, and so forth.

By and large, the media and the intellectuals of the West cherish pluralism. On the long haul, this has its effects both in society and in the church— effects to be explored in later chapters.

3. Philosophical or Hermeneutical Pluralism

This is, by far, the most serious development. Philosophical pluralism has generated many approaches[19] in support of one stance: namely, that any notion that a particular ideological or religious claim is intrinsically superior to another is *necessarily* wrong. The only absolute creed is the creed of pluralism. No religion has the right to pronounce itself right or true, and the others false, or even (in the majority view) relatively inferior.

This state of affairs is not the fruit of sophomoric relativism, or of the urgent need to redefine one's morals to justify one's sleeping arrangements. It is tied to some of the most complex intellectual developments in Western thought in the last twenty-five years. In particular it is bound up with the *new hermeneutic* and with its stepchild, *deconstruction*. The outlook that it spawns is often labeled *postmodernism*. I shall probe all three in the next two chapters. At the moment, a few clarifying explanations will suffice.

At one time "hermeneutics" was understood to be the art and science of biblical interpretation. The term was gradually extended to almost all kinds of interpretive acts, regardless of the object. At the same time, developments in Western intellectual thought kept emphasizing just how subjective all interpretation is. Eventually the expression "new hermeneutic" was coined to emphasize the break from the older approach; this label has in turn been displaced by "radical hermeneutics." Old-fashioned hermeneutics belongs to the "modern" era in which science, scholarship, and serious study were

---

18. Cf. John D. Woodbridge, "Culture War Casualties," *Christianity Today* 39/3 (March 6, 1995): 20–26.

19. Dr. Harold Netland, in a private communication, rightly says that "philosophical pluralism" is, in my usage, an umbrella term that embraces a variety of contemporary positions that are united in their opposition to the idea that we can know objective truth: e.g., ontological non-realism (there is no objective reality "out there" to be experienced and known); constructivism ("reality" is merely a construct of social experiences); perspectivism (we can never know reality as it is; the most we can know is reality from our perspective); various forms of relativism (truth, rationality norms, and the like are all relative to, or internal to, particular contexts).

thought capable of resolving most problems, of answering most questions, of understanding all of reality. Radical hermeneutics, by contrast, recognizes the subjectivity of interpretation, and how much of it is shaped by the cultures and subcultures to which the interpreter belongs.

But if old-fashioned hermeneutics belongs to the "modern" era, and we have now passed to radical hermeneutics, then we must be in the "postmodern" era. The roots of modernity lie in the Renaissance, and in the scientific revolution of the sixteenth and early seventeenth centuries. The world was understood to be a rational place; truth was there to be discovered. As naturalism took hold, God was either marginalized (in the deist understanding) or abandoned (the atheist perspective). Progress was seen to be almost inevitable; entire worldviews, including both Marxism and capitalism, were judged to be historically verifiable and believed to be developing according to a sort of natural law.

But postmodernity is less certain that there is any objective truth to be discovered. If all interpretation is culturally conditioned, reason itself may be nothing more than a tool of domination.[20] A Marxist or a capitalist historiography is merely one possible interpretation of the past. But if one cannot talk about the objective truth of the matter, then the interpretations are merely personal or at best culturally conditioned options. No interpretation can be dismissed, and no interpretation can be allowed the status of objective truth. To dismiss an interpretation presupposes you have some criterion to allow you to do so—and if an interpretation is merely one among many possible interpretations, it is pointless to argue for its unique worth or against the equal validity (or nonvalidity!) of another's interpretation. On the other hand, if you claim the criterion is the truth itself, you betray an old-fashioned bigotry, your enslavement to an eclipsed modernity. You have failed to recognize the subjectivity of all interpretations, the significance of the "turn to the subject."[21] The limits of the tendency is being recognized in some quarters, but a rationale for abandoning it seems, for many, hard to come by.[22]

David Tracy holds that all thinkers who embrace certain "emancipatory values" are "incontestably heirs of the modern era," as he is himself.[23] These

---

20. For a useful essay, see Thomas Finger, "Modernity, Postmodernity—What in the World Are They?" *Transformation* 10/4 (October/December 1993): 20–26.

21. This phrase is commonly used to refer to the basket of tendencies that focus less and less attention on either the author of the text (the concern of historical criticism and exegesis) or on the text itself (the concern of many of the more recent literary critics), and more and more on the subject, the knower, the reader.

22. The distinctions between modernity and postmodernity will be explored at some length in the next two chapters.

23. "Theology and the Many Faces of Postmodernity," *Theology Today* 51 (1994): 105.

"emancipatory values" include the democratic ideals of liberty and equality, a frank acknowledgment that the modern scientific revolution is "not just one more important event in Western culture" but "the watershed event that makes even the Reformation and Renaissance seem like family quarrels,"[24] ethical concern over the realities of "social location" (gender, race, class), and the world of nature and our place in it as the product of some evolutionary scheme. Not everyone defines "modernity" in quite this way, but this will do for the moment. Tracy's point, however, is that the "turn to the subject" has shown that modernity itself, far from being the last word, must be viewed as only one more tradition. To recognize this point does not mean that the modernists abandon the "emancipatory values" that constitute them modernists; it means, rather, that they become *post*modernists—i.e., they retain personal commitment to most of the values of modernity, while recognizing that modernity itself is an interpretative framework as fraught with subjectivism as all other frameworks.

> Any postmodern thinker who believes that she or he can now leave this ambiguous modern scene and begin anew in innocence is self-deluding. There is no innocent tradition (including modernity and certainly including modern liberal Christianity). There is no single innocent reading of any tradition, including this postmodern reading of the positive and negative realities, the profound ambiguities, of modernity.[25]

Of the many distinctions that have been attempted between modernism and postmodernism, perhaps this is the most common: modernism still believed in the objectivity of knowledge, and that the human mind can uncover such knowledge. In its most optimistic form, modernism held that ultimately knowledge would revolutionize the world, squeeze God to the periphery or perhaps abandon him to his own devices, and build an edifice of glorious knowledge to the great God Science. But this stance has largely been abandoned in the postmodernism that characterizes most Western universities. Deconstructionists have been most vociferous in denouncing the modernist vision. They hold that language and meaning are socially constructed, which is tantamount to saying arbitrarily constructed. Its meaning is grounded neither in "reality" nor in texts per se. Texts will invariably be interpreted against the backdrop of the interpreter's social "home" and the historical conditioning of the language itself. Granted this interpretive independence from the text, it is entirely appropriate and right for the interpreter to take bits and pieces of the text out of the frameworks in which they

---

24. Ibid., 105.
25. Tracy, "Theology and the Many Faces of Postmodernity," 106.

are apparently embedded ("deconstruct" the text), and refit them into the framework ("locatedness") of the interpreter, thereby generating fresh insight, not least that which relativizes and criticizes the text itself.

The new hermeneutic reaches back several decades; radical hermeneutics and deconstruction are a little younger; this analysis of the move from modernity to postmodernity is only a couple of decades old. Yet together they have exerted vast influence in every field of Western intellectual thought, touching virtually every intellectual endeavor.[26] If here and there a few thinkers suggest that during the past three or four years postmodernism became a spent force, several things must be said in reply. First, no other worldview has come along to displace it; second, its influence on certain disciplines is still on the ascendancy (as we shall see); and third, the sheer diversity of Western culture tends to nourish a kind of *de facto* postmodernity. In short, rumors of postmodernity's demise are greatly exaggerated.

Philosophical pluralism is the approach to cultural diversity that is supported by—and supports—postmodernity. Obviously, it transcends mere empirical data; it outstrips assumptions that cultural diversity is to be embraced and cherished. One of the principal arguments of this book is that *confessional Christianity cannot wholly embrace either modernity or postmodernity, yet it must learn certain lessons from both; it must vigorously oppose many features of philosophical pluralism, without retreating to modernism.*

B. The Impact of Philosophical Pluralism

Radical hermeneutics and deconstruction are complex and difficult subjects. It is tempting to think that at least some of their challenge owes not a little to a certain kind of intellectual arrogance that deploys technical language and sophisticated argumentation to keep the masses at bay, excluded from the fine tone and subtle spinning of the intellectual elite.[27] Whether or not this is too harsh an assessment, it is important to recognize something of the impact that philosophical pluralism has already made on our culture. Some of these points will be taken up at length in later chapters. At the moment it is necessary only to perceive something of what is at stake.

First, in one form or another these ways of looking at reality have made an impact on virtually all the humanities, and on not a few philosophers of science as well. Not only in English 101 are students introduced to Jacques Derrida and Stanley Fish, but in sociology, history, philosophy, law, educa-

---

26. See the important work by David Harvey, *The Condition of Postmodernity* (Cambridge, MA/Oxford: Blackwell Publishers, 1990).

27. See the provocative and analogous thesis of John Carey, *The Intellectuals and the Masses: Pride and Prejudice Among the Literary Intelligentsia 1880–1939* (New York: St. Martin's Press, 1992).

tion, anthropology, and even occasionally in philosophy of science. In every instance the net effect is predictable: while rightly decrying the hubris that thinks human beings can understand anything perfectly, that talks glibly about absolute truth without recognizing that all human knowledge is in some ways culture-bound, these movements unite in depreciating objective truth itself. Theory has thus buttressed both the empirical and the cherished pluralisms of the age, generating a philosophical basis for relativism. Moreover, unlike the old-fashioned liberalism, which took two or three generations to work its way down from the seminaries and the universities to the ordinary person in the pew, this brand of liberalism has made its way down to the person in the street in about half a generation.[28]

The result is what Stephen Carter calls a "culture of disbelief."[29] Carter has courageously and insightfully chronicled how we have moved beyond mere civil religion (to use the expression that Robert Bellah made popular by his famous 1970 essay)[30] to the place where modern politics and law trivialize all values, all religious devotion. This stance is now in the air we breathe. The extent to which it has invaded the church is troubling. Not less troubling, for the preacher of the gospel, is the extent to which it is everywhere assumed, especially by middle and upper classes, by the media and print elite, by almost all who set the agenda for the nation.

In this environment, it is not surprising that pollsters turn up all sorts of contradictory evidence. Thus while 74 percent of Americans strongly agree that "there is only one true God, who is holy and perfect, and who created the world and rules it today," fully 64 percent strongly agree or agree somewhat with the assertion that "there is no such thing as absolute truth."[31]

In the moral realm, there is very little consensus left in Western countries over the proper basis of moral behavior. And because of the power of the media, for millions of men and women the only venue where moral questions are discussed and weighed is the talk show, where more often than not

---

28. This fact makes the assessment of some popular conservatives sadly out of touch with reality. See, for example, Pat Robertson, *The Turning Tide: The Fall of Liberalism and the Rise of Common Sense* (Dallas: Word Books, 1993), which sounds more like optimistic hype announcing another run at the presidency rather than careful cultural analysis. The conservative backlash he perceives is itself profoundly pragmatic; there is little evidence that the underlying worldviews are changing.

29. Stephen L. Carter, *The Culture of Disbelief: How American Law and Politics Trivialize Religious Devotion* (New York: Basic Books, 1993).

30. Robert N. Bellah, *Beyond Belief: Essays on Religion in a Post-traditionalist World* (Berkeley: Univ. of California Press, 1970). According to my colleague John Woodbridge, the expression was first coined by Jean Jacques Rousseau in 1761–62.

31. See George Barna, *What Americans Believe: An Annual Survey of Values and Religious Views in the United States* (Ventura: Regal Books, 1991).

the primary aim is to entertain, even shock, not to think. When Geraldo and Oprah become the arbiters of public morality, when the opinion of the latest media personality is sought on everything from abortion to transvestites, when banality is mistaken for profundity because uttered by a movie star or a basketball player, it is not surprising that there is less thought than hype. Oprah shapes more of the nation's grasp of right and wrong than most of the pulpits in the land. Personal and social ethics have been removed from the realms of truth and of structures of thought; they have not only been relativized, but they have been democratized and trivialized. As a guest on a talk show dealing with pornography put it, "The great thing about our society is that you can have your opinion and I can have mine."

Even at the academic level, ethicists completely committed to pluralism are diligently attempting to create a consensus morality based on certain societal commitments: on the recognition that human beings are persons who demand mutual respect, for instance,[32] or on the assumption that reason is sufficient to evaluate the relative merits of concrete elements of competing moral systems, but insufficient to evaluate the moral systems themselves (since that would be a violation of philosophical pluralism).[33] Of course, all such attempts covertly re-introduce objective values; the question is whether the attempt is successful. Certainly none enjoys wide credibility.

Consider the impact of philosophical pluralism on the study of history. There are, of course, many competing schools of historiography, and pluralism is repulsed by some of them. As recently as 1983, Schlossberg was criticizing historians for interpreting what happened in the past as almost inevitable, the canons of inevitability determined by some philosophical stance.[34] The classic example, of course—nowadays a great deal less believable than a mere decade ago—is Marxist historiography, but there are many others. Each school of historiography was in danger of divinizing its own interpretation of the past, almost all of them entirely naturalistic. But today pluralism has taught at least some of them that each interpretation of the past

---

32. So H. Tristram Engelhardt, Jr., *Bioethics and Secular Humanism: The Search for a Common Morality* (London/Philadelphia: SCM Press/Trinity Press International, 1991). E.g., p. 140: "All that remains to ground a general secular morality . . . is the possible bond of mutual respect among persons." It is not difficult to demonstrate the appalling instability of so fragile a basis.

33. So John Kekes, *The Morality of Pluralism* (Princeton: Princeton Univ. Press, 1993). A similar attempt to salvage advantage out of both empirical and philosophical pluralism in the arena of literary criticism is found in Wayne C. Booth, *Critical Understanding: The Powers and Limits of Pluralism* (Chicago: Univ. of Chicago Press, 1979).

34. Herbert Schlossberg, *Idols for Destruction: Christian Faith and Its Confrontation with American Society* (Nashville: Nelson, 1983), 11–38.

is entirely subjective: *none* of them can claim any supreme tie to the "truth." Indeed, the pursuit of historical "truth" in any objective sense is a chimera.

Nowhere is this more easily seen than in the comparison of two editions of one famous book. In 1940 Mortimer J. Adler published his justly famous work, *How to Read a Book*.[35] In it he does not devote a specific section to the reading of history, but he includes such comments as these: " . . . one must be not only a responsive but a responsible listener. You are responsive to the extent that you follow what has been said and note the intention which prompts it" (240). Or again:

> I think that knowledge can be communicated and that discussion can result in learning. If knowledge, not opinion, is at stake, then either disagreements are apparent only—to be removed by coming to terms and a meeting of minds; or, if they are real, then the genuine issues can always be resolved—in the long run, of course—by appeals to fact and reason. . . . This maxim then requires [the reader] to distinguish between knowledge and opinion, and to regard an issue concerning knowledge as one which can be resolved (248–9).

In dealing with historical works it is important, Adler says, to compare historian with historian, in order to "discover the interpretation a writer places on the facts" (278)—a distinction no philosophical pluralist will allow. "You may even get interested enough to look into the original documents from which the historian gathered evidence" (279).

Granted, some of these formulations are, by current standards, hermeneutically naive. Certainly they bristle with the assumptions of modernism. But the really shocking change comes when we compare the 1972 edition, jointly written with Charles Van Doren. Now an entire chapter is devoted to the reading of history. Many useful things are said. But we are also told that a historical fact "is one of the most elusive things in the world."[36] If we must place history, "the *story* of the past" (italics theirs), somewhere on the spectrum between science and fiction, "then it is usually admitted that history is *closer* to fiction than to science."[37]

In short, philosophical pluralism has made an enormous impact on an astonishingly wide spectrum of disciplines. Some of this impact will be sketched out in later chapters of this book.

---

35. New York: Simon & Schuster.

36. 1972 edition, 236.

37. Ibid., 237. Of course, several interesting presuppositions lurk behind this "spectrum" as to the nature of science, but I shall briefly treat this subject in chaps. 2 and 3. At one point, where they treat biographies and autobiographies, Adler and Van Doren acknowledge that "we expect the author to be accurate, to know his facts." The work almost calls out for a little source criticism.

Second, philosophical pluralism has enjoyed remarkable success in engendering new forms of religious pluralism. I am referring now not merely to the multiplication of religions (a subset of empirical pluralism), but to one form or another of the view that all religions are really saying the same thing, or that all achieve salvation (however that is construed) with equal power and efficiency. The roots of this stance stretch back through Hegel to Feuerbach, but their influence has been catapulted ahead on the springs of contemporary intellectual developments.

It is worth pausing to place the impact of philosophical pluralism on religion within a historical framework. Recent developments in Western Christendom are racing in more than one direction. In a masterful essay, Leonard Sweet traces the course from the mid-1930s to the mid-1980s, especially in mainline Protestant churches.[38] The last stage, he contends, is characterized by a pair of reactions against modernism. On the one hand there is "antimodernism," i.e., various evangelical, fundamentalist, and charismatic resurgence movements, both outside and within the mainline denominations. On the other hand there is "postmodernism" under various guises (though it is less than clear that Sweet has a good grasp of the latter). The loss of objective truth and the extreme subjectivity bound up with most forms of postmodernism have called forth, in the religious arena, a variety of responses. These are most commonly reduced to three:[39]

1. Radical religious pluralism: Under the direct impact of philosophical pluralism, this stance holds that no religion can advance any legitimate claim to superiority over any other religion. Wherever any religion (save the religion of pluralism) in any detail holds itself right or superior, and therefore holds that others are correspondingly wrong or inferior, it is necessarily mistaken. Of course, the challenge from philosophical pluralism is not restricted to the experience of Christians, even though in most Western countries confessional Christianity is philosophical pluralism's primary religious opponent. Philosophical pluralism threatens *any* pretension of superiority, let alone exclusiveness, in *all* of the world religions that come in contact with it[40]—as indeed they will if they have adherents in the West.

2. Inclusivism: This stance, while affirming the truth of fundamental

---

38. Leonard I. Sweet, "The Modernization of Protestant Religion in America," in *Altered Landscapes: Christianity in America, 1935–1985*, ed. David W. Lotz, Donald W. Shriver, Jr., and John F. Wilson (Grand Rapids: Eerdmans, 1989), 19–41.

39. This analysis has been common since the 1970s, and especially in some of the work of John Hick. It is nicely summarized in Harold A. Netland, *Dissonant Voices: Religious Pluralism and the Question of Truth* (Grand Rapids: Eerdmans, 1991), 8–27.

40. See especially Harold Coward, *Pluralism: Challenge to World Religions* (Maryknoll: Orbis Books, 1985).

Christian claims, nevertheless insists that God has revealed himself, even in saving ways, in other religions. Inclusivists normally contend that God's definitive act of self-disclosure is in Jesus Christ, and that he is in some way central to God's plan of salvation for the human race, but that salvation itself is available in other religions.

3. Exclusivism: This position teaches that the central claims of biblically faithful Christianity are true. Correspondingly, where the teachings of other religions conflict with these claims, they must necessarily be false. This stance brings with it certain views of who Jesus is, what the Bible is, and how salvation is achieved. Normally it is also held that salvation cannot be attained through the structures or claims of other religions. It does not hold that every other religion is wrong in every respect. Nor does it claim that all who claim to be Christians are saved, or right in every respect. It does insist that where other religions are contradicted by the gracious self-disclosure of Christ, they must necessarily be wrong. Until the modern period, this was virtually the unanimous view of Christians. Christians who still hold to this view sometimes now cast it as a direct negation of both modernism and postmodernism; adherents of postmodernism are inclined to dismiss this stance as a reflection of bigoted fundamentalism, and in part a reaction to the sheer fluidity and uncertainty of our age.

There are, of course, other analyses. Even in the simple one I have just outlined, there are many possible points along the spectrum from exclusivism to consistent religious pluralism.[41]

Since it is radical religious pluralism that is the focus of this book, along with the intellectual movements that sustain it, it may help to provide a few examples. Probably the best known exponent of consistent religious pluralism is John Hick. Hick's many articles and books condemn the Christian "monopoly of saving truth," insisting that any sense of superiority is guilty of generating "the paradox of a God of universal love who has ordained that only the Christian minority of the human race can be saved."[42] As for other religions, Hick writes:

> Around the different ways of conceiving, experiencing and responding to the Real there have grown up the various religious traditions of the world

---

41. For example, under the first category we may place what S. Mark Heim (*Is Christ the Only Way? Christian Faith in a Pluralistic World* [Valley Forge: Judson Press, 1985], 111–14) would call "parallel pluralism"—the view that the Christian faith is right *for me*, while the Muslim faith may be right *for Muslims*, and so forth. Such a position can be reasonably adopted only when the truth claims of the respective religions have been relativized or abandoned or reinterpreted. See also R. Panikkar, *The Intrareligious Dialogue* (New York: Paulist Press, 1978), xviii.

42. John Hick, *Problems of Religious Pluralism* (New York: Macmillan, 1985), 99.

with their myths and symbols, their philosophies and theologies, their liturgies and arts, their ethics and life-styles. Within all of them basically the same salvific process is taking place, namely, the transformation of human existence from self-centredness to Reality centredness. Each of the great traditions thus constitutes a valid context of salvation/liberation; each may be able to gain a larger understanding of the Real by attending to the reports and conceptualities of the others.[43]

Langdon Gilkey attributes the rise of this radical religious pluralism to a "shift in the balance between what were called the requirements of faith and those of love." This has been accompanied by another shift: from an assumption of Western cultural superiority, we have moved to an assumption of rough cultural parities, and this "shift in cultural consciousness has in turn had a vast effect on our theological consciousness," moving us toward a consciousness of theological and religious parity.[44] Don Cupitt's recent book in defense of absolute relativism insists that all values are mortal and therefore transient, that even tragedy is cultural, and that there is nothing in the universe to assure us that life must make sense. What we therefore need is a "religion of the fleeting moment and the slipping-away meaning."[45] In defense of religious pluralism, von Balthasar argues that truth is "symphonic," reminding us that etymologically symphony means "standing together."[46] To support this position, von Balthasar resorts to the most breathtaking array of misinterpreted biblical texts torn from their context that I have ever seen.

In defense of radical religious pluralism, Harvey Cox finds support even in the failed predictions of bygone atheists.[47] Thus, if some of the eighteenth-century French *philosophes* predicted that religion, like all superstition, was fated for prompt extinction (Cox quotes Voltaire's well-known line: "Not until the last priest is hanged with the entrails of the last king will mankind finally be free"), and have obviously erred in their prognostications, nevertheless they were correct, Cox avers, "to foresee the disappearance of religion as an extension of that way of knowing the external world we now call magic or superstition."[48] In other words, religion cannot supply any answers

---

43. Ibid., 102. Cf. also his *Interpretation of Religion* (New Haven: Yale Univ. Press, 1988). Hick is discussed at length in part 2 of this book.

44. "Plurality and Its Theological Implications," in *The Myth of Christian Uniqueness*, ed. John Hick and Paul F. Knitter (Maryknoll: Orbis Books, 1987), 37–50, esp. 38, 39.

45. *The Time Being* (London: SCM, 1992).

46. Hans Urs von Balthasar, *Truth Is Symphonic: Aspects of Christian Pluralism* (San Francisco: Ignatius Press, 1972).

47. *Many Mansions: A Christian's Encounter with Other Faiths* (Boston: Beacon Press, 1988).

48. Ibid., 200. I should mention that Cox fails to note that a number of the *philosophes* were in fact deeply religious.

to questions that can be answered in an empirical way, but can provide answers to questions of human meaning and purpose. If Lenin predicted that his own brand of naturalistic Marxist thought would ultimately replace religion as a metaphysical worldview, his predictions seem less threatening today. But, Cox insists, insofar as Lenin was saying that religion must be understood not in isolation, but as tied to all of life, he was right—a clever reinterpretation that makes it unclear whether or not Cox espouses philosophical naturalism. Cox attempts a similar justification of Freud and Jung. All of this leans in support of a universal, secular meaning of religion. Even Bonhoeffer's famous aphorism—that to be a Christian is, in the final analysis, to be fully human—is appealed to, almost as if what Bonhoeffer meant was that to be human is to be Christian, or at least religious, whereas of course what he was really saying was the reverse: to be Christian is what makes us truly human.

Taking the long view, the pervasiveness of radical religious pluralism is astonishing.[49] Religious pluralists capture no denomination completely, but they dominate the discussion in many, and exercise important influence in many more. Even in Roman Catholicism, thought by many to be a bastion of conservativism on these points, some form of inclusiveness predominates in the North Atlantic wings, and this not infrequently veers off toward radical pluralism.[50] In the arena of academic theology and religious studies, which after all shapes the next generation of clergy, it is sometimes difficult to find someone of stature who will stand up and call this perspective into question. In academic biblical studies, postmodernism links with the "new" literary criticism to create endless "fresh" readings, many of them clever and parts of them insightful, even if, taken as a whole, their insight is more and more removed from reasoned and defensible anchorage in the text.[51]

Reading many of the documents of the 1993 Parliament of the World's Religions, one is struck by two features. First, the sheer diversity of mutually contradictory religions is fascinating, yet each is under pressure to avoid the one taboo: to say anyone else is mistaken. Second, the documents on which the delegates could agree are strong on global ecology (raised to higher status by linking it with a call to truthfulness and tolerance and labeling the

---

49. For a useful hint at some of the religious implications of postmodernism, see Philippa Berry and Andrew Wernick, eds., *Shadow of the Spirit: Postmodernism and Religion* (London: Routledge, 1993).

50. The "anonymous Christian" theory of Karl Rahner (a form of inclusivism) is well known, and I shall discuss it later. But some discussion goes beyond that: e.g., Ernest D. Piryns, "Current Roman Catholic Views of Other Religions," *Missionalia* 13 (August 1986): 55–62; Chester Gillis, *Pluralism: A New Paradigm for Theology* (Grand Rapids: Eerdmans, 1993).

51. I shall deal with this more substantially in chaps. 2 and 3. For an excellent example, one might read Francis Watson, ed., *The Open Text: New Directions for Biblical Studies?* (London: SCM Press, 1993).

result "global ethic") and one or two other "in" concerns, but in fact the documents contain so little of anything distinctively religious that any decent atheist could happily sign on.[52] Indeed, that is the final plea: "Therefore we commit ourselves to a common global ethic, to better mutual understanding, as well as to socially-beneficial, peace-fostering, and Earth-Friendly ways of life. *We invite all men and women, whether religious or not, to do the same* [italics theirs]."[53]

For those who espouse radical religious pluralism, there is no longer *any* heresy, except perhaps the view that there are heresies. Other ages have disagreed over just what constitutes a heresy, but the category itself was inviolate. For the first time in history, large numbers of people deny that theological corruption is possible. For these people, even to ask if there are any theological boundaries, let alone where they lie (in two senses!), is to flirt with sacrilege.

It is vitally important to recognize that philosophical pluralism has exerted a dramatic "softening" influence on many people who would disavow radical religious pluralism. It is hard, for instance, to deny the influence of pluralism on evangelical preachers who increasingly reconstruct the "gospel" along the lines of felt needs, knowing that such a presentation will be far better appreciated than one that articulates truth with hard edges (i.e., that insists that certain contrary things are false), or that warns of the wrath to come. How far can such reconstruction go before what is preached is no longer the gospel in any historical or biblical sense?

Or consider two recent books. One was written by a confessional Lutheran, Carl Braaten, who with unflinching courage repeatedly affirms the exclusive sufficiency of Christ, the need for God's grace, the uniqueness of Christian revelation. The book is littered with strong judgments like this: "When Raimundo Panikkar writes that Christ has other names—Rama, Krishna, Isvara, Purusha, Tathagata, and the like—we must disagree mightily."[54] Yet despite his courage in defending this line of argument, Braaten ends up proposing a model that "pictures Jesus Christ as the revelation of the eschatological fulfillment of the religions. The gospel of Jesus Christ does not destroy but fulfills the religions."[55] In other words, the assumption is that

---

52. This is not an exaggeration: only a very vague statement would be acceptable to the Theravada and many Mahayama Buddhist and Jain participants, who are of course explicitly atheistic.

53. Closing paragraph of the final, jointly signed Declaration, widely circulated in manuscript form before being published in newspapers and other media.

54. Carl E. Braaten, *No Other Gospel! Christianity Among the World's Religions* (Minneapolis: Fortress Press, 1992), 78.

55. Ibid., 80.

God has revealed himself in some sense in all religions, and the eschatological fulfillment of all such revelation is Jesus Christ. But there are several slippery steps in the argument. That there is "revelation" in *some* sense in all religions few Christian thinkers (except some in the Barthian tradition) would want to deny. Some would speak of the revelation implicit in the *imago Dei*; others would speak, quite dogmatically at that, of general revelation that can be found in non-Christian religions; still others of the residual revelation not destroyed by the overlay of false religion. But Braaten moves from this weak sense of revelation to a much stronger sense, in which these revelations are "fulfilled" in Jesus Christ much as the old covenant is "fulfilled" in Jesus Christ. But in the Bible, the fulfillment of the old covenant in Jesus Christ (e.g., Matt. 5:17–20) is the fulfillment of what systematicians have called special revelation, and "fulfillment" itself means not the satisfaction of religious and personal aspirations, but the arrival of the eschatological event to which the old covenant Scriptures pointed in promise and type. Although the Bible as a whole can sometimes speak of the gospel and of Jesus as bringing to fruition the *aspirations* of pagans who surround the covenant community, it does not speak of the gospel or of Christ as fulfilling their *religion*. Nor would the adherents of such religions see themselves in such light; indeed, they would be insulted at the suggestion.[56]

In the other book, Daniel Taylor rightly challenges what he calls "the myth of certainty."[57] The kind of pursuit of certainty and affirmation of it that pretends to omniscience to the point of idolatry. I shall have more to say about such idolatry later in this book. But so relentless is Taylor's disavowal of such Christians that they are caricatured and stereotyped: when people defend their worldview or some system of thought, they are simply defending their own fragile self-identity. Over against such people are the "reflective" Christians (by which Taylor refers to himself and to those who agree with him). This simple, not to say simplistic, antithesis is teased out throughout the book. At the end of the day, Taylor is forced to retreat to the simplest fideism, unchecked by any appeal to history or revelation or "fit." Some form of fideism, I shall shortly argue, is inevitable; Taylor's form is a long way

---

56. The problem is compounded when Braaten (ibid., 72) seems even more open to "the so-called religions of grace," viz., Bhakti Hinduism and Mahayana Buddhism. Here Braaten, possibly influenced by Emil Brunner, seems to be unduly swayed by the importance of *sola gratia* in confessional Lutheran perspective, without really coming to terms with the essential polytheism of Hinduism and the flickering pantheism that lies even behind Mahayana Buddhism. On the latter, see especially Masao Uenuma, "A Christian View of Prayer and Spirituality in Muslim Thought," in *Teach Us to Pray: Prayer in the Bible and the World*, ed. D. A. Carson (Exeter: Paternoster Press, 1990), 192–204.

57. Daniel Taylor, *The Myth of Certainty* (Grand Rapids: Zondervan, 1992).

removed from the argument of Paul in 1 Corinthians, with his insistence on historical facts attested by ample numbers of eyewitnesses; or of Luke, with his affirmation of "many convincing proofs" (Acts 1:3). Taylor is surely right to raise a gentle protest against the invincible arrogance of those who have never struggled. But where he comes out is, I suspect, much more indebted to philosophical pluralism than he himself recognizes. I doubt that it is a stable position.

In short, philosophical pluralism has triumphantly engineered the modern form of religious pluralism. By and large, this is not something with which contemporary Christians have come to terms.

Third, under the impact of radical hermeneutics and of deconstruction, the nature of tolerance has changed.[58] In a relatively free and open society, the best forms of tolerance are those that are open to and tolerant of people, even when there are strong disagreements with their ideas. This robust toleration for people, if not always for their ideas, engenders a measure of civility in public discourse while still fostering spirited debate over the relative merits of this or that idea. Today, however, tolerance in many Western societies increasingly focuses on ideas, not on people.

The result of adopting this new brand of tolerance is less discussion of the merits of competing ideas—and less civility. There is less discussion because toleration of diverse ideas demands that we avoid criticizing the opinions of others; in addition, there is almost no discussion where the ideas at issue are of the religious sort that claim to be valid for everyone everywhere: that sort of notion is right outside the modern "plausibility structure" (to use Peter Berger's term), and has to be trashed. There is less civility because there is no inherent demand, in this new practice of tolerance, to be tolerant of people, and it is especially difficult to be tolerant of those people whose views are so far outside the accepted "plausibility structures" that they think your brand of tolerance is muddleheaded.

In the religious field, this means that few people will be offended by the multiplying new religions. No matter how wacky, no matter how flimsy their intellectual credentials, no matter how subjective and uncontrolled, no matter how blatantly self-centered, no matter how obviously their gods have been manufactured to foster human self-promotion, the media will treat them with fascination and even a degree of respect. But if any religion claims that in some measure other religions are wrong, a line has been crossed and resentment is immediately stirred up: pluralism (in the third sense) has been chal-

---

58. The next few paragraphs are adapted from D. A. Carson, "Christian Witness in an Age of Pluralism," in *God and Culture: Essays in Honor of Carl F. H. Henry*, ed. D. A. Carson and John D. Woodbridge (Grand Rapids: Eerdmans, 1993), 38–39.

lenged. Exclusiveness is the one religious idea that cannot be tolerated. Correspondingly, *proselytism* is a dirty word. One cannot fail to observe a crushing irony: the gospel of relativistic tolerance is perhaps the most "evangelistic" movement in Western culture at the moment, demanding assent and brooking no rivals.

What is sometimes forgotten is that this vision of tolerance is, at one level, akin to the view of religious tolerance in some remarkably intolerant countries. In some Muslim countries, for example, it is perfectly acceptable to *be* a Christian; but it may be illegal and is certainly dangerous to *become* a Christian. What is overlooked is that genuine religious freedom necessarily includes the right to convert and to encourage others to convert. At the heart of such freedom is the assumption that ideas matter and must be argued out in the marketplace, and that individuals have the right to change their minds and adopt new positions even if everyone around them is convinced that their ideas are preposterous. Of course, these rights are still largely maintained in the United States and the Western democracies. By and large, however, they are not cherished, for the focus of tolerance has changed. Philosophical pluralism has managed to set in place certain "rules" for playing the game of religion—rules that transcend any single religion.

I do not for a moment mean that everyone plays by these rules. In fact, it is becoming clear that this third form of pluralism, philosophical pluralism, tends to militate, in time, against the first two. Instead of a rich diversity of claims arguing it out in the marketplace (i.e., empirical pluralism), in what Neuhaus calls "the naked public square,"[59] and instead of this diversity being cherished as the best way to ensure freedom and to pursue truth (cherished pluralism), the pressures from philosophical pluralism tend to squash any strong opinion that makes exclusive truth claims—all, that is, except the dogmatic opinion that all dogmatic opinions are to be ruled out, the dogmatic opinion that we must dismiss any assertion that some opinions are false. By way of reaction, various groups respond by becoming defensive. They circle the wagons and shout slogans. Small wonder, then, that Stanley S. Harakas can affirm that the prevailing worldview in America is not pluralistic (at least, not in the first and second senses, as I have labeled them), but atomistic and antireligious.[60]

When philosophical pluralism is allied, in the popular mood, with the notion of progress, so that those who disagree are often pictured as quaint

---

59. Richard John Neuhaus, *The Naked Public Square: Religion and Democracy in America* (Grand Rapids: Eerdmans, 1984).

60. "Educating for Moral Values in a Pluralistic Society," *Greek Orthodox Review* 29 (1984): 393–99.

vestiges of a bygone era, the pressure to conform is enormous, since the notion of "progress" has been a watchword of Western culture for at least two centuries. Recently, the idea of progress has come under vigorous and long-deserved attack.[61] Moreover, in university circles deconstruction itself is just beginning to be "deconstructed." But as far as I can make out, philosophical pluralism is still the dominant ideology, and it is proving to be enormously intolerant.

Several recent books betray the severity of the challenge. In each case the critics of "fundamentalism" tend to find the worst exemplars, and lump together under this rubric all who hold that objective truth and morality do exist—including those of us who think it is vitally important that people be allowed to disagree with or rebel against objective truth and morality. Because all "fundamentalists" are lumped together, they are all dismissed together as antipluralistic and even antidemocratic.

Consider, for example, the introductory essay in the third volume of the justly famous Fundamentalism Project, being published by the University of Chicago Press. Marty and Appleby write:

> If fundamentalism is defined and understood by the utterances and actions of its most radical proponents, then one may conclude that fundamentalism is essentially antidemocratic, anti-accommodationist, and antipluralist and that it violates, *as a matter of principle*, the standards of human rights defended, if not always perfectly upheld, by Western democracies. By this reading of fundamentalism, the battle lines are drawn clearly between fundamentalist and nonfundamentalist, mutual understanding is unlikely or impossible, and public policy studies like the present one are inevitably devoted to the defense of principles and lifestyles under assault by the forces of resurgent religious radicalism.[62]

Or here is Boone, with the same lack of sophistication in her analysis:

> Try as they might to be humble, to avoid pitfalls of intellectual pride—largely because the Bible tells them to, perhaps—fundamentalists are dogmatic and doctrinalistic because their doctrine of the text forces them to be. They are reading an inerrant text; what they read, and therefore what they *interpret*, must be inerrant.[63]

---

61. See especially Christopher Lasch, *The True and Only Heaven: Progress and Its Critics* (New York: W. W. Norton, 1991).

62. Martin E. Marty and R. Scott Appleby, eds., *Fundamentalisms and the State: Remaking Polities, Economies, and Militance*, The Fundamentalism Project, vol. 3 (Chicago: Univ. of Chicago Press, 1993), "Introduction," 5 (italics theirs). I am indebted to John D. Woodbridge for drawing this passage to my attention.

63. Kathleen C. Boone, *The Bible Tells Them So: The Discourse of Protestant Fundamentalism* (Albany: State Univ. of New York Press, 1989), 72–73 (italics hers). One cannot fail to note

The result is that tolerance is no longer a virtue; political correctness is in:

> In the past, PC [=political correctness] generally centered on issues that were quite substantive. The Victorians were prudish about sex because they were enthusiastic about bourgeois morality. In the fifties, many Americans were intolerant of any notion that seemed remotely "pink" (socialistic) because they assumed communism to be a major threat to their economic and political freedom. Today's PC, however, is intolerant not of substance but of intolerance itself. Thus, although the politically correct would have a great deal of difficulty agreeing on what constitutes goodness and truth, they have no trouble at all agreeing that intolerance itself is wrong. Why? Because no one deserves to be offended.[64]

Recently at an East Coast university, the most frequent term chosen in a word association exercise by non-Christians to describe a Christian was "intolerant." Doubtless some of this perception derives from insensitive Christians. But some of it derives from significant changes in what "open-minded" means. It no longer means that you may or may not have strong views yet remain committed to listening honestly to countervailing arguments. Rather, it means you are dogmatically committed to the view that all convictions that any view whatsoever is wrong are improper and narrow-minded. In other words, open-mindedness has come to be identified not with the means of rational discourse, but with certain conclusions. The irony is that Christians are a barely tolerated minority on most university campuses. In society at large there is growing documentation supporting the ominous rise in "a fragrance of oppression."[65] As Clark puts it, "Postmodern apologetic practice must face both the perspectivism that erases all truth and the political correctness that arbitrarily reinstates it."[66]

Fourth, the rising diversity in Western culture (empirical pluralism) and the concomitant loss of cultural consensus, coupled with the rising intolerance generated by philosophical pluralism, has produced what *Time* magazine calls "A Nation of Finger Pointers."[67] One of America's most astute observers describes the result: we have generated a "culture of complaint."[68] Eventually

---

that her dismissal of dogmatism is very dogmatic. Her comment must be fallacious for any reader to avoid a dogmatic acceptance of it!

64. S. D. Gaede, *When Tolerance Is No Virtue: Political Correctness, Multiculturalism and the Future of Truth and Justice* (Downers Grove: InterVarsity Press, 1993), 23.

65. See Herbert Schlossberg, *A Fragrance of Oppression* (Wheaton: Crossway, 1991).

66. David K. Clark, "Narrative Theology and Apologetics," *Journal of the Evangelical Theological Society* 36 (1993): 515.

67. *Time* 138/6 (August 12, 1991): 14–22.

68. Robert Hughes, *Culture of Complaint: The Fraying of America* (New York: Oxford Univ. Press, 1993).

his book, amusing as it is, becomes tiresome: the author's only solution is that people should try harder to tolerate each other and get along. In other words, his work turns out to be a colorful preachment in support of cherished pluralism, with occasional hints of philosophical pluralism thrown in.

Fifth, the rise of radical hermeneutics and of deconstruction has sapped the faith of many undergraduates and introduced a raft of new challenges to those interested in evangelizing them. Thus, Miss Christian goes off to the local state university, full of zeal and the knowledge of a few fundamental truths. There she will not find lecturers who will devote much time to overturning her truths. Rather, she will find many lecturers convincing her that the meaning in her religion, as in all religion, is merely communal bias, and therefore relative, subjective. No religion can make valid claims of a transcendent nature. Truth, whatever it is, does not reside in an object or idea or statement or affirmation about reality, historical or otherwise, that can be known by finite human beings; rather, it consists of fallible, faulty opinions held by finite knowers who themselves look at things that certain way only because they belong to a certain section of society. Miss Christian is told, a trifle condescendingly, that if her religion helps her, she should be grateful, but that no intelligent person this side of Derrida, Foucault, and Fish, could possibly believe that her beliefs have a transcendent claim on everybody everywhere. Thus, without overtly denying her faith, Miss Christian discovers that its vitality has been sapped. It has been relativized, trivialized, marginalized. Without ever having had a single one of its major tenets overturned by historical or other argument, the whole edifice of Christian truth has been detached from the objective status it once held. Miss Christian drifts off, and it may take years before she thinks seriously about Jesus again—if she ever does.

For similar reasons, evangelism among university students has changed a great deal since I was an undergraduate. If a Christian offered testimony thirty years ago, it was possible to get into a strong debate, sometimes even a heated one, over the validity of the truth claims that were being advanced. Part of intelligent Christian witness on a secular campus was, for example, to muster the arguments for the historical resurrection of Jesus, to display the veracity and coherence of the Scriptures, and to demonstrate the awesome wisdom and love in God's plan of redemption. You can, of course, do all these things today, but the first question is likely to be: "Yes, that's fine for you, but what about all the Hindus?" In other words, granted the empirical pluralism of our age, why should your particular brand of religion be thought better than anyone else's? And granted the philosophical pluralism of our age, your expression of belief, though very interesting and valuable for you and even, at times, compelling, is no more than the subjective product of your religious community. It is your depiction of religious experience, decisively shaped by who you are; it is reality for you, but it is not culture-transcending reality. Nothing is.

In the same way, a friend may listen to your testimony, and then smile quietly and say, "I'm so glad that your faith helps you. As for me, I don't really need it, and frankly I find it impossible to believe what you do. I enjoy your friendship, but please don't push your religion down my throat. We've each got to find our own way, and your way isn't mine."

Where do you begin?

C. The Impact of Correlatives of Pluralism

By "correlatives of pluralism" I am referring to a variety of societal trends that are partly causes and partly effects of pluralism. For example, the third one I shall mention, rising biblical illiteracy, contributes to pluralism in that there is a declining percentage of citizens who are so well read, biblically speaking, that they can recognize, let alone withstand, the negative features of pluralism's onslaught. They soon become part of the problem. On the other hand, the more philosophical pluralism triumphs in the land, the less incentive there is to read the Bible. In that sense pluralism contributes to biblical illiteracy. Most of what I shall introduce as the "correlatives of pluralism," as I have called them, have this kind of dual relation with one form or another of pluralism. My concern here is not to give a rich account of them, still less to analyze their relationships with pluralism, but to identify them briefly, as part and parcel of the broader challenge of pluralism, as part and parcel of movements that tend toward the gagging of God. A few of them will be more fully explored later in this book.

1. Secularization

Most social scientists do not think of secularization as one of the societal trends that tend toward the abolition of religion, but as one of those that tend toward the *marginalization* of religion. "By secularization we mean the process by which sectors of society and culture are removed from the domination of religious institutions and symbols."[69] In other words, religious institutions

---

69. Peter L. Berger, *The Sacred Canopy: Elements of a Sociological Theory of Religion* (Garden City: Doubleday, 1967), 107. For a detailed outline of how secularization proceeds, analyzed from a social science perspective, see David Martin, *A General Theory of Secularization* (New York: Harper & Row, 1978). For discussion of the theory, see Jonathan D. Harrop, "The Limits of Sociology in the Work of David Martin. Towards a Critique of David Martin's Sociology of Religion Centered on His Essay: 'Can the Church Survive?'" *Religion* 17 (1987): 173–92; and especially David W. Smith, "In Praise of Ambiguity: A Response to Jonathan Harrop's Critique of the Sociology of David Martin," *Religion* 18 (1988): 81–85. Cf. also Klaas Runia, "The Challenge of the Modern World to the Church," *Evangelical Review of Theology* 18 (1994): 301–24.

and symbols may survive and even flourish, but their influence in the culture at large is progressively diminished. As Wells puts it, "It is axiomatic that secularism strips life of the divine, but it is important to see that it does so by relocating the divine in that part of life which is private."[70]

The subtlety of this definition is crucial if we are to answer revisionist critics who assure us, as Nielsen does, that "secularity seems to be declining in influence."[71] One recent book has uncovered some important demographic sources that enable the authors to reconstruct probable "religious adherence" rates from 1776 on. The authors insist that the religious adherence rate doubled between the Revolution and the Civil War, from 17 percent to 34 percent, that it climbed to more than 50 percent by 1906, and to 62 percent by 1980. Along the way they debunk the importance of the Awakenings, and insist, against most strategists and ecumenists, that the most important factor in retaining or gaining a large "market share" is preserving a distinctive religious identity.[72] Despite its interesting statistics, the work is flawed by remarkable reductionism. But in any case, it is inadequate as an index to secularization as defined here unless the "religious adherence" quotient measured the degree to which religion shaped the national discussion. Polls have repeatedly shown that a large percentage of Americans (and other Westerners) still assent to such fundamental Christian beliefs as the existence of God, the importance of moral order, the deity of Christ, and the authority of the Bible, "but these beliefs appear to be stranded on the beaches of private consciousness. Certainly they are not appealed to in any debate over the shape of our corporate life."[73] One thinks of the oft-repeated summary coined by Guinness: "privately engaging, publicly irrelevant." In other words, sophisticated studies in the processes of secularization do not focus only on such brute statistics as the number of those who attend church services now and then, but also on the way religious commitment bears, or does not bear, on all of human life. What such studies show is that millions of Americans are

---

70. David F. Wells, *No Place for Truth*, 79. Wells distinguishes between secularization (a process dealing with the external and sociological) and secularism (that which concerns the internal and the ideological [80]); others make slightly different distinctions. But the distinctions do not concern us here.

71. Niels C. Nielsen, Jr., *Fundamentalism, Mythos, and World Religions* (Albany: State Univ. of New York Press, 1993), 153.

72. Roger Finke and Rodney Stark, *The Churching of America, 1776–1990: Winners and Losers in Our Religious Economy* (New Brunswick: Rutgers Univ. Press, 1992).

73. Wells, *No Place for Truth*, 81. This is not to say that there are no elements of contemporary secularization theory that do not need challenging. For example, Harvie M. Conn, "The Secularization Myth," *Evangelical Review of Theology* 12 (1988): 78–92, offers substantial evidence against the commonly held thesis that urbanization and secularization go hand in hand.

religious in certain ways, but that that fact has little bearing on anything they really judge important in their life.

Another way to get at this subject is to evaluate the national discourse. A century and a half ago it was impossible to engage for long in political or historical study without bringing up the subject of providence. It was important for thinking people to try to understand what God himself was saying in history, whether he was speaking the language of blessing or of judgment. Today, there is not a history department in the land that would approve a Ph.D. dissertation that tried to infer anything at all about providence.[74] Fewer than six decades ago, President Franklin Delano Roosevelt, at the height of the Great Depression, could tell his fellow Americans, in one of his radio fireside chats, "Our difficulties, thank God, concern only material things."[75] It is impossible to imagine any of the last half-dozen presidents saying anything similar.[76] The national discourse is taken up with economics, politics, entertainment figures, sports, disasters, occasionally international affairs, and crime—but nothing about God, very little about religion (except to snicker at its most painfully embarrassing hypocrites and failures), not even very much about such concepts as truth, courtesy, civility, honor, duty, moral courage—all of which sound vaguely quaint and old-fashioned in our ears. And when a religious topic, such as conversion, is treated at the academic level, the treatment is likely to be entirely constrained by social science categories committed to philosophical naturalism and utterly averse to "mysticism." The question of God's existence or reality in conversion is carefully bracketed out, prompting the reviewer of one recent book along these lines[77] to complain rather ruefully, "What difference would it make to social science if . . . the origin of the sense of god was God?"[78] The powers of secularization stalk the land.

The bearing of all this on the preacher of the gospel is obvious. We must not only declare the whole counsel of God, but do so in an environment where the subject is perceived to be vaguely or even explicitly irrelevant. In fact, if you seem too passionate about it, *you too* may appear to be vaguely irrelevant. To bridge this gap, many preachers succumb to the temptation to

---

74. Some would argue that the decisive nail in the coffin of any doctrine of providence was the Holocaust. Among Jewish theologians, that is a recurring theme. The argument has received relatively meager treatment by Christian theologians, though see Wolfhart Pannenberg, *Human Nature, Election and History* (Philadelphia: Westminster Press, 1977); Carl F. H. Henry, *God, Revelation and Authority*, 6 vols. (Waco: Word Books, 1976–83), 6:485–91.

75. Quoted by Dan Coats in *Imprimus* 20/9 (September 1991): 1.

76. The contemporary presidential "God bless you" or "God bless America" is no parallel.

77. Peter B. Stromberg, *Language and Self-Transformation: A Study of the Christian Conversion Narrative* (Cambridge: Cambridge Univ. Press, 1993).

78. David Atkinson, in *Expository Times* 105 (1994): 190.

become entertainers (for entertainment is one of the categories people *do* understand), or to the temptation to transmute the gospel into something that helps us in our perceived inadequacies (for endless self-focus certainly dominates the national discourse). Other preachers, more robust, dig in and condemn, and gather a group of like-minded conservatives around them, but make little impact on the land. What shall we do?

But if the effects of secularization have been severe in the pulpit and in the pew, in higher education they have been incalculable. This may owe something to the decline in the study of classical texts and in the respect for tradition that once marked the academy,[79] but it owes far more to what Marsden and Longfield and their colleagues, in an insightful analysis, identify as the measured marginalization of Christianity in the academy.[80] From a time when organized Christianity, or at least its ideals, exercised a leading role in the founding, development, and maintenance of the principal schools of higher learning, we have arrived at a point at which virtually all forms of Christianity are commonly ignored or even despised in the academy, and especially those forms that insist that there are objective truths and standards.[81]

Modern secularization is an extraordinary phenomenon. Almost every civilization in the history of the world has been undergirded by some sort of religious/philosophical outlook. Major exceptions, such as the Marxist nations, displaced the supernatural, but strongly imposed other values—"religious" in the sense that the individual was not his or her own measure, but was called upon to sacrifice everything for an almost transcendental value, certainly an ultimate value, namely, the inevitable triumph of socialism. From today's vantage, we can easily see how ephemeral that "religion" was, but at least it was moderately self-consistent. Western secularized society, by contrast, has no unifying commitment to a single "other" or "transcendent" value. By this I am not overlooking the obvious fact that much of Western culture espouses *de facto* naturalism (as did atheistic forms of Marxism). I mean, rather, to emphasize that there is no agreed-upon philosophy or outlook or value system or historical interpretation that binds the majority of the nation together, other than pluralism itself. If from a Christian perspective Marxism was an idol that needed to be overthrown, Western secularized

---

79. Amply if sensationally chronicled by E. D. Hirsch, Jr., *Cultural Literacy: What Every American Needs to Know* (Boston: Houghton Mifflin, 1987) and Allan Bloom, *The Closing of the American Mind: How Higher Education Has Failed Democracy and Impoverished the Souls of Today's Students* (New York: Simon & Schuster, 1988).

80. George M. Marsden and Bradley J. Longfield, eds., *The Secularization of the Academy* (New York: Oxford Univ. Press, 1992).

81. See George M. Marsden, *The Soul of the American University* (New York: Oxford Univ. Press, 1994).

society, for all its marginalized religion, is replete with myriads of individual idols, as each person thinks and does what is "right" in his or her own eyes, unwittingly conforming to the fragmented dictates of this secularizing age of pluralism.[82] How long such a culture can survive is still an unanswered question.

2. New Age Theosophy

So many books and articles have appeared in recent years describing one facet or another of the New Age movement that I need not describe it afresh.[83] The branches of this highly heterogeneous movement have certain features in common. Most visions of "god" in the movement are pantheistic; some are tied to ecology or to the more radical strains of feminism.[84] The aim is not to be reconciled to a transcendent God, who has made us and against whom we have rebelled, but to grow in self-awareness and self-fulfillment, to become self-actualized, to grow to our full potential, until we are rather more at one with the god/universe than we otherwise would be.[85] The focus, in short, is self; evil is reinterpreted and thus emasculated; and any notion of judgment imposed by a personal/transcendent God whose wrath has been and will be displayed, is utterly repugnant. Thus "spirituality," a popular notion that enjoys full scope even in the *New York Times Book Review*, is divorced from any biblically faithful worldview. Needless to say, there is no need for a mediator, let alone a suffering priest who takes our sin on himself.

There are at least two important implications for the preacher of the gospel. The first is that a person who is largely biblically illiterate but who has absorbed substantial doses of New Age theosophy will hear us to be saying things we do not really mean. If we talk about God, Spirit, new birth, power, abundant life, peace, joy, love, family life, conscience, faith, trust, and a host of other topics, they will all be nicely slotted into a New Age framework. Even words like "sin" will be read as "bad things" or perhaps "bad karma"— but not at all as something whose badness derives from its offensiveness to the God who has made us and to whom we must give an account. The entire

---

82. See J. A. Walter, *A Long Way from Home: A Sociological Exploration of Contemporary Idolatry* (Exeter: Paternoster Press, 1979).

83. Among the better ones are Russell Chandler, *Understanding the New Age* (Dallas: Word Books, 1988); James R. Lewis and J. Gordon Melton, eds., *Perspectives on the New Age* (Albany: State Univ. of New York, 1992).

84. E.g., Rosemary Radford Ruether, *Gaia and God: An Ecofeminist Theology of Earth Healing* (San Francisco: Harper San Francisco, 1992).

85. Peter Jones, *The Gnostic Empire Strikes Back: An Old Heresy for the New Age* (Phillipsburg: Presbyterian and Reformed, 1992) perceives not a few parallels between the New Age movement and ancient Gnosticism.

structure of thought of such a person guarantees that he or she will hear us quite differently from what we intend to say, what we think we are saying. "Sin" is a snicker word—that is, it conveys nothing of odium, but makes people snicker. Millions of men and women fornicate without the slightest qualms of conscience.

The second implication is that many ostensible believers inside our churches—some of whom are genuine believers and some of whom are not— have inevitably picked up some of the surrounding chatter and, being poorly grounded in Scripture and theology, have incorporated into their under- standing of Christianity some frankly incompatible elements. Remarkably smarmy notions of "spirituality" abound; very few ask, for instance, what a "spiritual" life looks like *according to the New Testament documents*.[86] In this framework there is going on, as Tinker puts it, a battle for the mind,[87] even though many have not perceived the nature of the fight.

3. Rising Biblical Illiteracy

In 1950 the Gallup organization asked the question, "Did you receive any religious instruction in your youth?" Only 6 percent of Americans answered negatively. When the same question was put to people in 1989, the figure had risen to 38 percent.

Many of us are so cocooned in our confessional churches, or we live in such relatively conservative parts of the country, that we really do not have any idea how serious this challenge has become. Two years ago I gave a series of evangelistic talks to a small group of scientists near Chicago, all with earned doctorates. From previous experience, I went in expecting that two-thirds of them would not even know that the Bible has two Testaments. I discovered that my estimate was a trifle low. Some churches that draw significant num- bers of university students take time, whenever they have a special service geared specifically to the outsider, to explain what prayer is, before public prayer is offered: many of those who attend have never prayed, or witnessed prayer. A few months ago I was on a television set for a couple of days, work- ing on two or three religious programs sponsored by The Learning Channel and *U.S. News and World Report*. I shared my faith, in some detail, with three people; I probably chatted with thirty others. I found only two who knew the Bible had two Testaments—and these two people had found out only during the previous few weeks, while working on the programs at hand.

In many parts of the country, we cannot assume any biblical knowledge on the part of our hearers at all: the most elementary biblical narratives are

---

86. Cf. the appendix to this volume, "When Is Spirituality Spiritual?"
87. Melvin Tinker, "Battle for the Mind," *Churchman* 106 (1992): 34–44.

completely unknown. Furthermore, the situation is getting worse, now that the Bible is all but excluded from our schools, is not systematically taught in most of our churches, and has been further sidelined with the demise of family devotions.

The rising impact of biblical illiteracy was brought home to me a couple of years ago in a rather vivid way. My son then attended grade 4 in a public school which, by most standards, is excellent. For their Christmas concert that year—or, more accurately, their Season's concert—there was not a single song that had anything whatsoever to do with Christmas or Hanukkah. By "anything whatsoever" I include not only explicitly religious pieces, but also songs of the "Jingle Bells" variety. I have never heard, in ten songs, so many eminently forgettable lines of well-sung poetry. It was all entirely harmless. But it was also a sign that the culture of disbelief is striking again. When I was a child, all of us sang Christmas carols at school, at home, and at church. It would have been hard to find a child who could not recite the words, "Veiled in flesh, the Godhead see / Hail, th' incarnate Deity." Today the schools are becoming silent; there is little singing at home, for it has largely been displaced by VCRs; and in the church, there is less and less congregational participation that ensures that people learn truths through song. In a fifth grade class of thirty students, not far from our home, the teacher asked if anyone knew who Moses was. Only one child could say *anything* about him. On another occasion in the same class, the word "sin" came up, and one child asked what the word meant. In some adult circles, if a biblical narrative is recognized at all, it is because they have seen an epic film—Charlton Heston playing Moses, perhaps. Didn't Moses have something to do with the Ten Commandments?

We are thus ensuring that an entire generation will be even theoretically ignorant of the most elementary structures of the Judeo-Christian heritage on which our civilization has been nurtured. Worse (from the perspective of the preaching of the gospel), they will not have the "hooks" on which to hang the appeals to the gospel that have been our staple. I recognize, of course, that with the rising empirical pluralism in the land, adjustments in the public school education system are inevitable, and in some instances desirable. But massive silence regarding all things religious, a silence fostered by our culture of disbelief, is not the best option. As Jewish talk-show host Dennis Prager puts it:

> Liberals are always talking about pluralism, but that is not what they mean.... In public school, Jews don't meet Christians. Christians don't meet Hindus. Everybody meets nothing. That is, as I explain to Jews all the time, why their children so easily inter-marry. Jews don't marry Christians. Non-Jewish Jews marry non-Christian Christians. Jews for nothing marry

Christians for nothing. They get along great because they both affirm nothing. They have everything in common—nothing. That's not pluralism.[88]

Or, more accurately, that's not the first kind of pluralism, i.e., empirical
pluralism, but it is most certainly the kind of culture postmodern philosophical pluralism wants to build.

4. Vague But Emphatic Appeals to the Cosmic Christ

The person who is usually credited with the expression "cosmic Christ,"
as it has come to be deployed in international theological circles, is Professor
Joseph Sittler, then of the Chicago Divinity School, in his 1961 address to the
Third Assembly of the World Council of Churches at New Delhi.[89] Building
on Colossians 1:15–20, where the word "all" is used six times, Sittler assigned
the "all" maximum reach, insisting that God's redemption is "cosmic in
scope," and that the Christ envisaged there is the "cosmic Christ." From this
lead, a number of writers have used the same expression in progressively complex ways. For example, Panikkar defends the view that "Christ" is found not
only in the historical Jesus, but also in certain strands of Hindu thought.[90]
One can find not dissimilar notions in Hans Küng, Karl Rahner, M. M.
Thomas, and many others.

More conservative exegetes have often pointed out that to base such views
on the Bible it is necessary to pick and choose the texts of the Bible, and then
interpret them outside their context. This is, of course, a form of deconstruction. No less disastrously, "Christ" is so divorced from the historical
Jesus that the term can be given almost any content one wishes—though certainly no New Testament writer had any such disjunction in mind. Thus what
texts are interpreted to say is *intentionally* distanced from authorial intent.

Whatever the problems inherent in such views, they are widespread in
mainline denominations. Where our witness touches men and women from
such backgrounds, or includes students enrolled in religious studies programs
in many universities, it is imperative that we address the distortion of the biblical portrait of the Lord Jesus Christ.

---

88. Cited in *Christianity Today* 35 (May 27, 1991): 40.

89. For a useful summary of the development of the expression, and a telling critique, see
Sunand Sumithra, "Conversion: To Cosmic Christ?" *Evangelical Review of Theology* 16 (1992):
385–97.

90. Raimundo Panikkar, "The Meaning of Christ's Name," in *Service and Salvation*, ed.
Joseph Pathrapankal (Bangalore: C.M.I., 1973), 242ff. Cf. also his 1964 book, *The Unknown
Christ of Hinduism: Towards an Ecumenical Christophany* (Maryknoll: Orbis Books, 1981).
Panikkar exegetes a passage from the Hindu Scriptures, *Janmadi Yasyatah*, which on his read-
ing speaks of the cause, power, and goal of all things, but leaves this cause/power/goal
unnamed. Panikkar names it "Christ."

5. The Sheer Pragmatism of the Baby Busters

The number of books and papers differentiating between "baby boomers" (people born between roughly 1945 and 1960) and "baby busters" (people born between 1960 and 1975) is now legion.[91] It is said that baby busters do not want to be lectured; they expect to be entertained. They prefer videos to books; many of them have not learned to think in a linear fashion; they put more store than they recognize in mere impressions. As a result, they can live with all sorts of logical inconsistencies and be totally unaware of them. (How many times have I tried to explain to a university-age young person who has made some profession of faith that it is fundamentally inconsistent to claim to know and love the God of the Bible, while cohabiting with someone? They can *see* they are doing what the Bible forbids, but when you press them to articulate the contradiction they scuttle into inconsistency without embarrassment.) They are cynical, not idealistic. They vehemently deny the existence of absolutes: that is their one absolute. Many have never *experienced* principled morality in the home. They have been brought up without a coherent vision or value system, and they have embraced pragmatism with a vengeance. Many of them are furious with the preceding generation (that's me and my generation) for being so crassly materialistic as to ruin the economy and dump a tax load onto their shoulders. On the other hand, they are no less materialistic themselves, and will vote for any candidate who promises to deliver more goodies while lowering taxes—precisely the same greedy stupidity that afflicted the generation they condemn. Pluralism is so much their creed that even when the strongest arguments are arrayed to explain, on biblical presuppositions, why morally "good" people should be rejected by the Christian God and assigned to hell, their emotions so rule their heads that very frequently no amount of argumentation is adequate. On the other hand, they tend to be interested in "spirituality" (very hazily defined), and on the whole tend to see themselves as occupying a fairly high place in the spiritual pecking order.

It does not take a great deal of imagination to see how people with such positions as these will have an enormous impact on the way the gospel is perceived, if it is preached in strictly traditional categories. The solution of some is to design what are in effect baby buster churches, or at least baby buster church services.[92] The problem, of course, is that unless the various components in the culture of baby busters is analyzed biblically and theologically, we

---

91. One of the most useful surveys is a fairly recent article in *Atlantic Monthly*. Neil Howe and William Strauss, "The New Generation Gap" (December 1992): 67–89.

92. E.g., Leith Anderson, *Dying for Change: An Arresting Look at the New Realities Confronting Churches and Para-Church Ministries* (Minneapolis: Bethany House, 1990).

will not know what elements we must confront and reform, what elements are morally neutral, and what elements should be commended and strengthened. But unless we engage in such reflection, we will either remain insensitive to the changing face of American culture (and thus serve only those churches that are found in very conservative parts of the country, or those churches with an aging population), or we will capsize to merely pragmatic considerations ourselves, and build so-called churches with a lot of happy baby busters and very few genuine converts pursuing the knowledge of God and growth in genuine holiness and service.

6. The Hegemony of Pop Culture

I do not want to succumb to the elitism that makes sharp distinctions between popular and high culture.[93] Nor can I quite bring myself to believe that the medium of television is so bad, intrinsically speaking, that even if all the programs were Christian, the medium itself is beyond redemption: so McLuhan, Ellul, and many others.[94] Granted, a great deal of what appears on television is rubbish; granted, this medium, deployed in an undisciplined way, can take over families, squash conversation, fertilize couch potatoes, discourage serious reading and thought, and pamper the desire to be entertained; granted, much that evangelicalism has attempted to do on television is theologically (not to say aesthetically) pathetic;[95] granted, a culture addicted to the visual presentation of data presents peculiar challenges to the proclamation of a God who is not only invisible, but who insists that the desire for visual security and certainty is one of the hallmarks of idolatry. Still, I think that one of the most fundamental problems is want of discipline. Homes that severely restrict viewing hours, insist on family reading, encourage debate on good books, talk about the quality and the morality of television programs they do see, rarely or never allow children to watch television without an adult being present (in other words, refusing to let the TV become an unpaid nanny), and generally develop a host of other interests, are not likely to be greatly contaminated by the medium, while still enjoying its numerous benefits. But what will produce such families, if not godly parents and the power of the Holy Spirit in and through biblical preaching, teaching, example, and witness?

---

93. See, for example the telling review of Kenneth A. Myers, *All God's Children and Blue Suede Shoes: Christians and Popular Culture* (Westchester: Crossway, 1989), written by William Edgar and published in *Westminster Theological Journal* 53 (1991): 377–80.

94. See, most recently, Simon Vibert, "The Word in an Audio-Visual Age: Can We Still Preach the Gospel?" *Churchman* 106 (1992): 147–58.

95. See especially Quentin J. Schultze, *Televangelism and American Culture: The Business of Popular Religion* (Grand Rapids: Baker, 1991).

The sad fact is that unless families have a tremendously stron[ ], they will not perceive the dangers in the popular culture; or, if they perceive them, they will not have the stamina to oppose them. There is little point in preachers disgorging all the sad statistics about how many hours of television the average American watches per week, or how many murders a child has witnessed on television by the age of six, or how a teenager has failed to think linearly because of the twenty thousand hours of flickering images he or she has watched, unless the preacher, by the grace of God, is establishing a radically different lifestyle, and serving as a vehicle of grace to enable the people in his congregation to pursue it with determination, joy, and a sense of adventurous, God-pleasing freedom.

Meanwhile, the harsh reality is that most Americans, including most of those in our churches, have been so shaped by the popular culture that no thoughtful preacher can afford to ignore the impact. The combination of music and visual presentation, often highly suggestive, is no longer novel. Casual sexual liaisons are everywhere, not least in many of our churches, often with little shame. "Get even" is a common dramatic theme. Strength is commonly confused with lawless brutality. Most advertising titillates our sin of covetousness. This is the air we breathe; this is our culture.

7. Rugged Individualism Veering Toward Narcissism

It is a commonplace in the literature that the United States, Australia, and to some extent Canada espouse individualism more strongly than most Western countries.[96] By contrast, although the Bible leaves ample scope for individuals, both precept and underlying assumptions make much more of corporate values than does our culture: the value of family and the importance of the covenant people of God as a body, are constantly reinforced.[97]

In one context, individualism breeds courage, an entrepreneurial spirit, individual heroism, self-denial, deferred gratification, and thrift. It may accent values such as duty, honor, and industry. But if for whatever reasons the cultural values change, individualism can easily become a factor that reinforces narcissism, self-indulgence, instant gratification, self-promotion, and greed. This change has been tracked and analyzed in a number of ways. Robert

---

96. Clearly this is a sweeping generalization. Quite apart from individual exceptions, there are numerous pockets within these countries (e.g., immigrant Chinese) which in this respect stand in marked antithesis to the broader culture.

97. Whatever its faults, the modern study that turned scholarly attention to the emphasis on the corporate in the Old Testament was H. Wheeler Robinson, *Corporate Personality in Ancient Israel* (Philadelphia: Fortress, 1964 [1935]). For a useful study of the place of the individual in the same corpus, cf. Frederick J. Gaiser, "The Emergence of the Self in the Old Testament: A Study in Biblical Wellness," *Horizons in Biblical Theology* 14 (1992): 1–29.

Bellah and his associates have shown that an older generation of Americans saw emotions as properly subject to larger values: commitment, duty, reason, honor. But this vision of things has largely been replaced by what they call the therapeutic model. Feelings and emotions assume extraordinary importance; individualistic self-fulfillment becomes the prime good. And often this self-fulfillment will be achieved, it is thought, by self-expression. What was formerly considered to be cheerful self-discipline and self-control is now dismissed with contempt as dangerous repression. Even marriage, formerly seen as in principle inviolate, is now merely a means to the end of self-actualization and self-fulfillment, to be readily discarded if emotional "needs" are not met. The habits of the heart have changed.[98] Granted that these developments have helped some people escape genuine repression, it takes a willful blindness not to see that far more societal damage has been caused than societal good.

Perhaps no one has put this more trenchantly than Lasch:

> In their emotional shallowness, their fear of intimacy, their hypochondria, their pseudo-self-insight, their promiscuous pansexuality, their dread of old age and death, the new narcissists bear the stamp of a culture that has lost interest in the future. Their outlook on life—as revealed in the new consciousness movements and therapeutic culture; in pseudo-confessional autobiography and fiction; in the replacement of Horatio Alger by the happy hooker as the symbol of success; in the theater of the absurd and the absurdist theater of everyday life; in the degradation of sport; in the collapse of authority; in the escalating war between men and women—is the world view of the resigned.[99]

The analysis of Yankelovich is scarcely different.[100] He thinks the change toward instant self-focus and self-gratification (in 1981 he thought this outlook controlled about 80 percent of the American populace) is so revolutionary that it is nothing less than a "world turned upside down." Many have noted that the conservatism of the 1980s was rather different from the conservatism of the Eisenhower 1950s. The adults of the latter decade had endured the Great Depression and World War II. Despite the menace of the cold war, they were determined to build families and communities, to leave something for their children. This too, of course, can be another form of selfishness, but the lingering assumptions of the inherited Judeo-Christian cul-

---

98. Robert N. Bellah et al., *Habits of the Heart: Individualism and Commitment in American Life* (New York: Harper & Row, 1985).

99. Christopher Lasch, *The Culture of Narcissism: American Life in an Age of Diminishing Expectations* (New York: W. W. Norton, 1978), flyleaf outlining the thrust of the chapters.

100. Daniel Yankelovich, *New Rules: Search for Self-Fulfillment in a World Turned Upside Down* (New York: Random House, 1981).

ture kept at least some of that selfishness in check. Such bonds were much loosened by the 1980s. Self-absorbed and lusting after personal fulfillment, the conservatism of that decade could happily live beyond its means and leave its debts for the children.[101] Some of its couples could engender long-delayed children they once thought of as encumbrances, but only by placing them fourth or fifth on their scale of priorities, after career, house, and two cars.

Individualism once allied with a societal assumption of objective truth and eternal verities could generate at least some men and women of courage, honor, vision; individualism allied with philosophical pluralism and the scarcely qualified relativism of postmodernity generates "a world without heroes."[102] The proponents of modernism and postmodernism alike "castrate, and bid the gelding be fruitful" (in the witticism of C. S. Lewis).

Inevitably, individualism has made an impact on the way religion is conceived. The spread of privatized spirituality, developed apart from a disciplined and disciplining church, doubtless fosters desires for personal connection with the transcendent, but, at the risk of an oxymoron, it is a personally defined transcendence. Privatized spirituality is not conspicuously able to foster care for others.[103] God, if S/He exists, must satisfy the prime criterion: S/He must meet my needs, as I define them. It is hard to resist the conclusion that this God is less the God and Father of our Lord Jesus Christ than a Christianized species of the genie in Aladdin's lamp. Having abandoned authoritative revelation and ecclesiastical tradition alike, many in this generation find it easy to adopt all sorts of absurd beliefs, provided only that they serve personal interests: this is the age when huge sums are paid to psychic counselors, when even *Time* lists crystal healing as a possible medical remedy, when an American president seeks guidance from astrologers.

Phillip Hammond goes so far as to argue that the emphasis on personal autonomy during the past two decades has brought about the "third disestablishment" of religion in America.[104] The first disestablishment was legal, embodied in the First Amendment; but although it had profound influence,

---

101. This is not to go along with cliché-ridden assessments of the 1980s advanced by the political left—"the decade of greed" and the like. The hard economic data do not, by and large, support the view that the 1980s were the worst of times economically, except for the very rich, or that most Americans were more greedy in the 1980s than in the 1970s: see the well displayed data in Richard B. McKenzie, *What Went Right in the 1980s* (San Franciso: Pacific Research Institute for Public Policy, 1994).

102. Cf. George Roche, *A World Without Heroes: The Modern Tragedy* (Hillsdale: Hillsdale College Press, 1987).

103. Cf. Robert Wuthnow, *Acts of Compassion: Caring for Others and Helping Ourselves* (Princeton: Princeton Univ. Press, 1991).

104. Phillip E. Hammond, *Religion and Personal Autonomy: The Third Disestablishment in America* (Columbia: Univ. of South Carolina Press, 1992).

it scarcely diminished the enormous influence of organized religion on the public sector. The second disestablishment (by "disestablishment" Hammond means "a qualitative change in the relationship between church and culture"[105]) had occurred by the end of World War I, in a progressive erosion of direct Christian influence, such that until about 1960 the relationship of Christian churches to the cultural core was more custodial than directorial. The third disestablishment, on which Hammond focuses his attention, springs from the emphasis on personal autonomy and its effect on the religious sphere. Personal autonomy has become an ideology that is suspicious of ecclesiastical loyalty and doctrine alike. The new generation does not readily think in terms of service to the church or to God, but in terms of what it can get out of it; they shop around for churches until they find a product they like. The churches themselves feel the pressure to respond to the "consumers" by taking polls to find out what they want.

It is hard to avoid the suspicion that even the contemporary penchant for discovering new victims is tied to modern species of individualism. We have entered an era of multiplying litigation, in which punitive compensatory damages are ardently sought, less out of a passion for dispassionate justice than out of passionate greed, out of vengeful pettiness that feeds on newly discovered forms of "victimization." *They* haven't been fair to *me*. Under the impact of philosophical pluralism, the new individualism believes that no ideology or value is intrinsically superior to any other, and therefore that no single *individual's* heritage is in any respect inferior. To think otherwise is to display cultural bias. There are not a few ironies, as Sowell reminds us:

> Any group whose past has not provided them with as many heroes, cultural contributions, or other glories as some other group's past now has a grievance against those who write history. Apparently a past to your liking has become an entitlement.
>
> It is not even considered necessary to demonstrate any reality before claiming that a group's "under-representation" in history books shows "exclusion" or "bias." Many of those who argue this way also loudly proclaim the many injustices suffered by the various under-represented groups. Yet, somehow, these pervasive injustices are not regarded as having inhibited the achievements of those who suffered them. Such is the self-contradictory vision of multiculturalists.[106]

---

105. Ibid., xiv.

106. Thomas Sowell, *Is Reality Optional? and Other Essays* (Stanford: Hoover Institution Press, 1993), 4.

8. Freudian Fraud

As scientism (as opposed to science) has sought to reduce human nature and conduct to matter, energy, time, and chance; as the social sciences have sometimes skewed data to arrive at conclusions that will undermine morality,[107] so the influence of Freud, whatever good it has produced, has been pervasive and often malign. Criticisms have gradually mounted, and have recently become extensive and well-documented.[108] Freud's influence extends well beyond those who would identify their brand of psychoanalysis as essentially Freudian. Directly or indirectly, it has fostered our therapeutic culture, in which the substitution of medical and quasi-scientific terminology for moral, ethical, and religious categories, to the enormous benefit of therapists and support groups, has bulldozed moral responsibility into the nearest landfill, and invented new "ailments du jour."[109] Once again, this is not to say that no positive advances have been made: such a conclusion would be both ignorant and mischievous. But the damage, as Torrey documents, is incalculable.[110]

The therapeutic culture has so invaded the church that some seminaries now have more students enrolled in counseling programs than are training to be preachers of the gospel. Some "evangelical" churches pride themselves on being "Twelve Step" churches, i.e., churches where the "Twelve Step" model of Alcoholics Anonymous is taken as the controlling model for support groups dealing with everything from addiction to obesity to codependency to problems with self-esteem. Relatively few pastors have both the training and the courage to deal with genuine problems in *biblical* categories that challenge the therapeutic culture at multiple levels.[111] In the realm of biblical scholarship, one can read learned essays with titles like "The Heuristic Value of a Psychoanalytic Model in the Interpretation of Pauline Theology."[112]

---

107. One thinks of the well-documented case of Margaret Mead (on which see a fuller treatment in chap. 5). More generally, see, for example, Robert J. Priest, "Cultural Anthropology, Sin, and the Missionary," in Carson and Woodbridge, *God and Culture*, 85–105.

108. See, for example, O. Hobart Mowrer, *The Crisis in Psychiatry and Religion* (Princeton: Van Nostrand, 1961); Karl Menninger, *Whatever Became of Sin?* (New York: Hawthorn, 1975); Jeffrey Moussaieff Masson, *The Assault on Truth: Freud's Suppression of the Seduction Theory* (Harmondsworth: Penguin, 1985); Robert C. Roberts, *Taking the Word to Heart: Self and Other in the Age of Therapies* (Grand Rapids: Eerdmans, 1993); and especially E. Fuller Torrey, *Freudian Fraud: The Malignant Effect of Freud's Theory on American Thought and Culture* (New York: HarperCollins, 1992).

109. The expression is that of Charles Sykes, in *Imprimus* 21/7 (July 1992): 1.

110. *Freudian Fraud*, see above n. 108.

111. See Robert C. Roberts, "Psychobabble," *Christianity Today* 38/6 (May 16, 1994): 18–24.

112. Robin Scroggs, *The Text and the Times: New Testament Essays for Today* (Minneapolis: Fortress Press, 1993), 125–50.

The point is that the Freudian model, locked in naturalism, has both reinforced and been reinforced by philosophical pluralism. The loss of truth and standards "out there," in objective reality, has encouraged this inward focus, this self-absorption. It is a long way from the perspective that teaches that the first commandment is to love God, and the second is to love one's neighbor—from which of course we must infer that the first sin is not to love God, and the second is not to love one's neighbor. It is a long way from the instruction of him who insisted that those who seek their own life will lose it, while those who take up their cross daily and follow him will find life, eternal life (Matt. 16:21–28; Mark 8:31–9:1; Luke 9:22–27).[113]

D. Summary and Reflections

In aiming for a measure of clarity in a confusing discussion, I have distinguished empirical pluralism, cherished pluralism, and philosophical pluralism. The first is merely a useful label for referring to the growing diversity in most Western countries. The reality is neither intrinsically good nor intrinsically bad, though clearly it spawns elements of both. The second category is cherished pluralism: the empirical reality is highly praised in many quarters as a fundamentally good thing, though many disagree, circle the wagons, and retreat to their own subculture. The third category, philosophical pluralism, is at bottom an epistemological stance: it buys into a basket of theories about understanding and interpretation that doubts whether objective truth is accessible, and locates most if not all meaning in the interpreter, not in the text or object interpreted. This step distinguishes postmodernity from modernity; an extension of this step is deconstruction.

The impact of philosophical pluralism on Western culture is incalculable. It touches virtually every discipline—history, art, literature, anthropology, education, philosophy, psychology, the social sciences, even, increasingly, the "hard" sciences—but it has already achieved popularity in the public square, even when its existence is not recognized. It achieves its greatest victory in redefining religious pluralism so as to render heretical the idea that heresy is possible. Tolerance is radically redefined, and masks a sometimes brutal intolerance, at times in the faddish categories of PC ("political correctness"). It has contributed to the destruction of gratitude, and turned not a few women and men into chronic whiners and finger-pointers. For the Christian, it has certainly altered some of the priorities that must be adopted in evangelism.

What I have called the "correlatives" of pluralism are no less significant. They are not exclusively causes of philosophical pluralism, nor are they exclu-

---

113. See Paul C. Vitz, *Psychology as Religion: The Cult of Self-Worship*, 2d ed. (Grand Rapids: Eerdmans, 1994).

sively effects. They are fellow travelers, and doubtless within various elements of society at any given time they are more one than the other. Eight were briefly described and discussed: secularization, New Age theosophy, rising biblical illiteracy, vague appeals to the cosmic Christ, the sheer pragmatism of baby busters, the hegemony of pop culture, rugged individualism veering toward narcissism, and Freudian fraud. The selection is arbitrary: it is based on personal impressions of what elements are important. But it would not take much imagination to extend the list.

Much of the rest of this book is an attempt to understand and evaluate these developments and to think our way forward from within the Christian framework. This is not the place to anticipate the discussion, but two things may usefully be said.

First, all but the most sanguine pluralists admit that there are immense dangers ahead and that signs of cultural decay abound. Where we differ is in both diagnosis and solution. But let no one doubt that although the issues discussed in this book are in the first instance intellectual challenges, and occasionally difficult intellectual challenges, they are fraught with practical implications for church and society alike. Writing of only one small part of the broader problem, namely the single-minded pursuit of individualistic "rights," Feder is not wrong to conclude:

> Absent a delicate balance—rights and duties, freedom and order—the social fabric begins to unravel. The rights explosion of the past three decades has taken us on a rapid descent to a culture without civility, decency, or even that degree of discipline necessary to maintain an advanced industrial civilization. Our cities are cesspools, our urban schools terrorist training camps, our legislatures brothels where rights are sold to the highest electoral bidder.[114]

Or as Colson puts it:

> As Dorothy Sayers observed:
> "In the world it is called Tolerance, but in hell it is called Despair ... the sin that believes in nothing, cares for nothing, seeks to know nothing, interferes with nothing, enjoys nothing, hates nothing, finds purpose in nothing, lives for nothing, and remains alive because there is nothing for which it will die."[115]

Second, it is imperative that we remind ourselves how innovative philosophical pluralism is. When Machen confronted the impact of modernism

---

114. Don Feder, *A Conservative Jew Looks at Pagan America* (Lafayette: Huntingdon House, 1993), 219.

115. Cited by Charles Colson, with Ellen Santilli Vaughn, in *Against the Night: Living in the New Dark Ages* (Ann Arbor: Servant Books, 1989), 93.

on Christianity, his driving point was that the liberalism of his day, whatever it was, was not Christianity at all, even though that was the way it paraded itself.[116] At least he recognized what was at stake, and addressed the fundamental issues. Today we must recognize that philosophical pluralism is not only non-Christian (though some Western pluralists think of themselves as Christians), but that the nature of the relativism it spawns and the worldliness that it engenders are in some respects qualitatively new, and must be addressed in fresh terms. Many generations have recognized how difficult it is for finite and sinful mortals to come to close agreement as to the objective truth of this or that subject, but this is the first generation to believe that there is no objective truth out there, or that if there is, there is no access to it. This necessarily changes the character of at least some of the debate.

For example, a bare fifteen years ago, Stephen Sykes, arguing that tolerance for theological diversity must not be adopted unquestioningly but must be justified by argument, wrote the following:

> A Christian Church which is aware of a wide variety of diverse theological positions and which deliberately decides not to adopt one of them, but rather to tolerate diversity, still has to offer a definite reason for doing so and to justify that reason in the face of objection.... Toleration of diversity itself needs to be justified theologically if it is to be able to claim any kind of integrity.[117]

Modernists may be impressed by the reasonableness of this argument; postmodernists will be entirely unimpressed. If their understanding of understanding is correct, if their deployment of radical hermeneutics is correct, the notion of a coherent theological position that a church adopts to the exclusion of others can never be more than a socially determined preference, which is scarcely what Sykes has in mind.

And that is the challenge.

---

116. J. Gresham Machen, *Christianity and Liberalism* (Grand Rapids: Eerdmans, 1923).

117. *The Integrity of Anglicanism* (New York: Seabury, 1978), 7–8; cited in Jerry L. Walls, "What Is Theological Pluralism?" *Quarterly Review* 5 (Fall 1985): 61.

Part One

—

HERMENEUTICS

Chapter 2

THE TAMING OF TRUTH: THE HERMENEUTICAL MORASS

All the challenges arising from postmodernism and philosophical pluralism are connected in some way with *hermeneutics*, with how we interpret things. Postmodernism is an outlook that depends not a little on what are perceived to be the fundamental limitations on the power of interpretation: that is, since interpretation can never be more than *my* interpretation or *our* interpretation, no purely objective stance is possible. Granted this conviction about the nature of the interpretative enterprise, philosophical pluralism infers that objective truth in most realms is impossible, and that therefore the only proper stance is that which disallows all claims to objective truth.

The study of hermeneutics has absorbed so much creative energy during the last few decades, sometimes expended by brilliant minds, that its complexity keeps multiplying. So far as hermeneutics is concerned, Mark Twain's famous quip cannot fairly be applied, but it does leap to mind: "The researches of many commentators have already thrown much darkness on this subject, and it is probable that, if they continue, we shall soon know nothing at all about it."

What follows, then, is the merest sketch, as fair as I can make it, of the most important developments. The following chapter will consider appropriate responses the Christian might offer, applauding what is surely on the right track and deploring what is merely naturalistic and finally nihilistic.

A. Modernity: Moving Toward the Morass

Generalizations about the march of history are almost always reductionistic. The patterns of history are rarely neat: remarkable contradictions coexist, and different groups within any one society can in some measure "belong" to remarkably different eras. In America, "young earth" science flourishes against a backdrop of naturalistic evolution; "King James Only" fundamentalists are fellow citizens both with those who purchase any translation that rolls off the presses, and with those who deny that objective revelation is a coherent concept; Bible Belt believers occupy the same decade as New England secularists. But provided they are not taken too absolutely, generalizations introduce some legitimate order to mere details, and thereby foster responsible evaluation.

So for convenience, it is helpful to join the many scholars who view Descartes as the transitional figure at the beginning of the period labeled modernity. In 1619 Descartes set himself the task of doubting everything, and from that stance trying to find some solid base of certainty on which he could build an entire philosophy. His pivotal work, *Discourse on Method*, published in 1637,[1] blazed a trail others followed. But we must not think that it was the result of pure, dispassionate thought. The revival of classical learning during the previous century and a half, the extraordinary political and social ferment of the seventeenth century, the relative freedom from monolithic ecclesiastical control achieved by the magisterial Reformation, and the dislocation caused by the barbarisms of the Thirty Years' War all doubtless contributed to the desire for certainty in shifting times.[2] And Descartes himself, of course, was trying to overthrow the skeptics of his day.[3]

Whatever the immediate incitement, the work of Descartes and his successors attempted to ground all knowledge in infallible reason. His famous axiom, "I think, therefore I am" (though generations of philosophers have questioned just how axiomatic it really is), served Descartes and his immediate followers well, providing a foundation on which to build. But a number of important developments ensued.

First, this formulation begins with the "I," the "knower," the subject, whose very existence is predicated on the mere fact that this subject "thinks." From this point on there is a fundamental disjunction between this subject

---

1. This has been published in many formats. One that is readily accessible is found in *Descartes, Spinoza*, Great Books of the Western World, vol. 31 (Chicago: Encyclopaedia Britannica, 1952).

2. See, for example, the discussion of Stephen Toulmin, *Cosmopolis: The Hidden Agenda of Modernity* (New York: Free Press, 1990), 70–71.

3. Cf. Richard H. Popkin, *The History of Skepticism from Erasmus to Spinoza* (Berkeley: Univ. of California Press, 1979), esp. 172–92. Of course, there were skeptics long before Descartes's day, but Descartes has the effect of teaching skeptics to pursue philosophical certainty. Cf. also E. M. Curley, *Descartes Against the Skeptics* (Cambridge: Harvard Univ. Press, 1978). How successful Descartes was in answering the skeptics of his day has been warmly debated. Certainly he was taken up later in quite different ways, e.g., by the Jansenists and by Spinoza.

and all objects. Of course, all other human beings, on this view, experience a similar subject/object distinction, and each one thinks of himself or herself as the subject. If what each subject "knows" differs with or even contradicts what other subjects "know," the objectivity of this knowledge will sooner or later be called into question. Not that Descartes himself envisaged such an outcome—but such an outcome is precisely what occurred. This is quite different from a view that holds that there is an omniscient God (who by definition truly knows everything), so that from his perspective all human beings are "objects," and all their true knowing is but a subset of his knowing. In other words, the Cartesian subject/object disjunction, by disallowing God at this foundational step,[4] unwittingly set the stage for a later rising skepticism.

Doubtless some have dealt with Descartes too harshly. Even his *cogito ergo sum* is not without merit. If it is meant as a deductive argument by which one proves one's own existence, it is fallacious. But if it is taken as a response to a skeptic, showing that there is something of which one can be certain—namely, the existence of a thinking subject—it seems hard to fault.[5] Nevertheless, Descartes's dictum generated a trajectory of thought, the Cartesian subject/object gap, that continues to this day as a fundamental problem in Western epistemology.

Second, increasingly the assumption for many thinkers in the period of modernity was that certainty, absolute epistemological certainty (and not just

---

4. This is not to say that Descartes was an atheist, but only that his fundamental axiom took nothing of God into account, even though he himself seems to have ascribed his findings to God. On the very night he embarked on his enterprise, November 10, 1619, he had three consecutive dreams that he imagined could only have come "from on high" (Norman Kemp Smith, *New Studies in the Philosophy of Descartes: Descartes as Pioneer* [London: Macmillan, 1952], 33, referring to information taken from Adrien Baillet's notes of Descartes's diary, which is no longer extant). Apparently he vowed that he would devote his life to this new science, and as thanks vowed to visit the shrine of Our Lady of Lareto (T. Z. Lavine, *From Socrates to Sartre: The Philosophic Quest* [Toronto: Bantam Books, 1984], 87). In a personal communication, Carl F. H. Henry comments, "It's noteworthy that modern philosophy takes its rise with a Jesuit in epistemic difficulty."

5. In a private communication, my colleague Harold Netland writes (I have slightly edited his note): "I find it fascinating that essentially the same move is made centuries earlier by Augustine (who is usually held up as a positive counter-example to the errors of Descartes) in his response to skepticism, a problem to which Augustine repeatedly returned. Augustine's formulation is *si fallor sum*—'If I am mistaken, then I am.' Augustine does not present this as an argument. His point rather is to show that there are certain things we can know directly, i.e., immediately and non-inferentially, in this case our own existence (cf. *Soliloquies* II.1.1; *On Free Will* iii.7; *On Tradition* xxxix.73; *On the Trinity* X.10; XV.12). I think both Augustine and Descartes are correct in pointing out that reflection upon the knowing process indicates that there are some things we can be certain of—even prior to bringing in the question of God and divine revelation."

a psychological feeling),[6] was not only desirable but attainable.[7] More and more, those who pleaded for categories like mystery or hidden truths were dismissed with scorn. One suspects that the emphasis on certainty sprang less from well-formed epistemological theory than from a skewed view of what certainty is. Descartes's famous expression "clear and distinct ideas" probably owes much to a mathematical paradigm of knowledge. The result is that for him, knowledge has the same degree of certainty attached to it that mathematics enjoys. Fueled by the intellectual achievements of the Enlightenment, by the scientific and manufacturing achievements of the industrial revolution, and by the economic achievements of empire and of rising standards of living, optimism grew among the intellectual élites during most of the nineteenth century, and in the population at large until the twentieth century. And this optimism triumphed as much in the epistemological arena as in any other: what we did not yet know, we soon would. Thus until fairly recently, the "quest for certainty"[8] was judged to be both inevitable and entirely salutary by most thinkers from the Western world. This quest for certainty was supported by seminal thinkers like Locke, Kant, and Hegel; it reached out to embrace almost every discipline.

In due course I shall argue that the quest for certainty is not entirely wrong. The (in)famous dictum of Leopold von Ranke in the nineteenth century, that history is nothing other than the discipline that discovers "*wie es eigentlich gewesen war*" (i.e., how it actually had been, what actually happened), can be read sympathetically.[9] But the fact of the matter is that as this quest for certainty manifested itself in various disciplines, it was increasingly characterized by more hubris than realism. This is not surprising: at the epistemological level God had been left out of the equation, making it impossible to cross the Cartesian gap.[10]

---

6. Cf. Lesslie Newbigin, "Certain Faith: What Kind of Certainty?" *Tyndale Bulletin* 44 (1993): 339–50.

7. This is not to deny there were other voices, some of which are given scope in chap. 3.

8. The phrase is John Dewey's: *The Quest for Certainty: A Study of the Relation of Knowledge and Action* (New York: Capricorn Books, 1929).

9. For an exposition of what it meant for von Ranke, and for a history of American history since then, see Peter Novick, *That Noble Dream: The "Objectivity Question" and the American Historical Profession* (Cambridge: Cambridge Univ. Press, 1988).

10. Novick's work (see n. 9) also shows that in the guild of historians, the "relativist critique" during the interwar years challenged the central, sacred passion for "objectivity," putting the objectivists on the defensive. This gave rise to a new synthesis after World War II and during the cold-war years, in which chastened objectivists criticized the objectivist critique by partially incorporating it. Novick argues that since that time the historical profession has witnessed the collapse of the postwar synthesis and has succumbed to confusion, polarization, and uncertainty, in which notions of historical objectivity have become more problematic than ever before. But that is to anticipate our survey.

Third, the way thinkers built up their knowledge and ordered it was commonly foundationalist—i.e., it was presupposed that one must adopt certain foundations for one's knowledge.[11] The foundations might be "self-evident" truths or incontestable sense-data, but only on the basis of such foundations can one certainly infer entire superstructures of thought that are then added to the foundations. Thus empiricists (building on sense-data) and rationalists (building on self-evident truths) alike are foundationalists.[12]

Fourth, characteristic of modernity is the confidence in method. Any particular subject-matter could be studied with confidence provided the foundations and the methods were in place. "Knowledge, truth, was now open to man: all he had to do, in any area of knowledge, was to apply the method. Man starts in ignorance and confusion, but by application of the method is led towards light and truth."[13] Tradition is largely irrelevant, and may be obscurantist; method is everything. A term which some espouse to describe modernity's linking of foundationalism with method is objectivism: adequate foundations plus appropriate method ensure a corpus of objective knowledge.[14]

Fifth, naturalism was in the ascendancy among the intellectual elite. In America in the nineteenth century, as in America and Britain in the eighteenth century, many intellectuals engaged in doxological science—science to the glory of God. But the times were changing. Not a few thinkers, though formally Christians, gravitated toward naturalistic explanations of everything, not least when they couched their explanations in a pious (and often implicitly deist) framework.[15] Philosophical naturalism was gradually winning: the only things to be taken into account in all human knowledge were matter, energy, time, and chance. It is not surprising, then, that in Peter Gay's influential treatment of the Enlightenment, the ultimate hero-protagonist is the

---

11. See especially Alvin Plantinga, "Reason and Belief in God," in *Faith and Rationality: Reason and Belief in God*, ed. Alvin Plantinga and Nicholas Wolterstorff (Notre Dame: Univ. of Notre Dame Press, 1983), 48.

12. Ibid., 358–59.

13. Andrew Louth, *Discerning the Mystery: An Essay on the Nature of Theology* (Oxford: Clarendon Press, 1983), 7. More broadly, see A. Schouls, *The Imposition of Method* (Oxford: Oxford Univ. Press, 1980). At a more popular level, see Jacques Ellul, *The Technological Society* (New York: Random House, 1967).

14. See Richard Bernstein, *Beyond Objectivism and Relativism: Science, Hermeneutics, and Praxis* (Philadelphia: Univ. of Pennsylvania Press, 1985), 8.

15. This is not to say that deism is a subset of theism, rather than of naturalism. But the drift from theism to teism was certainly accelerated by the rise of naturalism, just as naturalism was aided by the drift from theism to deism. One recalls Thomas Paine's famous dictum about rejecting "the Book of God's Words" for "the Book of God's Works" as the universal voice of revelation.

man perhaps most commonly associated with skepticism toward all things supernatural, David Hume.[16]

Sixth, many of these ideals of modernity found a home, and displayed their most amazing victories, in the natural sciences. The subject/object distinction, the passion for certainty and precision, the foundationalist nature (in the empirical tradition) of scientific research, the passion for well-defined method, the drift toward philosophical naturalism—all these features have been (and often still are) nicely displayed in modern science. This is not to deny that many of the roots of science lie in a distinctively Christian worldview,[17] a dimension often ignored or skated over in even the best treatments of the rise of science.[18] Rather, it is to acknowledge that the tremendous advances of modern science have been achieved within a framework of thought increasingly dominated by the characteristics of modernity. The triumphs of science have thus served, until very recent times, as modernity's prime trumpet blower.

Two consequences of these scientific triumphs demand notice. The first is the constant pressure felt by the "soft" sciences for more precision, more mathematics, more predictive successes, more technical language. Psychiatry, sociology, anthropology, and several other disciplines have felt the impact of physics and chemistry. Second, and more importantly, the successes of science within the worldview of modernity have fostered an important disjunction that went largely unchallenged until the last few decades. That is the disjunction between fact and opinion. Science, we were assured, deals with facts; some domains embrace a mixture of fact and opinion; still others reside almost completely within the contours of mere opinion. Science deals with facts; religion, it is (still) popularly believed, deals almost entirely with opinion.

It is not surprising, then, that toward the end of the nineteenth century and well into the twentieth, science was often associated with positivism in epistemology. Indeed, scientific knowledge became the model for all knowledge: data had to be obtained empirically, or they were suspect. Meanwhile

---

16. Peter Gay, *The Enlightenment: An Interpretation. The Rise of Modern Paganism* (New York: Knopf, 1967), passim, esp. 419: "Hume, therefore, more decisively than many of his brethren in the Enlightenment, stands at the threshold of modernity and exhibits its risks and its possibilities. Without melodrama but with the sober eloquence one would expect from an accomplished classicist, Hume makes plain that since God is silent, man is his own master: he must live in a disenchanted world, submit everything to criticism, and make his own way."

17. See especially R. J. Hooykaas, *Religion and the Rise of Modern Science* (Edinburgh: Scottish Academic Press, 1972); Malcolm A. Jeeves, *The Scientific Enterprise and the Christian Faith* (London: Tyndale Press, 1969); and especially Eugene M. Klaaren, *Religious Origins of Modern Science* (Grand Rapids: Eerdmans, 1977).

18. E.g., Herbert Butterfield, *The Origins of Modern Science 1300–1800* (New York: Free Press, 1965).

religion, relegated to the category of mere opinion, was necessarily based on "faith." Such "faith" was assumed to be making a bogus claim if it pretended to knowledge, which of course had to be empirically based. "Faith" was merely a privatized opinion. It had little to do with the public arena, and less and less claim on public learning or morals. It could be judged pious and even beneficial only if it remained private, a personal opinion, and in that guise seemed to exercise some socially useful influence in a person's life; it would be denounced as narrow and bigoted if it claimed universal applicability. Faith must be made subject to reason. "Reason must be our last judge and guide in everything," wrote Locke.[19] Locke's views on the relationship between faith and reason were complex and nuanced (he certainly did not want reason to be entirely freestanding). But his dictum was influential. Others ran with it, and where "reason" is then connected, not with logic and coherence, but with empiricism, faith is progressively squeezed to the peripheral and the private.

Seventh, modernity is characterized by the conviction that its findings achieve what Stiver calls "an ahistorical universality"—that is, that what modernity discerns to be the truth is "true for everyone, at all times, in the same way."[20] Indeed, Lyotard holds that modernity's prime characteristic is its dependence on "meta-narratives" (i.e., on universal "narratives" or accounts of reality, of the way things are), and these "meta-narratives" are objectively true: they transcend (or at least claim to transcend) time and circumstance.[21] These "meta-narratives" include Marxism, Hegel's theory of universal spirit, the post-Enlightenment view of progress, and, in theology, the view that we should accept as rational in the field of theology only what is judged rational by any reasonable and intelligent person[22]—which often means any person who adopts naturalistic presuppositions in the determination of what can be known.

These meta-narratives are breaking down: Marxists are not as plentiful as they used to be; Hegel's universal spirit eventually collapsed under the desks of Søren Kierkegaard and those who followed him; the idea that progress is

---

19. *Essay*, IV.xix.14.

20. Dan R. Stiver, "Much Ado About Athens and Jerusalem: The Implications of Postmodernism for Faith," *Review and Expositor* 91 (1994): 88.

21. Jean-François Lyotard, *The Postmodern Condition: A Report on Knowledge*, trans. Geoff Bennington and Frian Massumi, *Theory and History of Literature*, vol. 10 (Minnepolis: Univ. of Minnesota Press, 1984), xxiii–xxiv, 27–37.

22. See, for example, Bernard J. F. Lonergan, *Method in Theology*, Seabury Library of Contemporary Theology (New York: Crossroad, 1979), chaps. 1–2; David Tracy, *Blessed Rage for Order: The New Pluralism in Theology*, Seabury Library of Contemporary Theology (New York: Crossroad, 1979), 6–8. These examples are cited by Stivers, "Implications of Postmodernism," 100.

inevitable has been sandbagged by two world wars, the Great Depression, Vietnam, and dawning realization of the world's limited resources. Even the naturalist assumption in theology is being questioned. But as they break down, the sheer hubris of modernity is exposed. Doubtless many ages have suffered under the conviction that truth and a proper perception of reality are the peculiar prerogative of the contemporary thinker. Modernity raised this stance to a philosophical necessity, tied as it was to "science" and "progress" and method and naturalism.

Eighth, this framework of thought has massively influenced academic theology during the past quarter millennium or so. We can find the traces everywhere. The subject/object distinction meant that hermeneutics was understood as that science of biblical interpretation in which I, the subject, interpreted the text, the object. What was required was rigorous method, a point drilled into every doctoral student. As naturalism gained the ascendancy, the historical-critical method (that word again!), which implicitly assumed an increasingly naturalistic horizon, began to dictate what could or could not be "proved" from history by appealing to such method. Again and again theories of provenance or reconstruction were graced by such rubrics as "the assured results of modern criticism." Scientific terminology and attitudes became pervasive, not least in attitudes toward the "progress" of the discipline: previous ages were seen as ensnared in medieval allegory, Reformation dogmatics, or revivalist enthusiasm, whereas the theological theories espoused by modernity were thought to achieve ahistorical universality; and those who could not see their way to acknowledging the point were eccentric scholars at best, fundamentalists at worst.

It has to be said that the impact of modernity was felt only marginally less within conservative circles. True, conservatives did not so easily buy into passing critical theories and were less liable to succumb to philosophical naturalism, except in indirect ways. But they wrote many books on hermeneutics that presupposed a rigid subject/object distinction. Even in this century, some Bible colleges and seminaries have given the impression that rigorous training in Greek, Hebrew, and exegesis will almost guarantee an orthodox outcome in one's theology. Until very recently, some of them prided themselves in their ignorance of historical theology, judging it to be more or less a waste of time: learn how to do exegesis, and the right answers will be cranked out. There was almost no reflection on how the culture of our age affects us as we engage in interpretation. Thus if the conclusions of conservative theologians tended to be more in line with traditional orthodoxy than were those of more skeptical colleagues, the approach to the discipline of theology was on many fronts remarkably similar. These similarities are tied to dominant characteristics of modernity.

B. The New Hermeneutic

The danger of such a brief survey, of course, is that it gives the impression of monolithic agreement; invariably life is more complex. Before jumping into the twentieth century, it is worth pausing to recognize that many of the questions that now challenge us enjoy, in one form or another, a long pedigree.

Plato distinguished knowledge (γνῶσις) and opinion (δόξα), and firmly placed faith (πίστις) in the latter category.[23] Of course knowledge for Plato is not based on empirical observation, but is correlated with what is eternal, immutable, absolute. Knowledge means seeing precisely and clearly. Aristotle allowed more space for the empirical than did his mentor, but equally sharply distinguished true knowledge and wisdom from opinion and faith. When one leaps to the Christian era, however, although one of its greatest early thinkers maintained the neo-Platonic distinction between faith and reason, the priorities were reversed. Augustine loved to quote Isaiah 7:9 in Latin (mis)translation: "Unless you believe, you surely will not understand."[24] For Augustine, faith was based on God, his person, his authority. True knowledge is knowledge of the eternal, and it is acquired by faith in him who is eternal. Practical reason doubtless has its place, but it is an inferior place compared with believing, contemplative knowledge. For Augustine, faith precedes reason, faith seeks understanding (as his position is often summarily described).[25] But although by tying faith to the "knowledge" and not the "opinion" side of the equation he thereby transforms one of Plato's points, Augustine's position is possible only on the assumption of the Platonic dichotomy between faith and reason.

Still operating with the same dichotomy, Thomas Aquinas, introduced by his teachers to Aristotle, mastered the literary corpus of Aristotle and christianized him. Reason may precede faith; some true knowledge of God is possible apart from special revelation. Indeed, for Aquinas it is possible to demonstrate the existence of God, the soul, and immortality on the ground of empirical observation alone without any appeal to what would later be called special revelation. But this does not mean that for him natural revelation is salvific: it is clear in *Summa Contra Gentiles* that this is not the case. Moreover, the opening chapters of Book One show that at this juncture Aquinas is concerned to convince Muslims and others in error, and is therefore seeking common ground.

---

23. *The Republic*, Bk. VI.

24. *De libero arbitrio*, ii.6.

25. Viz., *fides quaerens intellectum*—though the expression itself appears not in Augustine, but in Anselm. On Augustine, cf. Dewey Hoitenga, *Faith and Reason from Plato to Plantiga* (Albany: State Univ. of New York Press, 1991), esp. chaps. 3–5.

Nevertheless, for Aquinas, knowledge of something and belief concerning that something are normally mutually exclusive categories: knowledge is based on what is self-evident, and is known with certainty. Normally beliefs are only probable: they are based on opinion. But if the authority is God himself, as when God has revealed something, then certainty is attainable.[26] Thus even if reason plays a more foundational role in the thought of Aquinas than in the thought of Augustine, there are limits to its power, and faith is vital if one is to be saved.

The thing to observe at this juncture is that although major Christian apologists and theologians could differ over something as fundamental as the relationship between faith and reason, the debate was entirely within the framework of a theistic universe, *and none of them doubted that certainty on some points was possible*. Not surprisingly, Luther, concerned as he was with *sola fide* in the context of the justification debates of the sixteenth century, and opposing as he was the many Catholic theologians who were Aristotelians and Thomists, insisted on the priority of faith.[27]

Abandoning theism, however, the English deists and their successors elevated reason over faith. As modernity progressed, the usefulness of faith in the obtaining of knowledge was increasingly depreciated, in proportion as reason gained esteem. *But above all, the realm of certainty was removed from any connection with faith, and left to reason and its devices.* Thus a mere generation after Descartes, Benedict de Spinoza insists that "the Bible leaves reason absolutely free." Indeed the Bible operates in a domain "entirely aloof from ordinary knowledge."[28] The Bible does not "aim at explaining things by their natural causes, but only at narrating what appeals to the popular imagination,"[29] using poetry and narrative to bend the wills of the naive masses. The truly enlightened thinker needs no such devices. The Bible "has no authority over the interpreter's mind. It may govern his actions, but only if he is somewhat unintelligent. If he is truly rational, reason alone will govern his whole life."[30]

Spinoza, in other words, was one of the architects of modernity. But with Immanuel Kant, there was injected into modernity a seed that would grow and grow and ultimately destroy it. No less than others in the movement of

---

26. See *The Summa Theologica of Saint Thomas Aquinas*, trans. Fathers of the English Dominican Province, rev. Daniel J. Sullivan, Great Books of the Western World, vols. 19–20 (Chicago: Encyclopaedia Britannica, 1952), Ia.1.108; Ia.12.12–13; passim.

27. Although in another context, of course, Luther could battle nominalists and Pelagians.

28. Benedict de Spinoza, *A Theologico-Political Treatise*, trans. R. H. M. Elwes (New York: Dover, 1951), 8–10.

29. Ibid., 90.

30. Ibid., 103.

modernity, Kant insisted on absolute intellectual autonomy.[31] But in *The Critique of Pure Reason*, Kant argued for a position that has become an axiom of postmodernism. He argued that the self does not so much discover what is objectively out there in the world, but "*projects* order creatively upon the world."[32] In a much quoted passage, Kant writes:

> Since ... nature's conformity to law rests on the necessary linking of phenomena in experience, without which we could not know any object of the world of the senses, in other words, such conformity rests on the original laws of the intellect, it sounds strange at first, but it is none the less true when I say in respect of these laws of the intellect: *The intellect does not derive its laws (a priori) from nature but prescribes them to nature.*[33]

Thus we can never really know what the world or life is like in themselves, because inevitably we see them through the patterns that our mind, the "transcendental ego," imposes. What we are given is "brute facts"; it is the "transcendental ego" that orders them so as to impose meaning. For Kant, even if we can never really *know* what the world is like, we can and must believe what we think we know of it as true. This response (for him) bridges the abyss. Doubtless some of Kant's successors, who rejected his second and third critiques, developed his theory in directions that would have appalled him, but the fact remains that "in Kant's philosophy, human consciousness begins to be not only the key for discovering reality, but the source of reality itself."[34]

The way had been opened for a struggle within modernity itself. It was not pursued quickly (it would take two centuries before the full implications would be teased out), but relentless developments within modernity were bound to call into question many of its fundamental tenets. This is not the place to trace these developments in any detail,[35] but a few jottings on a hand-

---

31. Immanuel Kant, "What Is Enlightenment?" trans. Carl J. Friedrich, in *The Philosophy of Kant*, ed. Carl J. Friedrich (New York: Modern Library, 1949 [1784]), 132–39.

32. To use the language of Roger Lundin, *The Culture of Interpretation: Christian Faith and the Postmodern World* (Grand Rapids: Eerdmans, 1993), 50.

33. Immanuel Kant, "Prolegomena to Every Future Metaphysics That May Be Presented as a Science," in *The Philosophy of Kant*, 91.

34. Thomas Finger, "Modernity, Postmodernity—What in the World Are They?" *Transformation* 10/4 (October–December 1993): 22. A helpful article on Kant's influence on later subjectivism and relativism is by Patrick Gardner, "German Philosophy and the Rise of Relativism," *The Monist* 64 (1981): 138–54.

35. See Lundin, *The Culture of Interpretation*, and Anthony C. Thiselton, *The Two Horizons: New Testament Hermeneutics and Philosophical Description with Special Reference to Heidegger, Bultmann, Gadamer, and Wittgenstein* (Grand Rapids: Eerdmans, 1980); idem, *New Horizons in Hermeneutics: The Theory and Practice of Transforming Biblical Reading* (Grand Rapids: Zondervan, 1992); Richard E. Palmer, *Hermeneutics: Interpretation Theory in Schleiermacher, Dilthey, Heidegger, and Gadamer* (Evanston: Northwestern Univ. Press, 1969).

ful of key figures may expose some of the contours of this developing critique within the bosom of modernity, and make clear what is new about the new hermeneutic.

Martin Heidegger attacked both the foundationalism that manifested itself in unambiguous subject/object distinctions (he was constantly critiquing the "transcendental subject") and the positivism that spoke of hard facts or brute facts.[36] His concern was to expose the many facets, the "hidden horizons," that are part of our perception of all Being. By "presencing the absent" he tried to show how death, care, and moods are philosophically ignored, but are constitutive of every subject (i.e., every knower). Subjects are never passive receptors of data and experience; that is to ignore complex horizons of our being. Both Kant's transcendental idealism and the positivism of nineteenth- and early twentieth-century science are epistemologically burying the world by a crude reductionism, the world which entirely embraces and saturates all human thought.[37]

Gadamer insists that one cannot escape from preunderstanding, prejudgments, traditions—all the things that one invariably brings to any interpretation. Quite impossibly, the Enlightenment had a prejudice against prejudice.[38] The most we can do is try to become aware of our prejudices and traditions by holding them up for inspection before other traditions.[39] Gadamer sees this as unqualified advantage: modernity deluded itself in thinking it was objective and without presuppositions, and its hidden presuppositions became more dangerous and distorting in precise proportion as they were unacknowledged. In the assessment of Bernstein,

> A pervasive theme in *Truth and Method*, and indeed in all of Gadamer's writings, is the critique of the Cartesian persuasion. Here, too, Gadamer is building on the work of Heidegger, who probed the phenomenon of the modern turn to subjectivity and traced it back to its Cartesian roots. The idea of a basic dichotomy between the subjective and the objective; the conception of knowledge as being a correct representation of what is objective; the conviction that human reason can completely free itself of bias, prejudice, and tradition; the ideal of a universal method by which we can first secure firm foundations of knowledge and then build the edifice of a universal science; the belief that by the power of self-reflection we can transcend our historical context and horizon and know things as they really are in themselves—all of these concepts are subjected to sustained criticism. In

---

36. Some of this attack is anticipated, in distinctly Christian guise, in Abraham Kuyper.

37. Heidegger, *Being and Time* (New York: Harper & Row, 1962 [1927]), esp. 191.

38. Hans-Georg Gadamer, *Truth and Method*, trans. and rev. Joel Weinsheimer and Donald G. Marshall, 2d ed. (New York: Crossroad, 1991), 270.

39. Ibid., 271–77.

this respect there are significant parallels (as well as striking differences) between Gadamer's and Heidegger's critique of Cartesianism.... [40]

Finally, in our look at key figures who critiqued modernity, we should briefly mention that in anticipation of some recent deconstructionists, the later *Wittgenstein* insisted that words have meaning only in the context of a form of life.[41]

It must be said at once that in some ways none of this was new. Sensitive thinkers have often wrestled with the fact that other minds of no less acuity have reached very different conclusions. In 1828, the early John Henry Newman wrote to Blanco White (who exerted some considerable influence on those who became the Tractarians) in these terms:

> We all look at things with our own eyes—and invest the whole face of nature with colors of our own. Each mind pursues its own course and is actuated in that course by ten thousand indescribable incommunicable feelings and imaginings. It would be comparatively easy to enumerate the various external impulses which determine the capricious motion of a floating feather or web, and to express in an algebraical formula the line it describes—so mysterious are the paths of thought. Nay, I might even be tempted to say that on no single point do any two individuals agree—no single object do their minds view from the same spot and in the same light. And this will of course hold good in religious matters. Necessary as it is, that we should all hold the same truths (as we wd. be saved) still each of us holds them in his own way; and differs from his nearest and most loved friends either in the relative importance he gives to them, or in the connected view he takes of them as in his perception of the particular consequences arising from them.
>
> Accordingly I trust I shall always be very slow to quarrel with persons differing from me in matters of *opinion* ..... *is what is a consistent Socinian a worse man than an orthodox believer? I* think him to be worse, but I wish my mind clear on the subject.[42]

It is important to recognize that Newman does not give up for a moment the existence of objective truth. Indeed, a case can be mounted that several of the Tractarians who resigned their Anglican orders and entered the Roman Catholic Church did so at least in part because they longed for certainty, unambiguous authority. The authority of Scripture was insufficient, in their

---

40. Richard J. Bernstein, *Beyond Objectivism and Relativism: Science, Hermeneutics, and Praxis* (Philadelphia: Univ. of Pennsylvania Press, 1983), 36.

41. Ludwig Wittgenstein, *Philosophical Investigations*, trans. G. E. M. Anscome, 3d ed. (New York: Macmillan, 1958), ##19, 23, 241 (cited also by Stivers, "Implications of Postmodernism," 98).

42. Kensington MSS. C. 2, cited by David Newsome, *The Parting of Friends: The Wilberforces and Henry Manning* (Grand Rapids: Eerdmans, 1993 [1966]), 88–89.

view, partly because it was being interpreted in various ways, and partly because the bishops of the Anglican Church, their natural home, seemed to be blowing an uncertain sound. One is tempted to detect something of a similar but altogether contemporary pilgrimage in Tom Howard and Richard John Neuhaus.[43]

But Heidegger, Gadamer, Wittgenstein, and others have pushed beyond this point. Not only is all interpretation contingent, but in most areas of life it is meaningless to talk about objective truth, objective interpretation. And so we arrive at the new hermeneutic. The expression itself was linked in the first instance most closely to the works of Ernst Fuchs and G. Ebeling, but is now used much more widely.

What is envisaged can be pictured, almost caricatured, easily enough. Ms. Smith sets herself the task of reading a text she has never read before—it might even be the Bible. In addition to all the education that she has enjoyed up to this point, she brings with her to the task the total package of who and what she is—her genetic makeup, the shaping of her mind by her culture, including her family life, the emotional shape she is in (which includes both long-term effects, perhaps from sexual abuse she suffered as a child, and short-term effects, brought on by, say, too little sleep, too much alcohol, and the breakup of a lingering affair), the pressures of her other commitments. She has never lived abroad and has no idea just how much she is a product of her age. She is blissfully unaware of most of the epistemic baggage she brings to the text. She happens to begin with the gospel of John, and has no idea that she is imposing, with considerable anachronism, assorted New Age biases on the text.

So how can one speak of a clear subject/object distinction? How can one imagine that the line of inquiry is a straight line from the knower to the text, and the line of data is the same straight line making the return trip? If someone else with quite different baggage were reading the same text, or if Ms. Smith were to read it again several years from now, or even tomorrow, she might "hear" something quite different. In fact, the text makes its own subtle impact on the subject, so that the subject who approaches the text tomorrow *cannot* be exactly the same as she was when she approaches it today. That inevitably means that the questions she asks of the text, and the kinds of answers she can hear, will be subtly altered from the questions she asked and

---

43. By contrast, two centuries earlier a former recusant, William Chillingworth, objected to Roman Catholic claims to infallible authority and defended the right to and importance of private judgment—though admittedly his arguments so tie faith to uncertainty that many of his Protestant colleagues were scandalized. See his *Religion of Protestants: A Safe Way to Salvation* (Oxford: Liechfield, 1638). I am indebted to Alan Hultberg for an unpublished paper on the subject.

the answers she heard on her first approach. Thus instead of a straight line from the knower to the text, what really takes place is better schematized as a circle, a hermeneutical circle: I approach the text today, the text makes its impact on me, I (slightly altered) approach the text again tomorrow, and receive its (slightly altered) impact, and so on, and so on, and so on. The so-called "dual aspect" of hermeneutics focuses simultaneously on text and interpreter.[44] It is what generates a question such as this: "To what extent and in what manner do texts determine and control their own interpretation and to what extent and in what manner is meaning determined by factors lying outside the text in the reading process?"[45]

On this showing, the aim of the exercise *cannot* be the discovery of the objective truth as to what the text "actually says": we simply do not have access to what it "actually says." For us there is no such thing; there is only *interpreted* "truth." The aim of the exercise, then, is not the discovery of objective truth, but *Sprachereignis* ("language-event," to use Fuchs's expression), or *Wortgeschehen* ("word-event" to follow Ebeling).[46] What they refer to is a serendipitous experience on the part of the interpreter that grants to him or her some new insight, an "Aha!" moment of "truth." What we are really coming to understand is ourselves. *"The text . . . becomes a hermeneutical aid in the understanding of present experience."*[47] For Fuchs, even the German word for "understanding" (*Einverständnis*) does not mean what most Germans mean by "understanding": it means something like "mutual understanding" or even "empathy," and is related to an entire experience rather than to conscious thought.[48] "Meaning" is less likely to refer to meaning in the text; indeed, some exponents of the new hermeneutic insist that the only "meaning" is what the subject "sees" or "understands." Certainly no tie is admitted between what the text "means" and authorial intent, not only because we have no

---

44. This is rather different from F. D. E. Schleiermacher, *Hermeneutics: The Handwritten Manuscripts*, ed. Heinz Kimmerle, trans. James Duke and Jack Forstman (Missoula: Scholars Press, 1977), who argues that intepretation must include both "grammatical interpretation" and "technical-psychological interpretation," the latter referring to the effort to apprehend the author's style and personality and distinctive language. But twentieth-century interpreters are no longer interested in the psychology of the author, but rather in the psychology of the interpreter: see Terry Graham, "The Dual Aspect Of Hermeneutics," *Studies in Religion* 22 (1993): 105–16.

45. Robert C. Culley, "Introduction," *Textual Determinacy: Part One*, ed. Robert C. Culley and Robert B. Robinson, *Semeia* 62 (1993): vii.

46. Cf. Thiselton, *Two Horizons*, 343–44—literally "language-event" and "word-happening."

47. G. Ebeling, *Word and Faith* (London: SCM, 1963), 33 (italics his).

48. Strictly speaking, *Verständnis* means understanding; *Einverständnis* means agreement, as one enters *into* understanding.

access to authorial intent other than through the text, but even more because different readers will interpret the text differently, i.e., they find different meanings "in the text," none of which can authoritatively be linked with authorial intent, and all of which are first and foremost meanings in the minds of the interpreters.

Clearly, we have entered a world very different from the world of modernity as previously described. The subject/object distinction has broken down. In this world, foundationalism is a washout;[49] the old distinction between fact and opinion is disappearing from view. The quest for certainty, precision, and ahistorical knowledge of objective truth is judged impossible. "Truth" is not an objective entity; the classic dikes between fact and opinion are springing leaks. Of course, not all the tenets of modernity have been sacrificed. Irrationally, philosophical naturalism (for most advocates of this radical hermeneutics), still holds sway; moreover, I must still say something about the place of science in this new model. But some variation of what once held the status of a minority report advanced only by a few intellectuals is now adopted almost everywhere.

How hard the new hermeneutic is pressed toward sheer subjectivity varies with the interpreter. Gadamer himself, as we shall see in the next chapter, advocated certain important safeguards. If the choice is between the stereotype of modernity and the stereotype of the new hermeneutic, the latter has a lot going for it: in many ways it conforms to our experience of cultural, intellectual, and religious diversity. The challenge, then, is this: once having entered this morass, precisely how can one continue to maintain that there *is* some objective truth "out there" that can serve as an anchor in the swirling currents? Or are we inevitably forced toward "radical hermeneutics"?

C. Radical Hermeneutics:
Deconstruction, Derrida, and Kindred Spirits

At the same time as the new hermeneutic was mushrooming, another movement was unfolding in France, seeded and watered at the beginning of the century by the great French linguist Ferdinand de Saussure. The "structuralism" he advocated has many complex components. For our purposes, it is enough to remember that according to the dictates of structuralism, a word that signifies enjoys no necessary connection with what is signified: there is an arbitrary element in words, an element established by mere convention (as the conversation between Alice and the March Hare reminds us). What a word signifies, then, depends on its place in the total language system, i.e., in

---

49. The destruction of foundationalism was the primary aim in Richard Rorty's first major book, *Philosophy and the Mirror of Nature* (Princeton: Princeton Univ. Press, 1979).

its *structural* position. The structuralist focuses energy on discovering the structure of the text—the linguistic structure not only of the immediate context but also of the overall language usage in a particular society.

Enter Jacques Derrida. He fully recognizes that he is going a stage beyond structuralism. In an important article, in which he recognizes some indirect indebtedness to Nietzsche, Freud, and Heidegger, Derrida argues that structuralism is simply not destructive enough.[50] The critic of other positions implicitly assumes a stance from which he or she criticizes. But that stance is itself a position, no less vulnerable to attack than the position being attacked. It appears, then, that all evaluations of or attacks upon any system of metaphysics are themselves presumptuous.[51]

In its various forms, deconstruction or "deconstructive postmodernism" (to distinguish it from less virulent forms of postmodernism, about which I shall shortly say more) implicitly adopts the more radical insights of the new hermeneutic[52] and some of the insights of structuralism, and goes beyond both. It boldly argues that there is no escape from the hermeneutical circle, none whatsoever. As for words, not only is their meaning constrained by other words (structuralism), but words are viciously self-limiting. In the strongest form of deconstruction, not only is all meaning bound up irretrievably with the knower, rather than with the text, but words themselves never have a referent other than other words, and even then with an emphasis on irony and ambiguity— the "plain meaning" of the text subverts itself. Language cannot in the nature of the case refer to objective reality. Words refer only to other words. If after hearing the sentence "The car across the street is blue," someone were to ask, "Which car?" the answer might be, "The vehicle just behind the panel truck," or "That one" (pointing with the finger). Strictly speaking, then, "car" in the first sentence now refers to the word "vehicle" with its modifers, or to the words that constitute the demonstrative expression "That one." One simply cannot escape the inability of language to refer outside itself. Rorty uses the

---

50. Jacques Derrida, "Structure, Sign, and Play in the Discourse of the Human Sciences," in *The Structuralist Controversy: The Languages of Criticism and the Sciences of Man*, ed. Richard Macksey and Eugenio Donado (Baltimore: Johns Hopkins Univ. Press, 1970), 247–72 (discussion with others occupies 265–72).

51. Of the various deconstructionists, probably Derrida is the most difficult to read, owing partly to a semi-technical vocabulary and partly to his love of paradox and irony. One of his least opaque contributions is "Passions: 'An Oblique Offering,'" in *Derrida: A Critical Reader*, ed. David Wood (Oxford: Blackwell, 1992), 5–35. This volume also includes a useful bibliography of Derrida's works. See also Hugh J. Silverman and Don Ihde, *Hermeneutics and Deconstruction* (Albany: State Univ. of New York Press, 1985).

52. Although a deconstructionist such as Derrida would deny that his enterprise is hermeneutical at all, since that label might suggest that there is a particular meaning to be recovered.

analogy of ancient cosmologists who held that the world rests on the back of an elephant. What, then, supports the elephant? Another elephant. And what supports that elephant? Yet another elephant. The support is nothing but elephants, all the way down. We may reject such a cosmology, but, says Rorty, that is the way it is with words: we have nothing but words all the way down.[53]

Add this perspective to the model of the hermeneutical circle, and one must recognize that texts are intrinsically incapable of conveying objective truth about some objective reality: they keep referring to other texts, and these, too, are in the hands of the interpreters. So not only must the notion of univocal meaning in texts be abandoned, but because meaning finally resides in the interpreter, there are as many meanings as there are interpreters, even if interpreters are multiplied indefinitely. That means no one meaning can ever be thought to be superior to any other meaning; there is no objective basis on which to evaluate them. Philosophy itself must be overthrown as the overseer of truth, for all philosophy uses words: it is bound up with "logocentrism" (the coinage is Derrida's), with word-centeredness, with the "myth" that words and rationality serve as the fulcrum on which true understanding swings.[54] Deconstruction, according to Derrida, is a "decentering" or removal of this fulcrum. Under deconstruction, the central focus of understanding is destroyed, and becomes "a nonlocus in which an infinite number of sign-substitutions come into play."[55]

Among the many inferences to be drawn is that the proper aim of literary criticism, of theology, and of all reading of "texts" (where "text" can refer to almost anything that is being interpreted) is to "deconstruct" merely traditional patterns and methods of interpretation. Long-defended interpretations may be nothing other than manipulative displays of power exercised by some group that is trying to enforce conformity to its heritage. Previously cherished criteria such as coherence and internal consistency are judged largely inapplicable. Instead, meaning is found in the free association of selective words and ideas within the text, even if the association of those ideas results in perceived meanings that destroy other ingredients of the text.

It is not that Derrida thinks texts are meaningless. Rather, he perceives in them a superfluity of meaning.[56] One of the purposes of deconstruction is to

---

53. Richard Rorty, *Consequences of Pragmatism: Essays 1972–1980* (Minneapolis: Univ. of Minnesota Press, 1982), xxxv.

54. Perhaps the most influential of Jacques Derrida's books is *Of Grammatology*, trans. G. Chakrovorty (Baltimore: Johns Hopkins Univ. Press, 1976).

55. Jacques Derrida, *Writing and Difference*, trans. Alan Bass (Chicago: Univ. of Chicago Press, 1978), 280.

56. Cf. also Edgar V. McKnight, *The Postmodern Use of the Bible: The Emergence of Reader-Oriented Criticism* (Nashville: Abingdon Press, 1988), passim.

pick apart a text so as to discover ways in which the text fails to communicate what some might think it is saying. Indeed, Derrida and other deconstructionists, such as Paul de Man, are often at pains to show how a text supports equally well two mutually incompatible interpretations.

A variation of deconstruction theory is found in the writings of Stanley Fish, whose work, unlike Derrida's attempts to reflect theoretical points in the form of his exposition, has the virtue of being readable. Many sociologists have argued that all human knowledge is inevitably tied to some social structure or other. Language itself is a phenomenon within the broader social structure. The way we evaluate things, regard institutions, think about people or programs or theories, is inevitably tied to the social fabric in which we ourselves are embedded.[57] Fish takes this insight to an extreme, and makes it determinative in the articulation of all meaning. Unlike classical hermeneutics, which locates meaning in the text, or the new hermeneutic, which locates meaning in the reader, Fish insists that "it is interpretive communities, rather than either the text or the reader, that produce meanings and are responsible for the emergence of formal features."[58]

Fish offers many illustrations, but one of the most intriguing is the following. One morning he was teaching two courses in the same classroom. The first was studying the relationships between linguistics and literary theory. Toward the end of the class period, Fish wrote on the blackboard the last names of a number of authors he was assigning the class to read:

Jacobs-Rosenbaum

Levin

Thorne

Hayes

Ohman (?)

For those in this interpretive community (i.e., the students of this class), the assignment was clear enough: they were to read the essays by Levin, Thorne, Hayes, and Ohmann in the book edited by Jacobs and Rosenbaum. Fish had put a question mark after "Ohman" because he could not at that moment remember whether that name was spelled with one *n* or two.

The students who entered for the second period were studying seventeenth-century religious poetry. Before they entered the room, Fish put a box around the names on the board he had just written down for the previous

---

57. Perhaps the classic book along these lines is that by Peter L. Berger and Thomas Luckmann, *The Social Construction of Reality: A Treatise in the Sociology of Knowledge* (Harmondsworth: Penguin Books, 1966).

58. Stanley Fish, *Is There a Text in This Class?* (Cambridge: Harvard Univ. Press, 1980), 14.

class, and wrote "p. 43" over this frame. As soon as they were settled, Fish told the students of this new class, this new interpretive community, that what he had written on the board was a poem not unlike those they had been studying. He asked them to interpret it. Predictably, Jacobs was taken as a reference to Jacob's ladder reaching up to heaven. Rosenbaum was German for a rose tree, a reference to the Virgin Mary, a rose without thorns. Thorne referred to Jesus' crown of thorns; Ohman was really "Oh man." Even the shape of the "poem" reminded some members of this interpretive community of the cross. Fish himself explains:

> As soon as my students were aware that it was poetry they were seeing, they began to look with poetry-seeing eyes, that is, with eyes that saw everything in relation to the properties they knew poems to possess. . . . Thus the meanings of the words and the interpretation in which those words were seen to be embedded emerged together. . . .
>
> . . . . Skilled reading is usually thought to be a matter of discerning what is there, but if the example of my students can be generalized, it is a matter of knowing how to *produce* what can thereafter be said to be there. Interpretation is not the art of construing but the art of construction. Interpreters do not decode poems, they make them.[59]

As Long nicely puts it, Fish's point "is that since his class on religious poetry was an interpretive community it operated as just such a community, using the text on the board as an occasion for bringing forth the meanings already present in the group under the guise of discerning meanings in the text. Indeed, there are no meanings as such *in* the text."[60]

Although there are many slants to contemporary deconstruction, certain core perspectives persist. Even Umberto Eco, who perhaps is the one who devotes the greatest percentage of his space to criticizing the interpretive theories of his colleagues and labeling them reductionistic, insists "that to reach an agreement about the nature of a given text does not mean either (a) that the interpreters must trace back to the original intention of its author or (b) that such a text must have a unique and final meaning. . . . But, even though the interpreters cannot decide which interpretation is the privileged one [what an older generation of interpreters would call the 'right' or 'correct' interpretation], they can agree on the fact that certain interpretations are not

---

59. Ibid., 326–27. The same example is cited by Thomas G. Long, *Preaching and the Literary Forms of the Bible* (Philadelphia: Fortress Press, 1989), 27–28. In a private communication, Kirk Allison comments, "Of course, Fish is claiming here that it *really wasn't* a poem (which he performatively made it to be), but rather a reading list. . . . [This example] might also say much about the state of poetry."

60. Ibid., 28.

contextually legitimated."[61] In other words, Eco thinks interpreters can largely agree on what interpretations cannot be accepted as "the privileged one," even while they cannot with precision and certainty agree on what can be accepted.

Limitations of space forbid describing the particular contributions of numerous other deconstructionist thinkers. A few of them will be introduced in the remainder of this chapter and in the next. What is clear is that the focus in interpretation has shifted from the author to the text to the reader. But now it is time to broaden the angle of vision and see how these approaches have made their impact on theology, and in particular on the interpretation of the biblical text.

D. The Disappearance of Objective Truth

It takes little effort to see how radical hermeneutics and deconstruction have provided some of the intellectual underpinnings for postmodernism. Of the eight characteristics of modernity outlined at the beginning of this chapter, only one survives into postmodernity: the widespread assumption of naturalism. Certainly the quest for certainty has gone, along with dependence on a single approved method in each discipline, all forms of foundationalism, and the confident assertion that the "truths" being discovered enjoy an ahistorical universality.[62]

This is true even if we pause to break down postmodernism into various subgroups. There are several ways of doing this. The simplest is to divide postmodernists into two groups—a destructive approach, and a constructive

---

61. Umberto Eco, *The Limits of Interpretation* (Bloomington: Indiana Univ. Press, 1994), 41.

62. It is this analysis that calls into question, I think, the neat breakdown proposed by Thomas C. Oden, *Two Worlds: Notes on the Death of Modernity in America and Russia* (Downers Grove: InterVarsity Press, 1992), and followed by Gene Edward Veith, Jr., *Postmodern Times: A Christian Guide to Contemporary Thought and Culture* (Wheaton: Crossway Books, 1994), 27–28. Oden argues that modernity reigned from 1789, the fall of the Bastille and the beginning of the French Revolution, to 1989, the fall of the Berlin Wall. But this fails to recognize that the move from modernity to postmodernity is primarily *epistemological*. The French Revolution, as significant an event as it was, marked the outworking of many kinds of religious, epistemological, economic, and political shifts; it did not decisively mark a fundamental shift in epistemology. The same could be said about the fall of the Berlin Wall. But although I would argue that my firm linking of postmodernity with epistemological issues is the most useful way of proceeding in our theological analysis of culture, I concede that the term was used with reference to art and literature in the 1960s, and with reference to architecture and style in the 1970s, before it came to be used with reference to radical hermeneutics and deconstruction in the 1980s. See Philip Sampson, "The Rise of Postmodernity," in *Faith and Modernity*, ed. Philip Sampson, Vinay Samuel, and Chris Sugden (Oxford: Regnum Books, 1994), 29–57.

approach.[63] The former is well exemplified in Derrida and, in theology, in Mark C. Taylor (about whom I shall shortly say a little more). The latter, the constructive approach, while self-consciously rejecting modernity, wants to avoid the drift toward intellectual nihilism that radical deconstruction is hard pressed to avoid. Thus David Ray Griffin, for example, tries to retain belief in the meaningfulness of history, and in fundamental distinctions between good and evil. But he achieves this feat by reposing confidence in process philosophy, which defines reality in terms of changing relationships. Inevitably he rejects the Christian insistence that God is omnipotent and omniscient, repudiates "supernatural infallible inspiration or revelation," insisting that God cannot know the future as that would entail "debilitating fatalism or complacent determinism."[64] Temporal divine creation is abandoned in favor of eternal process; consummation as the climax of history is eliminated as it involves an end predetermined by God himself. Human beings should entertain no hope for anything better than what is available to them right now.[65] It is hard not to see in this destruction of eschatology a perennial justification of the *status quo* on the knife edge of time.

This particular constructivist approach to postmodernism is typical. Unable to escape the siren call of postmodernity, yet unwilling to succumb to its most frightening implications, the constructivists insist that humanity does share some values and truths, in practice if not in theory, and, *mirabile dictu*, they turn out to support various "green" theories: pacifism, radical feminism, and Whiteheadian metaphysics. Some of the old agendas of modernity remain, but they are now recast. Nominally less strident because they are cast not in terms of truth, but in terms of equality, relationships, and tolerance, they resurface as politically correct items meeting all the demands of pluralism. This is not to say that all the appeals are wrong (whatever "wrong" means under postmodernity), but that the emperor has finally discovered he has no clothes, and that instead of getting properly suited up, he has grabbed a rag or two, an old bedsheet, and a soiled tissue, and has convinced himself he is setting the new fashion standards.

There are more exacting analyses of the varieties of postmodernity and of the responses postmodernity has called forth.[66] Moreover, I should

---

63. So, for example, David Ray Griffin, "Postmodern Theology and A/theology," in *Varieties of Postmodern Theology*, ed. David Ray Griffin (Albany: State Univ. of New York Press, 1989), 29–61; Carl F. H. Henry, "Reflections on Postmodernity," unpublished paper, a copy of which was kindly given to me by the author.

64. Griffin, "Postmodern Theology," 50.

65. On process theology, it is still useful to read Royce Gruenler, *The Inexhaustible God: Biblical Faith and the Challenge of Process Theism* (Grand Rapids: Baker, 1983).

66. One of the best succinct breakdowns is from Stivers, "Much Ado," 93: "I would identify at least six major postmodern families ... : (1) the hermeneutical philosophy based especially

acknowledge that some avant-garde intellectuals are already announcing the impending death of postmodernity. Certainly there are some *individuals* who have passed through postmodernity and emerged on the other side, casting about gamely for another worldview. But at the moment there is no pattern on the horizon to replace postmodernism, and as far as I can see the giant wave of the movement has not yet crested, or even come close. In any case, instead of exploring such matters I shall turn instead to three areas where postmodernity has made an impact of great importance for the themes of this book.

1. Theology

Perhaps the most useful analysis of the ways in which theology has responded to postmodernity is offered by Griffin, who identifies four postmodern theologies:[67]

a. A thorough capsize to deconstructive postmodernism, often espoused by literary critics in their readings of the Bible, with no reading ever declared incorrect or exclusively correct;

b. Liberationist postmodernism, which tends to divert attention from metaphysical questions in favor of urgent response to political and social injustices;

c. Constructive postmodernism, which argues that some sort of metaphysics is still possible, and which usually opts for some form of process theology;

d. Conservative or restorationist postmodernism, which accepts some of the insights from postmodernism (and from modernism too, for that

---

on the work of Hans-Georg Gadamer and Paul Ricoeur, which grew out of the traditions of both existentialism and phenomenology; (2) the thought of the later Wittgenstein; and (3) the philosophy of science characterized by people like Michael Polanyi, Thomas Kuhn, and Stephen Toulmin. To these may be added (4) the neo-Reformed epistemology of Alvin Plantinga and Nicholas Wolterstorff; (5) French post-structuralism, including the thought of Jacques Derrida, Michel Foucault, and Jean-Francois Lyotard; and (6) American neo-pragmatism, including the work of Richard Rorty, Jeffrey Stout, and Cornel West."

67. David Ray Griffin, "Introduction: Varieties of Postmodern Theology," in *Varieties of Postmodern Theology*, ed. Griffin, 1–7. His argument is nicely summarized by Millard J. Erickson, *Evangelical Interpretation: Perspectives on Hermeneutical Issues* (Grand Rapids: Baker, 1993), 102–3: "In theology, one could include the narrativist approaches of Hans Frei, George Lindbeck, James McClendon, and Stanley Hauerwas that bear a family resemblance to the thought of the later Wittgenstein; the revisionist theology of the Chicago school of Langdon Gilkey and the later David Tracy, which is heavily influenced by the hermeneutical philosophy of Gadamer and Riceour [*sic*]; liberation theology; and the anti-modernist approaches of theologians such as Thomas Oden." Cf. also the slightly different breakdown of Stivers, "Much Ado," 93.

matter), but argues that insights from the premodern period have been too long ignored. This stance is not simply a call to go backward, in that it does interact with and partially accept postmodern critique.

Of course, this is a somewhat artificial schema. Not all postmodernists are so easily categorized. Nevertheless, the most radical theologians are easy to identify, and some elements of their work must be grasped. For them, the radical deconstruction of Derrida must be adopted, and with it, for the most extreme of them, frank atheism—or, in the words of Mark Taylor, "the hermeneutic of the death of God." Taylor adds, "The insights released by deconstructive criticism suggest the ramifications of the death of God for areas as apparently distinct as contemporary psychology, linguistics, historical analysis."[68] Inevitably, this leads him to "an ontology of relativism."[69] Taylor is not alone. The brilliant German social philosopher Jürgen Habermas, finally cajoled into trying to spell out the implications of his postmodernism for theology, is only a whisker from functional atheism.[70]

But neither Taylor nor Habermas is the dominant voice of theological postmodernity. In America at least, that honor would have to go to David Tracy, and he is less easy to pin down. In a number of important books, Tracy argues that theology, a thoroughly hermeneutical enterprise, is nothing other than a particular approach to truth. Related to three publics (the academy, society, and the Church), theology is engaged in interdisciplinary "conversation" or "discussion" on human understanding, which includes the "mystery" of authentic human existence, the "transcendent" dimension of human thought. Such global and interdisciplinary conversation is the only thing that can save theology from mere ideology, which will inevitably be marginalized. Tracy insists there is no fleeing the Enlightenment: theology must work itself out in line with "secular standards for knowledge and action initiated by the Enlightenment."[71]

---

68. Mark C. Taylor, *Erring* (Chicago: Univ. of Chicago Press, 1984), 6.

69. Mark C. Taylor, *Deconstructing Theology* (New York: Crossroad, 1982), 45–65.

70. See Don Browning and Francis Schüssler Fiorenza, eds., *Habermas, Modernity, and Public Theology* (New York: Crossroad, 1992). Habermas argues that either theology is rooted in private experience and opinion, in which case its content is not defensible by public argument, or it presents its case in the public scientific terminology of the day, in which case its content is reducible to economics, sociology, psychology, and the like. For a lucid contrast between the thought of Habermas and the thought of David Tracy, cf. Anne Fortin-Melkevik, "Le statut de la religion dans la modernité selon David Tracy et Jürgen Habermas," *Studies in Religion/Sciences Religieuses* 22 (1994): 417–36.

71. David Tracy, *Blessed Rage for Order: The New Pluralism in Theology* (New York: Seabury, 1975), 8. This stance has been traced back to Schleiermacher: cf. Werner G. Jeanrond, "Theology in the Context of Pluralism and Postmodernity: David Tracy's

The Chicago theologian distinguishes his own from other methods of doing theology. Orthodox theology refuses to admit the impact of the Enlightenment, and in its pursuit of a corpus of unchanging truths has chained itself to a worldview now obsolete. Liberal theology does not fare any better: married to modernity, it lacks the critical awareness needed to overcome the easy identification of ostensibly Christian values with the values of the contemporary culture. Tracy praises neoorthodox theology for its recognition of the radically mysterious nature of God, but criticizes it for its tendency to agree with the Word of God without recognizing the diverse possibilities and limitations of human understanding when it comes to interpreting that Word.

By contrast, Tracy argues that the theologian he envisages

> is committed to what seems clearly to be the central task of contemporary Christian theology: the dramatic confrontation, the mutual illuminations and corrections, the possible basic reconciliation between the principal values, cognitive claims, and existential faiths of both a reinterpreted post-modern consciousness and a reinterpreted Christianity.[72]

Indeed, Tracy encourages the pursuit of possible meaning outside the Christian tradition. In two of his most important later works, Tracy shows how much he understands theology to be a fundamentally hermeneutical enterprise, *and how the inevitable result is a radical pluralism that cannot be denied, but can be experienced by participating in the discussion.*[73] The centrality of hermeneutics as the very essence of the work of theology for David Tracy is nowhere made clearer than in the work of his most assiduous commentator, Werner Jeanrond.[74]

What distinguishes the frankly atheistic postmodernism of, say, Taylor and Habermas, from the work of David Tracy? The question is not easy to answer. A superficial reading of Tracy might happily group him with the con-

---

Theological Method," in *Postmodernism, Literature and the Future of Theology*, ed. David Jasper (New York: St. Martin's, 1993), 144–45. Kirk Allison (in a private communication) is right: "Schleiermacher helped plow the field for the identity movement in 'German Christianity' in the 1920s, 1930s, and 1940s—generating some surprising and unintended fallout from the theological laboratory."

72. Ibid., 32.

73. David Tracy, *The Analogical Imagination: Christian Theology and the Culture of Pluralism* (New York: Crossroad, 1981); idem, *Plurality and Ambiguity: Hermeneutics, Religion, Hope* (San Francisco: Harper & Row, 1987).

74. See especially Werner G. Jeanrond, *Text and Interpretation as Categories of Theological Thinking*, trans. Thomas J. Wilson (New York: Crossroad, 1988). Cf. also the important essays in Werner G. Jeanrond and Jennifer L. Pike, eds., *Radical Pluralism and Truth: David Tracy and the Hermeneutics of Religion* (New York: Crossroad, 1991).

structive postmodern theologians (#c, above). Certainly he never openly embraces atheism. But his understanding of transcendental reflection is so tied to the mystery of (merely) human existence, his openness to all religions or none so evenhanded, and his focus on theology as essentially hermeneutical so all-embracing, that it is very difficult to see that much of what he has written would have to change if he were to espouse atheism openly. At the very least, one must conclude that, despite the immensely creative work that has emerged from his fertile mind, his commitment to philosophical pluralism is so total that, while his brilliance diverts us, he offers us no escape from the hermeneutical morass in which he frankly delights.[75]

2. Handling Texts

However it be defined, theology is inescapably bound up with handling texts. For the Christian, the primary text is the Bible. How, then, are biblical texts most likely to be handled by those who have drunk deeply from the wells of the new hermeneutic, of radical hermeneutics, and of deconstruction?

Theoretically, the new hermeneutic might teach an interpreter to be a little more aware of his or her cultural location, and thus engender humility and increased interpretive sensitivity.[76] In reality, it is increasingly common to assume that all interpretations are equally valid, and the excitement and value of the exercise depend on the novelty and perceived appropriateness (read "faddishness") of the "insights" thereby gleaned. The ego asserts itself ever more strongly.

If one wants a competent survey of the primary methods used by scholars engaged in biblical interpretation, one can scarcely do better than read a recent volume edited by McKenzie and Haynes, *To Each Its Own Meaning*.[77] This book assigns its essays into three sections. The first is "Traditional Methods of Biblical Criticism," where "traditional" primarily refers to the kinds of methods that grew up under modernity: source criticism, tradition-historical criticism, form criticism, and redaction criticism.[78] The second sec-

---

75. In old-fashioned terms, he appears to be not only an agnostic but a dogmatic agnostic. Granted the epistemological complexities, however, that does not mean he can be dismissed as a timid atheist!

76. In all fairness, however, the more reflective Christian thinkers have long recognized these dangers, even unaided by postmodernism: e.g., Carl F. H. Henry, *God, Revelation and Authority*, 6 vols. (Waco: Word Books, 1976–83), 5:395–408.

77. Steven L. McKenzie and Stephen R. Haynes, eds., *To Each Its Own Meaning: An Introduction to Biblical Criticisms and Their Application* (Louisville: Westminster/John Knox, 1993).

78. The exception is the first chapter, "Reading the Bible Historically: The Historian's Approach," which of course was a concern long before the rise of modernity. To the credit of

tion is called "Expanding the Tradition." Here there are essays on social-scientific criticism, canonical criticism, and rhetorical criticism. The "tradition" is being "expanded" in that these approaches are fairly new, yet they still aim to clarify or retrieve meaning *in the text*.

Significantly, the third section is titled "Overturning the Tradition." Now the focus is on structural criticism, narrative criticism, reader-response criticism, poststructuralist criticism, and feminist criticism. The ways in which these new "criticisms" *overturn* the tradition vary. Narrative criticism, for instance, may be nothing more than a formalized procedure for interpreting narratives—sorting out plot, principal characters, etc., which good readers do almost instinctively, with or without knowing the formalized procedures. Taken this way, narrative criticism overturns nothing. But in a fair bit of recent work, especially as applied to Old Testament narrative, narrative criticism unapologetically cuts through traditional source-critical boundaries in favor of final-form interpretation (and thus sets itself *against* source and redaction critical interpretations). In some instances it focuses so narrowly on the artistry of the narrative that any historical referent the story may ostensibly have is lost to view.[79] In this case the historian's reading is implicitly disavowed. In New Testament studies, one finds something of this overtone in the seminal work of Culpepper on the gospel of John, when he chooses the nineteenth-century novel as the narrative model by which he will read the Fourth Gospel.[80]

In what is the most delightfully written analysis of literary criticism applied to the gospels,[81] Stephen Moore concludes his treatment by showing that the most recent critical theory—I might label it postmodern criticism—does to Bultmann what Bultmann does to the New Testament: it demythologizes him.

To expand a little: The modernist quest constantly insisted it was trying to get back to the real Jesus. Bultmann came to the conclusion that there was

---

the author (J. Maxwell Miller), he does not reduce historical reading to the philosophical naturalism that some historians demand.

79. It would be wrong to slip by this point without acknowledging that radical hermeneutics and deconstruction have also made their impact on "the new historicism." The expression is usually taken to refer to an approach to the discipline of history that acknowledges that the historian works from a set of cultural axioms and personal biases, and so the reconstruction of the "history" is inevitably partial, personal, an act of interpretation, and (on the more radical side) only one interpretation of an infinite number of possibilities. But "the new historicism" is a slippery expression: see the excellent treatment by Brook Thomas, *The New Criticism and Other Old-Fashioned Topics* (Princeton: Princeton Univ. Press, 1991).

80. R. Alan Culpepper, *Anatomy of the Fourth Gospel: A Study in Literary Design* (Philadelphia: Fortress Press, 1983).

81. Stephen D. Moore, *Literary Criticism and the Gospels: The Theoretical Challenge* (New Haven: Yale Univ. Press, 1989).

nothing of historical certainty that one could reasonably say about Jesus, and saw this as a great advantage: one could then focus on the Christ of faith, while the Jesus of history slipped into the mists. Thus miracles, awkward sayings, implicit claims to divinity and the like were all demythologized: they were the works of later believers, forms of expression of a still deeper faith, and of little or no use to the examination of the historical Jesus. From his own perspective, Bultmann's demythologizing was "the radical application of the doctrine of justification by faith to the sphere of knowledge and thought. Like the doctrine of justification, demythologizing destroys every longing for security."[82] But as everyone knows, Bultmann's skepticism did not win the day. For "over the last three decades, the historical Jesus, helped to his feet initially by the post-Bultmannians and the New Quest, has made an impressive recovery from the beatings inflicted on him by earlier scholarship."[83] All of this pursuit of the historical Jesus, however, was undertaken with the goals and the tools of modernity. The aim was still to uncover "the truth" about what happened back there, and the tools were tradition criticism and redaction criticism. But while this was going on, modernity itself was being interrogated, its pretensions demythologized. Moore cites Huyssen:

> Postmodernism at its deepest level represents not just another crisis within the perpetual cycle of boom and bust, exhaustion and renewal, which has characterized the trajectory of modernist culture. It rather represents a new type of crisis *of* that modernist culture itself ... that we are not bound to *complete* the project of modernity (Habermas' phrase) and still do not necessarily have to lapse into irrationality or apocalyptic frenzy.... Rather than being bound to a one-way history of modernism which interprets it as a logical unfolding toward some imaginary goal ... we are beginning to explore its contradictions and contingencies, its tensions and internal resistances to its own "forward" movement.[84]

Moore concludes by laying down the gauntlet: "Relative to the cutting edge of secular literary study, historical criticism occupies one time warp, narrative criticism another. The question thus remains, What happens in gospel studies and in biblical studies generally once biblical scholars finally dispense with freeze-frames and action replays in order to participate fully in literary study in its high-risk present forms?"[85]

82. Rudolf Bultmann, *Jesus Christ and Mythology* (New York: Scribner's, 1958), 84.

83. Moore, *Literary Criticism*, 173.

84. Andreas Huyssen, *After the Great Divide: Modernism, Mass Culture, Postmodernism* (Bloomington: Indiana Univ. Press, 1986), 217, emphases and parentheses his; cited also in Moore, *Literary Criticism*, 173–74.

85. Moore, *Literary Criticism*, 178. A useful introduction to narrative criticism, especially as deployed in the Old Testament, is David M. Gunn and Danna Nolan Fewell, *Narrative in the Hebrew Bible* (Oxford: Clarendon Press, 1993).

Some might argue that there are already quite a number of postmodern biblical interpreters. One thinks, for instance, of the stimulating essays in a volume edited by Exum and Clines, *The New Literary Criticism and the Hebrew Bible*, introduced by the editors in these terms: "Whatever the reason, the message these essays convey, however subliminally, is that there are no holds barred, and no automatically inappropriate angles of vision upon our texts—and that even in centres of institutional power there are no longer any arbiters of what may and may not be legitimately and fruitfully said about our texts."[86] Charles Mabee holds that the diverse readings of the Bible constitute "biblical pluralism," and biblical pluralism "rejects any interpretation that makes the Bible itself the supreme object of religious faith, or better, any particular way of reading the Bible."[87] Seeley has written a book to deconstruct the four canonical gospels and Paul;[88] Moore himself has followed up his earlier work with a book that deconstructs Mark and Luke,[89] and another that deconstructs parts of John and Paul.[90] In the spirit of those who claim that most interpretations are in large measure statements of authority or manipulative control by those who belong to the interpretive community, Rowland and Corner offer a postmodern defense of liberation theology.[91] The essays that Watson has edited deal with the "Bible in a *post*modern world"—a Bible that is "a more surprising, demanding and interesting book than its rather bland modernist predecessor."[92]

So pervasive is the postmodern approach to texts and to theology, at least in North America and to a growing degree elsewhere, that some theologians are dismissed precisely because they conceive of theology as the pursuit of truth. Thus Placher's recent review of the first volume of Pannenberg's systematic theology[93] includes this trenchant remark:

---

86. J. Cheryl Exum and David J. A. Clines, *The New Literary Criticism and the Hebrew Bible* (Valley Forge: Trinity Press International, 1993), 13.

87. Charles Mabee, *Reading Sacred Texts Through American Eyes: Biblical Interpretation as Cultural Critique* (Macon: Mercer Univ. Press, 1991), 103.

88. David Seeley, *Deconstructing the New Testament*, Biblical Interpretation Series, vol. 5 (Leiden: E. J. Brill, 1994).

89. Stephen D. Moore, *Mark and Luke in Poststructuralist Perspectives: Jesus Begins to Write* (New Haven: Yale Univ. Press, 1992).

90. Stephen D. Moore, *Poststructuralism and the New Testament: Derrida and Foucault at the Foot of the Cross* (Minneapolis: Fortress Press, 1994).

91. Christopher Rowland and Mark Corner, *The Liberating Exegesis: The Challenge of Liberation Theology to Biblical Studies* (London: SPCK, 1990). Cf. the review by M. M. B. Turner, *Evangelical Quarterly* 66 (1994): 183–86.

92. Francis Watson, ed., *The Open Text: New Directions for Biblical Studies?* (London: SCM Press, 1993).

93. Wolfhard Pannenberg, *Systematic Theology*, vol. 1, trans. Geoffrey W. Bromiley (Grand Rapids: Eerdmans, 1991).

He seems to live in a world where some significant paradigms can be assumed: a world where Western tradition as a whole remains essentially unproblematic, where people generally seem to know what counts as a reasoned argument, and where theologians know what counts as "the theological tradition." One may envy that world or hate it, feel nostalgia for it, dream of restoring it or dismiss it as good riddance. But many of us trying to write theology in this country find it to be a world in which we do not live.[94]

3. Science

"But," someone may say, "doesn't the domain of science serve as a kind of reality check? After all, modernity achieved its greatest triumphs in the scientific arena, an arena in which, despite many setbacks, progress is still being made. Can modernity be so easily dismissed when the witness of science is brought to bear?"

Undoubtedly there are countless thousands of competent scientists who never or rarely doubt the "truth" that science produces. But philosophers of science, and scientists who read and think philosophically and theologically, recognize that science no longer holds the epistemological advantage it once did.

Less than half a century ago it was not uncommon to find scholars who felt that science was adequate not only for the recovery of hard facts and technological advancement, but also for the establishment of the most important human values.[95] Few would be so optimistic today. Nevertheless, because postmodernism has not displaced modernism, but has grown up out of it to challenge it and threaten it, one still finds modernist and postmodernist views of science side by side. One modernist voice, deeply committed to naturalism, thinks that the teaching of theology has no place in university life, though religious studies, understood as a social science concerned with collecting and explaining empirical data, has scientific validity and may be accorded a slot.[96] Inevitably, he has not gone unchallenged.[97] Another modernist voice,

---

94. William C. Placher, "Revealed to Reason: Theology as 'Normal Science,'" *Christian Century* (February 1, 1992): 195.

95. E.g., J. Bronowski, *Science and Human Values* (New York: Harper & Row, 1956).

96. So Donald Wiebe, *The Irony of Theology and the Nature of Religious Thought* (Montreal and Kingston: McGill/Queen's Univ. Press, 1991).

97. See P. Travis Kroeker, "The Ironic Cage of Positivism and the Nature of Philosophical Theology," *Studies in Religion/Sciences Religieuses* 22 (1993): 93–103. For a further exchange between Wiebe and Kroeker, see Donald Wiebe, "Argument or Authority in the Academy? On Kroeker on *The Irony of Theology*," *Studies in Religion/Sciences Religieuses* 23 (1994): 67–79; P. Travis Kroeker, "Reply to Donald Wiebe," *Studies in Religion/Sciences Religieuses* 23 (1994): 81–82. More generally, for a competent rebuttal of the kind of natural-

entirely contemporary (in time, at least, though certainly not in outlook) has apparently heard nothing of the challenges of postmodernism. Arthur Peacocke attempts to construct a "theology for a scientific age," but operates with a positivist view of science and an old-fashioned liberal-modernist view of theology, resulting in a Jesus who simply lights the way for us to become like him, but does not deal with sin and death.[98] If a century ago some committed to modernity could praise science for its discovery of facts, while praising literature for its ability to provide meaning, depict reality, and call people toward understanding and perfection,[99] Northrop Frye could argue very much the same thing within the last three decades.[100]

None of this, however, captures the direction of contemporary philosophy of science. Michael Polanyi[101] insists on the mysteriousness of our engagement with the outside world. Science takes its measurements, but always the measurements are theory-laden. We bring all of our experience to each interpretive act, including a range of anticipations that we have learned by experience. A blind man tapping a stick claims to feel what the stick is knocking against, not the pressure of the stick in his hand; the rower claims to feel the resistance of the water, not the pressure of the oar. The interpretive framework we always bring with us is tacit, and can never be wholly explicit. Polanyi insists that all human knowledge is either tacit or rooted in tacit knowledge; it is inevitably personal knowledge or personal knowing.

> This conception of knowledge as personal knowing departs in two closely related respects from the ideal of a strictly justifiable knowledge. It accredits man's capacity to acquire knowledge even though he cannot specify the grounds of his knowing, and it accepts the fact that his knowing is exercised within an accidentally given framework that is largely unspecifiable. These two acceptances are correlated within the effort of integration which achieves knowing.... The structure of knowing, revealed by the limits of specifiability, thus fuses our subsidiary awareness of the particulars belonging to our subject matter with the cultural background of our knowing.[102]

istic science that speaks of humans as "genetic survival machines" or the like, see Rodney Holder, *Nothing But Atoms and Molecules?* (Tunbridge Wells: Monarch, 1993).

98. Arthur Peacocke, *Theology for a Scientific Age: Being and Becoming—Natural, Divine, and Human* (Oxford: Basil Blackwell, 1990); 2d ed. (Minneapolis: Fortress Press, 1993).

99. E.g., the Victorian critic Matthew Arnold "Literature and Science," in *Prose of the Victorian Period*, ed. William E. Buckler (Boston: Houghton Mifflin, 1958), 499.

100. *The Educated Imagination* (Bloomington: Indiana Univ. Press, 1964), 32–33.

101. Perhaps his most important two books are *Knowing and Being* (Chicago: Univ. of Chicago Press, 1969) and *Personal Knowledge: Towards a Post-Critical Philosophy* (Chicago: Univ. of Chicago Press, 1958).

102. *Knowing and Being*, 133–34.

Polanyi is not calling into question the scientific method or the importance of experimentation and verifiable results. He is simply saying that such methods achieve nothing until they are integrated with tacit knowledge, not all of which is specifiable.

Polanyi is not for a moment suggesting that knowledge is purely personal, purely subjective. But he is certainly denying that scientific knowledge is *purely* objective and *exhaustively* verifiable. Nor is he the only thinker to take such lines: one thinks, for instance, of Norwood Hanson, Thomas Kuhn, Imre Lakatos, Paul Feyerabend, and Stanley Tambiah.[103]

The most influential of these is doubtless Thomas Kuhn, whose interest has been in tracing how one scientific theory succeeds and displaces another. Unlike many previous thinkers, Kuhn denies that theories are adapted and changed merely as more evidence accumulates. The reality, he says, is more complex. A theory will be maintained, despite its inability to handle some phenomena, and despite its contradictory elements, until another theory comes along that can handle everything the first one no longer could, plus a lot of additional information that has accumulated. And then, all of a sudden, there is a "scientific revolution": everyone or just about everyone in the field jumps to the new theory, the new paradigm.

According to Kuhn, the two paradigms are marked by *incompatibility*, *incommensurability*, and *incomparability*. Many of Kuhn's opponents have fixed on these words, treated them as if Kuhn meant the same thing by all three, and strenuously argued that such paradigms are not, for example, "incompatible": Newtonian physics, for example, can be seen as a subset, under specific conditions, of modern physics.[104] But Bernstein has shown, convincingly, that at this point Kuhn's opponents have not listened to him very well.[105]

---

103. Norwood Hanson, *Patterns of Discovery* (Cambridge: Cambridge Univ. Press, 1958); Thomas Kuhn, *The Structure of Scientific Revolutions*, 2d ed. (Chicago: Univ. of Chicago Press, 1970); Imre Lakatos, "Falsification and the Methodology of Scientific Research Programmes," in *Criticism and the Growth of Knowledge*, ed. Imre Lakatos and Alan Musgrave (Cambridge: Cambridge Univ. Press, 1970), 91–196; Paul Feyerabend, *Against Method* (London: New Left Books, 1975); Stanley Jeyaraja Tambiah, *Magic, Science, Religion, and the Scope of Rationality* (Cambridge: Cambridge Univ. Press, 1990). For a useful survey, see Thomas Guarino, "Contemporary Theology and Scientific Rationality," *Studies in Religion/Sciences Religieuses* 22 (1993): 311–22. None of what I have said is meant to deny that these thinkers adopt on occasion very different perspectives.

104. I am indebted to Scott Bonham for alerting me to the manner in which physicists sometimes use labels in ways not clearly distinguished by philosophers of religion. Within the physics community "Einsteinian physics" refers to relativity theory but not to quantum mechanics; "modern physics" embraces both. "Classical physics" refers to premodern physics (i.e., roughly pre-twentieth-century), and "Newtonian physics" is an acceptable equivalent, since Newton was doubtless the most important figure in constructing the framework.

105. *Beyond Objectivism and Relativism*, 80–87.

When Kuhn used the term "incompatibility," he was specifically attacking the earlier thesis that the relation between a more comprehensive theory and a less comprehensive theory could be analyzed in strictly logical terms: the less comprehensive theory could be logically derived from the laws and categories of the more comprehensive theory. The classic proof was, in fact, the relation of Newtonian physics to modern physics. But such an approach overlooks the elements of conflict and of transformed paradigms that actually pertain. Kuhn is, of course, perfectly aware that one can derive a close *approximation* of Newton's laws from modern physics—but that is just the point. Close approximation is not exactly the same thing. "Though an out-of-date theory can always be viewed as a special case of its up-to-date successor, it must be transformed for the purpose. And, the transformation is one that can be undertaken only with the advantages of hindsight, the explicit guidance of the more recent theory."[106] Strictly speaking, the two theories are logically "incompatible," i.e., the frameworks are different, and do not mesh; they are not mutually applicable.

As for "incommensurability," again Kuhn is taking on a specific point. He is not saying that the two paradigms are so incommensurable that physicists operating under one paradigm cannot communicate with physicists operating under another (as some of his detractors have said). Kuhn offers many examples where he is quite clear that two theories may have considerable overlap. What he denies is the implicit objectivist assumptions of his opponents. They argue as if there is an unknown and unacknowledged third and complete paradigm, corresponding to reality, of which the two scientific theories in question are subsets. In other words, his opponents assume the two are commensurable precisely because they both belong to a third, which corresponds with reality. This Kuhn denies. We have no independent access to such reality. Our understanding of reality will always be derivative, via the paradigms that constitute our most up-to-date science. Strictly speaking, then, the two theories in question are incommensurable, in the strictly limited sense suggested here. Kuhn takes a similar step with the notion of incomparability.

We can see, then, why Kuhn was initially met by a storm of opposition. Many philosophers of science had appealed to the ostensible progressive development of science for overwhelming support for a scientific distinction between rationality and irrationality. The later positivist argumentation depended absolutely upon such a view of science. But if science is not the accumulation of knowledge by addition and refinement, all carried out exclusively in the natural arena, but depends for its development, at least in part,

---

106. Kuhn, *Structure*, 102–3.

on Kuhnian "revolutions," then perhaps knowledge, whatever knowledge is, cannot be reduced, *even in the field of science*, to "scientific" rigor. There are subjective, whimsical, unanalyzable, paradigmatic constraints on all complex scientific theories.[107]

The importance of these developments to our topic cannot be overestimated. While some people on the street (and some scientists!) still think of science as the realm of indisputable fact, and religion as the realm of mere opinion, developments in the philosophy of science have shown, by one route or another, that anything complex in science is inevitably theory-laden, and all complex theories include components that are not themselves directly demonstrable by empirical means. Some Christians use these developments to argue for the plausibility of Christian truth claims. They argue, in effect, that if science depends on paradigms, models, inferences, subjective judgments and the like, then there is no automatic harm to Christianity if it resorts to similar arguments.[108]

But the thoroughgoing pluralists are unmoved.[109] They use exactly the same evidence, but reverse the flow of the argument. If the work of the "hard" sciences is parasitic on paradigms that can shift with time, then the degree of subjectivity inherent in these phenomena only confirms the pluralists' point. If even science is so subjective, then it is surely presumptuous for religion to speak of truth claims. Thus Paul Knitter insists that today "truth is no longer defined according to the Aristotelian notion of science: 'certain knowledge through causes.' Rather, 'modern science is not true; it is only on the way towards truth.' . . . On the personal level, truth is no longer seen as the pursuit of certainty but as the pursuit of understanding—ever greater understanding. This means that all 'true understanding' will be open to change and revision."[110] It comes as no surprise that he criticizes the law of noncontra-

---

107. Certainly the first presentation of Kuhn's theory (1962) was not without fault, nor was his second (1970). Kuhn himself has modified various points and made his theory more precise. See Frederick Suppe, ed., *The Structure of Scientific Theories*, 2d ed. (Urbana: Univ. of Illinois Press, 1977); Gary Gutting, ed., *Paradigms and Revolutions: Applications and Appraisals of Thomas Kuhn's Philosophy of Science* (Notre Dame: Univ. of Notre Dame Press, 1980). But today most philosophers of religion are quite right to acknowledge that in its main lines, Kuhn's theory has won the toss.

108. So, e.g., several chapters of Lesslie Newbigin's thoughtful book *The Gospel in a Pluralist Society* (Grand Rapids: Eerdmans, 1989). See also the generally excellent work of Earl R. MacCormac, *Metaphor and Myth in Science and Religion* (Durham: Duke Univ. Press, 1976).

109. The argument here is a development of my essay "Christian Witness in an Age of Pluralism," in *God and Culture*, ed. D. A. Carson and John D. Woodbridge (Grand Rapids: Eerdmans, 1993), 56.

110. Paul Knitter, *No Other Name? A Critical Survey of Christian Attitudes Toward the World Religions* (Maryknoll: Orbis Books, 1985), 32.

diction. Truth should be seen as relational: "What is true will reveal itself mainly by its ability to relate to other expressions of truth and to grow through these relationships."[111]

The point should now be very clear. Although not everyone is on the same page, although not everyone is committed to postmodernity, although not everyone thinks that no readings of texts are ever incorrect, although not everyone follows David Tracy in theology, and although not everyone follows Polanyi or Kuhn in science (after all, the sheer diversity that constitutes empirical pluralism is where I started this book), the fact remains that these movements are perceived to be on the cutting edge, and their influence in our culture is vast. Truth disappears, retreating before the culture of interpretation, dissolving in the mists of postmodernity.

E. Some Conclusions

Not surprisingly, ideas of such complexity and revolutionary significance have elicited a wide range of responses. Many are not explicitly aware of them, even though they are very substantially influenced by them. For example, in neighborhood Bible studies and adult Sunday school classes, where few could define postmodernism, one soon becomes aware that it is far more important for every opinion to be heard and praised than for the meaning of the text to be uncovered.

Intellectuals, not least evangelicals, have begun to recognize that there is a large measure of truth in postmodernity, at least in its critique of modernity, and are quietly attempting to incorporate what they can from the new hermeneutic and its stepchildren into a framework that would nevertheless leave a place for objective truth.[112] Others appeal to postmodernity to justify their firm and sometimes bitter reaction against the unnecessary dogmatisms and legalisms of a previous generation, without asking if they are sometimes in danger of throwing out the baby with the bathwater. They give the impression that they feel there is a specially high place in the spiritual sphere reserved for those who ask questions and say they don't know, and only low places for those who write or preach "so that you may know the certainty of the things you have been taught" (to use the words of Luke, 1:4).[113] Doubtless

111. Ibid., 219.
112. E.g., Grant R. Osborne, *The Hermeneutical Spiral: A Comprehensive Introduction to Biblical Interpretation* (Downers Grove: InterVarsity Press, 1991), esp. 366–411; Dan McCartney and Charles Clayton, *Let the Reader Understand: A Guide to Interpreting and Applying the Bible* (Wheaton: Bridgepoint, 1994), 283–84; Richard Lints, *The Fabric of Theology: A Prolegomenon to Evangelical Theology* (Grand Rapids: Eerdmans, 1993).
113. E.g., Daniel Taylor, *The Myth of Certainty: Trusting God, Asking Questions, Taking Risks* (Grand Rapids: Zondervan, 1992).

they have been burned by rabble-rousing preachers who focus on peripheries to generate a head of steam, and who prefer to be contentious about the gospel rather than to contend for the gospel. Postmodernity becomes a means of backing out of this insular world, without necessarily arriving at a stable and Christian epistemology oneself. Some Christian intellectuals are now openly taking opposite sides on the question as to whether it is wise or even possible to espouse a post-Christian faith.[114] Some informed Anglo-Catholics and Orthodox scholars now deploy a postmodern critique in order to establish the importance—indeed, the necessity—of working within "the Tradition."[115]

Some of these and other in-house responses to postmodernity I shall take up later in the book. What is of more immediate concern is the powerful drive toward radical religious pluralism to which these developments in the field of interpretation have contributed. If uncovering objective truth is well-nigh impossible (assuming objective truth exists!), how can one speak of an eternal gospel that was once for all entrusted to the saints (Jude 3)? If understanding absolutely depends on a framework that is shared by a community but with few outside that community, then how can one avoid the conclusion that some beliefs may be fine for a particular community, but should not be presented as demanding assent outside that community?

In short, the hermeneutical morass in which all of us struggle has been one of the defining points of the new religious pluralism. Before addressing other features of this drive toward pluralism, therefore, I shall try to build a small causeway out of the morass. Or if that is presumptuous, I shall at least try to indicate the location of some reasonably secure mounds within the morass. Unfortunately, there is little help for those who adamantly prefer the texture of quicksand.

---

114. See, for instance, the pair of articles, Paul Nisly, "A Word of Hope," *Faculty Dialogue* 17 (1992): 113–17; Samuel Smith, "Words of Hope: A Postmodern Faith," *Faculty Dialogue* 20 (1993): 131–45.

115. Andrew Louth, *Discerning the Mystery: An Essay on the Nature of Theology* (Oxford: Clarendon Press, 1983).

Chapter 3

ESCAPING FROM THE HERMENEUTICAL MORASS: "LET GOD BE TRUE, AND EVERY MAN A LIAR"

A. Introduction

In canvassing the substantial literature on the new hermeneutic, radical hermeneutics, deconstruction, and postmodernism, I have on several occasions found quoted a well-known poem by W. B. Yeats:

> Things fall apart, the centre cannot hold;
> Mere anarchy is loosed upon the world,
> The blood-dimmed tide is loosed, and everywhere
> The ceremony of innocence is drowned;
> The best lack all conviction, while the worst
> Are full of passionate intensity.

This feeling of lostness, of disorientation, is not the exclusive property of conservative evangelicals, Catholics, and fundamentalists. The *doyen* of an older style of biblical studies has recently bemoaned the loss of a "common universe of canonical theological discourse." He asks, "Is ours one of those situations in which 'Things fall apart; the centre cannot hold' because there is no one centre and often no centres. . . . [The] new pluralism can often become banal, trivial and pretentious, like a fish in that ocean [of the transcendent] always keeping its mouth wide open, afraid to shut it, and therefore never taking a bite."[1]

---

1. W. D. Davies, "Reflections on Thirty Years of Biblical Studies," *Scottish Journal of Theology* 39 (1986): 57. Cited also by William J. Larkin, Jr., "Culture, Scripture's Meaning, and Biblical Authority: Critical Hermeneutics for the 90's," *Bulletin for Biblical Research* 2 (1992): 174.

Quite apart from vague feelings of change and decay, all branches of confessing Christianity hold that there is more at stake than personal psychological comfort. Though in another context, Machen had put his finger on the practical point more than half a century earlier:

> The problem of the origin of Christianity is . . . an important practical problem. Rightly or wrongly, Christian experience has ordinarily been connected with one particular view of the origin of the Christian movement; where that view has been abandoned, the experience has ceased.[2]

By "one particular view of the origin of the Christian movement," Machen, of course, was referring to its professed supernatural origins, over against the reductionistic philosophical naturalism of the late modernism of his day. But if that modernism denied that what may be called the supernatural interpretation of the New Testament texts was correct, at least they agreed with Machen that a truth issue was at stake. If Machen's words are still relevant, the reason is worse: in some quarters it is denied that there is any (objective) truth issue at all.

Not for a moment would it be right for confessing Christians to bemoan the latest developments in Western philosophy and literary criticism *as if previous generations should be revered with sentimental nostalgia*. Modernism presented its own challenges to the gospel; so did the premodern period leading up to the Reformation (unless one thinks that the Reformation was simply an in-house squabble!); so has every age in every nation. Sometimes opposition has been ruthless and bloody; sometimes it has been condescending and civilized; not infrequently it has been seductive. But there has always been opposition. In the shifts currently taking place in our culture, it is salutary to remember that postmodernity virulently attacks the hubris of modernity—even if it displays more than a little of its own. Christians do not belong in either worldview. They must maintain their own vision. Not long before he died, Max Warren wrote:

> Reacting, and reacting rightly, against the dogmatic triumphalism of much past Christian approach to men of other faiths, it is all too easy to swing to the other extreme and talk happily of different roads to the summit, as if Jesus were in no particular and distinctive sense "the Way, the Truth, and the Life." Of course where this point is reached, the Great Commission is tacitly, if not explicitly, held to be indefinitely in suspense if not quite otiose. This is a view forcefully propounded by some Christians holding profes-

---

2. J. Gresham Machen, *The Origin of Paul's Religion* (Grand Rapids: Eerdmans, 1947 [1925]), 3. On the broader issue of the relation between Christian experience and the supporting claims, see Stephen Cox, "Theory, Experience and 'The American Religion,'" *Journal of the Evangelical Theological Society* 36 (1993): 363–73.

sorial Chairs in Britain and across the Atlantic. Are they right? Is courtesy always to preclude contradiction? Is choice now just a matter of taste, no longer a response to an absolute demand? Is the Cross on Calvary really no more than a confusing roundabout sign pointing in every direction, or is it still the place where *all* men are meant to kneel?[3]

However much both Warren and I are happy to answer his last question with an affirmative, such answers today are readily dismissed before they are given much of a hearing. The underlying hermeneutical issues, as the previous two chapters have shown, must be addressed. To some of these we now turn.

B. Preliminary Responses to Postmodernity

The severity of the challenge becomes clear when we picture two quite different Christian apologists approaching a thoughtful deconstructionist. The first Christian is an evidentialist. She may begin by marshaling various arguments for the existence of God, and proceed to demonstrate that the only adequate explanation of the biblical accounts of the resurrection of Jesus and of the change in his disciples is that Jesus in fact did rise from the dead. The deconstructionist listens with interest, but can find other explanations for the early belief in Jesus' resurrection. More importantly, he insists that his Christian interlocutor's passion to convert him is itself a function of the rather closed and old-fashioned society from which she hails. He is courteous, but unimpressed.

The second Christian apologist is one form of fideist, a particular kind of presuppositionalist. He has a name, partly because I cannot improve on the testimony of this man. John Cooper[4] was a philosophy major at Calvin College in the 1960s. There he learned to attack the alleged autonomy, neutrality, and vaunted self-sufficiency of all human reasoning. The aim was to hoist modernists with their own petard. This approach is fundamental to Abraham Kuyper's discernment of antithesis in science, to Hermann Dooyeweerd's transcendental critique of theoretical thought, to Van Til's presuppositionalism, and more generally to the various forms of Reformed foundationalism.[5] Eventually, however, Cooper began doctoral study under Paul

---

3. Max A. C. Warren, *I Believe in the Great Commission* (London: Hodder & Stoughton, 1976), 150–51.

4. John W. Cooper, "Reformed Apologetics and the Challenge of Post-Modern Relativism," *Calvin Theological Journal* 28 (1993): 108–20, esp. 108–9.

5. In one sense, it is also fundamental to what may cheekily be called the non-foundational foundationalism of Alvin Plantinga (whose work first caused a stir in the volume *God and Other Minds: A Study of the Rational Belief in God* [Ithaca: Cornell Univ. Press, 1967]) and Nicholas Wolterstorff (especially in his *Reason Within the Bounds of Revelation* [Grand Rapids: Eerdmans, 1976]). They reject foundationalism but hold that belief in God is "properly basic"—which

Ricoeur at the University of Toronto. The story may be continued in his own words:

> Gathering courage [at a Ricoeur seminar on hermeneutics], I trotted out my best Reformed arguments that reason and knowledge are not neutral but dependent upon basic commitments, presuppositions, and perspectives. I was ready for a fight, but everyone just stared at me as though I had announced that the Pope is Catholic. "Yes, yes ... go on," Ricoeur encouraged, interested in the validation of presuppositions. But I had nothing left except a personal testimony about my religious beliefs. My best Reformed philosophical arguments were mere truisms to these people. I'll never forget the consternation I felt.
>
> Times are changing. Modernism is dying, though its strength is not completely spent. By now the announcement of a new outlook, something called "post-modernism," has become a cliché.... At the heart of the new mood are principled pluralism and radical relativism.[6]

This does not mean that evidentialism has nothing useful to say, or that a Reformed apologetic is invalid. Moreover, some presuppositionalists would doubtless fault Cooper's understanding of presuppositionalism! I will not attempt to arbitrate on those debates in this chapter, except peripherally; I shall briefly return to them in chapter 4. What is reasonably clear, however, is that "standard" approaches to apologetics simply do not touch the committed deconstructionist.

Godly, effective Christian witness turns on much more than an intellectually responsible and biblically faithful apologetic. I shall say more along these lines in chapter 12. For the moment it is enough to issue a number of reflections on the new hermeneutic and deconstruction, and on some of their stepchildren.

1. While we deplore certain follies in postmodernity, it is vital to acknowledge a number of strengths.

There is of course irony in acknowledging (objective) truth in radical hermeneutics, but it will almost certainly bypass the postmodernist. In any case, our acknowledgment is not a cheap, psychological ploy to bring the

---

therefore can serve as an appropriate foundation. For useful discussion, cf. John Frame, *The Doctrine of the Knowledge of God* (Phillipsburg: Presbyterian and Reformed, 1987), appendix I, "The New Reformed Epistemology," 382–400. The classic foundationalism Plantinga rejects holds that basic beliefs must be either self-evident or incorrigible, and Plantinga argues that belief in God is neither. See further discussion in chap. 4.

6. Cooper, "Reformed Apologetics," 109. In a private communication, Kirk Allison tells me that one of his professors informed him that the professor does not espouse "the relativity of truth" but rather "the truth of relativity."

other person "on side," a mere courtesy perhaps: it is, rather, an *important* obligation, for there are in fact important things to learn.

All of us see things only in part, and never without some measure of distortion. To say this is not (I shall shortly argue) to succumb to absolute relativism. It is, rather, to admit a truth that many have recognized, but which has become clearer owing not least to our experience of empirical pluralism. Each of us is finite; none of us displays the attribute of omniscience. Our beliefs are shaped in part by our culture, language, heritage, community.

Of course, this is one of the reasons why the subject of contextualization has become ubiquitous in recent years. It has long been recognized that new churches, to become mature, must become self-governing, self-financing, and self-propagating: those were the measures of the old indigenous principle. Contextualization takes a big step further. It insists that believers must "do theology" from within their own culture, and not simply learn a system of theology developed in another culture. For most of us, I think, this has become almost axiomatic. We are aware of the abuses to which certain forms of contextualization can lead, and about which I'll say more in the last chapter; but we cannot reasonably doubt the importance of the phenomenon.

For the moment it is enough to offer an easy example. Believers in sub-Saharan Black Africa are likely to be less individualistic than their Western counterparts, to avoid deep dichotomies between the natural world and the spiritual world, and to think of death without the taboos that our culture places on it. These three cultural factors alone will have various influences on their theology, as they develop it from studying the Bible. They will likely find in Paul more corporate metaphors for the church than we do, and prove quicker at living them out. They will have less trouble with a comprehensive doctrine of providence, and will talk about death more frankly. Living as many Africans do in a still profoundly oral culture, they often prove more able to read and preach narrative parts of Scripture sensitively and tellingly; correspondingly, their ability to handle discourse is not impressive. Most Westerners have inverse strengths and weaknesses. It is not surprising, then, that we shall develop our respective theologies along somewhat different lines. If the new hermeneutic helps us along the path of humility, that is surely a good thing.

Indeed, in certain respects believers can embrace pluralism more lavishly than the secularists can. Our heavenly Father created a wonderfully diverse world: let us adore him for it.[7] He makes each snowflake different; we make ice cubes. Quite clearly, God likes diversity in the color of human skin—he

---

7. See some of the opening remarks by Jonathan F. Frothe, "Confessing Christ in a Pluralistic Age," *Concordia Journal* 16 (1990): 217–30.

has made people wonderfully diverse. Similarly, apart from the wretched sinfulness endemic to all cultures, one must assume that God likes cultural diversity as well. In the realm of knowing, we join the experts of deconstruction and of the new hermeneutic in insisting on human finiteness: more, we go further and insist on human sinfulness. The noetic effects of sin are so severe that we culpably distort the data brought to us by our senses to make it fit into self-serving grids. We are not only finite, on many fronts we are blind.

Moreover, we need to insist that *all* topics we deal with are *necessarily* culture-laden. Language itself is a feature of culture, and there are few topics we can examine very far without resorting to language. I simply cannot escape my cultural locatedness. Recognizing the need to preserve absolutes, yet perceiving the overarching and frankly relativizing influence of culture, some Christians have sought to escape the problem by suggesting that some core of basic Christian truths transcends culture. Take, for instance, the work of Charles Kraft[8]—an example I have developed more fully elsewhere.[9] Kraft thinks of the Bible as a casebook. The wise pastor or missionary applies the appropriate case to the culture at hand. Thus, in a society that is polygamous (his example), it might be wise to begin with Old Testament polygamy, perhaps with David and Solomon and their many wives, rather than with the monogamous ideal set out in the New Testament. When pressed to articulate what, if any, fundamental truths Christianity embraces that must be pressed on every culture, Kraft suggests there is a handful of non-negotiable, transcultural truths, such as "Jesus is Lord."

But Kraft, I think, has not gone far enough, and too far. He has not gone far enough in that even so basic a confession as "Jesus is Lord" cannot escape culture. For a start, it is in English. Moreover, we English-speaking Western Christians adopt common assumptions about the referent of the word "Jesus" (though Jehovah's Witnesses might not agree), and probably want to define "Lord" as well. For example, the instructed Christian will remember that "Lord" is often used in the Septuagint to refer to YHWH, and suspect that the confession "Jesus is Lord" includes not-very-subtle hints of Jesus' deity. Not all who take the confession on their lips will be saying so much; they will not be adequately instructed. But the problem is still more complex. If the confession were tranlated into Thai and uttered in a Buddhist Temple, it would probably be understood to imply that Jesus is inferior to Gautama the Buddha. This is because in Buddhist thought the highest state of exaltation

---

8. In particular, his *Christianity in Culture: A Study in Dynamic Biblical Theologizing in Cross-Cultural Perspective* (Maryknoll: Orbis Books, 1980).

9. D. A. Carson, "Church and Mission: Reflections on Contextualization and the Third Horizon," in *The Church in the Bible and the World*, ed. D. A. Carson (Exeter: Paternoster/Grand Rapids: Baker, 1987), 213–57, esp. 242ff.

is reached when nothing at all can be predicated about the person: the most exalted individual is neither hot nor cold, good nor bad, and so on. To predicate that Jesus is Lord, therefore, is to imply that Jesus is inferior to Gautama the Buddha, about whom nothing can be predicated. Thus not even "Jesus is Lord" can escape the grasp of culture. A similar analysis could be undertaken for any other fundamental truth that Kraft or anyone else advances as something that transcends all cultures. If truth can transcend culture (and I shall argue that in certain respects it does), it does not do so in any simple way. In this sense, Kraft does not go far enough.

But in another sense, Kraft goes much too far. If we can establish that truth can be objective and transcendent *even though it is necessarily expressed in culture-laden ways and believed or known by finite, culturally restricted people*—a perspective I shall briefly develop below—then the proposition "Jesus is Lord" can be judged absolute: even though it is expressed in culture-laden terms, there is nothing intrinsically inappropriate about the conclusion that countless other propositions may also be absolute, even though each of them is culture-laden.

This may become clearer if we analyze a little further what we mean by saying that "Jesus is Lord" is part of the culture-transcending heritage of the church everywhere. I mean something like this: The semantic content of "Jesus is Lord" as expressed and understood by an English-speaking believer who has at least some rudimentary knowledge of the Bible and Christian theology must be grasped and believed by men and women everywhere in every culture, however it is expressed and articulated within each culture. Of course, there are all sorts of ambiguities about this way of wording things. But my point is that if linguistics has taught us anything, it has taught us that whatever can be said in one language can be said in another, *even if not in the same way and brevity.*[10] What I as a Western believer mean by "Jesus is Lord" can be conveyed in Thai, to a Thai Buddhist. But it will not be conveyed, in the first instance, by a mere slogan. Christian understanding of the confession is dependent upon an entire worldview that takes in a personal/transcendent God, the revelation of the Scripture, understanding of who Jesus is, and so on. The initial Thai *mis*understanding turns on another entire worldview: an essentially pantheistic view of God, radically different understanding of

---

10. I refer here to the judgment of almost all linguists, but not necessarily to philosophers of language, e.g., W. V. Quine. See especially his essay, "Speaking of Objects," in his *Ontological Relativity and Other Essays* (New York: Columbia Univ. Press, 1969), 1–25; idem, *Word and Object* (Cambridge: MIT Press, 1960). For a sympathetic treatment of Quine's thought, see Alex Orenstein, *Willard Van Orman Quine* (Boston: Twayne, 1977); for a fuller and more critical work, see Lewis Edwin Hahn and Paul Arthur Schilpp, *The Philosophy of W. V. Quine* (LaSalle: Open Court, 1986).

revelation, relative or perhaps complete ignorance of Jesus, and so forth. To explain to the Thai what I mean by "Jesus is Lord" can be done, but not easily, not quickly, and not with mere slogans. Once there is a confessional Thai church, of course, the cultural barriers inherent in all Christian witness may be crossed more quickly.

I have not set up English as the *necessary* medium by which all other expressions of "Jesus is Lord" are to be tested. That would be the rankest cultural imperialism. I have used English in my example merely to personalize my argument. All I am saying is that if there is an objective standard of truth out there, the ways in which we confess it will vary enormously from culture to culture. Of course, all of this presupposes that there is some sense to the notion of objective truth in the first place, but I will not press that point here.

A further advantage gained from postmodernity is something to which I have already briefly alluded: the sustained attack on modernity, which in some of its manifestations was no friend of the Christian. This attack does not warrant that we all become "postmodern Christians," whatever that means. It means, rather, that just as Bolshevik Russia, after slicing off eastern Poland and invading the Baltic nations and Finland, could nevertheless become a cobelligerent with the Allies against the Nazis, so postmodernity has proved capable, in God's providence, of launching very heavy artillery against the modernity which, across four centuries, developed in such a way that increasingly it taunted confessional Christianity. The irony is delicious. The modernity which has arrogantly insisted that human reason is the final arbiter of truth has spawned a stepchild that has arisen to slay it. Consider, for instance, these strong words of David Tracy, no friend of confessional Christianity, inveighing against the tie between evolutionary theory and historical consciousness:

> The harsh word "barbarism" fits a culture all too willing to unite two of its greatest achievements—historical consciousness in the humanities and evolutionary theory in the natural and biological sciences—into a grand narrative that tells the modern story as one of an inevitable social evolutionary teleology leading up to and finding its glorious climax in us—the "Westerners," the "moderns." This grand, and finally, bogus narrative becomes the subconscious alibi for all the sins of moderns: for example in the *pecca fortiter* version of the "social Darwinists" (whose number, if not whose name, is still legion). This modern alibi-narrative exists as well in the quieter but finally no less violent forms of the neo-conservatives: Western culture *is* culture; Western classics *are* the classics: where is the Proust of Samoa, etc.? This narrative even drives the remaining liberal versions of the story: Soon all other traditions, all other cultures will quietly fade away as the grand social evolutionary schema of modern liberalism lulls all to rest with the

secret promise of making everything (and everyone) just one more expression of more of the same good liberal worldview.[11]

Nor is Tracy so naive as to think that postmodernity is the last word, or that all postmoderns are above reproach. Indeed, he says, with regret, that the "postmoderns sometimes seem more determined by ennui than by ethics. They are not, in fact, so much repelled by the ethical barbarism of modernity as bored by liberal modernity's 'gray-on-gray' world. This is perhaps an understandable aesthetic response to liberal modernity. But it is only that—a merely aesthetic response without the moral power of the great aesthetic and ethical traditions. . . ."[12]

Quite frankly, I think Tracy's own proposals will not fly. I suspect his epistemology will prove short-lived, and his appeal to ethics is constructed on sand. But he is both capturing and shaping a mood against modernity that is being heeded much more than were Christian analyses. The breakup of the monolith of modernity is not all bad.

Moreover, Christian thinkers have often mistaken their own tradition for the sum of all truth. Theology *can* become an agent of political correctness; Christian institutions *can* become corrupt; preachers *can* ratify the *status quo*, even when reformation is urgently needed. If deconstruction helps some to overthrow the hegemony of *mere* traditionalism, let us be thankful.

The frank calling into question of the finality of human reason in the enterprise of human knowing opens up for Christians the wide panoply of factors that enter into the knowledge of God. On this point I shall say more later, but it may be helpful to quote Sontag:

> Thus one of the chief metaphysical problems of Biblical studies is the place of ecstasy. In a rationalist and empiricist age, emotional involvement is often thought to be distorting, something to be removed in the interest of pursuing "truth." But what if it is the case that, at least where religious documents are concerned, a dispassionate approach may not yield the "truth," precisely because truth in such matters comes with inspiration?[13]

I do not think this is very well put, but the issues it raises are important, and surface more quickly precisely because of the impact of postmodernity.

We may consider one more gain, a mixed one. Michel Foucault argues (it will be remembered) that all interpretations advanced to others are in part an exercise in power. They control, define, sometimes manipulate. It is surely

---

11. David Tracy, "Theology and the Many Faces of Post-modernity," *Theology Today* 51 (1994): 106.

12. Ibid., 107–8.

13. Frederick Sontag, "The Metaphysics of Biblical Studies," *Journal of the Evangelical Theological Society* 35 (1992): 192.

important to acknowledge the element of truth in the point, and guard ourselves, for instance, against trying to manipulate people into the kingdom. At the same time, it is important to recognize that on Foucault's view even Foucault's view is manipulative and controlling, so we should not take it too seriously, less we find ourselves enslaved by it!

My first point, then, is that Christians have a vested interest in acknowledging that the new hermeneutic, deconstruction, and postmodernity say important and true things. Moreover, by acknowledging these things we may gain a hearing among some who would otherwise shut us out.

2. Practical experience with the way people actually communicate confirms that accurate communication is possible.

A few years ago I was teaching an evening course on hermeneutics, a course jointly offered by several of the seminaries in the Chicago area. Not very successfully, I was trying to set out both what could be learned from the new hermeneutic, and where the discipline was likely to lead one astray. In particular, I was insisting that true knowledge is possible, even to finite, culture-bound creatures. A doctoral student from another seminary waited patiently through two or three hours of lectures, and then quietly protested that she did not think I was escaping from the dreaded positivism of the nineteenth century. Deeper appreciation for the ambiguities of language, the limits of our understanding, the uniqueness of each individual, and the social nature of knowledge would surely drive me to a more positive assessment of the new hermeneutic. I tried to defend my position, but I was quite unable to persuade her.

Finally, in a moment of sheer intellectual perversity on my part, I joyfully exclaimed, "Ah, now I think I see what you are saying. You are using delicious irony to affirm the objectivity of truth." The lady was not amused. "That is exactly what I am *not* saying," she protested with some heat, and she laid out her position again. I clasped my hands in enthusiasm and told her how delighted I was to find someone using irony so cleverly in order to affirm the possibility of objective knowledge. Her answer was more heated, but along the same lines as her first reply. I believe she also accused me of twisting what she was saying. I told her I thought it was marvelous that she should add emotion to her irony, all to the purpose of exposing the futility of extreme relativism, thereby affirming truth's objectivity. Not surprisingly, she exploded in real anger, and accused me of a lot of unmentionable things.

When she finally cooled down, I said, rather quietly, "But this is how I am reading you."

Of course, she saw what I was getting at immediately, and sputtered out like a spent candle. She simply did not know what to say. My example was artificial, of course, since I only pretended to read her in a certain way, but what I did was sufficient to prove the point I was trying to make to her. "You are a deconstructionist," I told her, "but you expect me to interpet *your* words aright. More precisely, you are upset because I seem to be divorcing the meaning I claim to see in your words from your intent. Thus, implicitly you affirm the link between text and authorial intent. I have never read a deconstructionist who would be pleased if a reviewer misinterpreted his or her work: thus *in practice* deconstructionists implicitly link their own texts with their own intentions.[14] I simply want the same courtesy extended to Paul."

My point, then, is that in the real world, for all the difficulties there are in communication from person to person and from culture to culture, we still expect people to say more or less what they mean (and if they don't, we chide them for it), and we expect mature people to understand what others say, and represent it fairly. The understanding is doubtless never absolutely exhaustive and perfect, but that does not mean the only alternative is to dissociate text from speaker, and then locate all meaning in the reader or hearer. True knowledge of the meaning *of a text* and even *of the thoughts of the author who wrote it* is possible, even if perfect and exhaustive knowledge is not. That is the way things are in the real world—and that in turn suggests that any theory that flies in the face of these realities needs to be examined again.

Nor will it do to say that in the case of writings whose authors are still living incorrect interpretations can by challenged, but not in the case of writings by authors long deceased. For many scholarly enterprises the importance of authorial intent is still recognized, even while almost everyone tries to avoid the intentional fallacy. Thus in the latest circular from the International Organization for Septuagint and Cognate Studies sent to its members (July 10, 1994), a "Statement of Principles" is provided for their forthcoming new English translation of the Septuagint (NETS). The sixth principle reads as follows: "NETS translators will seek to reflect the meaning of the Greek text in accordance with the ancient translator's perceived intent, and as occasioned by the ancient translator's linguistic approach. . . ." Observe that the text is assumed to have a meaning; that although all translation (in this case from Hebrew to Greek) involves interpretation, it is assumed that the translator's intent can be perceived from the text that he actually writes. Why should such intent be less discernible in what is not a translation?

The general point has been recognized by many responsible philosophers. Against the threat of solipsism, or complete incommensurability, Stout

---

14. John M. Ellis, *Against Deconstruction* (Princeton: Princeton Univ. Press, 1989), 12–13, provides documentation as to how deconstructionists, when discussing their subject among themselves, "do not hesitate to state a position or to talk of correct and incorrect versions of that position, often asking directly whether a particular formulation is correct."

and Davidson have convincingly demonstrated that virtually any conversation presumes some degree of commonality and of mutual understanding. Almost always enough common ground exists to permit dialogue to commence and to continue. Quite apart from whatever criteria both sides agree constitute a sound or an unsound argument, it is also possible that extended conversation may help them discover and rectify their *dis*agreements regarding appropriate criteria. Stout argues that the intensity of our disagreements frequently blinds us to the range and depth of our agreements—which tend not to be noticed or commented on.[15]

Of course, this presupposes that misreadings are possible, whether of a map or a novel or an essay or the Bible. That very point is disputed: Crosman, for example, thinks that of the various kinds of misreadings, only the kind that finds an interpreter at odds with his or her own interpretive community (a very "weak" sense of misreading) can properly be called a misreading.[16] But even some constructive postmodernists are less skeptical. Thus Griffin argues that there are at least four hard-core commonsense notions shared by all humanity. By commonsense notions he means they are notions common to all humans; by hard-core, he means to set them off from "soft-core" notions that are not really universal, even though some take them that way.

> Included among the hard-core notions common to every person, I claim, are the following: (1) that the person has *freedom*, in the sense of some power for self-determination; (2) that there is an *actual world* beyond the person's present experience which exists independently of and exerts causal efficacy upon that person's interpretive perception of it; (3) that one's interpretive ideas are *true* to the degree that they correspond to that independently existing world; and (4) that, for a least some events, a distinction exists between what happened and *better and/or worse* things that could have happened.[17]

I confess I would not put some of it this way. Moreover, I have not yet inserted God into the discussion. My point is simply that even some postmodernists feel constrained to find common perspectives among interpreters, because the alternatives presented by the extreme positions are negated by our

---

15. Jeffrey Stout, *Ethics After Babel: The Languages of Morals and Their Discontents* (Boston: Beacon Press, 1988), esp. chap. 1; Donald Davidson, "On the Very Idea of a Conceptual Scheme," in *Post-Analytic Philosophy*, ed. John Rajchman and Cornel West (New York: Columbia Univ. Press, 1985), 129–44. Cf. also the essays in Paul Helm, ed., *Objective Knowledge: A Christian Perspective* (Leicester: Inter-Varsity Press, 1987).

16. Robert Crosman, "Is There Such a Thing as Misreading?" in *Criticism and Critical Theory*, ed. Jeremy Hawthorn (London: Edward Arnold, 1984), 1–12.

17. David Ray Griffin, "Introduction: Varieties of Postmodern Theology," in *Varieties of Postmodern Theology*, ed. David Ray Griffin (Albany: State Univ. of New York Press, 1989), 36.

common experience. All the more reason, then, to be suspicious of the claims of deconstruction, in which hermeneutical suspicion becomes a golden key.[18]

What Søren Kierkegaard said one hundred fifty years ago about the ascendency in Europe of Hegel's dialectical historicism and its devaluing of the individual is no less applicable to the rise of postmodernity:

> A passionate tumultuous age will overthrow everything, pull everything down; but a revolutionary age, that is at the same time reflective and passionless, transforms that expression of strength into a feat of dialectics: it leaves everything standing but cunningly empties it of significance. Instead of culminating in a rebellion it reduces the inward reality of all relationships to a reflective tension which leaves everything standing but makes the whole of life ambiguous: so that everything continues to exist factually whilst by a dialectical deceit, *privatissime*, it supplies a secret interpretation that it does not exist.[19]

3. The arguments of too many scholars turn on individualistic definitions and doubtful steps of logic that do not withstand close inspection.

Consider, for example, the recent book by Sandra Schneiders.[20] Although she despairs of redeeming terms such as "infallibility" and "inerrancy," she carefully embraces *and gently redefines* a swarm of other terms: as a Catholic, she thinks of herself as a "believer, that is, a participant in the Christian tradition that produced and claims as its own this book [i.e., the Bible] that it regards as scripture, that is, as the word of God that is inspired, revelatory, authoritative, and normative for the Church...."[21] It would take us too far astray to engage in detailed interaction with her revisions. But what she means by these words does not prevent her from taking some remarkable steps with the text of John 4. I give her summary in her own words: "Given the male tendency, pervasive in the Bible as elsewhere, to reduce women to their sexuality and their sexuality to immorality, I entertained an alternate possiblity about the [Samaritan] woman, namely, that she was not a whore whom Jesus

---

18. See especially Ben F. Meyer, "The Primacy of Consent and the Uses of Suspicion," *Ex Auditu* 2 (1986): 7–18. The same point is made with marvelous humor by N. T. Wright, "Taking the Text with Her Pleasure: A Post-Post-Modernist Response to J. Dominic Crossan *The Historical Jesus: The Life of a Mediterranean Jewish Peasant* (T & T Clark, Harper San Francisco, 1991). (With apologies to A. A. Milne, St Paul and James Joyce)," *Theology* 96 (1993): 303–10.

19. Søren Kierkegaard, *The Present Age* (New York: Harper & Row, 1962), 42–43. I am indebted to Bruce L. Edwards, *The Suicide of Liberal Education: Deconstruction in Academia*, Heritage Lectures, vol. 277 (Washington: Heritage Foundation, 1990), 9.

20. Sandra M. Schneiders, *The Revelatory Text: Interpreting the New Testament as Sacred Scripture* (San Francisco: Harper San Francisco, 1991).

21. Ibid., 196.

converted but a potential spouse whom he invited to intimacy" (294). Schneiders finds some literary "clues" to support her views. She then suggests that the Samaritan woman serves as a symbol for the Samaritan element in the Johannine community, "which understood itself as the New Israel, bride of the true Bridegroom, Jesus" (194). The dialogue about the five husbands becomes "symbolic discourse about the covenant. Jesus the prophet uses the familiar adultery/idolatry metaphor of the prophetic tradition to call Samaria to renounce its historical infidelity and to embrace the worship of the one God in spirit and in truth" (195).

This exegesis of John 4 is no longer rare among feminist interpreters, but doubtless it should get high marks for sheer creativity (one might almost suggest *creatio ex nihilo*). Quite apart from the fact that I remain unconvinced that one can read off the surface of the text as much detail about the Johannine community as many suppose, and quite apart from a series of exegetical and historical judgments Schneiders has taken that deserve detailed refutation, this reading is astonishing even on Schneiders's own terms. For she makes it clear that in her view "the episode in Samaria is, in all likelihood, not an historical event in the life of the earthly Jesus. . . . [It] represents a reading back into the public ministry of Jesus the Johannine community's postresurrection experience of the Samaritan mission and the influence of the Samaritan converts within the community of the fourth gospel."[22] Now if this is a created story with the purpose Schneiders assigns it, what does she mean when, "Given the male tendency, pervasive in the Bible as elsewhere, to reduce women to their sexuality and their sexuality to immorality," she entertains "an alternative possibility about the woman, namely, that she was not a whore whom Jesus converted but a potential spouse whom he invited to intimacy"? Schneiders is not claiming to uncover what "really happened" in an encounter between the historical Jesus and a historical Samaritan woman. As she stated, the story is fictional, and reflects pervasive male tendencies to reduce women to whores. Yet she "entertains an alternative possibility about the woman." What woman? Schneiders has in fact told a *different* story and *treated it as if it were an alternative reading of the story she has already dismissed.*

But my principal point, in this case, is that her hermeneutical approach enables her to take these remarkable steps while still holding that the Bible is "the word of God that is inspired, revelatory, authoritative, and normative for the church." The March Hare strikes again.[23]

---

22. Ibid., 186.
23. For a volume of Old Testament essays displaying a similarly creative imagination, see J. Cheryl Exum, *Fragmented Women: Feminist (Sub)versions of Biblical Narratives* (Valley Forge: Trinity Press International, 1993). The parentheses in the subtitle are Exum's. The ablest practitioners of deconstruction know exactly what they are doing.

This kind of transformation of terms is endemic to a fair bit of postmodern theology. It is pervasive, for example, in the work of Don Cupitt.[24] Nowhere is the problem more noticeable than in postmodernist handling of "truth"—but I shall say more on that subject in the next chapter.

4. Many deconstructionists slant the debate by appealing to indefensible antitheses.

They are inclined to do this in one of two ways. They may set up ostensible disjunctions that are capable of a measure of resolution, or they may set up an apparent antithesis by a rather manipulative emotional appeal.

The first is more common, and so it is easy to find examples. One of the most common is this: deconstructionists may insist on *either* absolute knowledge *or* complete relativism. Either we can know something truly and absolutely, or all so-called "knowledge" is nothing more than opinion, and thus relativized. The criterion is made rigid and extreme. As Juhl puts it, "Is this one of those cases in which an absolute demand has been imposed on a concept, in this case the concept of meaning, such that by its very nature our language is incapable of satisfying the demand?"[25]

An example of the difficulties inherent in language is commonly drawn from Archie Bunker. When his wife asks him if he wants his bowling shoes laced over or under, he offhandedly replies, "What's the difference?" So she tries to explain, in great detail, while the audience is howling with laughter because we perceive that what he means by "What's the difference?" is not "I do not understand the difference and would like you to explain it to me," but simply "I don't give a damn." Yet from this simple example, the deconstructionist Paul de Man, through complex reasoning, finally concludes, "Rhetoric radically suspends logic and opens up vertiginous possibilities of referential aberration."[26] One wants to say, "Give me a break." Archie's wife may not have understood the possibility of a double meaning, but the audience does, or it would not laugh. If Paul de Man were right to the degree that he thinks he is, no one in the audience would be howling with laughter: the joke depends on being able to see both senses and the discrepancy simultaneously. Perhaps people are not as dumb as de Man thinks they are. How does one responsibly move from a simple ambiguity, created for the sake of a joke and

---

24. See, for example, his *Only Human* (London: SCM Press, 1985) and *The Sea of Faith* (London: BBC Publications, 1984). Cf. Brian Hebblethwaite's response, *The Ocean of Truth: A Defence of Objective Theism* (Cambridge: Cambridge Univ. Press, 1988).

25. P. D. Juhl, "Playing with Texts: Can Deconstruction Account for Critical Practice?" in *Criticism and Critical Theory*, ed. Jeremy Hawthorn (London: Edward Arnold, 1984), 61.

26. Cited in ibid., 62–63.

instantly understood by a laughing audience, to "vertiginous possibilities of referential aberration"? We are being manipulated by a rigid and unacceptable antithesis.

This approach is disturbingly common. Thus Culler capably demonstrates that no human knowledge is ever absolute, exhaustive, beyond correction, and then concludes, "Since no reading can escape correction, all readings are misreadings."[27] What does he mean? If all he means is that human interpretations are in principle revisable, his statement is stale and uninteresting: that point has often been made, and long before the rise of deconstruction. What he means is much more. Culler intends to relativize *every* interpretation, and thus to remove meaning, or at least univocal meaning, from text. Instead of supposing that human interpretations may at least approximate to that meaning, to a lesser or greater degree, he has abolutized relativism. Of course, if his statement is then taken strictly (which is apparently what he wants), he has destroyed himself by relativizing his own absolutism. He would render impossible all communication from one mind to another mind by means of a text—including his own work.

Ellis has shown in dexterous detail how seriously flawed this line of reasoning is.[28] Moreover, there are many realms in which knowledge is surely unrevisable. This is true not only of many branches of mathematics (Pythagoras's theorem is as true today as it was two and a half millennia ago), but of many scientific discoveries as well. As Dembski has argued, general scientific theories are notorious for being revised or overturned, and so of course deconstructionists, not to say many philosophers of science, focus on them—just as in the literary field, deconstructionists tend to focus on poems, fiction, and parables. "But who seriously questions the efficacy of the smallpox vaccine in controlling smallpox or the capacity of morphine to suppress pain? And who thinks that our judgments on these matters are likely to change in the future?"[29] Of course, one may find better drugs than morphine, or discover hitherto unknown side effects of the smallpox vaccine, or uncover more of the mechanisms of its operation, but none of this calls in question the validity of the concrete claims made in these areas. And that at least raises the possibility of objective knowledge in other areas. But none of this is

27. Jonathan Culler, *On Deconstruction: Theory and Criticism After Structuralism* (Ithaca: Cornell Univ. Press, 1982), 178. One cannot help remarking that this is a rather categorical statement for a deconstructionist.

28. John M. Ellis, *Against Deconstruction* (Princeton: Princeton Univ. Press, 1989), 98–112.

29. Bill Dembski, "Truth with a Capital 'T'," *Transactions* 2/1 (February 1994): 3. Cf. further his *Incompleteness of Scientific Naturalism and Its Implications for a Scientifically Defensible Account of Intelligent Design in Nature* (Richardson: Foundation for Thought and Ethics, 1992).

allowed, in large part because the antitheses have been set up in forms super-ficially difficult to challenge.

A second example may be drawn from Derrida. Saussure, the father of modern linguistics, had argued that words, as linguistic signs, whether oral or written, are arbitrary. There is nothing that necessarily connects "tree" in English or *arbre* in French with any particular tree, or with the concept of treeness.[30] In his usage, *signifier* referred to the sound pattern or written form of the word, *signified* referred to the concept itself, and *sign* to the combina-tion of the two. The signifier, then, is arbitrary. What ensures that it has meaning are the *differences* between any one signifier and all other signifiers. For a competent English speaker, what gives "tree" its meaning is nothing intrinsic to the word itself, but precisely what it is not, i.e., how it differs from all other words (tea, three, thee, these, and so forth). In other words, "two signs *a* and *b* are never grasped as such by our linguistic consciousness, but only the difference between *a* and *b*."[31] This perspective generated his much-quoted claim, "*In the language itself, there are only differences.* Even more impor-tant than that is the fact that, although in general a difference presupposes positive terms between which the difference holds, in a language there are only differences, *and no positive terms.*"[32]

Part of this can be challenged, and Saussure himself backs down a little. But Jacques Derrida begins at this point, and develops it in ways never fore-seen by Saussure. Derrida says that the rigid maintenance of the distinction between the signifier and the signified gives the impression that there exist signifieds quite apart from signifiers.[33] Such a concept Derrida calls a "tran-scendental signified." Western philosophy, he contends, has been shot through with the assumption that these transcendental signifieds—God, con-sciousness, truth, intentionality, meaning, self, being—have some genuine reassuring existence apart from signifiers, and are actually present with us.[34] In reality, there is no escape from language. And each word is able to signify only because of the differences it sustains with all other words. Each signifier functions only because of its relationships with what it is not, with that from which it is distinct. "Nothing, neither among the elements nor within the system, is anywhere ever simply present or absent. There are only, every-

---

30. Ferdinand de Saussure, *Course in General Linguistics*, trans. Roy Harris (LaSalle: Open Court, 1986), 65–68.

31. Ibid., 116. In his defense, it should be noted that Saussure extends his theory to account for onomatopoeia and other apparent anomalies.

32. Ibid., 118 (emphasis his).

33. Jacques Derrida, *Positions*, trans. Alan Bass (Chicago: Univ. of Chicago Press, 1981), 19.

34. This theme constantly recurs in Derrida. See, for example, *Of Grammatology* (Chicago: Univ. of Chicago Press, 1976), 49.

where, differences and traces of traces."[35] So tightly bound is everything and every concept to language that Derrida recognizes that his implicit overthrow of Western metaphysics is forced to use the categories of metaphysics, since we have inherited no other. Moreover, if Saussure could say that difference is what enables signifiers to have meaning, Derrida goes further and insists that meaning is present only as an effect of linguistic difference.

Indeed, he invents a new word at this juncture, the French neologism *différance*, i.e., *différence* spelled with an *a*. What Derrida means by this is complicated,[36] but nicely laid out by Moore, who comments that *différance* is "Saussurean *différence* writ large."[37] It is not a thing, a being, but is everything that makes concepts possible in linguistic expression. The play of differences means than no single element can be simply present or absent itself, for any element achieves meaning by playing off all the things it is not.

At this point Derrida takes two crucial steps. First, he elevates the written word above the oral word. Most of us accept that oral speech is in some respects prior to writing. This is so not least in Christianity. Before there is the Bible, God speaks. God makes himself present through speech. Even the Son of God is called the Word (John 1:1). In the common assumptions of Western thought, speech signals presence; by contrast, writing hints at absence. This idea, which links speech and presence, Derrida labels "logocentrism" and condemns it as "an ethnocentric metaphysics. It is related to the history of the West."[38] If I understand him correctly, Derrida labels the hurley-burly of linguistic elements playing off one another to achieve meaning *writing*, and insists that this writing is necessarily antecedent to speech. Such writing is thus not the fossilization of speech, or a container for speech; rather, it is the necessary presupposition of speech. And second, as we saw in chapter 2, Derrida (and some other deconstructionists, for that matter) thinks that all language refers only to other language; it is incapable of referring to entitites other than language.

Such is one small part of the complex thought of the thinker who is usually thought of as the world's leading deconstructionist. My purpose in setting out these elements of his thinking is simply to provide another few examples of antithetical thinking gone amuck.

Let us begin with the claim that texts can only refer to other texts. Even Richard Rorty, who provided us with the assessment "It's all words, all the way down" (see chap. 2, above), offers these trenchant comments:

---

35. Derrida, *Positions*, 26.
36. Jacques Derrida, "Différance," in *Margins of Philosophy*, trans. Alan Bass (Chicago: Univ. of Chicago Press, 1982), 1–27.
37. Moore, *Poststructuralism*, 21–25, esp. 21.
38. *Of Grammatology*, 20.

As usual with pithy little formulae, the Derridean claim that "There is nothing outside the text" is right about what it implicitly denies and wrong about what it explicitly asserts. The *only* force of saying that texts do not refer to nontexts is just the old pragmatist chestnut that any specification of a referent is going to be in some vocabulary. Thus one is really comparing two descriptions of a thing rather than a description with the thing-in-itself. . . .

There are, alas, people nowadays who owlishly inform us "philosophy has *proved*" that language does not refer to anything nonlinguistic, and thus that everything one can talk about is a text. This claim is on a par with the claim that Kant proved that we cannot know about things-in-themselves. Both claims rest on a phony contrast between some sort of nondiscursive unmediated vision of the real and the way we actually talk and think. Both falsely infer from "We can't think without concepts, or talk without words" to "We can't think or talk except about what has been created by our thought and talk."[39]

A further connection is then often made, especially in American scholarship. From the assumption that texts cannot talk about "reality," it soon begins to appear that the only thing they can talk about is "their inability to do so."[40] Rorty quotes Gerald Graff's remark that "from the thesis that language cannot correspond to reality, it is a short step to the current revisionist mode of interpretation that specializes in reading all literary works as commentaries on their own epistemological problematics," and remarks:

It is in fact a rather long step, and a step backward. The tendency Graff speaks of is real enough, but it is a tendency to think that literature can take the place of philosophy by *mimicking* philosophy—by being, of all things, *epistemological*. Epistemology still looks classy to weak textualists. They think that by viewing a poet as having an epistemology they are paying him a compliment. They even think that in criticizing his theory of knowledge they are being something more than a mere critic—being, in fact, a philosopher. Thus conquering warriors might mistakenly think to impress the populace by wrapping themselves in shabby togas stripped from the local senators. Graff and others who have pointed to the weirdly solemn pretentiousness of much recent textualist criticism are right, I think, in claiming that such critics want to have the supposed prestige of philosophy without the necessity of offering arguments.[41]

---

39. Richard Rorty, as cited by Iain Wright, "History, Hermeneutics, Deconstruction," in Hawthorn, *Criticism and Critical Theory*, 89.

40. To use the language of Iain Wright, "History, Hermeneutics, Deconstruction," 90.

41. Richard Rorty, "Nineteenth-Century Idealism and Twentieth-Century Textualism," in his *Consequences of Pragmatism* (Minneapolis: Univ. of Minnesota Press, 1982), 154–56.

Obviously, fundamental errors of this sort are particularly egregious in texts purporting to convey historical information.[42]

Probably no one has done a better job than John Ellis at pointing out the flaws in Derrida's argument.[43] Derrida's charge that the entire Western tradition, including Saussure, is guilty of ethnocentrism in promoting speech above writing, is a major historical misunderstanding. Saussure openly opposed the ethnocentrism of Western linguists who had tended to elevate the written language above speech. They inevitably focused on cultures with a lengthy written tradition, and, focusing on written texts, developed their philology around written materials. Saussure reversed this by demonstrating that the oral language is the driving agent of change that ultimately establishes the shape of any language.[44]

As for arguing that writing is prior to speech, the countervailing evidence is abundant. To quote what Ellis marshals:

1. Speech quite clearly existed long before the *invention* of writing.
2. There still exist in the world languages that are spoken but not written, but none that are written without being spoken.
3. There are large numbers of individuals who speak without writing, but none who write without speaking (except when their physical capacity to produce speech is deficient).
4. There are many different forms of writing, but linguists of all persuasions agree that *no* form of writing in general use is adequate to record all that there is in language; intonation, stress, pitch, and other communicative features are not adequately dealt with even in the best writing systems. All writing systems are *in principle* only attempts to represent languages that *must* in varying degrees be incomplete.[45]

Derrida tries to cover himself without frankly admitting it:

If "writing" signifies inscription and especially the durable institution of a sign (and that is the only irreducible kernel of the concept of writing), writing in general covers the entire field of linguistic signs. In that field a certain sort of instituted signifiers may then appear, "graphic" in the narrow and derivative sense of the word, ordered by a certain relationship with other instituted—hence "written," even if they are "phonic"—signifiers. The very idea of institution—hence of the arbitrariness of the sign—is unthinkable before the possibility of writing and outside its horizon.[46]

42. See the useful book by V. Philips Long, *The Art of Biblical History* (Grand Rapids: Zondervan, 1994).
43. *Against Deconstruction*, 18–28.
44. Ibid., 19–20.
45. Ibid., 21.
46. Derrida, *Of Grammatology*, 44.

Ellis points out three holes in the argument. *First*, the idea that the institution of signs is unthinkable before the *possibility* of writing is useless. "To assert that as soon as speech arises, writing it down is possible, might *at best* be to argue for the *equal* status of speech and writing."[47] But that would not meet the exigencies of Derrida's insistence that writing is prior to speech, and in any case the evidence is against it. *Second*, Derrida has warped the meaning of the word "writing" by saying that the "only irreducible kernel of the concept of writing" is the "durable institution of signs." That is not true. "What is irreducibly essential to the idea of writing is the *visual* recording of the sign."[48] This key omission is what permits him to proceed to the *third* error, and it is the most important: he falls into a logical mistake. It is worth quoting Ellis at length:

> We begin with three terms: language, speech, and writing. The first contains the second and third. The question is now which of these last two has priority. Derrida is attempting to prove that the third has priority over the second, in the face of some obvious arguments to the contrary. To do so, he replaces the first triad of terms (language, speech, writing) with a different triad: writing, phonic, graphic. He substitutes the second triad for the first, and now writing has precedence over everything.
>
> It is not difficult to see what is wrong with this procedure. First of all, the nature of the phenomenon concerned has *not* been changed. If we decide arbitrarily to call language "writing," speech "phonic," and writing "graphic," we have not changed the relation of the three entities: what we ordinarily call "language" still stands in the same relationship to speech and writing whether we use these three names or the other three. Second, this procedure does, of course, involve a misuse of English. Language does *not* mean writing, and if we use "writing" to substitute for "language" we have misspoken.[49]

Derrida's real concern, of course, is a kind of moralizing condemnation of speech, because it seems to some to be closer to tying together language and reality or language and presence.[50] So Derrida brands it "logocentrism" and condemns it, and, in charged moralistic expressions, insists on the priority of writing.[51]

---

47. Ellis, *Against Deconstruction*, 23.

48. Ibid., 24.

49. Ibid., 24. The same problems exist, of course, in French, the language in which Derrida writes. Ellis's argument is not weakened by his reference to "misuse of English."

50. According to Derrida, speech commonly ties language and reality together more than writing does because "voice" is a metaphor for self-presence, before consciousness thinking clearly *before* thinking in language. I am indebted to Kevin J. Vanhoozer for clarifying this point for me.

51. For a detailed critique, see Ellis, *Against Deconstruction*, 30–66.

It would not be hard to show that a great deal of Derrida's thought resorts to extreme and sometimes duplicitous antitheses. From Saussure's insight that thought or concepts without words are impossible, and that formally words are arbitrary, and that (in a slightly exaggerated expression) the meanings of words turn on difference, what extreme and disputable inferences have been drawn! It is one thing to say, "Man does not live in relation to being as such, but in relation to being as it is present to him, and that means in language."[52] It is certainly appropriate to work through the difficulties language has in "presenting" being. It is another to resort to what Descombes calls "the grammatical reduction of ontological propositions."[53]

As a final example we may return to the illustration of Stanley Fish, introduced in chapter 2 of this book. It will be recalled that for one class he listed a number of authors to indicate reading assignments; for the next class, on seventeenth-century religious poetry, he asked his students to interpret it as a poem:

> Jacobs-Rosenbaum
> Levin
> Thorne
> Hayes
> Ohman (?)

Everything depended, according to Fish, on what the two "interpretive communities" brought to this "text." From this example, Fish denies that we go to texts like Scripture to find meaning, but to make it. There it is again: the hard antithesis.

The literary critic Robert Scholes is unconvinced by Fish's illustration. He writes:

> Suppose that what had been left on the blackboard was not simply a list of names in a vaguely emblematic shape. Suppose the text had taken the form of a prose statement of the assignment that read as follows:
>
> > For next Thursday read the essays in the Jacobs and Rosenbaum anthology by Levin, Thorne, Hayes, and Ohmann.
>
> If this were the case, would Fish have told the class that the text constituted a religious poem? If he had, would they have succeeded so splendidly in perceiving it as one? I think the answer to both questions is, "No." To any competent reader of English the prosaic quality of this sentence would make it

---

52. Robert W. Funk, *Language, Hermeneutic, and Word of God* (New York: Harper & Row, 1966), 51.

53. Vincent Descombes, *Objects of All Sorts: A Philosophical Grammar*, trans. Lorna Scott-Fox and Jeremy Harding (Baltimore: Johns Hopkins Univ. Press, 1986), 112–37.

difficult to perceive as poetry. I'm not saying it couldn't be done. I am say-ing it wouldn't be done.[54]

In other words, texts themselves normally contain many signals and hints as to how they are to be interpreted, and many of these are mastered as people learn to read. Fish has skewed the evidence by giving *misleading* clues to the community of interpreters. How then can his example illustrate his thesis? Moreover, as Long argues, " . . . encounters with Scripture itself have built up in the community of faith the expectation of Scripture's special character, rather than the other way around. The expectations a faithful interpreter brings to Scripture are not imposed upon those documents entirely from without but are derived from the history of the community's previous engage-ment with the Bible."[55] Relations among these three—Scripture, the (inter-pretive) community of faith, and the faithful interpreter—are far more complicated, as we shall see, than Fish's illustration suggests. It is simply reductionistic to adopt the position that Gellner charmingly parodies: "There is no meaning but meaning, and Hermeneutics is its Prophet."[56]

The second form of arbitrary antithesis is much cruder, and more explic-itly manipulative. It is the deployment of emotionally loaded words to stig-matize any reading that thinks there is objective meaning, and of equally loaded words to praise the ostensible freedom that belongs to the decon-structionist. Here is Derrida again:

> As a turning toward the presence, lost or impossible, of the absent ori-gin, this structuralist thematic of broken immediateness is thus the sad, *neg-ative*, nostalgic, guilty, Rousseauist facet of the thinking of freeplay of which the Nietzschean *affirmation*—the joyous affirmation of the freeplay of the world and without truth, without origin, offered to an active intepretation—would be the other side.[57]

Despite Culler's insistence that Derrida is not here saying one approach is better than another,[58] none but avid or ingenuous disciples of Derrida could read the original article and rush to that conclusion. As Wright puts it, "It is

---

54. Robert Scholes, *Textual Power: Literary Theory and the Teaching of English* (New Haven: Yale Univ. Press, 1985), 158–59.

55. Thomas G. Long, *Preaching and the Literary Forms of the Bible* (Philadelphia: Fortress Press, 1989), 29.

56. Ernest Gellner, *Postmodernism, Reason, and Religion* (London/New York: Routledge, 1992), 24.

57. Jacques Derrida, "Structure, Sign, and Play in the Discourse of the Human Sciences," in *The Structuralist Controversy: The Languages of Criticism and the Sciences of Man*, ed. Richard Macksey and Eugenio Donato (Baltimore: Johns Hopkins Univ. Press, 1970), 264 (emphasis his).

58. *On Deconstruction*, 132.

quite clear what the intention of this emotion-laden rhetoric is, and what in practice its effects have been: to stigmatize origin-oriented hermeneutics as fuddy-duddy, immature and destructive of individual freedom and creativity."[59]

5. Models from the hard sciences are of some, but limited, use. It is important to understand why this should be so.

There was a time when Christian thinkers drew close analogies between theology and the hard sciences. This of course arose in large part because they were wrestling with the challenges of modernity, as we must wrestle with the challenges of postmodernity. As a single instance of a very common attitude, consider this example from Machen:

> Theology, we hold, is not an attempt to express in merely symbolic terms an inner experience which must be expressed in different terms in subsequent generations; but it is a setting forth of those facts upon which experience is based. It is not indeed a complete setting forth of those facts, and therefore progress in theology become [sic] possible; but it may be true so far as it goes; and only because there is that possibility of attaining truth and of setting it forth ever more completely can there be progress. Theology, in other words, is just as much a science as is chemistry; and like the science of chemistry it is capable of advance. The two sciences, it is true, differ widely in their subject matter; they differ widely in the character of the evidence upon which their conclusions are based; in particular they differ widely in the qualifications required of the investigator: but they are both sciences, because they are both concerned with the acquisition and orderly arrangement of a body of truth.[60]

There are parts of this with which I would want to be associated today. Over against the endless subjectivism that finally grounds all theology in nothing more than personal experience, or, in contemporary categories, the limitations of individual perceptions, from any truly Christian perspective it is important to insist there are some facts out there on which all theology finally depends. Yet even the attempt to set this out begins to highlight critical differences.

Let us attempt a simple parallelism. Chemistry holds that the water molecule is made up of two hydrogen atoms and one oxygen atom: that is a fact. Of course, one may then comment on the isotopic oddity of "heavy water," and analyze the peculiar configuration of the orbitals of the electrons of the water molecule such that greater density is achieved at four degrees Celsius than at the freezing point, thus ensuring that lakes and rivers freeze from the

59. Wright, "History, Hermeneutics, Deconstruction," 87.
60. J. Gresham Machen, *What Is Faith?* (Grand Rapids: Eerdmans, 1946), 32–33.

top down; but the initial fact is still a fact, no more and no less. Similarly, theology holds that Jesus Christ rose from the dead, and that in resurrection form he was seen, touched, handled; that he ate and drank: that is a fact. Of course, one may then venture some exploration of the nature of the resurrection body, tie the resurrection of Jesus in various ways to the resurrection at the End and to the resurrection of Lazarus, and so forth; but the initial fact is still a fact, no more and no less.

Immediately one detects an array of differences between these two "facts." Confessing Christians will still want to insist that in both cases we are indeed dealing with facts, yet the differences call out for explication. At one level Machen was right, but although he hinted at some of the distinctions between theology and the hard sciences, he did not tease them out. Yet these differences lie at the heart of many contemporary disputes. The following brief comments do not take us very far, but may provide some helpful orientation.

First, the fact of the atomic constitution of the water molecule is universally recognized; the fact of Jesus' resurrection is not universally recognized. Amongst many contemporary scholars, that distinction is decisive: the former deals with fact or truth, while the latter is mere opinion and depends on "faith." Jeanrond quotes Habermas with approval: "Truth is that special coercion which leads to unforced universal acknowledgement; this however is connected with an ideal situation of discourse and that means a form of life in which free, uncoerced communication is possible."[61] Something like this is today widely assumed.

Yet observe two elements of Habermas's quotation. (1) He is careful not to allow truth to correspond to reality. Nor is truth the reality itself. Truth is not what is out there, what really exists, whether it is acknowledged or not. Rather, truth is "that special coercion" that wins universal assent, for whatever reason. No thoughtful Christian can be satisfied with that definition. (2) The words "unforced universal acknowledgement" are slightly ingenuous. Do the pygmies in equatorial rain forests acknowledge the molecular, let alone the atomic, nature of water? Does a five-year-old Westerner recognize the truth that water molecules are made up of two hydrogen atoms and one oxygen atom? Do *all* well-trained scientists buy into naturalistic evolution as the ultimate explanation of origins? But if Habermas were to modify his phrase to "unforced universal acknowledgement among the competent" or the like, then it becomes necessary to define "competent." And then may not

---

61. Jürgen Habermas, in *Hermeneutik und Ideologiekritik*, by Karl-Otto Apel, Claus v. Bormann, Rüdiger Bubner, Hans-Georg Gadamer, Hans Joachim Giegel, Jürgen Habermas; Theorie Diskussion (Frankfurt a.M.: Suhrkamp, 1971), 154; cited in Werner G. Jeanrond, *Text and Interpretation as Categories of Theological Thinking* (New York: Crossroad, 1988), 24.

Christians do the same? Who is competent to affirm the truth that Jesus rose from the dead? Does not the difference in the kinds of competencies required in the two cases take us back to Machen's observation, "in particular they differ widely in the qualifications of the investigator"? (3) Must the acknowledgement be at the present instant? Presumably, as more people are educated in the hard sciences, more people will recognize the nature of the water molecule. But by the same token, one day all will recognize that Jesus rose from the dead. Does that mean the fact of Jesus' resurrection is untrue until all acknowledge it?

If qualifications for knowing some things include moral and spiritual dimensions (a point I shall argue more fully in the next chapter), it is understandable why there is wider agreement in the hard sciences than in theology. Only a rationalistic view of theology would think otherwise. Most conclusions in the hard sciences make little demand on human beings in the moral and spiritual realms. In chemistry, the chemist remains more or less in control. This is not to deny that the chemist who is a thoughtful believer will recognize the externally given limits to and characteristics of water, acknowledge the Creator's wisdom in his design, and so forth. Rather, it is to say that chemists control and repeat their experiments, and their subject matter makes few moral demands on the experimenter. By contrast, if theology deals with a personal/transcendent God, the theologian begins by acknowledging his or her own indebtedness to and dependence upon that God. Christians who think about God do not control their subject; their subject makes his demands of them. In Christian theology, the theologian must begin by acknowledging that he or she is not in control. That is an insurmountable hurdle for many people—indeed, for all of us, apart from grace.

Second, we observed in the preceding chapter that some scholars have interpreted Kuhn's "scientific revolutions" theory to suggest that there are no brute scientific facts. All facts are theory-laden, and these theories may themselves be overturned. Thus, proponents of radical hermeneutics find themselves consoled that not even in science is there any objective meaning: all meaning resides in the interpreter, with all the subjectivity that implies.

Now, however, a strong reaction against that view is beginning to form. I have already cited Dembski's argument that the relativists love to appeal to general scientific theories, while in fact there are many concrete results in science that are not revisable. Others have taken up the philosophical challenge.[62] This is not to suggest there are not some difficult hurdles to cross in

---

62. E.g., Larry Laudan, *Science and Relativism: Some Key Controversies in the Philosophy of Science* (Chicago: Univ. of Chicago Press, 1990); Roger Trigg, *Reality at Risk: A Defence of Realism in Philosophy and the Sciences* (Sussex: Harvester Press, 1980).

the analysis of the ways in which language relates to the real world. It is to say that the contemporary reductionism is being challenged.

Third, especially in the hard sciences progress is made by *repeatable* tests. Even if we allow due place for Kuhn's "scientific revolutions," the fact remains (as he himself would acknowledge) that the accumulating evidence that eventually drives a scientific revolution is largely gleaned from repeatable tests. Scientific experiments are controlled, and can be repeated by other scientists in independent laboratories.[63] The explanations that seem best able to explain these testable results are given the widest credence. But nothing of this is true for theologians who are convinced the validation of their work lies in history. The tension, in other words, is not so much between science and religion per se, as between the domain of the repeatable and the domain of history. As Oden puts it:

> The heart of scientific method is verification. Historians cannot achieve verification, since the events have disappeared into the past. History cannot be reenacted. There is something amusing about the spectacle of historians seeking absolute verification. Proximate verification must depend upon the testimony of witnesses and the evidence of past documents fairly and honestly analyzed. The documents of ancient history are available largely on a chance (not a rational or equal or deliberate or extensive) basis, whereas evidences of physics are everywhere available for current experimentation. These factors limit historical inquiry so as to make it nonanalogous with physics. . . .[64]

Fourth, the scientific model so occupied Machen that, at least in these sorts of discussions, he tended to treat the Bible as a quarry. He would not have denied, of course, that among other things it is extraordinarily rich in the diversity of the genres of literature that are represented in it. This reality, however, further removes the task of the theologian from that of, say, the physicist. The sheer range of interpretive responsibilities laid on the shoulders of the interpreter of Scripture tends to shut down merely scientific models. And they plunge us back into the raging modern hermeneutical debate.

Fifth, despite all that I have said, especially when one rises above fairly small scientific discoveries, one's presuppositions enjoy rising importance.[65] Probably this is nowhere more dramatically obvious than in the subject of origins. In a powerful and influential book, Michael Denton attacks the theo-

---

63. Except, of course, in those rare instances when only one or two labs in the world would have the necessary equipment—as in the discovery of the top quark at Fermilab.

64. Thomas C. Oden, *After Modernity . . . What? Agenda for Theology* (Grand Rapids: Zondervan, 1990), 123.

65. See the thoughtful little book by Jan H. Boer, *Science Without Faith Is Dead* (Jos: Institute of Church and Society, 1991).

ry of evolution in most of its modern forms, insisting that the evidence for it is slight, flawed, and contradicted by too much counter-evidence. Then, as he draws his book to a close, he argues that he cannot accept some theory of creation, and so supposes there must be a better "scientific" explanation out there that will one day be discovered.[66] In other words, his presuppositional commitment to naturalism is so strong that even his own competent reading of the evidence cannot overturn it.

6. There are some models of approaching texts that glean the best from the new hermeneutic, but do not destroy all possibility of objective truth.

Although I have repeatedly used the expression "objective truth" in this book, it seems wise to clarify it at this point. By "objective" I mean "having extra-mental reality or validity."[67] Objective reality exists independently of individual or communal states of human consciousness; objective truth is distinct from individual or communal states of human consciousness and obtains regardless of whether anyone happens to accept it as truth.

The point to be made here is that there are models that allow for the valid insights of the new hermeneutic and of deconstruction without falling off the end into the extreme relativism and denial of objective truth that characterize postmoderns. We may briefly mention a few such models.

(1) Gadamer spoke of *Horizontsentfremdung* and *Horizonts-verschmelzung*, expressions that have come to be rendered by "distanciation" and "fusion of horizons." The idea is that if all the cultural "baggage" of a text is likened to one horizon, and all the cultural "baggage" of a reader is likened to another horizon, it is possible for the reader progressively to distance himself from his own horizon as he reads himself into the text, and thus finally so to "fuse" his own horizon of understanding with that of the text that some accurate transfer of information is possible, even if never perfect. As far as I can see, Gadamer is less than clear as to whether this model allows us to speak of objective truth.[68] But Thiselton and others have turned it to that use.

Obviously readers cannot distance themselves absolutely from their own baggage. But even if distanciation is never perfect, it can be remarkably effective. Such readers not only try to understand the social setting, meaning of words, cultural context, emotional overtones and symbolic associations of the text to be studied, but self-consciously distance themselves, so far as that is possible, from the automatic assumptions brought to bear by uncritical reading.

---

66. Michael Denton, *Evolution: A Theory in Crisis* (Bethesda: Adler & Adler, 1986).

67. The words are from Harold A. Netland, in a private communication.

68. See the discussion in Anthony C. Thiselton, *The Two Horizons: New Testament Hermeneutics and Philosophical Description* (Grand Rapids: Eerdmans 1980), esp. 314–19.

For example, readers of John 6:25ff., the bread of life discourse, will not only note the connection of the discourse with the feeding of the five thousand reported at the beginning of the chapter, and the background assumptions associated with "manna" generated by the Old Testament and adopted or revised in Second Temple Judaism, but they will also ask what associations "bread" has for first-century Jews living in their ancient homeland. For us, bread is something that comes in fifty or sixty varieties, usually wrapped in plastic, and obtainable from the shelves of the local supermarket. For first-century Jews, it was one of two staples: without it, you died. Moreover, first-century Jews lived in a largely agrarian world. They understood that almost everything we eat is supplied by something else's death. Meat comes from a dead animal; bread comes from dead wheat or barley. The only exceptions are a few minerals (e.g., salt). Suddenly words like these take on new force: "If anyone eats of this bread, he will live forever. This bread is my flesh, which I will give for the life of the world" (John 6:51). In the flow of the discourse, Jesus claims not only to be the antitype of the manna God provided under Moses, and the true significance of the symbol-laden miracle of the feeding of the five thousand, but the one who gives his life that others may live. Without his death, no one lives. He is the "staple" of all spiritual life, and he achieves this by his death. That last point is less than transparent to late twentieth-century urban, industrialized society. A little distanciation, a little fusing of our horizon with that of the first-century text, and it seems clear enough.

(2) A less complicated model is the "hermeneutical spiral" (the title of a recent book).[69] Instead of going round and round an endless hermeneutical circle, one can as it were "spiral in" on the truth, as one asks better questions of a text, and hears more accurate answers.

(3) A mathematical example I have sometimes used is the *asymptote*. A curved line may approach a straight line asymptotically, never quite touching it but always getting closer, so close, in fact, that all of differential and integral calculus—that branch of mathematics without which it would have been impossible to put human beings on the moon—depends upon such models of closeness. The model is useful precisely because it never touches the axis. In exactly the same way, we may not aspire to absolute knowledge of the sort only Omniscience may possess, but the "approximation" may be so good that it is adequate for placing human beings on the moon.

The point of all such models is that although none of us ever knows any complicated thing exhaustively, we can know some things truly. Our confidence in what we know may not enjoy the certainty of Omniscience, but it is not condemned to futility. Even a child may believe and understand the truth

---

69. Grant R. Osborne, *The Hermeneutical Spiral* (Downers Grove: InterVarsity Press, 1992).

of the proposition "God loves the world," even when the child's knowledge of God, love, and the world is minimal, and her grasp of Johannine theology still less (John 3:16). With patient study and increased learning and rising experience, a believer may come to understand a great deal more about the proposition "God loves the world" than does the child. The diligent student of John's gospel soon learns that "world" in John is usually a term that describes the moral order: human beings in rebellion against God. God's love is wonderful, in John 3:16, not because the world is so big, but because the world is so bad. Further study would show that God's love for the world is declared in a context that affirms his wrath upon the world (3:36), and this will lead to serious study of God, and of atonement passages in the Johannine corpus (e.g., 1 John 2:2). But would it not be incorrect to say that the child *misunderstands* the proposition? The proposition as John gave it, I would argue, is true; as grasped by the child, it is truly understood, even if not exhaustively understood. The child may have (and probably has) adopted some *false* associations along with her understanding—associating love, perhaps, with a good cuddle, or with a kind parent. But the heart of the matter is nevertheless rightly said to be understood, even if there is further explanation (and demonstration!) of God's love to come in the child's experience. The asymptote will draw closer to the axis. The child who grows to become a thoughtful and serious reader will learn distanciation and the fusion of horizons.

(4) Stanley Fish, we have seen, relativizes interpretations by emphasizing how much the interpreter's categories have been determined by the surrounding "interpretive community." But Paul Ricoeur's analysis is more profound. He too insists that there is a surplus of meaning in texts that transcends authorial intent; like Fish, he insists on assigning an important role to the stream of tradition (cf. Fish's "interpretive community") in which the interpreter stands. Philosophy, he repeats, does not begin empty-handed. But he insists that the text bridges the hermeneutical gulf between reader *and author*. Ricoeur constantly insists on a humble and attentive spirit before the text, and develops his interpretive theory so as to empower the reader the better to handle narrative and symbol and metaphor.[70] His work has been a powerful stimulus for one or two avowedly Christian thinkers.[71]

---

70. Ricoeur's works are voluminous. Among his more important ones, for our purposes, are *Interpretation Theory: Discourse and the Surplus of Meaning* (Fort Worth: Texas Christian Univ. Press, 1976); *Essays in Biblical Interpretation*, ed. Lewis Mudge (Philadelphia: Fortress Press, 1980); *Hermeneutics and the Human Sciences*, ed. and trans. John B. Thompson (Cambridge: Cambridge Univ. Press, 1981).

71. See especially Kevin J. Vanhoozer, *Biblical Narrative in the Philosophy of Paul Ricoeur: A Study in Hermeneutics and Theology* (Cambridge: Cambridge Univ. Press, 1990). Less insightful, but no less influenced by Ricoeur, is the work by Lynn M. Poland, *Literary Criticism and Biblical Hermeneutics: A Critique of Formalist Approaches* (Chico: Scholars Press, 1985).

It is not possible here to evaluate the contribution of numerous other thinkers, such as Michael Polanyi, whose theory of knowledge emphasizes the need for the observer to be committed to the notion of objective reality, and whose work has so greatly influenced Lesslie Newbigin.[72] Instead, it may be useful to reflect on a poem that many in my generation memorized when we were at school:

> It was six men of Indostan
>   To learning much inclined,
> Who went to see the elephant
>   (Though all of them were blind),
> That each by observation
>   Might satisfy his mind.
>
> The First approached the elephant
>   And, happening to fall
> Against his broad and sturdy side,
>   At once began to bawl:
> "God bless me! but the elephant
>   Is nothing but a wall!"
>
> The Second, feeling of the tusk,
>   Cried: "Ho! what have we here
> So very round and smooth and sharp?
>   To me 'tis mighty clear
> This wonder of an elephant
>   Is very like a spear!"
>
> The Third approached the animal,
>   And, happening to take
> The squirming trunk within his hands,
>   Thus boldly up and spake:
> "I see," quoth he, "the elephant
>   Is very like a snake!"
>
> The Fourth reached out his eager hand,
>   And felt about the knee:
> "What most this wondrous beast is like
>   Is mighty plain," quoth he;
> "'Tis clear enough the elephant
>   Is very like a tree."

---

72. Especially his *Truth to Tell: The Gospel as Public Truth* (Grand Rapids: Eerdmans, 1991), but also his *Gospel in a Pluralist Society* (Grand Rapids: Eerdmans, 1989). Cf. also Walter R. Thorson, "Scientific Objectivity and the Listening Attitude," in *Objective Knowledge: A Christian Perspective*, ed. Paul Helm (Leicester: Inter-Varsity Press, 1987), 59–83.

The Fifth, who chanced to touch the ear,
    Said: "E'en the blindest man
Can tell what this resembles most;
    Deny the fact who can,
This marvel of an elephant
    Is very like a fan!"

The Sixth no sooner had begun
    About the beast to grope,
Than, seizing on the swinging tail
    That fell within his scope,
"I see," quoth he, "the elephant
    Is very like a rope!"

And so these men of Indostan
    Disputed loud and long,
Each in his own opinion
    Exceeding stiff and strong,
Though each was partly in the right,
    And all were in the wrong!

So, oft in theologic wars
    The disputants, I ween,
Rail on in utter ignorance
    Of what each other mean,
And prate about an elephant
    Not one of them has seen!
        John Godfrey Saxe[73]

Despite the archaic elements that would make any self-regarding postmodernist groan (e.g., the assumption that seeing is believing, and the assumption that such a thing as an elephant actually exists), there is more than a little here to make a deconstructionist's heart leap for joy. But now let us apply some of the lessons learned under this point, and attempt an elementary exercise in deconstruction. *First*, why did these six blind men approach the elephant only once and then walk away (conveniently out of line with the body of the elephant, regrouping at a safe distance to continue their debate)? Why didn't each one hear the exclamations of the others and decide to follow the sound and feel what the others were feeling? Were they deaf as well as blind or just stupid? Why didn't they spiral in on the question at hand by going back to the elephant again and again? *Second*, how did each know he had an elephant at hand? One must suppose that a sighted person had

---

73. *The Best Loved Poems of the American People*, compiled by Hazel Felleman (New York: Doubleday, 1936), 521–22.

directed them to the elephant, so why didn't they ask the sighted person some questions? Clearly it is presupposed that they have asked enough questions to be directed to the beast. Granted their ignorance, why did they not engage in a little thoughtful distanciation, until they could more responsibly fuse the horizons of their understanding with that of the sighted person? *Third*, why did it not occur to any of them that the elephant might have been bigger and more complex than what any one of them had handled? Why did none of them wonder if his best knowledge on the subject was nothing more than an asymptotic approach to the truth, and that a further growth in understanding, a closer asymptotic approach, was available at the minimal cost of further exploration? *Fourth*, if these six men of Indostan had been mild postmodernists *who nevertheless held to the objectivity of truth*, but not to our access to it, then of course they would have understood that even the sighted person, elephantine scholar though he may have been, did not have an absolute and exhaustive knowledge of the elephant, however true that knowledge was. *Fifth*, this may have led the six blind men, after they had changed places several times and finally grasped (pun intended) at least something of the external dimensions and shape of the elephant, to contemplate that it was possible, owing to the superior hearing and smelling that their congenital blindness had bequeathed to them, that they could detect elements in the elephant's calls and smells that were overlooked by the sighted person. Thus although they constituted a peculiar interpretive community, it was not at all impossible that they should gain knowledge of the elephant shared by other interpretive communities (the sighted), and even contribute to the larger pool.[74] *Sixth*, the author is clearly writing from the perspective of one who is convinced that elephants exist, and that sighted persons, presumably others like himself, share his convictions. His poem thus becomes a manipulative exercise in power (shades of Michel Foucault) to manipulate theologians and other believers, for the author thinks he knows what an elephant looks like (or he could not be mocking the blind men) but does not claim to know what God is truly like. The analogy between the blind man and the theologians does not really work, but is merely an exercise in abusive power with words.

Thus a deconstructive reading of the poem may threaten deconstruction itself, without returning us to the hubris of modernity. It does not take much imagination to see how all of this applies to the business of interpreting other texts.

---

74. Cf. Vern S. Poythress, *Symphonic Theology: The Validity of Multiple Perspectives in Theology* (Grand Rapids: Zondervan, 1987).

7. Clearly the interpretive community, the nurturing community, the community of faith, plays an important role in an individual's understanding, but it is not necessarily a determinative or decisive role.

For Stanley Fish, as we have seen, the interpretive community is determinative; for Ricoeur, the tradition is very important, but not, I think, necessarily decisive. More importantly, the community that shapes the interpreter trying to read the text has itself been shaped by the text. It is helpful to remember four things.

First, the notion of an interpretive community is not, of course, restricted to, say, the heritage of Western confessing Christendom, or to the domain of theology. Marxist historians (before their recent drastic decline) constituted an important interpretive community. By and large, they could be counted on to read, say, Reformation documents in a way that squared with one branch or another of Marxist historiography. They could always find reasons to explain the most difficult texts in line with their own commitments.

So in this regard theologians are far from unique. Apart from the subject matter, Christian theologians differ from Marxist historians in another respect: we lay claim to a certain *experience* of God. In other words, what we lay claim to is not only a certain agreed understanding of certain texts, but a more or less shared experience of the living God. Nevertheless, from a purely epistemological point of view, it is difficult to see how Christians are under more influence from their own interpretive community than others are from theirs. This includes, of course, the interpretive community of, say, postmodernists, or of atheists (two groups which overlap, but are far from being identical). Father Brown could say, "You seem to like being atheists; so you may be just believing what you like to believe."[75] We might paraphrase: "You seem to like being postmodernists; so you may be just believing what you like to believe."

In other words, if the argument of Fish is pushed to the limit, it is self-destructive. It is hard to see how one can escape a kind of communal solipsism.

But *second*, the fact of the matter is that people do change their interpretive communities. Atheists become Christians, Hindus become Muslims, Capitalists become Marxists, and Marxists, even by droves, become Capitalists. Some changes involve an almost instantaneous transfer from one interpretive community to another, but this need not be the case. Evidence abounds of those who by reading and studying transfer themselves out of their interpretive community without yet joining another. In some cases, they may not yet be aware that another community that is very close to their new

75. G. K. Chesterton, *The Penguin Complete Father Brown* (Harmondsworth: Penguin Books, 1981), 372.

intellectual commitments actually exists. A community shapes those who are nurtured in it, but that does not mean that everyone in the community grows at exactly the same rate, or is equally submissive to the norms of the community, or is restricted from pushing back the established frontiers of the community.

Third, belonging to one or more overlapping interpretive communities is not only inevitable, *it can be a good thing*. Suppose the interpretive community in question is a group of sincere, committed, knowledgeable Christians. To put this in contemporary terms, this group has been shaped by the biblical text. This does not mean that all their understandings of the Bible are right or reasonable or true. It does mean that at least some of their number have spiralled in on the text again and again; they have taken pains to approach it asymptotically, believing or even fearing that they cannot approach it absolutely; they have tried, again and again, to fuse the horizon of their understanding with that of the text, as they themselves are being shaped by the community. And they have taught their findings to others in their community of faith and lived them out, thereby shaping the entire community of faith by the text. To be reared and nurtured in such a community is to grow up with tremendous advantages. By the grace of God, there may be a much earlier and deeper personal grasp of the message of Scripture than would be the case if the individual belonged to an entirely alien interpretive community.

Indeed, such an interpretive community may help many of those who are nurtured and shaped by it to avoid foolish and dangerous mistakes. This is, in part, the argument of Louth: belonging to an interpretive community is not only unavoidable, but for the Christian it is right and safe and good and rewarding to explore and think things out in the context of the lived Tradition.[76]

That does not mean it is *necessarily* a good thing. In my view, the Tradition to which Louth wishes to attach himself is at many points too far removed from the text of Scripture. All traditions tend to wander off in time. That is one of the reasons why constant checking and reformation are needed. Interpretive communities can also keep one from hearing the gospel: one thinks, for example, of societies that are tightly tied together by sets of cultural assumptions (e.g., the Japanese—though perhaps the ties are showing signs of loosening). One also thinks of the community of postmodern relativists! But that is why the Christian community must consciously seek its own reformation by conformity to the Word of God, and all that means for conduct, worship, service, creed, God-centeredness, repentance, faith, and so forth.

---

76. Andrew Louth, *Discerning the Mystery: An Essay on the Nature of Theology* (Oxford: Clarendon Press, 1983).

Finally, although I have tried to leave a large place for the role of the interpretive community, clearly I have cast the discussion on the assumption that there is some objective truth out there. It is this point that most postmodernists will want to challenge. Thus when Smith, who views himself as a postmodern Christian, responds to the charge that postmodernists display a profound skepticism about the possibility of any commonality of meaning, any truth, his response is more revealing than he thinks. He writes,

> On the contrary, postmodernist views of language are often rooted in a profound humility regarding the limitations of human understanding and the seemingly infinite possibilities of human speech. Most postmodernists assume that humans in community are every day arriving at commonality of meaning and truth (notice how much and how often they are talking intelligibly to one another?). For the postmodernist, meaning and perspective is [*sic*] shaped and understood in the context of interpretative communities, and this results in hope as often as despair, and in dialogue more than monologue (more meaning negotiated, less meaning assumed).[77]

Some of this is surely right. Over against individualistic readings, postmodernists in the Fish tradition lay considerable emphasis on commonality of meanings achieved in the community.[78] Why this should be tied to hope rather than despair is a little uncertain, unless it is assumed, on psychological grounds, that effective communication is an intrinsically good thing, regardless of what is said (would that be true of, say, the Nazi interpretive community?). What is at first very unclear is what Smith means by "arriving at commonality of meaning *and truth*." Is this *objective* truth, or is it merely the "truth" perceived (created?) by the community? If the latter, then Smith's interlocutor is right, except that the subjectivism is tied less to an individual than to an individual interpretive community. And at this point Smith gives the game away:

> ... one century [lives] according to the laws of Newtonian physics, or salvation through Church sacraments, or the belief that St. Paul had forbidden women to exercise leadership roles in the Church, and the next century by the laws of Einsteinian physics, or salvation through Luther's under-

---

77. Samuel Smith, "Words of Hope: A Postmodern Faith," *Faculty Dialogue* 20 (Winter 1993–94): 132–33.

78. In a private communication, Kirk Allison draws a parallel between this and Kantian transcendental categories. Kant argues that the mind shapes the multiplicity of sense data into an intuition (*Anschauung*) according to various categories, but without a priori regularity or distinctions (*an sich*). But surely, Allison argues, there could be no orderly world of such category-bound processing; it would have to be selected and shaped on a purely arbitrary basis. So also here.

standing of justification, or new understanding that contextualizes St. Paul's comments in favor of women assuming leadership roles in the Church. In fact, a short review of the history of the interpretation of the Bible reveals the Church changing its understanding of Jesus and important texts like the letters of St. Paul. Members of a given Christian community situated in a particular time and place have lived by the interpretations and understandings dominant for their particular time and place. The postmodern thesis that humans can assert only interpretations, not absolute knowledge, strikes me as a very orthodox recognition of the finiteness of human understanding.[79]

Note the antithesis: "only interpretations" versus "absolute knowledge." The reference to Newton and Einstein, as we have already seen (chap. 2), is naive. The question to ask is this: Are all the "interpretations" listed here, not least the mutually contradictory ones, equally acceptable to God? An atheist will be uncomfortable with such a question; a Christian *must* ask it. Is it enough simply to hold the beliefs of one's "Christian" community? How about the interpretive community of Jehovah's Witnesses? Mormons? Or how about, say, Muslims? Buddhists? Materialist Marxists?

I do not know how Smith would respond to such questions. If he draws the line somewhere, then of course I will ask him how he knows that is the place to draw it. At the very least he has then admitted the existence of objective truth, the denial of which is dangerous. If, in line with the central heritage of the Christian church, he ties that truth to the Bible, then one must push hard and ask which of the other interpretations can properly be justified and which must be ruled out by what the Bible says—or will he retreat again to some vague notion of equivalent value in all interpretations? If he denies that there is any way we can know that we are pleasing God, and that the best we can do is live in line with our interpretive communities, what possible excuse could he make for Luther breaking out of one community to start another? Was Luther right? How do we decide? If Smith hides behind the community in the face of such questions, then his interlocutor is basically right. And I would review with him the points I have already tried to make in this chapter and the previous one.

In short, I agree that all our understanding is interpretive, and that the interpretive communities in which we find ourselves are extremely influential. But this does not mean, on the one hand, that we cannot articulate objective truth, and on the other that our interpretive communities bind us utterly.

---

79. Smith, "Words of Hope," 133.

8. From a Christian perspective, an omniscient God who accommodates himself to talk in human languages introduces several new and important elements.

Without here trying to erect a defense of the existence of God, the theistic God of the Bible, I want now *to assume* the existence of God (I am, after all, a Christian!) and briefly explore how God's existence affects our understanding of understanding. The paths that could be taken are many, but here I want to mention two.

First, if God is a talking and acting God, not the withdrawn watchmaker of deist conception, there are some massive implications for our understanding of truth and communication. A few of these will be explored in the next chapter, including the role of the Holy Spirit. Here it is enough to draw out some implications of the fact that God, in Christian conception, is not only sovereign and transcendent, but also personal, a talking God,[80] one who can and does act. Nor does he restrict himself to forms of communication that only another omniscient being could comprehend. He chooses to talk in Hebrew, Aramaic, Greek, a priceless exhibition of "the scandal of historical particularity."[81] The magisterial Reformers developed a nuanced doctrine of "accommodation" to enable them to think through how the God who is described as transcendent, personal, and noncorporeal could be thought to speak in human words, and a contemporary restatement of that doctrine would be salutary today.

Because he chooses to communicate with finite mortals in their languages, God cannot possibly communicate *all* that he is and knows, but I cannot see how that is a barrier to his communicating *some* true elements of what he is and knows. Of course, we will misunderstand the communication in all sorts of ways, owing both to our finiteness and to our sinfulness. But the content itself is objectively true, a subset of what Omniscience knows, and cast in culture-laden forms that demand of modern readers that we attempt to fuse the horizon of our own understandings with that of the culture and language in which the deposit was given.[82] Moreover, this God not only knows

---

80. Cf. Alister E. McGrath, *Intellectuals Don't Need God and Other Modern Myths* (Grand Rapids: Zondervan, 1993), 19: "God is able to communicate with humans through human language. This belief is fundamental, to the point of being axiomatic, to Christian apologetics."

81. Frequently this notion is dismissed by postmodernist writers as docetic. I shall say more on this subject in the next chapter. For now it is important to say only that well-informed evangelicals today avoid any hint of thinking that the whole Bible was delivered by divine dictation, thus stripping it of its humanity. Sophisticated articulation of a theological understanding of inspiration that ensures that the result is simultaneously the very Word of God and the product of human minds is now so common that it is a little frustrating to discover how seldom modernists and postmodernists alike seriously engage it.

82. See Carson, "Church and Mission," 213–57 and esp. 342–47.

perfectly and in advance what *wrong* interpretations mortals will assign his words, he also knows that some later mortals will see true connections (meanings) in the complex of his words that the earlier mortals through whom he first spoke those words may *not* have seen, as they did not yet have enough information to build up entire typologies.[83]

If we are right in this understanding of God and his gracious self-disclosure, then we have additional reasons for speaking of "objective knowledge." There are some entailments.

(1) If God's self-disclosure in words is coextensive with the Bible, then the canon must be understood as establishing a principle of authority (as it has been understood through most of the church's history). It will not do, as in some contemporary canon criticism, to view it only as a hermeneutical tool, but not the locus of authority. (2) At the same time, recognition of the canon implicitly forbids an atomistic approach to texts within the canon. Brueggemann reflects both modernists and postmodernists (for different reasons) when he insists that the proper focus of biblical studies "is the specific text, without any necessary relation to other texts or any coherent pattern read out of or into the text."[84] As Vanhoozer says, "This approach is congenial to postmoderns because it focuses on 'little' stories rather than the 'great story'"[85]—i.e., the metanarrative (which occupies the next three chapters of this book). (3) More broadly, a view of God that understands him to be the Creator, to be sovereignly at work in the universe, and to have made us *imago Dei* "affirms that the divine creation and sustaining of the world is the foundation for epistemological confidence of whatever sort."[86] This becomes increasingly important as we recognize that postmodernists, for all their firm critique of modernism's confidence in foundations *and methods*, focus far more attention on hermeneutical questions (methods!) than on the texts

---

83. I think that something like this is what is meant by Augustine, especially in *De Doctrina Christiana* and in Book XII of *The Confessions*. A fascinating discussion of these points is found in E. D. Hirsch, Jr., "Transhistorical Intentions and the Persistence of Allegory," *New Literary History* 25 (1994): 549–67. But Hirsch confuses the issue by insisting that the texts themselves have no determinate meaning. Determinate meaning is authorial—but by "authorial" meaning Hirsch includes both the author and the reader who may be doing the "authoring." I do not see how this approach can fail to destroy the "principle of stability" that Hirsch is trying to preserve. I am indebted to Dr. Darrell Bock for some correspondence on these matters.

84. Walter Brueggemann, *Texts Under Negotiation: The Bible and PostModern Imagination* (Minneapolis: Fortress Press, 1993), 58.

85. Kevin J. Vanhoozer, "From Canon to Concept: 'Same' and 'Other' in the Relation Between Biblical and Systematic Theology," *Scottish Bulletin of Evangelical Theology* 12 (1994): 104.

86. Mark A. Noll, "Traditional Christianity and the Possibility of Historical Knowledge," *Christian Scholar's Review* 19 (1990): 399.

themselves. What has changed is not the focus on methods, but on (a) what the methods are, and (b) one's confidence in them. By contrast, Christian reliance on the words of a God who talks drives them to study *the text*, and not only methods for reading the text, or debates about whether the text exists.[87] But perhaps this conclusion can be demonstrated most easily by introducing the next point.

Second, we must think through how God views our finiteness, so far as he has disclosed that to us. Christians remain as finite as the local atheists, but their outlook on their finitude is bound to differ radically from that of the atheist if they hold that there is one Mind that does know all the truth. The really important thing is to know him, to be reconciled to him. Although this involves rational thought, more than rational thought is involved. God is more interested in eliciting from us trust, obedience, holiness, delight in his presence, humility of heart, than *merely* formal understanding (though he certainly wants that from us as well). Yes, we are finite, and therefore we must acknowledge, along with everyone else, that our presuppositions are not *self-evidently* true. Claiming to know him who is omniscient is not the same as being omniscient. Even if we claim that God's self-disclosure is reliable, and if we articulate a sophisticated doctrine of the truthfulness of Scripture, that does not mean that our doctrine is entirely and absolutely truthful. But because we claim that our beliefs about God do objectively reflect true reality, we do not cower behind our presuppositions as if nothing more can be said. We commend our knowledge of God with arguments; we insist that the presuppositions of others must change; we hold that it is the responsibility of all human beings to see if the entailments of their presuppositions really are the best "fit," or if they should be revised in the light of God's gracious self-disclosure not only in nature, not only in dramatic events, not only in Scripture, but supremely in his Son.[88]

Now all of these points would have to be argued out in great detail. That is not my purpose here. I am simply asserting that a Christian view of our finitude makes allowance for the valid insights from both modernity and postmodernity but succumbs to the worldview of neither. On the one hand, there is such a thing as objective truth; on the other, all human grasping of that

---

87. Cf. Bruce L. Edwards and Branson L. Woodard, Jr., "Wise as Serpents, Harmless as Doves: Christians and Contemporary Critical Theory," *Christianity and Literature* 39 (1990): 305: "The truth is that large numbers of readers in contemporary criticism are surfeited by the claims and counterclaims of that new hybrid among us, the 'criticist,' who spends as much time ruminating about how or whether a 'text' exists as he does writing to illuminate the meaning of the work itself."

88. For a brief treatment of the importance of tests of coherence, congruity, consistency, and comprehensiveness, see Osborne, *The Hermeneutical Spiral*, 407–8.

truth is necessarily interpretive, but it is not necessarily for that reason untrue or removed from objective truth. From this perspective, the Enlightenment was a kind of reductionism—or, to change the description, it was so bright a light that it blotted out the glories of the night sky.[89] And postmodernism, not least postmodernism with a naturalistic face, is another form of reductionism. Reductionism is displayed, for example, in the recent work of Clarke and Byrne. They rightly dismiss as reductionistic all comprehensive theories of religion that prove simplistic and incapable of explaining all religious phenomena (e.g., Hick's pluralism, Feuerback's reflection, Marx's materialism, Durkheim's social construct, Freud's projection), and then introduce another one: a Wittgensteinian "family resemblances" model.[90] All such analyses are necessarily limited because they operate exclusively "from below."

9. Postmodernism as a whole is characterized by astonishing hubris, by a focus on the self that is awesomely God-defying.

Understandably, sin is not a prominent factor in contemporary discussion of epistemology.[91] But the Bible insists (as we shall see in the next two chapters) that we are hopelessly self-centered and self-reliant. In God's universe, where he alone ought to be acknowledged as both the source and the end of all his creatures, not least those made in his image, our deep self-centeredness is rebellion; it is sin. This sinfulness has so deeply warped our personalities that, although none of us is as evil as we might be, no part of our personality is unaffected. Our choices, our judgments, our reasoning, our hopes, our affections—all are warped by this corrosive rebellion.

There is both a historical and a theological component to this hubris.

The historical component lies in the way most postmodernists are so adamant about their worldview being the only viable one. It is easy to demonstrate that "pretensions to be 'right' litter the pluralist agenda."[92] Their pretensions are often so strong that Oden rather scathingly concludes, "Their dogmatism itself is evidence that they are ultramodern, not postmodern."[93] In the first chapter I argued that philosophical pluralism is so opinionated that

---

89. See the analysis of Paulos Mar Gregorios, *A Light Too Bright: The Enlightenment Today* (Albany: State Univ. of New York Press, 1992).

90. Peter B. Clarke and Peter Byrne, *Religion Defined and Explained* (London: Macmillan, 1993).

91. An exception is William J. Larkin, *Culture and Biblical Hermeneutics: Interpreting and Applying the Authoritative Word in a Relativistic Age* (Grand Rapids: Baker, 1988), 293.

92. Alister E. McGrath, "Pluralism and the Decade of Evangelism," *Anvil* 9 (1992): 104, and the documentation there. Cf. also Peter Donovan, "The Intolerance of Religious Pluralism," *Religious Studies* 29 (1993): 217–29.

93. *After Modernity ... What?* 77.

it tends to drive out empirical pluralism; its plea for tolerance is so imperial that it is remarkably intolerant. By contrast, Christians ought to be simultaneously arguing for the truth of the gospel, and insisting that people have the right to disagree without fear of coercion.

But the theological component is more serious. The Enlightenment tried to make human beings the measure of everything; Rationalism elevated human reason to godlike status; existentialism debunked significance based on knowledge or status, and assigned it to human action, will, decision; now postmodernity insists there is no objective truth that can lay claims on us. At its root, postmodernity is deeply antiauthoritarian, as even its most astute exponents recognize:

> What, then, is the precise relationship of poststructuralism to historical criticism? As I see it, poststructuralism is temperamentally unsuited to be yet another handmaid (a French maid?) to historical criticism. Neither is poststructuralism poised to become historical criticism's slayer (historical criticism is much too massive for that, occupying entire city blocks at the national conferences; it crushes its enemies by sitting on them). Rather, in the context of biblical studies, poststructuralism would be historical criticism's id, the seat of its strongest antiauthoritarian instincts—historical criticism unfettered at last from the ecclesiastical superego that has always compelled it to genuflect before the icons it had come to destroy.[94]

Amusingly put, but deeply appalling from any Christian point of view. Having elevated self to the place where God is no longer needed, self now proclaims that language is inadequate to talk about objective reality, God included. Having damned interpretation for being manipulative, God, if he were to speak, becomes the arch manipulator. The gagging of God is complete. From a Christian perspective, this is not simply misguided, but lurks, tragically, at the heart of all that is evil.

10. Not a little postmodernism borders on the incoherent and is in fact more than a little sad.

That is a charge constantly put, in clear terms, by John Ellis.[95] The evidence in support of the contention is highly variegated. When a scholar as brilliant as Stephen Moore offers us a poststructuralist exegesis of John 4 that is full of the kind of word-association games that are trained out of the work of first-year exegesis students,[96] we are right to infer that something is amiss with the theory.

---

94. Moore, *Poststructuralism*, 117.
95. *Against Deconstruction*, passim, esp. 3–7, 13, 68–69.
96. *Poststructuralism*, 43–64.

Are we simply to be amused when two distinguished scholars cite a text to authorize the title of their book, and abuse the text in so doing? In the front material, McKenzie and Haynes render the closing words of the chief cupbearer to Pharaoh, "A Hebrew lad, servant to the chief of the bodyguard, was there with us, and when we told him our dreams he interpreted them for us, giving *to each its own meaning*" (Genesis 41:12; emphasis theirs). And so they call their book, *To Each Its Own Meaning: An Introduction to Biblical Criticisms and Their Application.*[97] The "own meaning" in the title refers to the various methods one may bring to bear in exegesis. These methods are sometimes judged mutually complementary, and sometimes mutually exclusive, both in their procedures and in their results, *when working on the same texts.* By contrast, the chief cupbearer is saying that Joseph interpreted the two dreams and assigned to each its own meaning, i.e., he rightly unpacked their individual univocal meanings, as was demonstrated by what then took place. Far from authorizing the approach of the volume edited by McKenzie and Haynes, the text serves as an instance that rather refutes it. No matter: contexts count for little these days.

LaFargue is not too cynical when he writes,

> The contemporary scene, dominated as it is by a plurality of contending viewpoints, fosters a style of discourse in which the merely rhetorical furthering of one's favored cause prevails; the substantive merits of the cause itself are too seldom themselves the subject of serious discussion and argument. One treats one's own allegiances, as well as those of others, as something ultimately irrational and arbitrary, not really susceptible to critical examination (even self-examination) and substantive discussion. In this situation, the allegedly indeterminate, "polysemic" character of the biblical text, and the necessity of a "fusion of horizons," easily become welcome excuses neither to take the otherness of the biblical text seriously nor to submit oneself to its challenges. The appearance and apparatus of interpretive research are used as occasions for furthering a cause, to which historical research in fact has only tangential substantive relevance. (Furthermore, what is in fact irrelevant erudition serves as a status badge, excluding from the conversation those who have every right to be included.) This is a formula for nondialogue and cynicism.[98]

---

97. Louisville: Westminster/John Knox, 1993.
98. Michael LaFargue, "Are Texts Determinate? Derrida, Barth, and the Role of the Biblical Scholar," *Harvard Theological Review* 81 (1988): 357. LaFargue is not arguing that there is no place for "fusion of horizons." In a footnote he writes: "I too would advocate the ultimate necessity of fusing ancient and modern horizons—otherwise, biblical interpretation become [*sic*] of merely antiquarian interest. I am simply arguing against a premature fusion of these two horizons" (357, n. 28).

Remembering that "texts" in discussion of postmodernism can refer to anything that is interpreted, one may usefully remark on the impact of postmodernism in nonliterary worlds. One thoughtful graduate student in art history at the University of Michigan remarked to me that it was painful for her to see how postmodernism could powerfully and sometimes usefully critique earlier movements, but did not seem to be taking us on to anything new. It is fundamentally backward-looking, not forward-looking. How could it be anything else? Postmodernism defines itself most clearly in terms of what it isn't—and that inevitably means a critique of the past. It has nowhere to go, for it has no vision of transcendent reality pulling us onward. It is all rather sad and pathetic.

I do not think Wright is too cynical when he concludes, "Deconstructive criticism will go away: it is in the nature of sudden reflex-movements of absurdist cognitive scepticism to be short-lived."[99] As a colleague of mine put it, left to itself, the academic side of these movements would probably die of boredom; unfortunately, the secondary cultural dissemination will probably carry on for some time.

C. Concluding Reflection

My doctoral dissertation treated the gospel of John and various elements in the Jewish background. When I faced my oral examiners, more or less prepared to defend the dissertation, Professor C. K. Barrett, after a few preliminaries, asked me this question: "Do you think John would have approved what you have written?"

I sputtered some sort of answer, and the discussion moved on. But I will not soon forget the shrewdness of the question. I wish I could be invited to answer it today, nearly twenty years later. At one level, the question was challenging me to defend how faithful to John my interpretation of what he wrote really was. At another level, it invited reflection on how John would see a much later use of his work, with all the historical and cultural distance that implied. Exactly how does one move from text to theology?

Perhaps that is for another book. But Professor Barrett's shrewd question raises all the issues bound up in the new hermeneutic and in radical hermeneutics, issues that have been developed along a problematic track by radical hermeneutics and deconstruction. The aim of this chapter has been to recognize, within a Christian framework, certain truths in postmodernity, without getting snookered by the entire package. The Scylla of modernity

---

99. Wright, "History, Hermeneutics, Deconstruction," 88.

and the Charybdis of postmodernity are equally uninviting to those who want to follow another Way, who are convinced that in a universe made by and for a personal/transcendent and omniscient God who talks, the only reasonable stance is that of the apostle Paul: "Let God be true, and every man a liar" (Rom. 3:4).

Part Two

—

RELIGIOUS PLURALISM

Chapter 4

HAS GOD SPOKEN? THE AUTHORITY OF REVELATION

In the first chapter of this book I surveyed the various kinds of pluralism currently growing stronger in most Western countries. I tried to draw distinctions among them, assess their relative strengths, and signal something of what this would mean for Christians. The most difficult challenge is philosophical pluralism, which unblushingly insists that all assertions of worldview and outlook that make exclusive truth claims are necessarily wrong. Especially is this prevalent in the religious arena.

Because so many elements of philosophical pluralism are irrefragably tied to hermeneutics—whether classical, new, or radical—I devoted the next two chapters to modern and postmodern developments in theories of interpretation and in deconstruction. "The myth sovereign in the old age was that everything means everything. The myth sovereign in the new is that nothing *means* anything."[1] Yet the fact of the matter is that although the siren call of postmodernity stands behind a great deal of contemporary religious pluralism, it does not stand behind all of it. Moreover, much of what it does stand behind resorts to arguments of other sorts. There are numerous species of religious pluralism, and although they can be conveniently grouped for some purposes, almost every species sports distinctives that must in some contexts be identified and acknowledged.

In the five chapters that comprise part 2 of the book, my purpose is to look at religious pluralism from the vantage of Christianity that aims to be

---

1. Thomas Howard, *Chance or the Dance?* (Wheaton: Harold Shaw, 1969), 14 (emphasis his).

141

faithful to Scripture. The first chapter, the present one, wrestles with questions of authority and revelation. The next two trace some high points on the Bible's plot-line to gain the bearing of the Bible's "story" on the subject, and then focus on a number of texts that are regularly judged to be focal in the debate. Radical religious pluralism cannot accept the Bible's portraits of Jesus, so the fourth of these five chapters considers him. The final chapter of part 2 outlines some of the reasons why responsible Christians cannot sit on the fence on these issues.

A. The World of Religious Pluralism

Philosophical pluralism in the religious arena has certain affinities to various forms of universalism, some of which have been around for a long time. In the third century, Origen moved in this direction, though on this and many other points the church departed from him. Essential to all forms of universalism is the view that finally, whenever and wherever "finally" is, no human being shall be lost; all shall be saved. This view became fairly popular in the nineteenth century. But in a careful taxonomy of universalist arguments, Bauckham draws attention to a fundamental distinction between that nineteenth-century outlook and the modern form. He notes that in the twentieth century, "exegesis has turned decisively against the universalist case."[2] In consequence, although most twentieth-century scholars recognize that many (especially New Testament texts) clearly teach a final division of humankind into saved and lost, the universalists have tried to put over against this evidence the biblical witness to the love of God, a love so absolutized that other strands of biblical witness are safely dismissed, or at very least held in suspension in the hope that universalism will be the final outcome.[3]

Cameron notes a second distinction between the universalism of the nineteenth century and that which is more prevalent today, one that is for our purposes more important than the first. The last century commonly held out universal hope *after death*. Many of the nineteenth-century universalists could thus hold to the superiority of Christianity while espousing universalism.

2. Richard J. Bauckham, "Universalism—A Historical Survey," *Themelios* 4/2 (1979): 48–54, esp. 52. In other words, although a few scholars still argue that the New Testament texts refer to a *temporary* hell to be followed by final salvation (e.g., M. Rissi, *The Future of the World* [London: SCM Press, 1972]), few find them convincing. For a more recent taxonomy and appraisal, cf. Henri Blocher, "The Scope of Redemption and Modern Theology," *Scottish Bulletin of Evangelical Theology* 9 (1991): 80–104.

3. So, for instance, Emil Brunner, *Eternal Hope* (Edinburgh: Lutterworth, 1954), chap. 17; and Karl Barth, *Church Dogmatics*, passim (see details below). G. C. Berkouwer, *The Return of Christ* (Grand Rapids: Eerdmans, 1972), 390–419, is not entirely dissimilar, though he is far more cautious and also distances himself from Barth.

People of other faiths or no faith would see the light eventually, after death if necessary, but see it they would. By contrast, contemporary religious pluralists are inclined to treat all religions of equivalent worth even during this life. That is the fundamental distinction between (older) universalism and (contemporary) religious pluralism: although in both cases people eventually end up in the same blessedness, in the latter they are in equivalent blessedness (and disadvantage, for that matter) even in this life.[4]

For all that they are differentiable, as a group, from nineteenth-century universalists, these pluralists, as I have suggested, emphasize quite different elements, some of which are mutually compatible and some of which are not. Earlier in the century, John Dewey argued that the way to reconcile religionists with naturalists is to recognize the fallacy held by both sides: both sides connect religion with the supernatural, one to embrace it, the other to reject it. Dewey wants to foster "a common faith" by grounding religion in the purely natural realm, by abstracting it from the supernatural. Along the way he redefines truth in pragmatic categories: it is what enables us to function with least conflict and most success in our environment (human or otherwise).[5]

Barth's move toward universalism (though he never fully embraces it) is by a redefined predestination. Jesus Christ is the one who was both rejected and elected: rejected in that God in Jesus has taken upon himself the rejection deserved by the human race, and elected in that Jesus is the Chosen One by whom the race is reconciled to God. Thus for Barth election is not a matter of God choosing some and not choosing others, but of God choosing Christ. The gospel is the good news that in Jesus the reconciliation of all human beings has already taken place. In him they are already elect, justified, and reconciled to God. But instead of inferring absolute universalism, Barth hesitates. He recognizes the reality of unbelief. The unbeliever is truly elect, but does not recognize this reality, and tries to change it. For Barth, the possibility that some might finally be condemned does not rest on their perverse freedom to reject what God has provided, but on *God's* freedom:

> To the man who persistently tries to change the truth into untruth, God does not owe eternal patience and therefore deliverance.... We should be denying or disarming that evil attempt and our own participation in it if, in relation to ourselves or others or all men, we were to permit ourselves to postulate a withdrawal of that threat and in this sense expect or maintain an *apokatastasis* or universal reconciliation as the goal and end of all things.... Even though theological consistency might seem to lead our thoughts and

---

4. Nigel M. de S. Cameron, "Universalism and the Logic of Revelation," *Evangelical Review of Theology* 11 (1987): 320.

5. John Dewey, *A Common Faith* (New Haven: Yale Univ. Press, 1934).

utterances most clearly in this direction, we must not arrogate to ourselves that which can be given and received only as a free gift.[6]

Even so, Barth holds out the possibility that all will ultimately be saved.[7]

J. A. T. Robinson argues for a modification of Brunner's position. The latter held that texts on hell and judgment and the final separation of the saved and the lost must be held in tension with texts holding out some larger hope or emphasizing the love of God. The texts, he insisted, are contradictory, but he hoped the universalist strand would prevail. Robinson, following Barth at this point, argues that the universalist strand is the truth as it is for God; the emphasis on heaven and hell "is the truth as it must be to the subject facing decision."[8] Thus the "truth" about heaven and hell degenerates to the purely utilitarian: it is in danger of becoming an empty threat, psychologically useful to bring about good behavior, but devoid of substance. Moreover, for Robinson it is hard to see how this view of God's love can be squared with the decidedly impersonal God Robinson espouses in his most (in)famous book.[9] Can an impersonal "ground of being" love anyone? Must love become benevolence? Or does the confusion simply reflect Robinson's shifting positions?

Jacques Ellul is not so restrained. Not only does he affirm that all will finally be saved, he frankly recognizes that this "is a scandalous proposition." It runs counter to our moral sensibilities (should Hitler and Stalin be saved?), it runs counter to the almost unanimous witness of the history of theology, and "the most serious objection . . . is posed by the biblical texts themselves."[10] Then, both disingenuously and confusingly, Ellul writes:

> As we proceed we must overcome these obstacles [!] and examine the theological reasons which lead me to believe in universal salvation, the texts that seem to speak against it, and a possible solution. But I want to stress that I am speaking about *belief* in universal salvation. This is for me a matter of faith. I am not making a dogma or a principle of it. I can only say what I believe, not pretending to teach it doctrinally as the truth.[11]

Ellul's "possible solution" is a combined emphasis on the love of God and on God's universal reconciling work in Christ, deploying some remarkable eisegesis as he proceeds. It is, in short, a Barthian reading without Barth's

---

6. Karl Barth, *Church Dogmatics* IV/3 (Edinburgh: T & T Clark, 1961), 477.

7. Ibid., 478; *Church Dogmatics* II/2 (Edinburgh: T & T Clark, 1957), 418.

8. J. A. T. Robinson, *In the End God* (London: Collins, 1978), 130. Cf. his earlier essay, "Universalism—Is It Heretical?" *Scottish Journal of Theology* 2 (1949): 139–55.

9. Viz., *Honest to God* (London: SCM Press, 1963).

10. *What I Believe* (Grand Rapids: Eerdmans, 1989), 188.

11. Ibid., 188–89 (emphasis his). I am grateful to Robert A. Krupp for reminding me of this passage.

sophistication, but sharing Barth's comfortable rejection of the laws of identity, excluded middle, and noncontradiction when it suits his purpose.

All of these discussions tilt toward universalism or quasi-universalism, without overtly espousing religious pluralism. Gilkey embraces the latter, and shows exactly what is at stake:

> ... the Christian churches have always known that religions were plural, that there were other religions than our own. This consciousness of plurality raised few theological problems, because the church was convinced on a number of grounds that Christianity was the only truly valid religion, the only effective "way." That we now speak of theological implications of plurality, and clearly intend *serious* implications, thus bespeaks a new sense of understanding of plurality, a new assessment of its meaning. This new understanding of plurality, therefore, includes and adds the concept of "parity," or of "rough parity," to that of plurality: we recognize, often against our will, that in some sense the sole efficacy or even superiority of Christianity are claims we can no longer make, or can make only with great discomfort. I assume we are all agreed on this, otherwise a serious discussion of diversity and its theological meaning would not be undertaken, nor would serious and authentic dialogue between religions be possible.[12]

The reasons for this change, according to Gilkey, are both theological and cultural. Theologically, the most important development "is the shift in the balance between what were called the requirements of faith and those of love; or, better put, a new asssessment of how God views these requirements."[13] Culturally, the Western world has recently undergone a shift "from a position of clear superiority to one of rough parity, and ... this shift in cultural consciousness has in turn had a vast effect on our theological consciousness—namely, the parallel shift toward parity."[14] Clearly, the changes in Western culture, not least the diminishing cultural triumphalism, have been influential. But as we shall see, this scarcely accounts for the fact that the first Christians not only lived in a pluralistic world, but they operated from a base

---

12. Langdon Gilkey, "Plurality and Its Theological Implications," in *The Myth of Christian Uniqueness: Toward a Pluralistic Theology of Religions*, ed. John Hick and Paul F. Knitter (Maryknoll: Orbis Books, 1987), 37 (emphasis his). See also Gilkey's important essays in his *Through the Tempest: Theological Voyages in a Pluralistic Culture* (Minneapolis: Fortress Press, 1991).

13. "Plurality and Its Theological Implications," 38. What Gilkey means by "how God views" such and such would be worth exploring, for such language seems to imply a personal God, very much at odds with, say, Buddhism. If Gilkey holds to a personal God (which may be doubted), doesn't this imply the intrinsic superiority of those religions that espouse a personal deity? And if he doesn't, then isn't the argument purely utilitarian—toothless if not meaningless?

14. Ibid., 39.

of perceived cultural *in*feriority. In any case, the result, for Gilkey, is the rejection of both exclusivism and inclusivism (as defined in the first chapter of this book), and the adoption of pluralism.

Nor is he alone. The most influential religious pluralist today is undoubtedly John Hick.[15] Hick's views have gradually evolved from those of a conservative Christian. In the seventies he came to the conclusion that if Christianity as popularly believed is true, other religions are correspondingly false, and that much of the human race is therefore damned to eternal perdition. He saw no recourse but to shift from *Christo*centrism to *theo*centrism, arguing that we should all come "to the realization that it is *God* who is at centre, and that all religions . . . including our own, serve and revolve around him."[16] Not surprisingly, this means Hick must "de-center" Christ and the incarnation. The latter must be taken as mythological and metaphorical, not as literal or definitive.[17] In time Hick came to see that even these proposals were not radical enough. He saw that he was still thinking and writing of God as personal, though some of the world's religions espouse an impersonal view of God. He was still a "covert theist" (as D'Costa charges[18]). Hick now prefers to speak of *Reality*-centeredness.[19] If all religions are salvific (whatever this "salvation" finally turns out to be), and some hold to a personal God and others to an impersonal God, then the great Reality behind both species of religion cannot be clearly identified one way or the other, so it is best to use some neutral term such as *Reality* or the *Real*. If this at first seems a little unrealistic (no pun intended), Hick replies with a Kantian distinction between the noumenal world and the phenomenal world. The latter is the world as it appears to human consciousness; the former exists independently of human perception or consciousness. Both theistic and nontheistic religions, he suggests, are nothing but phenomenal responses to the noumenal Reality. The actual belief systems do not correspond directly to Reality. The New Testament "heavenly Father" or the Qur'an's "Allah" is "mythological speech about the Real." He goes on:

15. Some of his most important works are listed in the bibliography. Perhaps his two most significant critics are Gavin D'Costa, *John Hick's Theology of Religions* (Lanham: University Press of America, 1987), and Harold A. Netland, *Dissonant Voices: Religious Pluralism and the Question of Truth* (Grand Rapids: Eerdmans, 1991).

16. John Hick, *God and the Universe of Faiths* (London: Fount, 1977), 131.

17. See especially his *Metaphor of God Incarnate: Christology in a Pluralistic Age* (Louisville: Westminster/John Knox, 1993). I shall return to this work in chap. 7. In due course, Paul A. Knitter followed the same course: see chap. 7, below, for references.

18. Gavin D'Costa, "The New Missionary: John Hick and Religious Plurality," *International Bulletin of Missionary Research* 15 (April 1991): 66–69.

19. See especially his *Interpretation of Religion: Human Responses to the Transcendent* (London: Macmillan, 1989).

I define a myth as a story or statement which is not literally true but which tends to evoke an appropriate dispositional attitude to its subject matter. Thus the truth of a myth is a practical truthfulness: a true myth is one which rightly relates us to a reality about which we cannot speak in non-mythological terms.[20]

John Hick is not the only one to have made this pilgrimage. Paul Knitter, with whom he has collaborated,[21] has followed a rather similar path.[22]

It is important to recognize that Hick's position has affinities with both modernism and postmodernism. When Robert Cook charged him with postmodernism,[23] the goad sparked off a response from Hick himself, and a surrejoinder from Cook.[24] Hick pointed out how various postmodernists have attacked his proposals as a typically *modern* metanarrative: there is one large, overarching explanation that claims to handle all religious phenomena, and that therefore fails to recognize the sheer diversity of opinion and outlook in the world. But Cook does not back down. Hick, he says, treats all the religions of the world exactly as a postmodernist does: he is deeply skeptical about the claims of any one of these religions to provide a metanarrative that truly explains reality. If Hick then goes on to provide his own metanarrative, this is really the problem of postmodernism itself: as soon as it makes an absolute claim that all truth claims are relative, it has forged its own metanarrative. Indeed, one might argue that to defend his view of religious pluralism, Hick has found it necessary to create his own anti-metanarrative metanarrative.

At very least, the exchange between Hick and Cook does highlight an important distinction. There are religious pluralists, like Hick, who spin a theory that becomes a criterion, a position, a place on which to stand; and there are others who argue that there is no such place, none at all: "there really is no such universally human position available to us."[25] But both groups are religous pluralists: that is, they unqualifiedly reject both exclusivism and inclusivism, and espouse the view that all religions are equally valuable (or equally valueless, for that matter), and none may be permitted to claim

---

20. Ibid., 248.
21. See especially John Hick and Paul F. Knitter, eds., *The Myth of Christian Uniqueness: Toward a Pluralistic Theology of Religions* (Maryknoll: Orbis Books, 1987).
22. See Paul R. Eddy, "Paul Knitter's Theology of Religions: A Survey and Evangelical Response," *Evangelical Quarterly* 65 (1993): 225–45. For a useful and sympathetic review article of some recent and important books in the area, see the lengthy contribution of Francis X. Clooney, "Christianity and World Religions: Religion, Reason, and Pluralism," *Religious Studies Review* 15/3 (July 1989): 198–207.
23. "Postmodernism, Pluralism and John Hick," *Themelios* 19/1 (1993): 10–12.
24. "Readers' Responses," *Themelios* 19/3 (1994): 20–21.
25. Gordon Kaufman, "Religious Diversity, Historical Consciousness, and Christian Theology," in Hick and Knitter, *The Myth of Christian Uniqueness*, 5.

priority or preference or superiority. Phillips is thus merely being consistent when on these premises he is not prepared to condemn child sacrifice in some remote tribe, simply because he does not properly appreciate what such a practice might mean to that tribe.[26]

In fact, not a few religous pluralists, even if they do not betray the technical sophistication of a Hick, nowadays espouse some vision of God beyond all human visions that is somehow related (equally!) to all of them. This perspective is sometimes seen as a great blessing. Thus the Roman Catholic scholar James Michael Lee writes, "Religious pluralism is a salvific blessing of the Spirit in that it enables persons to vastly expand their vision and their contact with the God whom no human endeavor can ever adequately contain."[27]

Hans Küng seems to skirt the border between inclusivism and pluralism.

> What, then, is demanded today of a basic Christian attitude toward the other world religions? Instead of an indifferentism for which everything is equally valid, let there be somewhat more *indifference* toward the alleged orthodoxy that makes itself the measure of the salvation or damnation of human beings, and wishes to make good its truth claim with instruments of power and force. Instead of a relativism for which there is no absolute, let there be more sensitivity for *relativity* in every human setting up of absolutes that hinders a productive coexistence of the various religions, and let there be more sensitivity for the *relationality* that allows every religion to be seen within its own web of relationships. Instead of a syncretism where everything possible and impossible is "mixed together," melted into one, let there be more commitment to a *synthesis* of all confessions and religious oppositions, which still take their daily toll of blood and tears, so that instead of war, hate, and dispute, peace may reign among all religions.

> In face of all religiously motivated impatience, one cannot demand too much patience, too much religious freedom. There should be no betrayal of freedom for the sake of truth, but at the same time there should be no betrayal of truth for the sake of freedom. The truth question must not be trivialized and sacrificed to the utopia of a future world unity and one world religion. . . . On the contrary, as Christians we are challenged to think through anew in a Christian-based *freedom* the question of *truth*.[28]

---

26. D. Z. Phillips, *Faith and Philosophical Enquiry* (New York: Schocken Books, 1970), 237.

27. "The Blessings of Religious Pluralism," in *Religious Pluralism and Religious Education*, ed. Norma H. Thompson (Birmingham: Religious Education Press, 1988), 57. I am grateful to Perry G. Downs for drawing this book to my attention.

28. "What Is True Religion? Toward an Ecumenical Criteriology," in *Toward a Universal Theology of Religon*, ed. Leonard Swidler (Maryknoll: Orbis Books, 1987), 237 (emphasis his). See further Hans Küng and Jürgen Moltmann, *Christianity Among World Religions* (Edinburgh: T & T Clark, 1986).

The only way to make much sense of this is to recognize that for Küng truth is not tied in any obvious way to notions of orthodoxy, but to that which is pursued. At face value, however, Küng sounds as if he is heading for religious pluralism in his first paragraph, and for inclusivism in the second.

In his most recent book, Schubert Ogden offers what he thinks of as a fourth position, one that lies beyond exclusivism, inclusivism, and pluralism.[29] The first two positions, exclusivism and inclusivism, Ogden lumps together under the designation "Christian monism," and rejects as being contrary to the standards of common human reason and experience, and an offence to Christian witness to Jesus Christ as the expression of God's primordial love for humanity. But pluralism does not fare well in his hands either. Arguments against "Christian monism," he says, do not entail the conclusion that pluralism is right. The pluralism position demands that there be material or substantial similarities between religions, and these are notoriously difficult to prove. Moreover, it is exceedingly difficult to adopt a pluralist position and then avoid a descent into religious relativism.

So Ogden proposes a crucial shift in Christology. Instead of holding that the possibility of salvation is constituted by the event of Jesus Christ ("a constitutive christology"), Ogden argues that the possibility of salvation is grounded rather in the prior and unbounded love of God, to which the event of Jesus Christ gives expression. Thus the possibility of salvation is not constituted by Christ, but is represented by Christ ("a representative christology"). This does not prove that other religions are true, but it does allow the possibility that Christianity and other religions alike can all be true insofar as they represent "the primordial and everlasting love of God."

Many questions might be raised against Ogden's proposal. For a start, it is not as all-embracing as he seems to think it is, for the religions that do not believe God is fundamentally personal have great difficulty with notions like "the love of God," and so cannot, on Ogden's premise, be "true." In other words, Hick has already eclipsed Ogden. Moreover, Ogden's understanding of God's love is so eminently unbiblical, as we shall see (chaps. 5 and 6), that one marvels at the hubris that still thinks it is Christian. Further, for the concerns of this chapter one must ask Ogden how he knows that God is loving, and that Christology can be "representational" (in his sense) and not "constitutive." Are biblical and theological pieces like some giant, ill-designed Lego set where one is free to pick up pieces and discard others, designing your own trucks and cranes and spaceships, your own gods and truths and salvations? With all respect, Ogden has not offered us a fourth option, but an

---

29. Schubert M. Ogden, *Is There Only One True Religion or Are There Many?* (Dallas: Southern Methodist Univ. Press, 1992).

inferior version of the third option. If one wants to be a religious pluralist, Hick is a considerably more rigorous thinker.

The tendencies of religious pluralism, in any case, are not in doubt. As Richard Lints put it, "The golden rule of postmodernism is 'Grant to all other religions the same presumption of truth as you grant to your own religion.' All religions are created equal."[30] For many pluralists that commitment actually injects a bias toward oriental religions that are characterized by syncretism, notably Hinduism. For others, religious pluralism has become so strong a credal point that any religion that claims monopoly or even superiority is outrageous. As McGrath observes:

> Let us hear one of Rosemary Radford Ruether's Olympian pronouncements on the relation of the religions. She clearly does not intend to enter into dialogue with her opponents when, like Zeus hurling a thunderbolt at those far below him, she delivers her verdict that "the idea that Christianity, or even the Biblical faiths, have a monopoly on religious truth is an outrageous and absurd religious chauvinism."[31] Yet the assumption that underlies the thinking of most of the contributors to *The Myth of Christian Uniqueness* is that a liberal pluralism does, in effect, have a monopoly on religious truth by allowing religions to be seen in their proper context. It alone provides the vantage point from which the true relation of the religions can be seen. Is this not also an "outrageous and absurd" imperialism? Ruether effectively treats her own religious position as privileged, detached, objective and correct, whereas that of Christianity (or, at least, those forms of Christianity that she dislikes) is treated with little more than scorn and sneer.[32]

Nor are the issues restricted to the narrowly religious: religion embraces all of life, so that fundamental questions of worldview and values are at stake, not least one's understanding of morals and of ethics. When religious pluralism triumphs, inevitably the common sins of humanity become defended as alternative lifestyles.

B. The Challenge of Authority

The subject is vast and complex; it regularly elicits books, not merely brief chapters. But the following seven points, of unequal weight, will have to serve.

---

30. *The Fabric of Theology: A Prologomenon to Evangelical Theology* (Grand Rapids: Eerdmans, 1993), 246.

31. McGrath is here quoting Rosemary Radford Ruether, "Feminism and Jewish-Christian Dialogue," in Hick and Knitter, *The Myth of Christian Uniqueness*, 141.

32. Alister E. McGrath, "The Christian Church's Response to Pluralism," *Journal of the Evangelical Theological Society* 35 (1992): 494.

1. Some frequently articulated views about revelation, and about the Bible in particular, must not go unchallenged.

It should go without saying that the authority of the Bible must be recognized by Christians. The church cannot exist and flourish without unreservedly embracing the Bible. But the central heritage of the church on this subject has come under increasing fire. It is not surprising therefore that Netland lists skepticism about the Bible as one of the contributing reasons for the rise of religious pluralism and the rejection of exclusivism.[33] In this atmosphere, to quote John 14:6 ("I am the way and the truth and the life. No one comes to the Father except through me") or Acts 4:12 ("Salvation is found in no one else, for there is no other name under heaven given to men by which we must be saved") proves nothing to those who are not already convinced.

This is not the place to set out a comprehensive doctrine of Scripture, cast in contemporary terms. In some measure, that has been adequately attempted—repeatedly so—during the past two decades.[34] With rare exceptions, the best of the works on Scripture written by confessional believers interact far more ably with the writings of skeptical opponents than do the efforts of the opponents when they discuss Scripture, usually without competent reference to the central tradition of the church or even to contemporary conservative scholarship.[35] Be that as it may, the debate cannot be set out again here, except to reinforce two points. (1) The God of the Bible is a God who acts and talks. He is personal. The Christian's view of the Bible is tied to the doctrine of God, who discloses himself in deeds and words.[36] (2) The Bible is simultaneously the product of God's mind and of human minds. Sophisticated treatments of inspiration are eager to avoid the assumption that God simply dictated the whole Bible, so that the human contribution was

---

33. Netland, *Dissonant Voices: Religious Pluralism and the Question of Truth,* 29.

34. From the many works that might be listed, see the essays in D. A. Carson and John D. Woodbridge, eds., *Scripture and Truth* (Grand Rapids: Zondervan, 1983); idem, *Hermeneutics, Authority, and Canon* (Grand Rapids: Zondervan, 1986); Roger R. Nicole and J. Ramsey Michaels, eds., *Inerrancy and Common Sense* (Grand Rapids: Baker; 1980); and the book by Ronald H. Nash, *The Word of God and the Mind of Man: The Crisis of Revealed Truth in Contemporary Theology* (Grand Rapids: Zondervan, 1982).

35. To take but one example, the important book by Sandra M. Schneiders, *The Revelatory Text: Interpreting the New Testament as Sacred Scripture* (San Francisco: Harper San Francisco, 1991), never interacts with conservative literature on this subject, except occasionally through the intermediary of a liberal critic.

36. For better or worse, I tried to tie God, revelation, the Bible, and hermeneutics together in an introductory yet fairly comprehensive way, in "Approaching the Bible," in D. A. Carson, R. T. France, J. A. Motyer, G. J. Wenham, eds., *New Bible Commentary: 21st Century Edition* (Downers Grove: InterVarsity Press, 1994), 1–19. See also Carl F. H. Henry, *God, Revelation and Authority* (Waco: Word Books, 1976–83), 3:403–28.

that of the secretary or the tape recorder and transcriber. That God's words, in verbatim quotation, are sometimes recorded, is clear; that the styles, themes, research, witness, emotions, commitments, and words of the human authors are frequently preserved is no less clear. The human engagement makes historical study of the Bible both possible and necessary;[37] the divine engagement ensures its veracity and authority. Theologians often speak of "concursive" theories of inspiration that picture God in his sovereignty, by whatever means, so superintending and preserving the human authors that what they wrote, while being precisely what they intended should be written, is nothing less than what God intended should be written. This duality of authorship is cast in various ways across the history of the church,[38] and sometimes (especially in the Patristic period) it is labeled "dictation."[39] (The latter term is accepted by no responsible conservative today, as an expression of God's primary means of bringing the Bible about.) Certainly it has an important bearing on what we mean by authorial intention, a point to which I shall briefly return later in this chapter.

If, then, the words of the Bible, while being the words of Ezekiel or of Matthew or of Paul, are also the words of God, then this is the place where we not only meet Ezekiel and Matthew and Paul, but where we meet God. If

---

37. This includes, of course, responsible attempts to understand the human author's social matrix, as the Sovereign Lord of history governs the social arena no less than the individual life. The danger is in thinking that social (or some other) analysis is sufficient explanation of the text, or in deploying notorious slippery and anachronistic social categories. For a responsible treatment, see Richard L. Rohrbaugh, "'Social Location of Thought' as a Heuristic Construct in New Testament Study," *Journal for the Study of the New Testament* 30 (1987): 103–19.

38. See, for example, the brief statement of Lints, *The Fabric of Theology*, 74–76; the many and well-known writings of Benjamin B. Warfield; or the relevant writings of the Puritan scholar John Owen, nicely outlined and summarized by J. I. Packer, "John Owen on Communication from God," in *A Quest for Godliness: The Puritan Vision of the Christian Life* (Wheaton: Crossway Books, 1990), 81–96.

39. Only rarely do contemporary authors deal with this topic; even more rarely do they deal with it seriously, though there is a substantial literature on it. Kathleen C. Boone, *The Bible Tells Them So: The Discourse of Protestant Fundamentalism* (Albany: State Univ. of New York Press, 1989), 29–34, insists that modern treatments disowning "dictation" (in the modern sense of that word) demand such verbal truthfulness that dictation is what is nevertheless in view. In the same way, she demands that "inerrancy" refer to an idealized picture and then criticizes evangelical ("fundamentalist") scholars for their sophisticated qualifications that treat textual criticism, matters of syntax, degrees of precision, and so forth as if they are wildly inconsistent—without reflecting on the fact that every word used to refer to a complex entity or doctrine could be similarly ridiculed (e.g., "God"!). She does not, for example, refer to sophisticated treatments such as Paul D. Feinberg, "The Meaning of Inerrancy," in *Inerrancy*, ed. Norman L. Geisler (Grand Rapids: Zondervan, 1979), 267–304. She repeatedly operates with caricatures and simply does not engage the thoughtful literature.

the qualifications to radical hermeneutics and deconstruction I put forward in chapters 2 and 3 are accepted, so that texts are not normally viewed as completely autonomous, the lines of C. S. Lewis come to mind:

> You stranger, long before your glance can light
> Upon these words, time will have washed away
> The moment when I first took pen to write,
> With all my road before me—yet to-day,
> Here, if at all, we meet. . . .
>
> —*Dymer*, I.1

In other words, if finite authors do think of their prospective readers, and in a sense communicate with them as their words are read, meeting them, as it were, over the written word (just as I am meeting you who read these words as you read them!), how much more must we recognize the intentions of God to meet with people over his words. I have very little idea of who you are, you who are reading this page; God has perfect knowledge of those who read his words.

From this base, then, I want to respond to six preliminary misconceptions or misconstruals of revelation, and in particular of Scripture.

First, it is quite mistaken to portray this high view of Scripture as a late creation of scholastic orthodoxy, or of Old Princeton Presbyterianism, or of a misguided use of Scottish Common Sense Realism. The implication, of course, is that we should return to a more primitive understanding of the Bible that will allow more latitude.

The mistake lies at four different levels. (1) At the historical level, it is now widely recognized that the best attempts to assign the notion of inerrancy to a very late stage of historical development[40] simply will not stand up to competent historical research that is intimately familiar with the primary documents.[41] If one insists that a high view of Scripture cannot or should not be maintained today, one should at least acknowledge that one is walking away from the ancient and central tradition of the church, and from the teaching of Scripture itself. (2) It has been repeatedly shown that, however dependent the Princetonians were on Scottish Common Sense Realism (and the extent has been exaggerated), their opponents were not less dependent. In other words, a high view of Scripture can hardly be made paradigmatically dependent on one philosophical outlook when those who denied that high view were not less dependent on the same outlook. (3) Further, the theory

---

40. Perhaps the best known is that of Jack B. Rogers and Donald K. McKim, *The Authority and Interpretation of the Bible: An Historical Approach* (San Francisco: Harper & Row, 1979).

41. See especially John D. Woodbridge, *Biblical Authority: A Critique of the Rogers/McKim Proposal* (Grand Rapids: Zondervan, 1982).

does not explain the Dutch or Germans who adopted a similarly high view of Scripture, and who in most cases paid no attention to Scottish Common Sense Realism or in some instances opposed it. (4) More importantly, the demonstration that a high view of Scripture recurs in every age of the church proves that this view is independent of particular philosophical paradigms. Better put, Christians have articulated more or less the same substantial view of the Bible, and on the same historical and exegetical grounds, regardless of the fact that they have lived in widely different times and cultures. If postmodernity has taught us anything, it has taught us that it is impossible for any "knower" to think outside of all paradigms, as an entirely "neutral" observer and thinker. The remarkable fact, then, is that substantially the same view of an error-free Scripture has recurred under so many cultural paradigms that it is irresponsible to try to "paradigm out" a high view of Scripture as if it were a late perversion.

Second, it is a misconception to treat the Bible as simply one of the classics, or on a par with the creeds, or freighted with the same weight, no more and no less, as other ancient documents such as the *Gospel of Thomas* or *The Manual of Discipline*. If the Bible is the locus of God's self-disclosure in words, it is privileged.[42] It follows that extrabiblical sources, whether ancient or modern, "are not independent counterbalancing sources of authority. The Bible's perspective is privileged, not ours."[43]

Failure to observe this point stands behind one of Barr's theses in his 1991 Gifford Lectures.[44] Against Karl Barth's well-known antipathy to natural theology,[45] Barr defends the importance of natural theology, not least on the ground that the Bible does (e.g., Psalms 19, 104, 119). But Barr's decisive step comes when he insists that natural theology must be allowed to critique the teachings of the Bible.[46]

---

42. Clearly this has a bearing on the changing face of authority across the centuries in the Roman Catholic Church, culminating in the promulgation of the infallibility of the pope in 1870 (and reconfigured again in Vatican II), but I cannot pursue such matters here. On the complex factors that moved Catholicism in these directions, see Bruno Neveu, *L'erreur et son juge. Remarques sur les censures doctrinales á l'époque moderne* (Naples: Biblipolis, 1993), and the important essay by Jacques Le Brun, "Autorité doctrinale, définition et censure dans le Catholicism moderne," *Revue de l'Histoire des Religions* 211 (1994): 335–43.

43. Richard B. Hayes, "The Church as a Scripture-Shaped Community: The Problem of Method in New Testament Ethics," *Interpretation* 44 (1990): 51.

44. James Barr, *Biblical Faith and Natural Theology* (Oxford: Clarendon Press, 1993).

45. Despite his denigration of natural theology, Barth occasionally makes some allowance for it: "God may speak to us through a flute concerto, through a blossoming shrub or through a dead dog" (*Church Dogmatics* I/1,60). But it is far from clear that Barth would allow such "speaking" to shape any part of the *substance* of his theology.

46. Barr, *Biblical Faith*, 150ff., passim. Part of the debate over natural theology turns on definitions. For some, natural theology is virtually indistinguishable from natural revelation.

Third, the approaches to the Bible spawned by a commitment to plural-ism and to comparative religions must be seen as the profoundly circular methods they are. Consider, for example, the recent work by Wilfrid Cantwell Smith.[47] Smith argues that "Scripture" and "text" should by no means be identified, since texts shape communities (even though communi-ties may interpret them differently over time), but it is the communities that make texts into scriptures.

At a certain level, that is surely true. Smith's analysis offers many intrigu-ing examples from the approaches to their respective scriptures found among Muslims, Hindus, and Jews. But surely Christians would want to argue that the text's influence on the community continues precisely because of its sta-tus as Scripture.[48] Moreover, in at least some instances the texts were recog-nized as Scripture as soon as they were first received. And in any Protestant understanding of the nature of the canon, the church did not confer "scrip-ture status" onto the biblical texts, but sought to discover, by articulated prin-ciples, which texts should be recognized as inherently having such status, and therefore to be included in the canon. From such a perspective, Scripture *must* be identified with certain texts. Smith's narrowly comparative approach does not really wrestle with the supernatural element in Scripture, so that his conclusion is entailed by the approach he adopts. His approach is not safer or less gullible or more responsible than those that follow the central heritage of the church on this point; it is merely narrower and more reductionistic. I cannot forbear to contrast the approach of Chesterton's Father Brown:

" ... I'm exactly in the position of the man who said, 'I can believe the impos-sible, but not the improbable.'"
"That's what you call a paradox, isn't it?" asked the other.

For others, natural theology suggests an entire system of thought based on natural revela-tion—and they argue that natural revelation does not provide sufficient content to authorize such theology (so Stephen R. Spencer, "Is Natural Theology Biblical?" *Grace Theological Journal* 9 [1988]: 59–72).

47. *What Is Scripture? A Comparative Approach* (Minneapolis: Fortress Press, 1993).

48. Of course, this is tied to the old debate about whether we should think of Scripture as *norma normans* ("the rule that prescribes") or *norma normata* ("the rule that is prescribed") by the church. In the former case, which I espouse, "the books within the collection are regarded as possessing an intrinsic worth prior to their having been assembled, and their authority is grounded in their nature and source." If so, "when once the principle of the canon has been determined, then ideally its extent is fixed and the canon is complete when the books which by principle belong to it have been written," even if "the making of the empirical canon required a long period of time and involved a complex historical process that progressed, not in a straight line, but in a zig-zag development" (Bruce M. Metzger, *The Canon of the New Testament: Its Origin, Development, and Significance* [Oxford: Clarendon Press, 1987], 283–84).

"It's what I call common sense, properly understood," replied Brown. "It really is more natural to believe a preternatural story, that deals with things we don't understand, than a natural story that contradicts things we do understand. Tell me that the great Mr. Gladstone, in his last hours, was haunted by the ghost of Parnell, and I will be agnostic about it. But tell me that Mr. Gladstone, when first presented to Queen Victoria, wore his hat in her drawing-room and slapped her on the back and offered her a cigar, and I am not agnostic at all. That is not impossible; it's only incredible...."[49]

Fourth, some criticisms of the Bible, written in astonishingly purple prose,[50] cannot be taken very seriously because they simply do not engage with the substantial serious literature that has accumulated during the last two millennia.

Even a moderate book, like the latest to be penned by John Barton,[51] drops far too many clangers. A collateral purpose of his book is to domesticate the Bible. After all, we are told, the Bible is not "a book written by the hand of God, which dropped from heaven." No one of my acquaintance claims it did: against whom is this directed? A straw man? Readings are offered that disparage various passages: Peter is implicitly condemned for his "satisfaction" at God's vengeful "striking down" of Ananias and Sapphira. We are assured that we cannot keep the Ten Commandments unless we restore slavery. Stories of miracles are regularly classified as legends. As one reviewer puts it:

> After all, miracles don't happen, do they? God doesn't direct the lightning, does He? Angels don't intervene in human history, and so on. Lightning strikes in accordance with scientific law, we now know. It can hardly have been pure chance that the king's "captains and their fifties" caught it, or didn't three times—so the story must be mere legend [2 Kings 1]. What do we reply to this? That it is superficial thinking. Let me give an analogy to illustrate this contention. My arm moves undeniably in accordance with known physiological principles; but that does not make it nonsense to say that *it moves at the instance of my will.* The discharge of lightning also is undeniably in accordance with known physical principles; but *neither does that make it nonsense to attribute it to the Divine will.* There is doubtless an intractable philosophical problem here; but most would agree that it is not solved by relegating the concept of will (or for that matter, angels) to the category of the legendary. Yet this is what in effect Professor Barton is doing

49. G. K. Chesterton, *The Penguin Complete Father Brown* (Harmondsworth: Penguin Books, 1981), 402.

50. See especially Robert P. Carroll, *Wolf in the Sheepfold: The Bible as a Problem for Christianity* (London: SPCK, 1991).

51. *What Is the Bible?* (London: SPCK, 1991).

(but without acknowledging it to his unsuspecting readers or perhaps even realizing it himself).[52]

But the most shocking claim advanced by Barton is this: "The fact that ground rules for effective biblical criticism are ... dependent only on good reasoning, means that for practical purposes the religious commitment of critics is entirely irrelevant to evaluating their work."[53] This is bad history, bad hermeneutics, and bad theology. It is bad history because, as Professor Barton knows well, "effective biblical criticism" has changed opinion constantly over the years (consider, for instance, the extraordinarily diverse opinions during the last two centuries of the quest and the new quest for the historical Jesus), and is now broken into many different schools of thought, not a few of which are mutually exclusive. It is bad hermeneutics because if the new hermeneutic has taught us anything, it is that no interpretation, including interpretation that claims "scientific" controls, is entirely neutral.[54] It is bad theology because it entirely ignores the Bible's own witness to our fallenness, the noetic distortion caused by sin, Pauline insistence on the work of the Spirit before the natural mind can understand the things of God (see chaps. 5 and 6 of this book), and more.

Fifth, inevitably a phalanx of interwoven critical decisions stands behind a fair bit of skepticism about the Bible. For instance, doubtless the majority of contemporary New Testament scholars date the Pastorals rather late, and see in them a kind of degenerative change from the purity of the Pauline gospel. But a substantial minority of scholars, not all of them espousing confessional Christianity, find many technical reasons for adopting the traditional position. My purpose here is not to mediate those debates; at a certain level, they become rather sterile. My point, rather, is that inevitably both sides of this particular debate link their interpretation to a substantial number of other critical decisions, so that ultimately one is very close to a worldview decision.

When the decision is made, in line with perfectly acceptable critical reasons, to read Scripture as Scripture, a different coloring may become obvious. For instance:

> We will benefit by the study of the Pastoral and General Epistles today because they represent a maturing, not a degenerating, phase of early Christian theological development. The crucial question before the churches then was: How, in a period of cross-cultural pluralism, syncretism, political alienation, and vast historical mutation, is it possible to pass the tradition

---

52. Douglas Spanner, in *Churchman* 108 (1994): 83.

53. Barton, *What Is the Bible?* 71.

54. Which, of course, is not the same thing as saying that no distinctions can be drawn between good and bad interpretations: see chaps. 2 and 3.

learned from the earliest Christians on to succeeding generations? How can we teach it accurately without distortions, and how can we defend it against interpretations that would profoundly diminish it? It is a life-and-death question that echoes in our situation today: Can the tradition be transgenerationally communicated amid a period of widespread social disruption?

It reveals a tedious lack of imagination to conclude that these writers' interest in historical continuity, unity, and tradition (which they solved successfully by means of ordination, the clear definition of apostolic teaching, a fierce struggle against heresy, and a stable church order) represented a disastrous setback in theology. If they had not done their job well in the period of the Pastoral and General Epistles, we would not be reading the rest of the New Testament now.[55]

Sixth, it is inadequate to view the Bible as nothing more than a collection of human responses to God, although that is a very common perspective among scholars who espouse many of the fundamentals of Christianity but who for one reason or another cannot bring themselves to adopt a high view of Scripture.

Several years ago I entered into lengthy correspondence with a gracious senior scholar over the nature of Scripture. His position was very much the sort of thing I have just described, yet his convictions on many other matters were entirely orthodox. Our letters went back and forth many times, often dealing with narrow technical matters, sometimes painting on a larger canvas. I doubt if I can deal better with the issue at hand than by printing parts of one of my letters to him, written toward the end of June 1990. I suppose I would not have written to him in exactly this vein if we were not so close in outlook on many doctrinal fronts.

In what follows, square brackets indicate attempts to smooth the flow or hide the identity of this senior scholar; the occasional footnote is explanatory.

Dear [Professor Smith],

Please forgive the inexcusable delay in my reply. The weeks have slipped by very quickly since you graced our home with your presence. I suppose I have been marshalling my strength[56] to complete one or two small projects before we leave on 12 July,[57] and so I have put some correspondence to one side.

---

55. Thomas C. Oden, *After Modernity . . . What?* (Grand Rapids: Zondervan, 1990), 146–47. This reading of the later epistles, or something like it, is of course a commonplace in the history of confessional Christianity. See, for example, R. W. Dale, *Fellowship with Christ and Other Discourses Delivered on Special Occasions* (New York: A. C. Armstrong and Son, 1892), chap. 4.

56. I had contracted typhoid a few months earlier.

57. We were at that time living in Cambridge, England.

In any case, thank you for taking the time to reply so fully. I think I understand your position a little better. At some points I agree with you fully; at others, I still have some questions.

(1) It is not so much that I disagree with what you say about what Scripture *is* and *does*. We will agree that the New Testament documents provide the primary evidence for the beginnings of Christianity, and that they *do* this because of what they *are*. As to what they are, I do not disagree that they constitute "a mirror of the convictions of the earliest believers." Nor would I dispute that, critically assessed, the "best and most plausible interpretation" of them was subsequently formulated in the historic creeds. My questions, I suppose, would be three-fold: (a) Does this not leave the gospel hostage to critical whim? Would it not be fair to say that many who share your view of Scripture so use critical tools that they could *not* say that the most plausible explanation of the NT documents was later formulated in the creeds? I think of, say, David Jenkins, or Helmut Koester, or Rudolf Bultmann, and countless more. Of course, if that is *all* that Scripture is, then we have little choice. But then I fear we make faith so hostage to the painfully faddish and idiosyncratic opinions of learned scholars that not only do few ordinary Christians enjoy access to knowledge by which to assess their scholars, but we lose whatever warrant we once had to encourage young preachers in the ministry of the Word to master the text and proclaim (with the strange mixture of humility and authority gained by those who stand *under* the text), "Thus says the Lord." (b) I cannot help [but think] that this sort of formulation enables the creeds to function more authoritatively than the Scriptures. I find this approach *historically* implausible. And if you were to reply that I have mis-read you, and that the creeds must always be placed under Scripture since demonstrably they are attempts at formulating what Scripture teaches, the first question I raised returns with a vengeance. Those whose critical acumen leads them to think that the creeds are pre-scientific, pre-critical syntheses can always find some other explanation of the biblical texts. (c) Above all, although I entirely agree that we must ask what the Scriptures *are*, and that it is entirely true to say that they represent the convictions of the earliest Christians, is that an *adequate* description of what they are? I shall return to the question of what the Scriptures are a little farther on. But if your description of what they are is adequate, it generates an interesting example of the first question. I think you would agree that the first Christians' convictions, represented in the New Testament documents, include the conviction that antecedent Scripture is truthful (leaving aside for the moment the problem of the closing of the OT canon, and restricting ourselves to thinking of "Scripture" rather than "canon"). For many reasons, I think that the most plausible explanation of this conviction is that the early Christians were right, and that their convictions in this area also prepared the way for the conceptualization of what became the NT Scriptures. Clearly, in this area you think the convictions of the first Christians were amiss. I hope we shall go on exploring why we disagree. But

the disagreement is a microcosm of much larger (and admittedly more significant) disagreements [with others] over, say, the resurrection of Jesus, the ὁμοούσιος formula,[58] and so forth. I look into an abyss, where each scholar claims his or her views are Christian, but where the diversity as to what [in the New Testament] is judged most plausible or critically ascertainable produces an endless variety of "canons within the canon."

It is in that sense that I wondered if this was not to "write off" the truth question too soon. My choice of words was unfortunate, my explanation too brief, and I am sorry if I offended you. When you say that the "truth-claims of the Christian creed are the whole point" of your definitions, I accept what you say without reservation. But the three questions still remain; and their bearing on what I was trying to say in my earlier letter may be put like this: Is it possible that defining what the Scriptures *are* so narrowly—as merely the convictions of the earliest Christians—already short-circuits the discussion? Is it not possible that the Scriptures are not only the convictions of the earliest Christians, but also divine self-disclosure from the God who speaks, however much he has used human agents with their own idiosyncratic styles and vocabularies and emphases to convey that revelation to us?

(2) I largely take your point that "inspiration" is a slippery word in the period from the first century B.C. right down to Jerome and beyond. I do *not* think that, as used during that period, inspiration *necessarily* [entailed] "free from error" or the like. The list of references even in the Fathers (provided, for instance, in Bruce Metzger's book on the canon)[59] is very interesting. If that is all the evangelical argument turns on, it is a broken reed.

But most knowledgeable evangelicals, I think, would acknowledge that they employ the term "inspiration" less according to its flexible use in the early centuries, than as a synthetic term governed by far more recent developments. They use it, in short, to refer to what they see as the work of God behind the production of Scripture; but the constituent arguments that support that synthesis are diverse. Implicitly, it seems to me, you recognize them when you say, "I believe that there is every likelihood that Jesus used Scripture just as his contemporaries did and most subsequent generations, right up to (say) the Enlightenment. But that doesn't convince me that we, with the knowledge that (for no merit of our own) we have been given, can do so." That you can write the first of these two sentences betrays that you think there is evidence that the NT writers, and Jesus himself, saw Scripture more or less as most evangelicals (and many others) do today. The diversity of the kinds of evidence that goes into this sort of assessment is easily overlooked. Wayne Grudem in his article in *Scripture and Truth*[60] tried to marshall some of it. Although I did not always think his way of reading the

---

58. I am referring to the later formula that led to the affirmations that Christ is of the same substance as the Father.

59. I was referring to Metzger, *The Canon of the New Testament*.

60. Ed. D. A. Carson and John D. Woodbridge (Grand Rapids: Zondervan, 1983).

evidence was convincing, nevertheless the array of kinds of evidence is impressive. With respect to the OT, the casual way in which Mt.22:43 (for instance) says "David, speaking by the Spirit," in order to ensure that readers will be reminded that what David said must be accepted (cf. John 10:35), surely says something about how the first Christians understood "Scripture." It is this large and somewhat complex construct, I think, that most contemporary evangelicals refer to when they speak of the inspired Scriptures, or the inspiration of Scripture. The usage is, doubtless, rather sloppy from an historical perspective; but it is surely one more term where it is necessary to distinguish between the use of a term in the first century, and the use of a term in subsequent theology. There is nothing inappropriate about such semantic developments, provided one does not try to read the later semantic range into the earlier occurrences, forgetting that it is the product of synthetic development. But I would nonetheless argue that the evidence for the existence of such a "high" view of Scripture in the first century is very strong, even if we summarize it or refer to it using some other rubric. And implicitly, as I have said, you seem to agree, even if you prefer to restrict the usage of the term "inspiration" to its early usage.

(3) If we agree, then, that the early Christians *did* have such a "high" view of Scripture, is it so *very* clear that "the attitude of the ancients . . . can't be adopted today with mental integrity"? Granted that some of the formulations of some of them are a bit strained, I confess I am surprised to be told that their *attitude* to Scripture can't be maintained today. Unless you mean something by their attitude that I haven't grasped, I do maintain it, or, I suppose, the next best thing. I would want to argue that just as controversy helped sharpen Christological formulations whose truth is nevertheless grounded in Scripture (as I think you would agree), so controversy on the nature of Scripture may also help sharpen the formulations of a bibliology whose truth is also grounded in Scripture. In others words the way I proceed to a formulation of the nature of Scripture is not inherently different from the way I proceed to a formulation of the nature of Christ. In that sense, I suppose my formulations re Scripture are not quite the same as those of antiquity, but I think my attitude is. Does this mean I have sacrificed mental integrity?

[Professor Smith], do you really believe that? All I can say is that I do not mean to do so. I think you would be loathe to charge, say, Helmut Koester with lacking in mental integrity because he reads the Christological evidence rather differently from the way you do; I imagine you would be distressed if he charged you with lacking mental integrity for the reciprocal reason. How is my case fundamentally different from these? If I hid my head in the sand and refused to consider or weigh the evidence, I could understand the charge, and I would plead guilty, in confusion and shame. But so far as I am aware, I have not done that. But my own case is insignificant. Surely you would not want to argue that, say, Westcott and Lightfoot (both post-Enlightenment men!) sacrificed their mental integrity. I do not see how my view of Scripture differs from theirs. (C. K. Barrett was here this year to give a lecture commemorating the work of Lightfoot, and praised his historical acumen while bemoaning his view of Scripture.) Nor am I suggesting that the Enlightenment should be ignored. Demonstrably, it has helped regain the *historical* dimension to Scripture, a dimension that Paul relies on (in, say, Rom. 4 and especially Gal. 3) in his response to the a-temporal approach to "law" presupposed by his opponents. But I am not persuaded that the Enlightenment was *all* gain. In any case, your internationally famous charity toward those with whom you disagree surely means that I have misunderstood what you are saying on this point.

(4) By the same token, the old saw that "it does remain a circular argument to defend the truthfulness of Scripture by a quotation from [Scripture]" is, in my view, a rather (dare I say it?) unfair caricature of what knowledgeable evangelicals actually do. Most of them are not resorting to cheap proof-texting. Rather, they mean to attempt to discover what Scripture *is* in order to articulate what it *does*. And surely part of the effort to find out what Scripture *is* requires that we read Scripture and see what it says of itself. That you acknowledge Jesus probably held the "high" view of Scripture espoused by his contemporaries suggests this is not an unintelligible or irresponsible approach. It must, of course, be coordinated with other approaches; and by itself it cannot *prove* anything about the nature of Scripture, since its own claims might be wrong, or misguided, or delusive, or whatever. But it is surely not viciously circular to use what Scripture says about itself and its truthfulness as one of the contributing elements that constitute a responsible doctrine of Scripture.

[. . .]

(5) I do not think that words carry greater "authority" than other possible modes of revelation. Indeed, I would insist that the greatest revelation is the "Word" incarnate. But I do think that words are less ambiguous than mere events. The burning bush was no more than an incitement to intellectual curiosity until God *spoke*. Even the resurrection of Jesus *by itself*, as dramatic as it would have been, surely required the articulation of its significance. That does not prove that God *must* have disclosed himself [in words]. But at least some revelations were in "speech" from God that was recognizably "human" (the voice Paul heard from heaven spoke in Aramaic!). If we agree that there is ample evidence that God has spoken, that at times he did speak, then there is nothing anomalous about the claim that the Scriptures themselves, while being the speech of David, of Paul, or whomever, is nonetheless also the speech of God. That, surely, is how the first Christians thought of Scripture.

I do not understand why you think that *if* the words of Scripture have this revelatory significance, "it is amazing that they have been transmitted as chaotically and carelessly as, in parts of Scripture, they evidently are." As for copyists' errors, there is nothing in Scripture to suggest that its texts *would* be so preserved, and all the evidence needed to demonstrate that such preservation never took place. As for other errors, I think I would need to know more about what you have in mind. I have read the lists of, say, Achtemeier and Barton with great interest, and I find them very diverse indeed.[61] I would say quite different things about many of their entries.

(6) I am not sure what you mean by saying, "Infallibility doesn't appear to me ever to be God's way with humankind at any level—and if it were we would certainly not be able infallibly to receive the infallibilities." In God's gracious self-disclosure in Christ, we read that he was tempted while remaining without sin. I have no reason to suppose that you would not accept this early Christian conviction was true. That does not mean Jesus was better understood for it, or that he thereby avoided charges of being in league with the devil himself. It seems to me that infallibility inheres in many of God's ways with humankind. But with the second part of your sentence I heartily agree. We are unable infallibly to receive what God has (infallibly or otherwise) provided. I have never for a moment thought otherwise. That, surely, is a function both of our finiteness and especially of our sin. That is also why I insist that no doctrine of the infallibility of Scripture can ever be infallible. But I do not see how our fallibility in any way jeopardizes the assumptions and claims ... of early believers that what God had revealed in Scripture could not be broken.

[...]

I fear I have taken up much too much of your time with this lengthy letter. I have greatly appreciated your willingness to respond to my probings. If I am wrong on this matter, I would like to be shown that I am wrong, since, as I have said, I do not hold that any doctrine of Scripture is itself infallible. But if at any point you feel you have had enough of this exchange, I shall not be in the least offended if you frankly tell me so.

I hope this finds you in good heart. Joy joins me in warm greetings.

As ever,
and etc.

2. The Bible's appeal to truth is rich and complex. It cannot be reduced to, but certainly includes, the notion of propositional truth.

Partly in response to the drumming denial of much truth in the Bible, especially propositional truth, some Christians have rightly stressed the importance of propositional truth.[62] The less informed sometimes speak as if there is no other kind. An alternative response has been to emphasize a

---

61. Paul J. Achtemeier, *The Inspiration of Scripture: Problems and Proposals* (Philadelphia: Westminster, 1980); John Barton, *People of the Book? The Authority of the Bible in Christianity* (London: SPCK, 1988); cf. also his *What Is the Bible?* (London: SPCK, 1991).

62. E.g., Henry, *God, Revelation and Authority*, vol. 3, chaps. 25–27. See also the useful book by Lesslie Newbigin, *Truth to Tell: The Gospel as Public Truth* (Grand Rapids: Eerdmans, 1991).

"mystical" or "spiritual" insight to which "scientific" or "rationalistic" or "secular" thought could not find access. Some forms of this argument make important contributions to Christian epistemology, as we shall see; as a more or less comprehensive solution, it fails rather badly.[63]

Certainly all thoughtful Christians, scholars or otherwise, recognize that adherence to propositional truth is not everything. We remember that even the demons can affirm the propositional truth of monotheism (James 2:19). Many passages from both Testaments tie truth and life together. For example, John's first epistle ties together the confession of certain Christological truths, love for the brothers and sisters, and hearty obedience to Jesus Christ. Karl Barth is in part getting at the same point when he dismisses the Christian religion, as religion, along with all religions, while still insisting that there is such a thing as true religion.[64]

When the influence of Christianity began to be felt throughout the Roman Empire, its appeal and impact lay in part in its linking of truth, religion, and ethics. At the street level, most pagans could be ever so religious without it making a scrap of difference in the moral arena (not unlike certain fringe segments of evangelicalism today). So strongly did the outlook of the Bible prevail that eventually it became a truism in Western culture that "religious" people (which usually meant those who claimed to be Christians) *ought* to be good. That is precisely why the media drool over the accounts of religious leaders who are hypocrites. Ironically, the fact that people think religious leaders ought to lead exemplary lives is unacknowledged testimony to the lingering influence of Christianity in our culture. Indeed, that view extends to other outlooks. For example, the furore over the deconstructionist views of Paul de Man ignited when some of his earlier writings were discovered, writings that show him to have been a Nazi collaborator. Defenders and accusers wrestled back and forth as to whether de Man's views should be dismissed once his moral life—or at least this moral element in his life—was called into question.[65] There is no little irony that the furore should be over the validity (read "truthfulness") of de Man's views *on deconstruction* (!), and

---

63. Karl Heim might be cited as one who leaned rather heavily on this approach, largely in an effort to respond to the impersonal and naturalistic pantheism rising in his day. See the important study by Rolf Hille, *Das Ringen um den säkularen Menschen: Karl Heims Auseinandersetzung mit der idealistischen Philosophie und den pantheistischen Religionen* (Giessen: Brunnen Verlag, 1990). But as Kenneth S. Kantzer puts it (in a private communication), "Karl Heim was a wonderful, godly Christian swept off his feet intellectually by the overwhelming flow of unbelief in Germany during the twenties and thirties."

64. *Church Dogmatics* I/2.3.

65. The most thorough brief treatment of this debate of which I am aware is an unpublished paper by Kirk Allison, "Blind-Sight? The Controversy Concerning the Early Belgian Writings of Paul de Man" (1988), a copy of which was kindly given to me by the author.

that the question should be raised at all because of the cultural impact of the Judeo-Christian heritage.

Christians, then, recognize that faithful Christianity concerns more than propositional truth. Morever, Christian scholars have long pointed out that at the linguistic level the "truth" word-group in the Bible covers a wide range of meanings.[66] It may mean "faithful" or "trustworthy" or "reliable," as well as "conforming to reality" or "propositionally veridical." Indeed, in some uses several of these meanings come together, e.g., 1 Kings 10:6, where the Queen of Sheba affirms that the reports of Solomon's greatness are reliable, i.e., they are propositionally true, precisely because they conform to the reality. Thus in every passage where the "truth" word-group is found, one must (to use the jargon of modern linguistics) figure out the "language game" that is being played to understand the term precisely.

Not only must the semantic range of "truth" be recognized, we must also see that the Bible contains more (though certainly not less) than propositions. Evangelical students at universities are often tweaked with some such question as this: "Are Jesus' words on the cross, 'My God, my God, why have you forsaken me?' an inerrant proposition?" The purpose of the question, of course, is to try to force the student to recognize that not everything in Scripture is easily described as "inerrant" or even "propositional," and therefore to force an acknowledgement that it is inappropriate to think of the whole Bible as made up of "inerrant" or "truthful" "propositions."

At a merely formal level, of course, that is correct. It is also misleading. For it is one thing to find an example of a sentence in Scripture to which some such term as "inerrant" does not easily apply, and another to infer that the Bible is errant. What believers mean when they say that the entire Bible is inerrant is that wherever the category (and in the theological arena it is a sophisticated category!) is applicable in the Bible, it prevails. To find some places where it is not directly applicable is not the same thing as finding places where it is applicable but is falsified.[67]

Very helpful is the analysis of Vanhoozer, following Austin.[68] They

---

66. See especially Anthony Thiselton, "Truth," *New International Dictionary of New Testament Theology,* ed. Colin Brown (Grand Rapids: Zondervan, 1978), 3:874–902; Roger Nicole, "The Biblical Concept of Truth," in Carson and Woodbridge, *Scripture and Truth,* 287–98.

67. I say "directly applicable," because on an historical reading of the passage one would argue that Jesus actually did say these words, and *that* he said them is true: i.e., the passage does not err in saying that he said these words. But that, of course, is an *in*direct application of the inerrancy category to this utterance.

68. Kevin J. Vanhoozer, "The Semantics of Biblical Literature," in Carson and Woodbridge, *Hermeneutics, Authority, and Canon,* 53–104, esp. 86–92. Cf. J. L. Austin, *How To Do Things with Words,* 2d ed. (Cambridge: Harvard Univ. Press, 1975).

distinguish three components of the total speech act: (1) the *locutionary act* is more or less the "meaning" of the utterance, in the traditional sense; (2) the *illocutionary act* is "what we do *in* saying something,"[69] and (3) the *perlocutionary act* is "what we bring about or achieve *by* saying something, such as convincing or persuading."[70] The interesting element, for our purposes, is the second: it can be useful to distinguish the *meanings* of utterances from their *force* or *function*. If an economist announces, "The stock market is beginning a slide," he is saying something that is either true or not true; at the same time, he is warning investors to get out of the market and switch to municipal bonds or some other investment. So with biblical warnings, whether cast as announcements or not.[71] Indeed, most speech acts lie somewhere along a scale from purely locutionary to purely illocutionary. Moreover, related complications arise from the way "facts" and "truths" are presented in different genres of literature (on which more below). Vanhoozer suggests that "inerrancy" be retained as a category wherever facts (e.g., historical claims) are at stake, but that "infallibility" be used to mean "that Scripture's diverse illocutionary forces will invariably achieve their respective purposes."[72]

Even these sophisticated distinctions beg for further qualification. The category of "inerrancy" as deployed by Vanhoozer is clearly useful. We cannot say that every passage of Scripture conveys the truth, but we can say that every passage is inerrant, i.e., never affirms in matter of fact what is false. But note: (1) Such a formulation raises again what constitutes a "fact." (2) In any case, some believers, for reasons not entirely clear to me, reject the term "inerrancy" simply because of its negative form, preferring something like "total trustworthiness" or the like. I have no profound objection, but confess to mild amusement when I remember other negative words with a long and noble theological heritage (e.g., "immutable," "aseity"). Vanhoozer's use of "infallible" to mean "that Scripture's diverse illocutionary forces will invariably achieve their respective purposes" is perhaps not sufficiently precise. Do the threats of eternal punishment designed to make people flee the wrath to come prove the Bible is *not* infallible if those threats fail in this purpose for some people? Doubtless there are ways of making Vanhoozer's useful proposals more comprehensive.

---

69. Vanhoozer, "Semantics," 86.

70. Austin, *How To Do Things with Words*, 109.

71. Even a "pure" warning (e.g., "Turn, turn, why will you die?") implicitly affirms one or more facts—in this case, that failure to repent will inevitably issue in catastrophic judgment. Indeed, the degree to which the implicit fact is believed is the degree to which the warning itself will be taken seriously.

72. Vanhoozer, "Semantics," 94.

But at this juncture, my point is that reflective Christians have always recognized these sorts of things, even if they have not analyzed them precisely
the same way or with equivalent rigor. They have always said that the Bible
is not simply a book of facts: however many facts it contains, Scripture's purpose is not simply to fill our heads with facts, but to bring us to the living
God. Moreover, when it comes to interpreting words like "truth" Christians
are as aware as anyone else that contexts shape the semantic weight carried
by a word. After all, they have heard countless well-meaning types rip John
8:32 out of context ("You will know the truth, and the truth will make you
free"), and treat the passage as dominical authorization for educational and
scientific programs designed to enlighten the benighted. The assumption is
that education saves. I would be the last one to belittle the advantages of good
education (an increasingly rare commodity in the Western world), but that is
not what John 8 is about. The flow of the argument in the chapter demonstrates that the freedom at issue is freedom from sin, and the truth that people
must know is who Jesus is and therefore all he discloses of the Father. So
Christians, having observed that "truth" passages in the Bible can be distorted, have a vested interest in getting them right.

But let us grant for the sake of argument that some Christians thinkers
have on occasion pressed propositional truth to such a place of preeminence
that other contributing perspectives are jeopardized. Fairness demands that
the inverse charge be levelled: as McGrath says, "Postmodernism has an
endemic aversion to questions of truth."[73] He goes on:

> But the need to have the truth question on the agenda is relatively easily
> argued. One method of approach might be the following. To the postmod-
> ern suggestion that something can be "true for me" but not "true" the fol-
> lowing reply might be made. Is fascism as equally true as democratic
> libertarianism? Consider the person who believes, passionately and sincerely,
> that it is an excellent thing to place millions of Jews in gas chambers. That
> is certainly "true for him." But can it be allowed to pass unchallenged? Is it
> as equally true as the belief that one ought to live in peace and tolerance
> with one's neighbors, including Jews? Should one tolerate the burning of
> widows on Hindu funeral pyres?[74]

It might be worthwhile to document the accusation that postmodern
writers display "an enduring aversion to questions of truth," with specific reference to the way Scripture's truth is commonly set aside.

---

73. Alister E. McGrath, "The Challenge of Pluralism for the Contemporary Church,"
Journal of the Evangelical Theological Society 35 (1992): 366.

74. Ibid. McGrath is here following Allan Bloom, *The Closing of the American Mind* (New
York: Simon & Schuster, 1987), 26.

Hauerwas's latest book[75] is a delightful read, partly because his language is so unrestrained, and partly because Hauerwas really does want to see the Bible exerting real influence among professing believers. Yet his solution is disastrously based. He charges both historical critics and fundamentalists with trying to say what Scripture means. To this alleged error he adds the influence of his favorite *bête noire*, namely, the fatal influence of the liberal democracies, which encouragd the individual Christian to forge his or her own private interpretation. The "primary contention" of Hauerwas's book is this: "*The Bible is not and should not be accessible to merely anyone, but rather it should only be made available to those who have undergone the hard discipline of existing as part of God's people.*"[76]

If this were simply a slightly purple passage deploring Western individualism, not least in interpretation, one could live with it. Certainly Hauerwas is disturbed by "North American Christians" who "feel no need to stand under the authority of a truthful community to be told how to read" (15). But what he really has in mind is Stanley Fish, and the denial that there really is a "text" with meaning out there. Communities create meaning; that is why Hauerwas wants individual believers to be part of a community in order to learn the meaning from the community—indeed, the community's meaning. Hauerwas goes so far as to say:

> If Paul could appear among us today to tell us what he "really meant" when he wrote, for example, 1 Corinthians 13, his view would not necessarily count more than Gregory's or Luther's account of Corinthians. There simply is no "real meaning" of Paul's letters to the Corinthians once we understand that they are no longer Paul's letters but the Church's Scripture. Such examples remind us, according to Fish, that texts only exist in a continuing web of interpretive practices. Therefore we cannot ask how we ought to interpret the text because we then assume that the text exists prior to such interpretive strategies (20).

Hauerwas ties this perspective to the Roman Catholic insistence that proper interpretation belongs to the community, in this case the "Office of the Magisterium"(21). Such a link is naive. Doubtless there are Catholic deconstructionists who think that is what is going on, but the traditional understanding of the place of the Magisterium has very little to do with interpretive communities *whose interpretations vary from community to community*. The Magisterium claims to give the true interpretation of the text, in the context of its responsibility to proclaim the entire deposit of faith with which

---

75. Stanley Hauerwas, *Unleashing the Scripture: Freeing the Bible from Captivity to America* (Nashville: Abingdon, 1993).

76. Ibid., 9 (emphasis his).

it is charged. Wittingly or unwittingly, Hauerwas is hostage to deconstruction theory, divorces meaning not only from authorial intent but even from text, and then makes an impassioned plea to submit to the community. While trying to "unleash the Scripture," Hauerwas ends up trying to gag God, denying God the possibility of disclosing any objective truth recorded in texts.

Hauerwas is not, in any case, as free from bias as to what the text means as he lets on. He writes, "Our failure to understand what Paul 'really meant' is not the problem. Our problem is that we live in churches that have no practice of nonviolence, of reconciliation, no sense of the significance of singleness; so we lack the resources to faithfully preach and hear God's Word" (8). How does Hauerwas know that that is what the problem is? Doesn't his assessment presuppose a certain interpretation—either private or belonging only to a certain Anabaptist strain?

If "community" exercises interpretive control for Hauerwas, "imagination" exercises much the same function in the latest offering from the prolific Old Testament scholar Walter Brueggemann.[77] Although this book is written in a more scholarly style than that of Hauerwas, it is primarily addressed to mainline churches where the Bible has been domesticated by historical criticism. Added to this is the "new pluralistic, postmodern situation" that places us "in a wholly new interpretive situation" (p. vii). Brueggemann wants to avoid the "ecclesiastical authoritarianism" of the post-Reformation church and of fundamentalism; equally, he wants to escape the barrenness of historical critical approaches, though he acknowledges that historical criticism is "a useful (and indispensable) tool" (p. viii). For him, the onset of postmodernism does not mean a new threat, but a new opportunity: the challenge to develop an "evangelical imagination."

"Evangelical" in this construct has little to do with "evangelicalism," one component of which is invariably certain doctrinal content.[78] Brueggemann insists that pre-Enlightenment understanding of Christian doctrine as normative for all human thought is gone; so also is nineteenth- and twentieth-century liberalism, which was white, male, and narrowly based in North Atlantic countries. In this postliberal, post-Christian age, doctrine has gone, along with certainty even in the scientific arena. The appropriate way to read the Bible is with a developing "evangelical imagination." Over against the self-deifying construals of reality foisted on us by secularism, thinking our way through the Bible with an "evangelical imagination" enables us to enter into continuing conversation with better ways of construing reality, ways that

---

77. *Texts Under Negotiation: The Bible and the Postmodern Imagination* (Minneapolis: Fortress Press, 1993).

78. See the discussion on the definition of "evangelical" and related terms in chap. 11 hereafter.

are in line with biblical faith. After all, biblical faith affirms that God created life, and that God brings about the consummation. All self-deifying tendencies must therefore be challenged, and "evangelical imagination" playing on the biblical text can help us in this regard, and help the preacher to use the Bible with power—though clearly the "power" at stake is more akin to the power of a fertile imagination than to the power of God's Spirit-borne truth in the human life.

The attractive part of this proposal is that Brueggemann implicitly recognizes that entire worldviews are at stake. Although he does not cast his work in this way, he is close to affirming that the worldview of secularism can only be challenged by an alternative worldview, not by bits of disparate truths. If that were all he is saying, I would utter a hearty "Amen." But because he has cast his proposal so strongly as the repudiation of truthful propositions, one is left with vague encouragement on the one hand, and profound disquiet on the other. What does he mean by saying that biblical faith affirms that God is the Creator and that God alone brings in the consummation? If he means this in any traditional sense, then he has made some propositional claims. How does he know them? Where did he learn them? By what authority does he put them forward? If, on the other hand, even these ideas are merely biblical construals to be set out to clash with the popular construals of secularism, but without any ontological reality, what authority do they have? Why not instead deploy the configurations of reality imagined in, say, the *Bhagavad Gita*, or in the Qur'an? Or in Mother Goose, for that matter, provided our imagination is stirred?

Clearly Brueggemann does not want to go so far. But he sets himself up for these sorts of questions precisely because he is terribly embarrassed whenever notions of propositional truth drift over the horizon. In his most recent essay,[79] he contrasts two views of human history that vie for contemporary allegiance. The dominant one, grounded in the Enlightenment, is what Brueggemann calls "the Henry Kissinger school" of history. History is a closed process; we manage the available pieces, assured that there are no new ones. Inscrutability and mystery are eradicated; we hold that "might makes right," and that the winners write the history. The older and now weaker alternative is what Brueggemann calls "the religious view of the historical process." In this view, all of life and history are in the hands of the gods or of God. We may propose, but God disposes; "in the end, human choice does not matter" (240). This "kind of supernaturalism" is precritical, is manifested in astrology, and destroys human freedom and responsibility. Over against these competing views of history, Brueggemann sets forth what he calls "the prophetic construal of history."

---

79. "The Prophetic Word of God and History," *Interpretation* 48 (1994): 239–51.

> It resists the modernist reduction that reduces history to power; it likewise resists the religious temptation of supernaturalism. It begins with astonished, unjustified, unargued speech of affirmation and celebration that asserts and testifies to the intrusion, surprise, discontinuity, gifts, judgment, newness, and ambiguity that are present in the midst of the human process. In other words, this theme insists on speaking precisely about those matters that the other two views of history want to deny, namely, the notion that astonished, unjustified, unargued speech is human speech, filled with daring *hutzpah* and focused on scandalous particularity. This speech is so daring as to specify concrete places where the presence, purpose, and reality of God's "otherness" make decisive inroads on the human process in either friendly or hostile ways. It names the places where intrusion, gift, ambiguity, and newness are present; and it gives those happenings the name of holiness, either holy graciousness or holy judgment (240–41).

These extraordinary human events, Brueggemann writes, include the promise of Isaac to Abraham and Sarah, the Exodus, the pronouncements of Israel's great prophets, and the ministry of Jesus. They are acts of God. "Accordingly, for all our interest in sociology and politics, the theme we strike is theological in nature and has to do with the character of God and the courage to bring this God to speech. What the prophets assert is that human processes and policies are, apart from this God, wrongly construed" (243).

There is much here that is wise. But note: (1) In focusing on the acts of God as opposed to other forms of God's self-disclosure, Brueggemann sounds uncomfortably similar to the older "biblical theology" school of G. Ernest Wright and others, who emphasized "the mighty acts of God" at the expense of speech. For Brueggemann, the acts of God are courageously brought to speech, but the speech is exclusively human. God does not appear to be a talking God. (2) In caricaturizing what he calls the supernaturalist view, Brueggemann confuses providence and fatalism, and tries to protect God's surprises, his freshness, his newness, by denying his sovereign and detailed control. *Yet the biblical witness, as we shall see* [in chap. 5], *amply testifies to both*. What authorizes Brueggemann to accept one and not the other? An older generation of theologians would have spoken of God as being, on the one hand, transcendent and sovereign, and on the other, personal and invasive—and not less than both. (3) What sets the agenda for what Brueggemann accepts? It does not appear to be truth in any enduring sense. It appears, rather, to be a kind of theologically flavored liberationism. (4) What the Bible offers is not *one* alternative worldview, or a different metanarrative that happens to be *true*, but a lot of stories: stories that reflect some acts of God, stories that can stimulate the imagination so as to provide foils for secular selfishness. This would be helpful if the imagination stirred by the stories were always tied to the same worldview and were always judged by some other standard than the imagination itself. But no such standard does Brueggemann have. His wonderful insights—and they are many—are accidentally useful.

Another way of handling the truth claims of Scripture is one that was briefly treated in chapters 2 and 3. Some forms of the New Criticism focus so narrowly on the world of the text, on textual forms and connections, that what the text ostensibly says about reality is elided.[80] Sternberg roundly condemns the kind of reading of biblical narrative that avoids history almost as a matter of principle: "Were the 'biblical' narratives written or read as fiction, then God would turn from the lord of history into a creature of the imagination with the most disastrous results. . . . Hence the Bible's determination to sanctify and compel literal belief in the past."[81] Any other approach is in danger of deifying language. In an essay still unpublished, Robert Eric Frykenberg shows how much of Old Testament religion is bound up with remembering the *historical* acts of God, i.e., the acts of God that took place in real history, in the past—so much so that large swaths of the faith of the Old Testament people of God is incoherent or deluded if they are mistaken on this point.[82] As Vanhoozer comments, "For the priest and teacher, language is the means for gaining access to reality and truth. But for the artist, language has become problematic and is in itself the new object of contemplation."[83] At some point, surely, one must say that fixation on the biblical text *divorced from the referent that the text itself demands* is a kind of idolatry. After all, "[i]f a belief performs the function of providing an object of devotion and an *all-pervasive* frame of orientation, then it is religious"[84]—and that includes beliefs about language and interpretation. One is reminded of the title of one of Klaus Bockmuehl's books: *The Unreal God of Modern Theology.*[85]

Others go farther. Kyaw Than writes, "Religion can only be understood from within. The sacred, transcendent, and infinite cannot be subjected to

---

80. Some forms of canon criticism indulge in the same reductionism. But the relationships between the New Criticism and canon criticism are complex. See J. Dickson Brown, "Barton, Brooks, and Childs: A Comparison of the New Criticism and Canonical Criticism," *Journal of the Evangelical Theological Society* 36 (1993): 481–89.

81. M. Sternberg, *The Poetics of Biblical Narrative: Ideological Literature and the Drama of Reading* (Bloomington: Univ. of Indiana Press, 1985), 32.

82. "History as Theodicy: A Redemptive Event," in *History and Belief: The Foundations of Historical Understanding* (forthcoming).

83. Kevin J. Vanhoozer, "A Lamp in the Labyrinth: The Hermeneutics of 'Aesthetic' Theology," *Trinity Journal* 8 (1987): 26.

84. William T. Blackstone, *The Problem of Religious Knowledge* (Englewood Cliffs: Prentice-Hall, 1963), 39. One thinks of the work of Northrop Frye, especially his *Great Code: The Bible and Literature* (Princeton: Princeton Univ. Press, 1957).

85. Colorado Springs: Helmers & Howard, 1988.

rational analysis."[86] Of course, the transcendent and infinite God of the Bible cannot be "subjected" to rational analysis if by that is meant that God becomes exhaustively analyzable, the subject matter that finite human minds are in some privileged position to evaluate. But if this God is as personal as he is transcendent, if he is a talking and acting God, if he chooses to address men and women made in his image in words they regularly use, then certainly part of the "understanding" of this God is bound up with reason, with "rational analysis" if you will. If much of the language used to talk about God is analogical or metaphorical, in itself that linguistic reality does not make what it conveys less truthful or restricted to some nonrational sphere labeled "within."[87] Than's reductionism aims to "paradigm out" rational analysis, and thus propositional truth claims. One might ask how he knows this, i.e., the basis on which he articulates this proposition about God. Is it true?

As Griffiths and Lewis point out, Hick falls into a similar trap when he insists that religious belief is "determined exclusively by large-scale cultural variables or small-scale psychological ones, and in any event by historical accident and not by a conscious attempt to apprehend and incarnate a true world view. . . . [T]he apparently conflicting truth-claims which form an important part of the major religious world-views are not really in conflict because they are not really truth-claims."[88] Granted the hermeneutical and other responses advanced so far, it is hard not to prefer the clarity of Chesterton's Father Brown: "'Well, I do believe some things, of course,' conceded Father Brown; 'and therefore, of course, I don't believe other things.'"[89]

We may consider one more example. In an influential book, Wilfrid Cantwell Smith distinguishes between belief and faith, arguing that the former is "non-Scriptural."[90] By "belief" Smith refers to faith that has a specific object. He delights in those passages of Scripture where πιστις ("faith") has no specified object, e.g., Hebrews 11:6, "And without faith it is impossible to

---

86. Kyaw Than, "Relations Between People of Different Faith Commitments," *Currents in Theology and Mission* 19 (1992): 23.

87. The best treatment of metaphor in recent years is that of Janet Martin Soskice, *Metaphor and Religious Language* (Oxford: Oxford Univ. Press, 1985).

88. Paul Griffiths and Delmas Lewis, "On Grading Religions, Seeking Truth, and Being Nice to People—A Reply to Professor Hick," *Religious Studies* 19 (1983): 78. John Hick's response, in *Problems of Religious Pluralism* (New York: St. Martin's Press, 1985), 94–95, despite its vigorous protest, surely confirms the point. Hick insists that differences in both myth and doctrine are "not of great *religious*, i.e., soteriological importance" (94, emphasis his); they are "alternative maps, in different projections, of the universe" (95).

89. Chesterton, *The Penguin Complete Father Brown*, 418.

90. *Belief and History* (Charlottesville: Univ. Press of Virginia, 1977).

please God"; or the repeated Synoptic "Your faith has made you whole." Where "to believe" or "faith" has a personal object (e.g., God or Christ), trust is at stake; where it has a propositional object (e.g., "if you do not believe *that I am*," John 8:24), what is at stake is recognition and acknowledgement of something, not "belief" in any modern sense. The purpose of this exercise is to drive to the conclusion that the many "faith" passages without an expressed object are open-ended, and must not be loaded with propositional or doctrinal content. Thus "faith" becomes the nonintellectual, transcendent form that achieves concrete expression in various intellectual forms that are necessarily tied to specific cultures. In an earlier work,[91] he argues that the "cumulative tradition" of a religious community must be sharply distinguished from the individual believer's internal and subjective faith. Only the latter is of vital importance; the external tradition is slow in forming, not binding, and culture-bound.

Smith's argument is terribly prejudicial. The breaches of logic in his position are tellingly and sometimes amusingly exposed by Nash and Netland.[92] So far as biblical evidence is concerned, it is a commonplace of Greek syntax that direct objects (and other parts of speech) are often omitted when they are to be inferred from the context. More importantly, for all that Smith warns against reading later credal utterances back into the faith-passages of the New Testament, he should take more pains to avoid reading a twentieth-century warmed-over Buddhist notion of faith back into the New Testament.[93] Contrast Machen, who argues at some length that the contrast between knowledge and faith "ignores an essential element in faith; and what is called faith after the subtraction of that element is not faith at all. As a matter of fact all true faith involves an intellectual element; all faith involves knowledge and issues in knowledge."[94]

In short: the Bible's appeal to truth is rich and complex. It cannot be reduced to, but certainly includes, propositional truth.

---

91. Wilfrid Cantwell Smith, *The Meaning and End of Religion* (New York: Harper & Row, 1962).

92. Ronald H. Nash, *Is Jesus the Only Savior?* (Grand Rapids: Zondervan, 1994), 60–68; Netland, *Dissonant Voices*, 117–20, 127–31.

93. Cf. Avery Dulles, *The Assurance of Things Hoped For: A Theology of Christian Faith* (Oxford: Oxford Univ. Press, 1994), 193: "Although propositions are not its true objects, faith may be called propositional inasmuch as its contents can, at least to a large extent, be expressed in propositions, such as articles of the creed and dogmatic definitions. To affirm the propositions is to affirm the faith, and acceptance of the faith, properly understood, prevents the believer from denying the propositions that express it."

94. J. Gresham Machen, *What Is Faith?* (Grand Rapids: Eerdmans, 1946), 40, passim.

3. There is an entailment: both orthodoxy and heresy are possible.

Such a view is terribly out of vogue. The necessary condition for a distinction to be made between orthodoxy and heresy is the existence of truth, truth that is sufficiently objective that it cannot be relativized by appeal to the individual or the interpretive community. Indeed, one wonders whether the primary motivation for the contemporary assault on the notion of objective truth is the passionate commitment to that religious pluralism which *must* obliterate distinctions between orthodoxy and heresy.[95] Of course, the existence of objective truth *by itself* is not a *sufficient* reason to advance the distinction between orthodoxy and heresy. But if this objective truth has as its content God-given specification of the conditions under which someone is saved, then tampering with such truth opens up the divide.

The subject is so important that I must return to it later (chap. 8). For now, I want to take note of just one related argument. In the exchange between John Hick and Robert Cook mentioned earlier, Hick writes, "I believe that one has only to meet spiritually outstanding individuals of the different world religions to recognize that within the context of their different belief-systems they are undergoing essentially the same salvific transformation from self-centredness to Reality-centredness."[96] In other words, if it is true, as Jesus says, "By their fruit you will recognize them" (Matt. 7:16), the "spiritual" fruit demonstrated by the outstanding proponents of each religion proves that each is "true." Therefore none can claim exclusive truth. Here the issue is not doctrine but life, not heresy but alternative religions. Even so, the appeal to "spiritually outstanding individuals" is so much a part of the contemporary appeal to "spirituality"—a notoriously vague term (see the Appendix)—that very similar issues are at stake. I have been dealing with truth and interpretation; at the moment, it is worth noting Cook's response to Hick on the narrower issue of fruit-attesting truth:

> I would like to say that I do not misunderstand Hick's position as he claims, but I do disagree with him. I am sorry if this is politically incorrect, but my own experience is that many are apparently moving along divergent paths. I well remember meeting a Hindu guru who was convinced that he was on his final incarnation, and being struck by the fact that he seemed close to achieving his goal—the total dissolution of personality. In fact, I was so shocked by the experience that I gave up practising transcendental meditation and

---

95. And in more cynical moments, one wonders whether the pluralists think their commitment to the proposition that there is no distinction between orthodoxy and heresy is true. If not, then their commitment is merely the opinion of the interpretive community constituted of pluralists; if so, then is the failure to believe it heretical?

96. "Readers' Responses," *Themelios* 19/3 (May 1994): 20.

attended a Christian mission at university where I met David Watson who impressed me as someone with an integrated personality, a sense of humour and an intangible sanctity of life. I became a Christian soon after. Surely, our beliefs must affect the way we work out our piety and it would, therefore, be very surprising to find, for example, a Zen sage like Yüan-wu who is admired for having said, "If you are a real man, you may by all means grab the food from a starving man"[97] living a life indistinguishable from that of Mother Theresa. Since I cannot agree with Hick on this point, I cannot agree with him on other related issues either, such as his assertion that Jahweh, Allah, Vishnu *et al.* must all be manifestations of the same ultimate reality because devotion to them produces the same life transformation (20).

4. The truth and authority questions must not be raised only against believers. They must be raised against religious pluralists as well.

By this I mean two things.

First, in the same way that confessing Christians are constantly challenged by pluralists to justify the authority of their position in a world characterized by so much demonstrable empirical pluralism, so pluralists themselves must be challenged to justify the authority of their position. They are claiming things about God, truth, the nature of reality. The question is, How do they know?

Second, there is an array of questions to be put to pluralists regarding their handling of the various world religions, their persistent reductionism of these religions' respective claims, the (in)coherence of pluralism's logic, and much more. The best accessible treatment of these topics in recent years, especially the discussion of Hick's position, is that of Netland.[98] I shall avoid repeating most of his arguments here, but I emphasize that they repay careful reading.

Perhaps the most powerful challenge in this regard is how the relativist can avoid destroying his own position. Any statement of relativism, whether grounded in culture, linguistics, or hermeneutics, is fundamentally self-destructive. For example, cultural relativism affirms that notions of truth and the structures of reason are so decisively shaped within the culture in which they are found that they are relative to that culture. But that means the proposition defining or defending cultural relativism, uttered within that culture, is no less relative; there is no particular reason why someone from another culture should adopt the position of cultural relativism.[99] But very

---

97. The quotation is reported by A. Watts, *The Way of Zen* (London: Penguin, 1990), 167.

98. Netland, *Dissonant Voices*, chaps. 5 and 6.

99. See especially Maurice Mandelbaum, "Subjective, Objective, and Conceptual Relativism," *The Monist* 62 (1979): 403–23. The argument is picked up and developed in Netland, *Dissonant Voices*, 175–76.

few pluralists have recognized the devastating nature of this criticism.[100] As Nash puts it:

> For Hick, truth is a function of geography, that is, where people happen to have been born. This idea, carried to its logical implications, would make Nazism, cannibalism, infanticide, and witchcraft true because they would all be a result of geographic and cultural conditioning. And Hick's position also implies that beliefs can be true and false at the same time, true for people conditioned in one way and false for others. Furthermore, it implies that the truth of pluralism is also a function of geographic and cultural conditioning.[101]

Moreover, why should we not see atheism as equally conditioned by culture? As Trigg observes, "Hick's argument, so far from encouraging us to give equal respect to all world religions, makes us wonder whether religion is any more valid than atheism."[102]

5. The selective and arbitrary ways in which many pluralists handle the biblical texts does not breed confidence in their interpretive ability. Too often their readings appear compromised by the philosophical commitment to pluralism.

The examples are legion; I here choose a small random sample. Perhaps in defense of these examples of egregious exegesis I should say that their perpetrators are justified, in their own lights, on one of two grounds: (1) Some (as in the first two examples below) have bought into some form or other of deconstruction: they may feel they have the right, even the duty, to rip texts out of their context and reconfigure meanings to suit their own world, using the results to criticize the text itself. In that case my point of departure in dialogue with them is reflected in chapters 2 and 3 of this book. But if they hold that their readings of the Bible are objectively true, then the crucial thing to do is to return to the text and show them they are mistaken. (2) Others (third example below) have bought into forms of destructive biblical criticism that divide asunder what God has put together. There is little possibility of dealing convincingly with their exegesis without tackling the critical issues in which they are enmeshed. The fourth example is a sublime case of slippery language; the fifth is so blatant an instance of postmodernist exegesis that it deserves to be recorded.

---

100. Langdon Gilkey is widely recognized to be one of the rare exceptions. See especially his "Plurality and Its Theological Implications," in Hick and Knitter, *The Myth of Christian Uniqueness*, 43–44 (cited in part 1 of this book).

101. Nash, *Is Jesus the Only Savior?* 96.

102. Roger Trigg, "Religion and the Threat of Relativism," *Religious Studies* 19 (1983): 298.

First example: Here is von Balthasar:

> It can be hard to carry out our task in the Church if we are alone with God and no one else understands. The only thing for it is to fight without moving an inch from the center of the mystery of Christ. . . .
>
> But what a tremendous panorama of freedom opens up for us from the vantage point of Christ's unity! "All things are yours," world, life and death, present and future, if "you are Christ's," for "Christ is God's" (1 Cor. 3:21ff.). The whole door opens on a single pivot; the plurality of all the forms in the world and in history, including death and the future, is accessible to the Christian's thinking and acting, if indeed he surrenders himself with Christ to God. . . .
>
> We think that God cannot do this. . . . [But w]hatever is in touch with itself at its origin cannot fail to know itself in the pluralism of perspectives and missions that spring from that origin. At root level they all meet and communicate.[103]

Thus, Paul in 1 Corinthians 3:21–23 emerges as the defender of contemporary religious pluralism.

What Paul has in mind, as judged by the context he himself provides for his words, is in reality not so broad. He has already established what the gospel is: it is the saving "message of the cross" (1:18), the message of "Jesus Christ and him crucified" (2:2). This message demolishes all human pretensions, precisely because it is so scandalously unexpected and destructive of our pride in being able to save ourselves: God in his "foolish" wisdom sends a Messiah who is barbarically executed, dying an odious death so that both Jews and Gentiles might go free. In the light of such divine self-abnegation, it is unthinkable that one-upmanship should prevail in the church. Not only so, but our ability to grasp the saving message has been effected by the Spirit (2:6–16). How then can we align ourselves with some figure or party in the church and play triumphalism games? Everything we have, we have received (4:7). So then, there should be no more boasting about men (3:21), i.e., about particular Christian leaders. They exercise distinct roles in the church, as God himself assigns the tasks (3:5–15). All of them belong to Christ (3:21)— as does everything else, this side of his triumph, whether the world or life of death or the present or the future. All these things appear to be of ultimate importance to finite mortals; in fact, they have all been relativized by Christ's triumph, and we are not to fear them. All of them are owned by Christ, they are controlled by him, and we are his—as he is God's (3:22–23). Thus to restrict ourselves to only one part of the heritage we have received in him, as

---

103. Hans Urs von Balthasar, *Truth Is Symphonic: Aspects of Christian Pluralism* (San Francisco: Ignatius Press, 1987), 86–87.

we do when we identify ourselves with only one leader in some narrow party spirit, is to miss the wealth of the inheritance he has secured for us. The point, in short, is to avoid a party spirit, and to appreciate the wonderful heritage secured by Christ as the messenger of the apostolic gospel. It is not an open-ended sanction of limitless pluralism.[104]

Second example: For Michael Barnes, religions are not competing ideologies but represent different ways of being human.[105] Following Cantwell Smith, he argues that "faith" and "beliefs" must be distinguished: the latter are the intellectual forms which faith takes within specific cultures and traditions (126). Feeling that his pluralism must be justified in the theological arena, he argues that the world has been redeemed in Christ, and is a new creation inaugurated with the outpouring of the Spirit. Thus the glorification of Christ cannot be constrained by the confines of the church, but is already being extended to all people (143). Similarly, the Spirit must be understood to be active within all religions (176).

But is the world ever identified with the new creation? Do not even those New Testament writers who speak most clearly of Christ's universal triumph (e.g., Paul in Col. 1:15–20) make sharp distinctions between those who are redeemed and those who are not? Do first-century Christians treat the pagan religions of their environment as alternative manifestations of the Spirit?

Third example: Scroggs tells how he and his wife led a retreat for women, dealing with the theme "Women in the New Testament."[106] Assuming the distinction between Pauline and deutero-Pauline literature, in the first lecture he talked about Paul's egalitarian theology, doubtless making use of such passages as Galatians 3:28. When in the second lecture he discussed "the more patriarchally oriented deutero-Pauline literature" (e.g., such passages as Col. 3:18–19; Eph. 5:21–23; 1 Tim. 2:8–15), some laypeople responded with, "Paul couldn't have written these passages"—which prompts Scroggs to conclude, "That judgment was echoed by the entire group. After all, biblical scholarship is simply codified common sense, and common sense is, fortunately, hardly limited to scholars."[107]

Surely Scroggs cannot be unaware how he has slanted the evidence. There are plenty of scholars, not less endowed with common sense than he,

---

104. See Gordon D. Fee, *The First Epistle to the Corinthians* (Grand Rapids: Eerdmans, 1987), in loc.; D. A. Carson, *The Cross and Christian Ministry* (Grand Rapids: Baker, 1993), chap. 3.

105. *Religions in Conversation: Christian Identity and Christian Pluralism* (London: SPCK, 1989), 131, 172, passim.

106. Robin Scroggs, *The Text and the Times: New Testament Essays for Today* (Minneapolis: Fortress Press, 1993), 261–62.

107. Ibid., 262.

who think that Paul wrote all thirteen canonical epistles that bear his name, and that it is possible to put together all the relevant passages that deal with women in such a way that the picture is consistent. The lay people were simply led to a predetermined conclusion by a clever scholar. Fair enough—but let us not then be so disingenuous as to suggest that the outcome was simply common sense.

Fourth example: Here I turn to an excerpt from the official statement of the International Missionary Council's second missionary conference, held in Jerusalem in 1928:

> We rejoice to think that just because in Jesus Christ the light that lighteth every man shone forth in full splendor, we find rays of that same light where he is unknown or even rejected. We welcome every noble quality in non-Christian persons or systems as further proof that the Father, who sent His Son into the world, has nowhere left himself without witness. Thus, merely to give illustration, and making no attempt to estimate the spiritual value of other religions to their adherents, we recognize as part of the one Truth that sense of the Majesty of God and the consequent reverence in worship which are conspicuous in Islam; the deep sympathy for the world's sorrow and unselfish search for the way of escape, which are at the heart of Buddhism; the desire for contact with Ultimate Reality conceived as spiritual, which is prominent in Hinduism; the belief in a moral order of the universe and consequent insistence on moral conduct, which are inculcated by Confucianism; the disinterested pursuit of truth and human welfare which are often found in those who stand for secular civilizations but do not accept Christ as their Lord and Saviour.[108]

At one level, interpreted very generously, there is nothing here to which to object. Yet note: (1) The question as to whether the revelation that has come to "non-Christian persons or systems" is a *saving* knowledge is not addressed. Indeed, it is specifically ducked: the writers insist they make "no attempt to estimate the spiritual value of other religions to their adherents." But that is the focal point of the debate. (2) Must any religion be *entirely* false for it to be disastrously wrong? Christians have long held to "common grace" (to use the Reformed category); they have never argued that persons or systems are as wicked as they might be. The real question is how the various positive values that the statement perceives in world religions *are related to those world religions as systems of thought*. A truth set in the wrong context,

---

108. "The Christian Life and Message in Relation to Non-Christian Systems of Thought and Life," in *The Jerusalem Meeting of the International Missionary Council: March 24–April 8, 1928*, 8 vols. (New York: International Missionary Council, 1928), 1:410–11. Probably it would be wiser to think of most of the writers of this document as inclusivists rather than pluralists, but the exegesis, as we shall see, is not better for that.

valuable as it may be intrinsically, can be damning. (3) The statement is larded with biblical phrases that cast a glow of sanctification over the document, but in several cases are misleadingly used. The "light that gives light to every man" (John 1:9) we shall return to in chapter 6. God has nowhere "left himself without testimony"—but that passage (Acts 14:17) does not refer to the merits of pagan religions, but, precisely in a context where Barnabas and Paul are dealing with pagan religions, appeals to God's faithful witness in nature: God "has shown kindness by giving you rain from heaven and crops in their seasons; he provides you with plenty of food and fills your hearts with joy."

Fifth example: At the 1993 Annual Meetings of the American Academy of Religion and Society of Biblical Literature, one scholar read a paper offering a postmodern interpretation of 1 Corinthians 8:1–6. He argued that in this passage Paul is a polytheist correcting the error of monotheism in the Corinthian church. One of my colleagues rose to his feet during the question period and asked the speaker if this was supposed to be a serious exegesis of 1 Corinthians 8. The speaker replied affirmatively. My colleague replied with words to this effect: "Then isn't it incumbent on you to justify your interpretation, which you confess to be idiosyncratic, by arguments that refute other readings and show yours to be right?" The speaker promptly responded that he was not claiming his interpretation was right or correct: how could he, if he was offering a postmodern reading? So my colleague continued, "I thought you might answer that way. Then what would you say if I read your paper and interpreted it as a defense of Pauline monotheism and an implicit rejection of postmodern thought?" The speaker responded, "You can interpret my paper any way you want to. What do you expect me to do? Have a foundation for my belief?"

I suppose he was consistent. He was also silly and tragic: the emperor has no clothes. We need a new collect: "From postmodern silliness in exegesis, and from the tragedy of bankrupt epistemology, dear Lord deliver us." One sympathizes with one reviewer's comments about a recent collection of essays on the Fourth Gospel: "The failure of most of the later authors in this collection to engage with alternative and conflicting explanations of the data they are studying is probably to be accounted for by the fact that they have not only lost interest in history: they have lost interest in argument as well. Is this perhaps because they believe that one interpretation is as good as another?"[109]

---

109. John Ashton's review, in *Biblical Interpretation* 2 (1994): 237, of Mark W. G. Stibbe, ed., *The Gospel of John as Literature: An Anthology of Twentieth-Century Perspectives* (Leiden: E. J. Brill, 1993).

6. However complex the subject, there are distinguishable paths by which a person may come to see the truth of the gospel and gladly come under its authority. The assumption behind all of them is revelation.

"We cannot spy out the secrets of God by obtrusive curiosity. Not even theologians of a technological era ... have any special radar for penetrating the mysteries of God's being and purpose."[110] I have been arguing that knowledge of God depends in the first instance on revelation, on God's gracious self-disclosure. But someone might then ask, How do we know that ostensibly divine revelation is what it claims to be? Are there not many competing claims?

The subject is extraordinarily complex, and the literature vast. It opens not only into detailed treatments of revelation, but of epistemology. Pretty soon the nature of God and of human beings is at issue, since one cannot say much about the *imago Dei*, in particular the role of the "image of God" in human knowledge, unless there is agreement about who the God is in whose image we have been made. It is not long before the question posed at the head of this section opens out into the entire body of Christian theology; for what is at stake is, finally, an entire Christian worldview. And discussion of that worldview has become even more difficult during the past two decades than it was in the past because postmodernism has convinced many of the absolute relativity of all truth claims, not least religious truth claims.

I shall restrict myself to four remarks.

First, against Kant, who (as we have seen) insists that one cannot by reason move from the phenomenal realm to the noumenal realm,[111] the apostle Paul is entirely prepared to infer from the created order God's existence, power, and divine nature (Rom. 1:20). Nor is this merely a matter of abstract doctrine for him: it is also a matter of evangelistic strategy and apologetic. According to Luke's witness, Paul openly and repeatedly drew such connections when he was evangelizing Gentiles (Acts 14:15–18; 17:24–29).

This fundamental distinction between Kant and Paul is as much as anything a difference in starting point. Kant begins from below, and wants human reason to be the test of all things. Paul begins with the personal/transcendent Creator-God of the Hebrew canon, and looks at reality from his perspective, insofar as God has disclosed it. God has left traces in his created work.[112] Elements of his nature "have been clearly seen, being understood from what has been made, so that men are without excuse" (Rom. 1:20).

---

110. Henry, *God, Revelation and Authority*, 2:8.

111. Into this realm Kant relegated God, the self, and things-in-themselves (i.e., essences).

112. Interestingly, the scientist-theologian Arthur Peacocke, whose views do not generally fall at the conservative end of the spectrum, takes up much the same argument in *Theology*

Second, Paul is not arguing that there is *saving* knowledge of God in nature, but that there is sufficient revelation in nature to rob human beings of excuses. In other words, from Paul's vantage point, the position of the atheist, or of a Kantian, or of a moral failure, is frankly inexcusable. Such people have already suppressed the truth that God has graciously given; their virulent insistence that there is insufficient evidence is already an index of a perverted mind that dares to make itself the final test of all things, instead of feeling itself rightly obligated to look at reality from the perspective of the Creator.

In an important argument on the use of reason in theology, Lints[113] distinguishes two kinds of rationality. The first is native rationality, i.e., the mechanisms of "belief formation" (117) that are part of human noetic structure, part of what it means to be made in the image of God. The second he calls cultural rationality, i.e., the structures of thought that are judged plausible in any particular culture, and that inevitably strongly influence what beliefs (including religious beliefs) an individual in that culture is likely to accept. Some beliefs, he argues, are irresistible, "in the sense that we do not decide to believe them" (121). Such irresistibility may be a function of our basic noetic structures; alternatively, for particular people it may be a function of cultural conditioning. Lints suggests that belief in God is "an innate human capacity" (125) that would drive all humans in the same direction, were it not for the suppression of that capacity caused by sin. Were it not for such suppression, "we would believe in God with the same kind of spontaneity that we believe in the external world around us. The difficulty we have with believing in God is part of the unnatural condition brought about by our willful rebellion against God" (125). This is in line with Paul's insistence that we have culpably suppressed the truth (Rom. 1:18); equally, it is in line with his insistence that the person without the Spirit of God remains blind to the gospel, while the person with the Spirit turns to the gospel and becomes a "spiritual" person (1 Cor. 2).[114]

Thus in a culture where a Christian outlook increasingly lies outside the accepted plausibility structures, individuals must by God's help overcome not only the impact of their sinfulness on their God-given noetic structures, but also the influence of their culture, if they are to accept the revelation God has graciously given. In a culture more decisively shaped by an inherited Christian outlook, the plausibility structures may favor Christian belief, while the

---

for a Scientific Age: Being and Becoming—Natural and Divine (Oxford: Basil Blackwell, 1990), 101–12.

113. Lints, *The Fabric of Theology*, 117–35.

114. In the terms of Calvin, *Institutes* I.2, the Spirit moves us to believe in God appropriately by stimulating the innate capacity which we all enjoy but which we have deadened by sin.

impact of sin on our "native rationality" will militate against such belief. From God's point of view, both our own sin and the sin that has driven our culture to adopt its limited plausibility structures (and the two loci of sin are not entirely separate, of course, since individuals constitute the culture) are blinding and morally reprehensible. On this accounting, the crucial issues are never narrowly epistemological: they are profoundly moral. As Williams puts it,

> But when Augustine told his tale of two cities, these were the city of "man," founded on the love of self, and the city of God, founded on the love of God. Augustine believed that human loves, most fundamental of all human desires, regulated life and thought. The will has a certain primacy over the intellect. It is whatever collides with the will that energizes reflection directed against God.[115]

Third, partly under the impact of postmodernism, the various "schools" of Christian apologetics have an opportunity to draw closer together than they have usually been in the past.

At the risk of oversimplification, let us restrict ourselves to presuppositionalism, rational presuppositionalism, and evidentialism. All three labels are loaded, and various proponents mean slightly different things by them. Moreover there is a tendency, especially among more popular writers, to caricature the other positions. Thus: (1) The presuppositionalist may charge the evidentialist with superficiality. You can line up evidence to support the truth of Christianity until you have exhausted yourself by your efforts, but no amount of evidence is sufficient to compel belief. Did not Jesus himself say that even if someone came back from the dead, they would not believe? Evidentialism simply does not understand the implications of human finitude or the profound noetic effects of the Fall—and both limitations are exacerbated by postmodernism. (2) The rational presuppositionalist is scarcely better. He acknowledges that there are controlling presuppositions, but thinks he can give adequate reasons to defend Christian presuppositions. Can a human being by reason find out God? (3) The rational presuppositionalist largely agrees with his presuppositionalist colleague with respect to the evidentialist, but then charges the presuppositionalist with vague irrelevance. If you cannot give reasons for the superiority of Christian presuppositions, will you simply offer a critique of everyone else's position and then sit around and wait for the Spirit to strike? Does not the record of New Testament preaching show that *reasons* were advanced in the bold advocacy of the gospel? Besides, doesn't the pressure of postmodernism drive us to the conclusion

---

115. Stephen Williams, "Revelation and Reconciliation: A Tale of Two Concepts," *European Journal of Theology* 3/1 (1994): 42.

that unless we provide reasoned argument why the Christian worldview is the true one, people will think of Christianity as just one more arbitrary option? (4) The evidentialist reminds her presuppositionalist colleagues that human beings, made in the image of God, are endowed with reason, and however corrupted those powers, God's truth must be set forth so as to appeal to that reason and to destroy alternative claims. Do not the canonical evangelists and other New Testament believers present the evidences in support of Jesus' resurrection, and take pains to debunk the denials? Moreover, precisely because postmodernism is so strong in the land, it is important to overturn presuppositionalist thought as a cop-out that inevitably ends in subjectivity and uncertainty. Proclaim the truth and support it with the fullest arsenal of evidences; it is God's truth, and by God's grace it shall prevail.

The debate has a long history, and a few lines will not begin to do justice to its complexities. A sympathetic reading of some recent proponents of each position, however, suggests that at least some of the fences that cordon off each position from the others are beginning to come down. Thus van den Toren, who is more aligned with evidentialism than anything else, breaks free from "cordoned off" evidentialism, precisely because he is wrestling with postmodernity.[116] He argues that the postmodernist rediscovery of the historical character of all human reasoning challenges what is an axiom among many Enlightenment thinkers: that only those truths can serve as a foundation for human reasoning which are directly accessible to all sane human beings. But this postmodern stress on the historical character of all human reasoning does not entail absolute relativity *unless epistemological foundationalism is true*, which says that truth must be found at the beginning of human reasoning. Van den Toren denies this is true, and proposes to account for human knowledge on the analogy of reading a book: more reading can progressively correct the misconceptions. So far he sounds like an updated evidentialist. But he then argues that the contemporary Christian apologist should insist that the Christian faith offers the only hermeneutical basis on which we can build an adequate understanding of reality. The Christian apologist asks for a "leap of faith" to the Christian worldview—in effect, for conversion that overcomes the bias against it.[117] At several points, he becomes aligned (unwittingly) with, say, Clouser, whose updated presuppositionalism, in the

---

116. Benno van den Toren, "A New Direction in Christian Apologetics: An Exploration with Reference to Postmodernism," *European Journal of Theology* 2/1 (1993): 49–64.

117. "This need for repentance, to overcome a strong ideological bias in the process of conversion, forms one of the necessary limits of the apologetical endeavor, which should be taken into account in order to approach the other realistically, combining proclamation and argument with a plea for repentance, the latter plea itself being strongly enforced by both proclamation and reasoning" (ibid., 61).

Dooyeweerdian frame, was published, astonishingly, by the presses of a Catholic university.[118] This is a confusing age.

In my view, some of van den Toren's essay is not yet very well thought out. But quite clearly, the impact of postmodernism is prompting revisions. As long as the modernist model of truth based on proper foundations and appropriate evidence and reason prevailed, a narrowly evidentialist approach (whether wise or unwise) was possible. It no longer is. Carl F. H. Henry has been known to tell his students, "There are two kinds of presuppositionalists: those who admit it and those who don't." Under the impact of postmodernism, the number of the latter is declining.

Probably Alvin Plantinga has been the foremost philosopher to argue that belief in God is "properly basic," i.e., that it does not deed some other foundation to be considered rational.[119] Plantinga shows, among other things, that everyone holds to *many* beliefs without proof (e.g., most of us believe in the existence of other minds, and in the continued existence of the world even when we are not perceiving it).[120] And if someone argues that it is immoral to believe anything without evidence, we may well ask what adequate evidence supports that view.

On the other hand, while presuppositionalism served as an important antidote to the sheer hubris of modernity, its narrowest forms, as Cooper found out in Ricoeur's seminar (see chapter 3 above), do not *justify* the Christian's worldview over against other competing worldviews. Indeed, the rhetoric of the narrowest forms of presuppositionalism

> may unwittingly aid relativism. In response to modernist claims of rational autonomy, some Reformed apologists have so strongly emphasized the relativity of reason to true faith and uniquely Christian presuppositions that the universal availability of any truth whatsoever has in effect been denied. What results is a kind of religious relativism. Truth is admitted to be completely system-relative, but only (Reformed?) Christians are acknowledged to have the right system. What follows is that unbelievers cannot really know anything at all in religion and morality or in nature and history, not even facts of everyday life. But this implies that non-Christians have good reason for adopting relativism or even agnosticism.[121]

---

118. Roy A. Clouser, *The Myth of Religious Neutrality: An Essay on the Hidden Role of Religious Belief in Theories* (Notre Dame: Univ. of Notre Dame Press, 1991).

119. See the bibliography. Most conveniently, see "Reason and Belief in God," in *Faith and Rationality*, ed. Alvin Plantinga and Nicholas Wolterstorff (Notre Dame: Univ. of Notre Dame Press, 1983), 16–93.

120. These two examples I have drawn from Ronald H. Nash, *Worldviews in Conflict: Choosing Christianity in a World of Ideas* (Grand Rapids: Zondervan, 1992), 90–91.

121. John W. Cooper, "Reformed Apologetics and the Challenge of Post-Modern Relativism," *Calvin Theological Journal* 28 (1993): 118.

Cooper goes on to argue that "standard" Reformed theology "does not paint itself into this corner," because "it affirms general revelation and common grace—God's providential maintenance of his Creation order and the remnants of the image of God in fallen human beings" (118). What must be articulated is "perspectival realism." Proper presuppositionalism "recognizes with postmodernism that understanding . . . is not an exercise of pure reason but unavoidably involves commitment-based and culturally-conditioned perspectives" (119). Nevertheless it insists, over against postmodernism, that there is one particular perspective that is objectively true, one that is tied to the omniscient God who really exists, who has made us for himself, who redeems his people, and who brings history and the universe to their planned and consummated end. To promote this perspective we simultaneously expose the incoherence of alternatives, and adduce reasons and evidences in defense of the Christian worldview, understanding that at the end of the day the transformation required for a person to adopt that worldview requires not only the revelation God has given in the public arena but also the work of the Spirit in the individual.[122]

At some point it becomes rather difficult to distinguish such presuppositionalism from the rational presuppositionalism of, say, Carl F. H. Henry or Ronald Nash. The former prefers to speak of "transcendental religious apriorism";[123] the latter has recently written on "worldviews in conflict."[124] Both have been dismissed as "Christian rationalists," but this tends to be sloganeering. The critical issue, I think, is how reason relates to presuppositions.

I have tried to spell out something of my (still tentative) approach, in somewhat different terms, in chapter 3. The contemporary apologist whose work is most rigorous in this area is John Frame.[125] Frame quietly distances himself from his mentor, Cornelius Van Til, at a number of significant points; more importantly, he writes with rare clarity and precision, and disabuses his opponents of a number of misconceptions. For example, he makes clear that he has no objection to the forceful presentation of evidences in Christian apologetics; what he objects to is the adoption (implicit or otherwise) of the assumption that evidences or reasons are neutral. He does not object to

---

122. It is this failure of postmodernists to provide a basis for "transcommunal" or "intersubjective explanations" that is both troubling and vexing. See, for instance, Nancey Murphy, *Theology in the Age of Scientific Reasoning* (Ithaca: Cornell Univ. Press, 1990); and the response by J. Wentzel van Huyssteen, "Is the Postmodernist Always a Postfoundationalist?" *Theology Today* 50 (1993): 373–86.

123. See especially *God, Revelation and Authority*, vol. 1.

124. Nash, *Worldviews in Conflict*.

125. John M. Frame, *Apologetics to the Glory of God: An Introduction* (Phillipsburg: Presbyterian and Reformed, 1994); idem, *The Doctrine of the Knowledge of God* (Phillipsburg: Presbyterian and Reformed, 1987).

appeals to extrabiblical data in apologetics, but refuses to assign them inde-pendent authority to which Scripture must measure up. His work marks the most mature melding of various components of apologetics I have seen so far.[126] This is not of course to say that distinctions in approaches cannot use-fully be made.[127] It is to say that the onset of postmodernism is fostering refinements in virtually every approach to apologetics, and the result might well be better integration than has been achieved in the past.

On the other hand, there are also new dangers. Plantinga's approach is well respected among many philosophers, but it is important to recall that all it secures is "epistemic permission"—i.e., if Plantinga's arguments are cor-rect, it is reasonable for him to claim belief in God without offering support-ing evidence. *But it says nothing whatsoever about "epistemic obligation"*—that you and everyone else ought to believe in God, indeed such and such a God, too.[128] In fact, it is easy to suspect that one reason why Plantinga's approach is so well respected is that, whatever its legitimate strengths, it unwittingly plays into the hands of postmodernists who are quite happy for you to find your own "properly basic" beliefs, provided you do not suggest that everyone ought to share them. But from the perspective of Christian witness, this could never be more than what is sometimes called "pre-evangelism."

Fourth, the way men and women come to know God is through his gra-cious self-disclosure in Scripture breaking in on their minds and hearts in the power of the Spirit. This requires not only the Spirit's work to remove our willful incapacity to believe and recognize the truth (even when we live in a believing subculture), but necessarily for anyone in the Western culture of philosophical pluralism it also requires Spirit-empowered willingness to adopt a quite different worldview.

These steps require interpretive changes; there is no alternative. And those interpretive steps are never *merely* rational (though they should never be less than rational); were they merely rational, then in our fallenness we would think our thought had domesticated God. Repentance can never be *merely* rational. Was it Gregory of Nyssa who said, "Concepts create idols. Only wonder understands"?

---

126. See also C. Stephen Evans, "Evidentialist and Non-Evidentialist Accounts of Historical Religious Knowledge," *Philosophy of Religion* 35 (1994): 153–82. I am grateful to Paul Feinberg for directing me to this essay.

127. See, for example, his own critique (in *Apologetics*, appendix A, 219–43, reprinted from *Westminster Theological Journal* 47 [1985]: 279–99) of R. C. Sproul, John Gerstner, and Arthur Lindsley, *Classical Apologetics* (Grand Rapids: Zondervan, 1984), itself a critique of Van Tillian presuppositionalism and a defense of evidentialism.

128. Cf. Harold A. Netland, "Truth, Authority and Modernity: Shopping for Truth in a Supermarket of Worldview," *Faith and Modernity*, ed. Philip Sampson, Vinay Samuel and Chris Sugden (Oxford: Regnum Books, 1994), 89–115.

Interpretation is our common human lot: our privilege, and our condition. . . . Theologians must resist eating fruit from the tree of Absolute knowledge. We must avoid the lust of the mind. Absolute knowledge is forbidden us, at least at present. And it is just as well: if we knew absolutely, we would become proud and complacent. Between absolute knowledge and relativism, however, there lies the alternative of poetic and interpretive rationality. There is in Scripture a determinate and dynamic structure of meaning that both gives and calls for thought.[129]

It has pleased God through the foolishness of the proclaimed message to save those who believe (1 Cor. 1:21). Christians overcome the baleful influence of the "great dragon"—"that ancient serpent called the devil, or Satan, who leads the whole world astray"—not only on the ground of "the blood of the Lamb," but "by the word of their testimony" (Rev. 12). They have no other offensive weapon than "the sword of the Spirit, which is the word of God" (Eph. 6:17).

Thus despite the best efforts we rebels can mount, God will not be gagged. We invent new ways of gagging God, of silencing him, of marginalizing or dismissing his revelation. But God has spoken, and by his Spirit through the Word still speaks.

7. What God has disclosed of himself in Scripture does not permit us to pick and choose.

On the other hand, it mandates that we interpret what he has disclosed within the constraints that he has himself imposed—i.e., with full recognition of the developing plot-line in Scripture, and of Scripture's highly diverse literary genres. Ignoring the former is typically the liberal fallacy; ignoring the latter is typically the fundamentalist fallacy.

I may begin with the latter. Scripture boasts many communicative acts: history, letter, proverbs, wisdom utterances, warnings, songs, questions, discourse, diatribes, gematria, apocalyptic, legal codes, moral exhortation, threats, promises, commands, laments, and so on. Some of these are recognized and recognizable genres; others are admittedly genres, but with very fuzzy borders. Some are genres found within several other genres. And genres have their own interpretive "rules," learned by observation and practice.[130]

---

129. Vanhoozer, "From Canon to Concept," 119.

130. Among the more useful work in this area is the writing of Leland Ryken. See especially his *Literature of the Bible* (Grand Rapids: Zondervan, 1974); *Words of Life: A Literary Introduction to the New Testament* (Grand Rapids: Baker, 1987); "Literature in Christian Perspective," in *God and Culture*, ed. D. A. Carson and John D. Woodbridge (Grand Rapids: Eerdmans, 1993), 215–34. For a useful appreciation, see Robert A. Weathers, "Leland Ryken's Literary Approach to Biblical Interpretation: An Evangelical Model," *Journal of the Evangelical Theological Society* 37 (1994): 115–24.

"Remembering this will provide the needed correction to propositional and metaphorical theology alike: the Bible does not merely give us atomistic propositions about God, nor free-floating metaphors, but ways of processing and organizing propositions and metaphors into meaningful wholes. The forms of biblical literature are the bridge between canon and concept we seek."[131] In the words of Gerhart: "With generic analysis, biblical theologians will understand themselves to mediate between genres."[132]

To offer an example, consider these lines from Jeremiah:

> Cursed be the day I was born!
> May the day my mother bore me not be blessed!
> Cursed be the man who brought my father the news,
> who made him very glad, saying
> "A child is born to you—a son!"
> May that man be like the towns the LORD overthrew without pity.
> May he hear wailing in the morning,
> a battle cry at noon.
> For he did not kill me in the womb,
> with my mother as my grave,
> her womb enlarged forever.
> Why did I ever come out of the womb
> to see trouble and sorrow
> and to end my days in shame?
>
> (Jeremiah 20:14–18)

Jeremiah is not really calling down God's curses on the head of the poor chap who, years before and quite innocently, broke the news of Jeremiah's birth to his dad. Nor is he seriously wishing that his mother would remain eternally pregnant, carrying around the dead fetus that would have been Jeremiah. This is the language of anguish and personal lament. It is more powerful than simply saying, rather prosaically, "I wish I had never been born."

But if we must be sensitive to the Bible's literary genres, we must be eager to embrace the whole Bible, recognizing the importance not only of the immediate context, but of larger contexts: the corpus (e.g., the Pauline epistles), the precise place in redemptive history, *and the canonical context*.[133]

---

131. Vanhoozer, "From Canon to Concept," 13.

132. Mary Gerhart, "Generic Competence in Biblical Hermeneutics," *Semeia* 43 (1988): 40.

133. Lints, *Fabric*, 293, following Edmund P. Clowney, *Preaching and Biblical Theology* (Grand Rapids: Eerdmans, 1961), 16, opts for the textual horizon, the epochal horizon, and the canonical horizon.

Because this chapter has gone on long enough, I forbear to give examples here, when two useful ones appear in the next chapter. They deal with the treatment of Genesis 3 and the nature of sin, and with some disastrously reductionistic contemporary treatments of the love of God.

C. Concluding Reflection

I have been arguing that Christians recognize the culture-relatedness of all truth, but that this does not jeopardize the objectivity of the revelation God has graciously provided in his Son Jesus Christ and in the Bible; that there are ways of thinking through how people come to know this truth, and the God who is its ultimate source; and that failure to recognize it for what it is—in short, failure to know God—is morally reprehensible, and marks a rebellion against the authority of the one who created us and who governs us. Several times I have hinted at the importance of adopting "the whole counsel of God," of recognizing the distinctiveness of an entire Christian worldview if the parts within it are to make much sense. That means not less than following and adopting the Bible's plot-line. In other words (to use the contemporary jargon), the Bible provides us with a metanarrative, a comprehensive "story" that provides the framework for a comprehensive explanation, a comprehensive worldview. In the next two chapters I intend to tease out some of the movements in that plot-line, and think through a few of their implications for Christianity's confrontation with contemporary religious pluralism.

Chapter 5

WHAT GOD HAS SPOKEN: OPENING MOVES IN THE BIBLE'S PLOT-LINE

I n one of his essays William Placher comments on a time when the theological use of the Bible presupposed a deep knowledge of what the Bible says.[1] The example he serves up is from the final pages of Calvin's *Institutes*, where the Reformer thinks through the issue of what Christians should do if they find themselves under a wicked ruler. Placher notes that Calvin reflects on Daniel and Ezekiel regarding the need to obey even bad rulers; he weighs the command to serve the king of Babylon in Jeremiah 27. He quotes from the Psalms, and he cites Isaiah to the effect that the faithful are urged to trust in God to overcome the unrighteous. On the other hand, he evenhandedly notes episodes in Exodus and Judges "where people serve God by overthrowing the evil rulers," and texts in 1 Kings and Hosea where God's people are criticized for being obedient to wicked kings. He cites Peter's conclusion before Gamaliel, according to Acts: "We must obey God rather than men" (Acts 5:29). From these and other biblical passages, he proceeds to weave nuanced conclusions. We should disobey what governement mandates if it violates our religious obligations. By contrast, Christians should not normally go around starting revolutions. But those who are in positions of authority should deploy that authority to deal with those who exploit others. Even violent revolutionaries may in mysterious ways perform the will of God, though of course they may be called to judgment on account of their evil.

---

1. William E. Placher, "Why Bother With Theology?" *Christian Century* 111/4 (February 2–9, 1994): 105.

Placher then comments:

> My point is not to defend all of Calvin's conclusions, or even all of his method, but simply to illustrate how immersion in biblical texts can produce a very complex way of reflecting within a framework of biblical authority, compared to which most contemporary examples look pretty simple-minded. We can't "appeal to the Bible" in a way that's either helpful or faithful without beginning to do theology. Theology begins to put together a way of looking as a Christian at the world in all its variety, a language that we share as Christians and that provides a context rich enough for discussing the complexities of our lives. Absent such a shared framework, we can quote passages at each other, but the only contexts in which we can operate come from the discourses of politics and popular culture.[2]

In his recent book on apologetics, Frame at one point offers an exposition of the "four most important things to remember about the Christian worldview," which he sees as antecedent to presenting the gospel. They are: "first, the absolute personality of God; second, the distinction between Creator and creature; third, the sovereignty of God; and fourth, the Trinity."[3] My interest at the moment is not the cogency of his choices. Rather, I observe that the categories by which Frame seeks to establish "the Christian worldview" are logical/systematic/philosophical. I certainly have no objection to such categories, and of course they are in line with Frame's specialist interest. But the fact remains that the Bible as a whole document tells a story, and, properly used, that story can serve as a metanarrative that shapes our grasp of the entire Christian faith. In my view it is increasingly important to spell this out to Christians and to non-Christians alike—to Christians, to ground them in Scripture, and to non-Christians, as part of our proclamation of the gospel. The ignorance of basic Scripture is so disturbing in our day that Christian preaching that does not seek to remedy the lack is simply irresponsible.

At the same time, the Bible is a very big and diverse book, and if *only* the story-line is plotted, a tremendous amount of material will be left out. What I have chosen to do is to draw attention to some turning points on the Bible's plot-line, and use the occasion of those turning points to draw a few connections with later biblical material related thematically to those turning points. Doubtless my choice is idiosyncratic; I am doing little more than priming the pump. But what primarily influences my choices in this chapter and the next is the challenge of religious pluralism that is constantly lurking in the background in part 2 of this book.

2. Ibid.
3. John M. Frame, *Apologetics to the Glory of God: An Introduction* (Phillipsburg: Presbyterian and Reformed, 1994), 34.

A. Creation

Because the legitimacy of an appeal to a doctrine of Creation is challenged by many mainstream scientists, and because large-scale issues of worldview are at stake, before turning to the biblical plot-line I must say something about the status of the current debate.

1. Although philosophical naturalism is far from dead, it is under assault.

Insofar as contemporary science buys into philosophical naturalism, not least in the complex questions surrounding the origins of the universe and the origins of the human race, it is tending to lash back with more heat than light. Thus some scientists *define* their discipline in such a way as to exclude those who leave any place for a Creator. For example, Dickerson, an expert in chemical evolution writes: "Science, fundamentally, is a game. It is a game with one overriding and defining rule. Rule No.1: Let us see how far and to what extent we can explain the behavior of the physical and material universe in terms of purely physical and material causes, without invoking the supernatural."[4] That is a remarkable definition, even though the attitude it betrays is a commonplace today in Western science. It does not allow that the evidence itself may point to God, *and that in science the evidence should be followed and tested wherever it leads.* The implication of Dickerson's first rule—an implication that is explicitly drawn out by not a few contemporary scientists—is that a researcher or scholar who advances evidence for, say, intelligent design or catastrophic breaks in natural selection or (above all!) a young earth, is simply not a scientist. He or she is not to be answered with evidence, but written off as a "non-scientist."

So perhaps it was not too surprising that *Scientific American* fired the science writer Forrest Mims as soon as they appointed him, simply because they discovered he was "a non-believer in evolution." It was not that he was going to be writing in that area, or that they judged any of his work to be incompetent. They simply did not want to be associated with anyone some of their readers might write off as a non-scientist. Johnson rightly concludes: "The Mims episode shows us that science is beset by religious fundamentalism—of two kinds. One group of fundamentalists—the Biblical creation-scientists—has been banished from mainstream science and education and has no significant influence. Another group has enormous clout in science and science

---

4. Richard E. Dickerson, "The Game of Science," *Perspectives on Science and Faith* 44 (June 1992): 137. Cf. the oft-repeated remark of Richard Dawkins, *The Blind Watchmaker* (New York: W. W. Norton, 1986), 6–7: "Although atheism might have been logically tenable before Darwin, Darwin made it possible to be an intellectually fulfilled atheist."

education, and is prepared to use it to exclude people they consider unbelievers. The influential fundamentalists are called Darwinists."[5]

Sometimes the science gets silly. In a recent edition of the *New York Times*, an article reporting on the field of palaeontology includes this sentence: "This [discovery] dramatically curtails the time available for life to have evolved naturally on earth, and could focus more attention on the disputed hypothesis that life originated. . . ."[6] How would you expect this sentence to be completed? Perhaps "that life originated by a creative act of God"? Here is the rest of the sentence: " . . . that life originated elsewhere in the universe and somehow reached earth from afar." Fred Hoyle strikes again. The "scientific" evidence does not seem to be working out too well on this planet, so we'll speculate about how well it must work out on some other planet. Brown's analogy is not unwarranted:

> Darwinism is in effect in somewhat the same position vis-á-vis fundamentalist Christianity that the Roman imperial religious cultus was vis-á-vis early Christianity in the days of persecution. The defenders of emperor-worship may have been very skeptical about its literal truth, but they furiously persecuted and repressed those who were unwilling to pay it the mandatory reverence. The same thing is true of Darwinism today: it furiously assaults those who fail to render it its worshipful due. (At least it does not throw us to the lions, for which one must be grateful.)[7]

The establishment of evolution as dogma[8] is a subset of the larger move to an *a priori* definition of science that rules out any consideration of the non-material, supernatural realm. One sometimes wonders if this move has been unwittingly abetted by the abundant use of metaphors in science, metaphors that make the physical world sound wiser, more benevolent, more "human" than it really is: chemical scissors, chaperones stabilizing and protecting polypeptides, solvent cage, optical molasses, DNA fingerprints, electron spin, read-only memory, squeezed light, natural *selection* (!), artificial intelligence, and so forth.[9] Be that as it may, one small but vociferous group of scientists, breaking away from the sterility of philosophical naturalism, has tried to tie

5. Phillip E. Johnson, "Unbelievers Unwelcome in the Science Lab," *Los Angeles Times* (November 3, 1990), Section B, 7.

6. Reported in the *Religion and Society Report* 10/10 (October 1993): 4.

7. Harold O. J. Brown, "Darwin on Display," *Religion and Society Report* 8/12 (December 1991): 2.

8. See Phillip E. Johnson, *Evolution as Dogma: The Establishment of Naturalism* (Dallas: Haughton, 1990).

9. My list is drawn from Anne Eisenberg, "Metaphor in the Language of Science," *Scientific American* 266/5 (May 1992): 144.

the New Age movement and Eastern mysticism to modern physics.[10] The attempt has not been very successful; the criticisms are severe.[11]

More importantly, reductionistic definitions of science are under assault because of rigorous philosophical work that cannot easily be gainsaid. Developments in hermeneutics, as we have seen (chap. 3), have demonstrated how much scientific theories, especially large-scale theories, are dependent on shifting paradigms. Moreover, rigorous work on the definition of science has shown that while it is relatively easy to identify instances of science (e.g., measurements of the half-life of a subatomic particle) and instances of nonscience (e.g., phrenology, palmistry, astrology), there are no "generally accepted necessary and sufficient conditions for drawing a line of demarcation between science and nonscience,"[12] and no warrant for arbitrary definitions that claim to rule out theological or philosophical concepts.

Above all, developments within the various disciplines of science are prompting rising numbers of scientists to be more circumspect in their claims. It may be helpful to list a few of these.

1. A number of very significant works have resuscitated the Argument from Design.[13] These contributions offer not only groundbreaking philosophical analysis of the issues, but study the scientific evidence in several areas: the origin and formation of the universe, the origin of life, the origin of major groups of organisms and the origin of human language. Strictly speaking, the argument for intelligent design requires less demonstration than scientific creationism: the latter, to be credible, must specify mechanism, limits to evolutionary change, duration, and so forth, while the former need demonstrate only that the order and complexity of the universe is an impossibility apart from design—not least within any timescale and mechanisms offered to us by evolutionary theorists.

On the matter of timescale, an interesting and amusing essay has recently been published on the challenge set by Huxley in his debate with Wilberforce in 1860. Huxley argued that six eternal monkeys (he actually used the word

---

10. Doubtless the most influential voice is that of Fritjof Capra. See especially his *Turning Point* (London: Flamingo, 1985) and *The Tao of Physics* (London: Flamingo, 1986).

11. See especially Ernest C. Lucas, "God, GUTs and Gurus: The New Physics and New Age Ideology," *Themelios* 16/3 (April/May 1991): 4–7, and the literature cited there.

12. J. P. Moreland, *Christianity and the Nature of Science: A Philosophical Investigation* (Grand Rapids: Baker, 1989), 56. The entire volume repays careful reading.

13. See William A. Dembski, "The Incompleteness of Scientific Naturalism and Its Implications for a Scientifically Defensible Account of Intelligent Design in Nature" (Richardson: Foundations for Thought and Ethics, 1992); idem, "Scientific Creationism and Intelligent Design," *Transations* 2/2 (May 1994): 1–4; and especially the essays in J. P. Moreland, ed., *The Creation Hypothesis: Scientific Evidence of an Intelligent Designer* (Downers Grove: InterVarsity Press, 1994).

"apes") tapping randomly on six eternal typewriters and supplied with unlimited paper would, given enough time, eventually produce a psalm, a Shakespearean sonnet, or even a whole book, purely by chance—and in the same way, molecular movement, given enough time, would produce the universe. Grigg has done the mathematics.[14] At the rate of one strike per second, ignoring differences between capitals and lower case letters (we have to give the monkeys one or two advantages), on a simplified keyboard, the average time it would take a monkey to produce the word "the" is 34.72 hours. To produce the twenty-third psalm, however, would take 9.552 x 101016 years, while the evolutionist's estimate of the age of the universe is about 15 billion years. Grigg goes on to show that the formation of DNA would take far, far more time, on any known mechanism, than the typing of the twenty-third psalm by our esteemed monkeys. More importantly, the theory that life can form spontaneously from nonlife postulates that proteins formed from peptides which formed from amino acids which formed from gases in a reducing atmosphere. But the biochemical reactions required to move from amino acids to peptides and from peptides to proteins are reversible: even infinite time will not do. In the body, the intervention of enzymes catalyse the reaction and inhibit reversibility. But enzymes are of course proteins, so one cannot postulate their presence in the primordial soup needed by biogenesis to make proteins in the first place.

Despite the effort of Richard Dawkins to prove that mechanisms are available to cross the necessary barriers to bring about life,[15] evenhanded analysis of his book demonstrates that he simply does not make a believable case.[16]

2. Several recent books have offered telling critique of evolutionists' theories of the move from nonlife to life. Denton's work (briefly mentioned in chap. 3)[17] is important precisely because he refuses to accept the alternative of special creation, and falls back on the hope that some other (materialistic) theory will replace current evolutionary thought some day. Johnson's book has circulated widely,[18] and is significant not only on account of its compe-

---

14. Russel Grigg, "Could Monkeys Type the 23rd Psalm?" *Interchange* 50 (1993): 25–31.

15. *The Blind Watchmaker* (London: Longman, 1986). The title, of course, comes from William Paley's argument, in the nineteenth century, that just as a watch does not come into existence by accidental processes but needs a watchmaker, so the complex mechanisms of life and of the universe itself could not have come into existence by accidental processes, but need a "watchmaker," i.e., God.

16. E.g., Howard Taylor, "Watchmakers Are Not Blind," *Evangel* 10/1 (Spring 1992): 26–29; Phillip E. Johnson, "The Religion of the Blind Watchmaker," *Perspectives on Science and Faith* 45 (1993): 46–48.

17. Michael Denton, *Evolution: A Theory in Crisis* (Bethesda: Adler & Adler, 1986).

18. Phillip E. Johnson, *Darwin on Trial* (Washington: Regnery Gateway, 1991).

tence, but also because Johnson invariably takes on his reviewers and critics, courteously but firmly refusing to allow a bad argument to slip past.[19]

3. While some physicists hope the discovery of the long-sought unifying equation will in principle explain everything in the universe mathematically, the rising discipline of chaos theory suggests that, even should such an equation be postulated, determinate development established by the laws of physics will prove more elusive.[20]

4. The brilliant Cambridge physicist Stephen Hawking has proposed that the universe, though not eternal, has neither beginning nor end.[21] Just as the surface of the earth is finite yet has no boundary or end (precisely because it is in the shape of a sphere), so many scientists have proposed that the universe is bounded: a space traveler would never escape the universe, but, if he or she traveled long enough, would return to the starting point. Hawking not only argues that the universe is finite, but that it is unbounded in imaginary time (imaginary numbers are the square roots of multiples of -1; they are important in the equations of quantum mechanics). Thus no act of creation at some point is needed, and therefore no doctrine of creation.

But Peacock argues that what we know of thermodynamics rules out Hawking's theory: the universe is running down, and there is no mechanism for charging it up again. Moreover, the relevant equations to which Hawking makes implicit appeal do not work at the beginning of real time (there is a "mathematical singularity").[22] Moreover, other "steady state models" have for some time been abandoned by most scientists.[23]

5. The dominant theory in the scientific community regarding the origin of the universe is the "big bang" theory: an original and unimaginably condensed particle of all matter/energy blew up and in time produced the universe that we observe. While there are books that argue whether or not this model can be squared with theism,[24] the theory itself is coming apart at the seams. Henry Morris amusingly suggests we should call it "the big bust." It

---

19. Thus when Stephen Jay Gould wrote a critical review of Johnson's book in *Scientific American* (July 1992), and that prestigious journal would not allow him to respond, Johnson published his response elsewhere, as "The Religion of the Blind Watchmaker" in *Perspectives on Science and Faith*.

20. See John Polkinghorne, *Reason and Reality: The Relationship Between Science and Theology* (London: SPCK, 1991), chap. 3.

21. *A Brief History of Time: From the Big Bang to Black Holes* (New York: Bantam Books, 1988).

22. Roy E. Peacock, *A Brief History of Eternity* (Wheaton: Crossway Books, 1990).

23. See the brief treatment by Hugh Ross, "Astronomical Evidences for a Personal, Transcendent God," in Moreland, *The Creation Hypothesis*, 146–48.

24. W. L. Craig and Q. Smith, *Theism, Atheism and Big Bang Cosmology* (Oxford: Clarendon Press, 1993).

is extremely difficult to square the commonly accepted date of the universe (about 15 billion years) with the estimate of the age of the universe calculated on the basis of big bang theory. Background radiation is smoothly distributed, while big bang theory predicts high variations. Big bang theory has not satisfactorily explained the formation of galaxies and larger structures. Evidence along these lines has been quietly circulating for years; some (evolutionary) scientists have argued that it has been suppressed.[25] Now it is emerging in news magazines[26] and popular books.[27]

6. Though their claims are sometimes exaggerated, young-earth creationists have accumulated pieces of evidence that conflict with old-earth models. The fairest researchers on both sides, I think, acknowledge conflicting evidence, and disagree over what to do with the evidence on the other side, and how strong it is.

For these and many more reasons, philosophical naturalism is decaying. It seemed wise to chronicle some of this, because some readers may not be aware that there is a significant debate, and that more and more a place is opening up again, even within the scientific community, for a competent articulation of the doctrine of creation.

2. Creation is the Bible's opening move in its plot-line.

In a currently circulating metaphor, the relation between science and religion has been likened to the relation between a boa constrictor and a warthog: the fight is to the death, and the victor swallows the loser.[28] Whatever scientists may think, it is certainly not the way Christians should think, whether they are scientists or not.

Some try to divide the turf occupied by the two: science deals with the material world, religion with the spiritual world, or some such similar dichotomy. If the Bible is allowed its say, that simply will not do. God made the world; he sent his Son to become a real man in this material world; he promises to wrap up history and transform this universe.

Yet for those who maintain that God and science occupy mutually exclusive turf, the sphere that is left to God, once science is finished, is very small. At one time appeal was made to God to explain everything that was not under-

---

25. E.g., Geoffrey Burbidge, "Why Only One Big Bang?" *Scientific American* 226/2 (February 1992): 120.

26. E.g., Michael D. Lemonick, "Bang! A Big Theory May Be Shot," *Time* (January 14, 1991): 63.

27. Russell Chandler, *Racing Toward 2001: The Forces Shaping America's Religious Future* (Grand Rapids: Zondervan, 1992), 56.

28. See Steve Bishop, "Science and Faith: Boa Constrictors and Warthogs?" *Themelios* 19/1 (October 1993): 4–9.

stood in the universe, and that was a great deal. As science progressed, William Paley and others appealed to God as the explanation of the gaps that science did not seem likely to fill. As the gaps shrank, so did God, prompting the much-cited remark of Laplace that he did not need the hypothesis of God.[29]

From the perspective of biblical theology, however, this debate was disastrously misguided. We may usefully distinguish an open universe, a closed universe, and a controlled universe. An open universe is espoused by animism. The spirits control most things, and the appropriate thing for human beings to do is to appease the spirits so that they may do things we want. Science is not possible because nothing is regular: the whims of the spirits are unpredictable, and even the sacrifices do not always work. In a closed universe, everything is explained by cause and effect at a purely material level. Science is possible; God is excluded. A modification of this model is espoused by deism. God set the whole thing up and established the principles of operation, but since then he has been rather removed from the scene, while he lets nature take its course. Science is possible, but there is little need to appeal to God, except for the initial act of creation.

The controlled universe reflected in the Bible, however, has God as both its creator and its sustainer/ruler. He creates it in an ordered way, and sustains and rules it in an ordered way, so that science is possible; but he is not bound by what he has created, so he is at perfect liberty to do things another way, with the result that miracles are possible. The Hebrew canon reflects human knowledge of the water cycle (Eccl. 1:7), but that does not prevent the biblical writers from preferring to say, on the whole, "God sends the rain" rather than simply "It rains." Jesus knows that the birds feed themselves, but he prefers to say that his heavenly Father feeds them (Matt. 6:26). Evidence abounds that the biblical authors could observe the natural order of things and speak phenomenologically, but they could as readily detect and speak of the providential hand of God behind that order.

Themes introduced by this opening move in the Bible's plot-line, then, include the following four:

First, that God creates the universe, while he himself is uncreated, establishes a particular relationship between God and the universe. "That God creates by his Word (Gen. 1; Isa. 41:4; 48:13; Amos 9:6; Ps. 33:6; cf. John 1:1–3) means not only that the universe is neither an ultimate necessity nor an inevitable divine emanation, but also that it is no act of sudden impulse or arbitrary will. Creation is the work of the omnipotent God who acts

---

29. The discussion of Christopher Kaiser, *Creation and the History of Science* (Grand Rapids: Eerdmans, 1991) shows that Laplace's remark was not uttered in defense of atheism, but as a judgment on the diminishing need of science to appeal to God's special actions to maintain a stable universe.

consciously and rationally."[30] The universe is neither an emanation from God, nor coequal with God. And since this is the beginning of the story, it is the beginning of a line, a direction, ultimately of a teleology: history does not go around in perpetual circles with no beginning and no end.

Such a view cannot be reconciled with, for instance, much first-century Greek thought, or with Hinduism or Buddhism (in their various forms).

Second, such universal creation establishes this God as the God of all. Later texts insist that God used an Agent in creation, of whom it is said that nothing that was made was made without him, and that all things were made by him and for him (John 1:1–3; Col. 1:15–17). God's universal power in creation becomes a constant stimulus to praise (e.g., Psalm 8), not least in the courts of heaven (Rev. 4:11).

Third, the text constantly reiterates that what God made was good (Gen.1:4, 10, 12, 18, 21, 25), even "very good" (Gen. 1:31). Such a view allows no fundamental dualism between spirit and matter such that spirit is good and matter is bad. The creation account not only insists on the goodness of the initial creation, but sets the stage for what goes wrong—for the development of the plot-line that issues in a Redeemer to set it to right. Ultimately that plot-line anticipates the restoration of goodness, even the transformation to a greater glory, of the universe gone wrong (Rom. 8:21), and arrives finally at the dawning of a new heaven and a new earth (Rev. 21–22; cf. Isa. 65:17), the home of righteousness (2 Peter 3:13).

Fourth, the creation account establishes certain structures. Not the least of these is the creation week culminating in the rest of God (Gen. 1:1–2:3) that serves to ground the Sabbath law in the time of Moses (Ex. 20:8–11) and is ultimately found to point to a "rest" that transcends both Sabbath and the "rest" that the covenant people found when they settled into the promised land (e.g., Josh. 11:23), a rest secured by a new "Joshua/Jesus" (Heb. 3:7–4:13; cf. Ps. 95; Jer. 6:16; Matt. 11:28). The creation account also introduces the first man and woman and their union, which is assigned an impressive sanctity against competing claims (Gen. 2:24). But this element, the introduction of human beings in the creation account, is so important for the developing plot-line, that I shall assign it the next two main headings.

The importance of these creation structures must not be overlooked:

> That which most distinguishes the concept of creation is that it is complete. Creation is the given totality of order which forms the presupposition of historical existence. "Created order" is that which is not negotiable within the course of history, that which neither the terrors of chance nor the inge-

30. Carl F. H. Henry, *God, Revelation and Authority*, 6 vols. (Waco: Word Books, 1976–83), 6:120.

nuity of art can overthrow. It defines the scope of our freedom and the limits of our fears. The affirmation of the psalm, sung on the sabbath which celebrates the completion of creation, affords a ground for human activity and human hope: "The world is established, it shall never be moved." Within such a world, in which "The Lord reigns," we are free to act and can have confidence that God will act. Because created order is given, because it is secure, we dare to be certain that God will vindicate it in history. "He comes to judge the earth. He will judge the world with righteousness and the peoples with his truth" (Ps. 96:10, 13).[31]

B. Human Beings

If human beings arose by chance from the primordial muck, if they descended from apes by a fortuitous combination of chance and the survival of the fittest according to the law of the jungle, then transparently what we should think of ourselves will be very different from what we should think of ourselves if the biblical account is true. The issue is not for our purposes some utilitarian question about which vision of reality seems to produce better people (although that consideration is not without importance), but which view is true, and what bearing the biblical view has on contemporary pressures toward pluralism.

In the academic arena today, perhaps the greatest pressures in defence of the essential amorality of human behavior and the essentially equivalent value of all human cultures come from anthropologists.[32] Increasingly, however, even materialistic forms of science acknowledge the uniqueness of human beings among the species. Only humans enjoy language facility with complex syntax. Although some sociobiologists want to assign even self-sacrificial and altruistic behavior to biological survival, a broader view is gaining ground. Only humans realize selfhood; in Barbour's words, humanity is a "biological organism and a responsible self."[33] Some of the pressures questioning the mechanistic models spawned by philosophical materialism are coming from

---

31. Oliver O'Donovan, *Resurrection and Moral Order* (Leicester: Inter-Varsity Press, 1986), 61.

32. See the documentation in Robert J. Priest, "Cultural Anthropology, Sin, and the Missionary," in D. A. Carson and John D. Woodbridge, eds., *God and Culture* (Grand Rapids: Eerdmans, 1993), 67–84. Cf. Roger Bastide, *Applied Anthropology* (New York: Harper & Row, 1973). There is not space here to discuss the relevent primate remains that bear on the discussion—Peking Man, Neanderthal Man, Cro-Magnon Man, and so forth. There is compressed evaluation of some of the more important literature up until about 1980 in Henry, *God, Revelation and Authority*, 6:197–228.

33. Ian G. Barbour, *Religion in an Age of Science: The Gifford Lectures*, vol. 1 (San Francisco: Harper San Francisco, 1990), 209.

postmodern, new age "spirituality." Although its conclusions ought to be questioned, its recognition that a purely materialist accounting of human beings is out of step with our experience may be welcomed. Here, for example, is Sprung, after describing a typically materialistic vision of humanity:

> A solemn and impressive story. But not an acceptable account of the way things are for humans. Held against Plato, Buddha, Nietzsche, something is awry. Science's world is not a world that offers a human being the right to live his or her life as a drama worth living. How is it that most of us don't sense the scientific world as an absurdity, as a perversity, as an inhuman conception? Because we must do so if we take it literally as the whole story. Somehow we defend ourselves against it. We all, laboratory scientists included, have vivial beliefs that so far have survived science. Do we not all have a sense of individuality, even of person when we talk of freedom or the sacred right of individuals to fulfill themselves in their own way? Isn't that the seed of thought of our social concept and of the way we understand ourselves?[34]

The Bible insists that human beings have been made in the image of God. The repetition in the text is impressively emphatic: "So God created man in his own image, in the image of God he created him; male and female he created them" (Gen. 1:27). We may specify six implications:

1. The content of "image of God" may be teased out inductively.

In other words, "image of God" is not a frequently used technical term with firm semantic borders, but a picture-expression dropped into the beginning of the Bible's story-line and used relatively infrequently thereafter. This does not empty the expression of content; it means the content must be specified from the story.[35]

Whatever else the expression suggests (some of which I will mention below), it distinguishes human beings from the rest of creation. On the one hand, like other creatures; we are part of the creation. From that perspective we are radically unlike God: only he is the Creator, only he is transcendent. On the other hand, unlike the rest of creation, we are made in God's image. Whereas much contemporary thought imagines God to be impersonal (see section D, below), the God of the Bible is a personal being who enters into personal relationships with persons that he has made. But that human beings

---

34. Mervyn Sprung, *After Truth: Explorations in Life Sense* (Albany: State Univ. of New York Press, 1994), 181. (Sprung coined the word *vivial* in an effort to ground a "vital" or "living" or "jointly regenerative" form of significant human consciousness in something other than science.)

35. For a useful systematic treatment, see Philip Edgcumbe Hughes, *The True Image: The Origin and Destiny of Man in Christ* (Grand Rapids: Eerdmans, 1989), esp. 1–69.

are "personal" cannot be all that is meant by "image of God," for the Bible boldly pictures God entering into personal relations with angels as well, while "image of God" language is restricted to human beings. The writer of the Epistle to the Hebrews draws attention to fundamental distinctions between angels and human beings, not least the wonderful fact that the incarnation brought the Son in human, not angelic likeness. There has arisen a Redeemer for fallen human beings, but not for fallen angels.

The least that "image of God" language suggests, in addition to human personhood, is that human beings are not simply hairless apes with cranial capacities slightly larger than those of other primates, but that we are accorded an astonishing dignity; that human beings are moral creatures with special privileges and responsibilities; that there is implanted within us a profound capacity for knowing God intimately, however much we have suppressed and distorted that capacity; that we have a hunger for creating things—not, of course, *ex nihilo*, but in art, building, expression, thought, joy of discovery, science, technology; that we have a capacity for personal relations with other persons.

2. The importance and dignity of human beings demand further reflection.

This dignity, both objectively and in our subjective grasp of it, depends on the significance of what we are (our nature and purpose) and what we do (the significance of our deeds and words and thoughts and relationships). The two, of course, are related.

It is hard to deny that the enormous influence of what some have called "selfism" today is a by-product of the loss of our self-identity as persons made in the image of God. At one level, selfishness has always been the core problem this side of the Fall. One could argue that war, hate, slavery, lust, covetousness, false religion and much more are inextricably entangled with self-focus. Individually and in our respective groupings, we tend to think of ourselves as at the center of the universe. Even God's significance is determined by his relation to me or to my peculiar group. It has taken the end of the twentieth century, however, to make self-centeredness a virtue; to interpret egotism as a strength, and whining self-pity a reason others must take yet one more course in sensitivity training; to ground every hint of instability or emotional disturbance or broken relationships in a disastrous loss of self-esteem. The tragedy is that this is both right and wrong. It is at least partly right in its analysis: loss of self-identity issues in meaninglessness, even despair. It is entirely wrong in its prescription: assertiveness training, endless exhortations to choose your own path regardless of others, foolish puffery to promote self-esteem based on very little. The older virtues, largely derived from the Judeo-Christian heritage, which promoted self-denial and service to others as joined alike to love for others and to personal growth, have been drowned in a deluge of selfism.

The irony is palpable; it was made clear by Jesus two millennia ago (Mark 8:34–38). Canonically, it is a lesson spelled out in many narratives: self-assertive insistence on finding one's own way brings chaos, while self-denial and a hearty submission to God's way retrieve purpose and fulfillment. Nowhere does it reach more eloquent portrayal than in some of the Wisdom Literature. Choosing to live in a purely naturalist world, "the Teacher" (NIV) plunged himself into immense projects, sex, work, pleasure, learning, reflection, unrelenting self-gratification. His conclusion could be the epitaph of secular humanism: "Meaningless! Meaningless! . . . Utterly meaningless! Everything is meaningless!" (Eccl. 1:2). There is, finally, only one way out of the Teacher's despair: a return to the theistic universe in which he was reared. "Remember your Creator in the days of your youth, before the days of trouble come and the years approach when you will say, 'I find no pleasure in them'" (12:1).

3. Human accountability to the Creator God not only grounds the biblical plot-line, but establishes the significance of our actions, and finally of our self-identity.

Here, if anywhere, the disastrous nature of the loss of a Christian worldview lies exposed. Degler has traced the impact of Darwinianism in American social thought.[36] It is all but impossible to deny that although the findings of the social sciences are presented with a show of impartiality, they are commonly constrained by profound commitment to Darwinian ideology. In the swings between nature and nurture, between debates as to whether our genes or our environment and culture are determinative in establishing who we are and what we do, two facts stand out: (1) in both cases, ideological commitment tends to skew the evidence; and (2) in both cases, the product is a relentless tendency to undermine the notion of personal responsibility and accountability.

Nietzsche could argue that abandonment of any notion of God was immensely liberating. "Once you said 'God' when you gazed upon distant seas; but now I have taught you to say 'superman.'"[37] But human history has rightly destroyed much of this form of arrogance. Since Nietzsche's day a succession of brutal tyrants and the wars they have spawned, ongoing strug-

---

36. Carl N. Degler, *In Search of Human Nature: The Decline and Revival of Darwinianism in Americal Social Thought* (Oxford: Oxford Univ. Press, 1991).

37. Friedrich Nietzsche, *A Nietzsche Reader* (Harmondsworth: Penguin Books, 1977), 242.

gles with racism, grinding poverty, urban violence, and the evils of massive bureaucracies have done much to temper enthusiasm for the notion that the death of God is a triumph of the human spirit. Indeed, it is death, human death, that spells the ultimate *finis* over human hubris, and "scientific humanism" (as opposed to "ethical humanism") is increasingly forced to come to terms with the fact. "Man is literally split in two," writes Becker; "he has the awareness of his own splendid uniqueness in that he sticks out of nature with a towering majesty, and yet he goes back into the ground a few feet in order blindly and dumbly to rot and disappear forever."[38]

Even as an undergraduate thirty years ago, when I lost my grandmother I learned that there are many different ways of viewing death. An atheist student in the next room offered his condolences, and then quietly added, "But I suppose it is different for you. When my grandmother died, I could not come to terms with the fact that I would never see her again."

One remembers a character in one of the novels of John Fowles, when he has learned that his girlfriend has died:

> Staring out to sea, I finally forced myself to stop thinking of her as someone still somewhere . . . but as a shovelful of ashes already scattered, as a broken link, a biological dead end, an eternal withdrawal from reality, a once complex object that now dwindled, dwindled, left nothing behind except a smudge like a fallen speck of soot on a blank sheet of paper. . . . I did not cry for her . . . but I sat in the silence of that night, that infinite hostility to man, to permanence, to love, remembering her, remembering her.[39]

Whether we opt for the social determinism of Margaret Mead or B. F. Skinner, in which society and environment cause human beings to do good and evil, or for the rising emphasis on a genetic basis for all behavior, the effect is the same: individual human accountability is decreased, and there are rising and impassioned pleas to force government to take responsibility for everything—both the research that will sanction more of these perspectives, and the changes that will allegedly solve our problems. Without doubting for a moment that both environment and genes, both nature and nurture, play important roles in human behavior, and without denying that govern-

---

38. Ernest Becker, *The Denial of Death* (New York: Free Press, 1973), 26. Some have argued that since the time of Becker we have tended to go one step farther. Unable to face the brute finality of the vision of death spawned by atheistic philosophical naturalism, and unwilling to return to a biblical perspective, a new generation puts faith in reports of out-of-body experiences and New Age mysticism. For a while, death was the last taboo in Western culture, and for many it still is; for others it is becoming an exploited sentimentality.

39. John Fowles, *The Magus*, 2d ed. (London: Jonathan Cape, 1977), 441. The passage is cited in a thoughtful essay by David Smith, "The Image of Humanity in Contemporary Culture," *Scottish Bulletin of Evangelical Theology* 10 (1992): 121.

ment may play useful though restricted roles in social betterment, Christians will want to remember two things: first, in terms of ethical behavior neither nature nor nurture is absolutely determinative, for individuals with the same background or carrying the same genes do head in different directions; and second, God is still on his throne, providentially governing this fallen world.

But the modern mood will not have it. Western societies, especially America, having sacrificed the notion of human accountability, foster a culture of victimization. In the words of the old Anna Russell song, "But I am happy. I have learned the lesson this has taught: That everything I do that's wrong is someone else's fault." The humorist P. J. O'Rourke is only slightly exaggerating when he writes, "The second item in the liberal creed, after self-righteousness, is unaccountability. Liberals have invented whole college majors—psychology, sociology, women's studies—to prove that nothing is anybody's fault."[40] Victimization is a growth industry: thousands of lawyers can't be wrong.

The repercussions are vast, even if they cannot all be accurately measured. In addition to fostering immorality and self-pity, in addition to sapping moral strength and emasculating conscience, the religious culture also changes:

> Unfortunately, victimization convinces men and women who should be looking for a Savior to search for a scapegoat. After all, if I am not to blame for what I do, the Cross is much ado about nothing. How hopelessly out of date the old spiritual sounds to us. "Not my mother or my father, but it's me, O Lord, standing in the need of prayer." Victims do not need God, just a sympathetic therapist or a good lawyer.[41]

This, too, is a form of idolatry. The words of Wells are not too strong:

> Why do people choose the substitute over God himself? Probably the most important reason is that it obviates accountability to God. We can meet idols on our own terms because they are our own creations. They are safe, predictable, and controllable; they are, in Jeremiah's colorful language, the "scarecrows in a cucumber field" (10:5). They are portable and completely under the user's control. They offer nothing like the threat of a God who thunders from Sinai and whose providence in this world so often appears to us to be incomprehensible and dangerous. . . . [People] need face only themselves. That is the appeal of idolatry.[42]

---

40. P. J. O'Rourke, *Give War a Chance* (New York: Atlantic Monthly Press, 1992), xxi.

41. Haddon W. Robinson, "Call Us Irresponsible," *Christianity Today* 38/4 (April 4, 1994): 15.

42. David F. Wells, *God in the Wasteland: The Reality of Truth in a World of Fading Dreams* (Grand Rapids: Eerdmans, 1994), 53.

With almost prophetic insight, C. S. Lewis wrote several decades ago:

> The ancient man approached God (or even the gods) as the accused person approaches his judge. For the modern man the roles are reversed. He is the judge: God is in the dock. He is quite a kindly judge: if God should have a reasonable defence for being the god who permits war, poverty and disease, he is ready to listen to it. The trial may even end in God's acquittal. But the important thing is that Man is on the Bench and God is in the Dock.[43]

How different is the Bible's outlook. God is praised in heaven because he is the Creator; by his will all things came into being (Rev. 4:11). And it is this truth that establishes our accountability. For we were made neither as an experiment, as toys, as robots, nor as utterly autonomous creatures. We were not only made *by* God, but *for* him. Thus not to acknowledge our dependency upon him and our purpose as established by him is already the deepest anarchy. To love God with heart and soul and mind and strength is, quite understandably, the first and greatest commandment; not to do so is correspondingly the first and greatest delinquency.

It is not just the bare fact that God has made us that establishes our moral accountability to him: after all, he made rocks, too. Rather, it is that he made us as moral, sentient beings; more, he made us in his image. Because other human beings are made in the image of the Maker no less than we, our relations with them, regardless of their station, are also constrained: "He who oppresses the poor shows contempt for their Maker, but whoever is kind to the needy honors God" (Prov. 14:31). In this fallen world order, human beings are "destined to die once, and after that to face judgment" (Heb. 9:27).

4. Our creation in the image of God ensures that human beings are endlessly restless if they suppress or deny this truth; it also makes possible true knowledge of the living God.

The skeptic committed to philosophical materialism must explain the recurring power of religion all over the world. Nor will it do to assign religion to the poor and ignorant. Perhaps the most telling and painful counter-example is the commune set up in Oregon in the seventies by the Bhagwan Shree Rajneesh, who had previously presided over a Buddhist commune in Poona, India. Although his literature spoke of living "together in a non-possessive way, neither possessing things nor possessing persons; people living together, creating together, celebrating together and still allowing each his own space; people creating a certain climate of meditativeness, of love, of living in that climate," the reality turned out to be different. The Bhagwan himself turned

---

43. *God in the Dock: Essays on Theology and Ethics*, ed. Walter Hooper (Grand Rapids: Eerdmans, 1970), 244.

out to be a pleasure-loving tyrant who collected Seiko watches and Rolls Royces. Most members of the commune saw him once a day, when he was driven past them in one of his vehicles. The reports of brutal physical abuse and degrading sexual activity were too extensively documented to ignore. Yet the members were on the whole an astonishingly well-educated group. An independent study established that the average age of the Bhagwan's disciples was just over thirty. Eighty percent came from middle- or upper-class backgrounds. Seventy-five percent had attended college; sixty-six percent had bachelor's degrees; twelve percent had earned doctorates. The president of the commune had been a systems analyst at IBM and Univac; the chief publicist had a Ph.D. from Yale.

The commune testifies to the desperate need for human beings to recognize themselves as more than a conveniently arranged collection of atoms. Why this human drive toward worshiping something beyond self? Christian theology locates the *multiplicity* of religions in the effluent from the Fall, as we shall see; but whence the drive to have religion at all? Rudolf Otto argued that it is easier to imagine that finite and fallible individuals would resist belief in a holy God, than that they would dream him into existence.[44] We should extend the argument farther: it is easier to imagine, on materialist principles, that human beings would accept death calmly, and see neither sense nor purpose in longing for some connection with transcendence, than to imagine, on the same principles, that human beings would be so incurably religious. The biblical answer is that we have been made in God's image, and however much we have abused ourselves as God's image-bearers until this innate capacity is distorted and twisted, at some deep level we hunger for its restoration, while scarcely understanding what that means. And so we multiply religious palliatives and placebos.

Whatever else is entailed by our status as God's image-bearers, Genesis 2 and 3 make clear that the capacity to know God intimately and commune with him lies near the heart of the matter: in the picturesque language of Genesis 3:8, the Lord God arranged intimate meetings with them "in the cool of the day." The shattering effects of the Fall (about which more below) then set the stage for the drama of redemption: God would make himself known to his loved and chosen people. Thus the purpose of the Exodus is that God would walk among his people and be their God (Lev. 26:11–13); the prospect of the new covenant is that God will be yet more intimately related to his people, his law written on their minds and hearts (Jer. 31:33; Ezek. 37:27); and the culmination of all is a new heaven and a new earth in which "God himself will be with them and be their God" (Rev. 21:3).

44. Rudolf Otto, *The Idea of the Holy* (Oxford: Oxford Univ. Press, 1923).

Thus the "image of God" language when it is first introduced is set in a framework of what it means to know God, and personal knowledge of God becomes one of the controlling themes that develop across the Scriptures. Within such a framework, it is entirely reasonable for Lints to write,

> God can be known because his self-revelation is comprehensible to his creatures. Our knowledge of God is always partial, but it is nonetheless authentic because it is inseparably linked to the divine disclosure and the fact that we have been created in the image of God. When God speaks, he can be understood by the divine image-bearers.[45]

5. Creation in the image of God also establishes a responsible perspective on the world of "nature."

In an age of "green" concerns, it is important to get this right. Doubtless the divine mandates to rule over the earth (Gen. 1:28) and to work and take care of the garden (Gen. 2:15) have been used by some as rationale for raw exploitation; doubtless, too, they have been used by others to condemn biblical faith as being exploitative in principle. But the issues are surely more subtle. A faithful reading places human beings in positions of responsibility and authority in God's universe; it assigns to the Fall the selfishness and suppression of God that exploits and rapes with little restraint. The issues of ecology are thus tied not only to who we are as beings made in the image of God, but also to the Fall. It is therefore difficult to generate a responsible theoretical approach to the "natural world" without careful reflection both on our role as divine image-bearers (so that we are not simply identified with the world, without remainder), and of our failures as rebels against the God who made us (so that our ecological failures are properly set against the background of the nature of sin).

What will not do is to adopt the stance of those who insist that human beings are no more and no less significant than other species on planet earth. Any other stance, they declare, is "speciesism," on analogy with racism.[46]

---

45. Richard Lints, *The Fabric of Theology: A Prolegomenon to Evangelical Theology* (Grand Rapids: Eerdmans, 1993), 63–64.

46. James L. Mays, "What Is a Human Being? Reflections on Psalm 8," *Theology Today* 50 (1994): 515, does not seem too harsh when he writes, "The answer, it is said, is to let nature be, to live in harmony and modesty within the sphere of life.... Every living creature is as valuable as humankind. Elephants have their rights. Humankind must learn to live in the great egalitarian democracy of nature. This argument too has its urgent rights against arrogant, greedy despoliation of the environment and raises the inescapable question whether we really want the kind of world we are making. But the solutions proposed are often tinged with the romanticism of urbanites who have no real experience of nature left to itself and who, in their real desires, have no intention of being left to nature."

At some point this concern for "green" becomes a kind of pluralism with respect to species. Just as religious pluralism insists that all religions are of equal value, so species pluralism insists that all species are of equal value. Moreover, just as the former generates a volume of politically correct propaganda, so does the latter. Indeed, the latter can itself become a new religion, an element of "gaia spirituality."[47] Whether this will have the effect, on the long haul, of elevating elephants to the level of human beings, or of lowering human beings to the level of the warthog or the flea, remains to be seen. On the face of it, the biblical account of human beings made in the image of God not only better accounts for the way human beings actually behave, but it better provides for a rationale for sustained responsibility with respect to the world in which God has placed us.

6. Canonically, Adam made in the image of God anticipates the new Adam who is the image of the invisible God.

Once again, something at the beginning points the way to the end. Christ as the second Adam is as much tied up with Christian anticipation of a resurrection body (1 Cor. 15) as with the justification we enjoy because of Christ's faultless obedience, even to the death of the cross (Rom. 5). Although his role as "the image of the invisible God" (Col. 1:15) is in certain respects unique, in other respects it provides a model of what redeemed humanity ought to be with respect to God, and one day will be.

C. Fall

On the subject of the Fall, four things must be said.

1. The significance of the Fall in Genesis 3 is most responsibly and significantly treated by tracing its effect and its interpretation across Scripture.[48]

At the end of the last chapter, I mentioned that one of the entailments of the high view of Scripture I was advocating was that responsible interpretation could not focus so narrowly on a single passage or narrative that it could generate interpretations with some show of plausibility *provided that only that*

---

47. See especially Steve Bishop, "Green Theology and Deep Ecology: New Age or New Creation?" *Themelios* 16/3 (1991): 8–14; Loren Wilkinson, "The Uneasy Conscience of the Human Race: Redeeming the 'Environmental' Movement," in Carson and Woodbridge, *God and Culture*, 301–20; idem, "Gaia Spirituality: A Christian Critique," *Themelios* 18/3 (1993): 4–8; Chris C. Parks, *Caring for the Creation: A Christian Way Forward* (London: Marshall Pickering, 1992).

48. Cf. Daniel P. Fuller, *The Unity of the Bible: Unfolding God's Plan for Humanity* (Grand Rapids: Zondervan, 1992), 175–86.

one text were considered. That text needs to be interpreted within its corpus, in full recognition of the epoch in which it is located within the redemptive historical framework Scripture provides, and in line with Scripture's unfolding of related themes. I indicated that one or two examples would be provided in this chapter. Here is the first; the second concerns the love of God (below).

A surprising number of books and essays have been written during the last decade or so on Genesis 3. There is a rising trend to interpret the narrative "positively" (as Mormons have been doing, in their distinctive fashion, for a long time!).[49] Most of those who take this step in the recent academic literature acknowledge that this is not how later Scriptures, least of all Paul, understand the significance of this chapter.[50]

That, surely, is important. Even the briefest survey of scriptural evidence is startling. The refrain of Genesis 5, "and he died," attests the triumph of the curse sin attracted in Genesis 3. The flood is sent because "[t]he Lord saw how great man's wickedness on earth had become, and that every inclination of the thoughts of his heart was only evil all the time" (Gen. 6:5). But although it offered the opportunity for a new beginning, the first reported event after the flood is Noah's drunkenness—new lapses attesting the continuing power of sin.[51] The opening section of Genesis ends with the account of the tower of Babel, a monument to human hubris.

When one scans forward more rapidly, the different genres of Scripture conspire to paint the same bleak picture of human fallenness. The Pentateuch's picture of Israel says much for God, but little for Israel. There is a relentless drift away from the God who redeemed them from slavery. At

---

49. E.g., Sam Dragga, "Genesis 2–3: A Story of Liberation," *Journal for the Study of the Old Testament* 55 (1992): 3–13; James Barr, *The Garden of Eden and the Hope of Immortality* (London: SCM Press, 1992). Cf. also Howard N. Wallace, *The Eden Narrative*, Harvard Semitic Monographs, vol. 32 (Atlanta: Scholars Press, 1985). These works, of course, are not all the same. Barr, for instance, argues that Genesis 3 is not about the entrance of sin or death into the world, but about a lost opportunity to achieve immortality, a notion which he says is not to be found exclusively in Greek thought. His work is full of suggestive insight, but the fundamental disjunction it offers—not entrance of sin and death but an account of lost opportunity to achieve immortality—is as unhelpful as it is unnecessary.

50. Other essays and books read Genesis 2 and 3 together in order to make a contribution to current literature on feminism. They are more or less evenly divided between those who think the texts are basically "liberating" to women and those who think they are "oppressive." Probably the former is more frequently tied to reconstructions of the putative earlier strata, the latter to the "final form." In true postmodernist fashion, one of the latest contributions argues, "Partly by virtue of its tradition history, Genesis 2–3 is irresolvably multivalent" (David Carr, "The Politics of Textual Subversion: A Diachronic Perspective on the Garden of Eden Story," *Journal of Biblical Literature* 112 [1993]: 594).

51. Cf. Anthony J. Tomasino, "History Repeats Itself: The 'Fall' and Noah's Drunkenness," *Vetus Testamentum* 42 (1992): 128–30.

the very moment of the giving of the law, the people, and Aaron himself, pant after false gods and construct their golden calf. Even after God has administered severe judgment, delaying entrance into the promised land by forty years, the rejuvenated people of God take only a couple of generations to sink into the wretched cycles described in the book of Judges. The closing line of that book, after accounts of nearly anarchic evil, almost provides a definition of sin and evil: "In those days Israel had no king; everyone did as he saw fit" (Judg. 21:25). Yet the period of the kings, though it produced some great leaders and admirable instances of faith and integrity, witnessed the rapid decline of the northern kingdom and the decay of the Davidic dynasty in the south, until the exile was inevitable. And even the greatest leaders—David, a man after God's own heart—can at times sink into miserable debauchery or inexcusable pettiness.

The prophets inveigh against sin constantly, calling the covenant community back to its promises. But they also condemn injustice in other nations, providing a prophetic counterpart to the Wisdom saying, "Righteousness exalts a nation, but sin is a disgrace to any people" (Prov. 14:34). The prophets also provide evidence that God is more interested in transformation of the heart than in merely formal and external conformity to rites and rules. The Wisdom Literature condemns living "under the sun" and embraces a lifestyle lived in "the fear of the Lord." Sin is folly, not only because of the horrible effects it produces in this life, but because it is anarchic rebellion against the God whose providential reign never goes into abeyance (e.g., Prov. 16). The Psalms depict sin in more personal, even psychological, terms. If they insist that sin is first and foremost against God (Ps. 51), they also powerfully depict personal shame, guilt, fear, unbelief, forgiveness, hope. Apocalyptic literature unfolds the cosmic and demonic dimensions of the struggle between good and evil, but never loses sight of the fact that God is on his throne, and will one day bring to an end all that is vile and accursed.

The four canonical Gospels depict sin in many complex ways. It cannot be forgotten that the first chapter of the first Gospel pictures Jesus as the One who comes to save his people from their sins (Matt. 1:21). Some scholars have argued that Matthew knows nothing of a notion of sin that embraces all people, but that assessment is surely naive. Because not everyone is as bad as the worst, it does not follow that some are unequivocally good. Because some actions and attitudes are described as good, it does not follow that those who perform such actions or adopt such attitudes do only what is good. More importantly, Jesus explicitly assumes a bleaker picture: "If you, then, *though you are evil*, know how to give good gifts to your children, how much more will your Father in heaven give good gifts to those who ask him!" (Matt. 7:11, italics added). John's gospel locates the heart of evil in unbelief and disobedience.

The Epistles provide an extraordinarily wide range of portraits of evil. Evil is failure to persevere in the new covenant brought to fulfillment in Jesus Christ (Hebrews). It is the despicable failure to put into practice what profession of faith properly entails (James). It is endless one-upmanship, arrogance, triumphalism (2 Corinthians 10–13). It is a power and a corruption that extends throughout all of Adam's descendants, but which no longer has controlling power over those who are in Christ. It rightly attracts God's wrath, yet this same God has graciously sent his Son as the unique sin-bearer (Romans).[52] Paul can provide an entire catena of texts to demonstrate human depravity (Rom. 3:10–18; see especially Ps. 5:9; 10:7; 14:1–3; 36:1; 53:1–3; 140:3; Eccl. 7:20; Isa. 59:7–8). Across the pages of the New Testament the united testimony of the effects of sin is devastating: we are dead in transgressions (Eph. 2); no one can turn to God unless he is drawn (John 6), and many others.

Obviously a great deal more could be spelled out, but this flavor of the evidence will suffice. If one were then to ask what relation such passages have with traditional categories such as "original sin" and "total depravity," a full account would have to provide the historical contexts in which these expressions arose. Certainly by themselves they can be misunderstood: original sin might suggest, to the uniformed, that sin was present at the very beginning, at creation itself; total depravity might signal that everyone is as evil as he or she can possibly be. Moreover, even when the expressions are properly understood, they do not entirely capture the subtlety, the texture, the variegation of the Bible's depiction of sin, a depiction that is multi-faceted precisely because it comes across in so many genres, with such rich vocabulary and form that it cannot be encapsulated in a doctrinal slogan or two.

But none of this means we can get rid of such expressions, either, or at least the truth they were originally meant to convey. For there is ample biblical evidence, for example, that we are "totally depraved"—that is, that the impact of sin on human beings reaches to every facet of our existence, our will, our bodies, our emotions, our imagination, our reason, our relationships. Doubtless the Bible says much more than this; it certainly does not say less. And though it is true that not all of this is explicitly laid out in Genesis 3, that is the chapter that begins this downward spiral, and many of the fea-

---

52. In the psychological interpretation of Paul's reading of Genesis 3, offered by Hamerton-Kelly, self or desire is played by Adam and Eve, the self's propensity for mimesis is played by the serpent, and the (Mosaic) law by the primal prohibition. It is desperately anemic, precisely because it is divorced from God. See Robert Hamerton-Kelly, "Sacred Violence and Sinful Desire: Paul's Interpretation of Adam's Sin in the Letter to the Romans," in *Studies in Paul and John: The Conversation Continues*, ed. Robert T. Fortna and Beverly R. Gaventa (Nashville: Abingdon, 1990), 35–54.

tures of sin that will be unpacked in sordid detail in later canonical writings are already there depicted *in nuce*.

2. Since the Enlightenment, there has been a sustained history of minimizing and even dismissing sin, or at least sin as described in Scripture.

In 1679, John Locke argued that before civilization, human beings lived in a perfect "State of Nature," completely free and utterly without guilt, simply because the rules and restrictions imposed by complex civilized societies did not exist.[53] There are parallels between this view and the Bible's depiction of Eden, but there are substantial differences. By the middle of the next century, Jean Jacques Rousseau pushed the thesis further. He insisted that society's rules of personal and sexual conduct *generate* the immorality and violence they are ostensibly designed to hold in check. Society's restrictions, competitions, boundaries, notions of property and the like conspire to incite men and women to conduct society, then judges them reprehensible. Before such restrictions, however, men and women ate and drank and indulged in sex on a whim. Disputes and rivalries, still less guilt, could not exist, because the property, territorial boundaries, and status did not exist. Therefore, what was needed was a return to nature. Of course, Rousseau was not writing in a vacuum. There are hints in his work that what he felt was needed in his own society was a powerful dictatorship that would strip the church of its wealth and power, and smash its ability to propagate inhibiting rules.

Rousseau's work fell on attentive ears. By the end of the century, the published reports of James Cook, the British naval captain and explorer, and of the French explorer Louis de Bougainville, on the quality of life in Tahiti, prompted many to wonder if Rousseau's state of innocence had been discovered in Tahiti's hedonistic culture. Bougainville certainly thought so. Thus a few years later when Fletcher Christian, an aristocrat, and the crew of the British naval vessel *Bounty* mutinied against Captain William Bligh, the trial of the captured mutineers caused a sensation around the world. Bligh's mission, in part, was to marry one of his aristocratic sailors into the Tahitian royal family, thus linking England and Tahiti politically, and to take detailed notes on the Tahitian system of government and societal structures, as a first step in colonizing the Polynesian islands. When Fletcher Christian mutinied, was he really revolting against a cruel, barbaric, and perhaps even insane captain who had to be stopped? Or had he seen paradise, and was really by his revolt implicitly condemning the British Empire, and even civilization itself?

---

53. John Locke, *Two Treatises of Government*, revised and introduced by Peter Laslett (New York: New American Library, 1963).

The next century witnessed the rise of socialist philosophy, which had more than a few connections with Rousseau's view of materialism, property, and what came to be called a "bourgeois mentality."[54] The rise of Freud confirmed for many the view that many of humanity's torments arise from frustrations caused by civilization's moral inhibitions. In the twentieth century, Margaret Mead went to Samoa, near Tahiti, largely to prove her doctoral mentor's thesis that culture, not heredity, determines human behavior. Like Cook and Bougainville earlier, Mead observed the hedonism of the island. She also uncovered patterns of behavior not mentioned by the early explorers, including bisexuality, minimal interest in the family, and much more commitment to communal living. Her book *Coming of Age in Samoa*[55] caused a sensation, as she openly advocated the elimination of Western possessiveness, monogamy, and sexual inhibition.

Cultural anthropology had thus struck a mighty blow against sin. It was soon argued that a culture might be illiterate, superstitious, even cannibalistic, and especially sexually permissive, but it could not be considered in any way inferior to our own. Other cultures, e.g., the Mayan, were regularly canvassed for their glory but not for their weaknesses. Mead clearly thought the Samoan culture was in many ways superior.

Whatever the combinations of factors that prompted the changes, our culture now has largely abandoned the extended family, and the nuclear family in some segments of our society is threatened. The divorce rate hovers around fifty percent. When two people decide to cohabit, there is very little consciousness of doing anything wrong.

In short, in many sectors of Western intellectual thought there has been a sustained diminishing of the notion of sin, not least (but by no means exclusively) in the sexual arena.

3. Almost as a counterpoint, an awareness of evil in the world, certainly never dead, has reawakened—though not usually characterized by a biblical worldview that sees sin with respect to God.

None of what I have said so far means there is no understanding of right and wrong at all. People who have inhabited a century with two world wars, endless regional conflicts, numerous brutal totalitarian régimes of both right and left, and mass starvation are hard pressed to conclude there is no such thing as evil. In some circles there has been considerable sensitivity to and

---

54. It must be emphasized, however, that although this was Rousseau's published view, it was certainly not the way he lived. See especially Paul Johnson, *Intellectuals* (New York: Harper & Row, 1988), 1–27.

55. Margaret Mead, *Coming of Age in Samoa: A Psychological Study of Primitive Youth for Western Civilisation*, 4th printing (New York: Wm. Morrow, 1967 [1928]).

even outrage in the face of social injustice, but little reflection on personal integrity, honesty, truth telling, and purity, and even less on how injustice of any sort relates to God.

In any case, evil is back in the news. In the cheap newspapers, exaggerated and entirely false shock serves only to titillate, and "sin" is a snicker-word. But serious news organs are rethinking a little. Lance Morrow's penetrating article in *Time*[56] does not come down very forcefully in defense of a biblical worldview, but at least such a worldview is not dismissed, and the weaknesses of some alternative stances are not ducked.

Careful research has documented cultural elements in Tahiti and Samoa that Mead and her precursors usually ignored or failed to understand.[57] Peter Heywood, an aristocratic crewman on the *Bounty*, assigned to compile the first Tahitian-English dictionary and become the spouse of a Tahitian royal, kept a diary. Not only did he emphasize that only the common people were hedonists, but that virginity was highly prized among the unmarried upper-class women, who were often guarded with chaperones. Not only were there two different classes, there were two races. The taller, lighter-skinned aristocracy suppressed the commoners ruthlessly. Even Bougainville noted the connection between hedonism and servility. Although he thought at first that sexual equality had created an egalitarian society, he soon noted that the class/racial distinction was absolute and tyrannical. Human sacrifices were not uncommon, and were drawn from the lower classes, except in the face of infanticide. One district chief sacrificed all eight of his children. Mead admitted she did not properly study the power systems in Samoa. She did acknowledge that the communal life of the lower class failed to provide much personal motivation or sense of responsibility. Responsible archaeologists and anthropologists have also begun to expose the cruelties, torture, and human sacrifice associated with ancient Mayan civilization.[58]

Although they are very much minority voices, the well-publicized works of Menninger and of Vitz[59] have begun to debunk the debunkers. The frequently expressed wonder that well-educated and civilized Germans could put up with the Nazi horror with little protest elicits this response from Steiner: "To *believe* the reports of Auschwitz smuggled out by the under-

---

56. "Evil," *Time* 137/23 (June 10, 1991): 48–53.

57. E.g., see John Chodes, "Mutiny in Paradise," *Chronicles* (February 1988): 10–13. See especially the careful exposé provided by Douglas Freeman, *Margaret Mead and Samoa: The Making and Unmaking of an Anthropological Myth* (Cambridge: Harvard Univ. Press, 1983).

58. Some of this is now filtering down to the popular media: e.g., Michael D. Lemonick, "Secrets of the Maya," *Time* 142/6 (August 9, 1993): 44–49.

59. Karl Menninger, *Whatever Became of Sin?* (New York: Hawthorn, 1975); Paul C. Vitz, *Psychology as Religion: The Cult of Self-Worship*, 2d ed. (Grand Rapids: Eerdmans, 1994).

ground, to credit the statistical facts before such credence had become irrefutable, was to yield in some measure to the monstrousness of the German intent. Scepticism ('such things cannot happen now, not at this point in man's history, not in a society that has produced Goethe') had its part of humane dignity and self-respect."[60]

None of this puts sin and evil into a biblical framework, but at least at the phenomenological level it is more candid than Rousseauist visions of reality. Harmon puts the German response to the Nazi Holocaust into a broader theological perspective:

> Having imbibed a humanitarian and therapeutic gospel, ordinary German civilians "knew" that basically good human beings could not do such a thing. One of the great ironies of our century must be that in the era in which more "hell on earth" has occurred than ever before, doctrines such as sin, hell, and the wrath of God have lost their meaning in the church on an unprecedented scale.[61]

In fact, one might argue that the *failure* to adopt Scripture's view of humans as being simultaneously important because made in the image of God, and desperately wicked because chronically in rebellion by nature and by choice, has played no small part in the butcheries of the twentieth century. Thus totalitarian forms of Communism argued that revolution would destroy the old structures, and the dictatorship of the proletariat would impose transforming structures on society, until the socialist New Man would appear—stronger, wiser, more generous, more productive. Since in Marxist theory such developments were judged inevitable, executing millions of men and women to assist inevitability on its way was morally inoffensive. The individual person is not worth much anyway: salvation lies in the socialist state. Thus while the Bible says that human beings are of great worth but morally depraved, Communism taught that human beings are of little worth but not intrinsically good or evil: they could be shaped by the state to become good, the socialist New Man, or easily liquidated if they stood in the way.

---

60. George Steiner, *Language and Silence: Essays 1958–1966* (London: Faber & Faber, 1967), 184.

61. Kendall S. Harmon, "Correspondence," *Expository Times* 105 (1994): 247. Perhaps it is worth adding, almost as an aside, that the *scale* of barbaric cruelty has doubtless been greater in this century than in any other, owing not least to the larger numbers of people and to the destructive power of modern arms and of modern "liquidation" techniques. It is not clear to me that modern war is intrinsically more evil than, say, the ravages of Genghis Khan. See the important book by John Keegan, *A History of Warfare* (New York: Knopf, 1993). Keegan is far more nuanced than Margaret Mead's astonishing assertion that war is merely an invention, nothing but learned behavior.

History has now pronounced its verdict. The socialist New Man is a chimera; he did not arrive, and will not arrive. And the dictatorial cliques did something worse: they denied that they too were fallen, and thus provided no checks and balances to stem their own iniquity.

But it is easy to talk about the errors, theological and others, of Communism. It is dangerously easy to succumb to trimphalism as we peer into the casket at its wake. But one must ask how much of Western culture is generating new barbarisms as we, along different axes and with different forms of government, adopt not dissimilar and equally unbiblical perspectives in our own societies: that human beings are not individually all that important, and, above all, that we are not wicked, and not accountable to ourselves, scarcely to the state, and certainly not to God. That is a subject to be briefly pursued in chapters 9 and 10.

4. From a Christian perspective we must get these matters right, for if our understanding of the human dilemma is substantially false, our grasp of the solution will be no less skewed by the contemporary agenda.

It is hard to imagine how this point could be too strongly emphasized.

At the personal level, taking on board what the Bible has to say about the image of God and the Fall and the central themes that flow from these beginnings will enable us to withstand the constant temptation to depreciate sin, or, equally bad, to excoriate only the sins that do not seem to be ours. It is easy to condemn war when I live in peace, to condemn racism when either I am the victim or I view myself as above the fray. But sin is nothing other than doing what God forbids (as in Genesis 3), or failing to do what he commands, and thus is in the first instance an affront to him, a ghastly declaration of independence by a dependent creature against his Creator. To see sin as it is inevitably related to God, and myself as a sinner, destroys self-righteousness, and for the first time discloses to our horrified eyes the sheer odium of such transgression. Sin can never be a snicker-word again. As Wright puts it, "I find it frustrating to read the work of religious pluralists because they tend to be so vague and inadequate on what salvation actually *is*. That seems to be largely because they ignore the Hebrew Bible's insight on the nature and seriousness of sin."[62] In the words of Father Brown:

> You may think a crime horrible because you could never commit it. I think it horrible because I could commit it. You think of it as something like an

---

62. Chris Wright, "The Uniqueness of Christ: An Old Testament Perspective," in *A.D. 2000 and Beyond: A Mission Agenda*, ed. Vinay Samuel and Chris Sugden (Oxford: Regnum Books, 1991), 113.

eruption of Vesuvius; but that would not really be so terrible as this house catching on fire.[63]

In the mainline churches of the Western world, sins have been gone for some time, except those few that our congregations like to hear disapproved. In the biting words of McGinley, describing her creation, the Reverend Doctor Harcourt:

> And in the pulpit eloquently speaks
> On divers matters with both wit and clarity:
> Art, Education, God, the Early Greeks,
> Psychiatry, Saint Paul, true Christian charity,
> Vestry repairs that must shortly begin—
> All things but Sin. He seldom mentions Sin.[64]

With sin gone, what need of a Savior? What need of theology? What need, finally, of a church? As Sweet comments, "With everything gone, there was little reason for people to stay."[65] Of course, it took a while for the churches to empty out; indeed, it is still happening. But the result should have surprised no one.

The more shocking phenomenon is that evangelical churches in many cases are tracking a similar path. Consider how many "conservatives" enjoy Robert Shuller. That brand of "gospel" cannot last. Weigh how many presentations of the gospel have been "eased" by portraying Jesus as the One who fixes marriages, ensures the American dream, cancels loneliness, gives us power, and generally makes us happy. He is portrayed that way primarily because in our efforts to make Jesus appear relevant *we have cast the human dilemma in merely contemporary categories, taking our cues from the perceived needs of our day*. But if we follow Scripture, and understand that the fundamental needs of the race are irrefragably tied to the Fall, we will follow the Bible as it sets out God's gracious solution to that fundamental need; and *then the gospel we preach will be less skewed by the contemporary agenda*. (What this means for our preaching, in practical terms, I will sketch in chapter 12.)

To put the matter bluntly: If you begin with perceived needs, you will always distort the gospel. If you begin with the Bible's definition of our need, relating perceived needs to that central grim reality, you are more likely to retain intact the gospel of God.

---

63. G. K. Chesterton, *The Penguin Complete Father Brown* (Harmondsworth: Penguin Books, 1981), 587.

64. Phyllis McGinley, *Times Three* (New York: Viking, 1961), 134–35.

65. Leonard I. Sweet, "The Modernization of Protestant Religion in America," in *Altered Landscapes: Christianity in America, 1935–1985*, ed. David W. Lotz, Donald W. Shriver, Jr., and John F. Wilson (Grand Rapids: Eerdmans, 1989), 39.

D. God

Three preliminary comments may properly restrict the expectations aroused by this section. *First*, this is no place to embark on a full-orbed doctrine of God. My concern here is to sketch only a few biblical themes and passages that bear on the nature and deeds of God, choosing in particular those that may address some of the questions raised by religious pluralism. *Second*, it is obvious that I might have started this chapter with God, rather than with Creation, the image of God theme, and the impact of the Fall. My reason for this choice is that strictly speaking Genesis 1, though it suggests much about God, is not primarily *about* God; it is about God's act of creation. Better put, it is about God in much the same way that the entire Bible is about God. There is not some key passage that deals with God systematically; rather, God discloses himself in works and words and relationships across the entire canon. The content of what we call "the doctrine of God" must ultimately be based in the total presentation of God in all the Scriptures. Packer's comment is helpful:

> But the status of the doctrine of God as a distillation from what we are told about the doings of God seems rarely to be perceived. Why is that? It is partly (I guess) because in catechisms and courses on systematic theology it is regularly dealt with first, . . . before any of God's acts come up for treatment; partly, too, because so much of it is couched in historic Latinized terms (aseity, omnipotence, omniscience, omnipresence, eternity, immensity, simplicity, transcendence, immanence, infinity, immutability, impassibility, invisibility, spirituality, coequality, coinherence) which do not obviously link up with the statements and speech-style of Scripture; partly, also, because the custom is to expound it as traditional ecclesiastical lore rather than display it as the constant implicate of the Bible's own narrative; and partly, I am sure, because so many have for so long followed Justin, Clement, Augustine, and Thomas in thinking of the foundations of the doctrine as laid by natural theology rather than by biblical exegesis. In truth, however, the doctrine of God stands on exactly the same footing as any other doctrine: it is as biblical teaching, and therefore as God's own testimony to himself, that it is to be received, irrespective of any support that rational argument and traditional status might give it. Though their support could confirm it once Scripture has established it, their support could never establish it in the absence of Scripture confirming it.[66]

So if I focus here on certain strands of the biblical witness, it is not because I find them more interesting than others, or because I think they are

---

66. J. I. Packer, "Theism for Our Time," in *God Who Is Rich in Mercy*, ed. Peter T. O'Brien and David G. Peterson (Grand Rapids: Baker, 1986), 5.

set out in Scripture with special emphasis that other elements lack, but because the handful that I gather are particularly needed to ward off some of the baleful influences of various forms of contemporary religious pluralism.

Third, one of the greatest attributes of God is his love. Certainly frequent appeal to God's love has been made in the name of religious pluralism, not to say universalism. But I shall reserve that topic for the next section.

Several characteristics[67] of God must be considered here.

1. God is transcendent, sovereign, and personal.

By transcendent, I mean that God exists apart from the creation that he made, and thus above space and time. Thus he is not in any way dependent upon his creation; he is self-existing—that is, he draws his own existence only from himself.[68] He is absolute. By sovereign, I mean that his power and rule are so extensive that, whatever the difficulties bound up with notions like "secondary causality," there is nothing whatsoever that takes place apart from his providential reign. By personal, I mean that God is not an impersonal force or power, but a being who interacts with other persons (whom he has made) as a person—with interchange, speech, "personality." That theologians and philosophers have difficulty drawing precise boundaries and definitions for some of these words (e.g., transcendence, person), and that God cannot be a person in *exactly* the same way that human beings are persons (since our personhood is inextricably linked to our finitude) does not diminish the biblical evidence that points in these directions.

Before surveying the evidence, however, it is important to recognize two things: (1) how rarely outside the Bible this combination of attributes is ascribed to God; and (2) *how in the rising press of religious pluralism, this understanding of God is never allowed.*

The transcendent and the personal are separated in most of the world's religions. In animism and polytheism, there are many personal spirits or gods, but none is absolute. Sometimes these religions supplement their gods, as it were, by appealing to fate—an impersonal absolute. Pantheistic religions adopt an absolute, but it is not personal. World religions are sometimes so

---

67. I hesitate to call them "attributes of God," for this expression does not apply equally to all those I discuss. In historical theology, an attribute of God is some characteristic such that without it God would cease to be God. That is true of the characteristics ("attributes") I group under the first entry. The second and third entries, though divine attributes lie behind them, are not themselves attributes in this sense, even though they are extremely important characteristics of God as judged by their repeated appearance from one end of the Bible's plot-line to the other.

68. An older generation of theologians referred to this quality in God as *aseity*—from the Latin *a se* ("from himself").

internally diverse that they fit into more than one of these categories. At one level Hinduism is clearly polytheistic, but much of Hindu outlook is finally pantheistic. Buddhism in its various branches is particularly difficult to label, but at no point does it adopt a vision of God as both absolute and personal. Contemporary science, with a frequent bias toward philosophical materialism, constantly tilts toward the impersonal absolute. In other words, persons are finally explained on an impersonal basis—bouncing molecules, statistically organized motion, chemical reactions in one's brain, and so forth.

Frame writes:

> Absolute personality! A personal absolute! I have not studied every non-Christian religion, and I would not wish to say that only Christianity holds to a personal absolute. There are variants of Hinduism and Buddhism that are sometimes described as "theistic." According to some African animistic religions, there is behind the world of spirits a singular personal being who holds all accountable. But it is certainly the case that the major contender for "absolute-personality theism" in our day is biblical religion.[69]

But my primary point here is that much contemporary religious thought is trying to undo this nexus. Thus in an extended review of a collection of essays that specifically disavows deism ("Deism is not on our agenda, for it cannot be denied that in the whole Bible—or in virtually all of it—God is one who acts, and acts by ruling or controlling"[70]), the editor of *The Expository Times*, C. S. Rodd, concludes, "Does not God today appear very much closer to the God of Deism than to 'the God who acts,' and is there not a need to come to terms with this God and his relation to the Kingdom?"[71] Deism leaves much more room for pluralism than the robust theism of the Bible. In any case, what the Bible says even about so central a subject as God is not in any sense normative for the editor of *The Expository Times*, if contemporary sensibilities prefer an alternative construal.

It is extraordinarily difficult to be clear in one's mind as to just what Rodd and many others who make the same move (at least Rodd is candid!) think

---

69. *Apologetics to the Glory of God*, 38. By "biblical religion" Frame means to include Christianity itself, "together with the Christian heresies. Christian heresies are religions influenced by the Bible, but which deny the central biblical gospel" (38, n.7). Here he includes not only those traditionally labeled heresies (e.g., Gnosticism, Arianism, Sabellianism, Jehovah's Witnesses, Mormonism), "but also the historic rivals of Christianity, namely, Judaism and Islam" (ibid.). I would myself differentiate Judaism, and observe that some of the Christian heresies deny the Christian emphasis on God as both absolute and personal (e.g., Gnosticism, Mormonism).

70. R. S. Barbour, ed., *The Kingdom of God and Human Society* (Edinburgh: T & T Clark, 1993), xi.

71. C. S. Rodd, "Talking Points from Books," *Expository Times* 105 (1994): 259.

they are doing. The difficulty does not arise out of their refusal to accept the Bible's normativity: they are perfectly frank about that. But the overt appeal to think of God in line with what appears acceptable to the contemporary spirit is a strange one—as if God changes with the cultural mood. If this is the approach, how on earth can one avoid domesticating God? Anything each generation does not like, it dismisses as uncivilized, or unenlightened, or unacceptable, and reshapes God to a more pleasing fancy. It soon becomes difficult to see how this differs very much from Kaufman's postmodernist insistence that theology does not describe or expound some being called "God" but is a "construct of the imagination which helps to tie together, unify and interpret the totality of experience."[72] In any case, the result here is a God not clearly personal, and, if absolute, sufficiently remote to be of little threat and of little use.

Another strand in contemporary thought, however, wants to emphasize God's personhood while dismissing his absoluteness. Process theology, in its plethora of forms, argues that God may be personal, but is certainly mutable and changing, himself (or itself) in process.[73] Some who have been traditional evangelicals, notably Clark Pinnock, are currently developing a very similar view of God (though in fairness to Pinnock he sharply distinguishes himself from process theologians by insisting that God created the universe, and that he could, but chooses not to, constrain his creatures).[74] Alternatively, some argue that the notion of a transcendent God is epistemologically unsupportable, and what is left of God is not entirely clear. Thus in a learned volume, Richard Gale argues that certain notions central to the heritage of Christian theism are in fact incoherent, in particular notions of a timeless eternal and therefore immutable God, of a God who is omniscient and omnipotent.

---

72. Gordon D. Kaufman, *An Essay on Theological Method* (Missoula: Scholars Press, 1975), 43.

73. From the substantial literature, one might mention the following representative works: John B. Cobb, Jr., *A Christian Natural Theology: Based on the Thought of Alfred North Whitehead* (Philadelphia: Westminster, 1965); Charles Hartshorne, *A Natural Theology for Our Time* (LaSalle: Open Court, 1967); Schubert M. Ogden, *The Reality of God and Other Essays* (New York: Harper & Row, 1966); Alfred North Whitehead, *Process and Reality: An Essay in Cosmology*, corrected ed., ed. David Ray Griffin and Donald W. Sherburne (New York: Free Press, 1979); Benjamin Reist, *Processive Revelation* (Louisville: Westminster/John Knox, 1992).

74. The various strands of this synthesis come together in a new book by Clark Pinnock, Richard Rice, John Sanders, William Hasker, and David Basinger, *The Openness of God: A Biblical Challenge to the Traditional Understanding of God* (Downers Grove: InterVarsity Press, 1994). I have to say, with regret, that this book is the most consistently inadequate treatment of both Scripture and historical theology dealing with the doctrine of God that I have ever seen from the hands of serious evangelical writers. Cf. the initial reviews in *Christianity Today* 39/1 (January 9, 1995): 30–34.

Worse, such notions, he insist, make God religiously unavailable: God is so totally "other" as to be entirely alien.[75]

Some of these works are learned and complex. There is not space here to address them adequately; in any case, some thoughtful responses have already appeared.[76] My interest here is only to sketch a little of the biblical evidence that supports the traditional Christian insistence that God is both transcendent and personal.[77]

(a) God as Person

The evidence begins in the opening chapters of the Bible. As for God's personhood, in the opening lines he speaks: God is to be thought of as a talking God. He not only talks so as to bring into being that which was not in being and which could not respond to him in a personal fashion, but he talks *with* the personal beings he creates. This is one of the great wonders and glories of the God of the Bible: he enters into relationships with the angels and with the human beings he has made. Nor is this relationship austere, still less mechanical. God is to be thought of as one who loves, who may become angry, who asks questions, gives commands, listens to praise and prayer, responds as he chooses to what other persons present to him. The evidence of this sort is so plentiful it scarcely requires listing. With but few exceptions, the narrative parts of the Bible have plot-lines that are incoherent apart from God's personal activity (and even in a book like Esther the God of the Bible is presupposed). The oracles of the prophets and the words of the psalmists alike find God speaking and listening to speech, betraying emotion, *engaging* with human beings. The Lord Jesus addresses God as his Father.

By far the most remarkable feature to the personhood of God, and one that is unique to Christianity (despite the best efforts of R. Panikkar to find something analogous in Hinduism) is the truth that God is a unity of three persons. Although very great objections have been raised against the doctrine

---

75. Richard M. Gale, *On the Nature and Existence of God* (Cambridge: Cambridge Univ. Press, 1992).

76. See, for instance, on process theology, not only the book by Royce Gruenler, *The Inexhaustible God: Biblical Faith and the Challenge of Process Theism* (Grand Rapids: Baker, 1983), but John S. Feinberg, "Process Theology," *Evangelical Review of Theology* 14 (1990): 291–334. See also Paul Helm, "Gale on God," *Religious Studies* 29 (1993): 245–55, and the rejoinder in the same issue by Gale (257–63). More generally, see Ronald H. Nash, *The Concept of God: An Exploration of Contemporary Difficulties with the Attributes of God* (Grand Rapids: Zondervan, 1983).

77. In another form, I have tried to canvas much of the relevant material elsewhere: see D. A. Carson, *Divine Sovereignty and Human Responsibility* (Grand Rapids: Baker, 1994 [1981]); idem, *How Long, O Lord? Reflections on Suffering and Evil* (Grand Rapids: Baker, 1990), chaps. 11 and 12.

of the Trinity, serious re-articulation of the doctrine has occupied not a few theologians in recent years. Although in particular it is often claimed that the entire construct is the product of patristic thinking too much divorced from the New Testament, the reality is that the relationship between the New Testament documents and the church fathers of the first four centuries is too complex for such swift dismissal.

A fair reading of the New Testament texts (a little of which will be attempted in chapters 6 and 7) finds the historical Jesus effectively claiming deity, and finds the earliest Christians affirming his deity (e.g., Phil. 2) and ascribing to him the worship offered only to God (e.g., Rev. 5). At the same time, though Jesus sometimes links himself in the closest ways with the Father and the Spirit, he is capable of distinguishing himself from them. And the New Testament does not hesitate to link Father, Son, and Holy Spirit into a web of distinctive relationships that together effect our salvation. These data cry out for some sort of explanation or synthesis or understanding. That several New Testament writers explicitly affirm that Jesus is God cannot reasonably be doubted; that they also distinguish Jesus from God cannot reasonably be doubted either.

Are there, then, hints of such a portrait of God in the Old Testament? Hints, certainly; a full-orbed exposition, certainly not. Historically, Christian thinkers have often pointed to the strange plural in Genesis 1:26: "Let us make man in our image." Yet were it not for the New Testament evidence, doubtless most readers would take it as a "royal we." In the light of the New Testament evidence, one pauses a little longer over it. More impressive is the fact that (at the risk of oversimplification) the prophets tend to envisage the coming eschatological hope in one of two ways: either Yahweh himself is coming to save his people, or he is sending his servant David. But in several remarkable passages these two come together. Especially in Isaiah 9:1–7 and Ezekiel 34, Yahweh and "David" are inextricably linked. If one holds that definable typologies also link the Testaments (as I do), then one pauses over the use of Psalm 45:6–7 in Hebrews 1:8–9.[78] Doubtless these and other passages could be explained (or explained away) if one ignores the canonical context; once admit that context, and the links become harder to dismiss. Moreover, in the Old Testament Scriptures various forms of divine agency, or, better put, various agencies operating in God's behalf, are on some occasions identified with God and on other distinguished from him. Several authors have recently argued that one or more of these agencies—Wisdom, the Word

---

78. See especially Murray J. Harris, "The Translation of *Elohim* in Psalm 45:7–8," *Tyndale Bulletin* 35 (1984): 65–89.

of the Lord, the Angel of Yahweh, the Son of Man—became the seedbed in which New Testament Christology flourished.[79]

If then the terminology of three "persons" united in one God is the fruit of post-New Testament reflection, reaching its most powerful early expression in the Cappadocian Fathers, it is not to be rejected simply because neither "Trinity" nor "person" is a New Testament category. The question to ask is this: What is the ablest and most convincing synthesis of the New Testament data on this subject? I do not know of a better one; indeed, that is what most orthodox theologians have decided throughout the history of the church. We shall of course recognize the limits of the language of analogy. We may search for useful parallels: for example, some have compared a person with multiple personalities all appearing serially in the one human being—but then (let us imagine) all three personalities appear in the one human being at the same time. Such analogs may help; they do not really explain. Packer's words are wise:

> But the Trinity is a divine mystery without parallel, and the certainty of its reality does not entail clarity as to what sort of a reality it can be. How then are we to testify to it? Despite all difficulties felt about the unscriptural word "person" we need, as it seems, to continue to use it, not because we fully know what it means to be a divine person in relation to two other divine persons, but because, as Augustine said, the alternative is to say nothing, and, as evangelicals know, only those who conceive the Father, Son, and Spirit as personal on the analogy of our own personhood will ever enter into the "I-thou" relationship of trust in the Father through the Son which is true biblical faith.[80]

The fundamental "I-thou" relationship is in God himself. The more one ponders passages such as John 5:16–30; 14:31 and 17:1–5, the more one sees that all of God's gracious self-disclosure in his Son, all of his purposes in redemption, are bound up with the Father's love for the Son and the Son's love for the Father. The Father's love for the Son results in his securing glory for the Son not less than what properly belongs to God, and the Son's love for the Father results in obedience that brings glory to the Father. God is personal not only in respect to his relations with other persons who are but creatures, but even in respect of his own complex Being.

---

79. E.g., Margaret Barker, *The Great Angel: A Study of Israel's Second God* (Louisville: Westminster/John Knox, 1992); Larry W. Hurtado, *One God, One Lord: Early Christian Devotion and Ancient Jewish Monotheism* (Philadelphia: Fortress Press, 1988); Paul Rainbow, "Monotheism and Christianity in 1 Corinthians 8:4–6" (D.Phil. dissertation, Oxford University, 1987); idem, "Jewish Monotheism as the Matrix for New Testament Christology: A Review Article," *Novum Testamentum* 33 (1991): 78–91; cf. Alan F. Segal, *Two Powers in Heaven: Early Rabbinic Reports About Christianity and Gnosticism* (Leiden: E. J. Brill, 1977).

80. Packer, "Theism for Our Time," 20.

Of the recent books on the Trinity, one of the most thought-provoking is that of Gunton.[81] He argues that the contribution of the Cappadocian Fathers was to understand "person" as "being-in-relation." Thus over against Arianism, Trinitarian theology insisted that being could be shared—a most un-Greek notion. "By insisting ... that God is eternally Son as well as Father, the Nicene theologians introduced a notion of relationality into the being of God: God's being is defined as being in relation."[82] Toward the end of his book, Gunton explores what this might mean in other areas, not least anthropology (what does it mean to be a "person"?) and creation. In each case he pairs "otherness" and "relationality," and the pairing is fruitful. To be a person is not to be an individual nor to be lost in a collective; it is to be both an "other" and in relation with others—that is part of what it means to be made in the image of God. The created order must not be construed in the categories of philosophical materialism, scientific deism, or immanentist pantheism: God is both "other" than the creation, and in crucial relation to it. Gunton's further reflections on freedom are important:

> For there to be freedom, there must be space. In terms of the relation between God and the universe, this entails an ontological otherness between God and the world.... Kierkegaard once observed that the only real alternative to Christianity is pantheism.... Atheism and deistic mechanism are in effect identical with pantheism, for all of them swallow up the many into the one, and so turn the many into mere functions of the one. There is, that is to say, no basis in any such unitary conception of God for freedom because there is in it no space between God and the world. Putting it another way, we can say that the logic of all unitarian thought is immanentist in the sense that it finally brings God and the creation too closely together; either the world is swallowed up in divinity, or its reality is the logical, and so necessitated, outcome of the way God is. By contrast, the doctrine of the Trinity allows for such space because it enables us to conceive the world as other than while yet in relation to God.[83]

---

81. Colin E. Gunton, *The Promise of Trinitarian Theology* (Edinburgh: T & T Clark, 1991).

82. Ibid., 8. I think I would prefer to say that the Cappadocians introduced the category of relationality to the discussion of "person" as applied to God, but by so doing they were truly unpacking elements of truth already present in the New Testament, elements that had not yet been adequately thought through.

83. Ibid., 132. Gunton further develops these insights in his later work, *The One, the Three and the Many* (Cambridge: Cambridge Univ. Press, 1993). For further reflections on "The Implications of the Doctrine of the Trinity for Theology and for Ordinary Life," see appendix B of D. Broughton Knox, *The Everlasting God* (Homebush West: Lancer Books, 1988), 129–46.

Neither the Bible nor the central heritage of the Christian church will allow us to think of God as impersonal (or, with Hick, indefinably neither personal nor impersonal).

(b) God as Transcendent and Sovereign

The evidence that God is to be viewed not only as personal but as transcendent and sovereign is no less striking. If he made the universe, then certainly he does not depend on it; no less certainly, he stands outside of time (at least as we know it), since all our notions of time are dependent on the motions of bodies in the created universe. God alone exists "from all eternity" (Ps. 93:2). He does not depend on human beings: "If I were hungry," God reminds the psalmist Asaph, "I would not tell you, for the world is mine, and all that is in it" (Ps. 50:12). Lest anyone misconstrue this to mean that God needs physical sustenance but not people to provide it, God adds, "Do I eat the flesh of bulls or drink the blood of goats?" (v. 13). Far from it: the proper relationship between human beings and their Maker is clear: "Sacrifice thank offerings to God, fulfill your vows to the Most High, and call upon me in the day of trouble; I will deliver you, and you will honor me" (vv. 14–15). Human dependency is established, even emphasized.

God alone is the "King eternal, immortal, invisible, the only God" to whom are due all "honor and glory for ever and ever" (1 Tim. 1:17). So foundational is this view of God that when Paul addresses the pagan Athenians it is basic to what he tries to get across *even before he makes any mention of Jesus* (Acts 17:24–25). Countless believers have had their vision of God restored by meditating on Isaiah 40–45, where God's transcendence, sovereignty, and personality pulsate through the text.

The texts that depict the range of God's sovereignty are similarly unrestrained. It is so unlimited that the Wisdom Literature insists, "The LORD works out everything for his own ends—even the wicked for a day of disaster" (Prov. 16:4). A man may plan his course, "but the LORD determines his steps" (v. 9). Even apparently "chance" events are under his sway: "The lot is cast into the lap, but its every decision is from the LORD" (v. 33). Nor are human intentions any less exempt: "The king's heart is in the hand of the LORD; he directs it like a watercourse wherever he pleases" (Prov. 21:1). Paul ties soteriological predestination and absolute providence together: believers were chosen in Christ, he writes, "having been predestined according to the plan of him who works out everything in conformity with the purpose of his will, in order that we, who were the first to hope in Christ, might be for the praise of his glory" (Eph. 1:11–12).

Such passages are well known. Less well known, perhaps, are those that depict God's sovereignty over evil. Where this occurs, the writer's aim is never to ascribe evil to God, but to make it clear that even evil cannot escape God's sway. No ontological dualism between good and evil is allowed. Sin and rebellion exist, but no matter how difficult the philosophical questions that are thereby called into being, the sweep of God's sovereignty is not curtailed or qualified. We must face these texts without flinching. The nations of Canaan, with the exception of Gibeon, opposed Joshua and were destroyed. "For it was the LORD himself who hardened their hearts to wage war against Israel, so that he might destroy them totally, exterminating them without mercy, as the LORD had commanded Moses" (Josh. 11:20; cf. the passages leading up to this text, viz., 10:8, 40; 11:15). Thus if the Israelites fought and destroyed the Amorites, it was in reality God doing it (Josh. 24:8; cf. Judg. 1:4, 7; 4:23; 20:35 ["the Lord defeated Benjamin before Israel"]). What we would call the bad blood between Abimelech and the citizens of Shechem is ascribed to an evil spirit sent by God, in order to avenge the savage butchery of the sons of Jerub-Baal (Judg. 9:23–24, 56–57; cf. 1 Samuel 18:10; 19:9; 26:19). Nor is God some merely tribal deity: if Naaman has enjoyed military victory, it is God's doing (2 Kings 5:1), and Nebuchadnezzar and Cyrus are both God's servants (Jer. 25:9; 27:6; 2 Chron. 36:22ff.), whether they are chastening or releasing the covenant people who have rebelled. God himself raises up the Assyrians, handling them as tools (Isa. 10:5ff.); similarly, he raises up the Babylonians (2 Chron. 36:17; Hab. 1:6). If entire cities are razed to the ground, it is because the Lord Almighty has "determined that the people's labor is only fuel for the fire, that the nations exhaust themselves for nothing," since these cities have been established corruptly (Hab. 2:12–13). The breakdown of social order may be a punishment from God himself (Zech. 8:10). An apparently casual circumstance is in reality God's doing (2 Chron. 22:7)—as much so as is revival (2 Chron. 29:36). Nor is it only circumstances and the movements of nations over which God is sovereign: his sovereignty extends even to the minds of the false prophets, even though those false prophets and the people they deceive are held accountable for the deception and for being deceived by it (Ezek. 14:9–10; cf. 2 Sam. 17:14; Ezek. 38:10,16; 1 Chron. 29:10ff.), since God has already disclosed his truth and established his covenant. Nor are such sweeping pictures of God's sovereignty limited to the Old Testament. In the Apocalypse, for example, it is repeatedly made clear that the authority of the dragon and of his beasts is "given" to them. This perspective reaches clearest form in Revelation 17:17: "For God has put it into their hearts to accomplish his purpose by agreeing to give the beast their power to rule, until God's words are fulfilled."

The question, of course, is how to bring together such evidence for the transcendence and sovereignty of God with the equally unquestionable evidence for his personhood, and, what is more, for the evidence of his love and goodness. But we must consider two more characteristics of the biblical presentation of God before reflecting briefly on how to hold these apparently disparate strands together.

2. God is offended.

If Genesis 1 and 2 establish (among other things) human accountability, and Genesis 3 establishes human guilt, the third chapter also introduces us to God's displeasure in response to human rebellion. God's sentence is death.

That is but the beginning of the terrifying biblical portrait of the wrath of God. The flood (Genesis 6–9) all but wipes out the race; the New Testament does not hesitate to warn us that the God who sent that catastrophic judgment has promised one more judgment, a judgment of fire, a judgment of apocalyptic proportions (2 Peter 3).

A very substantial part of the Bible's plot-line turns on God's wrath: when it is meted out, how he forbears to send it quickly, how his covenant people turn from him again and forget the earlier punishment. The entrance of the covenant people into the promised land is delayed for centuries because the iniquity of the people they were to displace was not so grievous that it called for their elimination (Gen. 15:16). When the time does come for them to enter, the Israelites are told that they are given the promised land not because of their righteousness "but on account of the wickedness of these nations. . . . Understand, then, that it is not because of your righteousness that the LORD your God is giving you this good land to possess" (Deut. 9:5–6). When God gives his people the law at Sinai, he repeatedly insists that he is "a jealous God" (e.g., Ex. 20:5). The point is not that God is capricious or selfish; the point, rather, is that he is God, the God of creation, the God who redeemed them from slavery in Egypt (Ex. 20:2): he has the *right* to expect allegiance from his creatures, *especially* his redeemed creatures. To pretend such allegiance did not matter would be a denial of his own deity.

Much of the Old Testament plot-line swings up and down, as the people repent and turn to God, or drift off toward idolatry, infidelity, and debauchery and bring wrath down on their own heads. Much of the message of the prophets is denunciation of sin, whether personal, social, or religious, and warnings of imminent judgment if there is no repentance. If they also foresee a time yet future when God will intervene climactically on behalf of his people, even such intervention is against the backdrop of a people who continually provoke God to his face, who love to embrace spiritual adultery (to use the language of Hosea). The tragic accounts of the judges, the cycles of the kings, the fall of both northern and southern kingdoms, are all part of this mosaic of divine wrath working out in history. God's wrath is so severe at the fall of Jerusalem and the transportation of the people that it was only by the Lord's mercies that they were not consumed (Lam. 3:22). Even when his wrath has not yet fallen on a people, God's purposes to deal with them in judgment and anger may be so fixed that he commands his prophets to cease praying for them (e.g., Jer. 7:16; 14:11; 15:1, 19b; cf. Rev. 22:10–11). And if God is the God whose salvation extends to the whole world, even to the Gentiles (e.g., Isa. 42:1–7), he is also the God who will not give his glory to another, or his praise to idols (42:8); so it is not surprising, conversely, that the prophets inveigh against pagan nations as well as the covenant community, and announce the imminent judgment of God upon them.

Even though God is pictured as the One who yearns for his people and pleads with them to turn (see below), never does this pleading descend into frustrated impotence. The nations may conspire against the Lord and his Anointed, but "[t]he One enthroned in heaven laughs; the Lord scoffs at them. Then he rebukes them in his anger and terrifies them in his wrath" (Ps. 2:4–5). From one perspective, the person or nation that defies God is nothing but a joke.

Although many have tried to contrast the "gentle Jesus, meek and mild" with the God of the Old Testament, the naked reality is that no one in the Bible is reported to talk as much about hell as Jesus. Yes, he weeps over Jerusalem, but his compassion does not prevent him from uttering the woes of Matthew 23. Peter's sermon on the day of Pentecost is an invitation to flee the corruption of the day (Acts 2:40): the "fleeing" is appropriate terminology precisely because, in line with the inherited theology of the Old Testament prophets, that corruption will surely bring judgment. Paul can describe the gospel he preaches as that which saves men and women from the coming wrath (1 Thess. 1:10). No New Testament writer has provided a more profound, terrifying, and yet strangely compassionate account of the wrath of God than Paul in Romans 1:18–3:20. And the last book of the Bible not only depicts, in apocalyptic imagery, horrific sequences of judgments, but speaks of "the wine of God's fury, which has been poured full strength into the cup of his wrath"; those who worship the beast "will be tormented with burning sulfur in the presence of the holy angels and of the Lamb. And the smoke of their torment rises for ever and ever" (Rev. 14:10–11).

The point that cannot be escaped is that God's wrath is not some minor and easily dismissed peripheral element to the Bible's plot-line. Theologically, God's wrath is not inseparable from what it means to be God. Rather, his wrath is a function of his holiness as he confronts sin. But insofar as holiness is an attribute of God, and sin is the endemic condition of this world, this side of the Fall divine wrath cannot be ignored or evaded. It is not going too far to say that the Bible would not have a plot-line at all if there were no wrath. From the perspective of the religious pluralist, this stance is unpardonable;

from the perspective of the biblical story-line, the pluralist's position is equivalent to idolatry, for it allows other gods to be raised to the status of the one true God, the Maker of heaven and earth, the final Judge, the universe's Sovereign, the One to whom we all, finally, must give an account (Heb. 4:13).

3. God provides for his own.

The account of creation already illustrates this truth. Human beings are not the inconsequential but fortuitous survival specimens of a savage struggle upward. Not only have we been made in the image of God, but initially we were placed in paradisal surroundings. God's generous provision for his image-bearers began with their creation.

Even after sin savages the relationship between human beings and their Maker, it is God who clothes them (Gen. 3:21)—the first instance of his peculiar care for and "covering" of his people. At issue is not only God's care displayed in providential rule over all of God's creation, but that special care that calls an Abraham (Genesis 12) and then watches over his ways, tests him and refines him (chap. 22), provides for the family in time of necessity (chaps. 37–50)—all in preparation of a new people, the children of Israel, from whom Messiah springs, and the means by which all peoples on earth will be blessed (Gen. 12:3). Such provision is displayed not only in the Exodus, but in the care of the people, despite their grumbling, before they enter the promised land; not only in the preparation of the tabernacle and its detailed stipulations but also in the related sacrificial system and priesthood by which the covenant people could continue their relation with God; not only in raising up the Davidic dynasty, with its promise of a mighty Redeemer to come, but in preserving it from obliteration in its darkest hours; not only in the return from exile, but in prophetic words that simultaneously call the people of God to renewed commitment to the covenant and anticipate the dawning of a new covenant (Jer. 31; Ezek. 36).

Here is the personal/transcendent God at work. But such work is so much the demonstration of God's love that further reflection can await the next section.

Concluding Reflections:

It is appropriate at this juncture to include a few reflections on questions that may have been stirred up by some part or other of this section, but which are best considered now that the pieces have been brought together.

(1) Aren't the strands in this interwoven portrait of God mutually incompatible? Does not logic force us to one of the proffered reductionisms—either an impersonal pantheistic God, or a finite personal God, whether that of process theology or that of Clark Pinnock?

If they are incompatible, it is important to see some of the things that are at stake. The first, of course, is that the Bible's witness to what God is like must be abandoned as a reliable revelation. As soon as one is permitted to pick and choose from its major emphases, sooner or later one must ask for the criterion on which the choice is made, or even why one should pick *any* of the major emphases. Alternatively, one may deploy hermeneutical heavy-handedness: constitute an interpretive grid out of the preferred part of the evidence, and use the grid to domesticate the rest of the evidence, the bits we don't like.[84]

There is no need for such drastic measures. Certainly there are great mysteries connected with the being of God, but that should not be surprising to any except those who want to be God themselves. Philosophically, compatibilism has long argued that there is nothing intrinsically contradictory about the notion of a transcendent, sovereign, personal God who interacts with finite, fallen, responsible, and accountable creatures. Certainly there are many biblical passages in which competing strands from this portrait of God come together with no self-consciousness of any impropriety: God's transcendent sovereignty never functions to eliminate or marginalize human accountability, or to transform God's image-bearers to the status of a robot, while human accountability and responsibility never make God absolutely contingent (e.g., Gen. 50:19–20; Isa. 10:5–19; John 6:35–40, 45–46; Acts 4:27–28; Rom. 9–10; Phil. 2:12–13). That there are extremely difficult philosophical questions associated with this outlook cannot be denied, but the solution cannot be to reduce the difficulty by adopting positions that outlaw half the evidence. It will not do, for example, to argue that God cannot know the future where the future brings decisions of free individuals. Not only do I not know exactly how "future" looks to a transcendent God (though at least some of the possibilities can be listed and explored),[85] the "free individuals" are never so free as to make God absolutely contingent. In any case, the Bible dares to speak not only of God's knowledge of the future, but even of the future of our thoughts and choices (remember Proverbs!). The Psalmist understood this: "Before a word is on my tongue you know it completely, O LORD. . . . Such knowledge is too wonderful for me, too lofty for me to attain" (Ps. 139:4–6). The Bible even assumes God has "middle knowledge," i.e., that he knows not

---

84. It is very difficult to avoid the conclusion that this is what is done by Pinnock and some of his colleagues in Clark H. Pinnock, ed., *A Case for Arminianism: The Grace of God, the Will of Man* (Grand Rapids: Zondervan, 1989). See especially John Piper, *The Pleasures of God: Meditations on God's Delight in Being God* (Portland: Multnomah Press, 1991), passim, esp. 70–74.

85. See especially the important book by Paul Helm, *Eternal God: A Study of God Without Time* (Oxford: Clarendon Press, 1988).

only what is, from our perspective, past, present, and future, but also what might have been under different circumstances (Matt. 11:20–24).

(2) But are there not *specific* difficulties that cannot be swept away by these vague generalities? What about the forty or so passages that speak of God "relenting" or changing his mind (e.g., Ex. 32:12; Job 6:29; Ps. 90:13)? What about the notion of the impassibility of God? If God is impassible, how can the Bible speak of his love and his anger in ways that are clearly related to his interactions with and responses to other persons?

Elsewhere I have tried to think through what the Bible says about God's relenting.[86] As for God's impassibility, a number of theologians have studied that subject a great deal during the past half-century or so. Certainly the influence of Greek thought has sometimes treated God as completely emotionless, dismissing the countless instances of the ascription of emotion to God in the Bible as cases of anthropopathy. I cannot agree. Where theology has taken that turn it needs to be corrected by the text of Scripture. The profound problem with that stance is that it runs the risk of depersonalizing God;[87] the problem with abandoning every conceivable understanding of impassibility is that it runs the risk of de-absolutizing him. I am inclined to be sympathetic to some such articulation of the doctrine as this:

> God is impassible, which means that no one can inflict suffering, pain, or any sort of distress upon him. Insofar as God enters into experience of that kind, it is by empathy for his creatures and according to his own deliberate decision, not as his creatures' victim. The words "of that kind" are important, for this impassibility has never been taken by Christian mainstreamers to mean that God is a stranger to joy and delight; it has, rather, been construed as an assertion of the permanence of God's joy, which no pain clouds. How the formula applies to the atoning sufferings of the incarnate Son is a special and open question, on which different views have been, and are, maintained. . . . The historical answer [to the question of what impassibility means] is: not impassivity, unconcern, and impersonal detachment in face of the creation; not insensitivity and indifference to the distresses of a fallen world; not inability or unwillingness to empathize with human pain and grief; but simply that God's experiences do not come upon him as ours come upon us, for his are foreknown, willed and chosen by himself, and are not involuntary surprises forced on him from outside, apart from his own decision, in the way that ours regularly are. In other words, he is never in reality the victim whom man makes to suffer: even the Son on his cross, where "a victim led, thy blood was shed," was suffering by his and the

---

86. Carson, *How Long, O Lord?* chaps.11–12. It is helpful to reflect on passages such as Isaiah 57:6; Jeremiah 4:28; 18:8; 26; etc.

87. A healthy antidote would include a careful reading of Piper, *The Pleasures of God.*

Father's conscious foreknowledge and choice, and those who made him suffer, however free and guilty their action, were real if unwitting tools of divine wisdom and agents of the divine plan (cf. Acts 2:23; 1 Pet 1:20).[88]

(3) Does not the portrait of God you have painted sanction genocide?

In this century of genocide, the question must be fairly faced. I have no formulaic response, but the following reflections may point a way forward. *First*, as awkward as it may appear, one cannot abstract the slaughter of the Canaanite tribes from the larger question of the wrath of God, of God's response to multiplying sin. If one excises large swaths of the Pentateuch and of Joshua, should one then excise all that Jesus says about hell, much of the Apocalypse, and so forth? Our first duty, surely, is to listen, and try to understand. *Second*, God's wrath, including that displayed in the extermination of Canaanite tribes, is tied, as we have seen, to the entire biblical plot-line. It is of a piece with the flood, the Exile, the destruction of Jerusalem, and of hell itself; conversely, it is tied as the dark side, the side of sin and hate and war and destruction, to the story of our redemption, stemming from the love of God intervening on our behalf, when he had no obligation to do so. It is tied to the importance God places on the distinctive holiness of his covenant people. I doubt that it is possible, let alone advisable, to try to disentangle this strand from the whole, without the whole unraveling. Chapters that announce God's love for the world insist on his wrath upon the disobedient (e.g., John 3:16, 36). In the biblical plot-line, the former has little sense or meaning without the latter. *Third*, the question is surely related to "epochal" or "salvation history" questions. The precise way that the covenant community is to interact with surrounding cultures is shaped in no small part by its location in the stream of redemptive history. The locus of the people of God was at that point a fledgling nation. That cannot be said of the church. The Crusades, however well motivated, were unqualifiedly wrong. But I am not sure this means we are following a "higher" morality. It means that just as the old covenant provided pictures of sacrifice—tens of thousands of slaughtered animals—which the church does not recapitulate today because it believes their antitype, the slaughtered lamb of God (Revelation 5) has brought such sacrifices to an end (Hebrews 9–10), so it provides pictures of God's wrath. The final wrath is yet to be poured out—not in Christians bearing arms to

---

88. Packer, "Theism for Our Time," 7–8, 16–17. He goes on to cite G. L. Prestige, *God in Patristic Thought* (London: SPCK, 1952), 7: "It is clear that impassibility [in Patristic thought] means not that God is inactive or uninterested, not that he surveys existence with Epicurean impassivity from the shelter of a metaphysical insulation, but that His will is determined from within instead of being swayed from without. It safeguards the truth that the impulse alike in providential order and in redemption and sanctification comes from the will of God."

slaughter neighbors, but in the apocalyptic end. So whereas Christians must wholly condemn genocide, as that word has any meaning today, we must not turn away from the theme of judgment, but tremble instead, remembering that judgment begins with the family of God (1 Peter 4:17).

(4) What bearing does this survey have on the question of religious pluralism?

I have repeatedly hinted at the point; it is time to state it explicitly. Religious pluralism of the sort that insists all religions are of equivalent value (the third sense of religious pluralism, as defined in chapter 1), where it does not resort to postmodern epistemology, inevitably attempts to latch on to a few elements in each religion as pointers either to a common religious thread in all religions, or to a greater (even if ineffable) Reality behind all religions. A certain plausibility for such a stance is achieved when themes are looked at piecemeal. But in this chapter and the next I am trying to show that when the Bible (which must be the Christian's foundation) is examined as a whole, and its themes and plot-line traced out—not least those themes that religious pluralists tend to espouse—the position of religious pluralism is from a Christian perspective utterly untenable. One may be a Christian, or one may be a religious pluralist in the third sense; one cannot be both. From the pluralist's perspective, the Christian must appear a bigot, unless "Christian" is redefined so that it has no necessary connection with Scripture; from the Christian's perspective, the religious pluralist, however sincere, is both misguided and an idolater.

E. The Love of God

If this book aimed at being a comprehensive theology, or a balanced treatment of all the major biblical themes, then a great deal of space would be devoted to this grandest of subjects. But because my purpose in this book is to think through how Christians should responsibly confront contemporary pluralism, my sights are a good deal lower. I shall, in any case, say a little more about it in the next chapter.

Part of what must be said in this section is what the love of God is not. Put more positively, we must see that what the Bible says about the love of God is much richer and more complex than the reductionistic appeal to God's love sometimes found in pluralist literature and in popular polemic (e.g., "I can't believe in a God who gets angry; I believe in a God of love").

I shall venture five points.

First, by way of clearing the air, it is not clear to me that a God who loves everyone and everything in exactly the same way—boa constrictors, Mother Teresa, Hitler, fleas, Michael the archangel, Augustine, the aurora borealis, Genghis Khan—loves anyone or anything at all. Or if he does, this singularly undiscriminating love is remarkably amoral. This sounds rather more like blind, impersonal benevolence. In fact, I am not even sure what "benevolence" might mean in such a sentence.

Second, what the Bible says about the love of God cannot adequately be studied by focusing merely on one or two word groups, or even on several (e.g., in addition to the "love" words, such words as *ḥesed* ["covenantal love/grace"][89] or χάρις ["grace"]. It turns no less on the entire biblical story-line. The God who made us and could have written us off, chose instead to pursue rebellious men and women across a long and tortuous history—men and women who often show they are fickle and prefer to think of themselves as the center of all things, and who find idols more congenial than knowledge of the living God. God's love is demonstrated in his dealings with Adam and Eve after the Fall, in his call and protection of Abraham, in his preservation of this fledgling people of God in a world of polytheism, dubious security, moral failure, and even famine. The establishment of the covenant with Israel is the result of God's invasive, intervening love; the gift of his Son is the supreme result of that same love.

Third, when John tells us that "God is love" (1 John 4:8, 16), he probably means more than "God is loving." It is the Johannine corpus, after all, that most clearly provides the pieces that result in the doctrine of the Trinity. It is John's gospel that insists the Father loves the Son, and the Son loves the Father (John 3:35; 5:20; 14:31). Long reflection on the relation between Father and Son, between Son and Spirit, between Father and Spirit, have in God's grace taught John a lesson: God is love. In other words, God is not only *capable* of loving, so that once something was actually created he had the capacity to love it, but that love is so much a part of his nature that it is rightly referred to as an attribute of God: without it, God would not be God. Of course, that is a meaningful confession only if God could love before there was anything external to himself to love (unless love is so drastically redefined as to include infinite self-absorption). But in all eternity the Father loved the Son; the Son loved the Father. God is one, but he is not solitary; it is of the essence of his triune nature that he has always been a God of love.

Fourth, the Bible speaks of God's love or of his care in several quite distinguishable ways. Failure to perceive these distinctions issues in sentimental generalities quite at variance with what the texts actually say. Apart from the affirmation of God's love for his Son, there are at least four (though the breakdown could be further extended):

---

89. Over against those who have argued that this word refers to relationships of obligation, see Francis I. Andersen, "Yahweh, the Kind and Sensitive God," in O'Brien and Peterson, *God Who Is Rich in Mercy*, 41–88.

(1) God loves the world, in the sense that he providentially rules over it with mercy, alike over those who hunger for him and over those who do not. He "causes his sun to rise on the evil and the good, and sends rain on the righteous and the unrighteous" (Matt. 5:45). God's profuse provision in the Garden is the first demonstration of God's love in this sense.

(2) God loves the world, with specifically salvific intent: "that whoever believes in him shall not perish but have eternal life" (John 3:16). "World" in John usually refers to the fallen moral order in rebellion against God. Thus God's love for the world is praiseworthy, not because the world is so big, but because the world is so bad. God does not love the world because it is attractive, but because he is love. If elsewhere believers are forbidden to love the world (1 John 2:15–17), what is in view is the selfish love of participation in all that is merely temporal and all that opposes God. By contrast, God's love for the world is self-sacrificial and costly.

This is of a piece with God's yearning stance toward rebels. So we read, "As surely as I live, . . . I take no pleasure in the death of the wicked, but rather that they turn from their ways and live. Turn! Turn from your evil ways! Why will you die, O house of Israel?" (Ezek. 33:11; cf. Jer. 3:12–13). This element of the story-line runs from Genesis to Revelation. The last chapter of the Bible includes the words, "The Spirit and the bride say, 'Come!' And let him who hears say, 'Come!' Whoever is thirsty, let him come; and whoever wishes, let him take the free gift of the water of life" (Rev. 22:17).

(3) God peculiarly loves his elect. "Because he loved your forefathers and chose their descendants after them," the Israelites are told, "he brought you out of Egypt by his Presence and his great strength" (Deut. 4:37). The people are told, "The LORD did not set his affection on you and choose you because you were more numerous than other peoples, for you were the fewest of all peoples. But it was because the LORD loved you and kept the oath he swore to your forefathers that he brought you out with a mighty hand and redeemed you from the land of slavery, from the power of Pharaoh king of Egypt. Know therefore that the LORD your God is God" (Deut. 7:7–9; cf. 10:14–15). At a time of national discouragement and moral slump, when the people frankly doubt God's special love for them as the covenant community, God addresses them through Malachi: "'I have loved you,' says the LORD. But you ask, 'How have you loved us?' 'Was not Esau Jacob's brother?' the LORD says. 'Yet I have loved Jacob, but Esau I have hated, and I have turned his mountains into a wasteland and left his inheritance to the desert jackals'" (Mal. 1:2–3; cf. Rom. 9:10–13). In other words, the second generation after the dramatic return from exile was sinking into callousness, apathy, broken promises, formality in worship, corrupt clergy—all of which issues Malachi addresses; but before he does so, he begins by calling on the people to trust God's special

covenant love for them. In the New Testament, Jesus lays down his life for his sheep (John 10); "Christ loved the church, and gave himself for up for her" (Eph. 5:25). Those God "foreknew" (i.e., foreloved), he predestined, called, justified, glorified (Rom. 8:29–30).

This strong strand in the Bible's story-line also begins in Genesis, in God's call of Abraham, in his establishing Isaac over Ishmael, and Jacob over Esau. It issues in the formation of the Israelite nation, and in the establishment of the church.

(4) Several passages speak of the love of God for his own people conditional on their obedience. Thus Jude exhorts, "Keep yourselves in God's love" (Jude 21). The unique relationship between the Father and the Son has never been tarnished because the Son's obedience has been perfect (John 8:29); he has obeyed his Father's commands and remained in his love (John 15:10). But that is to be our model as well: "If you obey my commands, you will remain in my love" (John 15:10). The general principle is foundational: "The LORD detests the way of the wicked but he loves those who pursue righteousness" (Prov. 15:9).

All of these ways of talking about the love of God could be expanded and tied together into the tapestry that constitutes the biblical plot-line. Granted that God is a person, it is surely unsurprising that there are different and complex ways of describing his love toward other persons who sustain varied and complicated relations with him.

Fifth, the theme of the love of God, as precious as it is, is not all that the Bible says about God, as we have seen. It is as irresponsible to talk about the love of God without considering the holiness, transcendence, and even the wrath of God as it would be, for example, to talk about his transcendence and omit consideration of his personhood, or to focus on his wrath without listening attentively to what the Bible has to say about his love.

In the light of these five points, to fall upon the theme of the love of God and base upon it some hope of universalism or even pluralism is utterly without defense. It does not consider fairly the various ways the Bible talks about the love of God, and examine them in their context; it does not attempt to think through how the Bible's emphasis on the love of God is tied to emphases on other divine attributes; if it reflects on love among the persons of the Trinity, it hesitates before embracing what the Bible says about the distinctive roles of Father, Son, and Holy Spirit and the uniqueness of this one God.

Moreover, these five points, together with the picture of God we have been building up from the biblical plot-line, disallow notions of God in which both human importance and divine inadequacy are established by God's love for us. For example, Brümmer writes, "If ... God *desires* our love, it would seem to follow that he also *needs* our love for this desire to be fulfilled.... Only by needing us can God bestow value on us and upon our love for him. If God does not need us, we become infinitely superfluous."[90] One can reach such unsatisfactory conclusions only by drawing inferences from selective scraps of the biblical evidence, never by paying attention to the whole drama.

F. Some Other Major Movements in the History of Redemption

So far I have done little more than pick up some of the narrative threads from the early chapters of Genesis, and run with them a little into the wealth of the canon. A full-orbed theology constructed to trace the patterns of redemptive history would have to treat at length a number of important themes (e.g., election, covenant, sacrificial system) and events (e.g., the call of Abraham, the Exodus, the onset of the monarchy).[91] Some critics minimize the significance of this history on the ground that particular history cannot possibly be universally authoritative. "The ecclesial community, moreover" write Farley and Hodgson, "is nonethnic, universal, and culturally pluralistic, so that purely ethnic, provincial, and culturally relative elements of scripture cannot be authoritative."[92] But the postmodernist commitments that drive these authors include the dogmatic insistence that the authority of Scripture derives not from its content, but from its power to excite new occurrences of "revelation"—i.e., to stir up the imagination to spark new understandings of openness to others. These "understandings" cannot be directly rendered into theological concepts—though apparently their postmodern approach can, or they could not have written their article.

Approached canonically, the Old Testament texts do not demand that modern believers adopt every cultural form found in its pages in fear of jeopardizing the authority of the text. One must instead ask the "epochal" or salvation-historical question: How do these texts and the events they relate contribute to the plot-line of the Scriptures? Where do they end up? To what do they point? I can do no more than prime the pump a little here, to show the kinds of turning points in the Old Testament that could be developed, with a special eye to responding to the pressures of pluralism. Some of these turning points have already been briefly mentioned in connection with other themes.

---

90. Vincent Brümmer, *The Model of Love* (Cambridge: Cambridge Univ. Press, 1993), 236, 242.

91. A start is made by Fuller, *The Unity of the Bible*, 251–402.

92. Edward Farley and Peter C. Hodgson, "Scripture and Tradition," in *Christian Theology: An Introduction to Its Traditions and Tasks*, 2d ed., ed. Peter C. Hodgson and Robert H. King (Philadelphia: Fortress Press, 1985), 75.

The call of Abraham and the ensuing narratives bring to sharp focus at least seven important themes that are taken up later in the Bible. (1) *Election*: God takes the initiative and chooses Abraham, a point to which later writers constantly return. This is precursor to a long list of "elections": the calling of the nation as such, the calling of individual prophets, Jesus' choice of the apostles (one of them a devil, John 6:70), the election of the people of God for salvation and for service. In Paul's emphasis, such divine initiative preserves the ultimacy of grace (Romans 9). (2) *Covenant*: Modeled on ancient near eastern treaties, the biblical covenants establish one of the frameworks that hold the Bible together, and the Abrahamic covenant (Genesis 15) is the first to deploy covenantal language and symbolism. Though the relationships among the biblical covenants are disputed, clearly the move from Abraham to the Sinai covenant ultimately issues in promise of a "new covenant" (Jeremiah 31; Ezekiel 36) whose advent is bound up with Jesus' death (Luke 22:20; 1 Cor. 11:23–26). (3) *Faith and obedience*: "Abram believed the LORD, and he credited it to him as righteousness" (Gen. 15:6). This verse assumes enormous importance in the New Testament.[93] It is used by Paul to demonstrate that faith and faith alone is what pleases God and is associated with God's pronouncement that a person is righteous (Galatians 3). It is set by James within the context of the Abrahamic narrative to show that genuine faith is never wanting in obedience, but inevitably issues in it (James 2). It is used in the epistle to the Hebrews to commend the persevering nature of genuine faith (Hebrews 11). (4) *Nation and land*: This is the beginning of the Hebrew nation, the first commitment to the land. Henceforth God's exclusive locus for mediating his salvation to the world is Israel—just as under the terms of the new covenant God's exclusive locus for mediating his salvation to the world is Jesus Christ. The detailed connections between the two are inevitably complex and disputed, but this main line is much emphasized.[94] (5) *Gentiles*: It is remarkable that the very first point where Abraham is introduced, where the fount of the Israelite nation is established, there too the other peoples are explicitly brought into view: "and all peoples on earth will be blessed through you" (Gen. 12:3), God declares to Abraham. Thus means and end are both in view from the beginning. If the focus for the next two millennia is on the Israelites, and if for much of that time the dominant covenant is that which is established at Sinai, there is no lack of hints and reminders, even within the Old Testament, of the larger perspective (e.g., Ps.

---

93. See Richard N. Longenecker, "The 'Faith of Abraham' Theme in Paul, James and Hebrews: A Study in the Circumstantial Nature of New Testament Teaching," *Journal of the Evangelical Theological Society* 20 (1917): 203–12.

94. See Wright, "The Uniqueness of Christ: An Old Testament Perspective."

72:17; Isa. 40ff.; Jer. 4:2). In that day, the "LORD Almighty will bless them, saying, 'Blessed be Egypt my people, Assyria my handiwork, and Israel my inheritance'" (Isa. 19:25). It is too small a thing for God's servant to restore only the fortunes of Israel: God makes him "a light for the Gentiles" to bring God's salvation "to the ends of the earth" (Isa. 49:6). Both Paul (Gal. 3:8) and Peter (in Luke's witness, Acts 3:25) see in the gospel of Jesus Christ the fulfillment of the promise to Abraham.[95] (6) *Family order and social justice*: In another passage recording God's dealings with Abraham, not only are all the peoples reintroduced, but also the beginnings of explicit concerns for family and social justice. As God contemplates the destruction of Sodom, he asks himself rhetorically, "Shall I hide from Abraham what I am about to do? Abraham will surely become a great and powerful nation, and all nations on earth will be blessed through him. For I have chosen him, so that he will direct his children and his household after him to keep the way of the LORD by doing what is right and just, so that the LORD will bring about for Abraham what he has promised him" (Gen. 18:17–19). From these small beginnings swell not only the social legislation of the Mosaic Law, but also the constant prophetic appeals for justice, integrity, compassion. For the covenant people of God, these are never ends in themselves, to be achieved and valued for their intrinsic worth apart from allegiance to the God of the covenant. But it is abundantly clear that this relatively minor point in the life of Abraham, accompanied by the total destruction of Sodom, sets the stage for the biblical concerns for family order and social justice, for a God who is never impressed by religious cant but who cries, "I hate, I despise your religious feasts; I cannot stand your assemblies. Even though you bring me burnt offerings and grain offerings, I will not accept them. Though you bring choice fellowship offerings, I will have no regard for them. Away with the noise of your songs! I will not listen to the music of your harps. But let justice roll on like a river, righteousness like a never-failing stream!" (Amos 5:21–24).[96] (7)

---

95. In this connection, it appears that Jean-Marc Heimerdinger, "The God of Abraham," *Vox Evangelica* 22 (1992): 41–55, has overstated his thesis. He argues that, unlike the Canaanite gods of the period—who were nature gods, war gods, tribal gods—God presents himself to Abraham as his *personal* God. Heimerdinger makes his positive point, but not his negative ones. Genesis 14:22 has God still sovereign over nature; the account of the defeat of the kings may not be an "epic work," but not only is God a personal protector and shield to Abraham (Gen. 15:1), but also his help in the battle is acknowledged in principle by the tithe paid to the priest of God Most High (Gen. 14:18–20). A little too much of Heimerdinger's position turns on arguments from silence.

96. For an excellent survey of some of the theological issues at stake in Old Testament concerns for justice, see some of the works of Christopher J. H. Wright in the bibliography, not least his "Ethical Decisions in the Old Testament," *European Journal of Theology* 1 (1992): 128–40.

Individual incidents: The most noteworthy, perhaps, are four, each of which is picked up in the New Testament: the tithes to Melchizedek (Genesis 14), the establishment of the covenant of circumcision (Genesis 17), the clear distinction between Isaac and Ishmael (Genesis 21), and the testing of Abraham, in which not only does Abraham's faith prove obedient, but God provides a substitute sacrifice (Genesis 22).

My interest in sketching these elements is to indicate, however briefly, how they are intertwined in the Bible's plot-line. That plot-line is coherent and progressively depicts a certain kind of God and a certain analysis of the human predicament and what is needed, and what God has done to repair it. It is utterly arbitrary (that is the kindest conclusion) to pick and choose some themes and ignore others—for example, to pick up the important emphasis on social justice but not on election, covenant, sacrifice, faith, and allegiance to and knowledge of God.

Limitations of space forbid me to attempt something similar with the Exodus narrative and the giving of the law; with the significance of the tabernacle, sacrifical system, and priestly roles; with the onset of the kingdom and the establishment of the Davidic dynasty; with the prophetic movement and its changing shape across the centuries. But the lessons would be very similar.

G. Other Readings of the Old Testament

Much of the cogency of the argument in this chapter turns on the reading of the Old Testament, and its thrusts toward the New Testament, that I have provided. Not surprisingly, others read the texts rather differently. Thorough interaction with all the major alternatives would treble or quadruple the length of this chapter, and, however indulgent the publisher may be, there are limits. So I shall briefly sketch four categories of alternative readings, and indicate the kind of direction I would take to respond to them had I more space. At this juncture I am explicitly eliminating discussion of the salvation of certain Old Testament individuals outside the covenant community, and its bearing on the salvation of individuals today who are without knowledge of Jesus Christ, as I shall take up that discussion in the next chapter.

1. Hick

Among biblical scholars, Hick's approach to the rise of religion, including the rise of religion reflected in the Old Testament documents, is a nonstarter, because it does not attempt exegesis of the texts in any sense. But because of his significant influence among those who are interested in religious pluralism, some mention should be made of his views.

In his wide-ranging Gifford Lectures,[97] Hick argues that there was a time in the "axial" period about the middle of the first millennium before Christ when the major world faiths came into being, largely in reaction to dissatisfaction with things as they were and in boundless belief in something limitlessly better. Such faith, such faiths, cannot be proved or disproved. They are all "religiously ambiguous" and open to wide varieties of interpretation. Hick admits that there is an element of projection in all discourse about religion, but holds that there is a Reality onto which all such projections are cast. The various inconsistencies, incompatibilities, and mutual contradictions among the world's religions are of little importance since there is no direct correlation between Reality and any particular religion's conceptions. What is important is that each religion produce "a shift from self-consciousness to Reality-consciousness."[98]

As I have canvassed Hick's general approach earlier in this book, I need not dwell on it here. What is added by Hick's Gifford Lectures to the structure of his total position is the argument that the origins of the major world religions is as he paints it. Quite apart from his rejection of revelation (in any traditional sense) and the unsubstantiated *a priori* implicit in his general thesis (what substantive reason can he give for affirming there is any Reality out there, not least one that correlates with nothing we know?), he must of course late-date many of the Old Testament documents. And he must deny that the plot-line of the Hebrew Bible in any way corresponds with reality.

2. Historical Reconstructions

Old Testament studies have generated many historical reconstructions that deny the plot-line found in the text as it stands has any cogency. The aging and in some ways moribund JEPD theory has proved the most enduring, but it does not stand alone.

(1) Mark Smith so arranges the Old Testament documents that as he moves from the period of the Judges through the monarchy to the Exile and beyond, he pens successive chapters explicating Yahweh's relationships with Baal, with Asherah, and so forth.[99] His thesis is that monotheism is a very late development.

(2) In a stimulating book, Freedman argues for the unity of the Hebrew Scriptures, against those who take them to be a heterogeneous collection of

---

97. John Hick, *An Interpretation of Religion: Human Responses to the Transcendent* (London: Macmillan, 1989).

98. Ibid., 373.

99. Mark Smith, *The Early History of God: Yahweh and the Other Deities in Ancient Israel* (San Francisco: Harper San Francisco, 1990).

writings.[100] Freedman groups the Hebrew canon into three parts: (a) the Primary History, consisting of Torah plus the Former Prophets; (b) the Latter Prophets; (c) the Writings. The first part focuses on "the moral and ethical relationship between creator and creature "[101] with the covenant presented in Deuteronomy at the heart. In line with most contemporary Old Testament scholarship, this he dates late, and so the fall of Jerusalem is by this means explained as the result of faithlessness toward the covenant. The second part, the Latter Prophets, supplements the first by providing more details and extending the history into the Persian period, thus including the restoration of the commonwealth, and above all the temple. The Writings, the most diverse collection, like the Primary History, stress that "the rules are the same and the possibilities are for either good or bad results."[102]

(3) Albertz divides the history of Israel into five periods (pre-state era, monarch, exile, postexilic period, Hellenistic period). In each period, he sets out a three-pole tension: more or less official religion, opposition, and, interestingly, family and personal cult. He strongly opposes the view that early Israel espoused an amorphous polytheism and only at a late date adopted monotheism, with Yahweh as God.[103]

Even this brief account of only three recent works shows how wide is the diversity in contemporary attempts to reconstruct Old Testament history. There are useful insights in all three, especially the latter two. But in each case the Bible's story-line is shifted, in the first two cases rather drastically. Smith has bought into an evolutionary approach to religions: the human race moves from animism to polytheism to henotheism to monotheism. How very different is the Bible's account, which begins with monotheism and, owing to the Fall, witnesses to the corruption of the knowledge of God and therefore to the rise of assorted false religions and false gods and distorted notions of the one true God. Freedman does not really integrate the Fall into his account, nor does he give much space to Abraham's significance, the recurring promises to Gentiles, and various messianic expectations. As a general rule, historical reconstructions that attempt to crowd so many of the Old Testament books into a relatively brief period from about Josiah to the end of the Exile tend to focus enormous attention on the fall and restoration of Jerusalem and its temple, and de-emphasize the earlier steps in the plot-line. And from a Christian point of view, of course, the plot-line must be contin-

---

100. David Noel Freedman, *The Unity of the Hebrew Bible* (Ann Arbor: Univ. of Michigan Press, 1991).

101. Ibid., 10.

102. Ibid., 99.

103. Rainer Albertz, *Religionsgeschichte Israels in alttestamentlicher Zeit*, 2 vols. (Göttingen: Vandenhoeck & Ruprecht, 1992).

ued into the new covenant if the old covenant is to be seen in its proper proportions. Similar things could be said about Albertz's work, despite the freshness of his focus on personal and family religion.

3. Thematic Readings

A substantial number of works set out to make the Old Testament relevant to contemporary mission and ministry. In the course of this endeavor, they delineate themes that can be taken into the pulpit or into theology texts. Almost all of them have to do with liberation.

Thus, Messer[104] argues that at least five Old Testament motifs for mission can be identified: (a) the global theme of universality; (b) the emphasis on rescue and liberation; (c) exhortation to Israel "to share God's love and liberation with all nations"; (d) recognition of "the antagonism against God's loving and liberating initiatives"; and (e) "God's compassion for the poor, the weak, and the outcast."[105]

Writing under the general theme of gospel and inculturation, Brueggemann points to "the *oddness of God* and the *oddness of Israel* as portrayed in the Old Testament."[106] The Old Testament narrative is odd "because it is the account of the liberation of the slave community from the grip of the empire," with no attention "paid to the needs of the imperial overlords." The narrative is "even more odd" in that "this non-generic God, whose name we are not yet told in the narrative, hears the slaves and heeds the pain, responds to it, and becomes enmeshed in it."[107] Again, Otto has shown that for Jürgen Moltmann the God of the Old Testament is primarily the God of the exodus, the God of liberation.[108]

This is all so terribly "with it." I am not for a moment suggesting that the themes that Messer, Brueggemann, and Moltmann find are entirely absent from the text. I am saying, rather, that they tend to get reduced to the horizontal dimension, *and they are abstracted from the Bible's plot-line*, such that their true significance and proportion are almost entirely lost.

104. Donald E. Messer, *A Conspiracy of Goodness: Contemporary Images of Christian Mission* (Nashville: Abingdon, 1992).

105. Ibid., 35–37.

106. Walter Brueggemann, "A Gospel Language of Pain and Possibility," *Horizons in Biblical Theology* 13 (1991): 97 (emphasis his).

107. Ibid., 98.

108. Randall E. Otto, "God and History in Jürgen Moltmann," *Journal of the Evangelical Theological Society* 35 (1992): 386.

4. Syncretism[109] in Israel

Many studies have commented on the degree to which nonprescribed and sometimes forbidden beliefs and practices crept into Israelite worship and belief. Recently, for example, Bloch-Smith has summarized the archaeological evidence showing that in many Judahite tombs there were left with the bodies a variety of provisions for the sustenance, safety, and supplication of the deceased in the afterlife[110]—this despite explicit prohibitions against consulting the dead through intermediaries (Lev. 19:26, 31; 20:6, 27; Deut. 18:10–11) and against feeding the deceased tithed food (Deut. 26:14). In a useful typology, Hess has summarized the biblical and archaeological evidence that at any given time there were often four distinguishable religious outlooks in the northern and southern kingdoms: (a) The religion of the prophets insisted that Yahweh alone be worshiped, and that the covenant between Yahweh and his people be honored. (b) Many of the kings and queens compromised such exclusiveness, tolerating and sometimes participating in the cults of neighboring pagan states, and entering into marriage alliances with the royals of those states. (c) Doubtless for many ill-taught ordinary Israelites Yahweh was the official or state deity, recognized to be more or less supreme, while they themselves sought out local deities, not least the local manifestations of Baal and Asherah, and sometimes also assorted household gods. (d) In certain more extreme cases, foreign deities were imported and (at least temporarily) forced on the nation by compromised and compromising royalty. One thinks, for instance, of Jezebel and Ahab in 1 Kings 18, and of Athaliah in 2 Kings 18.[111]

Having observed such phenomena, some authors tend to confuse description and prescription. Consider, for example, the approach of Goldingay and Wright to the Melchizedek narrative in Genesis 14.[112] Melchizedek blesses Abraham in the name of *El Elyon* ("God Most High"), Creator of heaven and earth (14:19). Abraham (properly "Abram" at this point) responds by taking

---

109. Although "syncretism" is a notoriously difficult expression to which to attach a precise definition (see Irina A. Levinskaya, "Syncretism—The Term and Phenomenon," *Tyndale Bulletin* 44 [1993]: 117–28), it retains usefulness to refer, rather vaguely, to attempts to merge alien or opposing practices or beliefs from diverse religious systems.

110. Elizabeth M. Bloch-Smith, "The Cult of the Dead in Judah: Interpreting the Material Remains," *Journal of Biblical Literature* 111 (1992): 113–24.

111. S. Hess, "Yahweh and His Asherah? Epigraphic Evidence for Religious Pluralism in Old Testament Times," in *One God One Lord in a World of Religious Pluralism*, ed. Andrew D. Clarke and Bruce W. Winter (Cambridge: Tyndale House, 1991), 5–33.

112. John E. Goldingay and Christopher J. H. Wright, "'Yahweh Our God Yahweh One': The Old Testament and Religious Pluralism," in Clarke and Winter, *One God One Lord in a World of Religious Pluralism*, 34–52, esp. 38–39.

an oath in the name of *Yahweh, El Elyon* ("the LORD, God Most High"), Creator of heaven and earth (14:22). "The implication seems to be that Abram and Genesis itself recognize that Malkisedeq (*sic*) (and presumably other people in Canaan who worship El under one manifestation or another) does serve the true God but does not know all there is to know about that God" (38). Two pages later they comment, "It is still the God worshipped within these other religions who is more fully known here, and it is apparently assumed that Israel can still learn from these other religions" (40). Noting some of the parallels between Israelite and Canaanite religions, they go on to say, "This is not to say that these institutions, ideas, or texts are unchanged when they feature within Yahwism, but that it was able to reach its own mature expression with their aid" (41). Moreover, "the Hebrew Bible does not explicitly base its condemnations of other peoples on the grounds that they believe in the wrong gods. Condemnation of the nations, where reasons are given, is usually based on their moral and social behaviour (see the oracles against the nations, e.g., Amos 1–2; Isa. 13–23). Condemnation of religious deficiency is reserved for the people of God (cf. Amos 2)" (42).

Almost all of this is right, and almost all of it is wrong, or at least questionable. When the Melchizedek passage is placed within the developing narrative within the book of Genesis, one can no longer think of monotheism emerging after endless struggles with pagan polytheism. It is far more natural in reading the account to suppose that there were still people who believed in the one true God, people who preserved some memory of God's gracious self-disclosure to Noah, people who revered the memory of the severe lesson of Babel. That Melchizedek should designate "God Most High" as "Creator of heaven and earth" points in the same direction: he was either a monotheist or a henotheist.[113] Of course, Abram was the one who received the special call to follow God and head up a race that would prove a blessing to all the nations of the earth. But that doesn't mean he was the only one who believed in the one true God. To use this account to justify the proposition that "apparently" Israel could "still learn from these other religions" is indefensible.

Certainly some of the institutions and ideas that characterized Israelite religion were shared with the surrounding pagan religions. That is almost inevitable: unless some group retreats into a hermitage and self-consciously sets out to do quite different things (and even then it is unlikely that every base will be covered), common rites (e.g., circumcision) and the like are not unlikely. But the question to be asked is what those rites symbolize in each religion, and how common beliefs function within the structure of their

---

113. The view that Melchizedek was a pre-incarnate appearance of the Son of God is based on a mistaken interpretation of Hebrews 7.

respective systems. To cast the Israelites as reaching "their own mature expression with [pagan] aid" is remarkable rhetoric. One might as well say that Jesus reached his own mature expression with the aid of the Pharisees. At one level, that is not entirely incorrect, but it so misrepresents the relationship that it is misleading. God's gracious self-disclosure is given to specific people in concrete historical situations: why should the historical connections be taken as a sign of necessary syncretism?

Common cultural and religious beliefs do not themselves justify syncretism: the interesting and important things are almost always where people differ. Where the point is not observed, as in the episode of the golden calf (Exodus 32–34),[114] terrible judgment ensues. Moreover, although the Hebrew Bible does not normally address the pagans and tell them they are worshiping the wrong gods, the impression Goldingay and Wright leave (perhaps unwittingly) is that it is acceptable for pagans to worship their own gods, provided that there is a reasonable amount of justice in the land. But the real reasons for biblical restraint when addressing the pagan nations are surely more nuanced. The primary locus of God's redemptive activity at that time (the "epochal" or "salvation-historical" question again) was Israel. And the Israelites are repeatedly told not only that Yahweh and Yahweh alone is *their* God, but that he is the *only* God, and that the gods of the nations are impotent idols (see especially Isaiah 40–55—chapters that Goldingay and Wright strangely designate "the most exclusivist and nationalist section of the Hebrew Bible"[115]).

It is important to remember that when Old Testament writers specifically address the challenges of syncretism, thinking through what may or could be learned from surrounding religions, their tone and emphases are very stern.

> The dominant concern of the opening eleven chapters of Deuteronomy is with idolatry. The ultimate claim on Israel was that they should acknowledge Yahweh alone as the living God. The monotheism of the shema (Deut. 6:4f.) was no armchair philosophy but a monumental challenge to all human polytheisms, and still is. The severity of the warnings against idolatry is not some hangover from primitive religion (to which culturally pluarilized [*sic*] western confusion consigns them) but are born of graphic awareness of what idolatry does to a society. It is not just an argument over how many gods exist. The shema does not say "There is only one God," but (in effect),

---

114. Cf. John N. Oswalt, "Golden Calves and the 'Bull of Jacob': The Impact on Israel of Its Religious Environment," in *Israel's Apostasy and Restoration*, ed. Avraham Gileadi (Grand Rapids: Baker, 1988), 9–18.

115. "Yahweh Our God Yahweh One," 50. Certainly it is one of the more exclusivist passages, but is "nationalist" the right tag for chapters full of hope for Gentiles?

"Yahweh alone is that one God," Yahwen as he is characterized in the rest of the OT, and specifically in the redemptive history of Israel recounted and celebrated in Deuteronomy. Once that living God and his claims are rejected, then the resulting vacuum is filled with gods that are destructive and cruel. The Baalism of Canaan which, through its fertility cults, sacralized sex and sacrificed babies (Deut. 12:31), is alive and well in our society, with its commodification of sex and the suffering of children in so many ways.[116]

When the people of God avoid syncretistic entanglements, it is a sign that the Lord is with them (Josh. 22:31). By contrast, when they oppress one another and follow other gods, it is because truth has perished (Jer. 7:28) and the people have rejected the word of the Lord (Jer. 8:9). Again and again Deuteronomy warns the people to be careful to follow all that the Lord has commanded, to avoid entanglements, including marriage, with the surrounding peoples, for fear of learning and following their ways (e.g., Deut. 4; 6:13–19; 7:21–26; 13:6–8). In part, the preservation of the covenant community depends on each generation carefully passing on to the next the exclusive greatness and covenant fidelity of Yahweh (chapter 6). The people are not even to inquire about how the surrounding pagans worship, lest they be tempted to follow them (12:30). "You must not worship the LORD your God in their way, because in worshiping their gods, they do all kinds of detestable things the LORD hates" (12:31). God's people are not even to have idols in their hearts (Ezek. 14:1–5). Some of the severity of Ezra and Nehemiah turns on the fact that the Exile was supposed to have obliterated any tendency toward compromise with idolatry, so that when residual hankerings reappeared, these leaders were struck with horror and fear.

In short, the reading of the biblical plot-line lightly sketched in this chapter seems amply justified. It is hard to see how it can be squared with contemporary religious pluralism. But we must pursue the line more fully into the Scriptures of the new covenant.

---

116. Chris Wright, "Deuteronomic Depression," *Themelios* 19/2 (1994): 3.

Chapter 6

WHAT GOD HAS SPOKEN: CLIMACTIC MOVES IN THE BIBLE'S PLOT-LINE

A. Introduction

Tracing the plot-line of the New Testament is at one level an easier and briefer job than tracing the plot-line of the Old Testament. Not only is the New Testament a fraction of the length of the Old Testament, but the historical period it covers in any detail is but a few decades long—even though, of course, it lights the path all the way to the consummation.

But there are two factors that complicate the task. The first is that a tremendous amount of contemporary discussion on pluralism turns on Jesus Christ. It seems best, therefore, to devote a separate chapter to it (chap. 7), and at the same time sort through charges that part of the New Testament is anti-Semitic, or alternatively that the New Testament advocates two covenants as legitimate approaches to God—one for Jews and another for Christians. The second complication is that although the plot-line is relatively simple, there are many texts from the New Testament corpus that have elicited hard questions, and that are being adduced to support some sort of religious inclusivism, or even religious pluralism. These require separate treatment. So following this introduction, I first sketch the plot-line, then respond to various critical questions, and finally I comment on disputed passages. As in earlier chapters, I make no pretense of being comprehensive, but deal with elements of the plot-line and particular passages and themes that are especially relevant to the subject of this book.

Some of the features of the New Testament's plot-line have already been introduced by running through them from their base in the Old Testament. Thus there is nothing that is utterly new about many features in the New

Testament: for example, the God-centeredness of its outlook; its concern to deal with human guilt and rebellion; its emphases on both the wrath and the love of God; its vision of history as a line that God ultimately directs and that is moving to the consummation; the significance, responsibility, and account-ability of God's image-bearers; the primacy of grace; and much more. In many instances these themes introduced in the Old Testament segment of the biblical plot-line are sharpened or heightened in the New Testament segment. Thus the love of God, a glorious theme in the Scriptures of the old covenant, takes on renewed life in the most concrete expression—God's gift of his Son, handed over to the odium of crucifixion so that God's people might go free. The wrath of God, terrifying though it is in Old Testament passages, now culminates in horrific visions of final judgment (e.g., Rev. 14:6–20). God himself, progressively revealed across the sweep of the Old Testament literature, is now simultaneously more clearly disclosed and, precisely because of that revelation, more mysterious: he is one God but not solitary, three "persons" who clearly interact with one another and with his creatures yet still but one God, the triune God.[1]

On the other hand, there are several themes cast up by the New Testament plot-line which, though they have roots in the Old Testament, play a far larger part in the unfolding drama than did their roots in the earlier stage—and, correspondingly, some prominent features in the Old Testament plot-line now fade away, or, more commonly, are transposed, as it were, to a new key. "Kingdom" no longer primarily conjures up a theocratic state in which God rules by his human vassal in the Davidic dynasty. It conjures up the immediate transforming reign of God, dawning now in the ministry, death, resurrection, ascension, and session of Jesus, the promised Messiah, and consummated at his return. Eschatology is thereby transformed. The locus of the people of God is no longer national and tribal; it is international, transracial, transcultural. If the Old Testament prophets constantly look forward to the day when God will act decisively, the New Testament writers announce that God has acted decisively, and that this is "good news," gospel, of universal, eternal significance and stellar importance. Thus kingdom, Christology, eschatology, church, gospel, become dominant terms or themes. Temple, priest, sacrifice, law, and much more are transposed; national and tribal outlooks gradually fade from view.

At this juncture it may be useful to mention three issues that anyone working in this area will soon confront.

First, for some the claims of religious pluralism are of such paramount importance that any exclusivistic claims or themes entailed by the New

---

1. Although as we have seen, words like "triune" and "Trinity" are not used.

Testament story-line simply have to be discounted. Thus T. V. Philip writes off election, covenant, anything distinctive in Christology, and ecclesiology as nasty impediments to true dialogue and honest religious pluralism.[2] He does not wrestle with questions of objective truth; he certainly does not work his way through competing worldviews. Pluralism is already the *summum bonum*; it is the god by which all other claims must be judged. Against such an outlook little of what I say here will be appealing. In dialogue with such a viewpoint I would probably begin with the kinds of topics raised earlier in this book. But even these two chapters (5 and 6) may help some who share Philip's outlook understand that for the Christian more is at stake than a few angular doctrines.

Second, in the world of New Testament scholarship relatively little attention is paid to the New Testament plot-line, owing primarily to the penchant for the piecemeal. In addition, this lack owes something to the studied conviction that the New Testament documents should primarily be read as the expressions of the religious convictions of diverse groups of believers— groups whose convictions were sometimes in contradiction with other groups of believers[3]—and not as parts of a whole. There is enough truth to this perspective that it must not be written off prematurely. Like the Old Testament documents, the collection that constitutes the New Testament *does* represent the beliefs of the writers and reflect the struggles in which they were engaged and the convictions they espoused. The New Testament documents are full of life: what, after all, would the alternative be? The product of abstruse theologians with no commitment to what they were writing? The dispassionate chronicling of events by "neutral" observers?

The real question is whether or not these documents are also mutually complementary, and, finally, nothing less than the Word of God, along the lines set out in chapter 4. If so, then however much we may legitimately try, for example, to delineate the distinctives of the Pauline corpus, or to set forth the peculiar contribution of Matthew, we are also under obligation to trace the principal story-line through the whole, and consider how the parts contribute to it. This means, for instance, that when a document like Matthew is found to be written later than, say, 1 Thessalonians, we will not automatically assume

---

2. *Christianity and Religious Pluralism* (Bangalore: United Theological College, 1988), 31–43.

3. E.g., John Reumann, *Variety and Unity in New Testament Thought* (Oxford: Oxford Univ. Press, 1991); James D. G. Dunn, *Unity and Diversity in the New Testament: An Inquiry into the Character of Earliest Christianity* (Philadelphia: Westminster, 1977). Cf. D. A. Carson, "Unity and Diversity in the New Testament: The Possibility of Systematic Theology," in *Scripture and Truth*, ed. D. A. Carson and John D. Woodbridge (Grand Rapids: Zondervan, 1983), 65–95.

that the line of developing thought is univocally from 1 Thessalonians to Matthew, if Matthew purports to be writing about a period considerably *before* the writing of 1 Thessalonians. We may rightly detect in Matthew distinctive ways of looking at things that betray the author to be a man of his times (aren't we all?). But not least because all four canonical evangelists explicitly make distinctions between what was understood and believed at the time of writing and what was understood and believed at the time they are describing (namely, the life, death, and resurrection of Jesus the Messiah),[4] it is imperative that we place the parts of the canonical story-line in their appropriate places.

Third, I should acknowledge that the ways in which the New Testament uses the Old in developing the story-line are extraordinarily complex. Quite apart from the fact that this is a subject that has corralled a great deal of scholarly attention in recent years, it has been one of my own interests,[5] and in time I hope to write something more substantial in the area than I have managed so far. The issues are not only narrowly technical (what form of text is cited? what does "to fulfill" mean?), but profoundly substantive. How is "the law" treated in the New Testament? How is it that the gospel of Jesus Christ can in some passages be said to be prophesied in the Old Testament and fulfilled in the coming and ministry of Jesus, and in other passages said to be hidden in the past and revealed in the coming and ministry of Jesus? Does Paul think of Adam as a historical figure? Does the writer of the epistle to the Hebrews think of the historical Melchizedek of Genesis 14 as truly immortal? And if someone were to answer "Yes" with respect to the Adam question and "No" with respect to the Melchizedek question (as I would), what are the grounds of the differentiation? What is typology? Or, more precisely, what kinds of typology are there, how do they operate, and what is their warrant? How, in short, does the Bible "hang together"?

But that must be the subject of another book. Although these and similar questions impinge on the subject at hand, they are not sufficiently important to the broad picture I am painting to warrant much consideration of them here.

---

4. E.g., John repeatedly draws a distinction between what the disciples understood at the time of Jesus (which he is narrating), and what he, John the evangelist, understands at the time of writing. That he does so shows he not only *can* make the distinction (and therefore should not be too quickly charged with anachronism), but that he has a vested interest in preserving it.

5. See the essays in D. A. Carson and H. G. M. Williamson, eds., *It Is Written: Scripture Citing Scripture* (Cambridge: Cambridge Univ. Press, 1988), and the relevant discussions in my commentaries on Matthew and John.

B. Elements in the New Testament Plot-line

1. Jesus and the Gospels

In their openings and closings all four canonical Gospels draw some care-ful connections toward the Old Testament. Matthew and Luke tie Jesus genealogically to the Davidic line; John ties Jesus not only to the God of creation, as God's agent in that creation (1:2–3), but to God as God's revealer, God's Word (1:1, 14, 18), and to the Old Testament as the ultimate tabernacle, the ultimate manifestation of the glory of God, the one to whom the law points (1:14–18). All four Gospels give place to John the Baptist as the forerunner and tie him to Old Testament promises of preparation for the coming of the Messiah himself. By announcing the good news and the nearness of the kingdom, Mark (as do the others in their own way) announces the dawning of something new, something that had been looked for for centuries. Connections with the Old Testament recur, sometimes in statements about Jesus' fulfilling this or that prophecy, sometimes in Jesus' own statements about his relation to something antecedent (e.g., the law in Matthew 5:17–20, the temple in Matthew 12). Three of the four Gospels include in their endings explicit commands regarding outreach to the entire world. However much Jesus focuses his own ministry on Israel, the expectation is aroused that what Jesus is bringing to pass is nothing less than the onset of the blessings to the Gentiles promised to Abraham two millennia earlier.

When one reads the Gospels rapidly, one after the other, again and again, one cannot but be struck by the towering figure of Jesus. Though they reflect the churches' convictions, the Gospels are not *about* the churches' convictions: they are about Jesus Christ. His excellence, his uniqueness, his authority, his compassion, his love, his wisdom, his holiness, all shine through passage after passage. What is important for the present discussion is to observe how these excellencies of Jesus are tied to the central biblical storyline, combining to create a whole worldview in which Jesus is the culmination of God's redemptive promises, the highest disclosure of God himself, the Word incarnate; Jesus is the one who saves us from our sin, who inaugurates the kingdom, and who will one day consummate it.

Examples are abundant. The birth narratives (Matt. 1–2; Luke 1–2) show that Jesus brings together two quite different orders: God and human beings. True, the ancient world of paganism had its share of accounts of miraculous births. What is staggering about the New Testament accounts is not so much their distinctive details, as important as they are, as the kind of God and the kind of human being that is presupposed. Without any crude account of gods sleeping with women, we find the "Holy Spirit" and "the power of the Most High" so overshadowing the virgin Mary that the "holy one" born to her will be called "the Son of God" (Luke 1:35). Of course, the expression "son of God" is applied to many others than to Jesus (e.g., Matt. 5:9), but the New Testament writers deploy various means to show that Jesus' sonship is unique. In any case, the significance of the birth narratives turns not simply on various technical expressions *but on the kind of God that is acting in this way, and on what it means to be a human being before Jesus is born as one.*

In a pantheistic universe, the birth narratives would not be particularly exciting; certainly they would not be spelling out anything unique. In a polytheistic universe, finite gods may impregnate women and produce all kinds of interesting progeny. But here is the one God, the transcendent/personal God, the Creator, the God disclosed in the Old Testament Scriptures, so working in one of his creatures, one of his image-bearers, that the resulting offspring is in the New Testament repeatedly said both to be God and to be a man. Not only does this divine/human person bring together the principal twin strands of Old Testament anticipation—in which on the one hand God himself lays bare his arm or comes down to his people to rescue them, and on the other that he sends "David" his servant to the rescue—but henceforth this divine/human person, while receiving the worship and homage due God alone (e.g., Rev. 4–5), achieves the reconciliation between human beings and God that had been so desperately savaged by the Fall.

We need to pause to reflect a little on the ways in which not only the Evangelists, but other New Testament writers as well, pick up on Jesus' unique status. We ought not confine ourselves to the relatively small number of passages in which Jesus is explicitly called "God" (e.g., John 1:1,18; 20:28; Titus 3:4–5).[6] We ought to remember a wealth of other phenomena: the proclamation of the Son as God's last word and the radiance of God's glory and the exact representation of his being in the prologue of Hebrews (1:1–3), an epistle which also insists on the humanity of Christ, both as a witnessed reality and as a theological necessity (chap. 2); Paul's penchant for taking verses from the Old Testament that refer to Yahweh and applying them without hesitation to Jesus;[7] Peter's capacity to do the same thing (cf. 1 Peter 3:14 and Isa. 8:12–13); Paul's insistence that "in Christ all the fullness of the Deity lives in bodily form" (Col. 2:9); the constant linking of "the Lord God Almighty and the Lamb" in the Apocalypse; the parables of Jesus in which implicitly he identifies himself with the figure in the parable who in Old Testament symbolism is none other than God; Jesus' remarkable question to

---

6. For a detailed treatment of the relevant texts, see Murray J. Harris, *Jesus as God: The New Testament Use of Theos in Reference to Jesus* (Grand Rapids: Baker, 1992).

7. Most recently, see Don N. Howell, Jr., "God-Christ Interchange in Paul: Impressive Testimony to the Deity of Jesus," *Journal of the Evangelical Theological Society* 36 (1993): 467–79.

his opponents, "Can any of you prove me guilty of sin?" (John 8:46)—attesting an astonishingly clear conscience; John's remarkable witness to the effect that Jesus takes on his own lips the divine title "I am," in self-conscious application to himself of the content and the context of passages in Isaiah where the title refers to Yahweh (see especially John 8).[8] And what must we make of God's declared purpose that all should honor the Son just as they honor the Father (John 5:23)? Indeed, "He who does not honor the Son does not honor the Father, who sent him" (John 5:23).

With most people, genuine greatness is associated with a certain unawareness of greatness. The alternative is gradually to become an arrogant poseur. What is so affecting about Jesus is that quite transparently he displays astonishing authority (e.g., Matt. 7:28–29), but is known for his gentleness and humility (11:29). For all that he goes to the cross, he sees himself as the focal point of history. When he insists that John the Baptist is the greatest person born of woman (i.e., up to that time), the context shows that Jesus holds John to be greater than Abraham, greater than David, greater than Solomon, greater than Isaiah, for the simple reason that to the Baptist was given the immense privilege of pointing Jesus out on the stage of history, of announcing the arrival of the promised Messiah (Matt. 11:9–11a). When Jesus goes on to insist that the least in the kingdom is greater than John the Baptist (Matt. 11:11b), the measure of greatness must be along a similar axis. In other words, the least in the kingdom is greater than John because anyone in the kingdom, living this side of the cross and resurrection, can point Jesus out with even greater clarity than did the Baptist.[9] But it is the fact that Jesus can talk like this that is so staggering. Suppose some speaker today began his remarks by announcing that the person who introduced him was the greatest person who ever lived, simply because that person had introduced him! The person who talks in such terms is either suffering such megalomania that he has lost touch with reality, or he has an identity that demands a second look. Quite apart from the sweep of the claim, it has the flavor of someone who does not have to prove anything because he knows who he is. Doubtless Paul understands this: the participle in Philippians 2:5–7 ("... Christ Jesus, who, *being* in very nature God, did not consider equality with God something to be grasped, but made himself nothing") should probably not be taken concessively ("*although* in very nature God") but causally: "... Christ Jesus, who,

---

8. See David M. Ball, "'My Lord and My God': The Implications of 'I Am' Sayings for Religious Pluralism," in *One God One Lord in a World of Religious Pluralism*, ed. Andrew D. Clarke and Bruce W. Winter (Cambridge: Tyndale House, 1991), 53–71.

9. Cf. D. A. Carson, "Matthew 11:19 / Luke 7:35: A Test Case for the Bearing of Q Christology on the Synoptic Problem," in *Jesus of Nazareth: Lord and Christ*, ed. Joel B. Green and Max Turner (Grand Rapids: Eerdmans, 1994), 128–46.

because he was in very nature God, did not consider equality with God something to be exploited, but made himself nothing."[10]

Then there is the astonishing quality of Jesus' love. It is not that he cannot utter the sternest denunications (e.g., Matt. 23); it is that he weeps over the city. It is not that he cannot speak of judgment, for in fact he speaks of hell more often than any other figure in Scripture; rather, it is that he provides a way of escape. It is not that he cannot operate as a man among men, and even find followers among the wealthy (e.g., Zacchaeus); rather, it is in his love for children, his care for the poor, the oppressed, the handicapped, the unclean, the outcast. This is of a piece with God who discloses himself in the pages of the Old Testament; now this same love is displayed in the most concrete form. And because, as we shall see, this love brings Jesus to the cross, New Testament writers so exult in the love of Jesus that the mere mention of his name or of one of his titles can prompt them to throw in an aside of exuberant praise: e.g., " ... I live by faith in the Son of God, *who loved me and gave himself for me*" (Gal. 2:20, italics added). Christian maturity can be measured by a believer's experiential grasp of the love of Christ (Eph. 3:16b–19).

With the coming of Jesus, "The kingdom of God is near" (Mark 1:15). In Jesus' announcement the verb "is near" should probably be taken spatially rather than temporally. God's reign is now "among you" (Luke 17:21), and is manifested not least in Jesus' rout of the powers of darkness (Matt. 12:28; cf. Luke 10:17–20). In some ways this reign is still hidden, unperceived by those without eyes to see. Thus it can be likened to yeast, performing its silent work. People are called to follow Christ, to believe in him, to believe the good news that the reign of God is present, even though the evidence in the natural world is still ambiguous and disputable. The kingdom is in conflict with the powers of darkness; the crowning and decisive victory occurs at the cross, which on the one hand is the hour of the power of darkness (Luke 22:53) and on the other is the accomplishment of Christ's atoning work. Disciples must pray for the consummation of the kingdom: "Your kingdom come; your will be done on earth as it is in heaven." Until that time, Jesus reigns: the most frequently quoted chapter from the Old Testament in the New is Psalm 110, which includes the words, "The LORD says to my Lord, 'Sit at my right hand until I make your enemies a footstool for your feet'" (Ps. 110:1). Before the Sanhedrin, Jesus insists he is coming back, and, conflating words from Psalm 110 and Daniel 7, declares, "And you will see the Son of Man sitting at the right hand of the Mighty One and coming on the clouds of heaven" (Mark 14:62).

---

10. See Peter T. O'Brien, *The Epistle to the Philippians: A Commentary on the Greek Text* (Grand Rapids: Eerdmans, 1991), 205–16.

These ways of looking at the kingdom precipitate three reflections.[11] *First*, we must ask ourselves how this dawning kingdom of God is in any substantive sense different from the kingdom of God that has always been in operation. God is the king of the whole earth: "dominion belongs to the LORD and he rules over the nations" (Ps. 22:28), and not just over Israel (Judg. 8:23; 1 Sam. 8:6). "The LORD has established his throne in heaven, and his kingdom rules over all" (Ps. 103:19). So what is it, precisely, that Jesus has inaugurated, if God's kingdom has always been operative?

One cannot fail to notice that even though Old Testament writers speak of the God's universal dominion, they can also on occasion speak of his *future* reign. According to Daniel, "the God of heaven will set up a kingdom that will never be destroyed, nor will it be left to another people" (2:44). Obadiah foresees a time when "Deliverers will go up on Mount Zion to govern the mountains of Esau. *And the kingdom will be the LORD's*" (21, italics added). But in what sense will this rule or reign of God be substantially different from what is already in operation? Or to put it another way, in what sense is Jesus inaugurating anything? Without some explanation, the pervasive sense in the New Testament of the *newness* of what is taking place, of the decisive dawning of God's salvation and of God's kingdom, is without apparent warrant.

McCartney provides an important part of the answer. He argues at length, and in the main convincingly, that the focus of newness lies in the fact that "Jesus received the kingdom as a *human*. . . . The arrival of the reign of God is the *reinstatement of the originally intended divine order for earth, with man properly situated as God's viceregent*."[12]

But there is another element of no less importance. In the relatively few passages that directly speak of God's rule or reign in the Old Testament (not to mention the many more that do not use "rule" or "kingdom" word-groups but that nevertheless depict or affirm God's sovereignty), the kingdom is extended over all, good and evil alike. Although the use of "kingdom" in the New Testament, and especially in the Gospels, can extend that far, as in the parable of the wheat and the weeds (Matt. 13:24–30), more characteristically the kingdom *is a subset under which there is life, forgiveness, truth, reconciliation with God*. Thus "unless you change and become like little children, you will never enter the kingdom of heaven" (Matt.18:3)—which suggests some are in it and some are not. Unless a person is born again, he cannot see or enter

---

11. Study of the kingdom has its own complex history. I cannot here interact with all the interpretive positions. For a recent survey, see Bruce Chilton, "The Kingdom of God in Recent Discussion," in *Studying the Historical Jesus: Evaluation of the State of Current Research*, ed. Bruce Chilton and Craig A. Evans (Leiden: E. J. Brill, 1994), 255–88.

12. Dan G. McCartney, "*Ecce Homo*: The Coming of the Kingdom as the Restoration of Human Viceregency," *Westminster Theological Journal* 56 (1994): 2 (emphasis his).

the kingdom (John 3:3, 5). Thus Paul can write, "For he has rescued us from the dominion of darkness and brought us into the kingdom of the Son he loves" (Col. 1:13). Something of the ambiguity of the situation is preserved in our Lord's explanation of the parable of the weeds (Matthew 13:36–43). Only the good seed "stands for the sons of the kingdom" (13:38); the weeds "are the sons of the evil one." Nevertheless, at harvest time the Son of Man sends out his angels "and they will weed out of his kingdom everything that causes sin and all who do evil" (13:41).

Thus the kingdom, viewed as that subset of the reign of God under which there is life, can be understood to be a bringing back into history of the final kingdom of blessedness that still awaits. It is appropriate to think in those terms, because the consummated kingdom has been guaranteed by the triumph of the Lamb (Rev. 5), which has occurred in history in the coming and death and resurrection and exaltation of Christ. The kingdom has truly dawned, and, as we shall see, if we do not yet enjoy the bliss of the consummated kingdom, we live in certain hope of its coming, and in conscious enjoyment of the presence of God mediated by the Spirit who is the down payment and guarantor of the glories to come.

These realities lead to a *second* reflection. The New Testament documents pulsate with a living tension between the "already" and the "not yet." The kingdom has already come; it is not yet here. It is terribly easy to distort this tension. Some will suppose that virtually all the blessings to be received have already arrived: they adopt an "over-realized" eschatology, and may deny that there is any resurrection ahead (e.g., 1 Cor. 15). Others act as if very little of triumph has yet occurred. With dour pessimism they grimly hang on for the end, and detect signs of its imminence in every war and dictator that comes along, even though Jesus warned that wars and rumors of wars will continue, and these are but the beginnings of sufferings (Mark 13:7–8). The fact of the matter is that "there is a precise meaning to this gap which opens up between the coming of the kingdom veiled in the vulnerable and powerless Jesus, and the coming of the kingdom in manifest power." This meaning is bound up with "the mission of the Church to the nations."[13] For "this gospel of the kingdom will be preached in the whole world as a testimony to all nations, and then the end will come" (Matt. 24:14). While Jesus reigns with all authority and commissions his followers to proclaim this good news and make disciples (Matt. 28:18–20), while the church already enjoys something of the delights and powers of the age to come, the kingdom advances without apocalyptic finality. Christians are constantly exhorted to watchfulness, patient

13. Lesslie Newbigin, *The Gospel in a Pluralist Society* (Grand Rapids: Eerdmans, 1989), 106.

endurance, faithfulness, discernment, boldness, willingness to suffer. God's grace is made perfect in our weakness. The followers of the Messiah who endured crucifixion are called upon to take up their cross and follow him. The world will hate believers as it hated their Lord, but some will be convicted, converted, justified, transformed. And one day the kingdom will come in the unimaginable glory of its consummation.

The *third* reflection is that the kingdom of God is no less the kingdom of Christ. Already in the Synoptic Gospels, while he commonly speaks of the kingdom of God or the kingdom of heaven, Jesus tells parables that speak of *his* (i.e., the Son of Man's) kingdom (e.g., Matt. 13:41). King Jesus is sometimes clearly differentiable from his Father (Matt. 25:31, 34, 40). In John 1:49 Jesus is the King of Israel; by John 18:36 he is speaking of "my kingdom." Paul teaches that all of the kingdom's authority is now mediated through Christ until no opposition is left (1 Cor. 15:24–25). In the words of the Apocalypse, "The kingdom of the world has become the kingdom of our Lord and of his Christ, and he will reign for ever and ever" (Rev. 11:15).

Clearly these kinds of data contribute to the trinitarian thought so pervasive in the New Testament. At the same time they constitute critical steps in the Bible's plot-line. These Christological and eschatological details are not unrelated to the bigger picture, nicely detachable wherever uncomfortable. The desperate plight begun in Eden now finds solution in Jesus: the opening chapter of the New Testament announces that he will save his people from their sins (Matt. 1:21). The prophetic anticipation of God's coming or David's coming to redeem the people of God comes to united fulfilment in the coming of Jesus. The promise that through Abraham's seed all the nations of the earth will be blessed, gradually expanded into a major theme in the Old Testament, now bursts into the Great Commission, the mushrooming growth of the Jewish church into the Gentile world, the spreading flame reaching across the Roman Empire and beyond, in anticipation of the climactic consummation of God's promises in the new heaven and the new earth.

There is no other solution to the wretched evil and guilt of sin.

That fact prompts one final observation about the contribution of the canonical Gospels to the Bible's story-line. Whatever their differences, however independent their stances, they unite in telling the story of Jesus so that the rush of the narrative is toward the cross. None of them downplays the cross. There is some variation on how much the resurrection is emphasized; there is only unanimity as to the place of the cross in the unfolding drama of redemption.

Some depreciate the contribution of the Gospels in this regard, observing that they do not contain any sustained discourse on the nature of the atonement, equivalent, say, to Romans 3:21–26. This judgment is without weight, *provided the Gospels are allowed to make their own contribution to the biblical story-line*, and are not expected to be something they are not. To be sure, there are explicit atonement texts in the Gospels: probably the most notable is, "For even the Son of Man did not come to be served, but to serve, and to give his life as a ransom for many" (Mark 10:45; cf. Matt. 20:28). But if the Gospels lack the profound reflection of Paul on this subject, it is because the gospel writers themselves are faithful to the disciples' slowness in coming to terms with the idea of a crucified Messiah. They simply did not expect that this one Messiah would gather in his person not only the kingly promises of the Old Testament, but the models of sacrifice bound up with the temple ritual, and the function of priest laid down by the Sinai covenant, and the slaughtered lamb foreseen by Isaiah. So they tell their story, and it is the story-line itself that drives the reader to the cross, asking constantly, "What does this mean?" Along the line the evangelists give hints, showing that at the time of writing they had come to terms with this question, even though none had been able to deal with the shattering disappointment of the cross at the time. For example, Matthew carefully connects Jesus' miraculous healings and exorcisms with the significance of the cross as well as with the fulfilment of prophecy (Matt. 8:15–17). Matthew, Luke, and John tie the first dawning of the disciples' understanding of the real nature of Jesus' mission to the resurrection appearances. Other New Testament books, especially Acts, unfold how the implications of the cross and resurrection were, under the Spirit's guidance, progressively discerned. A fresh way of looking at the antecedent revelation of the Old Testament was mandated; at the same time, if the cross and resurrection evoked a fresh look backward, it also opened up the future: the resurrection of Jesus is the firstfruits of the final resurrection that awaits all those who are in him (1 Cor.).

2. The Coming of the Spirit

Although this subject is wonderfully thought-provoking and evocative in its own right, here it is necessary for the purpose of sketching the biblical plot-line to say only three things.

First, although references to the Spirit abound in the Hebrew Bible, starting from the first chapter (Gen. 1:2), none of them unambiguously demands that we think of the Spirit as one with God yet differentiable from him. Some of the language could be read that way; never is that reading absolutely required. But as the New Testament opens, the reach of the language demands that one's understanding of God become enriched. Thus at Jesus' baptism, the Son who elsewhere in the Gospels and Epistles is so identified with God that he is to be worshiped with God, is here distinguished from the

Father who speaks of the Son in the third person: "This is my Son, whom I love; with him I am well pleased" (Matt. 3:17). In the same setting, the Spirit of God descends like a dove. None of this *by itself* absolutely demands full-blown trinitarian theology, but it is highly suggestive, and turns out to be a stage on the way toward the vision of monotheism that holds there is one God but that he has never been solitary.

Perhaps it is John's gospel that is the most demanding. The Spirit, the "Paraclete" (NIV "Counselor") succeeds Jesus in the lives of his followers (John 14:15–16). Though the Greek word for "Spirit" is grammatically neuter, when the referent is the Holy Spirit John sometimes treats the word like a masculine form—a further hint that John thinks of the Spirit in personal terms. Elsewhere the Spirit speaks, feels, is grieved. The Spirit, like Jesus, is sometimes virtually indistinguishable from God; indeed, the coming of the Spirit into the lives of believers is precisely what mediates the presence of the Father and the Son (John 14:23). Yet at other times, the Holy Spirit may be sharply differentiated from the One who sent him—which can be Jesus, the Father, or Jesus and the Father (John 14:16, 26; 15:26; 16:7). If the full panoply of biblical evidence regarding the Spirit and his status as a "person" of the Godhead is not quite as clear or as full as is the evidence in regard to the Son, it is not very surprising. By God's determination, all must honor the Son just as they honor the Father (John 5:23): the same determination is not repeated with respect to the Spirit. One of the Spirit's distinctive roles, rather, is to bring glory to Jesus (John 15:14).

Second, the Spirit is peculiarly tied to the heirs of the new covenant. Old Testament prophets sometimes present the time of the Lord's visitation of his people, the time of the anticipated new covenant, as the time when the Spirit will be poured out upon men and women, young and old, without the distinctions implicit in the essentially tribal nature of the old covenant (e.g., Ezek. 36; Joel 2; cf. Acts 2). Thus when in Acts the prophetic Spirit falls upon the church, mediating God's presence, enabling believers to speak with tongues and to perform deeds of power, forging the early links among Jewish, Samaritan, and Gentile believers, and gently nudging the church into an expanding vision of Gentile mission,[14] this is understood to be nothing other than what God himself had promised in Scripture. Moreover, the Spirit not only prompts us to look backward to God's earlier promises about his coming and work, but forward as well, for in Pauline thought the Spirit is the

---

14. Against those who read the Spirit's work in Luke–Acts in narrow perspective, see M. M. B. Turner, "The Spirit of Prophecy and the Power of Authoritative Preaching in Luke-Acts: A Question of Origins," *New Testament Studies* 38 (1992): 66–88; and especially his "'Empowerment for Mission'? The Pneumatology of Luke–Acts: An Appreciation and Critique of James B. Shelton's *Mighty in Word and Deed*," *Vox Evangelica* 24 (1994): 103–22.

ἀρραβών, the deposit and hence the guarantee, of the promised inheritance awaiting us in the consummation.

The work of the Spirit in the believer is life transforming. In the language of the Fourth Gospel, men and women must be born again if they are to enter the kingdom (John 3:3, 5), and in this respect the Spirit is like the wind: just as you cannot give an exhaustive account of the wind's origins and mechanisms even while you cannot doubt its effects, so you cannot give an exhaustive account of the Spirit's origins and mechanisms even while you cannot doubt his effects (3:9). In other words, the assumption is that the effects are inevitable, observable, undeniable.

Third, the Spirit is intimately involved in the business of enabling people to understand and know the truth of the gospel. The mechanisms of the Spirit's work in this regard are not easy to fathom. To the cynical, it is altogether too easy to dismiss any hermeneutical or epistemological role for the Spirit as an ill-defined appeal to mysticism. Nevertheless, there is such an abundance of evidence for these elements of the Spirit's work that the Bible's story-line would be greatly impoverished if they were stripped out.

It is vital to recognize that although little children can understand many parts of the Bible's story, the Bible itself is not a simple book. I am not now referring to the sweep of its contents, the profundity of its thought or the intricacy of its patterns, but to two other characteristics: (1) its recurring reversal of human expectations: the older serves the younger, the last is first and the first is last, the wisdom of the world is foolishness with God, the weakness of God is stronger than all human strength, the life-giving Son dies so that the death-deserving may live; (2) its developing patterns are subtle and interwoven: instead of *merely* propositional predictions, there are models, types, adumbrations. An entire cultus, complete with sacrifices, priesthood, tabernacle or temple, most holy place, altars, and more, point forward to the unique sacrifice of Christ, who is simultaneously sacrificial lamb and high priest; the Davidic monarch, God's vassal, establishes a kingdom that anticipates the ultimate "David." We come "to expect that redemptive patterns are largely implicit in the text, interwoven in and through the 'natural' history of the text. Is this not the reason for the frequent scriptural call for those who have eyes to see and those who have ears to hear (Deut. 29:4; Isa. 6:10; 11:3; 32:3; Jer. 5:21; Ezek. 12:2; 40:4; 44:5; Matt. 13:16; Mark 8:18; Rom. 11:8)?"[15] Add to these epistemic challenges our sinful self-sufficiency, such moral and spiritual blindness that we willfully prefer pictures of God and of ourselves that are wildly out of synch with the pictures that God him-

---

15. Richard Lints, *The Fabric of Theology: A Prolegomenon to Evangelical Theology* (Grand Rapids: Eerdmans, 1993), 284.

self paints, and we begin to understand why in John's gospel Jesus says, "No one can come to me unless the Father who sent me draws him" (6:44), and why Paul insists, "The man without the Spirit does not accept the things that come from the Spirit of God, for they are foolishness to him, and he cannot understand them, because they are spiritually discerned" (1 Cor. 2:14). From a biblical perspective, human fallenness is precisely why God's gracious revelation, whether general or specific,[16] is so often not seen for what it is. The light comes into the world, but people prefer the darkness to light, because their deeds are evil (John 3:19–20). When God speaks, there will always be some who say it thundered (John 12:28–29).

However much men and women are rightly held responsible to understand and obey what God discloses, in different ways several New Testament writers make it clear that only the Spirit of God enables them to meet this responsibility. The Spirit convicts them of their sin (John 16:7–11);[17] the Spirit is the agent who transforms "natural" people into "spiritual" people, the consequence of which is that for the first time they truly understand the things of God (1 Cor. 2).

We ought not imagine that this work of the Spirit is normally accomplished apart from observable means. That the Spirit is needed if the "natural man" is to understand the things of God does not prompt Paul to abandon preaching until the Spirit has opened the minds of his targeted hearers. Far from it: Paul recognizes that God is pleased through the foolishness of what is preached to save those who believe (1 Cor. 1:21)—preaching whose efficacy lies not in manipulative eloquence but in "a demonstration of the Spirit's power" (1 Cor. 2:4). Similarly, although the Spirit of truth leads the early apostles, after Jesus' resurrection, into a fuller grasp of the significance of Christ and his cross-work than they could have absorbed before those shattering events (John 16:12–15), the development of that understanding took place in the matrix of the earliest history of the church. In other words, as the church came to grips with who Jesus was and what he had achieved by his death and resurrection, as they came in time to accept Gentiles on an equal basis as participants in the new covenant (even though the Gentiles did not pledge themselves to observe all the strictures of the old covenant), as the church worked through (and not without dispute and bitterness) such hot topics as kosher food, circumcision, the sufficiency of Christ, the nature of

---

16. For the relevance of the distinction, see Bruce A. Demarest, "General and Specific Revelation: Epistemological Foundations of Religious Pluralism," in Clarke and Winter, *One God One Lord*, 135–52.

17. The precise meaning of this remarkably condensed passage is disputed. I remain convinced that what the "Counselor" does is drive home to individual sinners their profound guilt in regard to their sin, their righteousness, and their judgment.

faith, and the relation of the new covenant to the old, the Spirit led the church into the positions crystallized in the New Testament documents. Similarly, one of the ways the Spirit leads believers today into increasing understanding of truth is through the local church—i.e., the Spirit may work through the congregation to enhance the grasp of the individual believer.[18]

But none of this means that the Spirit's work can be reduced to oratory, early church history, or contemporary ecclesiastical enculturation. One could have all of these features and produce nothing of enduring worth. The addition of the Spirit's work is critical. The "spiritual man"—the person who has the Spirit of God—"makes judgments about all things, but he himself is not subject to any man's judgment" (1 Cor. 2:15). The idea is not that the person with the Spirit enjoys a perfect grasp of quarks, fusion, and molecular biology, but that his or her understanding covers the sweep of human experience, including both the knowledge of the profane person and the knowledge of the God-knower. By contrast, profane persons are not in a position to stand in judgment of the person with the Spirit (however much they may protest to the contrary), since the dimension given by the Spirit of God is a closed book so far as they are concerned (1 Cor. 2:14). Regardless of how numerous they are, the blind have no right to tell the sighted that the sighted cannot see.

What the New Testament says about the Spirit is much richer than the few matters itemized here. My present purpose, however, is modest and twofold: (1) I wish to emphasize that what the Bible says about the Spirit must be fitted into the Bible's plot-line, as contributing elements to what is disclosed of God and of the salvation he has achieved. The word "Spirit" is not to be stripped of its canonical connections and then attached to every vague contemporary usage, as if every occurrence has the same referent. (2) The Christian's ability to exercise faith in Christ Jesus and to grasp spiritual realities is the product of the Spirit's work. Therefore we do not dare restrict our epistemological categories to those of secularists. To do so would be to deny a central point in what distinguishes us as Christians; to ask us to do so would be tantamount to asking us to blaspheme.

3. The Contribution of the Epistles

Once again, the aim here is not to survey the theological contribution of one corpus—in this case, the Epistles—to the Bible, but to delineate some of the elements that contribute substantially to the Bible's story-line, in particular those elements that are relevant to contemporary discussion of religious pluralism. One very important topic in this connection is Paul's under-

---

18. So, rightly, Clark H. Pinnock, "The Role of the Spirit in Interpretation," *Journal of the Evangelical Theological Society* 36 (1993): 495–96.

standing of the relationship between the covenants. Does he think that there are two covenantal paths that lead to redemption, one for Jews and the other for Gentiles, as a large number of modern writers argue? But that topic I shall reserve for the next chapter. It will be sufficient here to draw attention to three sorts of phenomena.

First, many of the themes already introduced into the Bible at an earlier stage of the story-line are further developed in the epistles. Implicitly I have already argued along these lines by tracking forward from earlier stopping places. Thus it is not hard to find texts in the Pauline epistles that portray God as simultaneously transcendent/sovereign and personal, or that reflect powerfully on the love of God. One does not have to look far to find mature development of themes such as election, the nature of sin, the primacy of grace. Themes first developed with clarity during the ministry of Jesus receive profound theological treatment in the Pauline and Johannine epistles, not least the significance of the cross, and the eschatological tension between the "already" and the "not yet."

Witherington has recently shown that a great deal of Paul's thought is ultimately grounded in the Hebrew Bible and in the common account of Jesus and his life and mission. In particular, the apostle's thought is decisively shaped by four interrelated narratives: first, creation, Adam and Eve, the Fall, and what it meant for the world to go wrong; second, the people of Israel and their history in that world gone wrong; third, the death and resurrection of Jesus, which simultaneously arises out of the story of Israel and out of the account of God as Creator and Redeemer; and finally, the history of the early church as the first steps are taken to set the world to rights again.[19] Doubtless one may quibble with this or that minor point. The strength of Witherington's work, however, must not be overlooked: the primary features of Paul's thought are grounded in the antecedent movements of the Bible's plot-line. And some themes introduced earlier reach a climax of comprehensive exposition at Paul's hand. One thinks, for example, of Paul's treatment of the Fall.[20]

In fact, one of the most striking features not only of Paul's thought but also of some other New Testament epistles is the firm insistence that the Hebrew Bible makes sense, from a Christian point of view, only if the parts of the narrative are read in their proper chronological sequence. Thus, over

---

19. Ben Witherington III, *Paul's Narrative Thought World: The Tapestry of Tragedy and Triumph* (Louisville: Westminster/John Knox, 1994).

20. Not only passages such as Romans 1:18–3:20 and Romans 5 should be considered, but also Ephesians 2 — on which see, most recently, Peter T. O'Brien, "Divine Analysis and Comprehensive Solution: Some Priorities from Ephesians 2," *Reformed Theological Review* (forthcoming).

against conservative Jews who hold that the law of Moses properly exercises a hermeneutical control over the entire Hebrew Bible, Paul in Galatians 3 and Romans 4 is quick to observe chronological distinctions: Abraham was justified *before* he was circumcised (Rom. 4), and the promise to Abraham, including the blessings through his seed to all the nations of the earth, was solemnly and unconditionally made by God himself many centuries before the law was given. For Paul, the "Christian" reading of the Old Testament turns absolutely on a fair and careful examination of the Bible's plot-line.

But no epistle more forcefully than Hebrews insists that the Old Testament story-line, *properly read*, drives one toward Jesus. To this end, the elements of the Old Testament plot-line must be laid out in chronological sequence. Thus in 3:7–4:11 the author ties together God's rest at the end of creation week, sabbath rest, the promise to enter the land of promise and thereby find rest, the actual entry into the land under the leadership of Joshua, and the invitation, centuries later, to those already living in the promised land, not to harden their hearts but still to enter the rest of God. The point of this exercise is to argue that the promised land was not the culminating rest, and that the developing and recurring theme of rest in the Hebrew canon can only be properly understood if it is understood to point forward beyond itself. In Hebrews 7, the announcement of a priest in the order of Melchizedek, an announcement made centuries after the establishment of the Levitical priesthood, is understood to pronounce the obsolescence in principle of that Levitical priesthood—and of the law with which it is inextricably entwined. In Hebrews 8, the announcement of the new covenant in Jeremiah 31 is understood to pronounce the first covenant obsolete.

In short, among the plethora of rich theological themes developed in the epistles is the taking up and explaining of the antecedent biblical story-line.

Second, it is vitally important to recognize that the earliest Christians wrestled with pluralism from the earliest years of the church's birth.[21] The precise shape of the pluralism the church confronted doubtless varied from place to place throughout the Roman Empire, but enough is known about particular sites to give us some idea of what early Christians faced.[22] The

---

21. The next two or three pages are largely drawn from D. A. Carson, "Christian Witness in an Age of Pluralism," in *God and Culture*, ed. D. A. Carson and John D. Woodbridge (Grand Rapids: Eerdmans, 1993), 43–45.

22. See, among others, Bruce W. Winter, "Theological and Ethical Responses to Religious Pluralism—1 Corinthians 8–10," *Tyndale Bulletin* 41 (1990): 210–15; David W. J. Gill, "Behind the Classical Façade: Local Religions of the Roman Empire," in *One God One Lord*, 72–87; Clinton Arnold, *Ephesians: Powers and Magic* (Cambridge: Cambridge Univ. Press, 1989); Thorsten Moritz, "'Summing-up All Things': Religious Pluralism and Universalism in Ephesians," in Clarke and Winter, *One God One Lord*, 88–111; Colin J. Hemer, *The Letters to the Seven Churches of Asia in Their Local Setting* (Sheffield: JSOT Press, 1986).

imperial cult became increasingly important, with cities vying for the privilege of becoming *neokoros*—that is, being granted permission to build a temple to honor and worship a particular Caesar. A city like Corinth not only had temples in honor of traditional Greek deities such as Apollo and Neptune, but it also boasted a sanctuary of the Egyptian gods Isis and Serapis.[23] The many mystery cults entered their own mystical appeals. The goddess Artemis, cherished not only at Ephesus but in other parts as well (e.g., in Patras in northern Peloponnesus), demanded sacrifices in which large numbers of birds and animals were burned to death, the people enraptured by the spectacle and excited by the shrieks. Such sacrifices provided large quantities of meat. The healing gods, the fertility cults, the forms of religion bordering on pantheism—all made their appeals. Despite the fact that some classicists tend to purge the Greco-Roman tradition of all that might be judged ignoble, David Gill and others have graphically shown that at the popular level the "early church was addressing people who worshipped rocks, believed plants could be deities, had sacred animals, accepted ritual castration and prostitution. In addition there were the cults that we normally associate with the Roman empire: Jupiter and the other Capitoline deities, as well as the cult of the Emperor himself."[24]

This enormous potpourri was pluralistic—that is, it was not a conglomeration of mutually exclusive religious groups, each damning all the others. Rather, the opinion of the overwhelming majority was that the competing religions had more or less merit to them. True, many religious adherents judged that their favored brand was best; but probably most saw no problem in participating in many religions. Indeed, the cultural and religious diversity within the Empire, enhanced by the imperial decision to arrange "god-swaps" between the Roman pantheon and the gods favored by newly subjugated peoples, ensured that more and more religions made fewer and fewer exclusive claims. Jews were viewed as an intransigent exception. Not only could they not show what their God was like, but they were prepared to die to defend their particular views. The Empire therefore made a grudging exception in their case, and it extended that exception to Christians as well, at least for as long as the imperial powers thought of Christianity as a sect within Judaism. Certainly the pluralism of the Roman Empire was not driven by the engines of naturalism (though some thinkers, such as Lucretius, were philosophical naturalists). Even so, the religious world that nascent Christianity confronted was profoundly pluralistic, and from this fact we must draw an important observation.

---

23. According to Pausanias 2.4.7.
24. Gill, "Behind the Classical Façade," 87.

The locus of the new covenant community was no longer a nation (as was the old covenant community) but a transnational fellowship seeking to live out the new life imparted by the Spirit in a world that could not be expected to share its values. Moreover, this world, politically speaking, was not a democracy in which ordinary citizens could have much direct say in the organization and direction of the Empire. It is impossible to draw straight lines from their circumstances to ours. Nevertheless it is impossible not to recognize that in the current unravelling of Western culture our drift toward pluralism is casting up many parallels to the situation Christians faced in the first century. More precisely, we find in our culture two opposing hermeneutical effects. At one level our culture is departing from the heritage of Judeo-Christian values that so long sustained it, and so we are removing ourselves from the worldview of New Testament writers. At another level we are returning, through no virtue of our own, to something analogous to the pluralistic world the earliest Christians had to confront, and so in this sense the New Testament can be applied to us and our culture more directly than was possible fifty years ago. The fundamental difference, of course, is that the modern rush toward pluralism owes a great deal to the church's weaknesses and compromises during the past century or two, while the church in the first century carried no such burden. Moreover, the earliest Christians confronted their world from the position of the underdog; we are inclined to confront our world from the position of the once favored mascot who has recently become or is in the process of becoming the neighborhood cur, and expend too much of our energy on howls of protesting outrage. Even so, we shall be less morbid and despairing if we read the Scriptures today and recognize that the challenges of pluralism are not entirely new.

Third, once we recognize that the world in which the epistles were written was a world steeped in religious pluralism, the exclusive claims of the epistles take on an even starker hue. Thus, against the claims of other intermediaries, Colossians insists not only on the supremacy of Christ but also on the exclusiveness of his sufficiency. While others recognize many "lords," many (pagan) baptisms, a wide variety of "hopes" (i.e., diverse visions of the *summum bonum*), Christians recognize one Lord, one faith, one baptism, one hope, and one God (Eph. 4:4–6). While some Greek philosophers opined that there was "one god," this projected deity was almost always portrayed in pantheistic terms (one of the prime reasons why many Greek writers could alternate between "god" and "gods" without any apparent difference in meaning). They could speak of "one god" but could not confess that "God is One." Paul insists that the one God is the God and Father of our Lord Jesus Christ, the God of creation and of the old covenant, who has supremely disclosed himself in his Son (Rom. 1; 1 Cor. 8). One cannot read Revelation 2–3 without discerning the titanic struggle the early church faced from the multifaceted pressures of pluralism.

In the light of such pressures, whatever their source, they did not flinch. Paul is prepared to pronounce his solemn *anathema* on those who preach some other gospel (Gal. 1:8–9; cf. 2 Cor.11:4). Christian leaders are told they must "hold firmly to the trustworthy message as it has been taught" so that they "can encourage others by sound doctrine and refute those who oppose it" (Titus 1:9). In his first epistle, John insists that genuine believers embrace certain doctrine, exhibit principled obedience to Christ, and love other believers—and it is not best two out of three. Doubtless these tests are in the first place designed to reassure the genuine believers in the light of the pressures placed on them by the rising popularity of proto-Gnosticism. At the same time, John also uses them to exclude those who utterly fail in these areas. Christians must therefore be discerning and learn to "test the spirits" because "many false prophets have gone out into the world" (1 John 4:1).

Similar passages could easily be multiplied. But perhaps we can be satisfied with the conclusions of one scholar who compares the *public* ministry reflected in such passages as Acts 14 (Lystra), Acts 17 (Athens), and 1 Corinthians 8 (public cultic activities), with the *private* challenges faced by first-century believers (e.g., 1 Cor. 10:14–11:1). He demonstrates:

> (I) that religious pluralism was clearly the setting for the speeches in Lystra and Athens, (II) that preaching there took cognizance of, and interacted with, the religious views of the audiences *viz.* "popular superstition" and the natural theology of the Stoics and Epicureans, (III) that while the latter two reached a *rapprochement* with popular piety, the speeches in Acts reflect no such accommodation in spite of Roman imperial religious policy, and (IV) that Paul's discussion of religious pluralism in the two spheres aimed to help the church interact with it in such a way as to enhance its evangelistic task and fulfil its social obligations to society.[25]

Indeed, it is surely safe to conclude that, by and large, the New Testament writers did not readily distinguish the pluralism of the day from the idolatry of the day: the destruction of the one was the destruction of the other.

4. The Climax

"Perhaps Herodotus was a better chronicler of events than the authors of the Pentateuch," writes Lesslie Newbigin, "but what is distinctive in the Hebrew understanding of history is the belief that it has a goal. For Greek thought this was impossible since the essence of perfection is changelessness,

---

25. Bruce W. Winter, "In Public and in Private: Early Christian Interactions with Religious Pluralism," in Clarke and Winter, *One God One Lord*, 112.

and perfection cannot arise from the changes of human history. By contrast the Old Testament writers look forward to a glorious and terrible consummation of history."[26] The New Testament writers, far from disagreeing, sharpen the vision. Not only are we given apocalyptic glimpses of the new heaven and the new earth, but the resurrection of Jesus Christ is understood to be the crucial foretaste of the general resurrection that awaits us. The whole universe still groans under the curse earned by our rebellion, but, consequent upon the resurrection of Jesus, the gift of the Spirit serves as the down payment and guarantee of the transformation to come at the time of our "adoption as sons" (Rom. 8:23).

> To believe that the embodied Word rose again is to trust that the corruptibilities everywhere evident in the bodies we know—earthly and heavenly—will not have the last word. So the creed assures us in its bold statement, "I believe in ... the resurrection of the body," and through its inseparable companions, the return of Christ, final judgment, and everlasting life. Resurrection, Christ's and ours, is the hope by which we live and die and the light by which we see and serve.[27]

The climactic vision of the Bible (Rev. 21:1–22:5) pulls together not a few of the Old and New Testament themes long since introduced. The new heaven and the new earth is also the new Jerusalem, the community of the covenant people, and the antithesis to the other prominent city in the Apocalypse, Babylon the Great, the mother of prostitutes (Rev. 17). The notion of a new Jerusalem unveiled at Messiah's coming finds its roots in the return to Jerusalem and in the reestablishment of the city after the Exile. Already in the apocalyptic literature of Second Temple Judaism new Jerusalem is a place in which the saints rejoice and enjoy the glory of God forever (*Testament of Dan* 5:12), not just the old city rebuilt, but a new one built to a heavenly pattern (*2 Esdras* 10:49). Paul recognizes that the "mother" of Christians is "the Jerusalem ... above" (Gal. 4:26); the epistle to the Hebrews recognizes that believers belong to the city whose "architect and builder is God" (11:10). Those who remain faithful in Philadelphia are inscribed with "the name of the city of my God, the new Jerusalem, which is coming down out of heaven from my God" (Rev. 3:12). Then, in a change of imagery, we are assured that there is no temple in this city, "because the Lord God Almighty and the Lamb are its temple" (21:22). In other words, all forms of mediation of the knowledge of God are now unnecessary. If the city is built in the shape of a cube (21:16), it is because the entire city has become the

---

26. *The Gospel in a Pluralist Society*, 103.
27. Gabriel Fackre, "I Believe in the Resurrection of the Body," *Interpretation* 46 (1992): 52.

Most Holy Place, the very locus of the presence of God. And that, finally, is the point: all along God had promised to be the God of his people and to dwell with them, whether in the tabernacle (Lev. 26:11–13) or in the less mediated and more intimate form characteristic of the new covenant (Jer. 31:33; Ezek. 37:27). But now the consummation takes place: "Now the dwelling of God is with men, and he will live with them. They will be his people, and God himself will be with them and be their God" (Rev. 21:3). "They will see his face" (22:4). One could go on and mention the allusions to the tree of life in the garden (22:2), the bride imagery (21:2,15) drawn in the first instance from the Old Testament prophets, the "son" language (21:7), and so forth. What is clear is that John sees this as the culminating step in the Bible's story-line. That step brings the people of God into the most intimate relationship with him. God and the Lamb are at the center of everything; the delight and well-being of his people are predicated on enjoying him and worshiping him forever. Heaven would be hell without him; with him, in this unimaginably splendid degree of intimacy and glory, there can no longer be any possibility of death, mourning, or pain: "the old order of things has passed away" (21:4). By the constant references to the Lamb, the reader is inexorably reminded that whatever blessedness is to be gained has been achieved by Jesus Christ: the Apocalypse is profoundly Christocentric. As Reicke puts it:

> [T]he final combat led by Christ as the Word of God (19:13) ends with his triumph over all destructive powers in the cosmos including the devil (20:10). . . . Elements of the Genesis reports on creation return in [the final] vision, but throughout in connection with the glory of Christ. At the revelation of Paradise Regained the prophet sees to his delight the water of life streaming out from the throne of God and the Lamb, and trees of life producing different fruits every month (22:1–2). He understands that no physical light and no polarity between night and day will exist in this metaphysical context, but that God himself will enlighten his adorers (22:5) in analogy to the intelligible light by which creation first began (Gen 1:3). This perfect life and light (cf. John 1:4) is supplied by Christ, who lets the faithful approach the tree of life in the new creation (Rev 22:14).[28]

But this exquisite state of blessedness is not for everyone without exception. The book of Revelation anticipates redemption for people "from every tribe and language and people and nation" (Rev. 5:9): in that sense, the sweep is "universal," i.e., it draws in men and women without distinction. But never does it suggest that the sweep is universal in the sense that it draws in all without exception. Thus, the beast out of the sea, the antichrist, claims the

---

28. Bo Reicke, "Positive and Negative Aspect of the World in the NT," *Westminster Theological Journal* 49 (1987): 369.

worship of everyone except those whose names have been written in the book of life belong to the Lamb (Rev.13:8). The beast out of the earth, the false prophet, stamps all of them, so that those not stamped by him are opposed and killed. For his part, the Lamb writes his name and his Father's name on the foreheads of *his* people (Rev. 14), so that the wrath of God falls only on those not so marked (the imagery is drawn from Ezekiel 9, where God instructs a man with an inkhorn to place a mark on the forehead of all those deeply troubled over the sins of Jerusalem to protect them from the judgment that is coming on the city).

So it is not surprising that in the final vision humankind is divided in two. On the one hand: "To him who is thirsty I will give to drink without cost from the spring of the water of life. He who overcomes will inherit all this, and I will be his God and he will be my son" (Rev. 21:6–7). Here is eternal life provided out of sheer grace ("I will give to drink without cost"), working out in the lives of those who confess their utter need ("to him who is thirsty") and who by God's grace "overcome." On the other hand: "But the cowardly, the unbelieving, the vile, the murderers, the sexually immoral, those who practice magic arts, the idolaters and all liars—their place will be in the fiery lake of burning sulfur. This is the second death" (21:8). It is important to see that these categories include not only what we would label the sociopathic, but also the religious: "those who practice magic arts" include occultists, "the unbelieving" includes all who do not believe the gospel, "the idolaters" include all whose God is not the God who is there.[29]

The theme of cosmic reconciliation in Christ, especially prominent in Ephesians (1:9–10, 20–23; 2:10–22; 3:6; Col. 1:19–20), when examined in the total context provided by those epistles, not to mention the entire biblical plot-line, provides the same sort of bifurcation. Believers understood that God is ever the Lord of all the earth (e.g., Josh. 3:11), but the fact remains that in Old Testament times the nations were alienated from God's covenant community, while Israel herself was marred by factions, divided within herself, and often sold out to compromise and idolatry. The prophets well under-

---

29. To use an expression made famous by Francis Schaeffer. Pheme Perkins, "Theological Implications of New Testament Pluralism," *Catholic Biblical Quarterly* 50 (1988): 23, finds this division of humanity in the Apocalypse so offensive that she is prepared to write it off in a kind of counsel of despair: "Both apocalyptic visions like Revelation and gnostic revelations like *Apocalypse of Adam* foster sectarian loyalty and passion at the price of a universalistic ethos and realistic vision. But in the end, it is the faith and not the fanatic fervor of the martyrs which will sustain the church into the next century." But this not only overlooks how common in the Bible is the theme of the division of humanity, but it also ignores the plethora of extraordinarily tight connections between the Apocalypse and the plot-line of antecedent Scripture. In other words, Perkins adopts universalism and/or pluralism as her god, and correspondingly rejects whatever challenges or defies her deity.

stood that this wretched state of affairs could not go on forever. The day of the Lord would dawn, in both judgment and glory. "The LORD will be king over the whole earth. On that day there will be one LORD, and his name the only name" (Zech. 14:9). The messianic Prince of Peace will pacify not only the nations, but even nature (Isa. 11). Such Old Testament passages—and there are many—might properly be labeled cosmic reconciliation. The burden of Ephesians and Colossians is that such cosmic reconciliation has already begun in the work and ministry and church of Jesus the Messiah. The alienation between Jew and Gentile is overcome in the one new humanity (Eph. 2:10–16);[30] the alienation between God and rebellious human beings is also overcome (2:17–18). Thus it is the church, the body of Christ, which is the place Jesus fills (1:23); the church is the locus where, according to the eternal purposes of God, the world and the evil powers witness the cosmic reconciliation already introduced (3:6–12). But none of this means that no one without exception will be excluded. Ephesians 5:5 lists sins that keep a person out of the kingdom; the next verse insists that God's wrath falls on those who do such things. The "all things" of Colossians 1:19–20 are set in an epistle where the apostle is at pains to distinguish between true doctrine and abject error, between a true view of Christ and a compromised one, between the kingdom of darkness and the kingdom of the Son God loves (Col. 1:13). If all the new creation is united in Christ, it does not follow that all of the old creation participates in the new creation.

5. High Stakes in the Story-line

All of these elements, and more besides, constitute the Bible's story-line. Together they establish what the gospel is, that from which we are saved, the nature of the One to whom we must give an account, the relative importance of this world and the next so far as the focus of our hopes and investments is concerned, the desperate plight in which we find ourselves as we reject the grace of God, the wonders of God's grace along with the ineffable brilliance of his holiness, and much more.

Now if this entire vision is set over against the competing visions of the religious pluralists, we immediately discover that the issues dividing Christians from pluralists are not merely epistemological, or merely Christological (though they are not less than both), or reducible to any simple set of points. An entire vision of reality is at stake. One thing is very clear:

---

30. For the theme of the extension of salvation beyond the boundaries of Jews and Judaism as traced out in the Pauline *Hauptbriefe*, it is still well worth perusing Johannes Munck, *Paul and the Salvation of Mankind* (London: SCM Press, 1959).

it is quite impossible to be a Christian, in any responsible use of that term, and be a pluralist (in the third sense of pluralism, established in chapter1).

Moreover, each position, seeking to give an explanation of the world, must account for the other position. The pluralist must explain the Christian, and will doubtless conclude that the Christian is too tightly bound by tradition, naive in the area of epistemology, intolerant of other views, and so forth. The Christian response, while striving to address the pluralist's agenda in a responsible fashion, must also articulate how the pluralist will be perceived in the Christian's worldview. The pluralist is an idolater, worshiping the created world more than the Creator. He or she so relativizes God's truth that God's own Son becomes an incidental on the religious landscape, and his sacrificial death and miraculous resurrection become insignificant and unbelievable respectively. Pluralists are inconsistent in that they want to be understood univocally while insisting that ancient authors, let alone God himself, cannot be. They may have many religious experiences, but none of them deals with the heart of the human problem, the sin that is so deeply a part of our nature. In short, we must deal with massively clashing worldviews, and part of our responsibility is to explain competing worldviews from our vantage point. We cannot possibly engage at that level unless we ourselves have thoroughly grasped the biblical story-line and its entailed theology.

Finally, from the development of this plot-line it should be clear that event and word belong together. Even the most spectacular of God's saving actions in history would have been far more ambiguous than it is, if God had not also provided words of explanation and exhortation. On the other hand, the contemporary drift toward literary studies that focus *all* attention on the text and none on that to which the text refers is deceiving. At first glance these studies seem more "biblical." But words without events to which they refer are useless from the perspective of bringing real salvation (as opposed to mere ideas). So while it is important to remember that God is a talking God, he does not sit around all day and do nothing but talk. The Bible's story-line is therefore not to be admired the way one admires a well-crafted work of fiction.

C. Pluralism, Inclusivism, and the Plot-line

In the first chapter three commonly defined positions were outlined: exclusivism, inclusivism, and pluralism. Briefly, exclusivism is the view that only those who place their faith in the Christ of the Bible are saved; inclusivism is the view that all who are saved are saved on account of the person and work of Jesus Christ, but that conscious faith in Jesus Christ is not absolutely necessary: some may be saved by him who have never heard of him, for they may respond positively to the light they have received. And pluralism is the view that all religions have the same moral and spiritual value, and offer the same potential for achieving salvation, however "salvation" be construed.

At the time I may have given the impression that these are nicely defined positions with clear boundaries. The reality, however, is more complex. We have already seen that the pluralist category is occupied by several positions. For example, some argue that all religions are equally responses to a God who loves. But the notion of a God who loves presupposes theism or at least deism; certainly it will not apply to, say, most strands of Buddhism. So others, notably John Hick, defend a pluralism in which all religions equally reflect an unknown Reality about which we can postulate nothing, other than that he/she/it/they approves/is enmeshed in/stands behind pluralism.

But now we observe further that the category of inclusivism, no less than pluralism, embraces a packet of distinguishable positions.[31] At one end lies what we might call "soft" inclusivism. This view is barely distinguishable from exclusivism. It holds that people must place their faith in Jesus Christ and his redemptive work to be saved, but allows the possibility, the bare possibility, that God in his grace may save some who have never heard of Christ, assuming that in response to his grace in their lives they cast themselves in repentance and faith upon the God discernible, however dimly, in Creation. The exegetical basis for this view is slender, and will be discussed in the next section. At the other end of the continuum lies what might be called "hard" inclusivism. This view still insists that however many are finally redeemed, the basis of that redemption is exclusively the person and work of Christ. In that sense, this view is to be sharply distinguished from pluralism. Nevertheless, "hard" inclusivists put more emphasis on believing than on believing Christ. They may say that Christ is *ontologically* necessary for salvation, but that knowledge of Christ is not *epistemologically* necessary. People must respond in repentance and faith to whatever light they have, and should not, it is argued, be held responsible for light that they do not have. "Hard" inclusivists may actually intimate that exclusivism is so repugnant to them that if they find they cannot adopt inclusivism they might well prefer pluralism.[32] Such a position is not all that far removed from Karl Rahner's (in)famous "anonymous Christian" view,[33] in which people from any and all religions might in reality be "anonymous" Christians, saved by Christ without ever having heard of

---

31. See the useful typology of Harold A. Netland, *Dissonant Voices: Religious Pluralism and the Question of Truth* (Grand Rapids: Eerdmans, 1991), 264–77. My own differs from his more in form than in content.

32. Cf. Clark Pinnock, "Toward an Evangelical Theology of Religions," *Journal of the Evangelical Theological Society* 33 (1990): 362; John Sanders, *No Other Name* (Grand Rapids: Eerdmans, 1992), 106.

33. This famous expression is found in a number of important passages, not least the following, in Karl Rahner, *Theological Investigations* (New York: Seabury, 1966), 5:131:

him; it is not far removed from the qualified universalism of Neal Punt.[34] At some point, as one moves along this spectrum, it is hard to avoid the conclusion that the differentiating reason why some are saved and others are not is the degree of religious sincerity in one's faith, *regardless of the object of that faith*, even though the *efficacious* ground of saving faith is Jesus Christ, even if he is not recognized.[35]

In what follows, then, I shall offer some biblical and theological reflections on the cogency of several positions, beginning with some examples from the pluralist camp and moving into several positions from the inclusivist camp. In each case my reasoning emerges from the structure and priorities implicit in the Bible's story-line. My purpose is to focus on several fundamental approaches and positions; I shall reserve comment on a number of disputed biblical passages until the next section.

1. Major biblical themes cannot properly be dismissed on the basis of perceived social dynamics.

For example, Castelli argues that when a powerful figure such as Paul urges others to imitate him (e.g., 1 Cor. 11:1), he instantly divides his hearers or readers into conformists and nonconformists. While ostensibly urging unity, in reality Paul is enforcing hegemony. The exhortation to imitate him is inherently political and coercive. If Paul gives as his reason why others should follow him the proposition that he himself follows Christ, he has deployed a particularly egregious form of manipulation. By contrast, we should reinstate values of difference and independence.[36]

At the risk of an *ad hominem* argument, I might be tempted to respond by saying that when a powerful writer like Castelli urges others to adopt her view of independence, she is instantly dividing her hearers into conformists and nonconformists. While ostensibly urging difference and independence, in reality she is enforcing postmodernism. The exhortation to follow her

---

"Christianity does not simply confront the member of an extra-Christian religion as a mere non-Christian but as someone who can and must already be regarded in this or that respect as an anonymous Christian. It would be wrong to regard the pagan as someone who has not yet been touched in any way by God's grace and truth."

34. *Unconditional Good News* (Grand Rapids: Eerdmans, 1980).

35. Of the many who adopt some form of this position, see, in addition to those just mentioned, Molly Truman Marshall, *No Salvation Outside the Church? A Critical Inquiry* (Lewiston: Edwin Mellen Press, 1993); and Ralph C. Wood, "What Ever Happened to Baptist Calvinism? A Response to Molly Marshall and Clark Pinnock on the Nature of Salvation in Jesus Christ and in the World's Religions," *Review and Expositor* 91 (1994): 593–608. Wood's understanding of "Baptist Calvinism" is extraordinary.

36. Elizabeth A. Castelli, *Imitating Paul: A Discourse of Power* (Louisville: Westminster, 1991).

reasoning in this regard is inherently political and coercive. If Castelli
as her reason why she should be followed the supreme importance of independence and difference, this is a particularly egregious form of the sin of
anarchy, of silly sheep going their own way (Isa. 53:6). By contrast, we should
reinstate values of conformity to the God who made us, to whom we must
give an account, and who has graciously and supremely disclosed himself to
us in Jesus Christ.

Of course, such an *ad hominem* argument is inadequate as a comprehensive rejoinder to Castelli, but it does expose the inherent emptiness of arguments that reduce truth questions to matters of social dynamics. I cannot
decide if Castelli's argument is a self-conscious deployment of the tactics of
deconstruction, but that is the effect. In any case it is important to insist that
if Paul's theology is true, his urging that Christians follow him as he follows
Christ is an important and faithful call to discipleship, is pleasing to God, is
designed for the good of his hearers, and is ignored to their detriment. But
if Paul's theology is false, it does not follow that Castelli is justified: it would
simply mean that she is as exploitative as what she condemns. That is the
perennial problem of all such pluralism: it cannot consistently argue its case
without succumbing to the same kind of appeal to authority that it denounces.

2. More generally, it is entirely improper to attempt to destroy the Bible's exclusivism by admitting selective biblical evidence displaced from its location in the Bible's story-line.

My point is not simply that one must take all the Bible or none of it. The
issue is more complex.

Consider three recent works, the first popular, the other two scholarly. In
the first, Harpur argues that everybody will eventually get to heaven (however "heaven" be conceived).[37] He acknowledges that one might interpret the
Bible in an exclusivist way, but cavalierly dismisses such a reading with the
comment that one can interpret the Bible to make it teach anything you want.
In defense of his own view, he insists that there are many passages in the Bible
that make it clear that God's will and intention is to reconcile the entire cos-
mos, including every person who has ever lived, to "Himself/Herself." He
then quotes some passages on the love of God, pointing out that there will be
one fold and one shepherd, a new heaven and a new earth, and so forth.

Apart from the primary point I am making here, which I shall elucidate
in a few moments, one must surely recognize how irresponsible Harpur's
reading of the Bible is *as reading*. We have already observed how complex and
subtle are the ways the Bible talks about the love of God (chap. 5); these are

---

37. Tom Harpur, *Life After Death* (Buffalo: McClelland & Stewart, 1991).

es, the Bible speaks of one fold—more accurately,
herd, but in the context (John 10) the point is that
nstituted of believing Jews and believing Gentiles
to make up one flock. The context makes it abun-
are many people, both Jews and Gentiles, who do not
belong ⌐⌐   ⌐k. And the passage that speaks most clearly of the new
heaven and the new ⌐arth, Revelation 21:1–22:5, specifically mentions those
who are excluded (21:8). Harpur's reading is either the crudest form of deconstruction, or just plain incompetent.

Now we may consider the two more erudite works. Watson argues that
all persons are the benefactors of divine grace, but that Christians are called
to a "*disciplined* discipleship." The primary blockage to seeing this truth, he
argues, crops up when those who have been especially privileged to be the
heralds of God's grace view this universal commission less in terms of responsibility than in terms of privilege, and when emphasis is laid on faith in Christ
rather than on Christ himself "as the center of our spiritual understanding—
the anthropocentric aberration which ironically denies the incarnational presence of God in humanity as a whole."[38] What is remarkable about this book
is the way it jumps around: Scripture, historical theology, biblical theology,
contemporary thought, systematic theology—bits and pieces are pulled in
from all over the theological landscape in order to justify the thesis. It certainly makes for entertaining reading. But the work is undisciplined: it draws
pieces together, cutting them and trimming them until they form a pastiche
justifying the predetermined end, viz. a certain kind of pluralism.[39] Along the
way some extraordinary steps are taken, not only in exegesis, but in historical and systematic theology.

In a learned essay, Eugene Boring surveys the texts in the seven undisputed letters of Paul that might be interpreted to support universal salvation,
and how they have been interpreted in recent scholarship.[40] By and large he
is careful not to milk texts for too much.[41] His own proposal is that Paul's

---

38. David Lowes Watson, *God Does Not Foreclose* (Nashville: Abingdon, 1990), passim,
esp. 104.

39. I say "a certain kind of pluralism" because clearly some pluralists and some universalists would be very unhappy with Watson's position. Although he does not restrict salvation
to a Christian locus, he does restrict disciplined discipleship to that locus. I cannot imagine
that devout Buddhist monks or committed Muslim fundamentalists will be convinced by his
argument, and a pluralist like Hick will inevitably see this as one more form of Christian pater-
nalism.

40. M. Eugene Boring, "The Language of Universal Salvation in Paul," *Journal of Biblical
Literature* 105 (1986): 269–92.

41. E.g., in commenting on 1 Corinthians 15:22 ("For as in Adam all die, so in Christ all
will be made alive"), Boring fully acknowledges that the two instances of "all" are parallel only

soteriological language utilizes conflicting "central encompassing images," and that these images "necessarily involve him in conflicting language games."[42] Boring concludes:

> Paul affirms *both* limited salvation *and* universal salvation. Because they are affirmed together, the ultimate logical inferences belonging to each are never drawn. Paul affirms both human responsibility and the universal victory of God's grace. As propositions, they can only contradict each other. As pictures, they can both be held up, either alternatively or, occasionally, together, as pointers to the God whose grace and judgment both resist capture in a system, or in a single picture. And this is ultimately what Paul did.[43]

The cogency of this analysis can be supported or destroyed only by examining at least some of the relevant texts, and that I shall attempt below. What one immediately observes, however, is how quickly Boring is prepared to assign inconsistent thought to Paul, befuddled by his own choice of "central encompassing images" and unable to see that they have landed him in insuperable contradictions. And all of this is postulated without placing the Pauline arguments in the stream of redemptive history, without attempting to locate Paul in the expanding but certainly coherent pattern of Christian eschatology. On close examination, as we shall see, Paul can be understood to provide truly universalistic texts[44] *only by extracting them both from the theological contexts the apostle's writings provide, and from the biblical context in which those writings are embedded.*

Although the structures of the respective positions of Harpur, Watson, and Boring are quite different, this is the problem with all three works. Something that the Bible as a whole quite clearly teaches, again and again, in many of its diverse corpora, and an intrinsic part of the biblical story-line, is neatly sidestepped and implicitly or explicitly denied by the expedients of (1) focusing on texts that are declared to be universalist once they are wrenched out of their context (Harpur), (2) synthesizing bits of text and bits of theology so as to arrive at the desired conclusion (Watson), or (3) so interpreting the texts of one corpus that the author of that corpus is transformed into a

---

as they are qualified by "in Adam" and "in Christ" respectively, "so that in fact the contrast in v. 22 is between all who die and some who are raised in Christ" (279).

42. Ibid., 275.

43. Ibid., 292. In defense of Boring, one must say that his analysis is more evenhanded than that of, say, Peggy Starkey, "Biblical Faith and the Challenge of Religious Pluralism," *International Review of Mission* 71 (1982): 66–77: who lifts expressions such as "all things are yours" (1 Cor. 3:21) and "reconcile to himself all things" (Col. 1:20) and "new humanity" (Eph. 2:15 NRSV) out of their contexts and gives them enormous and independent weight.

44. By "truly" universalistic texts I mean those that affirm that every single person who has ever lived or will ever live is finally saved.

dialectical (read "inconsistent") thinker because he is enslaved by his own images and is incapable of understanding those images either within the context of his own expressed thought or within the context of the biblical story-line of which he is a part.

My point, however, is not that one must take all of the Bible or none of it, but that if one holds that only some parts of the Bible are worthy of our allegiance, one must articulate the criteria by which the decisions are made, and the grounds for holding that those parts deserve our allegiance. The Christian who holds that God has disclosed himself in the Bible must of course offer a defense of that position—something I briefly took up in chapter 4. But if someone steps back from that position, I want to know the basis on which that person tries to defend his or her theological position by appealing to *parts* of the Bible. For example, if you can prove anything from the Bible (Harpur), why on earth does he think his position is correct, and try to convince others of it? If his position in reality depends on extrabiblical outlook or reasoning, then I want to know the grounds on which he concludes that God is the kind of being he envisages. Or again, what finally authorizes the synthetic pastiche of Watson? Transparently, it is not the biblical story-line. How does he know that the picture he paints is the way things are? What is the principle by which he selects bits of text and theological reasoning so as to compose this particular picture? How do Paul's "central encompassing images" relate to the entire Bible, and to reality? And as for Boring, is he telling us that the ultimate reality will resolve a merely apparent contradiction? It does not seem so. It seems, rather, that, as far as Boring is concerned, the "encompassing images" Paul develops really are mutually contradictory—in which case why should we bother to hold to either of them, let alone both of them? Or if, instead, the "encompassing images" are in reality constrained by the contours of Paul's thought and by biblical theology, then perhaps Boring has pushed them much too hard, no longer allowing them to operate in their canonical context, and in fact they are not mutually contradictory—so that Boring's analysis is fundamentally mistaken.

In each case my point is the same. Why do these writers think that God is the sort of being they describe? The more one presses this sort of question, the more one is driven to the conclusion that the dominating influence is not respect for the texts, or evenhanded hermeneutics, or reverent submission to revelation, *but unqualified commitment to some form of pluralism or "hard" inclusivism.* And how could one possibly know that such a position is right? How could one possibly reform it? Even if someone were to come back from the dead to challenge our presuppositions, some would still not believe.

3. In particular, it is inappropriate for pluralists and "hard" in-
vists to appeal to the love of God, in such a way that they fail to listen
(a) to what the biblical texts actually say about the love of God, and
(b) to what else the biblical texts say that is contradicted by their
understanding of the love of God.

One of the most remarkable books guilty of this breach is the volume by John Sanders, which I have already mentioned.[45] Sanders frankly acknowledges that he has no very satisfactory response to the person who insists that the Bible really does teach the wrath of God, God's grace and sovereignty in election, crippling human depravity that includes noetic effects, and so forth. But he holds that many such doctrines are exegetically disputable. What is not disputable, he argues, is what the Bible says about the unconditional love of God, full of redemptive purpose. If we focus on that point, we are driven to some form of inclusivist position. Doubtless the crucial redemptive act was accomplished by Christ. But given the love of God that prompted it, it is surely inconceivable that God would then condemn millions and millions of people who have never heard the good news about that redemption. All the apparently exclusivist passages (e.g., John 14:6; Acts 4:12) he dismisses on the grounds that "it is not certain from these passages that one *must* hear of Christ in this life to obtain salvation. They simply say there is no other way to heaven except through the work of Christ; they do not say one has to know about that work in order to benefit from the work."[46] The same conclusion reached by Pinnock: "If God really loves the whole world and desires everyone to be saved, it follows logically that everyone must have access to salvation."[47]

Four points must be made.

First, we have already seen (especially in chap. 5) that the Bible speaks of the love of God in a variety of complex ways. One could similarly demonstrate that the Bible speaks of the will of God in several complex ways: as God's decree, God's desire, God's permission, and so forth. It is not easy to see how all that the Bible says about God's sovereignty, about God's transcendence, about God's love, and about God's goodness fit together. At bottom, the notion of a personal/transcendent God is fraught with difficult unknowns. But that the Bible actually does present God in such complex terms can be doubted only by those with a remarkable gift for reductionism.

---

45. *No Other Name*, (Grand Rapids: Eerdmans, 1992).

46. John E. Sanders, "Is Belief in Christ Necessary for Salvation?" *Evangelical Quarterly* 60 (1988): 246.

47. Clark H. Pinnock, *A Wideness in God's Mercy: The Finality of Jesus Christ in a World of Religions* (Grand Rapids: Zondervan, 1992), 157.

Not surprisingly, the nature and character of God are rich and complex. To take one strand of the theme of the love of God and so spin it that one arrives at flat contradictions with respect to the rest of the biblical evidence is either misguided or unconscionable. One of the most important hermeneutical constraints one should adopt in order to avoid such reductionism is this: Permit the various attributes and characteristics of God to function in your theology only in the ways in which they function in Scripture; never permit them to function in your theology in such a way that the primary data, the data of Scripture, are contradicted. Thus one must not infer fatalism from the sweeping biblical data about God's sovereignty; one must not infer that God is finite from the constant biblical portrayal of God personally interacting with finite persons. From God's knowledge and sovereignty we must not justify prayerlessness; from the exhortations to pray and not give up, we must not suppose God is coerced by our much speaking (compare Matt. 6:7–8 and Luke 18:1). Precisely because God is so gloriously rich and complex a being, we must draw out the lessons the biblical writers draw out, and no others.

Consider the response to the Lausanne Covenant (which adopts an exclusivist stance)[48] offered by Carl Braaten. Braaten insists that to hold this view is

> to teach as dogmatic truth and as a criterion for being faithful to the gospel of Jesus Christ that all of those who die or who have died without conscious faith in Jesus Christ are damned to eternal hell. If people have never heard the gospel and have never had a chance to believe, they are lost anyway. The logic of this position is that children who die in infancy are lost. The mentally retarded are lost. . . . [49]

But I suspect most of the evangelicals who signed the Lausanne Covenant would not argue that children who die in infancy and the mentally incapacitated are lost. Many of them would assert the opposite; some of them would say the Scriptures do not speak to that point clearly, but that they are willing to trust what we *do* know of the goodness and love of God. As for the fate of those who have never heard, Braaten himself, if I understand him aright, thinks those who reject Jesus Christ "are damned to eternal hell." So if a studious, moral, devout, God-fearing Muslim rejects Jesus Christ, Braaten thinks he is in the same position as the exclusivist thinks belongs to those who have not put their faith in Christ—but I am not sure he would use the motive language of his own position. The difference lies in whether or not those who

---

48. J. D. Douglas, ed., *Let the Earth Hear His Voice* (Minneapolis: World Wide Publications, 1975), 3–4.

49. Carl E. Braaten, "The Uniqueness and Universality of Jesus Christ," in *Faith Meets Faith*, ed. Gerald H. Anderson and Thomas F. Stransky (Grand Rapids: Eerdmans, 1981), 73.

have not heard of Christ are justly condemned. But about this I shall say more below.

A more hidden reductionism is found in Lesslie Newbigin's criticism of exclusivism. If it were true, he writes, "then it would be not only permissable but obligatory to use any means available, all the modern techniques of brainwashing included, to rescue others from this appalling fate.... If we hold this view, it is absolutely necessary to know who is saved and who is not, and we are then led into making the kind of judgments against which Scripture warns us."[50] I have benefited so greatly from the writings of Newbigin on the subject of pluralism that it grieves me to point out that these are bad arguments. They work only by taking certain facets of the exclusivists' position about God and salvation, ignoring the rest of their "package," and then drawing inferences that the exclusivists themselves never draw precisely because for them there is a fuller "package." Newbigin's argument, in short, is caricature, and I wish he would take as much care in describing the positions of people a little to the right of him as he obviously takes with people who are far to the left of him. I know no exclusivist who argues it is necessary for us to know exactly who is saved and who is not, or who would sanction brainwashing. The Arminians among them would insist on the importance of free will; the Calvinists, that it is God who saves by the preaching of the Word, so that brainwashing is not only counterproductive but usurps the place of God. Moreover, the same Scriptures that warn us against judgmentalism assure us that, in principle, believers are recognizable by their fruit (Matthew 7).

In short, the major thesis of the Sanders book, a central plank in the platform of the "hard" inclusivists, and a fair bit of the criticism of the exclusivists' position, are all profoundly flawed by theological reductionism and sometimes by rather offensive caricature.

Second, the texts that are most commonly cited to prove that God loves everyone without distinction and with a redeeming love are four, and on close inspection it is very doubtful that these four can bear the weight that is being made to rest on them. They are: 1 Timothy 2:3–4: " ... God our Savior, who wants all men to be saved and to come to a knowledge of the truth." Titus 2:11: "For the grace of God that brings salvation has appeared to all men." 2 Peter 3:9: "The Lord ... is patient with you, not wanting anyone to perish, but everyone to come to repentance." 1 John 2:2: "[Jesus Christ] is the atoning sacrifice for our sins, and not only for ours but also for the sins of the whole world."

---

50. *The Gospel in a Pluralist Society*, 173. Newbigin is apparently followed by Ken Gnanakan, *The Pluralist Predicament* (Bangalore: Theological Book Trust, 1992), 174.

There are two features in these texts that must be recognized. The first is that God's stance toward the world is commonly (i.e., not only in these texts, but elsewhere as well) presented as gracious, salvific. He is the God who takes no pleasure in the death of the wicked; he is the God who loves the world so much he sends his Son. What should be inferred from this sublime truth? Some infer that since God is omnipotent this redeeming love must eventually win all without exception—the universalist's conclusion. But that is to draw a conclusion that has to wipe out much of what else the Bible has to say; it is to create a grid from part of the data in order to filter out other parts of the data—and thus we return to my first point (above). Others infer that since God wants all to be saved, but that since not all are saved, God must be limited in knowledge and power. Methodologically, the same error is being committed. It is surely better to recognize that this is only one of the things that is said about God, his love, his holiness, his wrath, his purposes, and so forth, and to rejoice that God's stance toward his rebellious world is so redemptive when he could with perfect justice condemn us all, without drawing conclusions that contradict other parts of the primary evidence.

But in the second place, one must recognize that the "all" or "the whole world" or similar expressions in these texts cannot easily be taken to mean "all without exception." They mean something closer to "all without distinction." Thus if Titus 2:11 tells us that the grace of God that brings salvation has appeared "to all men," if we take "all men" to mean all without exception the statement is demonstrably false. In terms of the foundational "appearance" of the grace of God in the incarnation, the recipients were relatively few people, almost all of them citizens of one small vassal state at the eastern end of the Mediterranean; in terms of the existential "appearance" of the grace of God in the salvation of men and women, the recipients were a rising number of people in the Roman Empire, plus a few outsiders like the emissary from Candace's court (Acts 8), but the vast majority of human beings then living, to say nothing of those who lived before and after that time, had seen nothing of this "appearance" of the grace of God. In any case, the point of the Titus passage is that the grace of God has appeared "to all men *without distinction*," i.e., not to Jews only, but to Jews and Gentiles alike, without distinction, to slave and free alike, without distinction. So in the context, Christian slaves are told they are to live in such a way that "they will make the teaching about God our Savior attractive. For the grace of God that brings salvation has appeared to all men" (Titus 2:10–11).

Similar things could be said about other passages. For instance, 1 John 2:2 is almost certainly written against the background of the rising gnostic heresy, in which some people were claiming to be "spiritual" and to have an insider's special "knowledge" that others could not attain. These favored people, in the gnostic view, were intrinsically superior. To combat this profoundly unbiblical elitism, John finds it necessary not only to reassure the faithful believers that they, if anyone does, enjoy true "anointing" from God (e.g., 1 John 2:27), but to point out that Christ's cross-work is not just for "us" or for "our" sins, but also for the sins of the whole world without distinction.[51]

It is wonderfully reassuring to learn that Christ died for blacks as well as whites, for women as well as for men, for the educated as well as for the ignorant, for Arabs as well as for Jews, for the rich as well as for the poor. But to draw from such texts the inferences advanced by the "hard" inclusivists is without exegetical warrant.

Third, there is in any case a logical flaw in the connection that "hard" inclusivists draw between the love of God and human accessibility to salvation. Recall Pinnock's wording: "If God really loves the whole world and desires everyone to be saved, it follows logically that everyone must have access to salvation."[52] I have already indicated that in Pinnock's hands the protasis masks a number of important biblical complexities. But if we let it stand just as it is—and in certain contexts I would—then does the conclusion "logically" follow?

No, of course not. Assuming for the sake of the argument an Arminian understanding of what "God desires everyone to be saved" means (and with which Pinnock would agree), one immediately observes that most Arminians, historically speaking, have adopted a stance far removed from "hard" inclusivism. They hold that "God may desire the salvation of all men, *but* getting the gospel . . . to these people is *our* task."[53]

Fourth, I cannot escape the feeling that the entire presentation of Pinnock, Sanders, and most other "hard" inclusivists ends up, ironically, with a tragic distortion of the love of God. The tone of the Bible, as we have seen by sketching its story-line, is that if we human beings are lost, it is because of our sin. Our guilt before God justly earns his wrath. If we are not consumed,

---

51. The issues in this verse are extraordinarily complex. I have discussed them at length in my commentary on the Johannine Epistles in the New International Greek Testament Commentary series (forthcoming).

52. *A Wideness in God's Mercy*, 157.

53. Ronald H. Nash, *Is Jesus the Only Savior?* (Grand Rapids: Zondervan, 1994), 135. Moreover, as Nash points out (130–34), since Pinnock's God, unlike the understanding of God in mainstream Arminianism (let alone Christianity generally), is necessarily ignorant of the outcome of future free human decisions—including, presumably, the decision to have children, where they will live, what they will eat and read, and so forth—it is far from clear what Pinnock means by insisting that God must give access to salvation to all of them. He cannot even know how many will exist. Or is this universal provision of access effected by general revelation and/or by the *imago Dei*, regardless of how many human beings there are, what they are like, where they live, and so on? If so, Pinnock's argument needs much more substantiation.

it is of the Lord's mercy. If one sinner is saved, that salvation owes everything to the love of God. The love of God is presented as surprising, undeserved, unmerited, lavish. Yet somehow the "hard" inclusivists have turned the discussion around so that if God does not try harder, the blame for anyone perishing should be laid at his door. Thus what starts off as a defense of the love of God quickly turns into an indictment of God. Worse, the condemnation of guilty rebels that seems so transparently obvious in the Bible's story-line is now transmuted into a different kind of story, a "pity the perpetrator" story: they may be guilty, but if they do not have free access to a way of escape, surely it would be unjust to condemn them! How else can one understand this passage from Pinnock (not atypical, I fear)?

> The implication of popular eschatology is that the downtrodden of this world, unable to call upon Jesus through no fault of their own, are to be rejected for eternity, giving the final victory to the tyrants who trampled them down. Knowing little but suffering in this life, the unevangelized poor will know nothing but more and worse suffering in the next.[54]

This distortion of the love of God is in part accomplished, as we have seen, by pulling certain themes out of the Bible, creating a grid, and using that grid to eliminate or at least domesticate other biblical themes. Ironically, these inclusivists charge their opponents with the same vice, but their charge really will not stick. Thus Pinnock dismisses the picture of the sovereign God absorbed by most Christians who read their Bibles in terms like these: such a God has "to control everything like an oriental despot,"[55] he "forces [people] to enact the pre-programmed degrees,"[56] he is "virtually incapable of responsiveness";[57] indeed, "insofar as certain of its representatives have presented God as a cruel and arbitrary deity, orthodox theology badly needs revision and correction."[58] But who are these "representatives"? Most of them are simply faithful Christian teachers and preachers who are quoted by Pinnock without regard for their attempt to represent the balance and synthesis of the biblical portrait of God. Thus they say something about God's total omniscience and total omnipresence, and Pinnock immediately dismisses it as cruelty, arbitrariness, restrictiveness, fatalism, and so forth—even though the best of the writers thus cited disavow fatalism, or any hint of arbitrariness or cruelty on the part of God. They faithfully record what the Bible also says

---

54. *A Wideness in God's Mercy*, 152.
55. Clark H. Pinnock, ed., *The Grace of God, the Will of Man: A Case for Arminianism* (Grand Rapids: Zondervan, 1988), x.
56. Ibid., 20.
57. Ibid., 24.
58. *A Wideness in God's Mercy*, 19.

about God's personhood, his responsiveness, his love, and so forth, and acknowledge that it is not easy to keep all of these attributes together.

The fact of the matter is that one can avoid major error in one's doctrine of God only by keeping together what God has joined. It does no good to paint those who hold to God's unlimited sovereignty as ogres (especially when they themselves insist that such sovereignty never functions in Scripture to minimize human responsibiltiy or to turn God's love into play-acting), and then so react as to deny to God the full orb and sweep of attributes that the Scriptures assign him. Piper responds by "letting A. W. Tozer [certainly no Calvinist!] speak for thousands of us who know the God of total omniscience and total omnipotence, not as some lifeless philosophic idea, but as the all-satisfying Wonder and precious Father and Friend of our lives":[59]

> Omnipotence is not a name given to the sum of all power but an attribute of a personal God whom we Christians believe to be the Father of our Lord Jesus Christ and of all who believe on Him to life eternal. The worshiping man finds this knowledge a source of wonderful strength for his inner life. His faith rises to take the great leap upward into the fellowship of Him who can do whatever he wills to do, for whom nothing is hard or difficult because He possesses power absolute.[60]

4. Judging by the Bible's story-line, one must strenuously object to readings of Scripture that infer from every reference to God's sovereign activity among the nations, evidence of God's saving work among them.

According to Pinnock, the Bible "recognizes faith, neither Jewish nor Christian, which is nonetheless noble, uplifting, and sound." It is demonstrated not only in pre-Abrahamic believers such as Abel and Enoch, but in Ruth, Naaman, the Queen of Sheba, Cornelius, and others. "These were believing men and women who enjoyed a right relationship with God and lived saintly lives, under the terms of the wider covenant God made with Noah." And, "All who achieve holiness, whether in the church or outside it, achieve it not as a result of their own efforts but by the grace of God, which they received by faith."[61] Moreover,

---

59. *The Pleasures of God*, 73.

60. A. W. Tozer, *An Anthology* (Camp Hill: Christian Publications, 1984), 94. It is still eminently worthwhile to read the Puritan pastor and scholar Stephen Charnock, *The Existence and Attributes of God*. The original work was 1,100 pages long, and some reprints have all of it. A usefully abridged volume (800 pages!) was published in Grand Rapids by Sovereign Grace Publishers (1971).

61. *A Wideness in God's Mercy*, 92.

When Jews and Muslims, for example, praise God as the Creator of the world, it is obvious that they are referring to the same Being. There are not two almighty creators of heaven and earth, but only one. We may assume that they are intending to worship the one Creator God that we also serve. The same rule would apply to Africans who recognize a high God, a God who sees all, gives gifts to all, who is unchangeable and wise. If people in Ghana speak of the transcendent God as the shining one, as unchangeable as a rock, as all-wise and all-loving, how can anyone conclude otherwise than that they intend to acknowledge the true God as we do? . . . The proof that people commonly intend the same deity as Christians worship is seen when the Bible is translated into the languages of the world. The word "God" normally can be rendered by a word already known to the people in their own languages as referring to the same Supreme Being. People fear God all over the world, and God accepts them, even where the gospel of Jesus Christ has not yet been proclaimed.[62]

Suppose, then, that a religion is exceedingly alien to biblical faith. Pinnock comments:

Some question whether God would put up with a religion that was grossly deficient. Would God accept people whose beliefs fall far short of the complete truth? Yes, I think he would. For Scripture often hints at how merciful God is, even in the realm of religion. With liberality Yahweh permitted the nations to worship him in ways not proper for Israel to do (Dt 4:19). God allowed Naaman the Syrian leper, after his healing, to worship in Rimmon's temple because of the delicate circumstances he was in (2 Ki 5:18). Paul says that God permitted the nations to walk in their ways in past generations (Ac 14:16). . . . If God did not accept people whose religious faith was deficient, who among us could stand before him? . . . [H]ow can one fail to appreciate the noble aspects of the Buddha, whose ethical direction, compassion, and concern for others is so moving that it appears God is at work in his life? Gautama resembles the sort of "righteous man" whom Jesus told his disciples to receive (Mt 10:14). . . . I think we should not overemphasize the impersonal character of Buddha's faith. Of course, Buddhism is not Christianity and it does not try to be. But how does one come away after encountering Buddhism and deny that it is in touch with God in its way?[63]

How shall we respond to such reasoning?[64]

---

62. Ibid., 96–97.

63. Ibid., 101, 100.

64. It must be said that much of this sort of reasoning is encountered in the documents of Vatican II (especially *Nostra Aetate* and *Ad Gentes*) and related discussion. For a competent survey and evaluation, see John Nyquist, "The Use of the New Testament as Illustrated in Missiological Themes Within Selected Documents of the Second Vatican Council," Ed.D. dissertation, Trinity Evangelical Divinity School, 1991. See also David Wright, "The

First, the names on the list of people who in Pinnock's view prove that *faith* is critical, but not necessarily the *content* of Christian faith, are highly varied. The content of the faith of an Enoch, say, or of a Ruth, is surely tied to their particular locations in redemptive history. (What that may or may not say about those who today are "informationally B.C." I shall briefly discuss below.) It is far from clear to me that the Bible is interested in affirming that the Queen of Sheba is among the saved. I shall argue in the next section that Acts presents Cornelius as quite definitely not being among their number, until the gospel came to him.

Second, the argument is loaded with ambiguous sentences that are designed to tilt one's prejudices but do not really advance the argument. As we have seen, Pinnock writes, "All who achieve holiness, whether in the church or outside it, achieve it not as a result of their own efforts but by the grace of God, which they received by faith."[65] But what is meant by "achieve holiness"? If it means they are saved, then the sentence, stripped out of Pinnock's context, is formally correct (though the meaning of "church" in that case is somewhat alien to New Testament usage). But within Pinnock's context, the expression "All who achieve holiness" is clearly made to apply to those whose lives reflect some virtues that Christians uphold, even though the people in question are avowedly not Christians themselves. But what Christian has ever argued that all people are as bad as they could possibly be? Most believers speak of "common grace," or they embrace some other parallel theological component, to account for the fact that by God's gracious favor all kinds of people are restrained from many kinds of evil, and exhibit many different degrees of sanctity. But none of that means they are saved. Yes, one may agree that such people "achieve it not as a result of their own efforts but by the grace of God,"[66] but does it necessarily follow that such grace "they received by faith"? The point of "common grace" affirmations is precisely that much of God's grace is given "commonly," i.e., without reference to whether or not the individual exercises faith, or even exercises faith in some false deity. God commonly sends his rain upon the just and the unjust: that is a gracious gift that in no way demands the exercise of faith, still less orthodox faith, for its receipt. And the morally attractive features of Buddhism compel us not to "deny that it is in touch with God in its way."[67]

Watershed of Vatican II: Catholic Attitudes Towards Other Religions," in Clarke and Winter, *One God One Lord*, 153–71.

65. *A Wideness in God's Mercy*, 92.

66. Strictly speaking, unless one espouses a kind of "let go and let God" theology, this antithesis is troubling. It would be better to say that whatever effort such people put into the achieving of holiness, even that effort is the result of the grace of God.

67. Pinnock, *A Wideness in God's Mercy*, 100.

But the suggestion that Buddhism is "in touch with God in its way" is either cleverly misleading or fundamentally misguided. It is the sort of statement that is difficult to deny, but, like many ecumenical statements, the agreement is achieved by using language so fuzzy that people who disagree fundamentally over important things agree to the statement, precisely because they mean quite different things by it. Most branches of Buddhism do not think of God as a personal being at all. Does being "in touch with God in its way" simply mean that Buddhists are in touch with their conception of an impersonal deity as they conceive him? If so, the claim is the merest truism. But if, as the context seems to show, Pinnock means to suggest that by their altruism Buddhists really are in touch with the God and Father of our Lord Jesus Christ, albeit in a way that is seriously misconceived, then one wants to ask what is meant by being "in touch" with God. From a Christian perspective, whatever virtues one finds in Buddhism can ultimately be traced to God, and thus I suppose it is not wrong to say that Buddhists are in touch with God. But this no more means that Buddhists are saved than to say that staunch altruistic atheists are in touch with God means that they are saved.[68] Demarest is quite right when he says:

> On the basis of God's universal general revelation and common enabling grace, undisputed truths about God, man, and sin lie embedded to varying degrees in the non-Christian religions. In addition to elements of truth, the great religions of the world frequently display a sensitivity to the spiritual dimension of life, a persistence in devotion, a readiness to sacrifice, and sundry virtues both personal (gentleness, serenity of temper) and social (concern for the poor, nonviolence). But in spite of these positive features, natural man, operating within the context of natural religion and lacking special revelation, possesses a fundamentally false understanding of spiritual truth.[69]

Third, one must ask if it is so very clear that religions that on some axis or other refer to God in terms Christians recognize prove that they are referring to the *same* God. If having some characteristics in common were a sufficient criterion for sameness, one could prove that dogs are cats because both species have four legs and two eyes,[70] or that the God of Mormons is the God of Jehovah's Witnesses is the God of orthodox Christians because all three groups hold that in some sense God is the God and Father of our Lord Jesus

---

68. Cf. Ramesh P. Richard, *The Population of Heaven* (Chicago: Moody Press, 1994), 84–85.

69. Bruce A. Demarest, *General Revelation* (Grand Rapids: Zondervan, 1982), 259.

70. Richard, *The Population of Heaven*, 82–83, offers another example: "After a football win, one university fraternity got drunk with beer and water; another with brandy and water; another with gin and water; and a fourth with whiskey and water. Obviously, the common factor for the sophomoric drunkenness was the water from the university's water system!"

Christ. By this sort of criterion, Pinnock seems prepared to say that people believe in some *other* god only if their god is unlike the biblical God on every conceivable front. The question, then, is not whether or not both Allah and the God of the Bible are rightly designated the Almighty Creator—of course that is true—but whether or not the configuration of affirmations and denials about what God is like in the two cases warrant speaking of the same God. One can usefully speak of the common monotheistic heritage of Judaism, Christianity, and Islam, and identify common features in their respective doctrines of God, but one must at least ask whether, say, the pattern of how and why this God saves, including salvation's basis and conditions, is the same in the three systems of thought. If not, the commonalities belie differences that simply cannot be responsibly ignored.[71] "We must not conclude," writes Pinnock, "just because we know a person to be a Buddhist, that his or her heart is not seeking God."[72] True; but which God? At the end of the day, it is difficult to see how this criterion is anything other than the old assurance that it is sufficient to be religiously sincere.

Moreover, that the word for "God" already in use in the receptor language is often (though by no means always) used by Bible translators when the Bible is first put into that language can scarcely be thought to prove that God is the same being in both systems of thought. Even the slightest familiarity with the work of Bible translators around the world discloses that Christians sometimes have to work hard to fill available words with somewhat revised semantic content, and in some cases the receptor peoples strenuously object to Christians using their term for "God" (one thinks, for instance, of the banning of the use of the word "Allah" outside some Malaysian Muslim circles), precisely because *they* perceive a difference in referent even where some inclusivist Christians do not.[73]

Fourth, Pinnock's appeal to certain Scriptures is at least questionable. Doubtless some take Deuteronomy 4:19 to mean that God permitted the nations to adopt various forms of (idolatrous) worship that were forbidden to Israel,[74] but it is by no means clear that the sanction of the text goes quite so far.[75] Has God apportioned the worship of the sun and the moon and the stars to the other nations, or has he apportioned the sun and the moon and the

---

71. See Nash, *Is Jesus the Only Savior?* 113, on the inappropriateness of speaking of the description of the Ghanaian god in terms of "transcendence."

72. Pinnock, *A Wideness in God's Mercy*, 112.

73. Cf. Richard, *The Population of Heaven*, 80–84.

74. E.g., P. C. Craigie, *The Book of Deuteronomy*, New International Commentary on the Old Testament (Grand Rapids: Eerdmans, 1976), 137.

75. Cf. A. D. H. Mayes, *Deuteronomy*, New Century Bible Commentary (Grand Rapids: Eerdmans, 1979), 154.

stars to all the nations—and is particularly fearful of Israel following the distorting and destructive practices of the surrounding pagan nations?[76] Moroever, if God graciously allows Naaman to continue to go with his Master into the temple of Rimmon, and tip his hat, as it were, to the pagan god, on account of political considerations, it is in the context of a man who has come to believe that only the God of Israel is the true God, so much so that he even wants to pack home some of Israel's dirt as the base for his altar (2 Kings 5:17). In other words, it is difficult to see how this passage can serve to justify some generalizing principle about the adequacy of pagan faith.

5. Although Sanders and especially Pinnock often speak of the importance of faith, they rarely listen to what the New Testament has to say about the content of faith, about the object of faith.

Consider, for example, the following statements: "people can receive the gift of salvation without knowing the giver or the precise nature of the gift."[77] Inclusivism "denies that Jesus must be the object of saving faith."[78] "'Saving faith' . . . does not necessitate knowledge of Christ in this life. God's gracious activity is wider than the arena of special revelation. God will accept into his kingdom those who repent and trust him even if they know nothing of Jesus."[79] "Faith in God is what saves, not possessing certain minimum information."[80] "A person is saved by faith, even if the content of faith is deficient (and whose is not?). The Bible does not teach that one must confess the name of Jesus to be saved."[81] "The issue that God cares about is the direction of the heart, not the content of theology."[82]

Some of this argument is slanted by the form of the preferred antitheses. For example: "Faith in God is what saves, not possessing certain minimum information." At one level that is surely correct: merely possessing information, minimal or otherwise, does not save. Christians are not gnostics. On the other hand, the form of the antithesis may allow the unwary to overlook the fact that faith has content, or an object. Does faith in, say, a ouija board

---

76. Even if one decides that what is meant is that God apportions the worship of the heavenly array to the pagan nations, this may mean, within the context of the story-line (not least in Deuteronomy), no more than that God's sovereign sway extends even over the pagan nations and their false gods, but that is no reason for the covenant community who truly know God to follow in their path. In other words, the verse provides no optimism for the view that the worship of idols is an acceptable alternative approach to the one living and true God.

77. Sanders, *No Other Name*, 255. Note the loading implicit in "precise."

78. Ibid., 265.

79. Sanders, "Is Belief in Christ Necessary?" 252–53.

80. Pinnock, *A Wideness in God's Mercy*, 158.

81. Ibid.

82. Ibid.

save? How about sincere faith in astrology? Pinnock says it is "faith in God" that saves. But which God? The Buddhist impersonal God? And even if we assume we are dealing with the true God, does *all* faith in this God save, when we are told that even the devils believe?

Again: "The issue that God cares about is the direction of the heart, not the content of theology." At one level, I would strenuously agree. Yet at the same time, I would want to add that if the direction of the heart is truly right, one of the things it will be concerned about is the content of theology. Does Paul sound as if he does not care about the content of theology in Galatians 1:8–9? Does John, in 1 John 4:1–6? Far from resorting to antitheses, John purposely links sound doctrine, transparent obedience, and love for the brothers and sisters in Christ, as being joint marks of the true believer (and thus of true faith!).

I shall consider in the next section some texts that specify the content of Christian faith (e.g., Rom. 10:9–10). In fairness to Pinnock it is important to acknowledge that he insists on the importance "of making the historical facts about Jesus known everywhere . . . in order to clarify God's saving purposes for humanity and to motivate individuals to make their commitment to God in Christ."[83] But note carefully: such proclamation is not important so that men and women may be saved, but so that God's saving purposes may be clarified, and so that individuals may be properly motivated. For "we cannot reasonably suppose that a failure of evangelization that affects many millions would leave them completely bereft of any access to God."[84]

Although a few of the crucial texts will be examined below, already it is fair to conclude with Nash:

> I believe it is reckless, dangerous, and unbiblical to lead people to think that the preaching of the gospel (which I insist must contain specifics about the person and work of Christ) and personal faith in Jesus are not necessary for salvation. If we do not accept the inclusivist definition of faith, we cannot very well accept the rest of the inclusivist system.[85]

6. More subtle is the evaluation of the case of those who are "informationally B.C."

Not only "hard" inclusivists but also many "soft" inclusivists think this argument is persuasive. It runs like this: Even if (with the "soft" inclusivists) we think that in this age saving faith in Jesus normally has as its content, its object, the Jesus of the Scriptures, including both his person and his work, it

---

83. Ibid., 159.
84. Ibid.
85. *Is Jesus the Only Savior?* 126.

is clear that genuine believers (both Jews and Gentiles) before the coming of Jesus did not have to exercise faith *in Jesus* to be saved: they had not heard of the man Christ Jesus. Early enough along the axis of redemptive history, believers had not heard of many other things as well. Men and women responded in faith to such light as they had. Would not the same principle apply to people today who are "informationally B.C.," i.e., to people who, though they live this side of the decisive events connected with the life, ministry, death, and resurrection of Jesus, have never heard of them, and are therefore very much in the place of those who came before Jesus, and who consequently never heard of him?

This line of argument is very common.[86] Yet the argument is not as strong as at first appears. *First*, most of the pre-Christ believers are those who enter into a covenantal, faith-based relationship with the God who had disclosed himself to them in the terms and to the extent recorded up to that time. From the perspective of the biblical plot-line, there is some genuine continuity between such Old Testament saints and the New Testament saints (e.g., Rom. 1:1–2; 11; Phil. 3:3, 7, 9). Under the old covenant, institutions, sacrificial systems, entire priestly orders, were to be adhered to as part of obedient faith on the part of the people, but such institutions and systems also pointed forward, as we have seen, to Jesus Christ—to his sacrifice, his priesthood, the heavenly tabernacle, and so forth.[87] Inclusivists who draw a parallel between modern non-Christians who have never heard of Christ and such Old Testament believers overlook the fact that these believers on the Old Testament side were responding in faith to special revelation, and were not simply exercising some sort of general "faith" in an undefined "God." As Nash puts it, "How can Old Testament believers who had a significant relationship to special revelation and whose faith was tied to symbols and practices that looked forward to Christ provide warrant for treating unevangelized moderns as saved believers? If there is an argument here, I fail to see it."[88]

Second, some appeal more specifically to Old Testament "holy pagans" who are believers and yet who do not belong to the covenant community. Those commonly considered include Melchizedek, Jethro, Job, Naaman, and,

---

86. E.g., see Peter Cotterell, *Mission and Meaninglessness: The Good News in a World of Suffering and Disorder* (London: SPCK, 1990), 75; Chris Wright, "P for Pentateuch, Patriarchs and Pagans," *Themelios* 18/2 (January 1993): 3–4; Thorwald Lorenzen, "Baptists and the Challenge of Religious Pluralism," *Review and Expositor* 89 (1992): 57–58; Pinnock, *A Wideness in God's Mercy*, 161.

87. This essentially covenantal approach to the unity of Scripture could of course be modified to allow for the sensibilities of the more dispensationally minded: cf. Richard, *The Population of Heaven*, 117–26.

88. *Is Jesus the Only Savior?* 127.

from the New Testament, the Magi and Cornelius. I have already discussed Melchizedek; there is little to prompt us to think he was a pagan, holy or otherwise. And I have already mentioned Naaman. The status of Jethro is less than clear; for whom he was priest, and how far he came to follow Moses and his God, are not entirely without uncertainty. Cornelius I shall consider in the next section. Probably the Magi were pagan astrologers, all right. But they came seeking the prophesied Jewish king (which is scarcely the situation of modern pagans who have never heard of Jesus), and in any case the focus of the narrative is on who Jesus is (Matt. 2), not whether or not the Magi are to be viewed as among God's people. One could as easily infer from the narrative that their coming to see the baby Jesus demonstrates how God may sometimes use even the wrath and follies of human beings to praise him—in this case to provide a pregnant symbol of how his Son will someday meet the aspirations of Gentiles as well as of Jews—as infer that the Magi are true believers while still being pagans. Other suggestions—Abimelech, perhaps, or Balaam—are scarcely convincing examples of redeemed believers.

Third, in any case it is vital to recognize that even at its best, this argument is only a possible inference. As Phillips puts it, "But arguments by analogy are tenuous, and their probability depends upon the number of corresponding entities between the two analogies. The analogies from 'those who *had* not heard,' and perhaps from 'those who *cannot* hear,' have some points of correspondence with the case of 'those who *have* not heard,' but not enough for the confidence with which many evangelicals baptize the Untold."[89]

7. In some cases, the adoption of both inclusivism and postmortem evangelism[90] leads to an uneasy synthesis.

Probably Pinnock is the leading exponent of this combination of positions. Most of those who hold to postmortem evangelism are exclusivists: i.e., they hold not only that Jesus alone provides salvation, but that faith must consciously be placed in Jesus—and then meet the objections of those who think this condition is unfair to those who have never heard the gospel by postulating postmortem evangelism. But Pinnock adopts *both* inclusivism *and* postmortem evangelism. Nash goes so far as to say that these two positions are "logically incompatible."[91] I think that is a little too harsh: there is certainly nothing logically contradictory about holding the two views. On the

---

89. W. Gary Phillips, "Evangelicals and Pluralism: Current Options," *Evangelical Quarterly* 64 (1992): 242.

90. The view that those who have not heard the gospel in this life will have an opportunity to hear it and respond to it after death. We will return to this view briefly in chap. 13, dealing with annihilationism.

91. *Is Jesus the Only Savior?* 149.

other hand, it is very hard to see why anyone would want to hold both views simultaneously. If faith that is consciously focused on Jesus is not necessary for salvation, why should people be offered a further chance beyond death? Alternatively, if a further chance is offered beyond death, with the structure of the gospel clearly presented, why should people be thought disadvantaged if they do not hear the gospel in this life?

We begin to suspect that we are not dealing with a well thought out theological synthesis, backed by careful exegesis and evenhanded reasoning, but with a mindset that is no longer comfortable with the constraints established by the biblical story-line, but cannot quite let go of it.

D. Problem Passages

I have already surveyed a substantial number of relevant passages, whether in this or the previous two chapters, and I have no desire to canvass them again. Instead I will examine briefly a handful of passages of two sorts: those on which inclusivists tend to rely and those on which exclusivists tend to rely. Where it is relevant, I shall specify what the two parties make of these passages.

Matthew 7:14. By and large the biblical writers do not encourage speculation about the relative numbers of the redeemed. On an absolute scale, doubtless there will be a vast number drawn from every tongue and tribe and people and nation. Where the disciples ask the explicit question about numbers (Luke 13:23, "Lord, are only a few people going to be saved?"), Jesus sidesteps their curiosity and tells them to make every effort to enter *through the narrow door* (which suggests restricted access), for many "will try to enter and will not be able to" (Luke 13:24). Here in Matthew, Jesus' antithesis establishes proportions: "For wide is the gate and broad is the road that leads to destruction, and many enter through it. But small is the gate and narrow the road that leads to life, and only a few find it." Pinnock does not think "that this text about fewness can be used to cancel out the optimism of salvation that so many other verses articulate."[92] But are there any texts where the question of *relative* proportions is directly addressed and the proportions go the other way? Hermeneutically, one should not attempt to set aside texts that directly respond to a specific question by appealing to themes that answer the question, if they answer it at all, at best indirectly. Moreover, the proportionality envisaged by Jesus in this passage is entirely in line with the entire history of the people of God across the Bible's story-line.

Matthew 25:31–46. In line with many others, Pinnock takes "the least of these brothers of mine" (Matt. 25:40) in this parable of the sheep and the

92. *A Wideness in God's Mercy*, 154.

goats to refer to the poor and suffering.[93] If this identification is correct, then Jesus "wishes to say . . . that deeds of love done to needy people will be regarded at the last judgment as having been done to Christ, even though the Gentiles did not and could not have known it under the circumstances."[94] Certainly Jesus, not to mention the entire prophetic tradition before him, displayed wonderful compassion for the poor and suffering. Would-be disciples of Jesus today are not really following him if they ignore this fact. But in all fairness, that does not seem to be the likely interpretation of this parable. I have argued at length elsewhere that "the least of these brothers of mine" must refer to believers who are being opposed and persecuted for the gospel's sake.[95] Thus I do not accept some of the restrictive views: e.g., that the least of the brothers refers to Christian missionaries, or to some other group. One must remember that this Gospel has already established that Jesus' true "brothers" are his disciples (12:48–49; 28:10; cf. 23:8). "Good deeds done to Jesus' followers, even the least of them, are not only works of compassion and morality but reflect where people stand in relation to the kingdom and to Jesus himself. Jesus identifies himself with the fate of his followers and makes compassion for them equivalent to compassion for himself" (cf. Matt. 10:40–42; Mark 13:13; John 15:5, 18, 20; 17:10, 23, 26; Acts 9:4; 22:7; 26:14; 1 Cor. 12:27; Heb. 2:17).[96] This interpretation can be shown to fit the parable sequence at the end of the Olivet Discourse (Matt. 24–25); the alternative is irrelevant to the flow. Moreover, this interpretation takes into account the surprise expressed by both the sheep and the goats when Jesus makes his final pronouncements. If the interpretation preferred by Pinnock were correct, it is difficult to imagine why the sheep in particular would be surprised by the outcome.

Luke 15. The parables of this chapter, and especially the parable of the prodigal son, attract widespread interest from inclusivists. Thus Sanders concludes that "our unusual God loves his children, including those whom we may consider particularly ungodly. The church is still struggling to understand this great theme from the Bible."[97] At one level all must surely agree:

---

93. Ibid., 163–65.

94. Ibid., 164.

95. D. A. Carson, "Matthew," *Expositor's Bible Commentary*, vol. 8 (Grand Rapids: Zondervan, 1984), 518–23. Nor is this an idiosyncratic interpretation: it is in line with the majority of interpreters until the nineteenth century, and a number of recent scholars are returning to it. See Sherman W. Grey, *The Least of My Brothers, Matthew 25:31–46: A History of Interpretation*, Society of Biblical Literature Dissertation Series, vol. 114 (Atlanta: Scholars Press, 1989).

96. Ibid., 520.

97. *No Other Name*, 135.

the theme of God's undeserved and reconciling love constantly astonishes us, and must never be minimized. Nevertheless, it is important to remember the various ways the Bible talks about the love of God (see discussion in chap. 5). Moreover, in this parable it is not at all clear that the prodigal son represents pagans who have never heard the gospel! The "fatherhood of God" theme as applied to all human beings everywhere, so much a staple of classic liberal theology, is not supported by a single text from the canonical Gospels. And in any case the prodigal returns to his father with unqualified repentance. From a biblical perspective the amazing thing is that the father accepts him and does not throw him out. But there is no hint that the father sweeps into his household those who have neither repented nor wholeheartedly come under the father's authority and mercy, without conditions.

John 1:9. Whether we understand the text to say that "[t]he true light that gives light to every man was coming into the world" (NIV) or that "[t]his was the true light that gives light to every man who comes into the world" (NIVmg), the fact remains that this text connects the true light with "every man." Few texts have been more frequently cited by inclusivists than this one. This side of Vatican II, Roman Catholic theologians commonly insist that "the Christian's attitude to the religions of the world is one both of humility and respect, and of frankness in giving witness to Christ, the Word that enlightens every person . . . always ready to announce, always ready to be taught."[98]

Some take John 1:9 to refer to some element of general revelation, or of a sense of God, or of the ability to think God's thoughts after him, without in any way suggesting that such revelation is salvific.[99] I shall call that view in question in a moment. For "hard" inclusivists and pluralists, however, such an interpretation does not go nearly far enough. In a remarkable paper delivered to the John section of the 1993 Annual Meeting of the Society of Biblical Literature, R. Alan Culpepper argued that the gospel of John is inexcusably against Jews, and far too exclusivistic. Even the love command of John 13:34–35 needs to be modified by Jesus' teaching in the Sermon on the Mount about the importance of loving neighbors. Thus he argues that we simply cannot accept much of John's gospel. Since no interpretation is objective (note the postmodernist assumptions), we must choose interpretations and hermeneutical structures on the basis of the highest ethical beliefs of the Bible. (One might ask how, on postmodernist assumptions, one can possibly establish without arbitrariness what the highest ethical beliefs are.) Thus faithfulness

---

98. Pietro Rossano, "Christ's Lordship and Religious Pluralism," in *Mission Trends No. 5: Faith Meets Faith*, ed. Gerald Anderson and Thomas Stransky (Grand Rapids: Eerdmans, 1981), 34.

99. So, for instance, Demarest, *General Revelation*, 138, 228, 242.

to the gospel means fighting the text (note the assumptions of deconstruction). The Fourth Gospel demands faith, and it demands love. But what of those who display love but not faith, or vice versa? There is no answer; the two demands are irreconcilable at that level. (One wonders why the obvious solution, that both faith and love are demanded, is not canvassed.) A possible way forward is John 1:9: some notion or other of a cosmic Christ who illumines everyone without exception. This undermines even the hatred of Jews in John, encourages openness to other cultures and beliefs, and fosters a "hermeneutics of ethical responsibility."

Leaving aside for the moment the difficult question as to how one constructs an ethical system, and postponing till the next chapter the charge of anti-Semitism, and making allowances for the postmodernist rhetoric, how fair is this exegesis of John 1:9?

The short answer is that it is fundamentally mistaken, because the text is not being read in its context. The most thorough treatment in recent years is that of Miller,[100] who shows that the one coming into the world is almost certainly the Word, that is, Christ in common Johannine language. But that means the illumination in John 1:9 is tied to the incarnation, not to some inner or mystical light, that may, perhaps, be tied to the *imago Dei*. Miller also shows that in the context of the Johannine literature, where those who follow Christ are in the light and apart from him the whole world is in darkness (e.g., John 8:12; 12:46; 1 John 2:8; 5:19), it is extraordinarily unlikely that 1:9 should be read as universal salvific enlightenment. Miller writes,

> That John 1:9 teaches a universal enlightenment strikes me, by its contrast to the tenor of the whole of the Johannine literature, as an unjustifiable bolt out of the blue. It might be responded, of course, that bolt or no bolt, the text does not say that the light illumines only those it illumines, but that it illumines *every person*. I, in turn, would respond that the light does *in principle* illumine every person, and that this coheres with Johannine expression elsewhere, such as 12:32 where it is asserted that Jesus, when "lifted up," will draw everyone to himself, which, of course, is factually false though true in principle.[101]

It might be better and simpler to say that John 1:9 insists that the Word of God, the incarnate Jesus, enlightens everyone without distinction. The very next verses demonstrate that the shining of the light did not produce universal salvation.

---

100. Ed. L. Miller, "'The True Light Which Illumines Every Person,'" in *Good News in History*, ed. Ed. L. Miller (Atlanta: Scholars Press, 1993), 63–83.

101. Ibid., 79–80.

John 14:6. This verse is important to the debate because it not only affirms that Jesus is the way, the truth, and the life, but it articulates an exclusion principle: "No one comes to the Father except through me." Inclusivists and pluralists handle this passage in various ways. A thoroughgoing religious pluralist such as Bernhardt argues that passages like John 14:6, Acts 4:12, and Colossians 1:15–20 arose in specific contexts, and when those historical contexts no longer exist these texts should no longer be regarded as binding.[102] The assumptions are staggering. If there were such a God as the Bible suggests, he *could not* communicate anything definitive to us who are locked in space and time, for those conditions assure that things are constantly changing. Lorenzen says the text means "that according to *our experience* and according to *our knowledge* Jesus Christ *is* the true manifestation of the reality 'God', and that in and through him God has accomplished his *work of salvation* which has ontologically changed our world."[103] In fact, of course, the text says nothing of the kind. The text makes universalizing claims without superimposing phrases like "according to our experience" and "according to our knowledge"—ample evidence that Lorenzen's epistemology has been decisively shaped by postmodern considerations.

Sanders takes a different tack. He agrees that the text insists that all who are saved achieve salvation only because of the work of Christ. But he denies that anything is said or implied about epistemological recognition of that fact.[104] This is the distinction I mentioned earlier, common among inclusivists, between ontological necessity and epistemological necessity. There is a certain mechanical logic in the argument that has a superficial appeal, but it is fatally flawed (see below, on Rom. 10:9–10). On the face of it, in a book that constantly presents faith in Jesus as the only solution to the curse and wrath under which we operate (e.g., John 1:12; 3:15, 16, 36), John 14:6 is of a piece with this Johannine demand for faith in Jesus, and can be sidestepped by the inclusivists and pluralists only with the greatest implausibility.

Acts 4:12, etc. This passage is one of the most exclusivist texts in the New Testament: "Salvation is found in no one else, for there is no other name under heaven given to men by which we must be saved." Pinnock is not persuaded the verse should be read in an exclusivist fashion. He agrees that Jesus is doing something both wonderful and unique. In that sense,

> Acts 4:12 makes a strong and definitively exclusive claim about the messianic, holistic salvation Jesus has brought into the world. It is a salvation that is incomparable and without rival. It is available through no other name

---

102. Reinhold Bernhardt, *Christianity Without Absolutes* (London: SCM, 1994), passim.
103. "Baptists and the Challenge of Religious Pluralism," 59 (emphasis his).
104. *No Other Name,* 64.

than Jesus the Incarnate Son of God. But the text does not exclude from eternal salvation the vast majority of people who have ever lived on the earth.[105]

In part Pinnock relies on an argument Sanders develops for Romans 10:9–10: that strictly speaking this tells us that salvation is provided exclusively through Jesus, and that there is no other name under heaven given by which to effect such salvation, but it does not explicitly insist that people must know that name to benefit from the salvation, and it does not explicitly exclude those who have never heard. I shall evaluate the logic of that argument below. Bock concurs that on a strict reading this verse does not directly address the question of exclusivism, but he insists that Pinnock is too quick to see salvific overtones in such expressions as "God-fearing Greeks." Acts 4:12 is best understood in the broad context of messages such as those found in Acts 13 and 17; and these, he thinks, tell against Pinnock's interpretation.[106]

But we can surely go farther than this. In the context, the challenge to the apostles came about because they "were teaching the people and proclaiming in Jesus the resurrection of the dead" (4:2). When to these Jews, many of them doubtless sincere and devout, Peter responds with an exclusive formulation, he quite clearly cannot mean that although salvation, including the final resurrection, is brought about by Jesus and Jesus alone, it is not necessary for devout Jews to recognize that name in order to participate in the resurrection. Clearly, this does not *directly* address the fate of those who have never heard. But if Peter can speak in such exclusivistic terms to people whose heritage was steeped in the biblical revelation, would he have been somewhat more flexible for those whose religious heritage, from the vantage point of the Bible, is steeped in idolatry?[107]

Nash adds a simple but telling argument.[108] In two or three pages, he simply tries to see what Acts would look like if read right through with inclusivist lenses. Especially as one listens to the messages reported in the book, he tries to imagine whether what is actually said would be the sort of thing that inclusivists would say. For example, Peter says, in Acts 2:38, "Repent and be baptized every one of you, in the name of Jesus Christ for the forgiveness of your sins." Would an inclusivist assume that all of his hearers *need* to repent and be

---

105. Clark Pinnock, "Acts 4:12—No Other Name Under Heaven," in *Through No Fault of Their Own?* ed. William V. Crockett and James G. Sigountos (Grand Rapids: Baker, 1991), 107–15.

106. Darrell L. Bock, "Athenians Who Have Never Heard," in Crockett and Sigountos, *Through No Fault of Their Own?* 124.

107. Cf. also Hywel Jones, "No Other Name," *Foundations* 24 (1990): 23–31.

108. *Is Jesus the Only Savior?* 172–74.

baptized and have their sins forgiven? Would Paul's answer to the Philippian jailor, "Believe in the Lord Jesus, and you will be saved" (Acts 16:31), be quite so curt and decisive? After all, may it not have been the case that the jailor was already saved—a consideration all the more plausible in the light of his unexpectedly tender heart? How could an inclusivist state with Paul in Acts 20:26–27, "Therefore, I declare to you today that I am innocent of the blood of all men. For I have not hesitated to proclaim to you the whole will of God"? Why should Paul think himself guilty of the blood of others, assuming he had held his peace, if many of the others were already anonymous Christians? Nash concludes:

> And finally, had I been Paul and an inclusivist, I would have been totally shocked by what God said when he called me: "I am sending you to open their eyes and turn them from darkness to light, and from the power of Satan to God, so that they may receive forgiveness of sins and a place among those who are sanctified by faith in me" (Acts 26:18). This survey through the book of Acts makes it clear that Peter and Paul did not speak and act like inclusivists. Acts 26:18 helps us see that *God* does not speak or act like an inclusivist either.[109]

Acts 10:1–11:18. Peter begins his address to Cornelius and his household with the words, "I now realize how true it is that God does not show favoritism but accepts men from every nation who fear him and do what is right" (10:34–35). In Pinnock's view, this is the "crown jewel in the Cornelius story,"[110] and makes Cornelius "the pagan saint par excellence of the New Testament, a believer in God before he became a Christian."[111] Sanders infers from this passage, "Cornelius was already a saved believer before Peter arrived but he was not a Christian believer."[112]

But is that what the text says? If it is, then people who fear God and do what is right can have a saving knowledge of God. In other words, all that is necessary is some sort of (presumably reverent) fear and good works. Quite apart from the way that view is consistently challenged in the New Testament, it simply does not fit into the Bible's story-line. That is why the preachers in Acts are constantly preaching *in Jesus* forgiveness of sins and resurrection from the dead. It may be that the New International Version is slightly misleading. It holds that God "accepts" people from every nation who fear him and do what is right. If this "acceptance" is taken strongly, it might be taken by some to imply that God accepts them as forgiven people. Strictly speak-

109. Ibid., 174.
110. *A Wideness in God's Mercy*, 96.
111. Ibid., 165.
112. *No Other Name*, 254.

ing, however, the Greek says that everyone who fears God and obeys him "is acceptable δεκτός to him," or even "welcome" to him (cf. Luke 4:24, "no prophet is *accepted* in his home town"). It is never used in reference to whether or not a person is accepted by God in some saving sense.

The point of Peter's comment, in the context, is not to pass judgment on whether or not Cornelius is saved, but to conclude that in principle people from outside the Jewish race are acceptable to God, *as is evidenced from the fact that by the thrice-given vision of the sheet with its unclean animals Peter is assured he has not only the permission but the obligation to preach the gospel to people other than Jews, to the end that they too may be saved.* That this lies at the focal point of the account of the conversion of Cornelius is clear: the repetition of the story in Acts 11 is necessary precisely to reassure the Jewish believers in Jerusalem that Peter has not stepped out of bounds by entering a nonkosher house and preaching to Gentiles, even if the Gentiles, like Cornelius and his household, are God-fearers. And it is while Peter is preaching "the good news of peace through Jesus Christ, who is Lord of all" (10:36), and articulating the life and ministry and death and resurrection of Jesus (10:37–41), and insisting that the "everyone who believes in him receives forgiveness of sins through his name" (10:43), that the Holy Spirit falls on Cornelius and his guests, and their conversion is recognized by baptism.

As Richard observes, there are at least two conclusions to be drawn: "First, instead of a universal salvific will, Peter submits a universal salvific welcome to anyone from any nation. Second, there is also a particularity axiom—the reception of forgiveness for everyone is through Jesus' name and belief in Him"—not through an abstract "belief principle" without a specified object.[113]

Acts 14:16–17. In Lystra, preaching to a pagan audience Paul says, "In the past, [God] let all nations go their own way. Yet he has not left himself without testimony: He has shown kindness by giving you rain from heaven and crops in their seasons; he provides you with plenty of food and fills your years with joy." Pinnock infers from this "testimony" a great deal more than what the text actually says: "Elements of truth and goodness exist in pagan cultures like theirs because God has been with them and has not failed to reveal himself to them."[114] Indeed, "these people possessed truth from God in the context of their [pagan] religion and culture."[115] *A priori,* I am quite happy to accept that "elements of truth and goodness" exist in every culture: that is

---

113. *The Population of Heaven*, 64.

114. *A Wideness in God's Mercy*, 96.

115. Clark Pinnock, "The Finality of Jesus Christ in a World of Religions," in *Christian Faith and Practice in the Modern World*, ed. Mark A. Noll and David F. Wells (Grand Rapids: Eerdmans, 1988), 158.

the fruit of common grace, of the *imago Dei*, of general revelation. But that does not mean their sins are forgiven and they are saved. Certainly these people possess some truth from God, in that God does not leave himself without witness but declares something of himself even through nature (which is the point in the text)—but that is not a ringing endorsement of their pagan religion and culture, still less a sign that these people enjoy a saving knowledge of God.

If Paul says that God in the past let nations go their own way, we may concur that this restrained way of putting things reflects tact and sensitivity on Paul's part. But surely it is going too far to conclude, "This represents a gracious and understanding appreciation of their past and their culture."[116] That sounds like a modern, politically correct Paul; it is not what the text suggests. In fact, God letting the nations go their own way sounds very much like God giving people up to their own sinful ways (Rom. 1–2). In the past, God primarily directed his saving power to the covenant community of Israel, but this side of the cross he has now ordained that the good news of the gospel should be preached not only in Jerusalem and in all Judea and Samaria, but to the ends of the earth (Acts 1:8). That is the framework of the story into which this pericope fits.

Acts 16:31. In passing, it is important to remark how in this and other passages (see below on Rom. 10:9–10) there is remarkable emphasis on the content, the object, of faith: "Believe *in the Lord Jesus*, and you will be saved." Once again, it is far from clear that the New Testament encourages some sort of "faith principle" without the object of the faith clearly defined.

Acts 17:24–30. I shall return to Acts 17 in chapter12, when we consider how to preach the gospel to modern pagans. For the moment, it is enough to observe three elements in Paul's address to the Athenians from which inclusivists of various stripes derive comfort.

(1) In 17:24–27, God's creative power, his creation of the human race from one man and his providential rule over them were all done, we are told, "so that men would seek him and perhaps reach out for him and find him" (17:27). Cotterell argues that the passage simultaneously rejects all human religion that is committed to reducing God to the level of the superhuman, and yet "serves to show that creation is so ordered that in creation we may encounter God, and even find him."[117] Yet Cotterell is sufficiently careful with the text that he adds:

> There is a certain hesitancy evident in the words of Paul: there is a hope that "perhaps" people might reach out and find God. But again, reference to

---

116. *A Wideness in God's Mercy*, 32.
117. *Mission and Meaninglessness*, 67.

the context makes that hesitancy entirely appropriate: whatever might be the expectation or experience elsewhere, in the sophisticated metropolis of Athens the people had *not* found God. They had, instead, created gods. But the thrust of Paul's statement is clear: God's purpose in revealing himself in creation *was* salvific: some, at least, would find God. And in finding God they might expect to encounter, also, his grace.[118]

What is profoundly right about this paragraph is the recognition that there is nothing in Acts 17 to suggest that Paul was sanguine about the redemptive status of the Athenians. That is a marked improvement over the writings of most "hard" inclusivists. But Cotterell's further conclusion that "some, at least, would find God," needs careful weighing. Strictly speaking, the text does not say that some would find God by this means; it says, rather, that at least one of God's purposes in his providential rule is to lead people to know him. Clearly, that was the "hope." But the Athenians did not do so, at least by this means (see below); what is there that assures us that others did? On the face of it, God's creative power and providential rule establish what the pagan nations *ought* to learn, and their *obligation* to draw the right conclusions; and, in the context, these themes are used by Paul to prepare the ground for proclaiming Christ, at which point some do in fact believe (17:34). Moreover, it *may* be the case that God has in some cases opened the eyes of some people to recognize the existence and graciousness of their Maker and turn to him and in repentance and faith, imploring him for mercy. But the text does not say that this has taken place; certainly Romans 3:11 is not very encouraging. The least that must be said is that the passage offers no comfort for the view that there are millions and millions of pagan anonymous Christians out there.

(2) Because in Acts 17:28 Paul quotes a pagan poet, Pinnock concludes that this celebrates "the fact that such people as this have insight into the truth of God and his ways."[119] Is *that* Paul's point (or for that matter, Luke's)? We have already seen that no religion gets everything wrong: in that sense, it is doubtless correct, from a merely formal perspective, to say that pagan poets may well "have insight into the truth of God and his ways." But Pinnock thinks they are saved, acceptable to God; he interprets this verse as a "celebration" of "the fact that such people as this have insight into the truth of God and his ways." That is very wide of the mark. Paul is a sophisticated and educated preacher introducing his message to sophisticated and educated hearers: small wonder he uses pagan sources to bridge some gaps. I do the same thing all the time in evangelistic addresses to university students. I am more than happy to cite Martin Heidegger, Albert Camus, Bertrand Russell,

---

118. Ibid., 68.
119. *A Wideness in God's Mercy*, 96.

Jacques Derrida, Stanley Fish, Thomas Hardy, David Hume, and a host of others—sometimes in agreement, and sometimes in disagreement, but never with any suggestion that when I am in agreement I am implying that these are anonymous Christians. It is nonsense to conclude, with Race, that Paul here "acknowledges the authenticity of the worship of the men of Athens at their altar 'to an unknown God.'"[120] Otherwise, why does Luke record that some in the crowd turned from their false gods to the truth of the gospel (17:34)? One suspects that Race has not recently engaged in university evangelism.

(3) In verse 30, Paul comments, "In the past God overlooked such ignorance [i.e., the ignorance reflected in idolatry], but now he commands all people everywhere to repent." Pinnock takes this "overlooking" to mean that God in times past did not charge with guilt those who failed to trust him and come to terms with him out of ignorance.[121] But that is an astonishing inference. It would mean that the Athenians were better off before they heard Paul's preaching about Jesus: they were nicely spared any blame because they were ignorant, but now, poor chaps, for the first time they are held accountable. What Paul means, rather, is that God graciously overlooked their ignorance in the past, however culpable their ignorance was, for he did not punish them instantly, but in his forbearance "left the sins committed beforehand unpunished" (Rom. 3:25). Now, however, as salvation has been brought near, so also has judgment drawn close. That is a characteristic of realized eschatology in the New Testament: the blessings of the age to come have dawned, but concomitantly the dangers have increased proportionately. Thus in John's gospel the one who believes already has eternal life, but the wrath of God remains on the one who rejects the Son (John 3:36). If, in the past, culpable ignorance was graciously overlooked by God—not in the sense that he assigned no guilt, but in the sense that he bore with it—now it is inexcusable: "now he commands all people everywhere to repent" (17:30), and has backed up this demand with the threat of judgment threatening from the impending last day (17:31).

Romans 2:14–16. This is a rather difficult passage. The major interpretive options are canvassed in the major commentaries, and need not be summarized here. One interpretive option, widely popular these days, would in fact sanction at least some elements of the inclusivists' platform. If the Gentiles who do not have the law and yet who "do by nature things required by the law" (2:14) are pagan Gentiles with no access to the law of God, and if on occasion they actually live up to their consciences ("their consciences also bearing witness, and their thoughts now accusing, now even defending them,"

---

120. Alan Race, *Christians and Religious Pluralism* (Maryknoll: Orbis Books, 1982), 39.
121. *A Wideness in God's Mercy*, 101.

2:15), then surely we must see them as "devout pagans who, in the presence of sin, have been ashamed, have cried out in spiritual anguish, and confessed to whatever representation of the Holy Spirit they acknowledge."[122]

But even if the identification of the Gentiles here as pagans without knowledge of the law of God is correct, inferences like those just cited go way beyond the text. In Romans 2:14–16, Paul's point is that even people without the law show by their actions that distinctions between right and wrong are known to them. Like everyone else, they do experience crises of conscience. Sometimes their consciences actually defend them: no one, not even the pagan Gentile, is as bad as he or she might be. At other times, their consciences convict them. Paul's point, then, is that even those without the law must admit that distinctions between right and wrong are found everywhere, and everywhere people fall short and sometimes fail to live up to whatever light they have. That is very different from saying some pagans so live up to the light they have that they turn to God revealed in nature and call to him for mercy. The texts do not even hint at such a vision. Moreover, the burden of Paul's argument from 1:18 to 3:20 is to demonstrate "that Jews and Gentiles alike are all under sin" (Rom. 3:9).[123]

The most that could be admitted as a logical possibility—yet a possibility that the text does not set out to sanction, let alone defend—is that one might imagine some pagan, afflicted by conscience, crying to his Maker for mercy. That, I repeat, is not what the text *says*; but it does not absolutely shut the door to the possibility. Hence, even so conservative a writer as J. I. Packer can say:

> We may safely say (i) if any good pagan reached the point of throwing himself on his Maker's mercy for pardon, it was grace that brought him there; (ii) God will surely save anyone he brings thus far; (iii) anyone thus saved would learn in the next world that he was saved through Christ.[124]

Similar caution is voiced by others.[125] But this is not enough for Pinnock, who criticizes Packer for remaining uncertain "that God actually saves anyone in this way." Pinnock entertains no such uncertainties: "God most certainly does save people in this way. I do not know how many, but I hope for multitudes."[126] But the texts, as we have seen, are against him. To go no farther

---

122. D. Bruce Lockerbie, *The Cosmic Center* (Portland: Multnomah Press, 1986), 176. Lockerbie is taken up approvingly by Sanders, *No Other Name*, 235, and by many others.

123. For a detailed exegesis of these verses, see Douglas J. Moo, *Romans 1–8* (Chicago: Moody Press, 1991), 144–51.

124. J. I. Packer, *God's Words* (Downers Grove: InterVarsity Press, 1981), 210.

125. E.g., J. Herbert Kane, *Understanding Christian Missions*, 4th ed. (Grand Rapids: Baker, 1986), 135–36.

126. Pinnock, "The Finality of Jesus Christ," 159.

than Romans 2, Paul makes it clear that people are judged according to the light they have received, and no other—and that such light is sufficient to ensure universal condemnation. The text does not explicitly rule out the possibility for which Packer allows, but it does not explicitly sanction it either, and the place of this passage in the argument of Romans discourages Pinnock's drift from close adherence to the text.

Romans 10:9–10. Once again it is important to stress the content of the faith spelled out in these verses. Paul says that the person who confesses with the mouth "Jesus is Lord" and believes in the heart that God raised him from the dead will be saved. "For it is with your heart that you believe and are justified, and it is with your mouth that you confess and are saved." We are a long way from an abstract "faith principle" that does not have Jesus as its content. On the face of it, Paul thinks of Jesus not only as an ontological necessity, but as an epistemological necessity (cf. the comments on Acts 16:31, above).

But Sanders is not daunted. He concludes, "It is clear from Romans 10:9 that whoever confesses Jesus as Lord and believes in his heart that God raised him from the dead will be saved. It is not clear that whoever does not fulfill these conditions is lost. Paul simply does not specify how much a person has to know to be saved."[127] The matter, he insists, is one of logic. The text, he argues, is "logically similar" to the conditional statement, "If it rains, then the sidewalk will get wet" (cf. "If you confess Jesus as Lord and believe in your heart that God raised him from the dead, you will be saved"). If the protasis is true, the apodosis follows: if it rains, the sidewalk is wet, and if you confess and believe, you are saved. But it does not follow that if you negate the protasis, the apodosis is also negated. If it does not rain, it does not necessarily follow that the sidewalk is not wet, for it might have been soaked in some other way, e.g., by a sprinkling system. Similarly, if you do not confess with your mouth that Jesus is Lord, and if you do not believe in your heart that God has raised him from the dead, it does not necessarily follow that you are not saved.

At the level of logic, Sanders's conclusion is normally justified. Statements of the sort "If A, then B" do not guarantee the truth of "If not A, then not B," and that is what exclusivism demands. But there is one important exception. If all the members of class A are precisely identical to all the members of class B, then if the conditional statement "If A, then B" holds, so also does the conditional statement "If not A, then not B." In other words, if all those who confess with their mouth that Jesus is Lord and believe in their hearts that God has raised him constitute class A, and all those who are saved constitute

---

127. *No Other Name,* 67.

class B, then if the members of the two classes are the same, it is precisely true to say that if you do not confess Jesus as Lord and do not believe that God has raised him from the dead, you are not saved.[128]

In other words, what Sanders has done is *assume* that the two classes do not precisely coincide—which is, of course, nothing other than assuming his conclusion. Of course, exclusivists for their part must not simply assume the opposite. But in fact, it can be shown that the perfect coincidence of the two classes is precisely what Paul presupposes. This is clear not only from Paul's treatment of the entire biblical story-line, but from this chapter of his epistle to the Romans. At the beginning of the chapter, he experiences agony because the zeal of many of his fellow Jews "is not based on knowledge"— which certainly presupposes some epistemological needs. Verses 9 and 10 lead on eventually to a series of important rhetorical questions: "How, then, can they call on the one they have not believed in? And how can they believe in the one of whom they have not heard? And how can they hear without someone preaching to them? And how can they preach unless they are sent?" (10:14–15). For Paul, the impossibilities lurking behind these rhetorical questions "are exactly opposite of what inclusivists are proposing. For Paul, it is impossible to call on the true God without believing in Jesus."[129]

Sanders's appeal to logic fails.

D. Concluding Reflections

One could go on examining texts, but this survey will have to do. My primary point in these two long chapters is that the biblical plot-line establishes an entire worldview for Christians, and does not allow us to succumb to radical pluralism, or even to increasingly popular inclusivism. More rigorously philosophical defenses of exclusivism have been offered elsewhere;[130] my own concern has been to paint a broad biblical picture, stopping briefly at enough texts to establish credibility.

Christian efforts to expound that story-line, that biblical theology, and apply it to (post)modern settings must be undertaken with both humility and boldness: with humility, because an essential part of our beliefs is that we too were "dead in [our] transgressions and sins" and "like the rest ... objects of wrath" (Eph. 2:1, 3), and if we have been reconciled to God, it says much

---

128. This is an adaptation of the argument offered by Nash, *Is Jesus the Only Savior?* 145.

129. Richard, *The Population of Heaven*, 67.

130. See especially the very thoughtful paper by Alvin Plantinga, "Pluralism: A Defense of Religious Exclusivism" (so far as I know, still unpublished), which does not argue for the rightness or truth of Christian views, but shows that there is nothing wrong or immoral in an exclusivist position.

about his great grace, and nothing about our wisdom or goodness; and with boldness because, with Paul, we hold that we are debtors to all, and we cannot envisage that that truth which has been graciously given, both in the public arena of history and in the private watch of transformed experience—truth given by the self-disclosing, personal/transcendent, Trinitarian God of Christian monotheism, the God who will not finally be gagged—is of merely idiosyncratic relevance.

Chapter 7

GOD'S FINAL WORD

O urs is certainly not the first generation to call in question the finality of Jesus. Even without resorting to much "mirror reading," it is obvious that believers during the period when the New Testament was being written found their claims challenged by the world around them. In every century, minds both devout and profane have wrestled with the Bible's Christological claims, whether in reverent attempts at accurate articulation and reasonable apologetic, or in selective dismissal of those claims that any particular age finds peculiarly repugnant. Pelikan shows, for instance, how Christian thinkers in the third century adopted a variety of stances as they tried to reason from the finality of Christ to a new view of universal history.[1] Elsewhere, Pelikan rightly observes, "Regardless of what anyone may personally believe about him, Jesus of Nazareth has been the dominant figure in the history of Western culture for almost twenty centuries."[2] Granted this fact, Netland's conclusion is warranted: "No serious discussion of the relation of Christianity to other faiths can proceed very far without coming to grips with the towering figure of Jesus. Sooner or later, the blunt question put by Jesus to his followers—'Who do people say I am?' (Mark 8:27 NIV)—must be confronted."[3]

---

1. Jaroslav Pelikan, *The Finality of Jesus Christ in an Age of Universal History* (Richmond: John Knox, 1966).

2. Jaroslav Pelikan, *Jesus Through the Centuries: His Place in the History of Culture* (New Haven: Yale Univ. Press, 1985), 1.

3. Harold A. Netland, *Dissonant Voices: Religious Pluralism and the Question of Truth* (Grand Rapids: Eerdmans, 1991), 235.

The fact of the matter is that at least some people in every age have tried to make Jesus over into something that is acceptable to their frame of reference, something less than or even other than the robust picture painted by the New Testament writers. This tendency is not the unique preserve of exegetical amateurs or the culturally parochial: scholars engage in the same game, often advancing brilliant reasons in defense of what turns out to be a thoroughly ephemeral thesis. It would go beyond the parameters of this chapter to catalogue the major reconstructions cast up in the history of the church, even more to critique them. But if the history of life-of-Jesus research teaches us anything, it is that the latest historical reconstruction of Jesus rarely proves very enduring.

At the risk of a simplistic generalization, contemporary Christologies that break from the central tradition of the church may be broken down into two kinds, admittedly sometimes overlapping. In the one kind, the writer seeks to bring to readers some fresh interpretation of what really happened, of who the historical Jesus really is, of how we should think of Christian origins. The assumption is that people have got it wrong, at least in part and perhaps fundamentally, and this writing will begin to sort it out and put matters to right. The task is judged interesting and important for its own sake. In the other kind, the explicit assumption is philosophical pluralism, or some variation of it, and then the writer asks what kind of Christology would be necessary, or what kind of changes would have to be introduced into traditional Christology, in order to fit the "given" of that pluralism.

In this chapter I am primarily interested in the latter kind of work.[4] But I think it has to be admitted that the former has prepared the way for the latter. In other words, as Trocmé points out, the sheer multiplicity of ostensibly "historical" reconstructions has over time greatly eroded confidence in traditional Christological formulations.[5] With confidence eroded, the stage is set to construct whatever Christology seems needed to line up with whatever the priorities of the hour happen to be. At the moment, those priorities happen to be whatever is perceived to advance pluralism.

---

4. I do not here consider the positions of those who insist on a "high" Christology yet think that many are saved by this Christ even though they have no conscious knowledge of him. That sort of position is tied to numerous other questions and is discussed in the preceding chapter.

5. Étienne Trocmé, "Un Christianisme sans Jésus-Christ?" *New Testament Studies* 38 (1992): 336: "Il est bien vrai que, sans le voulour dans la plupart des cas, notre travail collectif a largement contribué à ébranler la doctrine christologique traditionelle et même à miner la place que Jésus-Christ occupait dans la piété et la catéchèse des Églises. Il est exacte que cet effet de sape continue sans que nous en ayons clairement conscience." He then bravely tries to turn this trend into a virtue.

In what follows, I shall try to show what is not negotiable for confessing believers, and why it is not,[6] and to survey and evaluate rather rapidly some of the Christologies currently being advocated by those who espouse some form of pluralism. At the end of the chapter I shall turn to one small aspect of this larger debate, but one that has become extraordinarily sensitive, for entirely understandable reasons: the charge that traditional Christology, not least that which is found in the New Testament, is anti-Semitic.

A. Pluralism in Search of an Acceptable Christology

In an important essay, Ziesler writes:

Christianity is an historical religion, that is to say, that it would quickly wither away if it were shown that Jesus never existed, or that he was substantially different in character from the New Testament picture of him, that he was simply a politically unsuccessful revolutionary, for example, or simply a magician. Claims that the portrayal of him in the gospels are seriously distorted are far from new, and equally far from showing signs of disappearing, and the Christian faithful are quite right to find such claims disturbing. If these claims were to be made good, then the whole of Christianity would become highly suspect. Christian faith is thus vulnerable to historical attack as not all faiths necessarily are.... When Dr. N. T. Wright ... decided that someone should answer the recent theories of Barbara Thiering, A. N. Wilson and John Spong, and undertook to do so himself, he rightly did so by mounting historical attacks on them. He did not content himself by saying "I read the crucial texts differently" nor by invoking his own or other people's Christian experience, but he rather argued that their historical methods and conclusions were faulty.[7]

In exactly the same way, the first and most important thing to say about Crossan's recent work[8] is that it is bad history. There is simply no way that the actual records can responsibly be dissected to prove that in reality the historical Jesus was a Cynic philosopher, and that even the accounts of Jesus' passion and death are nothing more than the creations of the church that needed such stories for its own existential purposes.[9] Even Crossan's dating

---

6. Cf. the useful article by Eberhard Hahn, "Die Einzigartigkeit Jesu Christi," *European Journal of Theology* 3 (1994): 137–44.

7. John Ziesler, "Historical Criticism and a Rational Faith," *Expository Times* 105 (1994): 270. The book by N. T. Wright to which he refers is *Who Was Jesus?* (London: SPCK, 1992).

8. John Dominic Crossan, *The Historical Jesus: The Life of a Mediterranean Jewish Peasant* (San Francisco: Harper San Francisco, 1991).

9. As one reviewer puts it, "In all these 500 pages of impeccable political correctness there is hardly one badly turned sentence. It is delightfully readable, the pace rapid, the text filled with useful information on recent anthropology, on the ancient world's social, economic, and

of the source material can be challenged at almost every point (e.g., he dates the "final edition" of the Fourth Gospel between 120 and 150 B.C.). Similarly, when Meyer criticizes Casey's reconstruction,[10] or Barnett challenges those who say Jesus was no more than a first-century rabbi and prophet,[11] the fundamental objections are in the historical arena.

One of the difficult features in such debates is that the positions adopted are often tied to a solid matrix of other positions, many of which are dubious but which have nevertheless achieved a certain status in the scholarly community. For example, when David Edwards tries to sort out what historians from different backgrounds could reasonably agree on regarding the historical Jesus, he first looks at what he calls the eight gospels: (1) "the Jewish gospel" of the earliest Christians, very largely lost, occasionally recoverable in patches of James, Jude, Revelation, and snippets of Luke-Acts; (2) Paul's gospel; (3) the early catholic gospel, preserved in Acts, Colossians, Ephesians, Hebrews, and the Pastorals; (4) Q; (5) Mark; (6) Luke; (7) Matthew; (8) John.[12] Well, perhaps. But insofar as his theological and historical reconstruction depends on this sequence, it is highly vulnerable to criticism, and not a little speculative. Breaking up Luke and Acts is not very reassuring. Many scholars, by no means only traditional "conservatives," are unpersuaded that Colossians, say, or the Pastorals, can be removed from the Pauline corpus. And cannot a book that is written slightly later than another describe a period slightly earlier than what is described in the other book? To tackle such questions, of course, involves one in detailed *historical* criticism, as time-consuming and difficult as that may be.[13] In any case, it is more than a little alarming that after he has finished listing the historical points he thinks are reasonably assured, Edwards has a Jesus *who is fundamentally removed from the Bible's story-line.*

political systems, on the Cynics, and so on. As historical-Jesus research, it is unsalvageable. Not that a long historical struggle has turned out to have been in vain, for there are no signs here of any such struggle's having taken place. Historical inquiry, with its connotations of a personal wrestling with evidence, is not to be found. There are no recalcitrant data, no agonizing reappraisals. All is aseptic, the data having been freeze-dried, prepackaged, and labelled with literary flair. Instead of an inquiry, what we have here is simply the proposal of a bright idea" (Ben F. Meyer, *Catholic Biblical Quarterly* 55 [1993]: 576).

10. P. Maurice Casey, *From Jewish Prophet to Gentile God: The Origins and Development of New Testament Christology* (Louisville: Westminster/John Knox, 1991); reviewed by Ben F. Meyer in *Catholic Biblical Quarterly* 55 (1993): 800–802.

11. Paul Barnett, *The Two Faces of Jesus* (Sydney: Hodder & Stoughton, 1990).

12. David Edwards, *The Real Jesus: How Much Can We Believe?* (London: Fount, 1992).

13. In the discussion between David L. Edwards and John Stott, *Essentials: A Liberal-Evangelical Dialogue* (London: Hodder & Stoughton, 1988), it is worth pondering how many of Stott's responses turn on historical considerations.

The same must be said of the recent work of Keith Ward.[14] This is doubly disappointing: first, because Ward seems to have capsized some of his earlier affirmations,[15] and second, because the motivating force behind the spill is clearly pluralism. Ward argues that we are approaching the Third Stage of religious thought. The First Stage was localized tribal religion; the Second Stage embraced the great scriptural traditions. This is now about to give way to the Third Stage, the stage of "convergent spirituality" in which each tradition can feel its way beyond itself, in dialogue with others, toward some new emergent truth. Thus the Bible gives us "not a final clear revelation of truth, but a mysterious signpost towards an unfolding understanding which is still in progress."[16]

Surveys of recent work in the area of Christology testify to how important the impact of pluralism is.[17] What follows is a mere sampling, followed by some brief reflections.

1. Hick: Incarnation as Metaphor

An earlier and well-publicized volume that was edited by Hick argued that the incarnation was a myth.[18] That volume kicked off a squall of responses, pro and con.[19] But now Hick wishes to take the argument in a slightly different direction. He argues that it is best to think of Scripture's description of the incarnation as a metaphor. The subtitle of his book displays the impetus for this move.[20] The argument of the closing chapters is that traditional notions of the incarnate Christ can scarcely avoid exclusivistic belief regarding revelation from God, and this is so unthinkable that it must be abandoned.

One of the intriguing things about this book is the way in which Hick handles the Bible. For example, in the chapter that argues that salvation

---

14. *A Vision to Pursue* (London: SCM Press, 1991).

15. The most important reviews in this respect are probably those of Robert R. Cook, *Themelios* 17/2 (1992): 16–17, and Jeremy Begbie, *Anvil* 9 (1992): 67–69. Cf. Ward's response in the same volume, 159–60. A sympathetic review of Ward is provided by the editor of the *Expository Times* 103 (1992): 161–63.

16. Ward, *A Vision to Pursue*, 153.

17. E.g., Lee E. Snook, *The Anonymous Christ: Jesus as Savior in Modern Theology* (Minneapolis: Augsburg, 1986).

18. John Hick, ed., *The Myth of God Incarnate* (London: SCM Press, 1977).

19. For example—Pro: Michael Goulder, ed., *Incarnation and Myth: The Debate Continued* (Grand Rapids: Eerdmans, 1979). One could argue that the volume by Casey, already mentioned, is in the same camp. Con: Michael Green, ed., *The Truth of God Incarnate* (Grand Rapids: Eerdmans, 1977); Brian Hebblethwaite, *The Incarnation: Collected Essays in Christology* (Cambridge: Cambridge Univ. Press, 1988).

20. John Hick, *The Metaphor of God Incarnate: Christology in a Pluralistic Age* (Louisville: Westminster/John Knox, 1993).

should be construed as human transformation, Hick begins by arguing that traditional Christianity has no real grasp of forgiveness at all. For if forgiveness has to be bought with sacrifice, it is scarcely worth the name. Besides, does not the recorded teaching of Jesus display him as one who assured people of forgiveness, contingent only on contrition and true repentance? Thus, in the Lord's Prayer we are simply taught to ask God for forgiveness. "There is no suggestion of the need for a mediator between ourselves and God or for an atoning death to enable God to forgive."[21] The same is true of the parable of the prodigal son (Luke 15:20–24).

What are we to make of this argument? At one level, what is so astonishing about it is the assumption that unless some particular point is explicitly mentioned on every conceivable occasion, it must be judged to be denied. If the Lord's Prayer does not explicitly mention atonement, it can only be because Jesus there envisages forgiveness from God quite apart from any notion of atonement. This is not merely a fairly surprising reductionism, but historical nonsense. It presupposes that Jesus, whose references to the Scriptures are repeated and complex, stands outside the Bible's story-line, which is full of references to sacrifice, sin, and death. Mark 10:45 ("The Son of Man did not come to be served, but to serve, and to give his life as a ransom for many") will doubtless have to be assigned to the creative power of the later church; the story-line of the four canonical Gospels, all of which press toward the cross, is of little historical significance. When Christians read their Bibles, the sacrificial system of the Old Testament, the arguments from, say, Romans 3, and from the epistle to the Hebrews, are all to be written off. In short, the Jesus Hick proposes is so unlike the Jesus of the New Testament that sooner or later one must ask why Hick bothers to quote the New Testament at all. Certainly he makes no attempt to listen to the balance of New Testament texts. One can only suppose that he continues to appeal to selective texts because he hopes to convince Christians that his views are "acceptable" because in some sense they are "biblical." But the narrowness and selectivity of his views are certainly not faithful to Scripture.

As Netland has shown,[22] Hick advances three principal reasons for rejecting the traditional understanding of the incarnation.

(1) Grasping as he does the uniqueness of the Christian claim, Hick concludes that if in fact "Jesus was ... the eternal creator God become man, then it becomes very difficult indeed to treat Jesus, the New Testament, and Christian faith as being on the same level as phenomena from other religious

---

21. Ibid., 127.
22. *Dissonant Voices*, 242–44.

traditions."[23] This is quite unlike the relativizing syntheses put forward by scholars from the history-of-religions school. For instance, Koester argues that the incarnation of Jesus is one of a piece with a large number of "incarnations" in the Graeco-Roman world: gods were not infrequently taking on human form.[24] But this conclusion can be reached only by overlooking the distinctive features of the Bible's claim. Not least of these is the way the incarnation is nestled into the Bible's story-line: we are dealing with complex monotheism, not polytheism; with a God who creates *ex nihilo*; with incarnation linked to atoning death as the answer to human sin; with a real resurrection attested by credible witnesses; and so forth. This "package" is utterly unique. But unlike Koester, Hick perceives what such claims mean, and cannot live with the entailments. So he opts for pluralism, and is forced to recast Christology.[25]

(2) Hick has become persuaded that the notion of one person who is truly God and truly a man is incoherent. "That Jesus was God the Son incarnate is not literally true, since it has no literal meaning, but it is an application to Jesus of a mythical concept whose function is analogous to that of the notion of divine sonship ascribed in the ancient world to a king."[26] It is true, of course, that "son of God" in *one* of its uses in the Bible is tied to the king who acts as the vassal for God. But the intriguing thing is that such language when applied to Jesus is pushed so hard that the Son does *everything* that the Father does, and the Father is determined that all should honor the Son even as they honor the Father (John 5:16–30). In any case, as Hick knows, incarnation is not dependent on "Son of God" terminology. It is the *logic* of the claim that he disputes.

I cannot canvass the intricate arguments here. But it is important to see that although all sides recognize unfathomable mystery in the doctrine of the incarnation, confessing believers insist that we are dealing with mystery, not

---

23. Ibid., 242, referring especially to John Hick's article, "Jesus and the World Religions," in *The Myth of God Incarnate*, 172. Cf. this in the same essay by Hick: "If Jesus was literally God incarnate, and if it is by his death alone that men can be saved, and by their response to him alone that they can appropriate that salvation, then the only doorway to eternal life is Christian faith. It would follow from this that the large majority of the human race so far have not been saved" (180). Cf. also John Hick, "An Inspirational Christology for a Religiously Plural World," in *Encountering Jesus*, ed. Stephen T. Davis (Atlanta: John Knox, 1988), 5–38.

24. Helmut Koester, "The Divine Human Being," *Harvard Theological Review* 78 (1986): 243–52.

25. I should perhaps add that there is an attractive clarity to Hick's thought on this and many other points. So much contemporary pluralism is woolly, sentimental, utterly devoid of intellectual rigor. But that is never true of Hick. Similarly, it is not true of Michael Ruse, "A Few Last Words—Until the Next Time," *Zygon* 29 (1994): 79.

26. Hick, "Jesus and the World Religions," 178.

contradiction, and have gone to great lengths to provide responsible exposi-
tions that are fair to the biblical evidence and that avoid logical potholes.[27]
Ironically, in another mood pluralists tend to criticize believers for failing to
recognize God's transcendence, for implying that mere words and credal confessions can capture him. Thus Wilfrid Cantwell Smith insists that there is
"no fundamental difference ... between a doctrine and a statue." The former is an intellectual image, the latter a visible and tactile one. All doctrines
are the product of human thought, and "[i]t is wrong for our intellects to
absolutize their own handiwork"; thus to absolutize our image of Christianity
is idolatry.[28] "For Christians to think that Christianity is true, or final, or
salvific, is a form of idolatry. For Christians to imagine that God has constructed Christianity ... , rather than that He/She/It has inspired us to construct it ... that is idolatry."[29] In Driver's words, "[I]dolatry is the insistence
that there is only one way, one norm, one truth."[30]

Stott's reply is worth quoting:

> In response, we certainly agree that God is the Transcendent Reality
> beyond all possible human imagination, apprehension or description. Words
> cannot capture, let alone contain, him. Because he is infinite, we shall never
> come to the end of him, but spend eternity exploring and worshipping his
> fathomless being. Nevertheless, to say that he remains a mystery is not
> incompatible with affirming that he has revealed himself. Moreover, his
> Word incarnate in Jesus and his Word written in Scripture have a norma-
> tive position for all Christian believers. It is somewhat extraordinary that
> the *Myth* contributors regard all Christians of all churches for two millen-
> nia, who have believed in the uniqueness of Jesus, as idolaters! If they are
> referring to "Christianity" as a human construct, then perhaps to absolutize

27. Apart from many classical treatments, see, for instance, Russell F. Aldwinckle, *More
Than a Man: A Study in Christology* (Grand Rapids: Eerdmans, 1976); idem, *Jesus—A Savior or
the Savior? Religious Pluralism in Christian Perspective* (Macon: Mercer Univ. Press, 1982);
Millard J. Erickson, *The Word Became Flesh: A Contemporary Incarnational Christology* (Grand
Rapids: Baker, 1991); Klaas Runia, *The Present-Day Christological Debate* (Leicester: Inter-
Varsity Press, 1984). Above all, perhaps, see Richard Sturch, *The Word and the Christ: An Essay
in Analytic Christology* (Oxford: Clarendon Press, 1991). Even at a more popular level, help is
readily available—e.g., Peter Lewis, *The Glory of Christ* (London: Hodder & Stoughton, 1992),
122–36. Responsible philosophical treatments include Stephen Davis, *Logic and the Nature of
God* (Grand Rapids: Eerdmans, 1983); Thomas V. Morris, *The Logic of God Incarnate* (Ithaca:
Cornell Univ. Press, 1986).

28. Wilfrid Cantwell Smith, "Idolatry in Comparative Perspective," in *The Myth of
Christian Uniqueness*, ed. John Hick and Paul F. Knitter (Maryknoll: Orbis Books, 1987), 56–
57.

29. Ibid., 59.

30. Tom Driver, "The Case for Pluralism," in Hick and Knitter, *The Myth of Christian
Uniqueness*, 216.

it could become an idolatry. To acknowledge the finality and absoluteness of Christ himself, however, is not idolatry but authentic worship.[31]

When pluralists can argue on the one hand that the incarnation is too mysterious to be convincing, and on the other that God is so mysterious that he should not be reduced to creeds and confessions that divide human beings up into discrete parties, one begins to suspect that it is not the evidence that is being allowed to speak, but the commitment to pluralism. In other words, Hick's second principal reason for rejecting the traditional understanding of the incarnation is in danger of collapsing into his first. In any case, sooner or later Christians will conclude, with Lints, "If the Scriptures declare that Jesus was God incarnate, then it may be incumbent upon the believer to wrestle with the question of *how* this is possible rather than *if* it is possible."[32]

(3) Finally, Hick finds support for many of his views in the more radical strands of New Testament scholarship. He therefore argues, on various critical grounds, that the notion of incarnation is a rather late development, that it was created out of whole cloth from the experience of the church, that Jesus never thought of himself that way, that the church moved in evolutionary steps from calling Jesus Master and Messiah to calling him Son of God to calling him God the Son, ending up with full Trinitarian formulae; and so forth.

No amount of evidence can be guaranteed to convince those who on philosophical grounds are persuaded that some position or ostensible fact must be dismissed. Yet it must be said that evidence is not lacking. The New Testament documents are not as easily relegated to a purely theological and certainly unhistorical dimension as some scholars think.[33] Though they are clearly confessional documents, they are not for that reason to be dismissed as historically unreliable.[34] As it would have been obscene for the first

---

31. John Stott, *The Contemporary Christian* (Leicester: Inter-Varsity Press, 1992), 302–3.

32. Richard Lints, *The Fabric of Theology: a Prolegomenon to Evangelical Theology* (Grand Rapids: Eerdmans, 1993), 134. Cf. further Helmut Burkhardt, "Jesus und die Gätter— Synkretismus einst und jetzt," *European Journal of Theology* 2 (1993): 31–38.

33. See, for example, Donald Guthrie, *New Testament Introduction*, 4th ed. (Downers Grove: InterVarsity Press, 1990); D. A. Carson, Douglas J. Moo, Leon Morris, *An Introduction to the New Testament* (Grand Rapids: Zondervan, 1992).

34. See, among many others, F. F. Bruce, *The New Testament Documents—Are They Reliable?* 5th ed. (Grand Rapids: Eerdmans, 1982); I. Howard Marshall, *I Believe in the Historical Jesus* (Grand Rapids: Eerdmans, 1979); R. T. France, *The Evidence for Jesus* (London: Hodder & Stoughton, 1985); Craig Blomberg, *The Historical Reliability of the Gospels* (Downers Grove: InterVarsity Press, 1987). At a more technical level, see Ben F. Meyer, *The Aims of Jesus* (London: SCM Press, 1979); idem, *Christus Faber: The Master-Builder and the House of God* (Allison Park: Pickwick Press, 1992); and many of the essays in the six-volume *Gospel Perspectives*, ed. R. T. France, David Wenham et al. (Sheffield: JSOT Press, 1980–86).

witnesses of the Holocaust to maintain careful neutrality about that to which they bore witness, so it would have been blasphemous for the first Christians to preserve careful neutrality about what they heard and saw in the Lord Jesus—both before his death and after his resurrection.[35] In other words, commitment and theological reflection, i.e., the faith stance of the Evangelists, cannot responsibly be used to devalue their testimony. In chapter 5, I summarized some of the New Testament evidence that supports the deity of Christ. Put into a broader framework, the evidence has been examined by various scholars who insist that the evolutionary model of Christological development simply will not fit the evidence: the development is more like that of organic growth, in which all the fundamental information that shapes the growth is encoded in the seed from the beginning.[36] Those who argue that the confession of Jesus as God is late—not earlier than the gospel of John[37]—have to ignore and "explain away" far too much evidence.[38] Nor will the classic liberal dichotomy between the historical Jesus (exclusively human, a Galilean peasant with some teaching gifts) and the ecclesiastical Christ (inflated out of all historical proportion by the hot wind of religious fervor) withstand much scrutiny: once again, doctrinaire commitments ignore the evidence.[39]

In some cases, the reason scholars dispute the evidence and insist there are Christological contradictions in the Scriptures and in the creeds is not only to dismiss select parts of the evidence but, more precisely, to authorize their overt deconstruction of the primary texts. That is one of Odell-Scott's strategies in his recent "de-constructive" attempt to rewrite Christology in order to accommodate pluralism, anti-supernaturalism, and our "post-

---

35. Of the many books on the resurrection see Murray J. Harris, *From Grave to Glory: Resurrection in the New Testament* (Grand Rapids: Zondervan, 1990); and at a more popular level, his *Three Crucial Questions About Jesus* (Grand Rapids: Baker, 1994), chap. 2.

36. See especially C. F. D. Moule, *The Origin of Christology* (Cambridge: Cambridge Univ. Press, 1977); I. Howard Marshall, *The Origins of New Testament Christology* (Downers Grove: InterVarsity Press, 1976); Richard N. Longenecker, *The Christology of Early Jewish Christianity* (London: SCM Press, 1970); and many of the essays in H. H. Rowdon, ed., *Christ the Lord* (Leicester: Inter-Varsity Press, 1982), and in Joel B. Green and Max Turner, eds., *Jesus of Nazareth: Lord and Christ* (Grand Rapids: Eerdmans, 1994).

37. E.g., James D. G. Dunn, *Christology in the Making: A New Testment Inquiry into the Origins of the Doctrine of the Incarnation* (Philadelphia: Westminster, 1980).

38. E.g., quite apart from the evidence briefly summarized in the previous chapter, one might focus on specific texts such as Philippians 2:6–11. See N. T. Wright, "γενόμενος and the Meaning of Philippians 2:5–11," *Journal of Theological Studies* 37 (1986): 321–53; Peter T. O'Brien, *The Epistle to the Philippians: A Commentary on the Greek Text* (Grand Rapids: Eerdmans, 1991), 186–271.

39. See Markus N. A. Bockmuehl, *This Jesus: Martyr, Lord, Messiah* (Edinburgh: T & T Clark, 1994).

patriarchal" values.[40] Religious pluralism, deconstruction, and political correctness make a heady brew.

In short, Hick's position can be made to stand up only if philosophical pluralism is the "given," such that no amount of biblical or textual or philosophical or theological reasoning can ever be permitted to stand against this "given."

2. Knitter: Theocentric Christology

Especially in his earlier writings in defense of pluralism, Knitter, as we have seen in chapter 4, followed Hick in arguing that we must move from a Christocentric to a theocentric perspective.[41] By this he hoped to remove what is unique to Christianity, and thereby open up greater reciprocity and dialogue between Christianity and other world religions. A necessary step is to show that Christ himself put God at the center of his thought. If so, then correspondingly it behooves us to develop a "theocentric Christology."

At a certain level, Knitter does not have to go far to gather evidence that is apparently in support of his thesis. After all, Jesus proclaims the kingdom *of God*; he prays to his heavenly Father; he insists, to Satan, that all must worship God alone. At a certain level, it is entirely appropriate to speak of a theocentric Christology.

But the cohesiveness of Knitter's position turns rather more on what he denies than on what he affirms. He adopts a common liberal reconstruction of the rise of Christology, an evolutionary model in which Jesus himself never thought of himself as divine, but the church gradually moved to the position that he was, and then attributed such belief to Jesus himself. Thus Knitter can dismiss any biblical counter-evidence to his thesis by appealing to the creative voice of the church. There is simply no way that textual evidence can ever be permitted to falsify his thesis. Moreover, Knitter holds that the New Testament preserves a variety of competing Christological trajectories, traced out as early Christians interacted with surrounding ideologies and religious perspectives, and that it is the part of wisdom today to continue developing a variety of Christologies as we interact with the world religions of our day. "Through such an open and critical dialogue with Hinduism, Buddhism, and

---

40. David W. Odell-Scott, *A Post-Patriarchal Christology*, American Academy of Religion Series, vol. 78 (Atlanta: Scholars Press, 1991).

41. Paul F. Knitter, *No Other Name? A Critical Survey of Christian Attitudes Toward the World Religions* (Maryknoll: Orbis Books, 1985). In two later essays, while not entirely overturning this stance, Knitter acknowledges that even this position does not go far enough to meet the pluralist agenda. See his "Toward a Liberation Theology of Religions," in Hick and Knitter, *The Myth of Christian Uniqueness*, 187–200; idem, "Theocentric Christology: Defended and Transcended," *Journal of Ecumenical Studies* 24 (1987): 41–52.

Islam, theologians of the theocentric model are open to new images of Jesus that will make him more meaningful to them as well as to persons of other faiths."[42]

The problem with this approach, of course, is that ultimately "Jesus" becomes a cipher. He is so plastic that he can be squeezed into any shape that will not cause umbrage. If Muslims, say, do not like the virgin birth, or Jesus' claims to deity as reported in the Bible, or his bodily resurrection from the dead, all these elements can be safely dropped in order to construct a Jesus who has been sanitized for these new partners in dialogue. But the question of truth will not go away. If Jesus really did rise from the dead, as all the early Christians believed, then it is false to dispense with this belief. If what the New Testament documents say about Jesus is to be read as a multifaceted composite, and not as competing and mutually conflicting trajectories, then there are clear boundaries to the plasticity of the portrait we may draw. If the classic liberal interpretation of the rise of Christology is fundamentally flawed, and must finally be dismissed as yet another effort to reconstruct Jesus in the image mandated by the contemporary cultural priorities, then Knitter's approach is simultaneously bad history, bad theology, and, from the perspective of the Bible's story-line, one more instance of catastrophic human rebellion against the God who insists that his intention is that all should honor the Son even as they honor the Father.[43]

We can look at Knitter's work another way. His approach to the Gospels is of no more than ephemeral scholarly value (however popular it may be for a while in some quarters). But worse, it wreaks havoc with the Bible's story-line. The Bible as a whole becomes nonsensical. Knitter is not revising some dispensable doctrine or restating an easily modified theological tenet. Rather, he is destroying the entire structure of Christian theology. For if major Christologies can be dropped and added to the canon at the urging of a theologian responding to the intellectual pressures of his or her age, such that the entire story-line becomes quite different, then there is no canon at all, except in a purely formal sense. There are no boundaries; there are no givens; there is nothing revealed that another generation may not subtract, no notion whatsoever that cannot in principle be added in. Of course, such problems rarely trouble committed pluralists, because for them Pluralism is god, and provided that god is satisfied it matters little what damage is done to other religions, such as Christianity. But in that case, of course, the pluralists would be a little more candid if they stopped referring to themselves as Christians.

---

42. Knitter, *No Other Name?* 181.

43. For a more extended critique of Knitter's Christology, see Netland, *Dissonant Voices,* 249–60; Mark Heim, "Thinking about Theocentric Christology," *Journal of Ecumenical Studies* 24 (1987): 1–16.

3. White: A New Moral Influence Theory

Strictly speaking, the focal concern of Vernon White in his new and important book[44] is not pluralism *per se*, but an inquiry into one particular facet of the doctrine of the atonement. That facet is sometimes referred to as "the scandal of particularity": How could a single event in an unimportant part of the Roman Empire two thousand years ago hold universal significance, throughout the world and time and even the universe?

The most common answer, as White acknowledges with admirable fairness, has been some form of the doctrine of penal substitution. White himself pursues another synthesis. He argues that "unless and until God himself has experienced suffering, death and the temptation to sin, and overcome them, as a human individual, he has no moral authority to overcome them in and with the rest of humanity" (39). Thus White argues for a real and indissoluble incarnation, but the cross becomes a subset of the suffering undertaken by that incarnation, rather than its primary purpose. This "model" grounds the possibility of salvation for every individual, and the necessary offering of such salvation to every individual (67). By his suffering God has acquired the necessary authority and power to transform our lives by standing alongside us and acting and operating through us (here White deploys Austin Farrar's notion of double agency). White finds inspiration for his views in several contemporary theologians, in "incorporation" language in Paul (we are "in" Christ), and in other suggestive echoes.

What fair appraisal can be ventured to this proposal? There is some sense in which God does, in fact, gain moral authority by the incarnation. The point is implicitly acknowledged every time preachers appeal to the incarnation or to Jesus' passion to provide the most astonishing model of self-abnegating love for the sake of others, as a ground for moral improvement. Paul explicitly offers such an appeal in Philippians 2:5–11. But surely it goes too far to suggest that God is *lacking* in moral authority *until* he becomes a suffering human being. Biblically and theologically, his authority is grounded in who he is; our responsibility and accountability to him is grounded in the brute fact that he made us, and made us for himself. White must discount the wrath of God, which repeatedly lies on the very surface of the biblical text. Moreover, because he sets his "model" over against those that deploy the categories of penal substitution, he must skirt "the teaching of the New Testament that the Lord Jesus Christ *is himself* our *justification, redemption, mediation and propitiation; he is himself the resurrection and the life*—he who is, who was and who is to come, the incarnate *I am* of the ever-living God" (to

---

44. *Atonement and Incarnation: An Essay in Universalism and Particularity* (Cambridge: Cambridge Univ. Press, 1991).

use the words of Torrance).[45] Nor is it clear how what the Bible says about the triune nature of God has much bearing or usefulness in White's model: modalism would do as nicely. The greatest expression of God's personhood would not be as-he-is-in-himself, but in becoming a human being. Once again we are being dragged away from the Bible's story-line. What purpose the sacrificial system of the old covenant? What purpose the temple, the priesthood, the promises? I am not suggesting that there is no validity whatsoever to White's "model," nor that it is reductionistic but harmless provided it is integrated with other lines of biblical thought on the complex ways by which our redemption was achieved. Rather, I am suggesting that the form of its reductionism once again destroys the fabric of Christian revelation.

4. Panikkar, Fox, and the Cosmic Christ

In an earlier chapter I briefly mentioned the thesis of Panikkar: "Christ" is found in other religions, not least in Hinduism, provided one looks in the right places.[46] The origin of the expression "cosmic Christ" is usually traced to Joseph Sittler in his 1961 address to the World Council of Churches Assembly meeting in New Delhi. That address was based not least on the occurrences of "all" in passages such as Colossians 1:15–20—issues that we have already examined and need not explore afresh. Panikkar developed the notion of the cosmic Christ along somewhat different lines. Christ, he said, cannot be identified with the historical Jesus; Christ is always more than Jesus, and therefore Christianity has no monopoly on Christ, even if it has a monopoly on Jesus. Since every religion develops some sort of link between the absolute God and human beings, it is appropriate to think of that link as "Christ." For Christians, doubtless the historical connection is Jesus; for others, Christ will be manifest as someone or something else. Christ is of course the only mediator, but he operates differently in different religions.

Apart from these seminal works, a number of "cosmic Christs" have been proposed. One thinks, for example, of Rahner's theology and its effluents, with many versions of the "anonymous Christian" theory (amply discussed in the preceding chapter); or of Schlette's proposal, to the effect that within the one world history one must distinguish two sacred histories, one general and one special, the latter with Israel and the church at the core, so that one may

---

45. Thomas F. Torrance, "The Atonement. The Singularity of Christ and the Finality of the Cross: The Atonement and the Moral Order," in *Universalism and the Doctrine of Hell*, ed. Nigel M. de S. Cameron (Carlisle: Paternoster, 1992), 233.

46. R. Panikkar, "The Meaning of Christ's Name," in *Service and Salvation*, ed. Joseph Pathrapankal (Bangalore: C.M.I., 1973), 235–63, esp. 242ff.; idem, *The Unknown Christ of Hinduism: Towards an Ecumenical Christophany* (Maryknoll: Orbis Books, 1981 [1964]). Cf. also his *Intrareligious Dialogue* (New York: Paulist Press, 1978).

speak of "non-Christian religions as the ordinary and the way of the Church as the extraordinary way of salvation";[47] or of the many writings of S. J. Samartha,[48] who urges that the Christian Scriptures be interpreted in the context of other Scriptures, in the hope that fresh interpretations will arise.[49] Sumithra offers a useful survey and critique.[50] Others who do not deploy the "cosmic Christ" terminology develop their thought in not dissimilar ways. For example, in the last chapter of one of his recent books, Wiles argues that one can claim that a genuine incarnation took place in Jesus of Nazareth while nevertheless abandoning claims to uniqueness and finality—which allows Christians to be faithful to their own heritage without denying the possibility that God is working salvifically in other religions.[51]

But one of the most intriguing developments is the takeover of the "cosmic Christ" category to serve the purposes of "green" and "Gaia" theology. The premier exponent is doubtless Matthew Fox.[52] In his earlier books Fox had scathingly attacked orthodox Christianity as guilty of matricide—the killing of Mother Earth. The charge is renewed here, and if Western culture in general and the church in particular is guilty of matricide, it is no less guilty "of ecocide, geocide, suicide and even deicide."[53] The religious language of the Christian heritage is taken over: "We have begun to put our hands in her [i.e., Mother Earth's] lanced side and in her crucified hands and feet" (16). Mother Earth is "very aware and sensitive" (18), while the church is "matricidal" and "sado-masochistic" (28). Conservative ("fundamentalist") Christianity is nothing but "Christofascism," and is charged with "a reptilian kind of energy and hatred" (40). This is one very angry man.

On the basis of a revelatory dream, which he sets over against all Christian revelation, Fox declares that out of the crucifixion of Mother Earth

---

47. H. R. Schlette, *Towards a Theology of Religions* (London: Burns & Oates, 1963), 74–75.

48. Most recently *One Christ—Many Religions: Toward a Revised Christology* (Bangalore: SATHRI and Wordmakers, 1992). On this one, see the trenchant and at times blistering review by D. Jebaraj, *Asia Theological Association Journal* 2/1 (1994): 69–75.

49. At one level, of course, the Christian would delight in the challenge, provided that rigorous exegetical and hermeneutical integrity be preserved on all sides. Then the differences amongst the major religions would become all the clearer!

50. Sunand Sumithra, "Conversion—to Cosmic Christ?" *Evangelical Review of Theology* 16 (1992): 385–97.

51. Maurice Wiles, *Christian Theology and Inter-religious Dialogue* (Philadelphia: Trinity Press International, 1992).

52. Of his many books, see especially *The Coming of the Cosmic Christ: The Healing of Mother Earth and the Birth of a Global Renaissance* (San Francisco: Harper & Row, 1988). An important review is by Margaret Brearley, "Matthew Fox and the Cosmic Christ," *Anvil* 9 (1992): 39–54.

53. Fox, *The Coming of the Cosmic Christ*, 17.

will come a new spiritual awakening. The Christian heritage is nonmystical, ascetic, concerned with sacraments and objective truth; what he is proposing is a mystical, creation-centered, right-brain experience. The historical Jesus as reconstructed by the church must be abandoned; the real Jesus is in fact a teacher of nondualistic creation mysticism.[54] But in the last analysis we must embrace the cosmic Christ, who represents "a true second coming, an ushering in of a spiritual and cultural renaissance that can heal the most poignant and urgent pain of our time—the crucifixion of Mother Earth."[55]

Despite the verve and wit of his writing, Fox is simply wrong on so many points it is hard to know where to begin. To argue that there is no "mystical" tradition within the heritage of orthodox Christianity is simply astonishing. His exegesis of biblical texts exhibits the kind and range of errors that a first-year seminarian would be worked over for—either that, or, more likely perhaps, his exegesis betrays a thorough commitment to the canons of postmodernity (but in that case, why is he so passionate about trying to convince the rest of us what *ought* to be?). There is no attempt to wrestle with the rising literature that places "green" concerns *within* the framework of the Bible's story-line and the matrix of Christian theology;[56] rather, there is an eclectic and emotional takeover of Christian terms, history, heritage, and language in order to serve an agenda fundamentally extra-biblical and finally anti-biblical. The real tragedy is that Fox's analysis of the human dilemma is unutterably shallow. Even when he makes telling points about the earth, the best of them can easily be brought under the framework of responsible Christian living in God's universe. But his thought, characterized by a kind of new paganism, does not deal with most of the human ills and sins that generate the very evils he is concerned about—and a lot of others to which he is curiously indifferent.

5. The Shamanized Jesus

This heading I have taken over from the title of an article by Douglas Groothuis in *Christianity Today*.[57] Groothuis points out that the New Age claims Jesus as one of their own: he is variously esteemed as Master, Guru,

---

54. All twenty-one of Fox's "running, experiential definitions of mysticism" (ibid., 47) he finds in his version of the historical Jesus.

55. Ibid., 83.

56. E.g., most recently (and after the book by Fox to which reference has been made), Loren Wilkinson, "The Uneasy Conscience of the Human Race: Redeeming Creation in the 'Environmental' Movement," in *God and Culture*, ed. D. A. Carson and John D. Woodbridge (Grand Rapids: Eerdmans, 1993), 301–20; idem, "Gaia Spirituality: A Christian Critique," *Themelios* 18/3 (1993): 4–8; and many of the works cited in those two articles.

57. 35/5 (April 29, 1991): 20–23.

Yogi, Adept, Avatar, Shaman. He belongs to "the spiritual hall of fame along with Buddha, Krishna, Lao Tse, and others."[58] In a lengthy and well-researched article in Canada's *Maclean's* magazine, we are introduced to some of the more important "New Age" movements and leaders in North America, including Hanne Strong's center in Colorado.[59] The range of options is formidable—crystals, meditation, home-grown Hinduism, psychic counselors, and on and on. "We of the federation of the intergalactic work together," coos trance-channeler Anne Morse to a packed center in Toronto where each person has paid $16 to get in. "And we are willing to work with you."[60] Within this ill-defined, utterly unverifiable, frequently manipulative theosophical smorgasbord, Jesus gets rewritten as one of the spiritual agents for change.

The more I read the New Age literature, the more I am struck by several facts. Almost none of it seriously wrestles with the *historical* and *textual* arguments put forward by serious Christians. New Age thought is insufferably fuzzy and inconsistent. Anything it likes or can use, it rips out of its historic context and redeploys with new content, often made out of whole cloth. It almost never deals with evil, because it is most commonly pantheistic—and religions that do not wrestle with the problems of human evil are blind beyond words. Worse, almost all of this multiplying thought is irremediably selfish. The aim of the exercise is self-fulfilment, self-actualization, serenity, productivity, power. God, if he/she/it exists, exists for me. And from a biblical perspective, it is this profound selfishness that lies at the heart of all human sin.

This is not to deny that some good is sometimes achieved by New Age religion. A person may go through an emotional experience that proves wonderfully cathartic where there has been, say, the suppression of many angry resentments that have proved emotionally crippling. But if the matrix of thought within which that emotional catharsis has been worked out is fundamentally wrong and untrue, then for all the good of the emotional release, the long-term damage that emerges from committing oneself to what is foundationally false far exceeds the gains. The emotional release *could* have come, for instance, from the joy of being forgiven and forgiving, from delighting in the experienced pleasure of the love of the personal/transcendent God (Eph. 3:14–21)—and in that case the advantages of the emotional release have been linked to thought that reflects the truth of the God who is there, the God who revealed himself in history, the God who sent his Son to reconcile broken

---

58. Ibid., 20.

59. "The New Spirituality," and related articles, in *Maclean's* 107/41 (October 10, 1994), 44–54.

60. Ibid., 47.

and rebellious sinners to himself. If the pleasure of emotional release is the sufficient criterion, little thought will be given to the broader ramifications. And that, of course, opens us up to deception from the devil himself, who loves to parade himself as an angel of light. The situation is becoming terribly sad and painful, for the vast majority of those involved in the movement have never been thoroughly exposed to an intelligent articulation of a truly Christian worldview.

That is why sometimes it is possible to make real inroads into a New Ager's life and thought with a little kindness and some basic summary of the *facts* about Jesus, and where he fits into the Bible's story-line—and what that story-line is. I shall return to the question of evangelism in chapter 12. My point here is that with the exception of his name, the Jesus of various wings of the New Age movement bears little or no relation with the Jesus of the Bible.[61]

Concluding Reflections

Changes in approach to Christology have been introduced so rapidly and so frequently that today many think doctrinal change is inevitable. As a result, some pluralists are standing back and self-consciously reflecting on the precise ways in which Christian theology, in particular Christology, would have to change if philosophical pluralism, their given, is to triumph.[62] But from a Christian point of view, one should not accept as binding on one's conscience any model of Christology, or of any other Christian teaching, that is not clearly taught in Scripture—and that means, among other things, in line with the basic plot-line of Scripture. One thinks of the wise words of Stephen Williams in his review of a book by Kettler: "I question whether we should make anything Christologically or soteriologically foundational that is not close to the surface of Scripture."[63]

At some point one sometimes detects an ignoble running away from the truth. The well-known words of Father Brown would not have to be greatly rewritten to be applicable in our day:

---

61. In the past, Christians have responded to the bifurcation between faith and history much loved by modernist critics by insisting that true history can be conveyed in a confessional statement, a faith statement. Now we must respond to postmodernist critics by insisting that true faith is in part the product of real history, i.e., that true faith is called into being because of God's gracious and unique self-disclosure in real history.

62. E.g., Leonard Swidler, *After the Absolute: The Dialogical Future of Religious Reflection* (Minneapolis: Fortress Press, 1990); Chester Gillis, *Pluralism: A New Paradigm for Theology* (Louvain/Grand Rapids: Peeters/Eerdmans, 1993).

63. The review is in *Themelios* 19/2 (1994): 32–33; the book being reviewed is Christian D. Kettler, *The Vicarious Humanity of Christ and the Reality of Salvation* (London/New York: University Press of America, 1991).

It's part of something I've noticed more and more in the modern world, appearing in all sorts of newspaper rumours and conversational catchwords; something that's arbitrary without being authoritative. People readily swallow the untested claims of this, that, or the other. It's drowning all your old rationalism and scepticism, it's coming in like a sea; and the name of it is superstition.... It's the first effect of not believing in God that you lose your common sense and can't see things as they are. Anything that anybody talks about, and says there's a good deal in it, extends itself indefinitely like a vista in a nightmare. And a dog is an omen, and a cat is a mystery, and a pig is a mascot and a beetle is a scarab, calling all the menagerie of polytheism from Egypt and old India; Dog Anubis and great green-eyed Pasht and all the holy howling Bulls of Bashan; reeling back to the bestial gods of the beginning, escaping into elephants and snakes and crocodiles; and all because you are frightened of four words: "He was made Man."[64]

B. Two-Covenant Salvation and the Charge of Anti-Semitism

Whatever appeals to pluralism people make when religions far removed from Christianity such as Hinduism and Buddhism are introduced, the same appeals take on new heat and urgency when Judaism is mentioned. This is not surprising, for Christianity arose out of Judaism, claiming to be the sole rightful heir of the heritage of the Hebrew canon. Conflict between siblings or close neighbors is often more spiteful than between distant opponents. Worse, whatever (relatively minor) opposition first-century Jews meted out on their Christian antagonists through the synagogue system, the Christian world has generated restrictions and pogroms and atrocities, culminating in a Holocaust so shockingly callous and vile that the whole world took notice. In the wake of such realities, how dare Christians insist that Jews must become Christians in order to be saved?

I shall venture four points to try to clarify the issues.

1. Not surprisingly, a substantial literature explores almost every facet of the debate.

This literature adopts a wide diversity of positions. A volume edited by Shermis and Zannoni tends to place Jewish-Christian dialogue within the larger framework of discussion about religious pluralism.[65] Others argue that

64. G. K. Chesterton, *The Penguin Complete Father Brown* (Harmondsworth: Penguin Books, 1963), 367–68.

65. Michael Shermis and Arthur E. Zannoni, eds., *Introduction to Jewish-Christian Relations* (New York: Paulist Press, 1991). See especially one of the essays in that volume, viz., Philip L. Culbertson, "The Seventy Faces of the One God: The Theology of Religious Pluralism," 145–73.

what Jews and Christians have in common is so important that they must join hands against the rising secularization of Western culture. Thus Novak insists that the greatest danger to Judaism and to Christianity alike is secularism and its antimetaphysics written into public policy.[66] But inevitably he asserts (though it is for him a relatively minor point) that "disavowal of proselytizing intent has been the indispensable precondition for Jewish-Christian dialogue."[67]

Mention of proselytizing[68] offers an excuse for a brief aside. Even the place alloted to proselytism differs greatly between Judaism and Christianity. Although there is plenty of evidence that people from a Christian heritage have at various periods of history become pious Jews,[69] and that people from a Jewish heritage have become pious Christians, it is fair to conclude that "Judaism has rarely if ever felt an absolute compulsion to win souls to the cause at all costs. Its theology has never prompted such a compulsion."[70] Probably this has been tied up with the racial component intrinsic to the locus of the people of God under the terms of the Sinai covenant. But this does not mean that most Jews have seen Judaism as one religion among many. Until the rise of the most liberal forms of Judaism, most Jews have thought of their heritage as the best. Jews in the heritage of Maimonides have tended to view Christians as idolaters. For their part, Christians at their most vital have felt that winning others to Christ is an intrinsic part of their faith. Christian theology is tied to an eschatological vision in which the gospel of the kingdom is preached throughout the entire world as preparation for the end. Christians cannot forswear notions such as witness, mission, evangelism, proclamation, whose aim is inevitably proselytism. And if Christians do not think that Jews are idolaters, they hold that Christianity is superior to Judaism—not because Christians are superior, but because they believe that the correct reading of the Hebrew canon leads to Jesus Christ as reported in the New Testament canon, i.e., that the line of divine revelation actually runs

---

66. David Novak, *Jewish-Christian Dialogue: A Jewish Justification* (New York: Oxford University Press, 1989), 8–9, 132.

67. Ibid., 129.

68. For convenience, I here use "proselytizing" to refer to all attempts to win someone from one religious position to another. By such usage, I mean to convey neither positive nor negative overtones. Other words—mission, witness, evangelism, sharing one's faith, proclamation, etc.—will carry different overtones in different contexts, and in some discussions need to be distinguished. At this point, however, I need a global term.

69. See especially Marcel Simon, *Verus Israel* (Oxford: Oxford Univ. Press, 1986), esp. 271–305.

70. Tony Bayfield, "Mission—A Jewish Perspective," *Theology* 96 (1993): 181. See further Scot McKnight, *A Light Among the Gentiles: Jewish Mission in the Second Temple Period* (Minneapolis: Fortress Press, 1991).

that way, and that it is a tragic failure not to recognize the point. Thus insistence by many Jews that for fruitful dialogue to take place Christians must disavow the intent to proselytize, doubtless seems an entirely reasonable demand to them; to most Christians, it sounds like an invitation to abandon something that lies at the heart of their faith. I am not sure that the two sides have always recognized the fundamentally different ways in which Judaism and Christianity assess proselytism.

In any case, if Novak represents the voice that tends to play down differences between Christianity and Judaism (without ignoring those differences) in order to achieve a greater good, there are certainly other voices around. A slightly different tack, often found in discussions between evangelicals and Jews, is to foster goodwill, to discuss differences candidly, to recognize the profound anti-Semitism that still lurks not too deeply buried in large swaths of Western culture, and to encourage Christians to recognize the intensely Jewish nature of their roots.[71] Some Christian writers in this camp gently but firmly insist that Christians cannot fairly be asked to abandon their calling to evangelize.[72] But it is perhaps more common today to find books and articles that trace anti-Semitism back to the fundamentals of Christianity, and especially to the New Testament itself.[73] Sometimes contemporary Jewish attempts to "reclaim" Jesus have sharply distinguished between this reconstructed Jewish Jesus and the Jesus of the New Testament.[74] Between these two poles are many books that adopt the tone of scholarly exploration, expressing a wide variety of opinions.[75] In a class by themselves stand several products of the pen of Neusner, who argues that Jews and Christians cannot be said, in any useful way, to share a common tradition. For Neusner, modern

---

71. E.g., A. James Rudin and Marvin R. Wilson, eds., *A Time to Speak: The Evangelical-Jewish Encounter* (Grand Rapids: Eerdmans, 1987). See also Marvin R. Wilson, *Our Father Abraham: Jewish Roots of the Christian Faith* (Grand Rapids: Eerdmans, 1989).

72. David F. Wells, "'No Offense: I Am an Evangelical': A Search for Self-Definition," in Rudin and Wilson, *A Time To Speak*, 20–40.

73. Perhaps the most virulent of these is Norman A. Beck, *Mature Christianity in the 21st Century: The Recognition and Repudiation of the Anti-Jewish Polemic in the New Testament* (New York: Crossroad, 1994). Cf. also Marcus Braybrooke, *Time to Meet: Towards a Deeper Relationship Between Jews and Christians* (London: SCM Press, 1990).

74. See the evenhanded assessment of Donald A. Hagner, *The Jewish Reclamation of Jesus: An Analysis and Critique of Modern Jewish Study of Jesus* (Grand Rapids: Zondervan, 1984).

75. E.g., see many of the essays in James H. Charlesworth, ed., *Jews and Christians: Exploring the Past, Present, and Future* (New York: Crossroad, 1990); Malcolm Lowe, ed., *People, Land and State of Israel: Jewish and Christian Perspectives* (Jerusalem: Ecumenical Theological Research Fraternity in Israel, 1989 [= *Immanuel* 22–23 (1989)]; idem, *The New Testament and Christian-Jewish Dialogue* (Jerusalem: Ecumenical Theological Research Fraternity in Israel, 1990) [= *Immanuel* 24/25 (1990)].

Jewish-Christian "dialogues" are pretty much nonstarters: they do not deal frankly and candidly with the profound differences that divide Jews and Christians. Christians believe in the incarnation of God in Jesus Christ, and in the death and resurrection of Jesus as the only basis for the salvation of men and women everywhere; Jews don't. Jews believe in the divine vocation of Israel, unchanged this side of the coming of Jesus, and that the Talmudic sage in some ways stands for the Torah incarnate, and promises sanctification; Christians don't. The way forward is for each side to try to enter empathetically into the perspectives of the other, while frankly acknowledging the unbridgeable differences.[76]

Whether one agrees or not with Neusner's view that no real dialogue has yet taken place, his view of the way forward is surely wise, provided each side is also allowed to try to convince the others in fair, open, courteous encounter. Otherwise dialogue degenerates into an excuse for fuzzy thought.

2. The Holocaust inevitably colors all contemporary discussion.

At one level, this is as it should be: it would be odious beyond words for the Holocaust not to affect us. But unless, with postmodernists, one feels one has the right to abandon the attempt to discover what texts meant in their time, we ought to try to find out what Paul meant, for example in Romans 11 or Ephesians 2, when he wrote without any knowledge of two thousand years of additional history, not least the history of the last six decades.[77]

The best and most careful thinkers on both sides, Jewish and Christian, have long recognized this. The great Jewish scholar Samuel Sandmel wrote, "Perhaps we might be willing to say to ourselves that it is not at all impossible that some Jews, even leading Jews, recommended the death of Jesus to Pilate. We are averse to saying this to ourselves, for so total has been the charge against us that we have been constrained to make a total denial."[78] In a careful article, Weinfeld works his way through the blistering charges of hypocrisy Jesus levels against the Pharisees in Matthew 23, and finds ample parallels in the rabbinic sources. He concludes:

---

76. Jacob Neusner, *Jew and Christian: The Myth of a Common Tradition* (Philadelphia: Trinity Press International, 1991); idem, *Telling Tales: Making Sense of Christian and Judaic Nonsense. The Urgency and Basis for Judeo-Christian Dialogue* (Louisville: Westminster/John Knox, 1993); idem, "The Jewish-Christian Argument in the First Century: Different People Talking About Different Things to Different People," in *The Law in the Bible and in Its Environment*, ed. Timo Veijola (Helsinki/Gättingen: Finnish Exegetical Society/Vandenhoeck & Ruprecht, 1990), 173–87.

77. This is precisely where Sidney G. Hall III falls short in his *Christian Anti-Semitism and Paul's Theology* (Minneapolis: Augsburg Fortress, 1993).

78. *We Jews and Jesus* (London/New York: Oxford University Press, 1965), 114.

To sum up, accusations of Pharisaic hypocrisy in the Gospels contain motifs identical with the accusations in the rabbinic sources. These are: 1) not practicing what one preaches; 2) ostentatiously wearing cloaks; 3) showing off phylacteries and fringes; 4) demanding the first place at dinner; 5) tithing trivial things. All these are denounced in rabbinic literature, a fact which shows that such a critique was prevalent in Judaism at the time when Christianity began to take shape.

It appears that the critique of Pharisaic hypocrisy was a common phenomenon in Judaism of the first centuries of the common era. When the authors of the Synoptic Gospels wrote about Pharisaic hypocrites, they were using material that was widespread in Pharisaic lore itself.[79]

In other words, the charge of "anti-Semitism" leveled against Jesus or against the New Testament writers is scarcely coherent, considering that (1) according to extant Jewish literature, some Jews charged other Jews with the same sins; and further, (2) Jesus himself and all or nearly all of the writers of the New Testament were Jews; and (3) more important yet, most of the "purple passages" of condemnation in the New Testament belong to a *biblical* tradition of prophetic denunciation (e.g., Isa. 1:4, 21; 30:9; 57:3–5; Jer. 3:6; 7:25–26; 9:26; 11:7–8; Hos. 1:2; 4:6; Amos 5:18–24; 6:1–7)—and of course that is entirely within the Israelite tradition.

This is not to dismiss the relevance of the Holocaust from hermeneutical consideration; it is to deny it the right to control *all* hermeneutic considerations. Proper hermeneutic influence arising from the Holocaust might include the following points: (1) Granted the deeply ingrained and odious anti-Semitism that seeps through much of Western culture, it is vital that extra care be taken with our translations of the Bible, so that translators do not unwittingly generate harmful impressions among the untutored or the bigoted. For instance, in the Fourth Gospel, after opposition to Jesus has coalesced into policy, John comments, "Therefore Jesus no longer moved about publicly *among the Jews.* Instead he withdrew to a region near the desert, to a village called Ephraim, where he stayed with his disciples" (John 11:54, emphasis mine). One might infer from this that all Jews were against Jesus, and that the village to which Jesus withdrew, Ephraim, was necessarily a Gentile center. In fact, all serious students of John's gospel know that John uses the expression "the Jews" in quite a variety of ways, sometimes, as here, to refer to the religious authorities in Judea—and in any case, Ephraim was a Jewish village.[80] Doubtless we need to take more care in our Bible

---

79. Moshe Weinfeld, "The Charge of Hypocrisy in Matthew 23 and in Jewish Sources," *Immanuel* 24/25 (1990): 58.

80. I am indebted for this example to James H. Charlesworth, "Is the New Testament Anti-Semitic or Anti-Jewish?" *Explorations* 7/2 (1993): 2–3.

translations. (2) What is often needed is *more* historical awareness of what went on in New Testament times, precisely so that we can see the nature of the struggle between the synagogue and the nascent church in its own light, and not in terms of later centuries of distortion and oppression. For example, when we are told by countless contemporary commentators that John's gospel is anti-Semitic because "the Jews" in that gospel often come in for a fair bit of shtick, why is it almost never pointed out that it is John's version of the passion narrative that lays most of the blame on Pilate, while by comparison the Synoptics lay more emphasis on the roles of the Sanhedrin and the Jewish crowds? If John is anti-Semitic, he certainly overlooked a number of remarkable opportunities for scoring points. The only way to help people think their way through these things is to place the New Testament documents firmly in their historical setting. (3) Similarly, the horrendous charge of "God-killers" and the like cannot possibly be hurled by Christians at Jews, if they have so much as begun to understand the biblical plot-line. For that plot-line shows that the crucifixion of the Son of God arose out of God's gracious response to the sin of the human race, not out of God's response to the sin of the Jewish race, or of those Jews who happened to be living in Jerusalem at the time. This is not to deny that certain Jewish *and Gentile* leaders were involved in a criminal conspiracy (see Acts 4:27); it is not to deny that some Jews in a frenzied crowd called down guilt on themselves and on their children (Matt. 27:25). It is to say that from a theological and canonical point of view they did on the immediate occasion what in principal the entire race does when confronted with God's gracious self-disclosure. Apart from his intervening mercy, we all shake our puny fists in his face and join Sinatra in the refrain, "I did it my way"—the essence of perversity in God's universe. From any distinctly Christian perspective, it is this universal sinfulness, not the sinfulness of the occasional Jewish players at the time, that is the more fundamental of the factors that brought Jesus to the cross. That is why we sing:

> Was it for sins that I had done
> He groaned upon the tree?
> Amazing pity! Grace unknown!
> And love beyond degree!

But if the New Testament writers cannot reasonably be charged with anti-Semitism, however much later readers have sometimes read anti-Semitism into the New Testament, can they at least be charged with anti-Judaism? That is, if there is no fundamentally racial tinge to their opposition, is there an unhealthy religious malice? That brings us to the next point.

3. Many contemporary scholars have adopted one form or another of a "two-covenant" theory: Jews are saved by one covenant, and Gentiles by another.

The exact shape of this theory varies a great deal from writer to writer, but in broad outline it is no longer rare. And owing, perhaps, on the one hand, to the pressure exerted by the popularity of philosophical pluralism, and, on the other, to the sensitivities called into being by the Holocaust, some writers emotionally ratchet up the stakes when they turn to this subject. One well-known scholar, in a recent popular publication, boldly insists that anyone who says a Jew is not saved if he does not espouse Jesus the Messiah is stooping to anti-Semitism (thus condemning Peter as an anti-Semite, Acts 4:12), and that he hates Christological readings of the Old Testament (thus condemning all the major New Testament writers).

There is often an unspoken assumption in such expressions, namely, that Christianity is something of a usurper, that Jewish interpretation has a kind of hermeneutic right of primogeniture. That must be firmly disputed, and on many grounds—not least the ground that modern Judaism in all its forms is, arguably, considerably farther removed from the Hebrew canon than Christianity is. As Neusner points out,

> When the rabbis of late antiquity rewrote in their own image and likeness the entire Scripture and history of Israel, dropping whole eras as though they had never been, ignoring vast bodies of old Jewish writing, inventing whole new books for the canon of Judaism, they did the same thing [as Christianity did]. They reworked what they had received in light of what they prepared to give.... [I]n Judaism of the first century to the seventh, every mode of piety would be refashioned in the light of the vast public events represented by the religious revolutionaries at hand, rabbi-clerk, rabbi-priest, rabbi-Messiah.[81]

One might quibble with some of this, but clearly any Judaism which, of necessity after A.D. 70, includes no sacrificial system, no priesthood, no tabernacle or temple, and no land, is a long way from the religion of the Sinai code. This does not prove that the Christian reading of the Old Testament is right: that must be established on its own terms. But it helps remove the assumption that Christianity is a usurper.

On the Jewish side, the "two-covenants" terminology is largely identified with Franz Rosenzweig.[82] He argues that Christianity may providentially be doing things that Judaism cannot do; that the daughter is not necessarily

81. "The Jewish-Christian Argument," 186.
82. Especially in his book *Star of Redemption* (New York: Holt, Rinehart & Winston, 1970).

the enemy of the mother; that the uniqueness of Israel's contribution does not automatically negate the uniqueness of Christianity's contribution; that the two together may thus prepare the way for the coming Messiah. Most Jews have not been prepared to follow Rosenzweig, especially in his deployment of two-covenant terminology, which violates so much of what many Jews hold dear. Recently Moran has taken up Rosenzweig, but abandons the two-covenant terminology.[83] In neither case will the proposals withstand close testing by the exegesis of the biblical texts.

In the Christian tradition, a large number of writers have extended the "old covenant"/"new covenant" terminology of Paul in 2 Corinthians 3 and implicit in Hebrews to speak of two covenants, both of them redeeming, one for Jews and the other for Gentiles. The number of writers is so large and the issues so complex that I can merely introduce them here. Lohfink argues that in 2 Corinthians 3:14 Paul is really saying that it is not the old covenant that comes to an end, but the veil that covers it. "The 'new covenant' is nothing else than the unveiled, no longer covered 'old covenant' which radiates God's splendor already contained in it."[84] Moreover, we must read Paul's words about the unveiling "as belonging to the topos of hyperbole" (40). The epistle to the Hebrews must be read in the light of this interpretation of 2 Corinthians 3:14 (41–44). That Romans 11:26–27 can speak of hope for an as yet unbelieving Israel presupposes God's love for this people, a love that he never renounces, and that is operative even during the period of their unbelief. Jews who do not believe in Jesus are not lopped off the olive tree: they are still loved on account of the patriarchs, but miss out on the blessings of being in the new covenant (48–74).

It is doubtful if many devout Jews will buy into this accounting of things: accepted they may be among the elect, but quite clearly at a second level, unless they become Christians. This sounds more like a liberal Christian reading than either a Jewish reading or a robust pluralist reading. More importantly, at almost every point, Lohfink's exegesis must be challenged. It is true that what is taken away in 2 Corinthians 3:14 is the veil—but "only in Christ is it taken away." In other words, from Paul's perspective, the true significance of the old covenant is rightly perceived only when one has come to terms with Christ.[85] And the epistle to the Hebrews repeatedly deploys a salvation-historical argument to prove that *already in the Hebrew canon* the

83. Gabriel Moran, *Uniqueness: Problem or Paradox in Jewish and Christian Traditions* (Maryknoll: Orbis Books, 1992), esp. 64–70.

84. Norbert Lohfink, *The Covenant Never Revoked: Biblical Reflections on Christian-Jewish Dialogue* (New York: Paulist Press, 1991), 39.

85. See especially Scott J. Hafemann, "The Glory and Veil of Moses in 2 Cor 3:7–14: An Example of Paul's Contextual Exegesis of the Old Testament—A Proposal," *Horizons in*

biblical writers announce the obsolescence in principle of the Mosaic covenant. Thus if, centuries after the establishment of the Levitical priesthood, Psalm 110 announces a priest in the order of Melchizedek, implicitly it is announcing the insufficiency of the Levitical priesthood—and therefore of the law with which it is inextricably entangled (Hebrews 7). If Jeremiah foresees a "new" covenant, "he has made the first one obsolete; and what is obsolete and aging will soon disappear" (Heb. 8:13). Eventually the conclusion is specifically drawn out: "The law is only a shadow of the good things that are coming—not the realities themselves" (Heb. 10:1). From a Christian perspective, that does not depreciate the law-covenant: it merely encourages people to recognize it for what it is, and not to take it for something else. To rely on it as if it were the ultimate in revelation, instead of grasping that to which it points, finally flirts with idolatry. That is why the author of the epistle to the Hebrews is so concerned about Jewish believers who have become Christians but who are tempted back to reliance on a code and structure that has in certain ways been superseded by developments in the history of redemption. Granted that this exposition is not very conducive to pluralist ideology, it seems to be a good deal closer to what Hebrews actually says than is Lohfink's summary.

In a recent study of Romans, Campbell offers many subtle and sensitive readings of the text, yet turns his interpretation in a way that betrays Paul.[86] He rightly observes that in Romans Paul does not insist that Christians and Jews should submerge their cultural identity in some supracultural ideal of (new) humanity. Both Jews and Christians are alike members of the Israel of God. "It is no accident that Paul refuses to give the term 'Israel' a wholly Gentile Christian or even a Gentile Christian and a Jewish Christian content. For him it still refers to all God's people and God determines in his election who these shall be!"[87] True enough—but the fact remains that at this point in redemptive history all such people belong to this Israel solely by virtue of faith in Jesus the Messiah. Others, whether Jews or Gentiles, are excluded. That is why, elsewhere, Paul sees his status as a Christian as in some ways qualitatively different from being a Jew and from being a Gentile: as a Christian, he has to flex in *both* directions to win both. To the Jew, he must become as a Jew; to the Gentile, he must become as a Gentile (1 Cor. 9:19–23). Campbell is trying to draw lessons from partial truths as if they were the whole story.

Biblical Theology 14 (1992): 31–49; and especially his larger work, *Suffering and Ministry in the Spirit: Paul's Defense of His Ministry in II Corinthians 2:14–3:3* (Grand Rapids: Eerdmans, 1990).

86. William S. Campbell, *Paul's Gospel in an Intercultural Context: Jew and Gentile in the Letter to the Romans* (Frankfurt a.M.: Peter Lang, 1991).

87. Ibid., 129.

Something similar happens in Siker's study.[88] Siker develops the following schematic:

> Paul, a Jewish Christian, uses Abraham to argue for Gentile inclusion within the promises of God.
>
> Luke, a Gentile Christian, also uses Abraham to argue for Gentile inclusion within the promises of God.
>
> John, a Jewish Christian, uses Abraham to argue for Jewish exclusion from God's purpose.
>
> Justin, a Gentile Christian, also uses Abraham to argue for Jewish exclusion from God's purposes.[89]

Siker argues that the church quickly forgot Paul's point, but that if we return to it then we will be prepared to abandon the exclusiveness that has characterized much of Christendom.

This is a substantial distortion of the texts. Because Siker has focused narrowly on some New Testament and early patristic texts, and is prepared to rip them out of their respective contexts so that they can form a neat catalogue of inclusion/exclusion statements, he gains some show of plausibility while forcing every single author of his principal four into positions that they explicitly disavow. Yes, Paul does use Abraham to argue for Gentile inclusion within the promises of God (especially Romans 4 and Galatians 3). More explicitly, however, he uses Abraham to argue that the salvation achieved by Jesus the Messiah is the fulfilment of God's promises to Abraham, which the law-covenant could never set aside. Salvation in Christ is open to Jew and Gentile alike; it is provided by grace, and received by faith. But this by no means suggests that *all* Jews and *all* Gentiles without exception are included within the redemptive promises of God: the critical point is Jesus the Messiah, and his relation to the antecedent promises and covenant. One could say something similar about Luke. True, there is some sense in which John in his eighth chapter uses Abraham to argue for Jewish exclusion from the purposes of God. But to put it so generically misses the Christological focus of the chapter. Those who do perseveringly believe in Jesus in the gospel of John are Jews: they are not excluded *because* they are Jews, nor is Abraham deployed to construct such an argument. John's point—or, rather, Jesus' point, as John reports it—is that if Abraham is rightly understood within the Hebrew Scriptures, he points in a variety of complex ways to Jesus the Messiah. The true children of Abraham are not Gentiles, with all Jews excluded, but those who share Abraham's faith and who recognize him to whom Abraham, canon-

---

88. Jeffrey S. Siker, *Disinheriting the Jews: Abraham in Early Christian Controversy* (Louisville: Westminster/John Knox, 1991).

89. Ibid., 193.

ically considered, pointed. That, of course, was also Paul's point, and Luke's point—and Justin Martyr's point, for that matter. Siker's schematic really will not work.

4. The various forms of "two-covenant" approach, for all the admirable motivation that stands behind them, cannot be aligned with the New Testament and may be guilty of an unacknowledged anti-Semitism.

There are three observations to make.

First, when the story-line of the Bible is followed, not least its New Testament dimensions, the fundamental issue is not race, but human response to God's self-disclosure. If our dilemma is as the Bible portrays it, we have no way out but by the solution that God himself provides. That is a truth issue, a revelation issue, a redemption issue, a Christological issue. Christians simply cannot yield on these fronts.[90]

Second, it follows from that same story-line, as we have traced it out, that salvation will not be enjoyed by every Gentile or by every Jew. But it will be enjoyed by some Gentiles and by some Jews. There are two implications: (1) One of the great omissions in contemporary discussion of Jewish/Christian relations is the place of Christian Jews. The subject is of extraordinary delicacy, arousing as it does intense discussion about the very definition of what it means to be a Jew. But the phenomenon of tens of thousands of "messianic Jews" will not go away. Most of them perceive issues of truth to be at stake (as well as other things). Most forms of the "two-covenant" theory, not to mention most forms of philosophical pluralism itself, have no categories to handle these converts in a reflective way. (2) Not all Gentiles in the Christian world are Christians. To our shame, many genuine Christians have been caught up in anti-Semitism, some passively (by refusing to oppose what is evil), and some actively (by participating in it). But it is surely profoundly mistaken to think of the Nazi Holocaust or the Communist pogroms as essentially a *Christian* persecution of Jews. Since the time of Constantine until the present decline, Christianity has enjoyed (and abused) a civil status in many countries of the world, Western and otherwise. Inevitably this generates many "cultural Christians" who are not Christians in any New Testament sense of the word. While Jews remember the Inquisition as a Christian persecution of Jews, Protestants, who suffered under it no less, remember it as a Catholic persecution of believers who simply wanted to follow the Bible as they understood it. History is notoriously messy. But from a Christian point

90. See the useful comments of Carl F. H. Henry, *God, Revelation and Authority*, 6 vols. (Waco: Word Books, 1976–83), 3:118–46.

of view, the dividing line is not race, or church, or culture, or heritage, but Jesus Christ—who he is, what he has done, how he calls out and reconciles men and women to God from every people and tribe and tongue and nation, and progressively transforms them in anticipation of the consummated glory on the last day.

Third, if the good news of the gospel is to be proclaimed to every tongue and tribe and people and nation, then it is to be proclaimed to Jews not less than to others. Not to offer such glorious good news would be a kind of racism in itself. "The church has not become an exclusively gentile possession. Precisely because the gospel stands athwart all ethnic claims, the church cannot erect a new racial boundary. The irony of this is that the late twentieth century, in order to avoid anti-Semitism, has advocated a position (the non-evangelization of Jews) *which Paul regards as precisely anti-Semitic.*"[91] Bloesch is right:

> [T]he church is betraying its evangelistic mandate if it withholds the gospel of salvation from the very people who gave us the Messiah and Savior of the world. Such an attitude could be construed as the worst kind of anti-Semitism because it means deliberately bypassing the Jews in giving out the invitation to the banquet of the kingdom (cf. Luke 14:15–24). Such an attitude could imply that the Jews are incapable or unworthy of receiving the blessings of the new covenant. Or it might suggest that they can best find God by adhering to their own laws and traditions, but this is to reinstate the dividing wall between Jew and Gentile that Christ tore down (Eph.2:14). Significantly the German Christians, those in the German church who sought to accommodate to Nazism, vigorously opposed missions to the Jews on the grounds of racial contamination.
>
> The New Testament is unequivocal that the Jews too should be included in the Christian mission; indeed, they even have priority over the Gentiles. Paul declared that the gospel "is the power of God for salvation to every one who has faith, to the Jew first and also the Greek" (Rom.1:16). The name of the Lord has to be carried "before the Gentiles and kings and the sons of Israel" (Acts 9:15). Our Lord said to his disciples on the eve of Pentecost: "You shall be my witnesses in Jerusalem and in all Judea and Samaria and to the end of the earth" (Acts 1:8).[92]

---

91. N. T. Wright, *The Climax of the Covenant: Christ and the Law in Pauline Theology* (Minneapolis: Fortress Press, 1992), 253 (emphasis his). Perhaps I should add that this does not require us to follow Wright at every point, including the collapse of every reference of Israel into the church (e.g., Rom. 11).

92. Donald G. Bloesch, "'All Israel Will Be Saved': Supersessionism and the Biblical Witness," *Interpretation* 43 (1989): 140–41.

C. Concluding Reflections

"In the past God spoke to our forefathers through the prophets at many times and in various ways, but in these last days he has spoken to us *by his Son*" (Heb. 1:1–2): the anarthrous prepositional expression suggests that emphasis is being placed on the nature or quality of this Son-revelation. In the past, God spoke: he has always been a talking God. But in these last days—the eschatological framework is inescapable—his final "Word," as it were, is his Son, Jesus Christ.

If this is true, to ignore him or to treat him as one option among many is to defy God our Maker and Judge. And one day we shall give an account to him.

If it is not true, then there is no value in claiming Christian allegiance at all. The whole is a sham, not one option among many.

In the light of such texts, there is no third alternative.

Chapter 8

ON DRAWING LINES, WHEN DRAWING LINES IS RUDE

I n this short chapter my purpose is not to embark on a new theme, but, assuming the thrust of the argument in the preceding four chapters, to reflect a little on how Christians must view the situation, and to ponder what kind of stance we must adopt, regardless of how unpopular it is likely to be.

Three features of contemporary religious pluralism, largely called into being by the impact of postmodernity, deserve notice.

First, it has been demonstrated that never before in the history of humankind have so many scholars in so many disciplines focused so much of their study, *not* on the disciplines themselves, but on the "metaquestions" thrown up by their disciplines.[1] This is scarcely surprising: with objective truth disappearing over the horizon of yesteryear, the drift toward introverted "navel gazing" should scarcely be thought remarkable. In response, Christian thinkers *must* be informed about such debates, and participate in them, but they must not be entirely given over to them, or they become part of the problem.

Second, postmodernity's penchant for the privatized opinion and the communal belief is quite ready to tolerate religion, but only if all religion is strictly relegated to the private or communal spheres. All religions must be evaluated pragmatically: How well do they function and what do they achieve within their respective interpretive communities? Postmodernity is not especially intolerant of religion, provided that no religion is permitted to talk

---

1. David J. Bosch, *Transforming Mission: Paradigm Shifts in Theology of Mission* (Maryknoll: Orbis Books, 1991), chap. 11.

of universally valid truth. Such talk would be intellectually compromised, culturally disrespectful, fundamentally untenable.[2]

Third, behind such issues is the question of revelation.

> Nothing is so unacceptable to the modern temper as religious exclusivity— rendered as doctrinal exactitude. But doctrine and dogma are the necessary accompaniments of revealed truth; they are verbal definitions of the particularization of the divine. That is, again, alien to the expectations of modern men and women, who prefer religious truth to be general. . . . [T]he present mood casts all religions into the melting-pot. The artefact which emerges resembles the human form, for it is a god made in the image of men's sensations, suited to the religion of humanity, indiscriminate in its affections, undemanding in its spiritual requirements, but extremely exacting when it comes to social ethics or political morality. . . . When modern Westerners encounter truly demanding religion—as in the Islamic revival—they are horrified. It dares to dictate the terms upon which men and women are to live out their existence; it speaks to its followers of the exclusive demands and religious observances of daily life. It is, in short, religion. That it is, in the judgement of some, not very agreeable religion, is all the more reason for resistance to the notion that all religions are essentially the same.[3]

These pressures make it difficult for many Christians to draw lines. How many of us want to be classified with fundamentalist Muslims? Why not emphasize the communal and pragmatic values of our faith, in order to gain respect and avoid unnecessarily offending the people of our generation? Why not defend "the truth" merely *as it appears to us*? After all, that is in fact what we are doing, isn't it—defending the truth *as it appears to us*? So why make offensive claims about the universality of truth claims? Why draw lines? It is painful to do so; it also seems impolitic. Why alienate people? Why should it be thought necessary to draw lines, when drawing lines is rude?

In these few pages, my concern is not how to proceed with the evangelistic task (see chap. 12), but to ponder briefly some of the reasons why drawing lines is utterly crucial at the moment.

A. Truth Demands It

I have tried to show that, whatever the genuine insights that can be gleaned from postmodern epistemology, it is finally unsuccessful in its attempt to deny the existence both of objective truth and of human access to

---

2. Cf. Harold A. Netland, "Truth, Authority, and Modernity: Shopping for Truth in a Supermarket of Worldviews," in *Faith and Modernity*, ed. Philip Sampson, Vinay Samuel, and Chris Sugden (Oxford: Regnum Books, 1994), 89–115.

3. Edward Norman, *Entering the Darkness: Christianity and its Modern Substitutes* (London: SPCK, 1991), 67, 69.

it. We may readily concur that human knowing is partial, but not that it is therefore necessarily objectively untrue; that our cultural baggage shapes our perceptions and categories, but not that no one from the culture may transcend those categories; that individuals belong to interpretive communities, but not that the individual in such a community, or even the entire community itself, cannot be reformed by information coming from outside. In some ways, Christians go farther than postmodernists: we insist on the noetic effects of sin. But on the other hand, we insist equally on the power of grace and the work of the Spirit through the heralded word of God to transform our understanding. Above all, because the God who has so graciously disclosed himself knows all things truly and exhaustively, we perceive that it is possible for his image-bearers to enjoy knowledge that is a subset of his. Moreover, we perceive that the strongest arguments of postmodernism in general and of deconstruction in particular are not securely based, and in many instances can be shown to be inconsistent at their core and finally self-destructive.

The entailment of such a stance is that however much we may defend the right of people to articulate their views, we must equally insist that some views are in error. However much the empirical pluralism in which we are enmeshed encourages us to shun the totalitarian imposition of any view, we must not succumb to the conclusion that all views are of equivalent worth and unworth, veracity and falsity. Thus we must strongly oppose Gilkey's assumption. After insisting that the new realities of pluralism all around us drive us to the conclusion that no religion can ever be viewed as superior to another, he writes, "I assume that we are all agreed on this, otherwise a serious discussion of diversity and its theological meaning would not be undertaken, nor would serious and authentic dialogue between religions be possible."[4] On the contrary: it is difficult to see how a discussion on his terms *can* be "theologically meaningful." There is much more likelihood of "serious and authentic dialogue" taking place between those who hold opposing positions, but who equally hold that objective truth is out there and is worth pursuing.

The drift away from this elementary point is disturbingly common in all branches of Christendom. Out of an important Christian center in Africa, for instance, comes the bold insistence that 1 John 1:1ff. shows that "God's supreme disclosure of Himself was not in a set of theological propositions, but in a life—a human life which could be seen, looked upon and touched."[5] But

---

4. Langdon Gilkey, "Plurality and Its Theological Implications," in *The Myth of Christian Uniqueness: Toward a Pluralistic Theology of Religions*, ed. John Hick and Paul F. Knitter (Maryknoll: Orbis Books, 1987), 37.

5. Kwame Bediako, in *Akrofi-Christaller Centre News* 15 (July–December 1994): 11.

the epistle that four times makes a *proposition* one of the central criteria that determine whether or not someone is truly a Christian (1 John 2:22; 4:2; 5:1, 5)? True, *mere* propositional belief is insufficient—but who says otherwise? The disjunction the African scholar sets forth is not only unnecessary reductionism, but serves to disparage one kind of truth found in the Scripture, namely, propositional truth. Or consider this piece from a contemporary Catholic scholar:

> Because of Christ all barriers have been broken down and "there is neither Jew nor Greek, there is neither slave nor free, there is neither male nor female; for you are all one in Christ Jesus" (Gal 3:28). He relativizes the importance of belonging to a particular race or social class and instead emphasizes the importance of sincerity and authenticity. God, he insists, is to be worshipped in spirit and in truth. God has certainly revealed himself in a special way through Israel and above all through Jesus, a revelation that is continued through his Church—but this does not mean that his Spirit, his truth, is confined. By his life and teaching, Christ attacked all exclusivism, underlining that it was the poor, the marginalized, the strangers, who would first enter the kingdom of heaven.[6]

This is an extraordinary mingling of categories, achieved because biblical passages are ripped out of their context and assigned new meanings. Galatians 3:28 certainly affirms that Jews and Greeks, slaves and free, males and females, are all alike justified by Christ; in that sense, Paul "relativizes the importance of belonging to a particular race or social class." But he does not replace the truth category by "the importance of sincerity and authenticity." True, God insists that he is to be worshiped "in spirit and in truth," but that lovely expression, in its context in John 4, far from authorizing "sincerity and authenticity" at the expense of truth, insists that true worship is tied to the eschatological fulfillment of the promises of the old covenant, bound up with Jesus himself, from whom they cannot be detached—as the better commentaries invariably demonstrate. Yes, Christ "attacked all exclusivism," if by that is meant that he attacked the notion that some people have an inside track with God, achieved by their piety or wealth or social standing. But Jesus himself made some remarkably exclusive claims himself: these the quotation ignores, driving its readers to a quite different conclusion by juxtaposing the sentence boasting the words "Christ attacked all exclusivism" with the denial that God's "Spirit, his truth, is confined." The constant, gentle pressure in the quoted paragraph—indeed, in much of the book—is carefully crafted to undermine confidence in the existence of objective truth.

---

6. John Patrick Brennan, *Christian Mission in a Pluralistic World* (Wilton: Morehouse, 1990), 58.

Or consider the following chain of reasoning by a leading evangelical theologian, Clark Pinnock. "Historically it was possible to identify heresy fairly readily because of the assumption that revelation was cognitive," he writes. But "belief in cognitive revelation, the prerequisite for recognizing heresy," has fallen on hard times, for various reasons that Pinnock enumerates.[7] This brings us "to the fundamental split among theologians in the modern period. Traditionalists of all kinds affirm the existence of a divinely authorized interpretation of the Christian story that makes it possible for them to solicit doctrines from it and identify error. Liberals of every type deny this possibility because they say there is no such thing as cognitive revelation."[8] "But how would one approach the question of heresy if the essence of Christianity were understood to be story?"[9] What is the way ahead?

> The answer lies in the fact that Christian revelation is already an *interpreted* story, genuinely historical and genuinely mythical. It is neither bare event nor mere experience but an integrated package of event and interpretation in one. By means of God's saving actions, God is communicating what God is doing to us. The interpretive dimension is not left up to chance. God reveals himself effectively through events. The interpreted story is carried down on the shoulders of the multiple mediating sources that portray a clear picture of God's word to humanity.
>
> Sound theology in this view is theology that is faithful to the biblically narrated story and articulates its meaning and significance in a way that respects its original integrity: Was Jesus raised from the dead? Is he now the exalted Lord? Has the Spirit been poured out? Did Jesus die for the sins of the world? . . .
>
> Alongside clarity about essentials, a diversity of interpretation is also possible. The work of formulating doctrine is a human response to the story and experiences change down through history. . . .
>
> Unsound theology would be theology that strays away from the canonical narrative, operates out of another story, and inhabits a different universe of meaning.[10]

Although I have tried to read this with the utmost sympathy, I am not certain that I understand Pinnock's argument: the categories strike me as a bit confusing. Because of the way he sets us up for his solution, Pinnock is apparently distancing himself from what he calls "cognitive revelation." He wants Christianity to be understood as a story, but recognizes that a story

---

7. Clark H. Pinnock, *Tracking the Maze: Finding Our Way Through Modern Theology from an Evangelical Perspective* (San Francisco: Harper San Francisco, 1990), 188.

8. Ibid., 189.

9. Ibid.

10. Ibid., 189–90.

needs interpretation. So he insists that "Christian revelation is already an *interpreted* story." This is eminently right, if by "interpretation" he is referring to what is found in the Bible, i.e., to the Bible's interpretation of the redemptive historical events it reports. The next lines sometimes sound as if this is what Pinnock means. For example, he writes, "The interpretive dimension is not left up to chance." Sound theology "is faithful to the biblically narrated story and articulates its meaning and significance in a way that respects its original integrity." My uncertainty springs from the fact that most Christians in this century have believed precisely that—so just what is it that Pinnock thinks he is correcting? If the report of the story and the interpretation of the story are both found in the Bible, we are returned, by another route, to cognitive revelation—though along with most generations of Christians we insist that Christian revelation is never *reductionistically* cognitive. Why so much effort to distance oneself from cognitive revelation, only to let it slip back into a central place by using other terms?

Moreover, I am uncertain what this sentence means: "[Christian revelation] is neither bare event nor mere experience but an integrated package of event and interpretation in one." The syntax of the sentence suggests that "experience" is parallel to "interpretation." But what would that mean? Whose experience? That of the biblical writer? Then a few lines on we are told, "Alongside clarity about essentials, diversity of interpretation is also possible." If this is referring to *our* interpretation of Scripture, which is nothing other than *God's* interpretation of events (and presumably of other things), there can be no objection. But if that is what is meant, we are surely back to cognitive revelation (among other kinds) whether we like it or not. "Unsound theology," we are told, strays away from the canonical narrative. In terms of *mere* story, Jehovah's Witnesses stay very close to the biblical narrative: is their theology sound? More broadly, the history of modern historical skepticism is predicated on the assumption that the "facts" of history must be reinterpreted. Fidelity to the biblical revelation demands that we remain faithful not only to the biblical "story," but to the biblical interpretation of that story. How can we do otherwise? Or does Pinnock now mean to include under the rubric of "canonical narrative" both the story and its biblical interpretation? But if so, how can he begin by distancing himself from cognitive revelation?

Perhaps I may be forgiven for thinking I am confused about what this passage means because the passage itself is confusing. It is difficult not to draw the conclusion that the passage is confusing because Pinnock is simultaneously trying to distance himself from cognitive revelation, while maintaining it. He appears to be embarrassed by propositional truth, while acknowledging in different terms that he cannot do without it. Such are the signs of the times.

One final example. Vaughan Roberts has written an article advising university chaplains in Britain how to handle students who sign the UCCF statement of faith.[11] Roberts assumes his readers will be uncomfortable with "the exclusive truth claims of the document."[12] One of his suggestions is that he and other chaplains adopt the framework of James Fowler and recognize that most people go through various "stages of faith." Adolescents usually pass through "synthetic-conventional faith" (the third stage on a six-step scale); some never get out of it. But many will be helped by recognizing that their current beliefs are just a stage connected with adolescence. This is a remarkable conclusion. Roberts has simultaneously (1) misappropriated Fowler, who would be the first to acknowledge that people much farther along his maturity scale might still hold to the authority and finality of the Bible; and (2) ducked any discussion of the truth claims themselves, by relegating them to an adjacent plane of discourse to do with stages of faith and degrees of maturity. Roberts thinks he is helping these students by refusing to deal directly with one of the very things the students themselves judge to be of great importance.

In all of these authors, one senses that doctrine is archaic, that truth is an obsolete category, that cognitive content purporting to reflect objective reality is more than a little embarrassing. But if the lines taken in this book are right, then the truth itself, however imperfectly we grasp it, demands that lines be drawn. It is refreshing to read such elementary clearheadedness as that found in the following lines:

> There is no faith relation with Christ free of doctrinal content. The knower must have some knowledge of the known, or no relation exists. That seemingly redundant and self-evident statement should underline the issue. Jesus Christ and our knowledge of Him are not in any sense coextensive. But one cannot have a relation with Him without knowledge, and that knowledge represents incipient doctrine....
>
> If one does *not* believe the truths concerning the Christ as revealed in Holy Scripture, one *cannot* have any authentic relationship with Him. Doctrine, we eagerly concede, does not in itself save.... But, on the other hand, one cannot truly worship Christ and seek to live as an authentic disciple and deny, denigrate, or neglect in any sense the biblical teachings concerning Him.[13]

---

11. UCCF = Universities and Colleges Christian Fellowship, originally Inter-Varsity Christian Fellowship. In Britain, this is certainly the largest and most productive of the various groups that work among university and college undergraduates.

12. Vaughan Roberts, "Reframing the UCCF Doctrinal Basis," *Theology* 45 (1992): 432–46.

13. R. Albert Mohler, Jr., "Response," in *Beyond the Impasse? Scripture, Interpretation, and Theology in Baptist Life*, ed. Robison B. James and David S. Dockery (Nashville: Broadman, 1992), 249.

But there is a second reason for drawing lines:

B. The Distinction Between Orthodoxy and Heresy Models It

The words "orthodoxy" and "heresy" are distasteful to those heavily influenced by classic liberalism, postmodernism, and radical religious pluralism. Sometimes the alternative is ruthless secularism; not less commonly, the alternative is dogmatic insistence that revelation is the common experience of all groups of human beings, and that what we need is not the theology of a religion but a "theology of religions."[14]

But I have already argued (chap. 4) that if one leaves any place at all for objective truth, however cautiously and imperfectly we may think we grasp it, we leave place for an ultimate distinction[15] between truth and error, and thus for a distinction between orthodoxy and heresy.[16] Even at the level of pragmatic experience, it is difficult to think of a single noetic plank in one religion that is universally recognized by all other religions to be the truth. That brute fact must, it appears, either drive us toward the unswerving relativism of principled postmodernism, and even to deconstruction, or, within a biblical framework, it will drive us to recognize afresh how badly our eyes have been blinded, and how urgently we need revelation—not only that in the public arena (e.g., the Bible and the public events surrounding the birth, ministry, death, and resurrection of Jesus), but that in the private arena as well (see 1 Cor. 2:5–16).

Here it is sufficient to comment on two specific tendencies that must be confronted.

First, even though much contemporary toleration for—indeed, delight in—what used to be called heresy springs from the climate of religious pluralism, a very substantial support for this attitude stems from some influential historical work done during the last century and a half. Against the traditional view—that the truth of the gospel was there from the beginning

---

14. To use the phrase invented by Paul Tillich toward the end of his life. See his tradition carried on in David J. Krieger, *The New Universalism: Foundations for a Global Theology* (Maryknoll: Orbis Books, 1991).

15. "Ultimate" in this connection means that the truth in view is objective truth, public truth, and not the private property of an individual or of an interpretive community.

16. The term "heresy" is sometimes bandied about so as to make it refer to any opinion different from my own! Most serious writers reserve the term to refer to such departure from the biblically disclosed truth that the salvation of the heretic must be called in question. The primarily noetic quality of such a category prompts many commentators to remark (1) that doctrinal issues are not the only ones that can put someone outside the camp; and (2) that the modern use of "heresy" must not be read back into the use of *airesis* in the first two centuries. See Michel Desjardins, "Bauer and Beyond: On Recent Scholarly Discussions of in the Early Christian Era," *Second Century* 8 (1991): 65–82.

but that this unified commitment broke down into various heresies during the first few centuries—several influential voices interpreted the earliest phase of the church quite differently. F. C. Bauer and the Tübingen school argued that from the earliest days there were mutually incompatible Petrine and Pauline factions that squabbled incessantly, and hence there was no original orthodoxy. Orthodoxy of a kind developed as the earlier disputes between the principal apostles and their followers slipped into the mists of history, and a new synthesis, early Catholicism, was forged. But this was not necessarily viewed as a good thing. Friedrich Schleiermacher insisted that the developing orthodoxy was nothing other than a wretched corruption of the pure teaching of Jesus by the baleful influences of Greco-Roman philosophy and law.

But the most influential figure on this subject in recent times has been Walter Bauer, who in 1934 published a book[17] that argues that at the beginning Christianity was a rich mixture of highly diverse and mutually contradictory beliefs, with views we now hold to be "heretical" being in the majority. The various factions in this potpourri of primitive opinion fought things out, and "orthodoxy" won: history is written by the victors, and conflicting evidence is suppressed. During the past decade or so, this stance has been taken up by some to justify a return to Gnosticism and other early heresies. Moreover, it has been reinforced by some of the ablest scholars working in the heritage of the history-of-religions school.[18]

Full-fledged rebuttal need not be attempted here, but a few comments may be useful. Like the majority of doubtful reconstructions, this one preserves a modicum of plausibility. Mature "orthodoxy" did not drop from heaven at Pentecost. The New Testament documents themselves, not least Acts, portray the steps by which the early church was led to some of its most important conclusions, not least how to reconcile the good news of Jesus with the law given by God at Sinai. Such steps did not take place overnight; they emerged in the context of debate (e.g., Acts 11, 15). Moreover, mature

---

17. Walter Bauer, *Rechtgläubigkeit und Ketzerei im ältesten Christentum* (Tübingen: J. C. B. Mohr [Paul Siebeck], 1934). The work finally appeared in English as *Orthodoxy and Heresy in Earliest Christianity* (Philadelphia: Fortress Press, 1971).

18. Not least Helmut Koester, especially in his "Gnomai Diaphorai: The Origin and Nature of Diversification in the History of Early Christianity," in *Trajectories Through Early Christianity*, ed. James M. Robinson and Helmut Koester (Philadelphia: Fortress Press, 1971), 114–57. This is not to say that Koester agrees in detail with Bauer. He prefers to think of diverse "trajectories" of development, some of which died out or were squeezed out, but which were there from the beginning. Differences of terminology and emphasis aside, however, Koester and others work in the Bauer tradition. For a broader survey of how Bauer was received, see Daniel J. Harrington, "The Reception of Walter Bauer's Orthodoxy and Heresy in Earliest Christianity During the Last Decade," *Harvard Theological Review* 77 (1980): 289–98.

"orthodoxy" emerged out of reflection on the documents of the Old and New Testaments in the light of fresh opposition and denials. Theological reflection and precision, ripening orthodoxy, are often triggered by heresy.[19] From such perspectives as these, one recognizes the danger of anachronism when what is later called orthodoxy is rather hastily read back into the New Testament. Insofar as the Bauer thesis warned against the danger, its influence was not entirely malign.

Nevertheless the Bauer synthesis has been severely (and rightly) criticized. Marshall points out that even the title of Bauer's book is a bit of a cheek: Bauer writes of *earliest* Christianity but begins his probe in the second century.[20] In his Bampton lectures, Turner demonstrates with great clarity the numerous flaws in Bauer's argument: his tendency to read more into the second- and third-century texts than is there, his reliance on arguments from silence,[21] his lack of clarity as to what "orthodoxy" and "heresy" might mean, and so forth.[22] More recently, Robinson has shown that the movements eventually judged heretical were neither early nor strong, contrary to what the Bauer thesis requires.[23] Robinson's work is so important (though regrettably still not widely known) that Desjardins concludes that his "points on the whole are well-taken and well-argued; he adds another row of nails to the coffin enclosing Bauer's thesis."[24] Moreover, other scholars have begun to examine second-century Christian thinkers afresh, asking questions, for example, about their degree of toleration for error. Such scholars have shown that "mainline" Christians of this period, for all their attempts to build bridges toward the pagan culture in order to facilitate evangelism, provide no exception to the fundamental stance of exclusivism.[25]

---

19. A useful book on the connections between the teaching of the New Testament and the formulations of the creeds is found in Gerald Bray, *Creeds, Councils and Christ* (Downers Grove: InterVarsity Press, 1984). One need not agree with all the details to appreciate as well the considerable insight in Arland J. Hultgren, *The Rise of Normative Christianity* (Minneapolis: Fortress Press, 1994).

20. I. Howard Marshall, "Orthodoxy and Heresy in Earlier Christianity," *Themelios* 2/1 (1976): 5–14.

21. As Hultgren, *The Rise of Normative Christianity*, would later put it: "[Bauer] creates a picture of conditions based on a reading between the lines of the texts we have—and ignoring the lines that we do have."

22. H. E. W. Turner, *The Pattern of Christian Truth: A Study in the Relations Between Orthodoxy and Heresy in the Early Church* (London: A. R. Mowbray, 1954).

23. Thomas A. Robinson, *The Bauer Thesis Examined: The Geography of Heresy in the Early Church* (Lewiston: Edwin Mellen, 1988).

24. "Bauer and Beyond," 72.

25. See especially Graham Keith, "Justin Martyr and Religious Exclusivism," *Tyndale Bulletin* 43 (1992): 57–80.

Thus even if it is anachronistic to read, say, fourth-century orthodoxy back into the New Testament (since the categories of fourth-century orthodoxy reflect fourth-century disputes), it is equally wrong to suggest that there are few ties between fourth-century orthodoxy and the New Testament, or, worse, that in the New Testament period Christians were uninterested in the distinction between truth and error, between what came to be called orthodoxy and heresy. We earlier saw that it is impossible to read, say, Galatians 1:8–9 or 1 John 2:22 or Hebrews 2:1–2 and fail to recognize that certain beliefs were viewed as nonnegotiable.[26] Outside those beliefs there was no salvation.

The *second* tendency that must be confronted is the habit of speaking of other religions with such respect, not to say reverence, that gradually the impression is given that the only religion that could ever be charged with anything questionable is one's own. Sedgwick is right to observe that "it is difficult to avoid the feeling that *liberal theology has become so deferential to other belief systems as to be in danger of losing its Christian distinctiveness.*"[27] One begins to have some sympathy for Chesterton's Father Brown when he is confronted with an interlocutor who says to him, "Surely you must understand that all religions are really the same." "'If they are,' said Father Brown mildly, 'it seems rather unnecessary to go into the middle of Asia to get one.'"[28]

That brings us to the nub of the issue. The second reason for drawing lines even when drawing lines is not "cool" (as my daughter and son would say) is that the New Testament documents model the distinction between orthodoxy and heresy, even if these terms are not deployed exactly in their English sense. Despite the faddish popularity of religious pluralism, despite the erroneous historical reconstructions of Walter Bauer and others, despite the common practice of treating other religions with more deference than a Christianity that tries to conform to the Bible, the fact remains that there is something disturbingly unfaithful about forms of expression that attempt to be more "broadminded" than the New Testament documents themselves. True, most who read these pages will want to avoid the kind of obscurantist "fundamentalism" that is less concerned with fundamentals than with fences.

---

26. Some scholars of more liberal tendency will read those texts as representing competing "orthodoxies"; those of more conservative tendecy hold that the texts are mutually complementary, and the reasons for stressing different components of nonnegotiable truth in different New Testament books have to do with the occasional interests which, under God, call those books forth.

27. Colin J. Sedgwick, "Where Liberal Theology Falls Short: A Response to the Revd Martin Camroux," *Expository Times* 104 (1992): 4 (emphasis his).

28. G. K. Chesterton, *The Penguin Complete Father Brown* (Harmondsworth: Penguin Books, 1981), 559–60.

But most who read these pages will not be tempted down that path, and so they scarcely need to be warned against it. It is a cheap zeal that reserves its passions to combat only the sins and temptations of others.

We are more likely to squirm when we read words like these:

> Do you agree with those who say that a spirit of love is incompatible with the negative and critical denunciation of blatant error, and that we must always be positive? The simple answer to such an attitude is that the Lord Jesus Christ denounced evil and denounced false teachers. I repeat that He denounced them as "ravening wolves" and "whited sepulchres,"and as "blind guides." The Apostle Paul said of some of them, "whose god is their belly, and whose glory is in their shame". That is the language of the Scriptures. There can be little doubt but that the Church is as she is today because we do not follow New Testament teaching and its exhortations, and confine ourselves to the positive and the so-called "simple Gospel", and fail to stress the negatives and the criticism. The result is that people do not reconize error when they meet it.
>
> It is not pleasant to be negative; it is not enjoyable to have to denounce and to expose error. But any pastor who feels in a little measure, and with humility, the responsibility which the Apostle Paul knew in an infinitely greater degree for the souls and the well-being spiritually of his people is compelled to utter these warnings. It is not liked and appreciated in this modern flabby generation.[29]

From this perspective, it is refreshing to come across a book with the title *The Cruelty of Heresy: An Affirmation of Christian Orthodoxy*.[30] In it the author offers a robust defense of the Trinity, precisely because he recognizes that fundamental issues of soteriology are at stake. Heresy is cruel: it does inestimable damage to human beings. It is not the mark of love; it is a reflection of blindness and rebellion.

If the truth of the gospel is alone the power of God unto salvation, the most loving thing we can do is to live it out and preach it out.

Though it pains me to bring them up, perhaps one or two further examples will clarify this discussion. In 1988, Hodder & Stoughton published a book of essays jointly written by the self-confessed liberal David Edwards and the self-confessed evangelical John Stott.[31] The format of the book permitted Edwards to set the agenda; Stott responded.[32] There is a tremendous

---

29. D. M. Lloyd-Jones, "Biblical Intolerance," *Banner of Truth* 371–72 (August/ September 1994): 55.

30. C. FitzSimons Allison (London: SPCK, 1994).

31. David L. Edwards and John R. W. Stott, *Essentials: A Liberal-Evangelical Dialogue* (London: Hodder & Stoughton, 1988).

32. In passing, I should comment that this format was perhaps unfortunate. It left Stott formally on the defensive. A more evenhanded approach would have been for each party to set

amount that is admirable about this volume. The mutual courtesy, the frankness of the debate, the clarity with which each side articulates its views are all praiseworthy. From a confessional perspective, it is refreshing to observe a believer with the acumen of a John Stott demonstrate how confessional Christians must not hover in the holy huddle but engage the broader world. Yet at the same time, one is struck by the way Stott insists on calling Edwards a *Christian*.

I do not want to be misunderstood. If "Christian" means something like "nice person living in the West," then of course Edwards is a Christian. If it means "member of an ecclesiastical body which in many respects clings to biblical beliefs, even if in other respects it is happy to depart from them," then again Edwards is not only a Christian, but an esteemed one. If "Christian" refers to someone whose views, on all sorts of relatively peripheral issues, many traditional Christians hold suspect, but whose commitment to the central cognitive and moral demands of the New Testament is unwavering, then whether or not Edwards is a Christian, at least the term is protected from too narrow and sectarian a definition. If "Christian" includes those who have unquestionably been converted by the power of God, but whose level of instruction is still abysmally low, the same conclusion may be drawn: there is much to be said for charitably giving the benefit of the doubt wherever possible.

But what shall we say of an instructed and thoughtful theologian who explicitly rejects the Fall, denies that human beings have any need for an atonement provided by a divine/human redeemer, discounts belief in the physical resurrection of Jesus, and concludes that "everything" in the gospel of John "must be questionable"? We are not in the realm of quibbling about the precise definition of inerrancy; we are in the realm of those truths without which Christianity is no longer Christianity. If, as Stott says, those who deny the bodily resurrection of Christ do not "forfeit the right to be called Christians,"[33] is there *any* specific disavowal that forfeits that right? What does Paul mean when he says, "And if Christ has not been raised, our preaching is useless and so is your faith. . . . And if Christ has not been raised, your faith is futile; you are still in your sins" (1 Cor. 15:14, 17)? It is no answer to observe that Paul seems to treat the Corinthians to whom he is writing as Christians, even though some of them at least have trouble with the resurrection, for his point is that if they persist in this unbelief they will show

---

the agenda for half the book, with the other party responding. For example, a robust articulation of some central Christian truth, in line both with the New Testament and with the mainstream of the church throughout its history, would leave the liberal position trying to articulate why it feels free to abandon it.

33. *Essentials*, 228.

to be Christians. In any case, Paul is dealing with relatively
ivers, not with theologians and doctors of the church.

Iain Murray puts his finger on the matter when he interacts with *Essentials*
and with one or two of its reviews:

> Here then is *the* crucial issue and it ought to be raised in reviews of *Essentials*
> because it is implicit in the whole nature of the dialogue.... How much do
> evangelical beliefs really matter?
>
> The *Themelios* editorial confirms the existence of a new standpoint
> within evangelicalism. What has to be assessed is whether this standpoint is
> the result of greater charity and less bigotry, or whether it represents a sur-
> render to thought which is alien to biblical Christianity. The issue, let it be
> understood, is not whether poorly-taught believers, knowing their sinful-
> ness and clinging to Christ and his words, will be saved; it is whether men
> who deny all evangelical beliefs can still go to heaven.... [34]

Something of the same difficulty attaches to a number of other books.
For example, while one deeply appreciates the tact, humility, and good spirit
Fackre displays in one of his recent works,[35] pretty soon one recalls the fundamental point Machen made more than half a century ago: At some point
one must face the fact that the kind of disavowals and denials one finds in
many branches of classic liberalism, and repeated by the major proponents of
religious pluralism, are much deeper even than the chasms between, say,
Russian Orthodoxy and American Pentecostalism, or between Roman
Catholicism and classic evangelicalism; we are dealing with "different religions," in the strongest sense of that expression.[36]

There is a third reason why lines must be drawn:

C. The Plurality of Errors Calls for It

This is one of the most sensitive issues now confronting the Western
church.

Faced with what many judge to be a veritable onslaught from secularism
and postmodernism, many voices contend that confessional Christians of all
sorts need to band together against the one common enemy. The expression
"confessional Christians" is usually taken to refer to believers who uphold a

---

34. Iain Murray, "Who Is a Christian," *Evangelicals Now* 4/4 (April 1989): 7. This precipitated some correspondence back and forth, which cannot be followed and evaluated here.

35. E.g., Gabriel Fackre, *Ecumenical Faith in Evangelical Perspective* (Grand Rapids:
Eerdmans, 1993).

36. So J. Gresham Machen, *Christianity and Liberalism* (Grand Rapids: Eerdmans, 1923).
The same point is made regarding Fackre in a review by H. O. J. Brown, published in
Christianity Today 38/4 (April 4, 1994): 99–100.

supernatural worldview and who are bound together by their common adherence to the ancient creeds, especially the Apostle's Creed, Nicea, and Chalcedon. Of the many voices that espouse this stance, perhaps the most articulate is that of Andrew Walker.[37]

Doubtless this call is prompted by the highest motivations of Christian witness. But the kindest accurate assessment is that it is hopelessly naive— indeed, it is naive in at least three dimensions.

First, it is naive at the historical level. It is naive about church history and about the hermeneutical enterprise that shapes the historical development of theological reflection. Let us begin with a hypothetical example. Would the robust thought of Ignatius in the early second century prove sufficient for combatting Arius in the fourth century, or Tetzel in the sixteenth? Most, I think, would answer negatively. We might argue about how Ignatius would develop his thought if he were suddenly confronted by Tetzel, or for that matter by Joseph Smith and the early Mormons. But the form of his theological reflection is so pointedly tied to the agendas of the second century that Ignatius can scarcely be permitted to serve as the proper fount of all later theology.

In exactly the same way, it is improper to suppose that Chalcedon is the infallible and sufficient credal touchstone for all time. That Chalcedon was of enormous importance as an attempt to think biblically and in a spirit of loyalty to the Scriptures, while answering the Christological aberrations of the time, few believers would question. But Chalcedon was not shaped to deal with questions of authority, justification, faith, and grace that so fully occupied the magisterial reformers. It is still less capable of dealing comprehensively with, say, the Mormons, or with the challenges of postmodernity, or with modern woolly notions of the meaning of spirituality. It remains an important and even a *necessary* touchstone, but it is not in every circumstance a *sufficient* touchstone.

Someone might interrupt this chain of thought and ask whether the same charge could be raised against the Bible itself. After all, are not, say, the New Testament writers so locked into their own history and culture, that they cannot possibly be expected to address problems and errors that did not crop up in their day? And does it not follow that the New Testament is therefore itself inadequate as a sufficient guide to heresy and as a response to it? But several responses can be offered. (1) From a Christian perspective, the New Testament writers, along with the rest of the biblical writers,

---

37. See his *Enemy Territory*, 2d ed. (Bristol: Bristol House, 1990); idem, ed., *Betraying the Gospel* (Bristol: Bristol House, 1988); idem, "We Believe," *Christianity Today* 35/5 (April 29, 1991): 25–27.

though necessarily locked in time and space and specific cultures, were so used by God that what they wrote was revelatory. Otherwise put, what they wrote that has been assembled as Scripture constitutes canon; not many would say that Ignatius or Ireneus enjoys the same status. By itself, this observation does not *directly* address the problem of how culture-bound material can properly be applied to another culture, but it does prompt us to wonder why fourth-century sources should be advanced as the ultimate touchstone, as opposed to the canonical material. (2) As reflected in the New Testament, first-century believers faced a wide diversity of problems and challenges, which in turn were addressed by a considerable diversity of writers. Thus, unlike the writings of one person, an Ignatius, perhaps, or a Eusebius, who is primarily occupied with one or two perspectives or challenges, the New Testament documents were written by many persons facing highly diverse challenges and occupying a variety of perspectives. The very diversity of the New Testament documents that some scholars take for a sign of intrinsic incompatibility of trajectories within earliest Christianity, others of less skeptical outlook take for glorious evidence of the richness of nascent Christianity and for a providential provision of a breadth of material adequate to guide the church in the future. Thus adaptation and application to another age can be achieved more naturally and with less artificiality than is likely when a single creed or a single writer is the touchstone. (3) As we have seen, the New Testament documents provide the culmination of a story-line begun at creation and achieving its climax in the Word made flesh in Jesus Christ—even if the culmination of the story awaits the Parousia. Of no other documents can that be said to be true.

Thus we do not deny that it is right to refer to the creeds; we do not deny that it is possible to make historical judgments relevant to our own day based in part on judgments that serious Christians made to similar aberrations in their day. But that does not mean that the creeds are the ultimate arbiter: they represent important but not final articulation of Christian truth at particular points in history. If Christians dissent from the creeds at any point, they must do so only because they have become convinced, on good grounds, that on some detail they diverge from a still higher authority, the authority of Scripture. But credal authority is derivative; the creeds themselves are *in principle* correctable, however cautiously this should be done. Doubtless in their own times they constituted criteria that were both necessary and sufficient. In later times, where other questions are being raised, they continue to provide necessary criteria (within the constraints just articulated), but not sufficient criteria.

Second, the position of Walker and those with him is naive about the present situation. It argues that in the West the *one* danger the church confronts, secularism, is so imposing and urgent that all other conceivable or actual dangers pale into such insignificance that they may be safely ignored, *unless they were already dealt with in credal form by the fourth century*. To put it that way makes the position seem faintly ridiculous; but I do not see how else the position can be fairly put. When one starts to list the major aberrations, even overt heresies, that have developed since the fourth century and that were not addressed in the early creeds, one marvels at the optimism of Walker's position. The dogma of the infallibility of the Pope was not promulgated until 1870; the sharpest divisions over grace and justification were precipitated at the time of the Reformation, and continue, in various forms, around the world; the widespread and fundamental retreat from the authority of Scripture is in large measure an offshoot of the Enlightenment, and it is a position adopted by many who formally subscribe to Nicea and Chalcedon. Moreover, neither Nicea nor Chalcedon set forth everything that was not *then* in dispute, but which had been disputed earlier and would be disputed again. For instance, neither insisted that there is an ineradicable connection between conversion and a changed life, even though many of the Fathers and certainly the New Testament writers addressed such matters. If the creeds are a sufficient criterion, the devil himself could sign on. In real life, on the street, in local churches, away from theological faculties and ecumenical discussions, these sorts of issues are often more urgent than Arianism—and they are treated very differently by groups that can agree on Nicea and Chalcedon.[38]

We should have learned these points by thoughtfully reading the New Testament. The New Testament does not provide us with a simple twenty-line creed set forth as the sufficient criterion for genuine faith. It emphasizes

---

38. Perhaps I should add in passing that doctrinal priorities look very different in different cultures. While working with the World Evangelical Fellowship, an extraordinarily diverse body, I discovered that evangelicals in India, where the prevalent religion is Hinduism, often look on Roman Catholics very differently from the way evangelicals look on Roman Catholics in, say, Colombia or Brazil. Catholicism itself is quite different in the two places, of course: a missionary environment will inevitably call forth a different stance than will a culture largely influenced by and frequently controlled by the ecclesiastical community. But quite apart from such differences, evangelicals who draw most of their converts from a Catholic population are going to look at Catholicism differently from evangelicals who draw most of their converts from an Indian population. The academic or ecumenical strategist who never engages in fruitful evangelism at all should allow more space for those working on the front lines. In public position papers sponsored by the world evangelical body, therefore, we tended to give greater say to the people who faced the majority group. Thus evangelicals in India would have greater say when it came to discussing Hinduism than would evangelicals in Spain or Venezuela; conversely, when it came to discussing Roman Catholicism, evangelicals in Italy or Costa Rica would be given a stronger voice than evangelicals in India.

different criteria in different situations. In the Christological arena, for instance, compare 1 Corinthians 12:1–3 and 1 John 2:22: the formulations are different because the truth that is being denied is different. But elsewhere the New Testament might emphasize the need for new birth (John 3) or the necessity of a transformed life characterized by love for brothers and sisters in Christ (1 John 3:14–15). These are not alternative criteria, as if one is free to pick and choose according to personal preference. From a theoretical perspective, they are cumulative; they are part of the package of what it means to live life under the terms of the new covenant. From an existential perspective, those criteria from which you currently seem most alienated are precisely the ones that are most immediately applicable. But in no case can it be said that one simple cognitive criterion fits all—i.e., that it proves to be a sufficient criterion in every instance.

Third, Walker's stance is naive about the prospects of success. For better and worse, Walker and others of his persuasion are addressing Western democracies steeped in individualism (especially in America and Australia) and rising pluralism (almost everywhere): do-it-yourself-religion is in. Thus while some will heed his call, more will hunker down into the security of the traditional group, and even more will do their own thing. The irony is that the call itself compounds the problem. It calls into being a new group that simultaneously identifies itself with an established group (Roman Catholics, say, or evangelicals) while criticizing it for being too narrow. Worse, far from sharpening theological reflection, it discourages it, by looking for a kind of lowest-common-denominator Christianity that will have as a long-term consequence the inability to think theologically at all.[39] Respectful mutual tolerance gives way to a hearty mutual declaration of universal Christian unity and fellowship (secularists excluded). It is very cozy and "in"; it is also short-sighted and, finally, dangerous.

For these three reasons, then, Walker's appeal is naive. But there are more sophisticated calls to engage with Christian tradition. Some of them combine well-founded good sense, and elements of the same naiveté just described. Consider the well-written and important work by Nathan Hatch, *The Democratization of American Christianity*.[40] One of the important theses of the book is that in the American setting the call for a return to the primitive Scriptures—i.e., an appeal to the Bible detached from tradition—was first launched by liberals who were seeking to disentangle themselves from what they thought of as the entrenched Calvinism of New England. Thus Hatch

---

39. This is not to say that on certain strategic issues there can never be a place for "co-belligerence" (to use one of Francis Schaeffer's expressions) with those with whom one disagrees on other issues. I shall take up that question in the next two chapters.

40. New Haven: Yale Univ. Press, 1989.

holds that in the American context the desire to free oneself from tradition is at heart a liberalizing tendency. Lints argues, "If he is correct, then it is ironically the case that insofar as this remains an essential thrust within evangelicalism, the movement will increasingly move away from the biblical text."[41]

There is a large element of truth in this analysis. Certainly there are evangelicals who think they can read the Bible *tabula rasa* and need learn nothing from tradition. For them, the warnings of Hatch and Lints are salutary. But one could argue that the three dimensions of naiveté outlined above surface again here. At the historical level, the kind of appeal to Scripture advanced by the more liberal party in New England a century and a half ago and the kind of appeal to Scripture advanced by more thoughtful evangelicals today are very different animals. The former thought, rightly or wrongly, that the Christian tradition had departed from Scripture, and that Scripture needed to correct it. The latter thinks that the best of Christian tradition is in line with Scripture, but that Scripture itself is frequently being put down, relativized, domesticated, and that return to the original fount is an essential part of Christian faithfulness. Liberalizing tendencies today are not usually associated with those seeking a return to Scripture. One could as easily draw attention to historical analogies in which there has come a rejuvenating and an enriching of Christian tradition, not some liberalizing trajectory, by a fresh appeal to Scripture (e.g., the best heritage of primitive Methodism, on both sides of the Atlantic). In other words, because of the changes in the culture, the historical analogy that Lints paints seems a little strained.

In short, the plurality of errors and heresies that our generation confronts demands that lines be drawn—thoughtfully, carefully, humbly, corrigibly, but drawn nonetheless. A single line against a bogeyman called secularism will prove inadequate. In this war the enemy advances on more than one front.

There is a final reason why lines must be drawn, lines of more than one kind:

D. The Entailments of the Gospel Confront Our Culture —and Must Be Lived Out

The issues before us are far from being purely cognitive. The pluralism that shapes our culture intrudes into every domain. If Christians are obligated to think through issues of truth and error, or orthodoxy and heresy, they are obligated to think no less about issues of right and wrong, morality and immorality, purity and impurity. Indeed, the two are intimately connected, for Christians hold that the most fundamental distinctions in the moral arena

41. Richard Lints, *The Fabric of Theology: A Prolegomenon to Evangelical Theology* (Grand Rapids: Eerdmans, 1993), 88, n. 7.

are upheld by revelation that is nothing less than propositional, revelation that is absorbed by cognitive faculties.

Related issues of public policy are extraordinarily complex. I shall treat them in a cursory fashion in the next two chapters. Here, it is enough to insist that the matter of drawing lines must be restricted to doctrine and cognitive truth. There are lines that need to be drawn in the arenas of speech, sexual behavior, self-discipline, materialism.

This is not to suggest that every church needs to start excommunicating everyone who has an affair, regardless of repentance, or who drives a BMW, regardless of a range of other factors, or who is overweight, regardless of physical disorder or an abusive background, and so forth. It does mean that the church, for all of its warm welcome extended to sinners like us, is in the business, by the power of the gospel, of changing sinners, preparing them for glory while teaching them how to live here. In a culture where acquisition is one of the chief goals, how do we help believers learn the privilege of self-denial? In a culture saturated with sexual titillation, how can we help Christians live lives of joyful monogamy?[42] By what means do we insist that genuine Christianity embraces all of life, not merely a set of cognitive positions? More broadly:

> Orthodoxy often requires us to be hard precisely where the world is soft, and soft where the world is hard. It means condemning the homosexual lifestyle and being labeled bigots. It means caring for AIDS patients though many think us fools. It means respecting the rule of law though our culture is increasingly lawless. It means visiting the prisoners who offend that law though our culture would prefer to forget them. In every way that matters, Christianity is an affront to the world; it is countercultural.[43]

In this framework, although church discipline is being thought through afresh by many Christian groups,[44] one of the areas where more thought is still needed is the manner in which churches that draw lines in the moral arenas—however graciously, humbly, gently, sometimes by degrees, but also firmly—are not only taking steps to align themselves with Scripture (and with the main strands of Christian heritage, for that matter), but are taking on the

---

42. Cf. the useful essay by Tim Stafford, "The Next Sexual Revolution," *Christianity Today* 36/3 (March 9, 1992): 28–29.

43. Charles Colson, *Against the Night: Living in the New Dark Ages* (Ann Arbor: Servant, 1989), 151–52.

44. E.g., Marvin L. Warkentin, "Church Discipline in a Pluralistic Society," *Direction* 12 (April 1983): 15–27; Won Yong Ji, "Witnessing to Christ in a Pluralistic Age: Theological Principle and Practice," *Concordia Journal* 16 (1990): 231–44; the essays in *The Ministerial Forum* 4/2, published by the Evangelical Free Church of America (Fall 1993).

culture. Such steps become not only a matter of nurturing and protecting the faithful, but of showing a pluralistic world what Christian living looks like. This will alienate some; under God's good hand, it will draw others, not least because the freedoms promised by pluralism are tearing society apart. In any case, we have little choice: elementary faithfulness demands it.

Part Three

CHRISTIAN LIVING IN A PLURALISTIC CULTURE

Chapter 9

NIBBLING AT THE EDGES: THE RANGE OF THE CHALLENGE

ollowing the introductory chapter of this book, which surveyed the field of pluralism and its impact on Western culture, parts 1 and 2 have brought us through two of its most difficult aspects. The first, embracing chapters 2–3, focused on hermeneutical and related questions; the second, embracing chapters 4–8, considered various facets of religious pluralism, from an avowedly Christian point of view.

In part 3, comprising only two chapters, we will consider the impact of pluralism on society at large: on government in a democratic society, education, marriage and family, law, the media, morals, art, economics, bioethics, and a host of related issues. The aim is not to be comprehensive—after all, many volumes are being published each year on each of these topics—but in this chapter to survey the sweep of the challenge, and in the next to articulate some priorities that Christians must be careful to maintain.

Two introductory remarks may prove helpful. *First*, there is widespread recognition that Western culture is in trouble. A very long chapter would be needed merely to chronicle the range of troubled reflection. Some of this is the work of avowed Christians writing out of their heritage: one thinks, for instance, of Schlossberg,[1] of Neuhaus,[2] and of Veith[3] who have been in the

---

1. E.g., Herbert Schlossberg, *Idols for Destruction: Christian Faith and Its Confrontation with American Society* (Nashville: Nelson, 1983). The title comes from Hosea 8:4: " ... they made idols for their own destruction" (NRSV).

2. Of the many books by Richard John Neuhaus, see perhaps his *America Against Itself: Moral Vision and the Public Order* (Notre Dame: Univ. of Notre Dame Press, 1992).

3. Gene Edward Veith, Jr., *Postmodern Times: A Christian Guide to Contemporary Thought and Culture* (Wheaton: Crossway Books, 1994).

vanguard of such warnings. But much of it is not. From front-rank scholars to newspaper "op-ed" pieces, people are ringing alarm bells. Thus Himmelfarb ponders the place of liberty in a highly pluralistic society.[4] She insists that a John Stuart Mill could in his day argue for a virtually unfettered principle of liberty only because he lived in a culture where certain virtues were assumed to be constant, virtues tied to broad cultural acceptance of common religious norms, traditions, laws, and a host of other resources of "civilization." She quotes Tocqueville: "How is it possible that society should escape destruction if the moral tie is not strengthened in proportion as the political tie is relaxed?"[5]

Op-ed pieces tend less toward philosophical underpinnings than to statistics and obvious societal trends. Thus the op-ed columns for the *Chicago Tribune* of July 23, 1994, under the banner, "The Coming Apart of America," observes that in 1993 "6.3 million children—27 percent—were living with a single, never-married parent." Fully 30 percent of all births and 68 percent of African-American babies were born to unwed mothers. The Census Bureau reports that between 1983 and 1993 there was a 70 percent increase in births to unwed mothers. The editorial concludes, "When adults, men and women, take flight from responsibility, families fail to form, children suffer and society, slowly and by degrees, comes apart."

Some books aim at particular phenomena in society. Thus Martha Bayle traces the development of popular music in this century from the early influence of the African-American tradition through the determinative 1960s to its current tendency to express the self-absorption and nihilism that in her opinion characterize "Generation X."[6] But whatever the level of the analysis, the perception that Western culture in general and American culture in particular has passed its zenith and is now in decline is widespread.

Second, although it is notoriously difficult to chart simple causes and effects at the societal level, few would be so bold as to deny that one of the factors that has powerfully contributed to the changes convulsing Western culture is the decline in Judeo-Christian assumptions, allied with (but emphatically differentiable from) the shift from modernity to postmodernity. The reasons for these developments, as we have seen, are many; not a few of them are morally neutral (e.g., immigration policies) or even beneficial (e.g.,

---

4. Gertrude Himmelfarb, *On Looking into the Abyss: Untimely Thoughts on Culture and Society* (New York: Knopf, 1994).

5. Ibid., 100. Her ideas are becoming better disseminated: cf. her essay, "Re-Moralizing America," *Wall Street Journal* (February 7, 1995): A20, where she comments, "I'm not even sure that a moral reformation is possible without the inspiration of a religious reformation."

6. *Hole in the Soul: The Loss of Beauty and Meaning in American Popular Music* (New York: Free Press, 1994).

the gradual self-destruction of the epistemology of modernity). The effects can also be helpful (e.g., less excuse for parochial blinders). But whether the causes and the effects of these changes have been beneficial or malevolent, it is vital to recognize that they are irrefragably tied to the rise of the various forms of pluralism, with all the shifts in worldview this implies.

The point can be made in a number of ways. Although he did not live long enough to treat postmodernism, one of Francis Schaeffer's major concerns was to tie the rise of Western culture to the rise of the fortunes of the gospel and of the Bible, and the decline of Western culture to the decline of the fortunes of the gospel and of the Bible.[7] Many have criticized Schaeffer for painting with too broad a brush. But no one could question Shuger's immense learning in her extraordinarily fine study of the impact of the Bible on the Protestant cultures of northern Europe during the Renaissance.[8] Her depiction of life and thought and conceptuality at a time when the Bible still shaped the entire culture contrasts vividly with the contemporary postmodern world, in which a biblical scholar can ask, "Why bother with biblical studies?"[9] At a time when "religious group and academy have for the most part gone their different ways, and where society as a whole follows a different path again, listening occasionally to the voice of the academy when it suits and almost never to the voice of religion,"[10] why bother studying the Bible? One can advance reasons of personal interest (as one can advance reasons for studying, say, Shakespeare or John Donne), but neither the culture nor the biblical scholars themselves usually perceive any reason grounded in the intrinsic authority and relevance of the Bible. In true postmodernist fashion, the author of this particular article can suggest nothing more than a new way of reading the Bible, in which we discover "a new kind of meta-narrative," one that is "dialogic"—i.e., biblical students become "purveyors of a vision of the possibility and necessity of conversation between communities of discourse," resisting "all totalising interpretations (like fundamentalism) and totalising claims for method (like fundamentalism)"[11]—though perhaps one may be excused for wondering if the dogmatism of his solution does not reflect a certain "totalising claim for method" that borders on a new fundamentalism.

---

7. See especially his *How Should We Then Live? The Rise and Decline of Western Thought and Culture* (Old Tappan: Revell, 1976).

8. Debora Kuller Shuger, *The Renaissance Bible: Scholarship, Sacrifice, and Subjectivity* (Berkeley: Univ. of California Press, 1994).

9. Mark Coleridge, "Life in the Crypt or Why Bother with Biblical Studies?" *Biblical Interpretation* 2 (1994): 139–51.

10. Ibid., 140.

11. Ibid., 150. I find it difficult to imagine that Coleridge has ever tried preaching this goal to a large congregation of tradespeople.

In short, what we are witnessing is what Senior calls "the death of a Christian culture."[12] One may quibble about just how "Christian" the culture has ever been—I shall say more on that point in a moment—but whatever the assessment of the past, there is less and less doubt that the inherited influence of a Judeo-Christian outlook has largely dissipated. In its place are a large number of groups trying to define America (or Canada, or England, or Germany, etc.)[13] in the light of these new realities. The informed postmodernists among them, holding that principles are nothing but preferences and that preferences merely hide the will to exert power, assault the ramparts of our culture's social and intellectual life.

The arenas in which this struggle is being fought out are many. What follows is an attempt to sketch a few of them.

A. Government

Most historians affirm that the United States was considerably more homogeneous, religiously speaking, in its first decades than it is now.[14] This is not to deny that the point has been overstated by some popular conservatives. Partly in reaction, the most recent well-received history of Christianity in America and Canada[15] goes out of its way to stress the diversity that was present at the beginning. After all, in many intellectual circles in the early years of the United States, deism was more highly prized than orthodox Christianity. Roman Catholics were putting down communities on what became the West Coast of America, and sending "coureurs de bois" through the Great Lakes and down the Mississippi, while Protestants were settling on the eastern seaboard. Conflicts among denominations were more intense than they are today. Nevertheless most of the early leaders of the emerging American nation were steeped in the Judeo-Christian heritage.[16] By this I mean that certain notions were part of the standard mental furniture for most

---

12. John Senior, *The Death of a Christian Culture*, 2d ed. (Harrison: RC Books, 1994).

13. Although much of the specific argumentation in the pages that follow interacts primarily with events and literature in the United States of America, it would not take much imagination to make appropriate transfers to other Western nations, and even to many non-Western nations that are heavily influenced by the West.

14. Much of the first part of this section is adapted from D. A. Carson, "Christian Witness in an Age of Pluralism," in *God and Culture*, ed. D. A. Carson and John D. Woodbridge (Grand Rapids: Eerdmans, 1993), 39–40.

15. Mark A. Noll, *A History of Christianity in the United States and Canada* (Grand Rapids: Eerdmans, 1992).

16. See, for instance, M. E. Bradford, *Founding Fathers: Brief Lives of the Framers of the United States Constitution*, 2d ed. (Lawrence: Univ. Press of Kansas, 1994); John Eidsmoe, *Christianity and the Constitution: The Faith of the Founding Fathers* (Grand Rapids: Baker, 1987).

Americans. God exists. He created all things, and we are responsible to him. Moral law exists, and is flaunted to our detriment. History is going somewhere; we must all finally give an account to God. Most held that divine providence was leading the nation.

If one links the major Protestant groups (apart from Unitarians) and Roman Catholics (still a fringe group on the eastern seaboard, numerically speaking), one may add common beliefs in God as Trinity, basic Christian assumptions in the realm of Christology, and the recognition that the fundamental human problem is sin. Moreover, not only were most of the early leaders on the eastern seaboard related in some way to the Protestant tradition, but it was within that tradition that seeds were sown that encouraged reflection on the differentiable but overlapping jurisdictions of church and state.[17] Perhaps I should add that the weakness of Noll's book, referred to above, is that although it faithfully and admirably chronicles the *diversity* of outlooks at the time of the founding of the nation, it rarely attempts to assess the relative weight and influence of the disparate contributions.

The point of these reflections is to underscore the fact that the roots of liberty and democracy as they found form in the United States were deeply embedded in the soil of a Judeo-Christian worldview, and were irrigated by wide reading in political theorists from Plato to Burke. When Russell Kirk calls us back to what he calls "America's British culture," this is the sort of thing he has in mind.[18] The loss of a central, unifying vision of the *summum bonum* was almost unthinkable in the early years. The Federalist Papers show that limited government was widely understood to be possible only where society was largely constrained by a moral consensus. John Adams went so far as to say that the system of government being adopted was "wholly inadequate" if that consensus did not exist. Even James Madison's remonstrance that religion flourishes best where there is no government interference did not take issue with this judgment. Madison, a Virginian, was referring to the Massachusetts Bay Colony, which until that time had operated in large measure as a theocracy. He was opposed to the intertwining of some denomination(s) with government, very much the sort of thing that characterized not only the Bay Colony but also England; he was not wrestling with the degree

---

17. A useful recent book on the subject is Douglas Kelly, *The Emergence of Liberty in the Modern World* (Phillipsburg: Presbyterian and Reformed, 1992). Tracing the rising distinctions from Calvin through Scotland (especially John Knox and George Buchanan), the English Puritans, and the Evangelical Awakening, Kelly recognizes other critical influences. But he rightly states, "Although by no means an exclusively or even originally Calvinist concept, limitation of governmental powers generally tended to exist where Calvinist influence had been strong" (113).

18. *America's British Culture* (New Brunswick: Transaction, 1993).

of religious diversity we face today. Moreover, despite occasional statements to the contrary, the virtues of a system of checks and balances were extolled, not on the grounds that unrestrained pluralism is an inherently good thing, but on the grounds that human nature is corrupt (certainly a Christian perspective) and that bad people must not be given too much power. Since we cannot be sure of thwarting bad people with good people, it is better to introduce a structure of checks and balances so that unfettered power never falls into the hands of one person or group without the possibility of nonviolent redress.

But we have arrived at a new situation. The original democratic ideals, far from being challenged by the loss of a controlling worldview, have actually been strengthened. Democracy has become not the best means of government *granted the general adoption of a certain worldview*, but the best means of government, period. That may or may not be true; what is certain is that the Founding Fathers never put the matter that way. Meanwhile, the culture itself has changed so massively that on every axis on which measurement occurs, we are in a very different situation from that envisaged by the framers of the Constitution. In race, language, religion (or lack of it), we are far, far more diverse than Thomas Jefferson or Patrick Henry could have imagined. While some, like Russell Kirk, eloquently appeal to the dominant cultural heritage at the time of the Revolution and for the century-and-a-half that succeeded it, many citizens today hold that such an appeal is racist, sexist, indefensibly Eurocentric, and so forth. In short, there is less and less commonality shared by the citizens.

The results are everywhere apparent. Apart from those rare occasions when we face a foe widely recognized as such—as in the Gulf War—we simply cannot pull together. The words of the English poet John Dryden (1631–1700) come to mind, when, ostensibly writing about the period of David and Absalom but in fact describing the decadent populace of his own day:

> God's pampered people, whom, debauched with ease,
> No king could govern, and no God could please.

Or, more accurately in our setting, competing "kings" please different segments of society, while competing "gods" display their weak-kneed subservience to the will of the people by catering to whatever seems faddish.[19]

For that is the real problem. With the ideal of democracy still in full bloom, but with no transcendent ideology or vision claiming a large proportion of the populace and imposing moral accountability, legislators frequently

---

19. Even *Time* has recently commented on the "emphasis on the nation's 'multicultural' heritage [that] exalts racial and ethnic pride at the expense of social cohesion" (138/1 [July 8, 1991]: 12–21).

have no higher vision than to garner votes. Majority rule is by definition moral law.

This combination of developments—the absolutizing of democracy and the triumph of both empirical and philosophical pluralism—ensures that excellence in government as measured by agreed criteria cannot easily be pursued. The provocative works of von Kuehnelt-Leddihn and de Jouvenel suddenly sound prophetic.[20] Over the last several decades, government power has been in the process of massive expansion. One doubts whether this expansion can be turned around by the periodic triumph of a particular party, because the moral consensus necessary for sustained restraint is no longer present. On the long haul, people without a controlling vision beyond economic advancement will simply vote for more. That "more" may mean a temporary tax-break, but only rarely will it mean a cut in services. The more we demand, the more government takes; the more it takes and the more it provides, the more we think it unthinkable that we could do without what is provided. Such a world allows no aristocracy of excellence, for there are no agreed criteria as to what is praiseworthy, and therefore no direction toward which the country as a whole "pulls." The apparent exceptions, baseball heroes, movie stars, and pop singers, are not real exceptions, for they achieve their status simply because they entertain us. When their entertainment value falls, they are easily shucked aside because their achievements are not something to strive after, to emulate, to duplicate. They are merely something to chortle over and admire briefly, as we reach for some more beer nuts and fondle the TV remote.

What is unsure is how long democracies can survive once they lose a controlling vision of the common good that extends beyond the merely pragmatic. It may take a long time—I certainly hope so—but it is hard to be optimistic. What seems so difficult for Westerners to grasp at the moment is that our problems are not merely economic (though many are tied to economics), but reflect the most fundamental questions of cultural cohesiveness. They touch all of life. They are as much tied to religion, philosophy, the family, heritage, direction, vision of the future, language, and everything else that contributes to any culture, as to the interest rate and the federal deficit.[21] With the loss of any public center, Tracy insists that the earlier debates about the public nature of public policy "are now spent." He goes on:

20. Erik von Kuehnelt-Leddihn, *Liberty or Equality: The Challenge of Our Time* (Front Royal: Christendom Press, 1993 [1952]); Bertrand de Jouvenal, *Du Pouvoir, Histoire Naturelle de sa Croissance* (Geneva: Edition du Cheval Ailé, 1945); idem, *Sovereignty: An Inquiry into the Political Good* (Chicago: Univ. of Chicago Press, 1957 [orig. 1955]).

21. One of the few to express this elegantly is Eric Voegelin, *The New Science of Politics* (Chicago: Univ. of Chicago Press, 1952).

The major discussion (and a far more difficult one) has shifted elsewhere: . . . Must we, therefore, resign ourselves to the absence of *any* public realm at all and the destruction of any "hard" notion of "publicness"? We would then be left with the failure of the pluralistic experiment: for the possibilities of pluralism for the public realm would have retreated to the realm of the private.[22]

How long, then, can democracy itself survive? What stance should Christians adopt in the current climate?

B. Religious Freedom

Although many conservative voices insist that religious freedom is being eroded, and others of more liberal persuasion appeal to the Constitution in order to promote additional freedom *from* the baleful influences of religion, some major thinkers have insisted that both perspectives are extremist and alarmist. In an engagingly written work, Garry Wills insists that it is impossible to disentangle religion from society at large, that the courts by and large exercise a mediating role between extremes, and that the separation of church and state has been a blessing that has strengthened religion, which in turn has in large measure been a progressive force in American society.[23] In a thoughtful historical review and analysis, Miller urges that freedom of religion is the "first liberty" not only in some chronological sense, but in a defining sense: religious liberty is so bound up with questions of the location of final authority that it has rendered possible the ongoing free debate about first principles that lies at the heart of American democracy.[24]

Certainly the concerns of the Founding Fathers had much to do with the desire to disavow and disallow all forms of established religion, in the technical sense of an Established Church (like the Church of England). I do not know of anyone today who seriously thinks that a particular denomination is a threat because it is successfully pressing to be recognized by the federal government as the official religion of America. Moreover, most commentators since Augustine have recognized that tensions between church and state cannot be entirely avoided this side of the Parousia.[25] But the situation we face today has been transformed by four factors.

---

22. David Tracy, "The Questions of Pluralism: The Context of the United States," *Mid-Stream: An Ecumenical Journal* 22 (1983): 277.

23. Garry Wills, *Under God: Religion and American Politics* (New York: Simon & Schuster, 1990).

24. William Lee Miller, *The First Liberty: Religion and the American Republic* (New York: Paragon House, 1988).

25. Cf. Robert N. Bellah, "Religion and Legitimation in the American Republic," in *In Gods We Trust: New Patterns of Religious Pluralism in America*, ed. Thomas Robbins and Dick Anthony (New Brunswick: Transaction, 1981), 37: "The very spirituality and otherworldliness

First, the sheer diversity of religions and of forms of irreligion ensures that the debate does not focus on the establishment of a Christian denomination as the official religion, but on whether *any* form of Christianity has the right to anything that might be perceived to be an advantage—and, derivatively, whether any form of *any* religion has the right to anything that might be perceived to be an advantage. None of the Founding Fathers envisaged a land where various forms of Christianity coexist with Mormonism, atheism, Buddhism, Islam, Jehovah's Witnesses, various New Age movements, and much more—a total of about 1,200 religious bodies, plus countless informal groups.[26] "The practice of liberty includes the knack of keeping out of each other's way, thus giving free play to the natural forces of social cohesion," writes Opitz;[27] but that becomes harder and harder to do when visions of the good clash at fundamental levels. The alternative is for every expression of religion to be exclusively private; at that point, getting in someone else's way is less likely. But as we shall see, this brings other dangers. Meanwhile, as Hunter argues, what we have in reality is a double standard, by which "secularistic faiths and ideologies" receive state support, especially through the educational system but also in the arts, because they are judged nonreligious.[28]

Second, the rising influence of government into every sphere of life ensures that conflicts between church and state are inevitable. For instance, in 1878 the Supreme Court, in *Reynolds v. United States*, upheld a federal law prohibiting polygamy against a Mormon challenge, on the ground that although the right to hold religious beliefs is absolute, the state has the right to limit the practice of religion in the interest of the public good. Probably few Christians would want to see that judgment overturned on the particular issue then being examined, even though casual extension of the principle could easily prove extremely troubling. Who decides what constitutes the "public good"? The 1947 Supreme Court decision, written by Justice Hugo Black, that neither federal nor state governments can "pass laws which aid one religion, aid all religions or prefer one religion over another" can become

---

of Christianity has provided a certain avenue for reducing the tension not always open to other historic religions: the differentiation of functions, the division of spheres. Yet no solution has ever dissolved the underlying tensions described by Augustine and Rousseau. The tendency has been for every solution to break down into religion as the servant of the state or vice versa."

26. See especially Dick Anthony and Thomas Robbins, "Culture Crisis and Contemporary Religion," in Robbins and Anthony, *In Gods We Trust*, 9–31.

27. Edmund A. Opitz, *Religion: Foundation of the Free Society* (Irvington-on-Hudson: Foundation for Economic Education, 1994), 242.

28. James Davison Hunter, "Religious Freedom and the Challenge of Modern Pluralism," in *Articles of Faith, Articles of Peace: The Religious Liberty Clauses and the American Public Philosophy*, ed. James Davison Hunter and Os Guinness (Washington: Brookings Institution, 1990), 54–73.

a powerful separatist tool in a society where federal funds and federal laws touch almost everything we do.[29]

The line taken by the Court has veered from side to side. In one of its more important rulings, the Court in *Lemon v. Kurtzman* (1971) synthesized from earlier decisions a three-part test. To be constitutional, a law must (1) have a secular purpose; (2) neither advance nor inhibit religion as a primary effect; (3) avoid excessive entanglement between church and state. The words "primary effect" can be slippery: for instance, the Court has upheld the right of towns to pass zoning laws that have the effect of forbidding churches to acquire land and build buildings, or even rent established buildings, provided this was not the *primary* effect of the law. On the other hand, in *Marsh v. Chambers* (1983) the Court decided not to apply the *Lemon* test when it rejected a challenge to Nebraska's employment of a legislative chaplain.

Often the basis on which a decision is reached is tied to governmental "largesse." And because governmental largesse touches almost everything, there is very little on which the courts may not rule. For example, in a small town a group of churches want to put up a stone engraving of the Ten Commandments on common ground in the village square. It makes no difference that, say, 95 percent of the people in the town have no objection, provided that their tax dollars are not used. The courts will reflect on the fact that this ground belongs to all the people; they are likely to observe that town employes will have to clean the stone, with the result that public moneys are being used to support a particular religion; and so forth. In others words, the extent of government reach means that some clashes are almost inevitable.[30]

Third, the increasing empirical pluralism and consequent privatization of religion may lead to the creation of what Hannah Arendt calls the "atomistic mass."[31] She argues that for totalitarianism to occur there must be the progressive elimination of intermediate structures in society, and consequently the growth of direct dependency of every individual upon the central goverment. Sooner or later totalitarianism becomes almost inevitable. Donovan,

29. Mr. Justice Black asserted (in *Everson v. Board of Education*, 1947) that the "First Amendment erected a wall between church and state. That wall must be kept high and impregnable. We could not approve the slightest breach." This "impregnable wall" Black justified, not on the intent of the framers of the Constitution as expressed in the Constitutional Conventions or in the state ratifying conventions, but on the experiment with religious liberty in the Commonwealth of Virginia. See Daniel P. Larsen, "Justice Hugh L. Black and the 'Wall' Between Church and State: Reasons Behind the *Everson v. Board of Education* (1947) Decision" (M.A. thesis, Trinity Evangelical Divinity School, 1984).

30. A more complex variation of this example is progressively teased out in Miller, *The First Liberty*.

31. See her treatment in *The Origins of Totalitarianism*, 2d ed. (Cleveland: World, 1958).

building on Arendt's thesis, demonstrates that one of the tragic legacies of the ACLU is that by fixating on the liberties of the individual *over against* the mediating institutions of society, and by weakening the latter by incessantly suing them, it has substantially reduced prospects for freedom.[32]

Colson has recently taken to quoting Lord Acton, often remembered by political science students for his famous dictum about the corrupting influence of power. Though it came later than they did, that dictum would have been heartily approved by the Founding Fathers: "Power tends to corrupt and absolute power corrupts absolutely."[33] Colson points out that Lord Acton set forth proposals as to how to *avoid* a situation where government assumes absolute power: "No country can be free without religion. It creates and strengthens the notion of duty. If men are not kept straight by duty, they must be by fear. The more they are kept by fear, the less they are free. The greater the strength of duty, the greater the liberty."[34]

Fourth, as the previous chapters have shown, the rise of philosophical pluralism and of secularizing tendencies, especially in the media and in the academy, project an image of believers as old-fashioned, quaint, ill-informed, red-necked, "fundamentalist"—and therefore needing to be tamed. The left demonizes the right, and the right returns the compliment—but the left holds virtually all the positions of leadership in the media and in the academy. In short, the culture of our age firmly opposes all claims to transcendent authority, with the result that there is often a bias against believers. No small irony rests in the fact that the Pilgrim fathers left England because they were not free to practice the truth, and then left Holland for America because they perceived that the amorphous tolerance they found there was in danger of corroding their love of the truth. As Gaede puts it, "[T]he Pilgrims were neither lovers of liberty nor religious imperialists, but people who sought the freedom to be a people of faith—a community. They did not seek freedom for freedom's sake, but for the sake of truth." In other words, "[B]oth the intolerance of England and the tolerance of Holland were a problem for these Puritans. Committed to truth, they wanted freedom to practice it.

---

32. William A. Donahue, *Twilight of Liberty: The Legacy of the ACLU* (London: Transaction, 1994). In an earlier and well-regarded volume, Donahue challenged the ACLU's reputation for nonpartisanship: see *The Politics of the American Civil Liberties Union* (New Brunswick: Transaction, 1985).

33. Sir John Emerick Edward Dalberg Acton, in a letter to Mandell Creighton, April 5, 1887. He goes on: "Great men are almost always bad men, even when they exercise influence and not authority: still more when you superadd the tendency or the certainty of corruption by authority. There is no worse heresy than that the office sanctifies the holder of it."

34. Cited by Chuck Colson in "Making the World Safe for Religion," *Christianity Today* 37/13 (November 8, 1993): 32.

Committed to truth, they were not willing to compromise it in the name of freedom."[35]

At the moment, we are not in a situation in which all freedoms are in imminent danger of collapse. But at least some signs are ominous; some would be funny, if they were not so pathetic. Thus in Chicago, on May 31, 1994, District Court Judge Ann Williams ruled that it is unconstitutional for Illinois schools to observe Good Friday as a holiday because the purpose of this holiday is to advance the Christian religion. Does Good Friday have more of such purpose than Easter? And if one were to introduce even a trace of historical perspective, one would have to wipe, say, Thanksgiving off the calendar as well.

It is worth noting, in passing, that the forms in which questions of religious pluralism arise in the United States are peculiarly tied to her constitutional history. This does not mean that questions of freedom of religion are not debated in other nations where the constitutional history is quite different. In another forum, for example, it would be worth following the argument on the blasphemy laws in the United Kingdom in the wake of the Salman Rushdie affair,[36] or reflecting on the struggles African intellectuals are having in nations where religious pluralism is an empirical but brute reality, often including a contest between Christianity and Islam.[37]

What is quite clear, I think, is that the rising pluralism, of various kinds, is one of the factors precipitating profound questions about the nature and security of religious freedom. What stance should Christians adopt?

Already it is clear that these questions are tied to the judiciary and to educational systems, so to these we briefly turn.

C. Law and the Judiciary

Here three observations will suffice.

First, a fundamental shift in our self-identity has left the nation in general and the judiciary in particular without any sense of obligation to transcendent authority. The result is pragmatism controlled by faddishness and political correctness.

A mere century ago, Supreme Court Justice David Brewer, writing for the majority opinion in the case of *Church of the Holy Trinity v. United States* (1892), insisted: "Our civilization and our institutions are emphatically

---

35. S. D. Gaede, *When Tolerance Is No Virtue: Political Correctness, Multiculturalism and the Future of Truth and Justice* (Downers Grove: InterVarsity Press, 1993).

36. See, for instance, the useful reflections by A. J. Rivers, "Blasphemy Law in the Secular State," *Cambridge Papers* 1/4 (December 1992).

37. See the excellent essay by E. O. Oyelade, "Islamic Theocracy and Religious Pluralism in Africa," *Asia Journal of Theology* 7 (1993): 149–60.

Christian.... From the discovery of the continent to the present hour, there is a single voice making the affirmation ... that this is a Christian nation."

But all this has changed. In a published lecture frequently quoted in law review articles (and recently discussed in an essay by Phillip E. Johnson, professor of law at the University of California-Berkeley),[38] the late Arthur Leff, professor of law at Yale University candidly exposed the contemporary problem.[39] Leff casts the problem this way:

> I want to believe—and so do you—in a complete, transcendent and immanent set of propositions about right and wrong, *findable* rules that authoritatively and unambiguously direct us how to live righteously. I also want to believe—and so do you—in no such thing, but rather that we are wholly free, not only to choose for ourselves what we ought to do, but to decide for ourselves, individually and as a species, what we ought to be. What we want, Heaven help us, is simultaneously to be perfectly ruled and perfectly free, that is, at the same time to discover the right and the good and to create it.[40]

As soon as someone mandates or prohibits something (e.g., "Thou shalt not commit adultery"), someone else says, in effect, "Says who?"—i.e., Who are you to prescribe for me? What gives you authority over me? Leff explains:

> Putting it that way makes it clear that if we are looking for an evaluation, we must actually be looking for an *evaluator*: some machine for the generation of judgments on states of affairs. If the evaluation is to be beyond question, then the evaluator and its evaluative processes must be similarly insulated. If it is to fulfil its role, the evaluator must be the unjudged judge, the unruled legislator, the premise maker who rests on no premises, the uncreated creator of values.... We are never going to get anywhere (assuming for the moment that there is somewhere to get) in ethical or legal theory unless we finally face the fact that, in the Psalmist's words, there is no one like unto the Lord. If He does not exist, there is no metaphoric equivalent.... The so-called death of God turns out not to have been just *His* funeral; it also seems to have effected the total elimination of any coherent, or even more-than-momentarily convincing, ethical or legal system dependent upon finally authoritative, extrasystematic premises.[41]

Leff argues that in a God-based system, God cannot be controlled or evaluated by human beings. Thus if adultery is wrong in this system, it is wrong

---

38. "The Modernist Impasse in Law," in Carson and Woodbridge, *God and Culture*, 180–94.

39. Arthur Leff, "Unspeakable Ethics, Unnatural Law," *Duke Law Journal* (1979): 1229–49.

40. Ibid., 1229.

41. Ibid., 1230, 1232.

because that is the way God has made things; adultery is "naturally" bad "only because the system is supernaturally constructed."[42]

As Johnson[43] points out, in articulating this relationship between natural law and divine authority Leff is relying on the philosophical Thomist tradition. So-called "natural law" is distinguished from divine law "because its commands are accessible to human reason even in the absence of divine revelation."[44] The reality of divinely authorized law could not be doubted by a theist like Thomas Aquinas; the only question was how much of it we could learn through natural reason, apart from special revelation. To a thoroughgoing naturalist, such "natural law" is unacceptable, because it entails the unacceptable premise of nature divinely created.

Naturalists are often happy to speak of "natural rights"; they are less comfortable with "natural obligations." If God is dead, and each human being becomes, in Leff's expression, a "godlet," every debate quickly descends to questions of competing "rights." If X has the "right" to an abortion because she controls her own body, and Y has the "right" to protect the "rights" of unborn children, who will adjudicate? If the pro-choice people insist on their rights, and the Constitution does not address the question of abortion one way or the other, then extensions of the Constitution have to be found. But the other side can do the same. As Johnson puts it:

> The modernist impasse, in other words, does not arise as long as all we are doing is proclaiming liberties. The problem for modernists is how to justify imposing obligations. Homosexuals have a right to be homosexuals, of course; but do employers who disapprove have an obligation to hire them? The poor have a right to public assistance, of course; but do the more fortunate and productive citizens have a right to refuse to pay when they think the tax burden has become unreasonable? The rights of all citizens must be protected, of course; but who are the citizens? What about infants, the unborn, foreigners, and animals? Who or what has the authority to tell us whom we ought to admit to the sphere of protection?[45]

The rest of Leff's lecture dismisses futile attempts to get around the impasse. Johnson goes one step further. Despite the impasse, Leff cannot avoid the conclusion that there is such a thing as evil, including such acts as napalming babies, starving the poor, buying and selling one another, and so forth. But Johnson follows this line more consistently:

> What Leff said is fascinating, but what he failed to say is more fascinating still. If there is no ultimate evaluator, then there is no real distinction

42. Ibid., 1231.
43. "The Modernist Impassed in Law," 183–84.
44. Ibid., 183.
45. Ibid., 185.

between good and evil. It follows that if evil is nonetheless *real*, then atheism—that is, the nonexistence of that evaluator or standard of evaluation—is not only an extraordinarily unappetizing prospect; it is also fundamentally untrue, because the reality of evil implies the reality of the evaluator, who alone has the authority to establish the standard by which evil can deserve to be damned. When impeccable logic leads to self-contradiction, there must be a faulty premise. In this case the logical connection is clear: because God is dead, "it looks as if we are all we have." Why not reexamine the premise? Why not at least explain *why* you refuse to reexamine the premise?[46]

Johnson then surveys and critiques one or two attempts to get around this reasoning, and concludes that they are intellectually bankrupt.[47]

The inevitable result is that judges make decisions that are in line with their politics, their prejudices, their cultural alignments, their value systems, without reference to anything that claims to be stable or in any sense culture-transcendent. The best of them are very clever people who can always use the Constitution to support their biases. They are, in short, a reflection of the philosophical pluralism reigning in the land; we should not expect otherwise.

Second, for various complex reasons, this is increasingly a time when judges rule. The people rule less and less, even through their duly elected legislators; unelected judges rule. Why?

The *New York Times* gives one answer: this is the result "when one person's civil rights are another's moral outrage."[48] When any piece of legislation that could be viewed as an advantage to any group offends some other group's notion of their "rights," an attempt at legal redress follows. As the nation becomes more diverse, the opportunities for such lawsuits multiply.

Of course, in theory the courts could exercise self-restraint and, apart from fairly explicit contravention of the Constitution, simply refuse to overturn legislation that had been duly passed. The effect would be that people who felt unjustly treated by the laws of the land would turn more promptly to their legislators. As it stands, the unelected branch of government draws more and more power to itself, because (1) the Supreme Court is procedurally the final step in the process of adjudication as to what the Constitution means; and (2) the Court has in recent decades exercised little self-restraint.

People on the political right often put the matter something like this:

> If we imagine a country with a democratically elected parliament but having a monarch, a king, or a queen whose sole voice can abrogate laws

---

46. Ibid., 187.
47. For further discussion of the relationship between morality and divine commands, whether naturally revealed or supernaturally revealed, see Paul Helm, ed., *Divine Commands and Morality* (Oxford: Oxford Univ. Press, 1981).
48. Sunday, 16 October 1994, 6.

passed by parliament and unilaterally enact others in their place, we would call that country's democracy a sham. We would probably say that it was, in the last and most important analysis, an intolerable absolutism. What if the king could not himself abrogate the laws of parliament and replace them with his own, but could appoint a select group of aristocrats to exercise that power? Would that be democracy? If these aristocrats were named for life, and the king himself could not remove them, this would no longer be an absolute monarchy, but an aristocratic oligarchy. Would that be significantly closer to true democracy than the absolute monarch?[49]

Third, as much as many conservatives might like it, this is not a period in which judges are going to restrain themselves by sticking as closely as possible to the original intent of the Constitution. That is the solution most commonly advanced. But it will not succeed, for at least the following reasons:

(1) The Constitution has been successively reinterpreted by various branches of government, sometimes with good effect, sometimes with bad, and there is no reason to think that the process will stop now. On the side most would consider good, the outstanding example is Lincoln's Gettysburg Address. A mere 272 words—and the Constitution was successfully re-interpreted. "Four score and seven years ago our fathers brought forth on this continent, a new nation, conceived in Liberty, and dedicated to the proposition that all men are created equal." Really? The Constitution said nothing about equality, and clearly tolerated slavery. Garry Wills rightly observes:

> [Lincoln] altered the document from within, by appeal from its letter to the spirit, subtly changing the recalcitrant stuff of that legal compromise, bringing it to its own indictment. By implicitly doing this, he performed one of the most daring acts of open-air sleight-of-hand ever witnessed by the unsuspecting. Everyone in that vast throng of thousands was having his or her intellectual pocket picked. The crowd departed with a new thing in its ideological luggage, that new constitution Lincoln had substituted for the one they brought there with them.... Lincoln had revolutionized the Revolution, giving people a new past to live with that would change their future indefinitely.[50]

Within the judiciary, one thinks immediately of the change from the 1892 Supreme Court Decision, quoted at the beginning of this section, to the present outlook. The literature chronicles scores of other examples.

(2) In any case, the nation has changed so much that if the Constitution is to retain its absolute authority, most Americans feel that it *must* be rein-

---

49. Harold O. J. Brown, "Our Chosen Tyranny, or The Illusions of Democracy," *Religion & Society Report* 11/7 (July 1994): 4–5.

50. Garry Wills, *Lincoln at Gettysburg: The Words That Remade America* (New York: Simon & Schuster, 1992), 38.

terpreted. One might argue that it would be better to amend the Constitution, but that is such a cumbersome process that it is unlikely to become the principal solution.

Let us suppose for argument's sake that the Justices became convinced that they should interpret the Constitution strictly in line with the framers' intent, so far as that can be discerned. Suppose, further, that the nation became, say, 35 percent atheist, 25 percent Muslim, 10 percent Hindu, 15 percent New Age, 10 percent Christian, and 5 percent miscellaneous. How could the demands of democracy and the demands of a strict reading of the Constitution in line with the framers' intent possibly be reconciled? Of course, we have not reached the percentages suggested, and probably we never will. But the fact remains that the demographic, ideological, religious, and cultural changes in the nation since the Revolution are so vast that *some* reinterpretation is virtually inevitable. That fact does not authorize *all* reinterpretations or *any particular* reinterpretation. It does warn against a simplistic call to the framers' original intentions.[51]

(3) There are at least a few ambiguities built into the Declaration of Independence and into the Constitution that call out for clarification—and inevitably such phrases will be "clarified" in slightly different ways at different times in the nation's history. The Declaration holds up "Life, Liberty and the pursuit of Happiness"; but what precise content is to be given to each of these three? Homosexuals may well think that freedom to promote their sexual orientation falls nicely under the last two items. The Constitution speaks of "life, liberty, or property" (Fifth Amendment), not as things guaranteed but as items protected from deprivation by the government itself, and even then what it is really promising is procedural fairness, equal treatment before the law.

The result is that different interpreters, judicial and otherwise, handle such expressions quite differently. Many appeal to the phrase "Laws of Nature" in the first sentence of the Declaration. The second sentence provides a definition: human beings are "endowed by their Creator with certain inalienable Rights," including "Life, Liberty and the pursuit of Happiness." Others point out that none of this is preserved in the Constitution, which neither mentions God nor includes such general "rights." Moreover, persuaded by the arguments of Leff, cited above, they think there is no place for a "natural law" reading of the Constitution. But perhaps most argue in an *ad hoc* fashion, well illustrated in a brief essay by Michael Kinsley. Kinsley is

---

51. A work that I have not seen—at this time of writing it is not yet published—but that promises evenhanded evaluation of the cases critical to religious liberty, is Terry Eastland, ed., *Religious Liberty in the Supreme Court: The Cases That Define the Debate over Church and State* (Grand Rapids: Eerdmans, 1995).

quite sure that Justice Thomas could abuse his belief in "natural law," yet at the same time he argues:

> All this is not to say that natural-law concepts have no role to play in constitutional interpretation. Many people, for example, find it hard to understand why freedom of speech must be extended to Nazis and others who do not believe in free speech themselves and would deny it to others if they could. The answer is that the Bill of Rights is based on the theory of natural law, not on the alternative theory of a social contract. You are entitled to these rights simply becuase you are a human being, not because you have agreed, literally or metaphorically, to honor them.[52]

Quite apart from the arguments advanced by Leff and Johnson, summarized above, Kinsley's argument, in its context, basically means that he supports natural law when it aligns with things he believes in, and rejects it when it doesn't. At the end of the day, one cannot quite rid oneself of the suspicion he wants to be a hermeneutical godlet.

But barring detailed exposition of the relevant phrases within the Declaration and the Constitution themselves, one must at least acknowledge that they are not transparent.

(4) Above all, judges are not going to exercise hermeneutical self-restraint for the simple reason that most of them are imbued with the same postmodernism that percolates through the rest of society. Of course, the degree of the infection, and even the extent to which a particular judge recognizes his or her own symptoms, varies from case to case. But we cannot reasonably suppose that the judiciary will be insulated from the most powerful intellectual movement in the Western world since the Renaissance.

Consider, for example, a recent book by University of Chicago law professor Cass Sunstein, who has been suggested as a possible candidate for the Supreme Court. His brilliance is widely acclaimed. In his recent book, Sunstein argues that, analogous to FDR's "New Deal," we need a "new deal" in First Amendment theory. His starting point, like FDR's, is that the current distribution of power and wealth is not guaranteed by the Constitution.[53] As one of Sunstein's reviewers puts it:

> Private parties, he argues, ought to understand that they maintain and use their wealth at the sufferance of the government, while their so-called property rights, also governmentally created, ought to be subject to adjustment in the interests of promoting greater political equality and political discourse. Of course, you might have some trouble with these notions if you believe (*as did many, if not all, of the founders*) that the right to property is a

---

52. "Judges, Democracy and Natural Law," *Time* 138/6 (August 12, 1991): 68.
53. *Democracy and the Limits of Free Speech* (New York: Free Press, 1993).

principle that precedes the formation of governments, which are formed to protect—not to redistribute—property.[54]

So we have arrived at a point where necessity is made a virtue: if we cannot tie ourselves to the framers' original intent (Sunstein insists we cannot), then creative reinterpretations are wide open, by which various perspectives can be "retrieved" from the Constitution even at the expense of what the Constitution says on the surface. We must deconstruct the Constitution while still appealing to its authority. The future becomes very bleak indeed.

Granted the accuracy of these observations and inferences—that changes in the culture ensure that few in the judiciary feel any obligation to any transcendent authority; that we live in an age when the unelected branch of government wields extraordinary power; that it is highly unlikely that judges will any time soon exercise much self-restraint in their reinterpretation of the Constitution—what stance should Christians adopt?

D. Education

Few would dispute the proposition that American educational standards are still declining. The same is true in many Western countries, though for reasons of focus I shall direct primary attention here. The addition of more and more money has not turned the tide. Educational fads have used our children as guinea pigs. SAT and GRE scores, with a few exceptional blips, continue to decline. In the name of freedom and tolerance, we have drifted toward a bland secularization of the system. Ethics, morals, and civics have often been judged much less important than sex education. Criticism is so widespread that it is not coming from only one segment of the political and social spectra. On the right, it would be hard to imagine a more incisive treatment than that of Thomas Sowell.[55] From a very different vantage point, Pearce wants education that will enhance the next stage of human evolution, and from that vantage point insists that too much television impedes vital neurological development, that daycare creates a dangerous sense of alienation from the surrounding world, that synthetic hormones foster premature sexual development, and so forth.[56]

I make no pretension here of surveying this complex field. My concern is merely to suggest some of the ways in which empirical pluralism and

---

54. Stephen B. Presser, in *Chicago Tribune* (October 31, 1993), section 14, p. 5 (emphasis mine).

55. *Inside American Education: The Decline, the Deception, the Dogmas* (New York: Free Press, 1993).

56. Joseph Chilton Pearce, *Evolution's End: Claiming the Potential of Our Intelligence* (San Francisco: Harper San Francisco, 1992).

390 ♦ The Gagging of God

philosophical pluralism have contributed to the situation. Four observations will have to suffice.

First, rising empirical pluralism has been one of the factors that have brought about changes in the classroom, changes sometimes enforced by the courts. Let us frankly admit that the challenges on this issue faced by the Supreme Court today are extraordinarily complex. When Muslim, Buddhist, Jewish, Orthodox, Roman Catholic, liberal Protestant, evangelical, agnostic, Satanist, and atheistic children all meet together in the same classroom, it seems slightly simplistic to appeal to the intentions of the Founding Fathers to support judicial restraint. I do not want my children inculcated with the doctrines of the Qur'an; I understand why Muslim parents may not want their children taught Christian doctrines. Theoretical solutions, such as telling children about many religions and about atheism, but advocating no position, are largely impractical wherever there are parents in the wings willing to sue at the slightest hint that their "side" has been unfairly represented. And how does one divide the time alloted to each religion? Should the division reflect the percentage of students in the class from each group? Would that not mean that curriculum would vary not only from school to school but even from year to year, owing to changing demographics? Should the Christian heritage receive extra attention because it has been so influential in the history of the nation? Does this mean that, say, Islam is proportionately slighted, and that therefore children from that heritage are in danger of losing their chief point of cultural self-identification?

Second, owing in part to the dilemma just outlined, and in part to philosophical pluralism and an assumed postmodern outlook, another course has frequently been followed, that is more troubling yet. Many schools say nothing whatever about religion, or only extraordinarily bland and misleading things. Such silence is a totally irresponsible approach to the teaching of history, for historically religion has had a determinative role at many turning points in the nation's history. The contribution that postmodernism plays in this is straightforward. Since all writing of history is interpretation, and all interpretation is subjective, there is less effort to present the actual "facts" of the case (after all, there are no "brute" facts, no uninterpreted facts). It is more important, then, to present what seems socially useful, what will insulate a school from the threat of lawsuits, what is in line with the dominant forces of the contemporary culture and thus with what is "politically correct."

The implications are massive. Marsden and others have ably documented the rise of secularizing forces in the universities.[57] The same pressures abound

---

57. George M. Marsden and Bradley J. Longfield, eds., *The Secularization of the Academy* (New York: Oxford Univ. Press, 1992); George M. Marsden, *The Soul of the American University: From Protestant Establishment to Established Nonbelief* (New York: Oxford Univ. Press, 1994).

in many elementary and secondary schools, although the extent of the process varies greatly around the country. The result is that although philosophical pluralism is commonly presupposed, students are not taught in a manner that enhances the empirical pluralism in which we live, but in a manner which squeezes religious distinctions to the periphery in favor of the primary importance of other things: either triumphant secularism, or narcissistic forms of religion where the entire aim of the exercise is to do your own thing. In this sense, as Olneck puts it, "[P]luralism, properly defined, does not characterize the practices, organization, or ideology of the American public schools, nor is it likely to in the foreseeable future."[58] There is a bland sameness to what is presented, a lowest-common-denominator approach that is not really tolerance, since nothing is presented that needs to be tolerated. Everything that could conceivably be offensive, and therefore might *need* to be tolerated and thus serve as a test case for tolerance, is edited out.[59]

Are there any alternative ways forward? Olneck has no doubt. He goes on:

> [A]uthentic pluralism must in some fashion recognize the identities and claims of groups *as groups*, must facilitate or at least symbolically represent and legitimate the collective institutional and cultural lives of groups, and must enhance the salience of group membership as a basis for participation in society, though not necessarily as a basis for distributive outcomes or life chances. Authentic pluralism in schooling also requires, to the extent that valued cultural differences among groups are real, that pedagogy, curricular form and content, and modes of assessment be congruent with and preserve these differences, so long as the groups in question wish this to be so.[60]

Olneck's solution reflects what is in many circles wonderfully politically correct. Away with the monopoly of Eurocentric, male-dominated culture. "Authentic pluralism" demands curricular and other pedagogical changes that please the groups targeted, i.e., the changes must be kept in place "so long as the groups in question wish this to be so." This seems to be the rising approach in the areas of literature and history. On paper, it is not entirely bad. But because there are only so many hours available for each course, whenever new content is added something else must be taken out. At what

---

58. Michael R. Olneck, "Is Pluralism Possible in American Public Education?" in *The Challenge of Pluralism: Education, Politics, and Values*, ed. F. Clark Power and Daniel K. Lapsley (Notre Dame: Univ. of Notre Dame Press, 1992), 252.

59. From this perspective, some essays extolling tolerance as a liberal virtue seem rather naive: e.g., Roger Cresswell and Peter Hobson, "The Concept of Tolerance and Its Role in a Pluralist Society, with Particular Reference to Religious Education," *Journal of Christian Education* 98 (September 1990): 23–30.

60. Michael R. Olneck, "Is Pluralism Possible in American Public Education?" 252.

point do we veer toward the tribalization of education, and the cantonization of society? Is there any special place to be given to learning what has been the dominant cultural influence in America to this point? Similar questions could be asked in many Western countries.

At time of writing, the National Education Standards and Improvement Council, set up by the Clinton Administration,[61] is due to prescribe what students in grades five through twelve are supposed to know about American history. Not a single one of the thirty-one standards set up mentions the Constitution. Paul Revere is unmentioned; the Gettysburg address is briefly mentioned once. On the other hand, the early feminist Seneca Falls Declaration of Sentiments receives nine notices. Joseph McCarthy is mentioned nineteen times; there is no mention of the Wright brothers, Thomas Edison, Albert Einstein, Robert E. Lee; Harriet Tubman receives six notices. The Ku Klux Klan is mentioned seventeen times; the American Federation of Labor comes up with nine appearances. The role of religion, especially Christianity, in the founding and building of the nation is totally ignored; the grandeur of the court of Mansa Musa (King of Mali in fifteenth-century Africa) is praised, and recommended as a topic for further study.[62] Such standards are linked in the minds of many with "outcome-based-education" (OBE). If the "outcomes" were well balanced and not less than thoroughly cognitive (though hopefully more than cognitive), there would be few objections. But OBE has become a lightening-rod issue precisely because in the hands of many it explicitly minimizes cognitive tests and competency skills, while focusing much more attention on attitudes, group conformity, and the like. In other words, granted the postmodernism that grips many educational theorists and the political correctness that shapes their values, this begins to look like one more experiment in social engineering.

The situation is so serious that many pundits are commenting on it (though with no observable change thereby being effected). One of the best of these is the essay by Robert Brustein, which includes this memorable if slightly hyperbolic sentence: "The time is nigh when 8-year-olds will have more knowledge about Native American totem rituals than about the multiplication table and will be better instructed in how to use a condom than in how to apply the rules of grammar."[63]

---

61. "At time of writing" refers to the fact that, with the dawning of a Republican Congress in January 1993, there may be some changes instituted in this Council or in the standards it erects.

62. The synopsis is conveniently chronicled in the *Religion & Society Report* 12/1 (January 1995): 3, which concludes its report by observing, "One of the incidental problems created by this sort of thing is that it is becoming virtually impossible to write satire. When reality becomes this bizarre, it can no longer be parodied."

63. "What Price Correctness?" first published in *Partisan Review* and often reprinted. I found it in the *Chicago Tribune Magazine* (January 16, 1994), section 10, pp. 10–14.

In the religious arena, instead of going for highly diverse coverage of the religious options offered in American culture, education specialists treat religion (and especially Christianity) as if it never played a significant part in American life. If Christianity exists today, it is primarily something to be dismissed or ridiculed. Study after study has validated this point. In 1986, Paul Vitz pointed out that in social studies texts for grades 1 to 4, twenty-five of the forty books examined have no reference in either word or image to any American religious activity whatsoever. Of the remaining fifteen books that preserve some religious reference, seven mention religion only in the past, whether Spanish mission life or Puritan influence. Not one of these textbooks mentions that Christianity is a powerful influence, numerically speaking, in the land today. In twenty-two basal readers for grades 3 to 6, there is not one story in which a central motif or important motivation reflects or derives from Judaism or Christianity. Many stories treat animals; others touch on archaeology, fossils, even magic; there is occasional occult reference, and the odd story that refers to the religion of American Indians. In the essay on Martin Luther King, Jr., there is no mention as to how Christian ideas or the life of Jesus influenced him. In ten high school history texts containing over 450 events considered important, only three referred to religion: (1) the landing of the Pilgrims in 1620; (2) the passage of the Toleration Act in 1649; (3) the settling of the Mormons at Salt Lake in 1847.[64]

But suppose, for argument's sake, that changes could be effected such that religion, and especially Christianity (for it is still the dominant religious heritage), would henceforth get a fair shake. Suppose that various cultures and racial heritages received proper emphasis, without despising or depreciating the Western cultural heritage.[65] In the present climate, I cannot imagine how such changes could be brought about; but if they could, would they be adequate? Should they satisfy us?

The fact of the matter is that even if such curricular matters were nicely sorted out—an eventuality that would prove the age of miracles is not yet over—they could be taught from quite different perspectives. Broadly speaking, we might say that they could be taught from (1) a naturalistic/atheistic perspective (whether or not the teachers were atheists, they might teach from so naturalistic a vantage point that they might as well be atheists); (2) a pantheistic perspective, which would keep Hindus and New Agers happy; (3) a theistic perspective. But if the latter, one could imagine a Jewish slant, a

---

64. Paul Vitz, *Censorship: Evidence of Bias in Our Children's Textbooks* (Ann Arbor: Servant, 1986).

65. Presumably every student, in addition to wide exposure to a variety of "ethnic" cultures and histories, would have to master E. D. Hirsch, Jr., *Cultural Literacy: What Every American Needs to Know* (Boston: Houghton Mifflin, 1987), or some other such work!

Christian slant, or a Muslim slant. Thus even if we conjure up in our mind's eye this marvelous curricular reform—and doubtless at least *some* of it is achievable by political action—the most serious question is not one of curriculum but of personnel: Who will be teaching this material, and from what vantage point?[66] I suppose a few especially capable teachers might manage the kind of professed neutrality that would make it very difficult for students to guess the teacher's own stance. But would that satisfy, say, devout Muslim parents? Or devout Christian parents?

Third, the revolution in our classrooms brought about in part by philosophical pluralism and its attendant devils is most poignantly reflected in the sacrifice of ethics. I do not mean that a course called "ethics" used to be on the high school curriculum, and now it is gone. Rather, it used to be that home, school, church, the society at large, still resting, unwittingly, on Judeo-Christian assumptions, tended to reinforce one another in a wide array of ethical issues. Nowadays they often pull apart, or worse, in some instances none of them does anything very positive.

The larger questions concerning ethics in our society will be briefly considered below. At the moment my focus is on the manner in which the subject is or is not taught. Ethics has largely been replaced by "values clarification" or the like. Teachers—or, better, "facilitators," since in this subject there is very little content to teach—encourage students to discover and clarify their own values by asking questions. There are at least four fundamental problems with this approach. First, decreasing numbers of students have been given any sort of grounding at home or church. This pursuit of their "own" values tends therefore to be nothing more than an opportunity to go along with the drift of the age, the very thing most of them are doing anyway with respect to clothes, music, topics of conversation, and so forth. Second, there is no attempt to help students think through the roots or grounds or principles of values. The facilitators tend to ask, "What would you do if ... (e.g., you were in a lifeboat with four people and there were only enough food for two to survive)?"[67] Apart from the fact that this sort of question is far removed from the experience of most young people, it might stimulate useful discussion *if the grounds of the choices were made clear.* If the basis is nothing more than pragmatics or personal preference, it is unsurprising that character is not built up. Third, questions of entirely different orders of significance are treated with the same tone, the same groundless probing of what students would "feel comfortable" doing. Whether it is ever right to

---

66. Though it is somewhat dated, it is still worth reading Gordon H. Clark, *Historiography: Secular and Religious* (Nutley: Craig Press, 1971).

67. See especially Peter Kreeft, *Back to Virtue* (San Francisco: Ignatius Press, 1992), chap. 1.

cheat on an exam, and whether it is right to have an abortion, are presented as if they belong to the same order of significance.[68] And fourth, from a Christian point of view, this sort of approach is a flagrant denial of human sinfulness, which assumes that vice has to be combated. Virtue will not be achieved merely by encouraging people to clarify their "own" values, for we all, like sheep, go astray; we have turned to our "own" way—and that is almost a definition of sin. As a friend of mine puts it, we are all highly original sinners.

On this front, then, the schools have fared miserably. A small number of influential voices are making this clear. One thinks of Kilpatrick's *Why Johnny Can't Tell Right from Wrong*,[69] or of Bennett's *Book of Virtues*,[70] both of which are circulating widely. But while applauding these books, and without wanting to sound too negative, I confess I am not sanguine about what they will achieve, and this for four reasons:

(1) The most difficult challenge is the question of foundations. The Rutherford Institute and other groups of Christian lawyers have been telling us how much we are still legally allowed to do in the schools, if we have the will. Essays and books are being written on how to teach virtues without facing a constitutional challenge. All of this is better than nothing. *But it does not address the challenge of foundations.*

For example, Dick lays out "various streams of thought" in regard to religious and moral education, i.e., various ways to construe the task:

> 1) teaching of religion which attempts to impose Judaeo-Christian values on *everyone*, whether or not they so desire; 2) teaching *about* religion which acknowledges religion in an academic sense but does not acknowledge man's spiritual needs; 3) non-religious morals instructions, which, like the first alternative, attempts to inculcate a certain set of morals without careful scrutiny and without choice; 4) moral education with its relativistic emphasis on process and its possibility of leaving children wandering in a vacuum; 5) an approach, not widely used but acceptable to people of various faiths, which utilizes a knowledge of moral development, which insists on academic teaching *about* religion and which acknowledges man's spirituality. This

---

68. Cf. Christina Hoff Sommers, "Teaching the Virtues," *Imprimus* 20/11 (November 1991): 3: "The teacher asks the students, 'How do you feel about homemade birthday presents? Do you like wall-to-wall carpeting? What is you favorite color? Which flavor of ice cream do you prefer? How do you feel about hit-and-run drivers? What are your feelings on the abortion question?'"

69. William K. Kilpatrick, *Why Johnny Can't Tell Right from Wrong: Moral Illiteracy and the Case for Character Education* (New York: Simon & Schuster, 1992).

70. William J. Bennett, ed., *A Book of Virtues: A Treasury of Great Moral Stories* (New York: Simon & Schuster, 1993).

approach does not attempt to indoctrinate. It calls for questioning, analysis and decision-making.[71]

The first option will certainly face a constitutional challenge; the third might, but in any case irate parents will in many school districts make this option impossible to pursue. The second is a gain in curriculum, but probably by itself will affect morals very little. The fourth is common, and worse than ineffective: it is positively corrosive. Dick opts for the fifth option. But it is hard to see how in reality it is anything other than a combination of the second and the fourth options, since no foundation is laid. The assumptions about human nature are so naively naturalistic that one marvels at the optimism.

(2) In particular, the optimism seems unwarranted because there is little support from the home. In many parts of the country, if you call together any group of public elementary school teachers who are Christians, you will find them troubled by what children in grades 4 and 5, or even 2 and 3, are watching on television or in cinemas. Most of them have seen R-rated movies, usually with their parents; some have seen X-rated films, usually as videos, at home. Many of the same parents, who are terribly concerned that schools do not manipulate their children in the moral arena and are pulling for their children to make good grades, have simply not thought through these incongruities. One does not generate responsible citizens with values-clarification at school; equally, one does not generate responsible citizens by extolling morally unfounded virtues at school, while having them flouted in the home. If greed, cheating on taxes, broken marriages, self-centeredness, and promiscuity are not opposed at home and displaced by the corresponding and opposite virtues of generosity, integrity, fidelity, self-denial, and purity, institutional changes will matter fairly little.

(3) The schemes of Kilpatrick and Bennett are worth pursuing, and certainly they produced some fruit in the past. Kilpatrick in particular contrasts what is taught in school today with what was taught in the past. What he and Bennett do not adequately face, I fear, is the fact that when stories of virtue were taught in the past, even when they were not overtly Christian, they were read in an atmosphere where a Judeo-Christian worldview predominated. The morals of the stories were unthinkingly grafted into that stalk. But in most of the country, as we have seen, that stalk has been hacked away until it is little more than a stump, sometimes a buried stump. One should not oppose what Kilpatrick and Bennett are calling for; may God speed their efforts. But one should not be so naive as to think that what they are offering is "the solution."

71. Judith Dick, "The Morals Maze: Religious and Moral Education in the Public School System," *Direction* 12 (1983): 38.

(4) At the end of the day, everything comes back to the teacher in the classroom. And where are such teachers formed? Where do they gain their values?

I have known many fine teachers; I am profoundly grateful how many gifted teachers my children have been exposed to, within the public system. Endless lashing of teachers, many of whom serve in difficult situations with little support from the home, is counterproductive. But if the intellectual movements collectively labeled postmodernity enjoy anything like the power I think they do, there is little reason to suppose that the rising generation of teachers will be immune to them. The only ones who will not be swept along by the tide will be those with some other anchor, some other perspective, some other worldview, that enables them to buck the tide.

Fourth, arguably the growth of government, especially federal government, in the arena of education has itself had a stifling effect on education. When quotas become more important than quality, when fiscal largesse fosters the extraordinary managerial incompetence one finds in many educational establishments (budgets go up while the percentage of budgets devoted to teachers' salaries goes down), when "race-norming" (test scores are "adjusted" according to race)[72] is encouraged, when financial aid is tied to certain forms of political correctness, one recognizes that the impact of pluralism on the educational system has come about not only by direct means, but also indirectly through categories already discussed: government, visions of religious freedom, the law and the judiciary.[73]

Out of such concerns as these, then, Christians are among the leaders of those scrambling to find solutions. Home schooling? Christian schools? But then are we not obligated to sanction the rising press for Muslim schools? A voucher system? Reforming the public system, either by state or local action? What shall we do?

E. Economics

Branches of economics have so proliferated that even expert economists have difficulty mastering more than a few of them. I do not claim special competence in the area, and certainly neither profundity nor originality. But one of the problems economists face is that their subject matter is tied not only

---

72. Minority groups should be outraged at this scandalous and racist practice, which on the long haul results not only in "dumbing down" the entire system, but in loss of self-respect among the minorities.

73. Perhaps the person who has done the most to blow the whistle in these areas is George Roche, *The Fall of the Ivory Tower: Government Funding, Corruption, and the Bankrupting of American Higher Education* (Washington: Regnery Gateway, 1994).

to "things" like consumables and gold; and to indexes like mortgage rates, tax rates, and stock markets; and to historical patterns that can be analyzed, such as recessions, bull markets, and social welfare; but to *people*. The former categories are complex enough;[74] but people are more complex yet. Not only are they frequently unpredictable, but our understanding of their nature, their significance, their eternal destiny, their habits, their sins, their joy, their generosity, their social behavior and much more clearly affects our estimate of the *significance* of what they do. To put the matter another way, standard economics textbooks often focus on "positive" economics, i.e., what "is" rather than what "ought to be." As Ian Smith puts it:

> This dichotomy is based on the positivist view that facts per se are in principle independent of values; there is a "logical gulf" between descriptive and evaluative sentences. Hence the result that Bible study is irrelevant for understanding modern economic behavior.
>
> However, if it can be demonstrated that ethical considerations pervade economic analysis, then there is clearly scope for biblical values to shape economic descriptions. Indeed, there is now wide acknowledgement that at least in the humanities and social sciences the sharp positive-normative distinction is fallacious. In practice many economists recognize the ubiquitous intrusion of value considerations. It is difficult, for example, to remain dispassionate when advising on public policy. Also, language is replete with implicit values. While Lionel Robbins protests that surely "equilibrium is just equilibrium," as Joan Robinson points out, "disequilibrium sounds uncomfortable, goods sound good, exploitation wicked, and sub-normal profits rather sad." Furthermore, description may often be motivated by normative considerations. Poverty, for example, might be studied in order to contribute to its alleviation.[75]

So in this brief section I am not directly interested in the broad field of economics *per se*, nor in traditional disputes about whether Christians should support the economic "right" or the economic "left,"[76] but to reflect a little,

---

74. One of the simplest ways for economic novices to glimpse at least elements of the complexities, without reading several economics textbooks, is to read the justly famous essay by Leonard E. Read, "I, Pencil," first published in 1958 and reprinted numerous times, most recently in *Imprimis* 21/6 (June 1992): 1–3.

75. Ian Smith, "God and Economics," in Carson and Woodbridge, *God and Culture*, 168–69.

76. Although it is true that during the last half-century evangelicals in the Western world have more often than not been tied to the economic "right" than to the economic "left," their history and the issues are quite complex. In the wake of the Great Awakening, evangelical Methodists tended toward the left and reform, while evangelical Anglicans and Presbyterians tended toward the right. At the end of the last century and the beginning of this one, modernism in theology generated forms of faith that denied the creeds while identifying

from a Christian vantage, on the impact of pluralism and its correlatives on economic factors. Three observations will suffice.

First, with the widespread cultural diminution of transcendent values, and, more generally, of values other than those in the economic arena, several ugly things take place. One form or another of greed becomes an unacknowledged virtue. A substantial component of governmental self-justification is in terms of economic performance—how the economy is faring, and what the government is "doing" with its grotesque budget. The dominance of economics stripped of transcendent or moral values virtually ensures terrible evils at both ends, i.e., in the government and among the people.

Among the people, poll after poll shows a clear majority voting for lower taxes and increased benefits, or, at very least, no diminution of benefits to the particular group that is voting. The simplest arithmetic shows this cannot go on. In other words, the people demand deficits, and elected officials, eager above all to maintain their jobs, happily acquiesce. Because we have lost certain cultural values—self-reliance, minimal debt, financial integrity all the way from personal finances to national finances—it is difficult to see how this can easily be reversed. I am not saying that only a Christian outlook would prevent it. The cultures of Japan and Germany, arising from the ashes of the war and, in the case of Germany, remembering the desperate inflation of the Weimar Republic, produced a generation that had zero tolerance for extended debt. But here, the weakening of moral values, the rising empirical pluralism that has set group against group, the destruction of many mediating structures in our society, the individualism that in this arena approves restraint as a principle "but not for me," combine to nurture a culture of greed.

In the government, money is not only what sustains the bureaucracy but what lubricates the engines of power. Well-documented studies list the billions and billions of wasted dollars (often ideologically directed),[77] and the encrusted rules can go so far beyond what makes life safer and fairer that

---

Christianity with social concern. It is not surprising that evangelicals responded by stressing credal truths and distancing themselves from social concern as the *identifying* characteristic of Christianity. Moreover, with Marxism tying atheism to state control, many Christians linked theism and economic freedom. Similarly, suspicions of mega-government when that government enforces changes in schools and other institutions that many Christians want to preserve as they were, inevitably prompts many Christians toward the economic "right." But the fact of the matter is that Christians at their best have always been at the forefront of "hands on" compassion and social concern. Current disputes among them have more to do with the "how to" question, than with the question as to whether it is imperative for us to help the poor. See especially Craig M. Gay, *With Liberty and Justice for Whom? The Recent Evangelical Debate over Capitalism* (Grand Rapids: Eerdmans, 1991).

77. See James T. Bennett and Thomas J. DiLorenzo, *Destroying Democracy* (Washington: Cato Institute, 1985).

businesses now spend about five billion worker-hours per year in government paperwork demands. The lowest estimate I have seen for the cost of compliance to government regulations is that it doubled between the late 1970s and the late 1980s.[78] Did we double our security during that time?

My suspicion is that the moral resolve needed is simply not there, in the streets or in Congress. I hope I am wrong.

Second, only belatedly are we coming to recognize that economics, far from being an independent discipline, is intimately tied, whether we acknowledge it or not, to the broadest questions of worldview.[79] Even if we are merely trying to manipulate the "is" components while refusing to ask the "ought" questions, we are betraying what our worldview is. We can be grateful, then, for a little book that tries to explain the rudiments of economic thought, but within a broadly Christian framework,[80] and for a perceptive historical analysis that ties economic theory in the West, across the centuries, to the prevailing worldview.[81] The last two chapters of this historical analysis study what it means for us to enter "a world of postmodern economics." Of the many insights offered, I mention only two. Increasingly, postmodern economic theorists recognize that in real life government does not work by moving from rational plans to systematic implementation. In the real world, there are incremental adjustments, and these are worked out in line with the worldview of the administrators themselves. It cannot be otherwise. But if Christian values are ruthlessly eliminated from the deposit of administrators' values, then the government becomes massively unrepresentative for all believers. This would scarcely matter if the government were small and touched few facets of its citizens' lives; it is an inescapable reality for citizens who quite literally cannot escape government tentacles in almost all that they do. At the extreme level, some theorists now argue that postmodernism justifies the view that there are *many* plausible economic theories, and it is foolish and even arrogant to justify only one of them. Won't this make for interesting policy-formation?

---

78. Cf. Richard W. Duesenberg, "Economic Liberties and the Law," *Imprimus* 23/4 (April 1994): 1–4.

79. On the piecemeal nature of a great deal of Western thought, cf. Joseph Mitsuo Katagawa, *The Christian Tradition: Beyond Its European Captivity* (Philadelphia: Trinity Press International, 1992), 235: "One of the predicaments for Christianity and all other religions alike in our time is the ambiguity of the definition of religion that is based on the provincial Western convention of dividing human experience into a series of semiautonomous pigeonholes (e.g., religion, aesthetics, ethics, law, culture, society, politics, economics)."

80. John A. Sparks, ed., *Reader on Economics and Religion* (Grove City: Public Policy Education Fund, 1994).

81. Robert H. Nelson, *Reaching for Heaven: The Theological Meaning of Economics* (Lanham: Rowman & Littlefield, 1991).

On a narrower front, Olasky has shown that welfare that is narrowly economic in its analysis and provisions but that is stripped of other ideas with which social concern, both private and public, was once related, is simply bound to fail. The seven other ideas he lists are: affiliation, bonding, categorization, discernment, employment, freedom, and belief in God.[82] One or two of these are tentatively being resurrected in some states (e.g., insisting that those on welfare who are healthy be employed); the rest are largely ignored.

Third, it is far from certain that economic vigor can be long sustained simply by making it god. Some broader consuming vision may well suffice; economic vigor itself will not.

The generation brought up during the Great Depression and the Second World War, still in measure steeped in the much-maligned Protestant work ethic, resolved to work hard and provide a more secure heritage for their children. And, in measure, they did. But the children, for whom the Depression and the War belonged to the relics of history, had nothing to live for but more "progress." There was no grand vision, no taste of genuine want, and not much of the Protestant work ethic either.[83] Soon the war in Vietnam became one of the central "causes" of that generation, but scarcely one that incited hard work, integrity in relationships, frugality, self-denial, and preparation for the next generation. That '60s generation, the baby boomers, have now gone mainstream—but with a selfishness and consumerism that outstrips anything their parents displayed. There is no larger vision.

Contrast a genuine Christian vision that lives life with integrity now because this life is never seen as more than the portal to the life to come, including perfect judgment from our Maker. At its best, such a stance, far from breeding withdrawal from the world, fosters industry, honest work for honest pay, frugality, generosity, provision for one's children, honesty in personal relationships and in business relationships, the rule of law, a despising of greed. A "Protestant work ethic" of such a character I am happy to live with. Of course, a couple of generations later, when such a Christian vision has eroded, people may equate prosperity with God's blessing, and with despicable religious cant protest that they are preparing for eternity when in their heart of hearts they are merely preparing for retirement. But a generation or two after that their children will expose their empty fatuousness. In any case, what has been lost is a genuinely Christian vision.

---

82. Marvin Olasky, *The Tragedy of American Compassion* (Wheaton: Crossway Books, 1992). One might also usefully consult Marvin Olasky, Herbert Schlossberg, Pierre Berthoud, and Clark H. Pinnock, *Freedom, Justice, and Hope: Toward a Strategy for the Poor and Oppressed* (Westchester: Crossway Books, 1988).

83. Cf. Chuck Colson and Jack Eckerd, *Why America Doesn't Work* (Dallas: Word Books, 1991).

This is not to say that such a vision will *ensure* prosperity. When it is a minority vision it may ensure nothing more than persecution. In any case, other unifying visions may bring about prosperity as well, as we have seen. From the perspective of the Bible, prosperity is never the ultimate goal, so that is scarcely troubling. What is troubling is a measuring stick in which the only scale is measured in terms of financial units.

So what public stance should Christians adopt?

F. Ethics and Morals

It has recently been reported in a number of organs that in 1944 New York City had 150,000 more inhabitants than it does today (1994), fifty years later. Fifty years ago, 97 percent of all children were born into two-parent families; today, that is true of only 50 percent. In 1944, forty people died of gunshot wounds; today, the same figure is reached every ten days. Fifty years ago, one hundred babies were sent to orphanages; today, thousands of babies are abandoned, some merely dropped into trash cans.

Such statistics, shocking as they are, are but the proverbial tip of the iceberg. Today, the cold war is over, the economy is in reasonably good shape,[84] inflation is under control, the unemployment rate is at an acceptable level and still declining—and America is undergoing profound malaise. The reason is partly fear: fear of what drugs are doing, fear of crime, fear of delining standards, fear of the future. At heart, there is a moral vacuum, a restlessness that betrays the loss of vision. The outcome is documented in book after book.[85]

Hans Küng has put his finger on at least one of the fundamental problems:

For our grandparents, religion—Christianity—was still a matter of personal conviction. For our parents it remained at least a matter of tradition and good manners. For their emancipated sons and daughters, however, it is becoming increasingly a matter of the past that is no longer binding—*passé et dépassé*, passed away and obsolete. Moreover, there are parents today who observe with perplexity that morality has vanished together with religion, as Nietzsche predicted. For, as is becoming increasingly clear, it is not so easy to justify ethics purely rationally, by reason alone, as Sigmund Freud and others wanted to do; we cannot explain why freedom under any circumstances is supposed to be better than oppression, justice better than avarice, nonviolence better than violence, love better than hate, peace bet-

---

84. Though it should be noted that the median income is declining, even as average household income has increased—for obvious reasons.

85. See not least Cal Thomas, *The Death of Ethics in America* (Waco: Word Books, 1988).

ter than war. Or more brutally: why, if it is to our advantage or contributes to our personal happiness, we may not lie, steal, commit adultery, or murder; or even why we should simply be "fair."[86]

Well said! But the issues are still more complex. In a highly pluralistic society (both empirically and philosophically) we must steadfastly reject "the philosophically and sociologically impossible notion that in a pluralistic society the state can and should be neutral on all matters of morality about which there is disagreement among the people, lest the values of some be imposed on others. This notion, a half-truth at best, leads to the establishment of the beliefs of the most secularized, materialistic, and hedonistic elements of the population as normative,"[87] as Canavan says. Canavan's point is that neutrality simply does not exist. He cites the case of *Belmont v. Belmont*. A divorced and remarried father applied to the New Jersey Superior Court for custody of his children on the ground that his former wife, who held custody of them, was living in a lesbian relationship that he judged deleterious to the well-being of the children. The court "found him to be suitable as a custodian in all respects," but denied his application anyway. It ruled that "the mother is not to be denied custody merely because of her sexual orientation. Her sexual preference and her living arrangement with her lover are only two of the many factors to be examined in determining the best interests of the children." As Canavan observes:

> In so ruling, the court committed the State of New Jersey to the proposition that a homosexual union is, or can be, as acceptable a one in which to raise children as is a heterosexual one dignified by matrimony. This is something more than a decision to leave sexual preferences up to individuals. It is a public stand in regard to the institution of the family.
>
> The point is that there is inescapably a public morality—a good one or a bad one—in the sense of some set or other of basic norms, in the light of which the public makes policy decisions. . . . [This is not] the advent of a truly neutral state but the replacement of one view of man, and the ethic and the legal norms based on it, by another view.[88]

I offer two final observations.

---

86. Hans Küng, "To What Can We Still Cling?" in *Humanizing America's Iconic Book*, ed. G. M. Tucker and D. A. Knight (Chicago: Scholars Press, 1982), 40.

87. Francis Canavan, "Pluralism and the Limits of Neutrality," in *Whose Values? The Battle for Morality in Pluralistic America*, ed. Carl Horn (Ann Arbor: Servant, 1985), 160.

88. Ibid., 162–63. Cf. also the useful essay by Brenda Almond, "New Occasions Teach New Duties? 3. Seven Moral Myths," *Expository Times* 105 (1994): 164–67. This particular myth she calls "the myth of neutrality." This point is no less true regarding homosexuality than with a number of other issues: see George Grant and Mark A. Horne, *Legislating Immorality* (Chicago: Moody Press, 1993).

First, if under the impact of pluralism public morality is declining, the continued drift toward privatized religion is a fertile soil in which to water the rapidly multiplying and universally encroaching roots of self-esteem. A few see the danger,[89] but not many. The drive to sort out life's problems and my happiness along the axis of self-esteem banishes truth questions, makes feeling good about yourself more important than having a clear conscience, insists that your opinion of yourself is more important than God's opinion, and fails to deal with objective guilt. In the Scriptures, a right knowledge of yourself is contingent on having in the first place a right knowledge of God.

Second, one particular field of ethics, bioethics, is mushrooming on every hand, owing in large measure to the advancing medical and especially genetic technology.[90] But bioethics does not have a hope of gaining decisions beyond the pragmatic unless there is established a firm basis in who and what human beings are in God's universe. Euthanasia, abortion, cloning, genetic engineering, allocation of resources—none of these can possibly escape relegation to the domain of private opinion unless convincing arguments are advanced that sweep across wide numbers of people.

What stance, then, should Christians adopt? What kind of mission should we pursue?

---

89. E.g., Paul C. Vitz, *Psychology as Religion: The Cult of Self-Worship*, 2d ed. (Grand Rapids: Eerdmans, 1994). Joanna and Alister McGrath, in their book *The Dilemma of Self-Esteem: The Cross and Christian Confidence* (Wheaton: Crossway Books, 1992) try to domesticate the category of self-esteem to Christian priorities and make some good points, but they are too indebted to secular outlooks to perceive where they are getting duped by the category itself. See the important review by David Powlison in *Westminster Theological Journal* 55 (1993): 368–71.

90. For useful discussion, see John F. Kilner, *Life on the Line: Ethics, Aging, Ending Patients' Lives and Allocating Vital Resources* (Grand Rapids: Eerdmans, 1992); Allen Verhey and Stephen Lammers, *Theological Voices in Medical Ethics* (Grand Rapids: Eerdmans, 1993); Nigel M. de S. Cameron, "Bioethics and the Challenge of the Post-Consensus Society," *Ethics and Medicine* 11/1 (1995): 1–7.

Chapter 10

THE VISION THING

President George Bush is alleged to have said that he had difficulty with "the vision thing." Presumably he meant that although he felt competent to handle the day-to-day responsibilities of the highest political office in the United States, and might have some gut feeling for where things should go, he did not think that the ability to articulate and forcefully expound a unified vision of where to go and how to get there was his forte.

For any number of reasons, many Christians similarly feel that they can participate in this little corner or that, but that in the face of the extraordinary complexities cast up by the new pluralisms they find it difficult to articulate a more comprehensive vision. It would be presumptuous to think that one short chapter can do so. But in what follows I hope to (1) clarify some of the issues that Christians must think through on the way toward the articulation of a vision, (2) outline and evaluate some of the practical steps currently being taken, and (3) insist that there is a priority that must not be assigned some lesser value.

A. Preliminary Issues That Must Be Faced

It was H. Richard Niebuhr who developed the dominant typology of possible responses to culture: (1) Christ against culture, (2) the Christ of culture, (3) Christ above culture, (4) Christ and culture in paradox, (5) Christ the transformer of culture.[1] Which paradigm one judges to be the most faithful description of what should prevail has in the past turned as much on the

---

1. *Christ and Culture* (New York: Harper & Row, 1956).

historical situation of the observer as on the observer's exegesis of the Bible. Even in any brief period, more than one of these paradigms may prevail, at least in different groups, and occasionally, in rapid succession, in the same group. Indeed, it is arguable that the balance found in the New Testament on the early Christians' view of the state was achieved, in the providence of God, partly through different perceptions, during the first century, of the Roman Empire. In the Apocalypse, the Empire becomes the very embodiment of evil; Luke/Acts goes out of its way to persuade Roman leaders that the Christian movement is not politically dangerous; Paul can argue that the powers that be are ordained of God. These positions are not as irreconcilable as is sometimes suggested.[2] For example, for all that the Apocalypse sees the Roman Empire in demonic terms, it also insists that God is still finally in control and will triumph in the end, in part through the faithful "witness" (which borders on martyrdom) of God's people. In other words, if the "Christ against culture" theme is abundant in the Apocalypse, "Christ above culture" and "Christ the transformer" of culture are not entirely absent.

Whatever paradigm is emphasized, Christians in the West must relate that paradigm to three realities:

1. Christian thought is eschatological thought.

This means at least three things.

First, the ultimate solution to society's problems is the Parousia; the ultimate Christian hope is the new heaven and the new earth. Christians cannot compromise on this point. However deeply they may feel the need to do what they can to improve society, their frame of reference is not the same as, say, that of the free market purist who holds that Nirvana can be achieved by reducing government input in the marketplace, and letting free market forces drive everything. Nor can it be the same as the naturalistic socialist who not only exercises incredibly naive faith in statist solutions, but whose horizons are limited by the shrouds of mere temporality. But I shall say a little more about this at the end of this chapter.

Second, virtually every form of Christian eschatology preserves some notion of the tension between the "already" and the "not yet." Although that might not be the language used, all sides agree that Christians almost invariably speak, on the one hand, of what God has done in Christ Jesus once for all, and on the other of what he will do at the coming of Jesus in the end.[3] On

---

2. See the suggestive but sometimes overly disjunctive arguments of Klaus Wengst, *Pax Romana and the Peace of Jesus Christ* (Philadelphia: Fortress Press, 1987).

3. Cf. Gabriel Fackre, "Eschatology and Systematics," *Ex Auditu* 6 (1990): 101–17; and especially Geoffrey W. Bromiley, "Eschatology: The Meaning of the End," in *God and Culture*, ed. D. A. Carson and John D. Woodbridge (Grand Rapids: Eerdmans, 1993), 67–84.

the one hand, Christ is already reigning, and Christians rejoice to be under his rule; on the other hand, the whole universe groans in travail waiting for his rule to begin in an uncontested fashion.

However framed, it is this tension that generates not a few of the Christian's conundrums about the state. We cannot expect complete success in our efforts to reform the state; we may on occasion meet dismal failure. So what should we do?

Christians have given very different answers to this question. Some, such as those in the classic Anabaptist mold, thought it best to withdraw from the public arena. They maintained a sharp distinction between the church and the world, recognizing that the church is the only contemporary institution that goes into eternity. They were interested in winning others to Christ; they did not see much point in wasting their energies in trying to reform the world. A few voices still advocate withdrawing from the public arena today (Romans 8; Revelation 19).[4]

Other Christians, while not advocating unqualified withdrawal, have sometimes in fact largely withdrawn from the "culture wars" for a variety of theological or pragmatic reasons. Theologically, some have been so convinced that Jesus is coming back soon that the urgency of world evangelism devoured them. Consequently they devoted relatively little thought or energy to the benefits they might have brought to society at large. They did not even consider the possibility that some of the good influence they might have exerted could in the long run enhance their evangelistic efforts. They tended to think such ventures were distractions from the primary focus. Pragmatically, some Christians have lived in times when the truth seemed to be swamped by some rising heresy. What the times called for, therefore, was a supreme effort along this front, the truth front, leaving little energy for anything else. That accounts, in part, for some of the stances adopted in the first half of this century as evangelicals combated what is now a rather old-fashioned and decaying liberalism.

Many other Christians have recognized the long heritage of Christian social involvement. They remember how the early church not only looked after their own, but fed many outsiders as well, and quietly tried to exert influence for good in the larger society. They remember the ideals of St. Francis of Assisi, the concern for the poor displayed by the Reformers, Wesley's letter-writing campaign to abolish slavery, Whitefield's orphanage. In America, they recall, none less than Jonathan Edwards developed a sophisticated out-

---

4. E.g., Wayne Walden, *God's Government: In Defense of Political Abstinence* (Plymouth: Living Books, 1989).

look as to how Christians should be actively promoting the good of the broader society.[5]

More recently a small but articulate group of Christian writers and thinkers variously labeling their position "theonomy," "Christian recon-struction," or "Dominion theology," have interested themselves in the chal-lenges facing Christians living in an increasingly hostile state, and have advocated lines which, though they have affinities with earlier movements, cut an independent swath across the theological landscape. Their emphases vary, but the following summary would be fair to most of them. God's law, revealed in the Sinai code, continues in force unless some element of it is explicitly suspended or abrogated. Rightly interpreted, that law lays out principles of economics and justice that are binding on people everywhere—indeed, because it is God's law, so it is all moral law, by definition. Some theonomists go further, and argue that at the beginning of her history America was truly a covenant nation. In 1777, for instance, the State of Delaware required of its elected political representatives this oath: "I, [Name], do profess faith in God the Father, and in Jesus Christ His only Son, and in the Holy Ghost, one God, blessed for evermore; and I do acknowledge the holy scriptures of the Old and New Testament to be given by divine inspiration." The reason that this and similar oaths were not incorporated into the Constitution is that Roger Williams's Rhode Island, which allowed much more political "free-dom," became the model for the dominant voices in the constitutional assem-bly. Instead of adopting one or other of the Trinitarian oaths found in several states, the assembly was led by these influential voices—Gary North does not hesitate to speak of their "conspiracy"[6]—to invest final authority in the people: "We the people. . . ." Thus Americans broke their solemn covenant with God. The way back is to repent and reaffirm their covenant, by revising the current Constitution, which is hopelessly compromised. Theonomists are often accused, wrongly, of wanting to impose Old Testament penal codes on contemporary offenders, against the will of the vast majority of the pop-ulace. In fact, what they argue is that by the preaching of the gospel and the adoption of this interpretation of the Bible, the nation should, and one day will, repent and reaffirm the covenant. Old Testament sanctions will then be the will of the people and the law of the land. This view of the future, of course, is tied to a firm conviction of the rightness of postmillennialism.

It would be inappropriate to evaluate each of these stances here. Even to begin to do so would embark us on some of the most complex issues of exe-

5. See especially Gerald McDermott, *One Holy and Happy Society: The Public Theology of Jonathan Edwards* (University Park: Pennsylvania State Univ. Press, 1992).
6. Gary North, *Political Pluralism: The Myth of Pluralism* (Tyler: Institute for Christian Economics, 1989).

gesis, hermeneutics, history, and theology, demanding a quite different book. For instance, if I were to disagree with theonomy, I would have to specify, in some detail, why I think postmillennialism cannot be adequately defended from Scripture (even though I cheerfully acknowledge that some very mature and competent Christians, not least most of the Puritans, have held that view), why theonomist elevation of law and covenant to controlling categories is indefensible, why their understanding of the fulfillment theme is misjudged, and so forth. In the historical arena, I would have to ask if the Trinitarian oath in Delaware and other states is adequate evidence to defend the proposition that America was originally a covenant nation; if, *mirabile dictu*, the Constitution were one day amended to restore biblical covenant language, it could ever be amended back again (like the repeal of Prohibition); or if instead the Old Testament sanctions on heretics would be invoked so that those advocating such a step would have to be executed. In that case I would have to ask if theonomist commitment to democracy at the moment is purely pragmatic (which is certainly a defensible position), and so on.[7]

Doubtless I should identify my own biases. Although I sympathize with the Anabaptist insistence that the church is the "called out" community that must be sharply differentiated from the "world" (in the Johannine sense of "world"), I cannot advocate withdrawal from the political arena. Most Anabaptists (Hutterites and similar communities excluded) think it imperative to do good in the larger society; the sole arena from which they think they should withdraw is the political. In a democratic society, this stance is, in my view, fatally flawed, and may be flawed anyway: the importance of serving as "salt and light" cannot be restricted to private altruism and fenced off from societal structures. In any case, I sympathize deeply with the mainstream

---

7. Since I have used theonomy as an example of the sorts of questions that would have to be addressed in any responsible large-scale treatment of different Christian eschatologies, I should note some of the relevant literature. In defense of Reconstruction, in addition to *Political Polytheism*, already noted, one might usefully read Rousas J. Rushdoony, *The Institutes of Biblical Law* (Nutley: Craig Press, 1973); Gary North, *Dominion and Common Grace: The Biblical Basis of Progress* (Tyler: Institute of Christian Economics, 1987); Gary North and Gary DeMar, *Christian Reconstruction: What It Is, What It Isn't* (Tyler: Institute of Christian Economics, 1991); Greg L. Bahnsen, *No Other Standard: Theonomy and Its Critics* (Tyler: Institute of Christian Economics, 1991); Gary North, ed., *Theonomy: An Informed Response* (Tyler: Institute of Christian Economics, 1991); Kenneth L. Gentry, Jr., *God's Law in the Modern World: The Continuing Relevance of Old Testament Law* (Phillipsburg: Presbyterian and Reformed, 1993). Useful responses or discussions include William S. Barker and W. Robert Godfrey, ed., *Theonomy: A Reformed Critique* (Grand Rapids: Zondervan, 1990); Wayne G. Strickland, ed., *The Law, the Gospel, and the Modern Christian: Five Views* (Grand Rapids: Zondervan, 1993); Bruce Barron, *Heaven on Earth? The Social and Political Agendas of Dominion Theology* (Grand Rapids: Zondervan, 1992); T. David Gordon, "Critique of Theonomy: A Taxonomy," *Westminster Theological Journal* 56 (1994): 23–43.

Christian heritage of Christian, evangelical involvement. Moreover, the Protestant, largely Reformed view that God has ordained the state with legitimate functions that should be honored and strengthened, even while its abuses are opposed, I largely accept. Even where a state is not Christian at all, it is always true that righteousness exalts a nation, but sin is a reproach to any people.[8] This means that seeking the good of the city or state where I live (Jer. 29:7) becomes part of my responsibility, precisely because I have spheres of responsibility which, in a fallen world, are often in tension. This fundamentally eschatological tension cannot be avoided this side of the Parousia. It may be more or less acute in different times and places, but it will not disappear until the end.[9] I differ from this tradition when evangelism and the centrality of the church are somehow lost to view, and the reform of society becomes all devouring. Suddenly I find myself siding with the Anabaptists afresh—but on this I shall say more at the end of this chapter.

This means, then, that we should not invest all political or social activity with "kingdom significance." Although "kingdom" can refer to the unlimited sovereignty of God, in the New Testament the word more commonly refers to that invasive aspect of his sovereignty under which there is eternal life. Everyone is under the kingdom in the first sense, whether they like it or not; only those who have passed from the kingdom of darkness to the kingdom of God's dear Son (Col. 1:13), those who have been born from above (John 3:3, 5), are under or in the kingdom in the second sense.[10] There are implications here for how we should speak of "kingdom work." As Myers puts it:

---

8. This stance can be tied to theological notions such as common grace, the *imago Dei*, divine providence, final judgment, and other essentially biblical structures of thought outlined in chapter 5 of this book. It can also be shown that some of the New Testament wrestling with the relation between the people of God and the state is also tied to Jewish reflection on the universal laws for the descendants of Noah and other related categories: see Markus Bockmuehl, "Public Ethics in a Pluralistic Society? Lessons from the Early Church," *Crux* 28/3 (September 1992): 2–9.

9. It is not surprising, then, that many of the essays in Richard John Neuhaus and Michael Cromartie, eds., *Piety and Politics: Evangelicals and Fundamentalists Confront the World* (Washington: Ethics and Public Policy Center, 1987), betray assorted eschatological stances and tensions, even though only rarely are these brought to attention and examined.

10. This sort of understanding of the "kingdom" in the New Testament is not necessarily at loggerheads with more recent discussion that affirms the word as a "tensive symbol"— i.e., "the kingdom of God" does not refer to a single entity, but evokes a complex range of notions rooted in the understanding that God is king. See Norman Perrin, *Jesus and the Language of the Kingdom* (Philadelphia: Westminster, 1976), esp. 29–34; and especially R. T. France, "The Church and the Kingdom of God: Some Hermeneutical Issues," in *Biblical Interpretation and the Church: Text and Context*, ed. D. A. Carson (Exeter: Paternoster, 1984), 30–44.

As we noted, today it is common to hear Christians referring to any thing worth doing as being "kingdom work." Sometimes this may be done out of a sense of guilt. That is, they feel they really ought to be spending more time studying the Scriptures or praying, but after all, their PTA meeting or their letter to the editor about the Route 288 extension or their volunteering at the public library is *kingdom* work.

I would like to present a case that the activity of Christians in the culture is not usually kingdom work in the sense it is assumed to be, nor is it redemptive in any useful sense of the word. But it is nonetheless imperative for us to be active in the culture, not because we are saved, but because we are created. Pursuing an understanding of and engagement with our culture is necessary for Christians because we must first bow to God as Creator, to thank him for the goodness that remains in his fallen creation, to live creatively, that is, in keeping with the patterns and norms he has established for creation, even as we eagerly await the advent of a new creation.[11]

This may be put too strongly, but it is saying something important. To put it a little differently, our volunteer work in the public library or our efforts to redirect Route 288 may in part be motivated by our Christian beliefs, and thus truly be said to be the product of the fact that we are children of the kingdom. Moreover, some of our actions along these lines may have the unwitting effect of opening people up to the gospel, so that in due course they become believers: in that sense, we have engaged in kingdom work. Further, since all of God's sovereignty is mediated through Christ (1 Cor. 15; Heb. 1:1–3), work that is undertaken in his name and for his sake may, I suppose, usefully be called "kingdom work." Nevertheless, the dominant use of "kingdom" in the New Testament suggests that we would often be wise to restrict categories like "kingdom work" to the promulgation of the gospel. When we are told, "Boldly and without hindrance [Paul] preached the kingdom of God and taught about the Lord Jesus Christ" (Acts 28:31), the context shows that Luke was not picturing the apostle protesting about the condition of the Appian Way, but preaching the gospel, which alone is the power of God unto salvation, i.e., it alone brings people into the kingdom.

Third, it is surely worth noting that at this moment in our history Christian eschatology is the only eschatology around that is worthy of the label. Its principal competitor for much of this century has been Marxist eschatology. This system claimed scientific basis and thus inevitability: "revolutionary man" would produce the Marxist "new man" in the utopia that was just around the corner. If Marxist eschatology is now just about dead, it is not because its defenders came to see how seriously it ignored the Christian

---

11. Ken Meyers, *Christianity, Culture, and Common Grace*, Mars Hill Monographs (Powhaten: Berea Publications, 1994), 3.

doctrine of sin and the Fall, or how reductionistic and naively optimistic its naturalism and economics were, but because these and similar oversights eventually brought down the whole system with a crash—but not before countless millions of human beings were butchered, tortured, liquidated, controlled, enslaved, and degraded. Whatever good Marxism produced—and it sometimes produced some short-term good, especially when it opposed particular evils—little can be set against this record of barbarism. So Marxist eschatological hope has largely faded.

And nothing has replaced it. More precisely, there are lots of small-scale eschatologies around, i.e., small groups prognosticating about this or that ultimate future. There are lots of short-term hopes around, usually tied to economic progress or a "green" world. There are individualistic eschatologies tied up with various forms of the New Age movement—ill-defined expectations of self-actualization and self-fulfillment both here and after death. But there is no large-scale eschatology that has captured much of the public mind, that is placarded in the public arena and that shapes public discourse.

This is the time for Christians to be drumming home some fundamentals as part of our witness in the larger world. Whatever fine points we express or even fight over in our own Christian communities, on the larger scale we should be hammering away at a few basic points. It is painfully disappointing to find many clerics and Christian gurus, on the few occasions they find themselves asked for a Christian outlook on this or that question, unable to deliver themselves of more than a few ethical platitudes veneered with Christian vocabulary. We must constantly say that we were made by God and for him; that all of us will have to give an account to him; that our Creator is our Judge; that the grace we ourselves have received in Christ Jesus impels us to good works, but that our ultimate hope for the future is the end of history, a new heaven and a new earth that only God himself can bring about; that human hubris stands humbled not only before our individual deaths, but before the deaths of civilizations and finally of the world itself; that a society that does not recognize these points finally becomes grotesquely self-serving and exposed to the judgment of God.

2. Democratic government generates peculiar challenges.

In a centralized and highly autocratic government, it may be extremely difficult for the average citizen to effect substantive changes in policy and direction, for he or she is unlikely to have access to "the corridors of power." But if the leadership suddenly changes, or radically changes its mind—one thinks of the "conversion" of Constantine—government policy may be radically redirected overnight. Conversely, ordinary citizens can make a difference in a democracy, even a representative democracy, especially if they are willing to engage in a little organization. But on the other hand, other blocks of the populace can organize, too, so that on most domestic issues change is incremental, or, if it is more rapid, it is because pressure has been building for some time and then it is suddenly released by a combination of popular uproar and a change in the elected officials.

There are several entailments, two of which are important for the present discussion. The first I have already mentioned: in a form of government where citizens have the right, indeed the obligation, to participate, Christians have a responsibility in the public arena that must not be ducked. The second is more difficult. Insofar as a government is democratic, its direction cannot quickly change in very substantive ways unless public opinion is changed.

And that is the problem. Under certain circumstances, public opinion can change very quickly: consider how promptly almost the entire nation approved of entrance into World War II once Pearl Harbor had been attacked. Moreover, where there is an external threat, citizens who in other areas might have very diverse opinions will usually coalesce around the primacy of defense. At the moment, in the United States and in some other Western nations, the cold war is perceived to be over: there is very little external threat, and therefore little cause to rally the troops. The several regional conflicts are judged by most citizens to be too distant and too far removed from America's interests to risk many American lives. Meanwhile, the diversity in the nation has been rapidly multiplying, and now blossoms into full flower because there is very little cause, external or internal, for common vision. Even the "civil religion" of which Bellah wrote a quarter of a century ago is an enfeebled tradition increasingly distanced from the biblical archetypes Bellah identified: exodus, chosen people, promised land, new Jerusalem, sacrificial death, rebirth.[12] Having survived the Nazis and the Communists, having shown that liberal democracies can withstand totalitarian regimes, many Western nations now wonder if they can defend themselves against themselves. At what point do the virtues of freedom, pluralism, and individualism, begin to tear the nation apart, unless those forces are tamed by the virtue of a unifying vision?[13]

If there are few substantive changes that can be made in a democracy without changing public opinion, then seeking the welfare of the nation, especially among a citizenry that embraces highly diverse and mutually

---

12. Robert N. Bellah, *Beyond Belief: Essays on Religion in a Post-Traditionalist World* (Berkeley: Univ. of California Press, 1970), 186.

13. Cf. Arnold J. Toynbee, *A Study of History*, one-volume ed. (Oxford: Oxford Univ. Press, 1972), 155: "The malady which holds the children of decadence fast bound in misery and iron is no paralysis of their natural faculties as human beings but a breakdown and disintegration of their social heritage."

contradictory stances, entails the obligation to try to change public opinion. How that might be done we shall briefly consider below. But there is little doubt, surely, about the aim.

3. If we live in a pluralistic democracy, tensions inevitably arise between our obligation to persuade others of the truth and rightness of what we believe, and the obligation to allow them to disagree—not least because we want to be allowed the freedom to disagree with others.

The nature of the tensions can be articulated in some rather uncharitable ways. For example, Capps writes:

> It is important to recognize that *democracy* (defined as "government by the people" and/or as "rule by the majority") and religious *fundamentalism* have never been good candidates for partnership. The way each is structured makes them always somewhat suspicious of each other. For fundamentalism advances a dualism—an absolute distinction between the saved and the lost, a cosmic battle between good and evil—that is impossible to reconcile satisfactorily with the inviolate democratic conviction that the basic fact about the human condition is equality.... [Fundamentalism] has remained on the margins because much of its deepest motivational energy involves instincts and impulses that run contrary, and are antithetical, to the spirit of democracy. An operational, functioning civil religion is fostered when the shared ideals and aspirations of a people are identified, and can be accorded some national creedal legitimation. It is not easy, therefore, to nationalize a religious perspective that is motivated to rescue a select minority of people, a group within a group, from the wrath that will be visited upon the others. The major obstacle is that such religious motivation is not easily homologized to cherished constitutional principles safeguarding "equality of conditions."[14]

This is not well put. For a start, "fundamentalism" in Capps's usage covers so wide a variety of stances that his analyses require repeated qualification. More importantly, democracy in the minds of most of the Founding Fathers was not to be built on some ideal of "equality of conditions" for all

---

14. Walter H. Capps, *The New Religious Right: Piety, Patriotism, and Politics* (Columbia: Univ. of South Carolina Press, 1990), 213. Cf. similarly Donald Atwell Zoll, *Twentieth Century Political Philosophy* (Englewood Cliffs: Prentice-Hall, 1974), 94: Attempts to show that Christianity and democratic theory are compatible are "fraught with philosophical difficulties, not the least of which is the obligation to show how religious eschatology is reconcilable with the relativistic appetitive foundations of popular democratic thought." Ironically, other writers have sometimes shown how much Western democracy owes to biblical thought: most recently, see Robert Jewett, *Paul: Apostle to America* (Louisville: Westminster/John Knox, 1994), 112–27.

people, but on a handful of quite different assumptions, one of which was that power is so corrosive and human beings are so power-hungry that it cannot safely be left in the hands of one group or party without possibility of recall, challenge, and change. Democracy is a means of dispersing and redirecting power.

What is right in Capps's point—though he does not quite put his finger on it—is that thoughtful Christians can never assign to democracy the same sort of value that a secularist might. Democracy for us can never be an *ultimate* good. Democracy is not always right; democracy can never define right and wrong; democracy cannot establish what the truth is; democracy is not some God-sanctioned mandate disclosed in Scripture. Politicians who appeal endlessly to "the great wisdom of the American (Canadian, British, French, German, etc.) people" are demagogues who either cannot be trusted or cannot think very clearly. The primary reason why Christians will want to support democracy is because in a fallen world it is usually[15] the best way to ensure long-lived freedom, dignity for the individual human being (who is, after all, God's image-bearer), forms of legislative and judicial redress, equitable taxation (or at least the means of reforming the system now and then), and above all freedom of conscience and of speech. These may not be *absolute* goods: doubtless the sons of Korah, for example, would have loved to claim freedom of conscience. But in our experience of the tensions under which we must live until the Parousia, we rejoice to strengthen everything that serves, even imperfectly, to promote justice, human dignity for God's image-bearers, peace, and freedom to herald the gospel.

That means thought must be given to the nature of democracy, the notion of the public good, the limits of governmental power, and the like. A handful of seminal thinkers—Rawls, Novak, Sennelt, Newbigin, and a few others—have been nicely summarized and examined in a recent book,[16] so I need not repeat and evaluate their arguments here. One of their points is that diversity, what I have called empirical pluralism, has some potential for *preserving* democracy, precisely because the competing stances vie for public acceptance. That is surely correct. They are perhaps less helpful in explaining how the arbitrating power, the government, especially a highly invasive government, can be restrained from itself becoming the powerful sponsor of

---

15. I say "usually" because the sad record of imposed democracies shows that when there is little heritage of freedom, little access to information and opportunity for open discussion and free debate, little experience at compromise and respect for law, little loyalty to promulgated constitutions, and deep tribal loyalties, democracies quickly break down, sometimes in barbaric, catastrophic fashion.

16. Richard J. Mouw and Sander Griffioen, *Pluralisms and Horizons: An Essay in Christian Public Philosophy* (Grand Rapids: Eerdmans, 1993).

a shrine so empty[17] that it offends all but the secularists; or how Christians can be strengthened in their *obligation* to feel the eschatological tension which requires a certain loyalty to Caesar but reserves ultimate loyalty only for King Jesus and must decide when Caesar demands too much. But at least they are trying to think through these issues calmly. The fact that there are no final resolutions this side of the Parousia is what we should expect: it is the product of this eschatological tension, which does not absolve us from thought and hope, but simultaneously fosters homesickness for heaven and seeks the good of the nation and impels us onward.

B. Some Practical Suggestions That Have Been Advanced

Although some have offered suggestions as to how to order a pluralistic society, the fact of the matter is that by and large there has been much more analysis of the problems than creative proposals for the way ahead. And some of the proposals, from a Christian perspective, are very thin. For example, in the analysis of Stivers a fair bit of our "culture of cynicism" can be traced to the "unprecendented [*sic*] nature of technological power," which has "two consequences: (1) symbolic meaning is destroyed; (2) power has itself become a value."[18] This analysis owes more than a little to Jacques Ellul. Moreover, ethical meaning "arises in the limitations placed on power. The values of freedom, justice, love, and equality all place limits on acting out of individual or collective self-interest."[19] What, then, is the way ahead?

> A genuine revolution against a technological civilization must be first a cultural one and it must start with the individual. Despite the facade of individualism, a technological civilization is at base thoroughly collectivistic. Politics is so heavily laden with technique that it cannot possibly be the place to start. The rediscovery of meaning will not come by resurrecting traditional values. It will come from the attempt to live out as nearly as possible an ethic of non-power. A sense of history is indispensable and in this con-

---

17. The expression is adapted from Michael Novak, *The Spirit of Democratic Capitalism* (New York: Simon & Schuster, 1983), 53: "In a genuinely pluralistic society, there is no one sacred canopy. *By intention* there is not. At its spiritual core, there is an empty shrine. That shrine is left empty in the knowledge that no one word, image, or symbol is worthy of what all seek there. Its emptiness, therefore, represents the transcendence which is approached by free consciences from a virtually infinite number of directions" (emphasis his). If Novak means what he says, then he needs to clarify further how his Christian commitment bows to absolute authority in certain respects and his political commitment bows to that which seems to relativize that authority in another respect. Perhaps I have not understood him, but it seems to me as if the tension is too easily elided.

18. Richard Stivers, *The Culture of Cynicism: American Morality in Decline* (Oxford: Blackwell, 1994), 175.

19. Ibid.

text, so is a knowledge of traditional values. Because the meaning of all values comes from the context of their application, the knowledge of past values can only be a rough guide to the future.

Such an ethic of non-power and freedom must be negative, exist in opposition to the morality of power, morality without meaning. It is not an ethic being applied to a neutral situation. It is an ethic that must find some tiny crack in a structure of near total power. Were it ever to attempt to become a morality, rather than an ethic of individual love and freedom, it would be swallowed up by the very civilization it had chosen to oppose.[20]

The *analysis* offers some useful points, though they are scarcely radical. The *solution* is much weaker. It is plagued by two problems. (1) It is far from clear that such individualism and self-restraint are sufficient for restoring meaning, purpose, freedom. (2) It is even less clear how, even supposing they would prove effective, they are to be brought about. "A sense of history" may prove of help to intellectuals; how will the rest be encouraged to read? Of course, if there is some massive program to motivate people in that direction, then by Stivers's criteria we have retreated to the collective society and lost the battle. In any case, can meaning and purpose long be maintained in a culture without some appeal to a transcendent vision or standard or goal?

From a Christian perspective, neither the analysis nor the solution, for all their insight, adequately deals with the nature of the human dilemma, which is tied to our alienation from God, our sin.

In what follows, then, I catalogue some of the suggestions that have been put forward, primarily by Christians (though others than Christians have supported many of them). They are not directly *gospel* solutions (e.g., "Spend more time and energy on evangelism"): I shall say more about that toward the end of this chapter. The list is suggestive rather than exhaustive. The first entry, a long one, wrestles with theoretical frameworks as to how to make our way and exert a godly influence within this culture. The remaining suggestions offer a sampling of more concrete proposals, including disputed calls as to the way forward. Here and there I include brief evaluation.

1. There is a rising call for evangelical public policy.

This call takes various forms. Numerous groups are stressing the minimalist (but nevertheless important) values of civility, courtesy, engagement. Thus Hunter, who fears that our pluralism could become violent, and who likens the diversity in American culture to the diversity that has brought about the conflicts in Lebanon, Ireland, and the former Yugoslavia,[21] sees the way

---

20. Ibid., 181.
21. James Davison Hunter, *Before the Shooting Begins: Searching for Democracy in America's Culture War* (New York: Free Press, 1994).

forward in terms of self-restraint and lowered expectations. What is needed is "modesty in politics," a recovery of "the languages of public argument" and of "the art of argument and persuasion," and a frank realism that does not expect too much.[22] Whether or not he is too alarmist in the first place, the proffered way ahead will likely be taken up by those who love empirical pluralism, and be viewed as an invitation to compromise by those who do not, unless more substantive reasons are advanced in defense of this appeal.

Others have advocated a national coalition of evangelicals and Roman Catholics, aiming for a moral front that will have real clout in the nation. Perhaps the best example of such a call is the volume edited by William Bentley Ball.[23] Certainly the recent encyclical by Pope John Paul II[24] includes much with which evangelicals would wish to identify. It restates four strands to a Catholic theistic ethic. The first is the importance of personhood, and a person's relatedness to the being of God. The dangers of totalitarianism and of democracy alike, once moral absolutes and the dignity of the person are denied and governments recognize no subjection or accountability to God, are apparent. The second theme is that goodness as a category opposed to evil is grounded in the character of God. Where worship of God is absent, secular power and secular morality are constantly in danger of corruption and callous inhumanity. The third theme is that goodness triumphs over evil in the lives of the faithful through the power of the Spirit, who enables us to live up to the moral standards laid down in the Old and New Testaments. The fourth is that the moral life of believers is inevitably tied to the worship of the Christian community, which is empowered to witness to the moral life through proclamation, and especially through participation in the Eucharist.

Apart from relatively insignificant details, there is little here that most evangelicals will have difficulty with until the last point, where the Eucharist receives a stress that most of us think should be reserved for "the spirituality of the Word." But the challenge is more complex. Most evangelicals are entirely happy with what Francis Schaeffer used to call "co-belligerency" on select issues: e.g., abortion, the importance of persons, the social importance of the family, and much more. We will disagree on some social/moral issues

---

22. Ibid., chap. 9, "Beyond the Culture War: What It Will Take," 227–44. Though certainly not wrong, the thinness of these proposals is probably what generates a higher percentage than usual of vague sentences like this one: "Democracy must be reinvented in every generation and for the circumstances in which each new generation finds itself" (243).

23. *In Search of a National Morality: A Manifesto for Evangelicals and Catholics* (Grand Rapids/San Francisco: Baker/Ignatius Press, 1992).

24. *Veritatis Splendor: Encyclical Letter Addressed by the Supreme Pontiff Pope John Paul II to All the Bishops of the Catholic Church Regarding Certain Fundamental Questions of the Church's Moral Teaching* (London: Catholic Truth Society, 1993).

(e.g., gambling). But recent evangelical/Roman Catholic pronouncements in this area have, ironically, done more to set back co-belligerency than to advance it. Instead of focusing on the agreed social issues, some evangelical and Roman Catholic theologians have agreed to use ambiguous language to project an image of *theological* agreement where both sides mean quite different things. Those who think that the theological issues are of minor importance in comparison with the social issues, and who feel that theological differences should be buried in order to confront the common foe of secular humanism, are delighted. In my view, they are, at best, naive. Candor, integrity, and even the moral issues are not advanced by uses of language that mask profound differences. Substantial numbers of evangelicals quite frankly feel confused and betrayed by these agreements. They point out that no generation ever defends the truth on only one front, and if the price paid for common statements on, say, abortion, is sacrifice of the evangelical understanding of the gospel, the price is too high.[25]

At this point it may be helpful to make three distinctions:

(a) One must distinguish between agreement on specific issues and agreement across a broad plain. If there is any hope of sustained cooperation between evangelicals and other groups on any part of the social or political agenda—whether the group is Catholic, Mormon, Jewish, or for that matter the ACLU—it will be achieved by articulating the areas of agreement *and nothing else*. Various individuals and subgroups will inevitably try to make the agreement seem broader than it is, in order to win points for their agendas. The result will almost always be further fragmentation. If we are serious about certain cultural agendas, the aims must be clear, specific, and limited.

(b) One must distinguish between strategies designed to win favor for certain values that are faithful to the Christian heritage, and strategies designed to help more believers become active in influencing society for good. The former provide fertile ground for inter-group cooperation in order to achieve certain specific goals; the latter are best handled entirely within confessional communities. To put this in the framework of the recent evangelical/Catholic dialogue, efforts to arouse a united front on specific moral issues may prove fruitful, but efforts to urge tight general alignment between two quite different groups in order to form a general public policy are doomed to frustration, suspicion, and resentments.

(c) More generally, one must distinguish between espousing philosophical pluralism as an ultimate good, and defending empirical pluralism as a

---

25. It is gratifying to note that *Christianity Today* 39/3 (March 6, 1995): 52–53 reports that the evangelicals who signed ECT (= "Evangelicals and Catholics Together: The Christian Mission in the Third Millennium") have published a clarifying second document that less ambiguously retains evangelical commitments.

pragmatically useful ally in the preservation of democracy. The former is an implicit denial of the transcultural claims of God himself, while the latter recognizes that in a fallen world there may be many reasons for fostering and preserving a form of government that allows the articulation of ideas we hold to be wrong. Failure to recognize this distinction is one of the reasons for the feeling of dissonance one experiences in reading Thiemann's call for a public theology.[26] On the one hand, he urges that Christians must exert an influence in the culture, trying to find a way "to influence the development of public policy without seeking to construct a new Christendom or lapsing into a benign moral relativism."[27] This line of thought presupposes that there is a "given"—a Christian content, a Christian worldview, some Christian truth—that we must urge on the world, even as we avoid the impression we wish to impose it on the world. Here, then, Christians are being encouraged to wield proper influence while not violating the empirical pluralism that characterizes our culture. On the other hand, Thiemann insists that the primary resources we have in engaging the world have to do with modeling how theology is done: theology, Thiemann says, is a communal, formative (i.e., it helps us establish our self-identity), critical, and public activity, and that is exactly the nature and value of public discourse.[28] This line of thought allows for no "given" at all, no substantive content, no Christian truth, but only whatever merit may be found in our form of discussion. Here is the implicit adoption of philosophical pluralism as an ultimate good. The confusion is palpable. Most of the early appeals for the separation of church and state in America were *for* freedom of conscience and *from* the legal establishment of the supremacy of a particular denomination; they were certainly not designed to keep believers from exerting influence, and most emphatically were not designed to deny the existence of objective truth.[29]

Probably the evangelical who has thought most deeply about how to go about forging a public philosophy in a pluralistic culture is Os Guinness.[30]

---

26. Ronald F. Thiemann, *Constructing a Public Theology: The Church in a Pluralistic Culture* (Louisville: Westminster/John Knox, 1991). His title is somewhat misleading, as the book itself is a collection of independent essays, some of which have only the remotest connection with the title.

27. Ibid., 43.

28. Ibid., 166–73.

29. See, for instance, William R. Estep, *Revolution Within the Revolution: The First Amendment in Historical Context, 1612–1789* (Grand Rapids: Eerdmans, 1990). The work has some serious historical flaws not directly related to the point being made: see the review in *Westminster Theological Journal* 54 (1992): 204–7.

30. Of his many writings, see especially *The American Hour: A Time of Reckoning and the Once and Future Role of Faith* (New York: Free Press, 1993), especially chap. 13, "Tribespeople, Idiots, or Citizens?" (239–57).

Whether or not one agrees with each step of his argumentation, the sanity and realism of his call are impressive, combined as they are with uncompromising Christian convictions. Guinness argues that traditional American ideals (e.g., openness, dynamism, self-reliance, toughness, risk-taking, egalitarianism, enterprise) presupposed shared ideals such as honesty and loyalty, and even a shared public philosophy. But with the move to postmodernism, the shared public philosophy has evaporated. Either we must find a new center, or we must learn to live in peace without a center. The latter route is likely to degenerate into chaos, or into soft or hard totalitarianism. Hence the urgency of seeking a new public philosophy.

Guinness proposes to build this philosophy around the First Amendment. Christians ought to articulate a vision of religious freedom that does not instantly seek the advantage of *our* religion. We must forcefully argue for a "chartered pluralism," a freely chosen compact of religious liberty characterized by three R's: the *right* to believe and practice any religion or none; the *responsibility* to guard this right for everyone, not least those with whom we most disagree; and *respect* meted to everyone, especially those with whom we disagree. Theologically, we must act this way and help to build this vision out of our view of human beings, God's image-bearers, in God's universe, even if others accept the vision but not the theological underpinning; practically, this calls for civility, "principled participation," and "principled persuasion."

What the outcome will be, Guinness does not pretend to know. He outlines various possibilities: drift toward further liberalism coupled with the seduction of continued and increased prosperity; gradual decline materially, culturally, spiritually, morally, and in terms of power and influence; takeover by some demagogue; and revitalization of the entire culture through spiritual revival and reformation. His argument is that regardless of the outcome, which we cannot predict, we ought to pursue such a public philosophy simply because it is right and wise.

Quite a number of people are arguing along these lines today. It may be the wisest course, but it is imperative that we see how difficult a course it is.

It is difficult internally—that is, within the evangelical camp—because it can easily be interpreted as being at cross-purposes with other pressing needs. At one level, many of us would very much like to recapture some of the values from our recent past that we have largely sacrificed. When journalist Cal Thomas, for example, argues as much,[31] his book is at least in part an argument (or even a diatribe) against the reigning liberalism. But the polarization in the country is great enough that many of his opponents will wonder if he wants them crushed, legally stopped, judicially thwarted, or at very least

---

31. *The Things That Matter Most* (New York: HarperCollins, 1994).

destroyed at the polls. Precisely how does this square with a public policy in which the rights of all sides to present their views, especially their religious views, is carefully nurtured and guarded? Conversely, while we argue in defense of a public policy such as that which Guinness expounds, how do we simultaneously say that we think that some religious opinions are wrong, dangerous, or even evil? For there is not much value in preserving the public philosophy if we cannot utilize it.

Here Christians face serious disadvantages. We saw in the first chapter how philosophical pluralism has transformed the nature of tolerance. For complex reasons, tolerance has come to be identified with pluralism. Those who do not espouse philosophical pluralism are beyond the pale; they are thought to be rejecting tolerance, and therefore are regarded intolerantly. With rare exceptions,[32] pluralists no longer think that tolerance is displayed by the person who argues that position A is correct and position B is incorrect, but who defends anyone's right to defend position B. Rather, pluralists think tolerance is displayed only by those who say there is no one right position (except, of course, for the position of philosophical pluralism itself).

The least this means is that in the arena of religion, Christians must constantly articulate *and display* the nature of true tolerance. While we insist that objective truth exists, that the personal/transcendent God can be known, that religious claims in conflict with Christ are necessarily false, we must also publicly and repeatedly disavow coerced belief and insist on the right of others to disagree with us. We must do this precisely because we are being misunderstood on this point, and that is because our hearers live in the postmodern world and many have therefore shifted to the new meaning of tolerance.

It is useful to remember that other approaches to pluralism and tolerance are possible—and instructive. Consider this report:

> Although not called by that name, pluralism has existed in the small country of Switzerland more or less from its beginnings. What it means is that where there is a majority of French-speakers, schools are conducted in French. German- or Italian-speaking parents have the possibility of establishing private schools for their children (as do speakers of English and other languages). In the largely Catholic cantons, there is Catholic religious instruction in public schools, and Protestant children, as well as those of other religions or none, are excused. The situation is reversed in the majority Protestant cantons. In the mixed cantons, it varies from community to community. Pluralism in the United States means that absolutely every school in every town in every state must be rigorously sanitized from any

---

32. E.g., Ian S. Markham, *Plurality and Christian Ethics* (Cambridge: Cambridge Univ. Press, 1994).

and all elements of any religious tradition that could possibly be inconsistent with any child or adult anywhere near. . . . Pluralism in Switzerland means that the local population has a right to its traditions, but does not impose them on dissenters, and that tolerance prevails. Pluralism in the United States means that the local population has no right to any tradition and that intolerance prevails. The new translation of *E pluribus unum* is "One size fits all."[33]

Of course, America has had a different history, enjoys a different constitution, and a peculiar history of judicial rulings. But one also suspects that there is such a vicious attachment to personal "rights" here that, just as the first casualty of war is truth, so the first casualty of perpetual insistence on rights is civility mingled with genuine tolerance.

At the same time, the arena in which Guinness and some others most commonly speak of constructing public policy is religion, and in some ways this arena is somewhat easier to manage than others. There are plenty of other contexts in which intolerance is rife. I am thinking not merely of intolerance in some parts of the scientific community, supremely but not uniquely attested by the Mims case,[34] but of something more difficult yet: situations where disagreements over the direction of things issue in laws and judicial rulings that one side or the other holds are fundamentally unacceptable. The two sides cannot agree, and the nature of the issue is such that to "live and let live" would be viewed by one side as intolerable betrayal. Of course, in many disputes both sides connect their own positions to utopian ideals. To sacrifice their vision would be to sacrifice utopia. But even if we were to agree that America will never be utopia, and that there is an urgent need for realism as to what political machinery can actually achieve, the different directions pursued by different segments of our society make neutrality almost impossible. One side or the other will "win."

Consider, for example, the recent book by Engelhardt.[35] A self-confessed secular humanist, Engelhardt offers careful distinctions in the notions of what "secular" and "humanism" might mean, and rejects any identification of sec-

---

33. *The Religion and Society Report* 12/2 (February 1995): 7.

34. In the Mims case, described in chapter 1, a qualified science writer was dropped from a prestigious scientific journal, *Scientific American*, simply because he admitted privately that he was "not a believer" in evolution—even though the column he was writing had nothing to do with evolution. The case caused considerable furor, but the editor of *Scientific American*, far from backing down, canceled the column to avoid legal problems, then started it up again after the flap had died down. The Mims episode has been amply discussed, perhaps most usefully by Jerry Bergman, "Censorship in Secular Science: The Mims Case," *Perspectives on Science and Religion* 45/1 (1993): 37–45.

35. H. Tristram Engelhardt, Jr., *Bioethics and Secular Humanism: The Search for a Common Morality* (Philadelphia: Trinity Press International, 1991).

ular humanism as an antireligious or nonreligious philosophy. A sensitive postmodernist, he recognizes that the loss of moral authority has been brought about not only by the decline in the authority of Judeo-Christian values, but also by the utter incapacity of mere rationality to bring about an agreed value system. He is one of the rare critics to recognize that "if God is silent" then "reason is impotent."[36] What we must have is some method or stance by which the moral strangers who make up many of the nations of the Western world can collaborate. In much of the book, Engelhardt thoughtfully evaluates and gently dismisses the alternatives, before offering his own proposal in the last chapter. What he offers is a morality based on being human, a morality focused on human consent. Moral authority derives from the consent of the consenting. What we are offered, then, is an extreme form of liberal individualism. As a stance, it is neither for nor against any particular religious outlook. If one woman consents to an abortion or to surrogate motherhood, there lies the moral authority: we have no right to impose some external moral authority.

But there are at least three problems with this public philosophy, two that most of us should recognize, and a third that Christians (and some others) will insist on. *First*, even if we were to agree that consenting individuals should not normally be forced to adopt a stance that did not gain their full consent (and some would reject such a position), the actions of the consenting individuals so often have such massive impact on the broader culture that those who disagree may feel that the issue involved is not a matter for the individual alone but for the public. Consider pornography, for example. A very strong case can be made for allowing maximum freedom of expression. But if that freedom is used to churn out millions of copies of sexually explicit material that one segment of society feels is corrosive, evil, and destructive of the family and of society's well-being, then however difficult pornography may be to define, they will be committed to taming it, limiting it, even if they cannot utterly destroy it. Moreover, even in the case of euthanasia, many are concerned about what its widespread practice, even if it were carefully controlled, would eventually do to our perceptions of human beings, of human dignity. In other words, there are profound problems with the individualism implicit in this philosophy.

Second, there are problems associated with the notion of "consenting individuals." As one of his more perceptive reviewers has noted, Engelhardt's case might be more secure if society were composed of nothing but consenting adults. But if some parts of society think that the embryo has rights, then questions about abortion and surrogate motherhood are raised. "How can he

36. Ibid., 119.

claim that his social philosophy is morally neutral in this matter? Why should his insistence on the rights of the consenting individual or consenting individuals to carry out a certain project take precedence over my conviction that non-consenting individuals have rights?"[37] And at what point does the notion of "consenting" kick in? What of pedophilia?

Third, from within a Christian worldview one may pragmatically agree that on many matters in a fallen world individuals should be permitted to go their own way. But we must still insist that Engelhardt's philosophy is not religiously neutral. In fact, it lies close to the heart of what thoughtful Christians understand the fundamental definition of evil to be: human beings, made in the image of God, denying the rights of their Maker to establish the proper course of their lives and their living, denying, if possible, his very existence, and seeking to establish a moral order on the basis of such a denial.

In short, the call for public policy, important as it is, is also complex, and we should not get our hopes up too high. When society is divided not only by differing perspectives within a single worldview, but by fundamentally clashing worldviews, then although people of good will from all sides will find a way forward with appropriate tolerance for alternative points of view, with no clear winners and losers, on some issues winning and losing is inevitable. At that point, the aim of any group in a pluralistic democracy is to frame their point of view in such a way as to carry the majority vote. But if that becomes the determining goal on *every* issue, instead of forging compromises and a *modus vivendi* wherever possible, then *every* issue is a win/lose issue, and the hope of widely accepted public policy on *any* issue will dissipate.

All of this is another way of saying that our eschatological location "between the times," between the "already" and the "not yet," leaves us with complex issues that must be worked out in each generation. For all that we must think hard about these issues, it does no good to give the impression that integrity combined with hard thought will solve them all.

Granted, then, that on many issues we are not going to be able to achieve widely acceptable public policies, we must nevertheless think through what stances are most likely to move in our direction the public policy that already exists. By "public policy" I am now referring not only to positions taken by government, but to values widely accepted in the culture at large, which doubtless influence not only government but education, the media, economics, ecology, freedom of religion, and much more. Three stances come to mind:

---

37. Stephen Williams, in *Themelios* 19/1 (1993): 29–30.

a. We must boldly, courteously, incessantly, confront public philosophies that are unchristian.

We often forget how temporary and faddish such movements can be. Much of this century has been governed, in the Western world, by Freudianism, Marxism, and evolution. Freudianism is certainly not dead, but it is no longer regnant. The sustained assaults it has received are now being noted even by the popular media.[38] Psychology is still horribly locked into "selfism," but even that stance is increasingly under attack.[39] In its quest to be a world-dominating philosophy, Marxism is a spent force. And now, as we saw earlier, there are signs that evolution itself is coming under competent attack.[40]

Such assaults must be maintained. They must be well directed. Sometimes they require courage: they can cost you promotions, advancement, even your job. Even though we can praise what is good in it, postmodernism should be exposed to the same sort of ruthless analysis that it deploys against earlier intellectual movements.

b. We must hold the state and other social institutions accountable.

Legislatures develop a certain life of their own. Once passed, laws achieve such awesome power in the hands of many bureaucrats that questions of justice, fairness, even of common sense, get squeezed to the periphery. Philip Howard has documented in explosive detail how asinine laws can be. For example, Mother Theresa's Sisters of Charity were about to open a home for the homeless in New York, when they were told they would have to install a $100,000 elevator, which the Sisters would never use since their order demands that they avoid such modern conveniences. After a year-and-a-half struggle, the Sisters of Charity simply walked away from the project, having concluded that the $100,000 could be better spent on soup and clothing for the urban poor. Government "won"; the poor lost.[41] Christians have enormous stakes in holding government to account. We should be courteous but firm leaders in the field, not stooping to cheap demagoguery to establish our own reputations by feeding the anger of the masses, but coolly exposing what

---

38. E.g., Paul Gray, "The Assault on Freud," *Time* 142/23 (November 29, 1993): 47–59.

39. E.g., Paul Vitz, *Psychology as Religion: The Cult of Self-Worship*, 2d ed. (Grand Rapids: Eerdmans, 1994).

40. See also Phillip E. Johnson, "Shouting 'Heresy' in the Temple of Darwin," *Christianity Today* 38/12 (October 24, 1994): 22–26.

41. Philip K. Howard, *The Death of Common Sense: How Law Is Suffocating America* (New York: Random House, 1994). Many books preserve smaller numbers of examples: e.g., Bruce L. Shelley, *The Gospel and the American Dream* (Portland: Multnomah Press, 1989).

is foolishness or wickedness, and offering suggestions as to how to improve the system.[42]

Similar exposés of other sectors are no less important. Twenty years ago Os Guinness's *The Dust of Death*[43] proved to be an insightful and influential critique of movements then current, some of which are now in fuller flowering. Rusher, Medved and others offer documented examination of television and other mass media.[44] Following the public roasting of Dan Quayle, after his remarks on Murphy Brown, the issue he raised, however opportunely or not, is being publicly addressed: When are "regular" families portrayed on TV? Why are most romantic scenes between a man and a woman, including pregnancies (as in Murphy Brown's case), pictured outside the bounds of marriage?[45] In the educational arena, the Rutherford Institute in Charlottesville, Virginia, and especially a book by its director, John Whitehead,[46] detail how many religious rights are still preserved by law and in the courts—far more than the average school principal knows about. The book is a goldmine of useful advice for the concerned parent.

c. We must work harder than we have been working at being persuasive.

Most who will read these chapters live under some form or other of democracy. That means, in the end, that we must persuade a lot of people on a lot of points. In a democracy, if you cannot do that, you lose. The point has been powerfully made by John Stott.[47]

Suppose, instead, that by powerful manipulation of electoral forces you manage to win sufficient strength in the legislature that you can ram through some cherished legislation. Let us suppose the country is America, and the issue is abortion on demand. Suddenly you have enough support in Congress that you might be able to ram through a constitutional amendment banning

42. A brief but amusing example that deserves wider circulation is an essay by Jonathan Mills, "Plato's 'Formalismgate': A Dialogue on the Cover-Up of the American Judiciary's Theological Rationales for 'Strict Separation,'" *Crux* 28/3 (September 1992): 27–33.

43. London: Inter-Varsity Press, 1973.

44. William A. Rusher, *The Coming Battle for the Media: Curbing the Power of the Media Elite* (New York: Wm. Morrow, 1988); Michael Medved, *Hollywood vs. America* (New York: HarperCollins, 1992).

45. See, especially, Barbara DaFoe Whitehead, "Dan Quayle Was Right," *Atlantic Monthly* (April 1993): 1–21. Whitehead demonstrates, from study after study, that family dissolution harms children and shatters the social fabric. The two-parent home is the best defense against despair, social destruction, poverty, and crime.

46. John W. Whitehead, *The Rights of Religious Persons in Public Education* (Wheaton: Crossway, 1991).

47. *Issues Facing Christians Today* (Basingstoke: Marshall, Morgan & Scott, 1984). See also John Senior, *The Death of Christian Culture* (Harrison: RC Books, 1994).

abortions except, let us say, in cases where the mother's life is in danger. Would this be a major victory for righteousness?

History warns us that at the very least we should be careful before we wave our triumph banners. In a passion of concern, America approved Prohibition almost three-quarters of a century ago, and when the gangsters and the cheats had finished, the country repealed the amendment. Suppose, then, that a constitutional amendment putting to rest *Roe v. Wade (1972)* passed Congress. Let us further suppose that, much to everyone's surprise, two-thirds of the States approved the amendment within five years: what would happen? First, there would be a rapid rise in the number of illegal abortions. Then the media would relate endless gory stories of how some poor woman lost her life to a back-door abortionist. It would not be surprising if in a few years the same fate awaited this amendment as awaited Prohibition: repeal.

Does this line of argument suggest that it is folly to suppose that effective change can be legislated? Not at all. It is simply a reminder that our deepest social problems are pre-political. They are cultural; they are embedded in worldviews that are fundamentally alien to the Judeo-Christian heritage. It may be wise and godly to aim for legislative change anyway. But unless changes are effected in the outlook of the nation at large, in many cases it won't be long before the changes are themselves reversed.

Of course, that is one of the fundamental differences between our time and that of the great British leaders who transformed much of British culture by legislation in the wake of the Evangelical Awakening. The abolition of slavery, penal reform, the abolition of child labor, the formation of the first trade unions, and much more, were pushed through Parliament by converts such as John Howard, the Earl of Shaftesbury, and others. But the point to observe is that these people were increasingly viewed as at the forefront of social betterment. The tides of history were with them, not least because the Awakening continued to bring in countless thousands of fresh converts. In most of the Western world, the tides of history are currently against us, and our legislative efforts often seem to others to be knee-jerk conservativism, not the high-water mark of desirable reform.

From a Christian perspective, it is pleasant to contemplate some of the changes that would be effected by massive revival and reformation. But we are not to despise the day of small things. Some changes may be possible by wisely choosing the tone and terms of the debate. For instance, on the abortion issue, a number of voices are pointing out that if the issue is constantly cast in terms of the rights of the woman versus the rights of the unborn child, the proabortion position is likely to win. The pro-life supporters are not helped by the handful of violent individuals who shoot abortion doctors and their receptionists. But if the debate is cast more broadly—if we keep asking what kind of society we want to become, if we point out that there are more crisis pregnancy centers in the land than abortion clinics, if we recount the documented psychological damage done to millions of women who have undergone abortion, if we demonstrate that abortion has proved a remarkably ineffective means of reducing the number of single-parent families—a constitutional amendment might be possible that would limit abortions, if not abolish them, *and get that amendment to endure and not be repealed.* Although I am uncertain that this would be the outcome, I am quite certain that on many fronts we need to work harder at being persuasive in the public arena than we have been.

Similarly, I suspect, on a host of other subjects: the terms of the debate need recasting. For example, if school prayer is seen primarily as a "separation-of-church-and-state" issue, conservatives will never win, and it is less than clear in my mind that they should. If the issue becomes one of constitutional freedom of speech for everyone, there just may be a way forward. The aim, in any case, is to be winsome and persuasive.

2. There are increasing numbers of voices advocating reform from within.

Many of these are explicitly set over against patterns of confrontation. Thus Briner offers fairly detailed plans on how to get better movies made and call forth better television programs. He calls for believers to excel in the academic world, to participate in the visual arts, and so forth.[48] Along with the debates about school vouchers, there are numerous appeals to get involved with public education and transform the structures from within.[49] Other disciplines boast similar appeals.

In most cases there is every reason to applaud the efforts and enthusiasm of those who are making the appeals. It is one way forward, one form of obedience to the injunction to be "salt" and "light." More doubtful is the hidden assumption in many such books and articles that if more of us would just get involved we could turn this whole culture around. The optimism is astounding. Realism does not demand that we gather up our marbles and retreat to our holy huddle in a sulk. It does demand that while we seek to be faithful, we do not entertain unreasonable expectations at a time when the cultural trends are drifting away from us.

---

48. Bob Briner, *Roaring Lambs: A Gentle Plan to Radically Change Your World* (Grand Rapids: Zondervan, 1993).
49. E.g., Brian V. Hill, "Educational Responses to Modern Pluralism," *Evangelical Review of Theology* 16 (1992): 82–96.

3. There is rising emphasis on the family and on other mediating social structures.

"The sanctity of family life as a decisive biblical concern raises a whole cluster of logically related contemporary issues including adultery, divorce, prostitution, and the lax media handling of moral permissiveness and casual sex." So writes Carl Henry,[50] and he is right. Most of us are familiar with James Dobson and the "Focus on the Family" enterprise. In Britain, similar emphases on the importance of returning to relationships of integrity is found in a recent publication of the Jubilee Centre.[51]

For all that we should applaud these courageous efforts, it is important to recognize that the restoration of the family cannot be achieved by legal fiat or moral exhortation, however important good laws and moral exhortation may be. In a highly structured and largely uniform society, like that of, say, Japan or Saudi Arabia, certain forms of family cohesion can be achieved. Neither pattern is an option in individualistic and now highly pluralistic America, or, for that matter, in many other Western countries. One can imagine some legal changes for the better—e.g., changes in the tax code that would make it financially advantageous to be married, rather than single and living together—but the fundamental problems are not going to be resolved by such small-scale changes, however desirable they might be, and however hard we should press for them.

4. There is a rising call to return to local government, along with a demand for diminution of the federal government.

That is one of the calls of Charles Murray.[52] Insofar as emphasis on local government fosters a greater degree of participation, it is also one of the appeals of Bellah,[53] who argues that a good society is one in which there is a widening of democratic participation. I agree with Bellah's point in theory, but doubt that it will take us very far *in a country that is as pluralistic as this one*. The wider the participation, the more thoroughly our differences not only of detail but over entire worldviews come to light. And while it is an axiom of democracy that the business of government should always be transacted at the lowest possible level, one of the reasons for the federal activism lies in

---

50. *The Christian Mindset in a Secular Society* (Portland: Multnomah Press, 1985), 103.

51. Michael Schluter and David Lee, *The R Factor* (London: Hodder & Stoughton, 1993). Cf. also M. Schluter and R. Clements, *Reactivating the Extended Family: From Biblical Norms to Public Policy in Britain* (Cambridge: Jubilee Centre Publications, 1986). The Jubilee Centre has advocated a similar approach in penal reform: see Jonathan Burnside and Nicola Baker, ed., *Relational Justice: Repairing the Breach* (Winchester: Waterside Press, 1994).

52. *In Pursuit of Happiness and Good Government* (New York: Simon & Schuster, 1988).

53. Robert N. Bellah, *The Good Society* (New York: Vintage Press, 1992).

the fact that, as we have seen, with empirical pluralism on the rise and with the intermediate structures slowly decaying, the federal government is precisely what keeps the country together. The only question is, At what cost?

5. There are still more than a few debates about what kind of "economic justice" Christians should be arguing for.

Kim Hawtrey's paper[54] begins with an old Polish joke: "Capitalism is the exploitation of man by man. Communism is the reverse." Doubtless both parties will feel equally insulted. Behind the humor, however, is a serious point. At the risk of simplification, Hawtrey points out that there are two opposing views of economic justice at stake.[55]

The first, the "commutative school," thinks of economic justice in terms of the fairness of the procedures. People in like circumstances should receive similar treatment. The emphasis is on the fair transaction: both parties should be satisfied, for there is a kind of mathematical equity in it. Justice is measured by "the rules of the game, not the results of the game."[56] The focus is on just procedures, not outcomes. Maximum freedom and minimum interference are cherished. This is the sort of view defended by F. A. Hayek and Milton Friedman.

The second, the "distributive school," associates justice with equity of outcome, not with equity of procedure or process. Justice is judged to be violated if there are enormous disparities in the distribution of wealth. Justice is measured by the results of the game, not its rules. In fact, justice under this model is best served by *tilting* the rules in order to bring about the desired outcome. Inevitably, this approach depends on heavy state intervention. To fail to perceive the justice of this approach is regularly taken by its proponents to betray a severe lack of compassion.

This is not the place to adjudicate the relative merits and demerits of these competing visions, except to say that both sides are in danger, in different ways, of overlooking human fallenness. In a virtually free economy, even where there is enormous social cohesion and a tradition of integrity, sooner or later trusts will form that monopolize markets and introduce wild distortions. Where integrity breaks down, trusts become cabals. Competition can be excluded by controlling the supplies, threatening the market, fixing the prices, even by cheap thuggery. That is why most "free marketers" insist, despite their position, that there must be enforced legislation to combat

---

54. Kim Hawtrey, "Economic Justice: A Twin Axiom Framework," *Reformed Theological Review* 50 (1991): 98–105.

55. This is, of course, a very considerable oversimplification. But it will do for our purposes, which are concerned to make clear the different views of justice that are at stake.

56. Hawtrey, "Economic Justice," 99.

monopolizing trusts, fraud, false advertising, and other abuses. To that end, of course, the market is not free; and that is a good thing, for otherwise some free *fallen* people will inevitably abuse the freedom. And one must still decide what to do with the poor who for good and bad reasons find they cannot compete in a system whose processes are just. Precisely where and how should compassion be added to justice?

For its part, the distributive school overlooks the evils that develop in people who are perpetually dependent on the handouts of the state. Worse, it underestimates the impact of the Fall on complex governmental structures designed and manned by sinners.[57] Inefficiency, bureaucracy, bloated overhead, and sometimes outright corruption combine to such an extent that it is not at all clear that government programs of this sort actually help many people over the long haul (after all, the percentage of people below the poverty line has actually increased in the years since President Johnson announced the Great Society), even though many individuals are helped. Equally bad, this approach tends "to underestimate the connection between wealth creation and distribution, which in practice is a dynamic, two-way process such that one cannot tamper with the distribution of income today without seriously affecting the manner, and rate, at which it will be created tomorrow, since to do so may merely 'kill the goose that laid the golden egg.'"[58] Thus what starts off as apparently the moral high ground—i.e., the appeal to structured compassion—often turns out in practice to be inefficient and corrosive, the progenitor of new kinds of *in*justice.

Whatever economic structures are advocated, Christian thinkers cannot afford to ignore the effects of the Fall in *either* system. We can never afford to lower standards of procedural justice, and that includes accountability, an emphasis on integrity, firm punishment for the corrupt; and simultaneously, we can never afford to adopt a stance without compassion, however greatly we may disagree as to what practical course that compassion demands we follow.

6. There is a considerable heritage of small but significant actions.

What I have in mind is the letters people write to their representatives in Congress, the faithful witness they bear while serving on the local school board, the work they put in for Habitat for Humanity, the time and energy they devote to strategic letters (e.g., to Letters to the Editor columns in the local newspaper), the help offered to organizations that circulate important

---

57. One cannot help but feel these are deep deficiencies not only in the economic theories of this school, but also among not a few Christian theoreticians—e.g., Stephen Charles Mott, *Biblical Ethics and Social Change* (New York: Oxford Univ. Press, 1982).

58. Hawtrey, "Economic Justice," 102.

information that would not otherwise be circulated, and much more. At the local level, this is often the most strategic sort of thing that can be done.

But although all of these things have their value and must certainly not be despised, Christians will also want to insist that from an eternal perspective there is something more important yet.

C. First Things First: The Priority of the Gospel

Although it is possible to read substantial parts of the Bible politically,[59] and certainly its central message so affects all of human existence that every sphere is transformed, including the political, the social, the economic; yet if the message of the Bible is understood to exhaust itself in, say, the political sphere, the Bible has been distorted. If the political sphere is understood to be primary in the Bible, the Bible has been domesticated.

Of the many useful tests of particular "readings" of the Bible, one of the best was emphasized in chapter 5: How well does this reading reflect the Bible's story-line? If an interpretation is unfaithful in this area, it is faddish and unreliable, however many insightful points it may generate along the way. That means, for any Christian reading of the Bible, that the gospel is central, the gospel that reconciles lost men and women to the God who made them and whose image they bear, the gospel that justifies them and transforms them in this life and prepares them for the new heaven and the new earth. Berger is right:

> Faith in the gospel of Christ is constitutive of the church. The church is the community that embodies this faith. Apostasy occurs when other content is deemed to be constitutive of the Christian community. At that point, the community becomes something other than the church of Christ. Of all the so-called "marks of the church," the central and indispensable one is that the church proclaims the gospel and not any other message of salvation. . . . The underlying question . . . has not changed at all: Is it the gospel of Christ that constitutes the church, or is it a "different gospel"?

It seems to me that we face precisely this question in American Christianity today—nothing less—and it is an awesome question. Compared to this question, the different moral and political options available to us pale not into insignificance (because Christians are in the world and responsible for the world) but into what Dietrich Bonhoeffer called "penultimacy": the ultimate question is the question of salvation. Thus the issue I want to address now is not—emphatically not—the substitution of one cultural or political agenda for another. Rather, it is the issue of placing

---

59. See, for instance, Richard Bauckham, *The Bible in Politics: How to Read the Bible Politically* (Louisville: Westminster/John Knox Press, 1989).

any such agenda into the place that is reserved for the gospel in the faith and the life of the church.[60]

For our materialistic culture, passionately focused on the comforts of this life and the pleasures of the now, this calls for the urgent restoration to our vision of the ultimate importance of heaven. Against Marxist critics who insist this is nothing but religious escapism, Conyers has shown that the eclipse of heaven in Western thought has resulted in a much shallower analysis of life and death than was found in our earlier heritage.[61] Our compass has lost its north pole, and jerks uncontrollably and arbitrarily in any and every direction. We have set ourselves free from the looming reality of heaven and hell and found ourselves lost in moral disarray, mired in cultural and individual purposelessness.

Serious Bible readers have always recognized this. Did not Jesus insist that his followers store up their treasures in heaven (Matt. 6:19–21)? Did he not frankly warn them, "Do not be afraid of those who kill the body but cannot kill the soul. Rather, be afraid of the One who can destroy both soul and body in hell" (Matt. 10:28; Luke 12:5)? "What good is it for a man to gain the whole world, yet forfeit his soul? Or what can a man give in exchange for his soul?" (Mark 8:36–37). Not only does Scripture insist that we are "destined to die once, and after that to face judgment" (Heb. 9:27), it announces that all of history is directed toward the new heaven and the new earth—or hell. More precisely, it is directed toward a renovated universe in which "the one who sits on the throne and the Lamb" are at the very center of everything. Life here and now that is not shaped and controlled by this perspective is not merely frivolous, it is culpably rebellious.

The gospel is the good news of how God reconciles his rebellious image-bearers to himself by the death and resurrection of his Son. This good news properly entails transformed living that touches all our horizontal relationships, but which is never reducible to horizontal relationships. The proclamation of this gospel that has freed us and prepared us to meet our Maker is our joyous privilege and solemn responsibility. When the discharge of this mission is met with God's blessing, it produces men and women who are ready for both this life and the next.

Thus Christian mission can never be reduced to preparing people for this life. It can never be properly Christian if all that it aims to do, if all that it

---

60. Peter L. Berger, "Different Gospels: The Social Sources of Apostasy," in *American Apostasy: The Triumph of "Other" Gospels*, ed. Richard John Neuhaus (Grand Rapids: Eerdmans, 1989), 8.

61. A. J. Conyers, *The Eclipse of Heaven: Rediscovering the Hope of a World Beyond* (Downers Grove: InterVarsity Press, 1992).

accomplishes, is to effect some reforms in government, or to improve social, moral, and economic standards. I cannot imagine a church profoundly shaped by Scripture that will not want to reform government and improve social, moral, and economic standards. But if that is all the church is trying to do, if it is all that individual Christians are trying to do, they have lost their moorings. There is a primacy to preparing people to meet God which, though its horizon is eternity, will also change how people live here and now. To put the matter another way, the notion of realized eschatology is ridiculous unless it is predicated on futurist eschatology. The ethics and values of the End cannot be brought back into the present if there is no End.

So we are driven back to proclamation, evangelism, mission. And that priority flies in the face of philosophical pluralism. Not surprisingly, then, there is much opposition, some of which I have already considered in previous chapters. It is enough here to conclude with two observations.

First, it is vital that we draw the right lessons from the Great Commission. An influential book by Harry Boer,[62] argues that so far as the evidence from Acts goes, the early church did not evangelize out of a self-conscious obedience to the Great Commission. There is no committee formed to chart a course, no incitement to preach and witness on the grounds that we have been commanded to do so. Rather, effective evangelism takes place because believers simply cannot stop talking about their new-found knowledge of God by faith in Jesus the Messiah. It takes place because the Holy Spirit emboldens and empowers a Peter, and directs the leaders of the church in Antioch to set aside Saul and Barnabas for a particular mission. It takes place because in God's providence persecution breaks out in Jerusalem, the believers are scattered, and wherever they go they talk. It takes place because God prepares Cornelius and Peter, at opposite ends of an evangelistic encounter as it were, and brings them together—and it is unclear which of them is more surprised. Why then is so much modern missionary recruitment dependent on appeals to the Great Commission?

Bosch takes the next step in the argument. Historically, he argues, certain texts or themes are characteristic of the understanding of mission in different periods of the church's history. John 3:16, he tries to show, is characteristic of the patristic understanding of mission; Luke 14:23 of the Catholic medieval period; Romans 1:16–18 of the Protestant Reformation. In each case, the choice of the peculiar texts or themes is inevitably tied to cultural and theological factors dominant at the time. In the modern period, the Great Commission texts are tied to the influences of Enlightenment and "modernity," including

---

62. Harry R. Boer, *Pentecost and Missions* (Grand Rapids: Eerdmans, 1961).

the undisputed primacy of reason, the separation between subject and object, the substitution of the cause-effect scheme for belief in purpose, the infatuation with progress, the unsolved tension between "fact" and "value," the confidence that every problem and puzzle can be solved, and the ideas of the emancipated, autonomous individual.... The entire Western missionary movement of the past three centuries emerged from the matrix of the Enlightenment. On the one hand, it spawned an attitude of tolerance to all people and a relativistic attitude toward belief of any kind; on the other, it gave birth to Western superiority feelings and prejudice.[63]

Many writers have tied the church's use of the Great Commission during the last three centuries to feelings of manifest destiny and to colonial exploitation. And some, on that basis, also call for a moratorium. Hunsberger turns Boer's argument in another direction: *"In the reporting of Jesus' final words in the Gospels and Acts we should see not a command for the early churches to obey, but an affirmation of what they found themselves doing."*[64]

What shall we make of this?

(a) There is clearly more than a little truth to Boer's analysis of Acts. But regrettably, he has set his analysis in a disjunctive framework that is slightly distorting. In the Bible, when God visits his people in a powerful way and they are characterized by zeal, godliness, and witness, there may be less self-conscious, programmatic obedience and more obedience that grows out of a delighted God-centeredness. One might similarly argue that there is no evidence in Acts that the earliest Christians met one another's physical needs, or kept themselves from adultery, because they self-consciously and programmatically decided to obey other specific injunctions of Jesus. It was unthinkable that they should do otherwise. But it does not follow that they would therefore fail to acknowledge that Jesus had in fact left some injunctions in this regard. Moreover, the earliest believers, all converted Jews and proselytes, took some time to wrestle with the challenges set by extension of the gospel to the Gentiles and thus with the relation of the gospel to the Jewish Scriptures. Just as even within the New Testament period it took some time for Christians to come to stable conviction on many of these points (witness the Jerusalem Council, Acts 15, and related passages), so also the universality of the Great Commission was in measure an unexplored "loose end" for many believers. At one level, this was a marginal problem at the time: just as brand new converts today may be witnessing happily and enthu-

---

63. David J. Bosch, *Transforming Mission: Paradigm Shifts in Theology of Mission* (Maryknoll: Orbis Books, 1991), 339–44, esp. 342, 344.

64. George R. Hunsberger, "Is There Biblical Warrant for Evangelism?" *Interpretation* 48 (1994): 135 (emphasis his).

siastically (and sometimes tactlessly!) from the day of their conversion, without having yet so much as heard of the Great Commission, so the rapid expansion of the early chuch ensured there was no shortage of converts in precisely that position.

In short, Boer's thesis is tied too much to an argument from silence, and is short on nuance. Even so, insofar as he is right, it suggests that the greatest incentive to evangelism, witness, and mission emerges from a church's deepening knowledge of God. It may be dangerous to make the call to mission turn on *mere* obedience *at the expense of a robust personal faith and knowledge of God*. But none of this warrants the view that the Great Commission texts are not really commands at all, or are at best mere affirmations of what the church is already doing. Doubtless they will serve as affirmations and confirmations if the church is engaged in witness and mission; they must serve as commands and even rebukes if the church is not.

(b) At the risk of introducing some thoroughly unresearched and uncontrolled evidence, I must relate evidence gathered by purely anecdotal means. Recently I have been asking many people in "vocational" ministry about their sense of "call." What brought them to this place? The number of people in my thoroughly arbitrary sample who say they enter the ministry or missionary service out of self-conscious obedience to the Great Commission is very small. Far larger is the group that talks about the dawning (or sudden) sense of the ineffable beauty and importance of the gospel, beside which everything else fades away. Many Christian witnesses date their "call" from such experiences. Thus, although it is true that mission conferences in evangelical churches often focus a disproportionate amount of time on the Great Commission, I suspect that what has in fact called many of the best and most fruitful of missionaries from this generation is in fact something else: a sudden or growing grasp of the excellencies of Christ.

(c) Those who wish to tie all evangelism and mission to imperialism forget the power and source of the initial expansion of the gospel. As Waldron Scott puts it, that early movement was undertaken by "a first-century band of believers witnessing from the underside of history," and the commission on which it is based "has captured the imagination of numerous emerging Third World missionary societies today, most of whom are as powerless and oppressed as their apostolic predecessors."[65]

(d) We are all people of an age, and doubtless many missionaries during the last three centuries were inflicted by a sense of colonial superiority.

---

65. "'No Other Name'—An Evangelical Response [plus rejoinders and a surrejoinder]," in *Christ's Lordship and Religious Pluralism*, ed. Gerald H. Anderson and Thomas F. Stransky (Maryknoll: Orbis Books, 1981), 96.

Wherever exploitation is found, it is to be regretted, condemned, repented of. But the generalities found in some of the current literature that looks back on the past is terribly prejudicial. It is, in fact, bad history, tied to a thesis the facts really won't fit, or will fit in only some cases. For example, British missionaries to India typically found in the colonial authorities their strongest opposition. Colonial powers were often far more interested in power, trade, control of trade routes and primary resources, than in gospel expansion, and saw the missionaries as nuisances and hindrances. The courage, perseverance, sacrifice, integrity, and suffering of many of these men and women should not be demeaned by comfortable scholars banging away on their word processors, analyzing history into neat little patterns. Life is too complex. A Jonathan Edwards, serving Indians on the American frontier, frequently fought with state authorities on behalf of justice and compassion for the Indians he sought to evangelize.

Moreover, insofar as missionaries during the period of modernity were compromised by the presuppositions of their age, surely it behooves us to humble ourselves and ask what are the presuppositions of *our* age that are compromising *us*? What kind of missionaries is postmodernity shaping? That is not a cynical question. The impact of postmodernity may in God's providence help us to come to a proper grasp of contextualization and globalization, the theme of the last chapter of this book. But as far as I can see it has not called forth much self-sacrifice, much zeal for the truth, much passion in prayer and preaching.

The problem of illegitimate appeals to culture or to the history of culture in order to curtail or limit mission and evangelism has always been with us. In the first century, Paul and Silas faced crowds that were not only racist but who threw their weight around by trying to manipulate the cultural biases (e.g., Acts 16:21). Thoughtful Christians must be aware of these pressures, must repeatedly examine themselves and their motives, and must finally stand unmoved.

Second, the articulation of the gospel must be undertaken in a spirit of compassion. In the present climate, the need for this seems to be a declining priority. The reasons are complex and tragic, but therefore call all the more urgently for attention.

Part of the problem is that while the left demonizes the right, the right returns the compliment. Certainly we have had ample opportunity in this book to observe some of the ways in which the left demonizes the right. Moltmann offers another choice example:

> Thirty years ago, we thought that fundamentalism, as old-fashioned and outdated, as repressed and primitive as it is, would soon disappear. Today it looks as though it, and not modernism, will determine the shape of the com-

ing century. At the end of this century we will hand over the conflict between modernism and fundamentalism without having resolved it.[66]

There it is: "old-fashioned," "outdated," "repressed," "primitive." Moreover, Moltmann is not talking about the extreme lunatic fringe. He is talking about the entire conservative spectrum of Christianity that has stood over against modernism for a century, but paints it with lurid colors. Moreover, he strips it of content, for in this article he paints it with the same brush used to portray "fundamentalism" in Islam.[67] Moltmann's perception of who is winning has less to do with great gains in social acceptance of "fundamentalists," but in great losses by the various branches of liberalism—though that is another issue. My only point here is that there is no want of writers quick to demonize the right.

But the right demonizes the left in equally lurid hues. After one has finished reading a broad spectrum of conservative Christian writers, each graphically depicting the decline in values or the shattering of families or the corruption of justice or decaying of Western culture, one becomes aware of two facts: (1) Books of this sort sell well and circulate widely, precisely because there is fear in the land, and these books give voice to that fear and articulate its causes. We look back, sometimes with nostalgia and sometimes with anger, because we are frightened to look forward. (2) Only rarely do these books breathe compassion. We are frightened, and we are in a mood to blame people and damn them.

One of the reasons for Francis Schaeffer's influence was his ability to present his analysis of the culture with a tear in his eye. Whether or not one agrees at every point with his analysis, and regardless of how severe his judgments were, one could not responsibly doubt his compassion, his genuine

---

66. Jürgen Moltmann, "Christianity in the Third Millennium," *Theology Today* 51 (1994): 83.

67. Part of the problem, of course, is changing definition. At the turn of the century, "fundamentalism" referred to that movement which insisted that there are definable "fundamentals" to the Christian religion without which Christianity is no longer Christianity. "Fundamentalism" and "evangelicalism" were, in the English-speaking world, used almost interchangeably. By the mid-1950s, fundamentalists positioned themselves on the right wing of almost every political and social axis, and frequently defined themselves by what they were *against*, while evangelicals, whose core beliefs were scarcely different from those of the fundamentalists, were more broadly distributed over the various axes, and preferred to identify themselves by what they were *for*. More recently, in the general media "fundamentalism" has been stripped of all doctrinal content whatsoever, and is used to refer to that religious attitude, regardless of the religion, that seems to the media (and sometimes their perception is correct) to be characterized by bigotry and hatred. Cf. John Fea, "Understanding the Changing Facade of Twentieth-Century American Protestant Fundamentalism: Toward a Historical Definition," *Trinity Journal* 15 (1994): 181–99, who divides the period into four phases.

love for men and women. Too many of his would-be successors simply sound like angry people. Our times call for Christian leaders who will articulate the truth boldly, courageously, humbly, knowledgeably, in a contemporary fashion, with prophetic fire—and with profound compassion. One cannot imagine how the kind of gospel set forth in the Bible could be effectively communicated in any other way. Those of us who address crowds today, whether in person or in books, serve the One who, on seeing large crowds, "had compassion on them, because they were like sheep without a shepherd" (Mark 6:34; cf. Matt. 9:36).

Part Four

Pluralism Within the Camp

Chapter 11

FRAYING, FRAGMENTED, FRUSTRATED: THE CHANGING FACE OF WESTERN EVANGELICALISM

Throughout this book I have been arguing that pluralism is many-faceted. Each facet demands its own kind of investigation. One of the facets that so far has received only brief allusion is the pluralism within evangelicalism itself. The four chapters of part 4 treat various aspects of this subject. Chapter 11 surveys the ground, highlights some of the more important challenges within the camp, and ventures a few suggestions as to an appropriate response. Chapter 12 reflects on some of the priorities our evangelism must take, bringing together the concerns of the first two parts of this book (on radical hermeneutics and religious pluralism), the challenges of part 3 (how to act responsibly as Christians in a decaying and increasingly hostile culture), and the changing shape of evangelicalism set out in this chapter. Chapter 13 picks up one particular doctrinal area, final punishment—an area in which current developments within evangelicalism doubtless reflect greater diversity, greater pluralism if you will, than anything the movement experienced half a century ago. The last chapter, chapter 14, argues that, from a worldwide perspective, although some of the diversity within evangelicalism is dangerous, some of it is salutary, and seeks to chart a way forward with responsibility to God, fidelity to Scripture, and hope.

A. The Challenge of Definition

Giving definition to evangelicalism is not only difficult, but is growing even more difficult as a wider and wider group of people apply the label to themselves. It may be, as some have suggested, that the term will eventually so lack definition as to be theologically useless—much like the term "Christian" today, which, in Western countries, may mean no more than that someone is not a Muslim or a Hindu or the like, and not an atheist. The term is exceedingly plastic and runs into many molds shaped by local history. So it is (some argue) with evangelical and evangelicalism. In that case, we must ask what group we are talking about before we can begin to talk about the group.

Part of the problem is that the measure of the term can be taken along several axes. Thus Marsden writes:

> First, evangelicalism is a conceptual unity that designates a grouping of Christians who fit a certain definition. Second, evangelicalism can designate a more organic movement. Religious groups with some common traditions and experiences, despite wide diversities and only meager institutional inter-connections, may constitute a movement in the sense of moving or tending in some common directions. Third, within evangelicalism in these broader senses is a more narrow, consciously "evangelical" transdenominational community with complicated infrastructures of institutions and persons who identify with "evangelicalism."[1]

Marsden himself makes clear that the "conceptual unity" to which he refers is a doctrinal summary. Evangelicals typically emphasize (1) the Reformation doctrine of the final authority of Scripture; (2) the real, historical character of God's saving work recorded in Scripture; (3) eternal salvation only through personal trust in Christ; (4) the importance of evangelism and missions; and (5) the importance of a "spiritually transformed life."[2] Evangelicals may differ sharply over how even these doctrines are put together, but on this axis there are some basic common doctrines. His point is that there are several competing axes.

It may assist our evaluation of the current status of evangelicalism if we briefly weigh some of the ways in which it is presently defined.

(1) As a starting point for this discussion, I will begin by summarizing an essay that I wrote several years ago in which I raised the question of evangelical self-identity.[3]

---

1. George M. Marsden, *Evangelicalism and Modern America* (Grand Rapids: Eerdmans, 1984), ix.

2. Ibid., ix–x.

3. D. A. Carson, "Evangelicals, Ecumenism and the Church," in *Evangelical Affirmations*, ed. Kenneth S. Kantzer and Carl F. H. Henry (Grand Rapids: Zondervan, 1990), esp. 349–54.

The term "evangelical" is colored with different shadings in various parts of the world. In North America until very recently, it was used to refer to Christians who are loyal to both a formal principle and a material principle. The formal principle is the truth, authority, and finality of the Bible. The material principle is the gospel as understood in historic evangelical Protestantism. While not wanting to minimize the theological and ecclesiastical differences in that heritage, we might summarize that heritage in terms such as these: We insist that salvation is gained exclusively through personal faith in the finished cross-work of Jesus Christ, who is both God and man. His atoning death, planned and brought about by his heavenly Father, expiates our sin, vanquishes Satan, propitiates the Father, and inaugurates the promised kingdom. In the ministry, death, resurrection, and exaltation of Jesus, God himself is supremely revealed, such that rejection of Jesus, or denials of what the Scriptures tell us about Jesus, constitute nothing less than rejection of God himself. In consequence of his triumphant cross-work, Christ has bequeathed the Holy Spirit, himself God, as the downpayment of the final inheritance that will come to Christ's people when he himself returns. The saving and transforming power of the Spirit displayed in the lives of Christ's people is the product of divine grace, grace alone—grace that is apprehended by faith alone. The knowledge of God that we enjoy becomes for us an impetus to missionary outreach characterized by urgency and compassion.

This summary, or something like it, most evangelicals would happily espouse. This sort of approach tightly ties "evangelical" to "evangel" (εὐαγγέλιον), the gospel of Jesus Christ. Yet in that essay I acknowledged that this sort of definition must take into account several points, which I here summarize and at one or two points slightly revise.

(a) In many parts of the world, the word *evangelical* has different overtones. In Germany, *evangelisch* refers to what is Protestant over against what is Roman Catholic, and is almost indistinguishable from Lutheran, whether liberal or conservative. But when a German resorts to *evangelikal*, there are overtones of the sectarian, not least because the term is normally associated with groups outside the recognized state churches. Traditions can cross national boundaries, so it is not surprising that the recently merged Lutheran denomination in the U.S. retained the word "evangelical" even though large swaths of the denomination would identify themselves with what is classically "liberal."

(b) In Anglo-Saxon heritage, *evangelical* is tightly tied to the movement's response to several defining theological and ecclesiastical developments in our history. Historically, evangelicals have rejected "high church" theology: that is, they have stressed the sufficiency and finality of Scripture over against a too-ready appeal to tradition; they have emphasized the finality of Christ's atoning death over against any sacramentarianism that appears to jeopardize that exclusiveness; and they have emphasized the priesthood of all believers as being of the essence of the new covenant, over against all sacerdotal claims to the contrary. Equally, as the impact of the Enlightenment favored deism and so-called "higher critical" views that had the effect of depreciating the authority of Scripture, evangelicals defined themselves by identifying strongly with the universal church's historic commitment to Scripture. Thus evangelicalism "came to be thought of as a movement characterized by low churchmanship, a high view of Scripture, and evangelistic zeal."[4]

(c) Many self-confessed evangelicals happily apply the label to many who would not use it to refer to themselves. Thus many confessional Lutherans and Presbyterians are suspicious of the label because of the cultural or ecclesiastical associations they perceive in many who call themselves evangelicals. They think of themselves as reformed, or simply Lutheran. Similarly, "evangelical" is not a self-identifying label for many charismatics who nevertheless fit the theological grid sketched above. At one level, this is unfortunate, not least because it has encouraged many scholars to try to define evangelicalism in nontheological categories, as we shall see. But it is surely useful to have some term to refer to believers who, whatever their doctrinal and ecclesiastical differences, wholeheartedly agree on the kinds of fundamentals I have briefly articulated, especially if some of these fundamentals are the foci for a great deal of contemporary skepticism and denial.

(d) A more difficult problem for the merely doctrinal definition is how to handle inherited "folk" religion. Many polls disclose that millions of people would happily "sign on" to most or all of the elements in the doctrinal summary I provided. But such polls cannot begin to assess whether such beliefs are deep, personal, and life controlling, or merely shallow, inherited, and of indifferent power.

(e) A further problem has arisen in that, as I noted at the beginning of this section, a wider and wider spectrum of people now apply the label "evangelical" to themselves. For example, as recently as 1975 an observer as astute as Martin Marty could insist that evangelicals and fundamentalists, however much they may disagree on many points, are equally committed to an inerrancy view of the Bible.[5] Many self-styled evangelicals now affirm the "infallibility" of Scripture (which at one point could not be distinguished

---

4. Ibid., 351.

5. Martin E. Marty, "Tensions Within Contemporary Evangelicalism: A Critical Appraisal," in *The Evangelicals: What They Believe, Who They Are, Where They Are Changing* (Nashville: Abingdon, 1975), esp. 173.

from its inerrancy), but not its inerrancy. The former category is now often taken as referring to the Bible's truthfulness exclusively in matters of "faith and practice." The "faith and practice" formula at the time of the Reformation was an *inclusive* category, over against the claims of the Roman Catholic Church to have the right to prescribe in these areas. Their modern scions sometimes wield the expression in an *exclusive* way, thus denying that the Bible is reliable on whatever subject it chooses to speak.

But this is only one dimension of the changes within evangelicalism. In ethics, doctrine, tolerance levels, and mores, evangelicals now admit much more diversity than their forebears three or four decades ago could have admitted. The point is so important that it earns separate treatment below. Here the point is that the changes inevitably render more complex all attempts to define evangelicalism.

(f) For many evangelicals the term is almost synonymous with "true Christian." If evangelicalism is irrefragably tied to the "evangel," and the evangel is the sole means by which men and women come to a saving knowledge of the living God, then we are only a whisker from concluding that nonevangelicals are non-Christians, in any biblically useful sense of "Christian." At the same time, evangelicals are as quick as anyone else to acknowledge that God sometimes works his saving grace in the lives of people with remarkably little understanding of the evangel. I suppose we would want to say that if this has been a genuine experience of grace, substantial understanding will come with time. But that introduces distinctions between the immature and the mature and raises questions about just how inconsistent a person may be before one concludes that what they understand to be the gospel simply isn't. Doubtless in the clear cases some of us might be willing to venture an opinion; in the doubtful cases, virtually none of us would be.

Suppose, then, that someone drops one or two of the historic distinctives of evangelicalism and calls the hybrid, say, "liberal evangelicalism," or "Catholic evangelicalism." To say such people are *not* evangelicals sounds too much like saying they are not Christians. But if they are Christians, many evangelicals would want to apply the word evangelical to them. Thus is born the pressure to apply the term to those who hold some positions not traditionally evangelical, but whose experience of grace can scarcely be denied. Properly speaking, the question then becomes, How much of the historic evangel can be abandoned before it is no longer evangelicalism? Out of this semantic potpourri emerge categories like (i) "consistent evangelical"—a category that is meaningful only if "evangelical" refers to a theological position, not to an experience of grace; (ii) "liberal evangelical"—a contradiction in terms if "liberal" refers to major matters of doctrine as "evangelical" is historically defined, but a combination that is usually achieved by stripping "evangelical" of most doctrinal content in favor of a fairly sentimental experience of grace; (iii) "Catholic evangelical"—which either means one is staunchly evangelical (doctrinally) while trying to remain a member of the Catholic church, or, more commonly, that one is trying to marry evangelical experience with Roman Catholic views of sacrament, priesthood, and liturgy; (iv) "confessional evangelical"—another way of insisting that the term "evangelical" is most useful when it has doctrinal content in it, but one which skirts "conservative evangelical" on the ground that "conservative" might be taken socially or politically, which may be an entirely different thing.

For reasons that will become increasingly apparent, I hold that "evangelical" and "evangelicalism" are most useful when they are held to their etymology in the evangel, "the gospel [God] promised beforehand through his prophets in the Holy Scriptures regarding his Son" (Rom. 1:2–3), on the assumption that such an "evangel" is held with firmness and sincerity of heart. In this light, evangelicalism as a movement must be seen to be determined by its center, not by its outermost boundary—and even that center must, in the light of its own confession, constantly be held up to the examination of Scripture. Contemporary evangelicalism, consistent or confessional or otherwise, embraces a wide range of people (including some who would not readily apply the label to themselves), but not all of their theological opinions. But I fully recognize that in the long run this understanding of the label might not prevail. In that case, there may come a time when it will be best to abandon it. But that time is not yet.

(2) Some writers deploy "evangelical" and "evangelicalism" strictly in a theological sense, often associated with the theology of "the Evangelical Awakening," (known in America as the "Great Awakening"). Perhaps the ablest exponent of this view is the late Dr. D. Martyn Lloyd-Jones. In three addresses first delivered to IFES[6] students in 1971,[7] he set forth his case. Beginning with the opening verses of Jude, Lloyd-Jones argued that sometimes the most urgent thing that Christian leaders can do, even when they much prefer to do something else, is urge fellow-believers "to contend for the faith that was once for all entrusted to the saints" (Jude 3). For Lloyd-Jones, the definition of "evangelical" he was defending was much more than a word game. "My whole contention," he said, "is that for us to assume that because we have once said that we are evangelical, therefore we must still be evangelical now and shall always be, is not only to misread the teaching of the

---

6. International Federation of Evangelical Students, the body that links together various national IVCF-related student groups.

7. Reprinted in D. M. Lloyd-Jones, *Knowing the Times: Addresses Delivered on Various Occasions, 1942–1977* (Edinburgh: Banner of Truth Trust, 1989), 299–355, and still worthy of careful reading.

New Testament, but to fail completely to grasp and to understand the great lessons which are taught us so clearly by history" (303). His argument is that people and movements change their character while the labels stay the same; that the initial dangers are subtle and at the periphery of things; that the danger was clearly present in New Testament times and has occurred repeatedly across history. He brooked no defense of being "too narrow, too rigid, and too detailed in definition" (307). But the opposite danger, he felt, is more obvious at the moment—"the danger of being so broad, so wide, and so loose that in the end we have no definitions at all" (309). Lloyd-Jones's concern, of course, is not the preservation of the label "evangelicalism," but the preservation and promulgation of the "evangel," the gospel.

In times of fuzzy thinking, we cannot too often be reminded of such points. Yet if pressed, doubtless Lloyd-Jones would have been the first to insist that our touchstone is not the Evangelical Awakening, but the Bible. Put differently, our attempts to "contend for the faith that was once for all entrusted to the saints" must never be cast as *merely* a conservative call to an earlier period of the evangelical movement (however much we think that period captures parts of the biblical message we are in danger of overlooking), but to the Bible itself. In principle it recognizes that parts of the movement may at any time be in error, and that all things must constantly be brought back to Scripture: that is the importance, of course, of the "formal principle" of evangelicalism to which I earlier referred.

The entailment of Lloyd-Jones's view, of course, is that much that calls itself evangelicalism today is not, or is only inconsistently so. That judgment, of course, will trouble all social scientists and historians struggling to define evangelicalism on a purely empirical base.

(3) Some have attempted a mixture of beliefs and practices as the defining genius of evangelicalism. Perhaps Bebbington's "four qualities that have been the special marks of Evangelical religion" have been the most frequently quoted: "*conversionism*, the belief that lives need to be changed; *activism*, the expression of the gospel in effort; *biblicism*, a particular regard for the Bible; and what may be called *crucicentrism*, a stress on the sacrifice of Christ on the cross. Together they form a quadrilateral of priorities that is the basis of Evangelicalism."[8]

Bebbington's discussion of these categories has much to commend it,[9] however much the labels themselves leave something to be desired. What is missing, I think, is the way evangelicals themselves have often seen an organic

---

8. David Bebbington, *Evangelicalism in Modern Britain: A History from the 1730s to the 1980s* (Grand Rapids: Baker, 1992 [1989]), 2–3.

9. Especially pp. 5–17.

wholeness to their beliefs and practices, and that at the center is a profound passion for submitting everything to the Bible. In that sense, what Bebbington calls "biblicism" (an ugly way of putting it) might properly come first. Of course, some other groups make the same claim (e.g., Jehovah's Witnesses), but emerge with a very different theology. Bebbington tries to avoid the trap by specifying "crucicentrism."

More fundamentally, Bebbington's quadrilateral is capable of being abused at two other points.

First, the emphasis on "the special marks of Evangelical religion" focuses on what might appear anomalous, as compared with some other traditions, giving the impression (however unwitting) of mere sectarianism. Because the focus is on what is distinctive, one might get the impression that evangelicals care nothing about, say, the Trinity, or Christology, or the importance of pursuing heaven and fleeing judgment. On the contrary, evangelicals adopt the early creeds.

Second, because the four points of the quadrilateral are so general, the precise nature of evangelical conflict with theological alternatives is sometimes obscured. Few leading evangelicals are particularly interested in debates over the precise definition of, say, inerrancy, *for their own sake*, but because sooner or later such definitions have an enormous bearing on Christology, justification, the nature of salvation, what we think of sin, and much more. Thus, if the "conversionism" and "activism" of evangelicalism have been concerned to deny the efficacy of merely formal religion (as well as to remain faithful to Scripture on these points), the "biblicism" and "crucicentrism" are nothing other than attempts to remain faithful to the gospel disclosed in Scripture in a sweep of areas where the tides of opinion were against such matters.

Perhaps I should add that I am troubled by not a few historical judgments in the book that I think are misleading. For example, Bebbington links the "Cambridge Trio" (A. J. Hort, J. B. Lightfoot, and B. F. Westcott) with S. R. Driver (Regius Professor of Hebrew at Oxford) and others as those whose "magisterial work" allayed fears that criticism was close to unbelief.[10] But Westcott certainly and Lightfoot probably adopted the historic view of Scripture, even if their colleague Hort was prepared to admit errors. Thus Westcott and Lightfoot were in a very different camp from Driver. Thoughtful evangelicals were not alarmed at "criticism" when the results were aligned with the conclusions of Westcott and Lightfoot; they were alarmed at "criticism" because so many who touted the expression were undermining belief in Scripture—not only in fine points (which is of course

---

10. Ibid., 186.

where unbelief begins) but in the very fabric of its thought. That Driver could argue—not very successfully, in my opinion—that the form of Old Testament criticism in which he indulged was entirely compatible with orthodoxy[11] was part of the "double-think" at the time, however well-intentioned, and was also an astonishing indication of how little theological integration Driver himself attempted. But my point is that Bebbington's analysis, lumping together a Westcott and a Driver, betrays a failure to recognize the evangelical concern for the *outcomes* of "critical" study. Inevitably one can find some ignorant evangelicals who damned all "criticism." But the observation is superficial. Many on the "left" end of criticism liked to think, because they belonged to the "modern" world, that their work was properly based, methodologically sound, and universally valid. It took work that was equally solid to demonstrate how culturally bound it was, how methodologically unsound, how philosophically committed—every bit as committed as evangelical scholarship. But none of these lines of thought are followed up, with the result that the picture of evangelicals at the turn of the century, and the nature of their primary concerns, is somewhat skewed.

(4) More helpful is the work of David Wells. Wells rightly points out that "evangelicals have always been *doctrinal* people."[12] But he argues that since World War II, "three centers to evangelical faith have emerged"[13]—not geographical centers but ideological centers that develop in part chronologically. These three he calls: (a) The confessional. The firm conviction that evangelicalism must be defined by what is believed, and that what is believed should be biblical, still governed the movement. (b) The transconfessional. By this, Wells refers to the emergence of managers, television personalities, and entrepreneurs, replacing theologians and thinkers; "everywhere the importance of theological belief is being replaced by the importance of effective strategy, proficient fund-raising, and the bold building of personal bases of power and influence."[14] (c) The charismatic. Wells is not concerned to evaluate Pentecostalism and the charismatic/renewal movements *per se*, but to point out that what they have in common is that

---

11. *An Introduction to the Literature of the Old Testament*, 8th ed. (Edinburgh: T & T Clark, 1909), viii–xiii.

12. David F. Wells, "'No Offense: I Am an Evangelical': A Search for Self-Definition," in A. James Rudin and Marvin R. Wilson, eds., *A Time to Speak: The Evangelical-Jewish Encounter* (Grand Rapids: Eerdmans, 1987), 22.

13. David Wells, "On Being Evangelical: Some Theological Differences and Similarities," in *Evangelicalism: Comparative Studies of Popular Protestantism in North America, the Bristish Isles, and Beyond, 1700–1990*, ed. Mark A. Noll, David W. Bebbington, and George A. Rawlyk (New York: Oxford Univ. Press, 1994), 390.

14. Ibid., 392.

[they] are forms of evangelicalism that are not primarily theologies. Both arise centrally from a spiritual intuition about the presence of the Holy Spirit. Both, therefore, have an entirely different place for biblical confession, as compared with those whom I am calling confessional evangelicals, and both have an entirely different way of relating matters of diversity to that of theological confession. Here, biblical confession arises not as a thing in itself but as an adjunct to the experience of the Holy Spirit; this experience of the Holy Spirit provides the ground on which charismatics desire to meet others, whether Catholic or Protestant.

The almost secondary role that theology has played in the charismatic movement coincided with the habits that have emerged among the transconfessional managers of the evangelical empire, and in this sense they have found themselves on the same wavelength as the charismatics.[15]

And all of this, of course, has been compounded by the impact of postmodernism, which is highly suspicious of doctrinal claims of a transcendental or cross-cultural character, and quite open to fluent talk of experience, and to efficiency and success.

Much of this analysis is very shrewd. There is a great deal of evidence to support Wells's central contentions. But for my purposes here, two caveats might not be out of place.

First, Wells paints with a broad brush. The result is that there is little attempt to deal charitably with the countless faithful ministers and lay Christians who have never heard of postmodernism, who are decidedly suspicious of pomp and imperial splendor, and who self-consciously try to elevate the authority of Scripture above personal experience, even their own. What percentage of the movement they make up, I have no idea. But they deserve respect and encouragement (as Wells doubtless would agree).

Second, there are other facets to the changing face of evangelicalism that Wells does not treat. His focus has tended to be on the popular and the semipopular. But one could equally argue that there have been some remarkable changes in the theological and intellectual leadership of evangelicalism. Some of these I will briefly explore below. Sweeney examines various "models" that have been used to chart the move from evangelicalism to neo-evangelicalism and finds all of them inadequate in some degree. For example, Sweeney cites a letter Wilbur Smith wrote to Carl Henry in April, 1961, saying, "I greatly regret to have to say that the atmosphere here at [Fuller] is nothing like what you and I knew it to be when the school was started."[16] Sweeney comments, "While this may simply be the complaint of one beginning to find himself on

---

15. Ibid., 392.

16. Smith to Henry, 25 April 1961. Folder 20, Box 16, Collection 8, Records of *Christianity Today*. Billy Graham Center Archives, Wheaton.

the intellectual outskirts of a progressively more scholarly seminary, it seems more likely a serious reflection of intergenerational vicissitudes within the neo-evangelical movement."[17] He adds, "Current neo-evangelical historiography, then, fails to grasp the magnitude of the identity crisis that the sources themselves suggest."[18] Sweeney goes on to delineate a kind of "schizophrenia" between a strand in historic evangelicalism that wanted to embrace all of true Christianity, and another that insisted on the nonnegotiability of evangelical truth. He concludes:

> The strange schizophrenia of modern evangelicalism owes to the increasing tension between historic evangelical ecumenism and historic evangelical thought. Because theological modernism divided evangelicalism's ecumenical heritage, the neo-evangelicals were forced to decide between an exclusive fellowship within the harbor of historic evangelical doctrine, and historic evangelical piety on the sea of American pluralism. While the founders opted for the former, the story of the unraveling of neo-evangelical identity is the story of their scions setting out to sea.[19]

This is very astute. It is reflected in the widely recognized clamor for academic recognition among many of the younger evangelical intellectuals, in their drumming criticism of evangelical "fathers" (like immature adolescents who cannot allow any opinion other than their own to be respected), in their persistent drift from biblical authority, and, increasingly, from other doctrines as well. But most of them still want to call themselves evangelicals: that is their power base, that is their prime readership, and it is that group that funds many of the colleges and seminaries where they teach.

What this suggests, then, is that there are as many problems among evangelical intellectuals as in evangelical populism, if of a slightly different sort. In both cases, the product is less and less "evangelical" in any useful historic or theological sense.

(5) Among many historians and some theologians, there is a growing tendency to reduce the theological component in evangelical definition to the vanishing point, emphasizing instead a variety of cultural, institutional, and personal factors. Typical of this approach is the work of Lints, who leans not a little on an essay by George Marsden.[20] Lints argues that an approach at

---

17. Douglas A. Sweeney, "The Essential Evangelicalism Dialectic: The Historiography of the Early Neo-Evangelical Movement and the Observer-Participant Dilemma," *Church History* 60 (1991): 83.

18. Ibid.

19. Ibid., 84.

20. George M. Marsden, "Evangelicalism in the Sociological Laboratory," *Reformed Journal* 34/6 (June 1984): 20–24. See also Marsden, *Evangelicalism and Modern America*, passim. Marsden and Lints are not alone in this perception. See, for example, the contributions

defining evangelicalism in doctrinal terms fails on three grounds: (a) it does not adequately account for the diversity of the movement; (b) the conceptual definitions "often fail to differentiate evangelicals sufficiently from nonevangelicals"[21]—i.e., there are many believers who would not call themselves evangelicals but who are so according to the doctrinal standards that most self-confessing evangelicals erect as defining. These first two points I have already discussed, and need not review again. But above all, according to Lints, (c) "the doctrinal criterion is in fact tangential rather than central to the essence of the movement. Put simply, the evangelical movement is not held together by a confessional or theological framework. Clearly certain theological beliefs are important to evangelicals, but they do not inhere in any larger theological construct that could be accurately identified as 'evangelical theology'"[22]—unlike confessional traditions such as Lutheran, Reformed, Presbyterian, Holiness, and the like. "In reality, it is a diversity of theological frameworks that more nearly captures the essence of evangelicalism. The movement's unique identity is defined to a considerably greater extent by cultural, institutional, and personal factors than by a narrow set of common doctrinal beliefs."[23] Lints cites Marty:

> Where local congregations are hugely successful, they are so as clienteles or constituencies, not as confessional expressions. . . . It is hard to picture a member of the Crystal Cathedral having chosen membership because its pastor and its official status are part of the Reformed Church in America. If a member leaves in disaffection, it will not be because of that Reformed tie but because some other minister or some other channel appeals more.[24]

How shall we evaluate this approach to defining evangelicalism? Seven brief remarks may clarify the issues.

First, there is some truth to this analysis. Especially in the evangelicalism of the past three decades or so, there are growing components very largely disconnected from any theological definition. But it is far from clear to me that such diversity prevailed in any large-scale way earlier. The question, then, is whether we should struggle to preserve what is godly and disciplined by Scripture in the movement, and insist on attaching such elements

---

by Dayton in Donald W. Dayton and Robert K. Johnston, eds., *The Variety of American Evangelicalism* (Downers Grove: InterVarsity Press, 1991).

21. Richard Lints, *The Fabric of Theology: A Prolegomenon to Evangelical Theology* (Grand Rapids: Eerdmans, 1993), 30.

22. Ibid., 30–31.

23. Ibid., 31.

24. Martin Marty, "The Clergy," in *The Professions in American History*, ed. Nathan O. Hatch (Notre Dame: Univ. of Notre Dame Press, 1988), 85: cited in Lints, *The Fabric of Theology*, 31.

to the "evangelical" label, rather than resorting so quickly to sociological categories.

Second, relying on Martin Marty's quip about the Crystal Cathedral really is a bit naughty. I imagine that if you asked five hundred evangelical leaders in America whether the theology preached at the Crystal Cathedral could properly be called evangelical at all, four hundred or four hundred fifty would roundly deny it. There are overtones here of trying to prove a case by appealing to the outermost fringes.

Third, I am frankly astonished that anyone could think that evangelical theology is more diverse than denominational theology or the theology of a certain broadly based heritage. Published Presbyterian theology today varies from Westminster confessionalism to flat-out anti-supernaturalism, with every conceivable stopping-place in between. And off on one side, ordained Presbyterian ministers insist that Sophia is a feminine expression of God, adopt pantheistic views, and espouse reincarnation. What is called Reformed thought is just as varied; the holiness and charismatic traditions scarcely less so. In any case, it is always unfair to compare the best of one tradition with the worst of another.

Fourth, if Lints is comparing the latest brands of so-called evangelicalism with the doctrinal uniformity of major traditions a century-and-a-half ago (which seems to be the case at one point),[25] then the comparison is unfair. The theological diversity within contemporary evangelicalism ought to be compared with the theological diversity within contemporary forms of the Christian heritage. But even if we were to allow the denominational heritages to make appeal to a time one hundred fifty years ago, we would have to remind ourselves that not a few denominations were at that point combating deism. And if instead Lints were to counter that he is only talking about *confessional* denominational heritage, then I would reply that evangelicalism at its best is *confessional* evangelicalism—and in that case, of course, we presuppose that what we are talking about is doctrinal standard, not institutional or social grouping.

Fifth, it cannot be said too strongly that the leaders of the movement whenever evangelicalism was struggling to make its voice heard after some dire setback—as, for instance, in the modernist/fundamentalist controversies at the turn of the century and beyond—did not understand their mission the way Marsden and Lints and others describe it. They understood what they were setting out to do in *theological* terms. Of course, they might have been entirely mistaken in their own motivations, but that is scarcely a charitable reading. Such a reading reminds me of certain reconstructions of the

---

25. Lints, 32–33.

Reformation. Marxist historiography, for instance, has often tried to explain the entire Reformation in terms of economics and class conflict. Certainly one cannot ignore the social and economic pressures on all integrative thought. But it must be said that Luther, Calvin, Zwingli and Hubmeier did not think of their tasks in such terms, and more recent work eschews Marxist reductionism. Similarly, then, Lints and the others are doing a disservice to those who at times have been patriarchs and matriarchs of evangelicalism, by relegating to the periphery what the leaders themselves saw as central. At the end of the day, that is surely bad history. If one wants to argue that much of *contemporary* evangelicalism has lost its theological moorings, that is another matter. But then one should say that until recently evangelicalism has tried to define itself primarily in theological categories, and that that emphasis seems to be changing among many who still attach themselves to the label. But to read the entire history of the movement in terms of the most recent developments of some wings of it is to fall into historical anachronism.

Sixth, although it is true that evangelicalism cannot offer the same sort of comprehensive theology that, say, Lutheranism or Presbyterianism can, this is surely one of those situations where "you win some and lose some," and it is disingenuous to focus only on what you lose. There is surely some place for trying to isolate the common strands of theology found among theological traditions that are self-consciously striving to be biblically faithful. It is an especially important task when the climate of opinion is against this inherited and shared body of truth, lest the faddish theologians win by a "divide and conquer" technique that tries to squeeze to the periphery every opinion that challenges them. That is why during the last century or so the ablest of evangelical theologicans, from many denominational heritages, have tried to show how evangelical convictions are not only mandated by Scripture, but have been central to the belief of faithful Christians in many centuries and traditions. Machen's famous judgment, that theological liberalism is an entirely different religion, was of course astute, but it was possible precisely because he was focusing on the *commonalities* enjoyed by the various theological traditions. If there is a "lowest common denominator" flavor about such discussions at times, charity demands that we recognize that evangelical leaders often adopted this approach to pull together a larger pool of committed and faithful Christians from a much broader base than could be provided by the struggling "remnant" in denominations in which they were increasingly marginalized.

Part of the problem is that the "remnant" has now coalesced into various groupings, some of which cherish *only* the lowest common denominator. To that extent, Lints is right. But that, I think, is part of the doctrinal declension bound up with this postmodern age—a doctrinal declension scarcely less remarkable within more narrowly confessional denominations. Small and tightly constituted denominations and associations of churches have often (but not always) been better at preserving their heritage, but often at the expense of a certain introverted cultural isolationism that has left them ill-equipped to evangelize. But the evangelical leaders in times of conflict have been evangelical *and* Presbyterian, evangelical *and* Baptist, evangelical *and* Reformed, or whatever. They did not deny their differences, and in their own contexts they emphasized them. But they perceived that the common "enemy," the common denial of historic Christianity, demanded concerted effort and a frank recognition of the great realities they held in common. Even today, not a few recent and avowedly evangelical theologies openly engage other stances *and adopt some more specific denominational heritage as well.* Thus Erickson's work has Baptist flavor, Oden is in the Wesleyan tradition, McGrath in the Anglican tradition, and Williams in the charismatic tradition. None of this in itself makes any of their works less "evangelical."

That brings us to the *seventh* point. Lints adopts this stance at least in part because one of the theses of his book is that the evangelical unity forged at the beginning of this century to combat modernism has left a couple of troubling legacies, the most important of which is that "the distillation of the gospel into a simple core led to the subsequent abandonment of a rich theological vision."[26] The recovery of rich, theological reflection today, then, demands that we work and think within a certain tradition, and eschew the "lowest common denominator" approach that has afflicted so much of evangelical thought.

A glance at the index of this book will show how indebted I am to Lints at many points, so it troubles me to disagree with him so profoundly on this point. I think he has bought into a flawed historiography of evangelicalism. At a certain level, of course, he is right: evangelicalism in its worst forms, or in its "lowest common denominator" forms, or in its purely populist forms, is unlikely to breed theologians of the fourth rank, let alone the first. But whereas such evangelicalism sometimes flourishes in parachurch groups, evangelicalism at its best also flourishes in the bosom of particular theological traditions, often enough as a purifying agent that calls Christians back to what is basic and nonnegotiable. If denominational life or comprehensive theological traditions are themselves the answer, why did they so frequently come unstuck in the conflict with modernism?

I fear we are being offered unfortunate and unnecessary disjunctions: either a comprehensive theological heritage, or evangelicalism. Rose-colored glasses are donned to look at the former; reductionism is deployed to examine the latter.

---

26. Ibid., 39.

More importantly, Lints offers his critique because he rightly perceives that evangelicalism (as defined by sociological categories) has in recent decades squandered so much of its theological heritage that it is becoming harder and harder to define it primarily in theological terms. He does this in order to *strengthen* the role of theology among confessing believers. But there are not a few others who are using the same sociological categories in order to *weaken* evangelicalism's historic theological distinctives. If they can convince enough people that evangelicalism has *always* been primarily a movement defined not by beliefs and doctrines, but by other concerns, then it becomes easier to stretch the label "evangelical" to include more and more people today who ignore those doctrinal distinctions.

For example, a writer-theologian from a well-known parachurch organization phoned me a few months ago saying she was deeply troubled because she had been asked by her head office to prepare some papers on Christology that reflected the full range of "evangelical" opinion on this subject. This organization wanted to ensure that its statements were comprehensive enough to take in everyone who is "evangelical." But precisely because "evangelicalism" these days includes more and more theological nonsense, while still retaining a label that is associated in the minds of many people with a set of convictions, what seems to be an open-minded courtesy to include fellow "evangelicals" becomes an open-ended slide into heresy. The confusion between the sociological use of "evangelical" and the theological use of "evangelical" contributes powerfully to that end. Add to this the subtle cultural pressures applied by the prevailing philosophical pluralism, and it becomes obvious that only thoughtful recognition of the dangers and wholehearted will to oppose them will prevent us from being snookered by the culture once again. While many historians and theologians seem to be taking an angry glee in exposing how the evangelical leaders of the last two or three generations were unwittingly seduced by aspects of modernist culture, must we not ask to what extent these critics are themselves being seduced by aspects of the postmodernist culture?

(6) In addition to the hyphenated evangelicalism I discussed above under the first point, one commonly hears another combination: "denomination evangelicals." Methodist evangelicals, Anglican evangelicals, Presbyterian evangelicals, and so forth, all clamor for discussion. Usage varies, but usually this expression surfaces when the denomination is very broad, perhaps encompassing many from one or more of the liberal traditions, and some from "high church" traditions. Over against these components in the denomination, one group, of various size and consistency, label themselves "denomination evangelicals." By this they usually mean that they value the denominational heritage they have received, but they feel that it has gone astray where it has abandoned one or more of the basic tenets of evangelicalism, and therefore of the Bible itself. When these "denomination evan-

gelicals" first spring up, they almost always think of the "basic tenets" primarily in doctrinal terms. Very often these evangelical wings feel their task is nothing other than to restore the gospel, the evangel, to denominations that once blazed with its glory.

With time, these movements within a denomination can end up almost anywhere, and this very fluidity casts its own shadow back on what "evangelical" comes to mean. In Anglican evangelicalism in England, for instance, although the percentage of evangelicals is impressive as compared with sixty years ago, it is becoming less and less clear what "evangelical" in "Anglican evangelical" means. For some, it is still a confessional category, and what is at stake is the gospel itself. For many others, Anglican evangelicalism is merely one form of the gospel; "Anglican" is elevated above "evangelical." Thus, one such Anglican evangelical recently wrote that what is needed in the Church of England is a certain kind of leadership without which "Anglican evangelicalism will probably (and sadly) become less Anglican and more partisanly evangelical."[27]

If "evangelical" in such an evaluation refers only to an ecclesiastical party indifferent to theological distinctions or convictions, while "Anglican" embraces all that is good and faithful to Scripture and to Scripture's God, that is a sensible and prophetic judgment. On the other hand, if "evangelical" refers to biblically defined truths more faithfully embraced by one segment of the Anglican community than by others, then it is a formula designed to weaken fidelity to Scripture and to the God who has disclosed himself in Scripture. New reports indicate that at the most recent conference of fifteen hundred "Evangelical Anglican leaders," held at Westminster Chapel (of all places) on January 6–7, 1995, one "evangelical" bishop devoted his paper to an attack on Scripture, while the Archbishop of Canterbury, Dr. George Carey, often dubbed "evangelical,"[28] voiced his enthusiasm for united evangelistic efforts in which "the Catholic, Liberal, Evangelical and Charismatic traditions merge to work together to bring the Good News to this land."[29] If Dr. Carey had simply argued that each of the four traditions has something to learn from the others, no one could reasonably object, even though such a pronouncement would be unbearably trite. But the paramount issue is, "What is the gospel?"

As it stands, the Archbishop's utterance is one of three things: (a) wondrously and intentionally woolly—i.e., recognizably nonsense because the "Good News" (= gospel = evangel) is simply not the same for the four parties.

---

27. David Holloway, "What Is an Anglican Evangelical?" in *Restoring the Vision: Anglican Evangelicals Speak Out*, ed. Melvin Tinker (Eastbourne: MARC, 1990), 34.

28. Though oral reports indicated that he no longer calls himself that.

29. The report has appeared in several places, not least *English Churchman* 7394 (January 20 and 27, 1995): 1.

Some liberals, for instance, reject theism in favor of deism, or even of pantheism. In this light, Carey's statement is nothing but an expedient encouragement that seemed like the politically correct thing to say; or (b) more or less true if all four parties so dilute what their heritage holds to be central that the gospel is utterly inoffensive—but in that case it is not the gospel taught in Scripture; or (c) guilty of assuming that the gospel is something other than what "the Catholic, Liberal, Evangelical and Charismatic traditions" teach, some ineffable "other" perhaps, that somehow manages to get itself articulated in mutually exclusive ways that are all equally valid—much like Hick's "Reality" manages to stand behind all the gods. Postmodernists and people who care little for clarity or logic will be pleased. But in none of these three cases can "evangelicalism" that has any hold on its doctrinal heritage thoughtfully embrace the Archbishop's enthusiasm. His utterance and declension are sad beyond belief.

(7) In the last decade we have begun to find "postmodern Christians" and "postmodern theologians" and "postmodern evangelicals." What might such expressions mean?

They might refer to one of three kinds of believer. (a) They might refer to believers who hold to the truthfulness of the central biblical teachings, but who try to interact with and witness to late-twentieth-century postmodernists. In that sense, I suppose I am a postmodernist evangelical. (b) They might refer to many a sincere evangelical who has unwittingly bought into a number of postmodernist values. Their own beliefs may be orthodox, and their values at first glance unimpeachable. But suddenly the question as to whether truth is communicable from culture to culture comes up, or something about the exclusiveness of Christ, or perhaps a tough case of discipline where there has been extreme moral delinquency—and suddenly the heretofore unarticulated commitments to postmodernity surface with a vengeance. (c) They might refer to people who hold to the evangelical heritage in some sense, but who insist they can knowingly fit it into a postmodern epistemology.

Under this latter category, we must distinguish two groups. The first is so powerfully committed to postmodernism that, protestations aside, it is difficult to see how they are truly evangelical. I provided one or two examples in chapter 3. The second accepts a slightly modified definition of postmodernism that allows for Christianity to be objectively true. With postmodernism as more generally held, it rejects objectivism and positivism; with only a handful of self-described postmodernists, it also rejects relativism, and actively seeks a new paradigm—still, in my view, with limited success.[30]

These, then, are some of the challenges in defining contemporary evangelicalism. But the problems are not merely definitional.

B. Selfism

In the pages that follow, I shall sometimes offer some rather negative judgments about the state of evangelicalism in the Western world. Precisely because so many books and articles have belabored such points in recent years, I need not repeat all the evidence here, but merely summarize some of the widely perceived trends, in order to establish a platform to say a few things that are less commonly observed.

But before launching into the negative, it is important to keep things in perspective by offering three observations. *First*, the progress of the evangel on a worldwide basis during the past one hundred years should be cause for great thanksgiving. More Muslims have come to Christ in Iran during the last fifteen years than in the previous one thousand years. Conservative estimates put the number of Christians in China at sixty million—a sixtyfold increase over the number of "Christians" of all stamps in China in 1950. At the turn of the century, Korea had no Protestant church, and was deemed by many experts to be impenetrable. Korea is over 30 percent Christian today, with something like seven thousand churches in Seoul alone. The nation with the highest number of Muslims in the world, Indonesia, has also witnessed the greatest number of Muslims converting to Jesus Christ. Africa has at least ten times as many Christians today as it did in 1900. This does not mean there are no problems in any of these areas. Some of the "conversions" are doubtless spurious. The level of Bible knowledge and Christian experience is sometimes disturbingly shallow, making the transition to the next generation an extremely perilous affair. Even so, it would be both unrealistic and ungrateful not to rejoice in what God has done.

Second, even within Western Anglo-Saxon countries there has been some cause for gratitude. In the wake of the various forms that the modernist/fundamentalist battles took at the beginning of the century and beyond, outside of Southern Baptist circles there were almost no leaders of evangelical conviction with bona fide advanced degrees. The degrees by themselves may mean little, but the loss was also a crude measurement of the loss in intellectual leadership in the movement, in the nation, in the training facilities for helping to form a new generation of pastors. Then Westminster Theological Seminary was founded, followed by Fuller and a substantial number of others, the best of which maintain standards at the M.Div. level second to none in the nation. The Tyndale Fellowship in England provided incalculable assistance to new generations of students from around the world who were seeking advanced training in biblical studies. The level and quality of evangelical publications today far exceeds what existed half a century ago. (In every case, of course, there are disappointments. Some of the newly founded seminaries have already drifted from their moorings. Some of the rising generation of Christian scholars have become more interested in academic acceptablity than in the progress of the gospel. Publishing houses crank out a discouraging quantity of piffle along with substantial work. But the fact remains that by God's grace there have been gains.) One of the reasons we have been slow to perceive the positive gains is that the extraordinary rate of decline in the culture as a whole has left us with a perception of a *net* loss that influences our assessment of evangelicalism itself.

Third, one cannot thoughtfully read the Bible without perceiving that in this fallen world there will always be struggle, and the shape of the opposition will vary constantly, whatever the commonalities. The danger for Christians who are fixated on the present and are too little aware of either history or what the Bible says is that they become depressed or exhilarated by relatively superficial assessments of the current state of affairs. During the "Year of the Evangelical" (1976), any number of evangelical leaders made the most outrageous comments about how the movement was poised to take over, clean house, bring in renewal and reform, decrease crime and corruption, and so on and so on. Quite apart from the sheer stupidity of such pronouncements—I cannot think of a faster way to provide incentives to the millions of Americans who loathe or are utterly indifferent to the agendas of vociferous evangelicals to organize effective opposition—the statements were born out of raw power, not humility; out of "can do" aggression, not a sense of dependency on the Spirit of God; out of ignorance of how fast popularity (and unpopularity) can shift; out of sublime indifference to the dangers of corruption in our own hearts, let alone the hearts of others, with the result that strategy is reduced to the political arena alone; out of rosy-eyed misreading of America's past. Conversely, now that the media seem to dump on evangelicals above all others, we forget how often the church has been in declension before. While regretting and trying to change some current trends, and while repenting of our own sins (which are many), it is vital that we maintain a certain sense of historical proportion, refusing to follow the siren voices that call us to despair or rage.

Despite such preliminary attempts to maintain a sense of perspective, it is difficult to avoid the conclusion that profound *selfism*—self-centeredness elevated to an unrecognized principle of interpretation—governs not only much of Western culture, but, of more interest to us at the moment, much of the Western church. This is one of the major themes in a string of recent evangelical critiques of the Western church, especially in America.[31] They agree that the church is too pragmatic, hedonistic, relativistic, given to emotion rather than thought, and, in short, self-centered. As Lints finely writes:

> This fascination with the self gives rise to the new focus of theodicy for modern evangelicals—unhappiness. How can there be a God if we are not happy all the time? Evil has become a private emotion, and the new gospel is that God offers to heal us of that privatized evil. The church exists to make people feel comfortable and happy. This is simply hedonism baptized with Christian rhetoric. We have come a great distance from Edwards's vision of theology as reflecting the glory of God, a glory that is also the chief end of humankind.[32]

The evidence is everywhere.

In a former age, insatiable desire was understood to be a principal source of frustration, something to be opposed. Now it is to be cultivated as the engine that drives economic development. The endemic consumerism of the age feeds our greed, and even defines our humanity: we are not primarily worshipers, or thinkers, or God's image-bearers, or lovers, but *consumers*. "Consumerism itself has become a kind of addiction. The more toys we acquire the more frequent and expensive they need to be to produce the old high. The shift from finding identity in what we produce to what we possess, from a work ethic to a consumption ethic, at once exalts the pursuit of happiness and guarantees its ultimate futility."[33]

When Postman wrote the introduction to his important book *Amusing Ourselves to Death*, he set forth the stance he adopts by contrasting the warnings of George Orwell's *1984* and Aldous Huxley's *Brave New World*:

> Orwell warns that we will be overcome by an externally imposed oppression. But in Huxley's vision, no Big Brother is required to deprive people of their autonomy, maturity, and history. As he saw it, people will come to love their oppression, to adore the technologies that undo their capacities to think. . . . What Orwell feared were those who would ban books. What

---

31. E.g., Os Guinness, *The Dust of Death: A Critique of the Establishment and the Counterculture and a Proposal for a Third Way* (Downers Grove: InterVarsity Press, 1973); Bruce Shelley, *The Gospel and the American Dream* (Portland: Multnomah Press, 1989); Os Guinness and John Seel, eds., *No God But God: Breaking with the Idols of Our Age* (Chicago: Moody Press, 1992); Michael Scott Horton, *Made in America: The Shaping of Modern American Evangelicalism* (Grand Rapids: Baker, 1991); David F. Wells, *God in the Wasteland: The Reality of Truth in a World of Fading Dreams* (Grand Rapids: Eerdmans, 1994).

32. *The Fabric of Theology*, 326.

33. John Ortberg, "Happy Meal Spirituality," *Christianity Today* 37/6 (May 17, 1993): 40. Much of Ortberg's essay is based on Christopher Lasch, *The True and Only Heaven: Progress and Its Critics* (New York: W. W. Norton, 1991).

Huxley feared was that there would be no reason to ban a book, for there would be no one who wanted to read one. Orwell feared those who would deprive us of information. Huxley feared those who would give us so much information that we would be reduced to passivity and egoism. Orwell feared that the truth would be concealed from us. Huxley feared that the truth would be drowned in a sea of irrelevance. Orwell feared that we would become a captive culture. Huxley feared that we would become a trivial culture, preoccupied with some equivalent of the feelies, the orgy porgy, and the centrifugal bumblepuppy. In *1984*, Orwell added, people are controlled by inflicting pain. In *Brave New World*, they are controlled by inflicting pleasure. In short, Orwell feared that what we hate will ruin us. Huxley feared that what we love will ruin us. This book is about the possibility that Huxley, not Orwell, was right.[34]

Even if we make allowances for the exaggerations in their created "worlds," there is little doubt that at the moment, Huxley's vision is closer to fulfillment in the West than Orwell's.

Four decades ago de Jouvenel compared and contrasted the claims of capitalism and socialism and concluded that we are invited to choose between them on the basis of which is better able to increase our level of consumption. "Nothing quite so trivial has been made into a social ideal."[35] As Schlossberg observes,

> materialism is thought to signify the desire for consumer goods, the meaning that led Huxley to refer to the Sears Roebuck catalog as the "Newest Testament." The legitimacy of such desires may be judged in part by our ability to satisfy them. All true needs—such as food, drink, and companionship—are satiable. Illegitimate wants—pride, envy, greed—are insatiable. By their nature they cannot be satisfied. In that sense materialism is the opium of the people. Enough is never enough. Greater quantities are required for satisfaction, and each increment proves inadequate the next time. That is the horror of the giant in John Bunyan and the wicked witch in C. S. Lewis who give their victims food that causes greater hunger. The idolatries that promise wealth without end draw adherents as the tavern draws alcoholics. . . . That is the sense in which the love of money is the root of all evils (1 Tim.6.10).[36]

---

34. Neil Postman, *Amusing Ourselves to Death: Public Discourse in the Age of Show Business* (New York: Penguin, 1985), vii–viii.

35. Bertrand de Jouvenel, *The Ethics of Redistribution* (Cambridge: Cambridge Univ. Press, 1951), 46–48.

36. Herbert Schlossberg, *Idols for Destruction: Christian Faith and Its Confrontation with American Society* (Nashville: Nelson, 1983); 107–8. The entire chapter, "Idols of Mammon" (88–139), deserves thoughtful reading.

This does not mean that no economic system can ever be said to be better than another. It means, rather, that when a system is judged purely on the basis of its ability to feed consumerism, no thoughtful Christian can ever responsibly espouse the criterion as a Christian value. That means that today, when government programs in Britain and the United States are being cut back, even if one espouses the desirability of such steps on the grounds of efficiency, fiscal responsibility, or sheer financial necessity, it is troubling that most of the criteria being appealed to in the debate are the products of a fundamentally materialistic outlook.

This development in the broader culture is all too easily mirrored in the church. Initially one thinks of the "prosperity gospel" of the so-called "faith" movement ("name it and claim it"), connected with Benny Hinn, Kenneth Hagin, Kenneth Copeland, Paul Crouch and others. But their views, as popular as they are in certain strands of televangelist land, are so bizarre that no one with a scrap of theological smarts should consider them evangelicals in any useful sense of the term.[37] Harder to identify is the kind of evangelical who formally espouses the historic faith but whose heartbeat is for more and more of this world's goods, whose dreams are not for heaven and for the glory of God, but for success, financial independence, a bigger house, a finer car.

More alarming still is the consumer mentality in the heart of mainstream evangelicalism. If left unchecked it will evacuate the heritage.[38] One worries, for instance, about strategies that are nothing but marketing techniques.[39] Doubtless one could argue that this is merely a matter of terminology, that all of us need to be aware of the profiles of the people around us whom we wish to evangelize. After all, don't I myself argue along similar lines (chaps. 12 and 14 of this book)?

But the differences are important. For a start, *words* are important. As soon as you start referring to outreach as a "marketing strategy" you not only change the perception of what you are about, but the rules that operate. There may be *some* legitimate overlap, and the church marketeers will bleed them to death. But there are also enormous differences, and the imposition of consumer categories obscures them. In any case, there is a fundamental difference between trying to learn from Acts 17 how to be culture-sensitive as we go about declaring the good news of Jesus Christ to people who are perishing without him, and thinking of the church as a corporation that must

---

37. The most rigorous treatment is that of Hank Hanegraaff, *Christianity in Crisis* (Eugene: Harvest House, 1993).

38. Cf. Kevin Offner, "American Evangelicalism: Adrift with Amnesia," *Regeneration Quarterly* 1/1 (1995): 6–9.

39. E.g., George Barna, *Church Marketing: Breaking Ground for the Harvest* (Ventura: Regal Books, 1992).

market its product to potential consumers. Crossing the cultural barriers to communicate the gospel "that was once for all entrusted to the saints" (Jude 3) is one thing. But as we have seen, if we control our evangelism by analysis of market "needs" the result is virtually always a domesticated gospel.

> Today [unlike the time of Augustine] the church also announces that "the good life" is found in Christ, but we have so completely reinterpreted the meaning of that classical phrase that for many people, the good life means little more than personal peace and prosperity. As a result, we have readjusted the gospel message so that it offers health and wealth rather than power over greed and pride.[40]

Perhaps the most damning evidence comes in the little things. When church music directors never fail to tell their choirs to "go backstage" to get ready, it is not hard to discern the tentacles of the entertainment industry controlling our vocabulary and our thoughts. When serious Christian journals publish articles with titles like "Will There Be Baseball in Heaven?"[41] one can be quite certain that the author has not thought very deeply on Revelation 4–5, 21–22. When churches advertise themselves in the newspaper with lines like, "We feature entertaining worship"—an exact quote, I am afraid—one scarcely knows whether to laugh or weep. When a recent graduate of the seminary in which I teach writes and tells me of his struggles in an evangelical church to help people to see that in small-group Bible study the *primary* aim is not to ensure that everyone ventures an opinion that can never be gainsaid, but that the *primary* aim is to discover what Scripture says and to work out how to apply it to life, one smells more than a whiff of postmodernist decay. When ministerial students are asked about their sense of call to ministry, and the best they can muster is, "I think I would feel fulfilled doing that kind of work," selfism has struck again.

Small groups in a church can do a great deal of good. They can foster genuine fellowship, serve as centers for exhortation and intercessory prayer, deepen knowledge of the Bible, model Christian graces from older Christians to younger ones, inculcate principles of inductive Bible study. Wuthnow shows how small groups can develop a sense of taking responsibility for one's faith, and can strengthen the desire to support others.

> But because they are of value in these ways, [small groups] can also inadvertently emphasize some aspects of spirituality at the expense of others. Individual responsibility may result in faith being focused too much on the needs and interests of the individual. When this happens, it may also encour-

---

40. Richard J. Foster, "The Good Life," *Christianity Today* 31/18 (December 11, 1987): 23.

41. David Holmquist, in *Christianity Today* (January 10, 1994): 29–33.

age each individual to do his or her "own thing" to the extent that faith becomes highly relativistic. Informal norms of support and encouragement may also work against the hard efforts actually required to develop one's spiritual muscles. Small groups, therefore, reinforce the emphasis in American religion on taking responsibility for one's faith, but may alter (or even undermine) this emphasis at the same time.[42]

The truth of the matter is that the consumer mentality authorizes people to judge all matters religious and theological by the simple criterion of whether or not they have been "helped"—and the only people equipped to assess whether or not they have truly been helped are the people who claim to have been helped. Questions of truth, long-range effects, and purpose are all shunted aside.

The pursuit of a feeling of being "helped" is bound up with the current passion for "self-esteem." The importance of self-esteem in order to achieve anything and gain wholeness has so been drummed into us that even Christians who should know better have bought into it.

> The bottom line is that no agreed-upon definition or agreed-upon measure of self-esteem exists, and whatever it is, no reliable evidence supports self-esteem scores meaning much at all anyway. There is no evidence that high self-esteem reliably causes anything—indeed lots of people with little of it have achieved a great deal in one dimension or another. . . . I am not implying that high self-esteem is always negatively related to accomplishment. Rather, the research mentioned above shows that measures of self-esteem have no reliable relationship to behavior, either positive or negative.[43]

Vitz's point is not that there is no place for thinking Christianly about "self-worth." Indeed, Christians will ponder the fact that they are God's image-bearers, that they are loved by their Maker in the most self-sacrificial way possible, and much more. But the therapeutic culture, designed to make people feel helped, has taken over.[44]

A few months ago I was in another country addressing some hundreds of missionaries. As I was at lunch with one missionary couple, the question of

---

42. Robert Wuthnow, "Small Groups and American Religion," in *"I Come Away Stronger": How Small Groups Are Shaping American Religion*, ed. Robert Wuthnow (Grand Rapids: Eerdmans, 1994), 347.

43. Paul Vitz, "Leaving Psychology Behind," in Guinness and Seel, *No God But God*, 97.

44. Cf. Os Guinness, "America's Last Men and Their Magnificent Talking Cure," in Guinness and Seel, *No God But God*, 111–19; Robert C. Roberts, "Psychobabble," *Christianity Today* 38/6 (May 16, 1994): 18–24. Contrast the extraordinarily shallow and piecemeal use of Scripture advocated by Edward P. Wimberly, *Using Scripture in Pastoral Counseling* (Nashville: Abingdon, 1994).

"rebirthing" came up. Somewhat defensively at first, and then openly, the husband told me his story. He came from an abusive background; the notion of "father" was entirely distorted for him. As a college student he trusted Christ, but never really felt or delighted in the love of God or the love of Christ. Then, some months before I arrived, an "evangelical" professor gave some talks on rebirthing which this missionary attended. He said that people from abusive homes should close their eyes and imagine themselves as they were emerging from their mothers. Picture Jesus standing there, ready to catch you up into his arms. You emerge, and he cuddles you, cleans you up, loves you, caresses you. Do you not see how all your life Jesus has been loving? The missionary told me that he broke down and wept and wept, and from that moment his life had become more integrated. He had become better able to give and receive love; for the first time he felt loved by Jesus. What was wrong with that, he wanted to know. The Bible does not teach rebirthing, but it does affirm the love of God, and if this technique helps you experience it, what fair criticism can be offered?

So many things could have been said. I had no desire to "crush a bruised reed" or "quench a smoking wick." I replied along these lines:

"I cannot help but be glad if your life is truly more integrated. I have talked with enough people from abusive backgrounds to have some idea of the terrible struggles you have gone through, and doubtless will go through. If in truth this experience really does teach you more of the love of God, I shall not be the first to criticize.

"But I have to tell you that at best you have experienced second best; and at worst you have been seduced to idolatry. Bear with me, and I shall try to explain.

"My dear brother, all the emotional catharsis, all the tears, all the healing integration, might well have been yours *along biblical lines*. You might have meditated long on Ephesians 3:14–21, praying along with Paul that God would give you the power, together with all the saints, to grasp how wide and long and high and deep is the love of God, to know this love that surpasses knowledge. You might have read and re-read the passion narratives. Where, after all, according to God's gracious self-disclosure in Scripture, is the greatest manifestation of his love? Is it not in the incarnation and the cross? Might not a godly pastor taking you back to the cross have brought you to the same tears, but with the anchor of God's Word authorizing them?

"For the fact of the matter is that you now associate your emotional release not with the cross, but with rebirthing techniques. You will be less inclined to think of the gospel as that which is the power of God unto salvation. You will think of the gospel as providing some sort of pardon, and rebirthing techniques as providing healing, power, restoration. All the associational links are wrong. They are diverting. They bring you some measure of relief, while distracting you from the cross.

"And if you ask, 'Why be so fussy as long as I am genuinely healed, or at least substantially improved?' then you have brought yourself to the very heart of my argument: the primary criterion for what is right and true and valuable cannot possibly be whether or not you feel helped. This does not mean that the gospel of Jesus Christ crucified *can't* help you: it can, and does, and will. It means that the content of that gospel cannot be determined or approved simply on the basis of whether or not you *feel* helped. For if that were the case, would not the archenemy, whose love of deception is well known, have a field day 'helping' people, and helping people feel helped, provided the result is that they are diverted from the cross? If he is clever—and he is—the danger will not be perceived at once. Like a spacecraft swiftly speeding off course by only a degree or two, this kind of trajectory ensures that in time you will miss the mark by millions of miles.

"And that is why I insist that at best you have experienced second best; at worst, you are being seduced into idolatry."

In short, the selfism that is characteristic of Western culture dominates more than a little of the church's life and thought and values and priorities as well. As always, there are wonderful, humbling exceptions. But the direction is not encouraging. Clowney's conclusions are not too strong:

> The world cannot be sacralized by the fiat of the new theology to form the community of love Christ came to establish. The world lacks the new life of the Spirit who sheds abroad the love of Christ in human hearts. It cannot be governed by the spiritual structure of Christ's kingdom. It is the church that possesses the Spirit, and indeed is possessed by the Spirit to manifest on earth now the realities of heaven and the age to come. The politics of the kingdom demand that Christians take seriously the structure of the church as the form of the people of God on earth. Today the church stands not so much as an institution as a ruin. Preachers of another gospel are not only tolerated; they control the church. The church is in Babylonian captivity to secular goals and values. While radical theologians serve the political left, there is no lack of conservative preachers to proclaim a fascist nationalism in the name of Christ. No longer does the church's ministry of mercy bear witness to the compassion of Christ's gospel. Instead, Christians spend on extravagant luxuries the funds Christ has entrusted to them for the relief of the poor and needy.
>
> The deep fellowship of love that joins the Lord's people finds little expression in churches that meet for one brief hour of formal boredom every Sunday morning. Evangelism has been shifted by default to para-ecclesiastical organizations, many presenting a truncated gospel, and most by their

very specialization detaching the gospel from the life of a serving and loving community.[45]

C. Relevance and Kitsch

I must confess immediately that I find the treatment of this subject difficult. That is because while some self-confessed evangelicals seem to be saying that the pursuit of relevance is the only responsible way to maintain growth and reach a lost world, others view the word "relevance" as utterly profane, and almost a definition of theological compromise. I am not quite happy with either side of this debate, until the issue is properly defined. So I shall begin by trying to set out what is at stake, and then turn to some evaluation.

1. The Nature of the Challenge

When selfism becomes sufficiently common, serving the perceived self-interests in a congregation or in a community can become part of ecclesiastical policy. In its most virulent form, that is what the relevance is all about: shaping policy and priorities and even doctrine so as to accommodate the self-interests and self-defined needs of those affected. Since so much selfism abounds, it is scarcely surprising that a fair bit of the current interest in relevance is so corrosive.

But there is another side to the matter. Most Western nations, not least the traditionally Anglo-Saxon ones, betray signs of rapid change. As we have seen again and again in this book, many aspects of Western culture are mutating. Churches that are faithful to the apostolic gospel are sometimes also the ones that are loyal to a culture becoming increasingly *passé*. In such a situation *cultural* conservatism can easily be mistaken for *theological* conservatism, for theological orthodoxy. In an age of confusing empirical pluralism and frankly frightening philosophical pluralism, in an age that seems to be stealing from us the Judeo-Christian worldview that prevailed for so long, it is easy to suppose that retrenchment and conservative responses on every conceivable axis are the only responsible courses for those who want to remain faithful to the gospel.

In various ways I have tried to show in this volume that such a course is neither wise nor prophetic. Sometimes it is not even faithful. The church may slip back into a defensive, conservative modernism that is fundamentally ill-equipped to address postmodernism. We shall see in the next chapter that the challenges of widespread biblical illiteracy demand, among other things, that we begin "farther back" in our articulation of the gospel—i.e., it is

---

45. Edmund P. Clowney, *The Politics of the Kingdom*, Mars Hill Monographs 3 (Powhatan: Berea Publications, n.d.), 9.

becoming more and more necessary to expound the Bible's story-line, the main lines of a Christian theistic worldview. Cultural conservatives may think of this as succumbing to the demand for relevance; I think it is prophetic wisdom, demanded by the the Scriptures themselves.

Others have seen the danger. Thus Bayly writes that "today" is

> the missing element in a great deal of contemporary evangelical theology. The facts as God has revealed them in His Word (the Bible) are there, but they are not focused upon today. Instead, most evangelical theology is oriented toward yesterday.
>
> But yesterday is past. The slings of the Hodges and B. B. Warfield and Robert Dick Wilson may have slain giants in their day. But they are dead.
>
> And today's giants are different. It is no disrespect toward these men and their learned, godly contemporaries that we should pass over the stones they so carefully chose and shot home to their targets. New stones are needed to slay new giants, although these new stones must come from the same river bed: the Word of God.[46]

If we ignore his rather strained metaphor, his words, written about three decades ago, still have surprising relevance to more than a few conservative churches. D. Martyn Lloyd-Jones, whom no one could accuse of being guilty of hasty relevance and kitsch, issues similar warnings. Observing Paul's flexibility in 1 Corinthians 9:19–23, he contrasts some modern preachers:

> They are slaves to phrases. I have observed that certain young men who have developed a new interest, for instance, in the Puritans, start speaking and writing as if they lived in the seventeenth century. That is quite ludicrous. . . .
>
> Let me sum it up in modern terms by asserting that it is always our business to be contemporary; our object is to deal with the living people who are in front of us and listening to us.[47]

Of course, Lloyd-Jones then goes on to warn against the merely faddish and manipulative. And that, of course, is what raises the problem. Some of those who are dismissed by the orthodox as being compromised by their pursuit of relevance insist that they are entirely faithful to the gospel—indeed, more faithful than some of their critics, since at least they are learning to share it and proclaim it in an effective and fruitful way.

Thus we are developing two very different assessments of the more innovative strands of evangelicalism. One side is nicely exemplified by David Wells. So far as he is concerned, we have arrived at a sad state of affairs where

> at the psychological center of much evangelical faith are two ideas that are also at the heart of the practice of democracy: (1) the audience is sovereign,

---

46. Joseph Bayly, *Out of My Mind* (Wheaton: Tyndale House, 1970), 96–97.
47. *Preaching and Preachers* (London: Hodder & Stoughton, 1971), 136–38.

and (2) ideas find legitimacy and value only within the marketplace. Ideas have no intrinsic or self-evident value; it is the people's *right* to give ideas their legitimacy. One implication of this belief is that the work of doing theology ought not to be left to an intellectual elite who may think that they are gifted for and called to do such work and may consider the discovery of truth to be an end in itself. Rather, it should be taken on by those who can persuade the masses of the usefulness of the ideas.[48]

To succumb to such temptations, Wells argues, is to distance oneself from the Son of God, "who never once tailored his teaching to what he judged the popular reception would be—unless he was an exceedingly poor judge of what the crowds and religious leaders had in mind as they heard him."[49]

By contrast, Mouw looks at the same evidence and reaches a rather different conclusion:

> It would be impious to disagree with Wells's main point, given the way he states his case. Jesus certainly wasn't a crowd-pleaser who tested the winds of public opinion before he said anything. Having agreed with the way Wells describes Jesus' approach, though, we can still wonder whether Wells hasn't pressed too quickly over some very important issues.[50]

Mouw could strengthen his case. Theologians have often remarked how amazingly flexible Jesus was. His approach to blind Bartimaeus was not the same as his approach to Zacchaeus; his handling of Nicodemus was not precisely parallel to his handling of the rich young ruler; his treatment of the Pharisees was not the same as his treatment of the Canaanite woman. One could argue that Jesus was astonishingly flexible precisely because he knew how to make his message relevant in every case—and whether or not that message was accepted or rejected.

So is contemporary evangelicalism displaying innovative creativity as a function of evangelistic zeal, or toadish captivity to whatever is novel, now that its interest in truth has so sadly waned, in order to titillate the masses?

Inevitably, one can find some examples of both. But if the trend is toward the latter—and I think it is—we must nevertheless be careful not to draw two premature conclusions. (1) We must not suggest that the motives of those involved are necessarily bad. Human hearts being what they are, doubtless wicked motives abound on all sides of this discussion. But if we conclude (and I think we must) that the tide of evangelicalism is drifting toward more and

---

48. David F. Wells, *No Place for Truth: or, Whatever Happened to Evangelical Theology?* (Grand Rapids: Eerdmans, 1993), 207.

49. Ibid., 215.

50. Richard J. Mouw, *Consulting the Faithful: What Christian Intellectuals Can Learn from Popular Religion* (Grand Rapids: Eerdmans, 1994), 7.

more pragmatism, as often as not the reasons lie less with self-conscious desire to transform the gospel into something it is not, or with a self-centered wish to appear to be on the "cutting edge," as with a desire to be "fruitful" in ministry. (2) We must not suggest that the alternative is a kind of rugged traditionalism that has not learned to live later than the 1950s, or perhaps in some cases the 1930s or even the 1870s.

It may be helpful at this point to glance at a couple of examples.

The first is Leith Anderson's racy *Dying for Change*.[51] As these sorts of approaches go, Anderson is on the conservative edge of the push for change (which is also one of the reasons why he is in considerable demand). Formally, at least, Anderson is aware how easy it is to sacrifice revelation for relevance, or vice versa. "The uncompromising balance must be maintained, forfeiting neither relevance nor revelation."[52] "My task," he writes, "is to take the Bible and make it relevant to those who listen."[53] Most of the book is given over to pop ethnography and pop sociology. The burden of his proposal is that as we learn the statistical profiles of "baby boomers" and "baby busters,"[54] we learn how to shape our churches so that we do not automatically alienate the people we want to win. There is a fair bit of "street smarts" in the book that should not be ignored by thoroughgoing traditionalists. But I come away from the book, and from the two public occasions where I have heard him speak and have watched him answer questions, with two disturbing questions.

(1) Despite the avowal of submission to biblical authority, it is unclear how such submission works out in practice. Anderson does not make clear where the profiles of, say, baby boomers, should call for correction, reformation, even outright opposition, and not the reshaping of the local church. Twice I have heard people ask him, in effect, "What elements in these profiles, if any, do you regard as not morally neutral, and not morally positive, but morally reprehensible, in the light of God's Word, and therefore in need of fundamental correction?" In neither case could he provide an example— though examples, as we shall see, are not hard to come by. I fear this reflects either a shallow grasp of the Bible and of theology, or an unwitting degree of respect for the categories of the social sciences that *de facto* domesticates the Bible, while formally upholding it.

---

51. Minneapolis: Bethany House, 1990.

52. Ibid., 119.

53. Ibid., 15.

54. There is a vast literature on the subject. One might usefully read Wade Clark Roof, *A Generation of Seekers: The Spiritual Journeys of the Baby Boom Generation* (San Francisco: Harper San Francisco, 1993); and George Barna, *The Invisible Generation: Baby Busters* (Glendale: Barna Research Group, 1992).

(2) More frightening is the impression that the social sciences hold the key for church renewal and growth. The assumption seems to be that we are basically okay theologically, spiritually, morally, in our prayers and passion and understanding, and that if we just add this component we are bound to see fruit. The solid core in this outlook is that we *do* need to understand the people to whom we minister. The falseness is that such understanding and the adaptive change that springs from it guarantees spiritual growth. It may be something God uses, and in that case God is to be thanked, for he is the Author of all good gifts, not least knowledge, including knowledge of demographic profiles. But he may withhold his blessing: he has certainly done so before. Blessings are not guaranteed by reading Gallup reports. Worse: the emphasis on awareness of the social sciences tends to divert people from things that are forever basic: the truth of the gospel, a living walk with the living God, love for men and women, an eternal perspective, hatred and fear of sin, a passion for holiness, a profound desire to see Christ exalted. Not for a moment am I suggesting Anderson lacks these things: that would be impious judgmentalism. But I worry when these things are not front and center.

Probably the best known and most widely imitated "seeker-sensitive" church is Willow Creek. A couple of decades ago, Hybels set out to discover why people in his area did not attend church. The music was too old-fashioned; the services were too boring; the language was old-fashioned and irrelevant; and so forth. Out of concern to evangelize, Hybels established "seeker services" on Sunday that dispense with creeds and hymnals and most corporate singing, but hum with drama, music groups at a professional quality, and a message that aims to address people where they are. Somewhat more traditional services, for the committed Christians who attend, are held midweek, and hundreds of small groups provide Bible studies, prayer times, help to particular groups (e.g., divorced persons, the mentally handicapped). Three times a year Willow Creek sponsors a conference to explain to the five hundred or so church leaders who attend just how it is done. There is now an association of over seven hundred Willow Creek-style churches.

Hybels himself acknowledges that some of his "followers" go way too far. His primary concern is not that others do what he does, but that others get to know their own community and thereby tear down the barriers that make communication of the gospel more fruitful. Hybels feels he is returning to the New Testament pattern; critics accuse him of succumbing to the modern passion for relevance and unwittingly leaving the full-orbed gospel of Christ behind.[55]

---

55. A useful introduction to the debate, including the responses of Hybels to his critics, is found in Michael G. Maudlin and Edward Gilbreath, "Selling Out the House of God?" *Christianity Today* 38/8 (July 18, 1994): 20–23, and other articles in the same issue. Cf. also

One cannot listen long to Hybels in person without recognizing his personal commitment to Christ and to the gospel, his passion to see men and women converted and genuinely transformed. It must be said, too, that compared with some experiments Willow Creek is still remarkably conservative. And whatever the "entertainment" factor in the Sunday meetings, and however many spurious conversions, there are still so many genuine ones that one must not criticize too quickly, or on the wrong grounds. To take an easy example: While a great deal of outreach occurred in American churches up until the 1960s or 1970s through Sunday services and Sunday schools, the fact is that many who become believers today first make contact with Christians in "seeker-sensitive" churches through divorce-recovery workshops, athletic teams, various support groups, and the like.[56]

Yet where does it stop? Liberal churches have long since airbrushed "sin" and related terms out of their vocabulary.[57] Now many so-called evangelical churches are running down the same course. In an interview, James Hunter said,

> To be perfectly blunt, sin is being redefined within the evangelical tradition. What was sinful a generation ago is no longer sinful today. When confronted with this reality, evangelicals will more or less trivialize their heritage by saying, "Those behaviors were not really sinful, but a mere religious and social quirkiness of our forebears." ... Contemporary society is more permissive than that of the past, and the evangelical community is being affected by that permissiveness.... [T]here is less and less continuity with the past.[58]

Surveys show that the moral behavior of self-confessed "evangelicals" is heading in the same direction as that in the broader culture: we simply lag a little behind. "Vision statements" from many churches today are entirely at the horizontal level (apart, of course, from the mandatory God-clichés). A relatively new organization called Leadership Network has recently been running conferences under the banner "The Church in the 21st Century." At the most recent one for which I have reliable data, the speakers were Leith Anderson (mentioned above), a Fortune-500 executive called Max De Pree,

---

Russell Chandler, *Racing Toward 2001: The Forces Shaping America's Religious Future* (Grand Rapids: Zondervan, 1992), 246–55.

56. That is one of the prime points Leith Anderson makes in *A Church for the 21st Century* (Minneapolis: Bethany House, 1992).

57. I am not minimizing how difficult it is to get across the notion of sin to a postmodern generation for whom sin is merely a snicker-word. The issue is not so much the precise vocabulary deployed as the burden of what is said. I shall say more on this subject in the next chapter.

58. Interview in *Ministry* (Winter 1989): 10.

476 ◆ The Gagging of God

a consultant in human development by the name of William Bridges, trend analyst George Barna, psychologist Larry Crabb, and the president of United Theological Seminary, Leonard Sweet (scarcely a bastion of evangelical conviction). The chair of Leadership Network, Bob Buford, prides himself in the fact that the Network does not get into doctrine or theology. According to various news reports, the Network's president, Fred Smith, Jr., bases the philosophy of the Network on Jesus' parable of the talents: "We think the Master is entrepreneurial. He said, 'Handle your resources, work your talents.' We want to get the Master a better return on the giftedness of people. We want to be a broker between what God has designed them to be and what they are."

This is scary. And I have purposely avoided taking the *worst* examples of this kind of thinking in my files.

2. Evaluation

(a) Study after study has shown that pursuing relevance may achieve a certain instant "success," but is frequently the advance warning to bitter declension. Liberal churches thought they were being terribly relevant in the '30s, the '50s, the '60s—and virtually without exception they are in massive decline.[59] As Guinness puts it,

> In addition, relevance has a false allure that masks both its built-in transcience and its catch–22 demand. Dean Inge captured the transcience in his celebrated line "He who marries the spirit of the age soon becomes a widower." But it was Simone Weil who highlighted the catch–22: "To be always relevant, you have to say things which are eternal."[60]

(b) Although it is surely right to ask how best to communicate the historic gospel to each generation and culture, evangelicalism is gradually sacrificing the concomitant commitment to truth. While protestations of inerrancy abound, increasingly there is so little grasp of biblical theology that the merest proof-texting can justify almost anything—like the nonsense from the Leadership Network just quoted above. Texts are abstracted both from their immediate context, and from the Bible's story-line.

(c) Although we must communicate the gospel in categories that are not in the first instance alien to the people we are addressing, our whole aim must be to get them to think and know God in the categories that he has himself

---

59. See especially Dean R. Hoge, Benton Johnson, and Donald A. Luidens, *Vanishing Boundaries: The Religion of Mainline Protestant Baby Boomers* (Louisville: Westminster/John Knox, 1994), esp. 200–201.

60. Os Guinness, *Dining with the Devil: The Megachurch Movement Flirts with Modernity* (Grand Rapids: Baker, 1993), 63.

provided. *Our* analysis of human needs must be based on the Bible's identification of human needs, even if it is necessary to show how the Bible's presentation of human need is connected, often in ways they did not expect, to the ways human beings define their own needs. Otherwise the gospel itself will always get perverted with time. This stance, surely, is reflected in apostolic forms of ministry. Paul communicated with the Athenians, but the aim of his discourse was to create an entirely different worldview. As Horton puts it, "Instead of taking a marketing survey of Corinthian attitudes and developing a gospel that would address 'felt needs,' Paul told the Corinthians what their real needs were, whether they were felt or not."[61] What is at stake, I fear, is a fundamental loss of confidence in the gospel.

(d) The focus on needs easily generates more need. Guinness refers to an analyst who has commented that a generation ago, "*problems* existed only in mathematics or chess; *solutions* were saline or legal, and *need* was mainly a verb. The expressions 'I have a problem,' or 'I have a need' both sounded silly." But "needs" today are "socially respectable and even fashionable."[62] I can testify how my children are put under some pressure from school counselors because they do *not* feel abused, rejected, facing crushing problems, and so forth. "To be ignorant of one's own needs has become the unforgivable anti-social act."[63]

But the implications are profound. If emphasis on needs uncovers (or generates!) more and more needs, at what point do we shift gears and think in terms of *others'* needs? In terms of service? In terms of death to self-interest? If Christianity is primarily a religion in which God exists to meet my needs, how can it be truly God-centered? How can we avoid the rising number of "specialists" who cater for the rising number of confusing needs?

(e) Despite the entirely salutary concern to communicate the gospel to complete outsiders, is there not another way beside Willow Creek? Are we unwittingly contrasting dead orthodoxy with imaginative programming, as if there is no alternative?

In my experience, there are churches where public service after public service is full of the presence and glory of God. Such churches may take special pains to communicate clearly to a generation that no longer knows the language of Zion (even that metaphor would be obscure to them!), but they somehow are drawn to the God who discloses himself among these people. The prophetic Word brings conviction of sin, and they "fall down and worship God, exclaiming 'God is really among you!'" (1 Cor. 14:25). Even the

---

61. Michael S. Horton, "Corinthian Distractions," *Modern Reformation* (March/April 1993): 23.

62. *Dining with the Devil*, 65.

63. Ivan Illich, *Disabling Professions* (London: Marion Boyars, 1977), 72.

Lord's Supper can be celebrated in a kerygmatic fashion to some who attend but do not participate: by this means we may *proclaim* the Lord's death until he comes (11:26). "Guest services," more common in Anglo-Saxon countries outside America and Canada, can be helpful and fruitful: I shall say more of them in the next chapter.

(f) There is something important about being the *church*, about being Christ's *community*. We will stand out; we will be different from the rest of society. The individualism of "seeker services" easily obscures this truth, and caters to the individualism that is profoundly rooted in a number of Western countries. Although their categories sometimes make me cautious, Hauerwas and Willimon do not go too far when they write:

> The challenge facing today's Christians is not the necessity to translate Christian convictions into a modern idiom, but rather to form a community, a colony of resident aliens which is so shaped by our convictions that no one even has to ask what we mean by confessing belief in God as Father, Son, and Holy Spirit.
>
> The biggest problem facing Christian theology is not translation but enactment. No doubt, one of the major reasons for the great modern theologians who strove to translate our language for modernity was that the church had become so inept at enactment. Yet no clever theological moves can be substituted for the necessity of the church being a community of people who embody our language about God, where talk about God is used without apology because our life together does not mock our words. The church is the visible, political enactment of our language of God by a people who can name their sin and accept God's forgiveness and are thereby enabled to speak the truth in love. Our Sunday worship has a way of reminding us, in the most explicit and ecclesial of ways, of the source of our power, the peculiar nature of our solutions to what ails us.[64]

(g) In all our concern to get things "right," there is the hidden danger of professionalism. Not for a moment am I suggesting that Christian leaders should be *un*professional. I detest, for example, the kind of public services where ministers prattle on with shallow patter and self-conscious asides, where little is planned and clichés are the highest form of verbal reverence. But mere professionalism projects an image a long way from the cross. It sacrifices something of the passion of, say, 1 Corinthians 2:1–5 or 2 Corinthians 5. It draws plaudits from admiring hearers, but humbles no one, least of all the minister. In our desires to maintain or attain a certain professional status at a time when ministerial credibility is in decline, we have lost something

---

64. Stanley Hauerwas and William H. Willimon, *Resident Aliens* (Nashville: Abingdon, 1989), 170–71. The passage is cited in another useful essay: John Bolt, "Some Reflections on Church and World, Worship and Evangelism," *Calvin Theological Journal* 27 (1992): 96–101.

even more important: passionate God-centeredness, passionate gospel-centeredness.[65]

(h) The specialization in our seminaries and churches at the hermeneutical level plays into the hands of the dictatorship of the present, or at least the "over-privileging" of the present. Thiselton shrewdly observes that we have traditionally assigned the task of describing what the biblical texts "meant" to biblical scholars, left the organizing of that material to the systematicians, and assigned to experts in pastoral theology the responsibility of determining what in the text "can meaningfully address the present."[66] We might add that we then give to the pastors the task of putting it into practice. The result is that for the practitioners the present is "over-privileged."[67] One might add that this division of labor, common under modernism, is exacerbated under postmodernism, in that the findings of the biblical scholars and theologians are more and more easily relegated and ignored as the product of private opinion or an (old-fashioned) interpretive community: what *works* is what has value.

We simply must smash down the various bifurcations. We must have theologians who are pastors and evangelists; we must have evangelists who think biblically and theologically. There is enough fault to go around on this item. One suspects that seminaries are badly in need of a massive rewriting of curriculum—not to reduce the "theoretical" content, but to integrate theory and practice, Greek and homiletics, Pauline theology and evangelism, Wisdom Literature and counseling, systematic theology and communicating worldviews, church history and spirituality, and so forth.

(i) One wonders what the long-term effects of the pursuit of relevance will be. If we think about people long enough as "consumers" or "prospects" or "seekers" or "targets" or "respondents," how will that affect our perception of God's image-bearers? How will it affect our theology of the impact of the Fall, and of the sovereignty of grace? How will it affect our commitment to the primacy of the Bible's story-line—our need to be reconciled to

---

65. Cf. V. James Mannoia, "The Perils of Professionalism," *Faculty Dialogue* 13 (1990): 7–20. Incidentally, I suspect that one of the reasons why in God's good purposes Hybels has seen as much fruit as he has is that he evinces this passionate God-centeredness in his own living, his own personal priorities. It is perhaps unwise to speculate, but I suspect that he would have seen no fewer genuine converts (though probably smaller numbers at his large Sunday meetings) if his concern to reach those untouched by the gospel had been challenged in somewhat more traditional channels.

66. Anthony C. Thiselton, *New Horizons in Hermeneutics* (London: HarperCollins, 1992), 604–11.

67. A somewhat similar analysis is offered by James A. Speer, "'Dynamic Field Theologizing': An Agenda for Theological Education," *Trinity World Forum* 19/2 (Winter 1994): 1–4.

God, to escape hell, to have our guilt dealt with? How will it affect our view of our own ministry? How will it affect our vision of the church thirty years from now?

(j) Finally, when preaching based on the individual's perception of his or her needs is linked with contemporary trends in pluralism, we are asking for conflagration. Ten years ago, Guinness declared, "We have reached the stage in pluralization where choice is not just a state of affairs, it is a state of mind. Choice has become a value in itself, even a priority. To be modern is to be addicted to choice and change. Change becomes the very essence of life."[68] The result is the tendency to become conversion-prone.[69] People may "trust" Christ in the hope that he will meet their needs, but an unspoken assumption is borne along with this "faith": if trust in this Christ does not work out as advertised, one is always free (and perhaps even obligated) to try something else on offer.[70]

D. Playing Loose with the Bible

As reflection on selfism (section B) led naturally to reflection on relevance (section C), so an evaluation of the current pursuit of relevance leads us inexorably to the present section. Despite formal affirmations of Scripture's authority and even inerrancy, a great deal of contemporary evangelicalism does not burn with zeal to be submissive to Scripture. That, of course, has been the flip side of the discussion on relevance.[71] Lindbeck writes, "Playing fast and loose with the Bible needed a liberal audience in the days of Norman Vincent Peale, but now, as the case of Robert Schuller indicates, professed conservatives eat it up."[72]

---

68. Os Guinness, *The Gravedigger File* (Downers Grove: InterVarsity Press, 1983), 96.

69. Ibid., 102.

70. For further discussion, see Douglas Webster, *Selling Jesus: What's Wrong with Marketing the Church* (Downers Grove: InterVarsity Press, 1992).

71. Two recent books by David Wells document the alarming drift: *No Place for Truth* (see n. 47), and *God in the Wasteland: The Reality of Truth in a World of Fading Dreams* (Grand Rapids: Eerdmans, 1994).

72. George A. Lindbeck, "The Church's Mission to a Postmodern Culture," in *Postmodern Theology: Christian Faith in a Pluralist World*, ed. Frederic B. Burnham (San Francisco: Harper San Francisco, 1989), 45. The remark is astute, for it does not say that Schuller is conservative (there is very little in his messages that should associate him with evangelicalism), but that professedly conservative audiences think he is fine. The remark is all the more shrewd in the light of the fact that Lindbeck himself sees doctrine in purely functional terms, i.e., in terms of providing "communally authoritative rules of discourse, attitude and action" (George Lindbeck, *The Nature of Doctrine: Religion and Theology in a Postliberal Age* [Philadelphia: Westminster Press, 1984], 18).

One of the most stunning studies in this respect examined all the essays in *Leadership Journal*, a respected evangelical spinoff of *Christianity Today*, between 1980, when it began, and 1988. It showed

> that less than 1 percent made any obvious attempt to root the answers in anything biblical or doctrinal—despite the fact that many of the problems addressed are addressed directly in Scripture. Instead, the answers were taken heavily from the insights of the managerial and therapeutic revolutions.[73]

In many of the media presentations (though not all), the problem is still worse: the Bible is not merely ignored, but perverted.

But the problem is not restricted to pastors, televangelists, laypeople, and evangelical journalists. It can be found among "evangelical" theologians as well.[74] For example, in two recent books Stanley J. Grenz rejects the "propositionalism" in "modern evangelicalism's" approach to Scripture.[75] He does not fairly assess how affirmation of the Bible's truthfulness has been characteristic of believers throughout church history until the modern and post-modern periods, or evaluate how numbers of contemporary evangelical scholars want to uphold the propositional truthfulness of Scripture where propositions are offered us, while still recognizing other dimensions of truth (see the discussion in chap. 4, above). He prefers the direction illumined by Schleiermacher,[76] arguing that the three sources or norms for theology are Scripture, tradition, and culture. This is, to say the least, decidedly unhelpful. Quite apart from the extraordinary complexities of linking Scripture and tradition in this way, the addition of culture is astonishing. One might hazard a guess that Grenz has read enough to recognize that the interpreter cannot escape his or her own culture, and therefore has put down culture as a norm or source of theology, without recognizing the minefield he has created for himself (see the first two parts of this book). His openness to Tillich's method of correlation is not reassuring. With the best will in the world, I cannot see how Grenz's approach to Scripture can be called "evangelical" in any useful sense.

---

73. David F. Wells, "The D-Min-ization of the Ministry," in Guinness and Seel, *No God But God*, 181; and for detailed analysis, see his *No Place for Truth*, chap. 3.

74. One might gain some idea of the range of ways in which Scripture *functions* for various theologians by reading Robert K. Johnston, ed., *The Use of the Bible in Theology: Evangelical Options* (Atlanta: John Knox Press, 1985)—but that is a slightly different (though related) question that cannot be pursued here.

75. *Revisioning Evangelical Theology: A Fresh Agenda for the 21st Century* (Downers Grove: InterVarsity Press, 1993); *Theology for the People of God* (Nashville: Broadman & Holman, 1994).

76. *Revisioning Evangelical Theology*, 70.

One observes, too, the common elevation of praxis above Scripture in some forms of "evangelical" contextualization—and sometimes a knee-jerk reactionary traditionalism by way of response (see chap. 14).

Some churches try so hard to be user-friendly and relational that the Bible is implicitly ignored or depreciated. In one evangelical church that I recently attended, the morning's skit came in three secenes that devoured about fifteen minutes. The closing lines on true love and friendship emerged from a scene in which one woman was giving comfort and love to another who had just had a miscarriage. The latter thanked her for not quoting verses like Romans 8:28 at her, but just loving her. Now I realize that quoting verses "at" someone can be done in an insensitive and triumphalistic fashion. Yet the fact remains that no Christian who passes through deep waters draws much comfort from God until he or she realizes that God really is in control, God really does love his own people, God really is wise and good, God really can use pain in this fallen world in remarkable ways.[77] To turn people away from such God-centered truths to appeal to purely human comfort I might have expected from a liberal church; it is crushingly disappointing in a church that nominally retains its evangelical statement of faith.

One observes the decline of family and personal devotions and the rising number of self-confessed evangelicals who assume the gospel but devote themselves to *relatively* peripheral issues that become their premier passion: debates over Lordship salvation, spiritual warfare, counseling, home schooling, divorce and remarriage, abortion, Christian schools, Gothard seminars, social drinking, debt-free financing, charismatic issues, tastes in music and corporate worship, sex education in public schools, church polity, church discipline, ecology, women's ordination, and much more.

An important book on this subject is Mark Noll's *The Scandal of the Evangelical Mind*.[78] The opening line is already much cited: "The scandal of the evangelical mind is that there is not much of an evangelical mind."[79] Step by step, Noll traces the anti-intellectualism that has afflicted much of the history of evangelicalism, interacting with the "proof texts" that ostensibly justify such a stance (e.g., 1 Cor. 1), gradually building a damning indictment. Yet perhaps it would not be unfair to suggest that his evidence reflects a more serious departure from the Bible than even he recognizes. For all that I resonate with the main thrust of Noll's work, I have two serious reservations.

---

77. Cf. D. A. Carson, *How Long, O Lord? Reflections on Suffering and Evil* (Grand Rapids: Baker, 1990).

78. Grand Rapids: Eerdmans, 1994.

79. Ibid., 3. Others have recently taken the same approach, e.g., Os Guinness, *Fit Bodies, Fat Minds: Why Evangelicals Don't Think and What To Do About It* (Grand Rapids: Baker, 1994).

First, certain historical analyses do not ring quite true. For example, Noll praises Jonathan Edwards for his intellectual leadership and profoundly God-centered thought (1703–58) and then criticizes him for promoting notions of revival that ultimately turned aside from intellectual endeavor. Noll writes:

> Edwards, in a full range of metaphysical, psychological, and epistemo-logical works, alongside a small library of theological and biblical writing, was responsible for the most God-centered as well as the most intellectually subtle reasoning in all of American evangelical history. Yet Edwards was also a promoter of the revival that pushed American evangelicalism in a direction that made it unable or unwilling to benefit from his own intellectual work.[80]

Is this quite fair? For a start, this does not adequately distinguish God-given revival, which Edwards espoused, from the revivalism that developed a century later.[81] Unless one were to argue that it is always wrong to support revival, for fear of what it might turn into, this assessment is surely a bit skewed. One might as well argue that it is always wrong to defend loving God with one's mind, for fear of how intellectualism regularly puffs up, while only love builds up.

Second, and more importantly, while Noll rightly excoriates the anti-intel-lectualism that characterizes a wide swath of contemporary evangelicalism, especially in the populist approaches of some leaders, and easily marshals evidence that would sometimes be funny if it were not so sad,[82] it seems to me he overlooks the most serious loss of a truly biblical mind. It is the loss of biblical outlook among Christian intellectuals.

In other words, I worry less about the anti-intellectualism of the less educated sections of evangelicalism than I do about the biblical and theological illiteracy, or astonishing intellectual compromise, among its leading intellectuals. Evangelicalism has many sons and daughters whose primary vocation is the life of the mind: writers, thinkers, scholars, academicians, researchers— in field after field. They are not inferior to other thinkers in similar fields. But with rare exceptions they have not made the impact they might have because their grasp of biblical and theological truth has rarely extended much beyond Sunday school knowledge. In the main, they think like secularists and bless their insights with the odd text or biblical cliché. They cannot quite be

---

80. Ibid., 80–81.

81. Cf. Iain H. Murray, *Revival and Revivalism: The Making and Marring of American Evangelicalism 1750–1858* (Edinburgh: Banner of Truth Trust, 1994).

82. Even here, I think, Noll is in danger of overstating his case. There is a considerable body of literature, all of which Noll knows, that denies "that fundamentalism at the turn of the century was inherently antagonistic to the life of the mind." See D. G. Hart, "Presbyterians and Fundamentalism," *Westminster Theological Journal* 55 (1993): 331–42, esp. 332, and the literature there cited.

accepted by the secular guilds (unless of course they keep their mouths shut completely about their faith), and they cannot revolutionize intellectual life in the West because they do not think like consistent Christians who take on the *status quo* and seek to replace it with something better.

The fault is not theirs alone. The modern explosion of knowledge has resulted in many specializations, and it is becoming more and more difficult to become competent in several fields. Above all, the problem lies in the pulpit. Too few preachers have so married content and passion that they have taught their people to think biblically and love and honor God passionately. The books on many church bookstalls are a disgrace—thousands of pages of sentimental twaddle laced with the occasional biblical gem. There is very little effort to build up a biblical mind in our churches—and after all, Christian intellectuals attend our churches, too, and if they are not shown what the contours of Christian thinking look like there, where will they learn it?

Noll and others often cite Jesus' injunction to love the Lord your God "with all your heart and with all your soul *and with all your mind* and with all your strength" (Mark 12:30) as if that justifies all intellectual effort expended by a Christian. John Piper, in a private conversation, thoughtfully commented that he was unsure what the passage means: What precisely does it mean to love God with one's mind? It is not obvious. This is not the place to embark on a full-scale exegesis. Remembering, however, that the "heart" in biblical thought is not so much the seat of the emotions as the seat of thought and of the whole person, both "loving God with your heart" and "loving God with your mind" are bound up with thinking the right things about God. They cannot simply be equated with all intellectual endeavor undertaken by a Christian, even though such endeavor must be undertaken *coram Deo*. But whatever the full sweep of this injunction, it cannot mean less than a God-inspired delight in all of God's thoughts insofar as he has disclosed them, and a God-given determination to dethrone all competing systems of thought and bring them into captivity to the gospel (cf. 2 Cor. 10:5). And that requires constant, thoughtful, Bible reading, theological reflection, interaction with Christian thinkers from the past, humble assessment of the currents of our age and courageous determination not to become their slave.

It is precisely here, I fear, that many evangelical intellectuals have failed. Perhaps it would not be too harsh to wonder if some of Noll's fellow historians have missed the boat. Consider Stout's recent biography of George Whitefield.[83] Stout's thesis is that the key to Whitefield's "unprecedented success in marketing religion in the eighteenth century" (!) lies in the fact that

83. Harry S. Stout, *The Divine Dramatist: George Whitefield and the Rise of Modern Evangelicalism* (Grand Rapids: Eerdmans, 1991).

Whitefield became an actor preacher as opposed to a scholar preacher. This thesis governs the entire book: George Whitefield was above all an actor. Stout speaks of Whitefield's conversion as a contrived experience copied from the Puritans, but neglects the obvious transformation of his character. He regularly belittles Whitefield's interest in theology, but does not thoughtfully weigh the doctrinal content of whole sermon after whole sermon. The best-known Whitefield scholar of this century has responded:

> This book also abounds with outright errors of fact. This reviewer has marked his copy with the term "false" written in the margin where these mistakes occur and has done so more than three hundred times. For instance, Stout confuses Howell Harris the Welsh evangelist with Gabriel Harris, a businessman of Gloucester. He pictures Whitefield as arriving at his open-air meetings, proud to be conveyed there in William Seward's grand carriage, but Seward tells us that upon being converted he had sold his carriage—this before he ever knew Whitefield. He speaks of Whitefield as putting on his revivals in town after town, but Whitefield never referred to the results of his work as "revival" and virtually never used the word. He would have used the term, as biblically-oriented people have ever done, only as a description of a work done by God. He charges that Whitefield's pronunciation was so poor that he spoke of the "Lord God" as the "Lurd Gud," yet Whitefield's preaching won the high praise of such masters of the English tongue as Lord Bolingbroke and the Earl of Chesterfield.[84]

But the most problematic element of Stout's reconstruction is not its historical errors of detail, but its reductionistic stance. All of Whitefield's "success" is finally attributed to his acting ability. There is almost nothing left over for other causes; there is certainly no place for the Spirit of God. Of course, the Spirit of God customarily uses means, so that after the fact one can sometimes trace those means and thank God for them. But none of that strand of thought appears in Stout. In short, the work is profoundly secular.

In a fascinating exchange of letters, Stout graciously takes on some of his critics (whose Christian commitments he shares) and is rewarded with a reply from Iain Murray.[85] Stout's *apologia* turns on several points, the most important of which is that his "primary intended audience" was "the professional academy and university students" who, he alleges, before Stout's biography, simply ignored Whitefield. "Professional historians are not interested in Dallimore's (and my) faith claims, but they are interested in social, cultural, and intellectual significance. So those are the terms in which the biography

---

84. Arnold Dallimore, in *Baptist Review of Theology* 3/2 (1993): 69.
85. *Banner of Truth Magazine* 378 (March 1995): 7–11.

was framed."[86] After acknowledging the peculiar difficulties Christian scholars face in the secular academy, the burden of Murray's reply is this: "But surely, to write the lives of eminent Christians with minimum notice of the things which meant *most* to them, and without which their lives cannot be understood, is to mislead?"[87]

In short, Stout is asking Murray how a Christian voice can be heard in the secular academy at all, unless Christians are willing to "play by the rules" of the academy. Murray is asking if they so much confine themselves to these rules that they succumb to the same reductionism characteristic of secular minds—or, otherwise put, How does such work do any good, unless it exerts influence to move unbelievers away from their secular minds?

Or consider the Epilogue to Hatch's brilliant treatment of American Christianity.[88] The central thesis is easily put. The instincts of fundamentalism/evangelicalism/Pentecostalism are "populist rather than those of upper-class conservatism,"[89] and are the outworking of a principle of democratization that refuses to be cowed by voices of authority. In his closing lines, Hatch writes:

> Following the long tradition of democratic Christianity in America, Fundamentalists and Pentecostals reject modernity as it is expressed in high culture but remain stalwart defenders of modern attitudes as they build popular constituencies with the most innovative techniques. They will not surrender to learned experts the right to think for themselves. For two centuries Americans have refused to defer sensitive matters of conscience to the staid graduates of Harvard, Yale, and Princeton. They have taken faith into their own hands and molded it according to the aspirations of everyday life. American Christianity continues to be powered by ordinary people and by the contagious spirit of their efforts to storm heaven by the back door.[90]

Clearly there is more than a little truth in this assessment, and certainly the work is well crafted. Yet in the end we are treated to another case of thoroughly secular reductionism. No place is allowed for the work of God in the Second Great Awakening (1857–58), for the rise from the ashes of evangelicalism in the wake of the the the modernist-fundamentalist debates, and so forth. The whole thing can be ascribed to one simple social/psychological premise, one monocausational explanation. The entire approach is horizontal.

---

86. Ibid., 9.
87. Ibid., 11.
88. Nathan O. Hatch, *The Democratization of American Christianity* (New Haven: Yale Univ. Press, 1989). Epilogue: "The Recurring Populist Impulse in American Christianity" (210–19).
89. Ibid., 219.
90. Ibid.

Not for a moment am I minimizing the difficulties of getting published by a university press if one steps outside these bounds. On some issues and in some kinds of writing, this strikes me as a wise strategy. I am simply saying that this sort of approach, consistently deployed, will win academic plaudits from the guild of secularists, but it is not a conspicuous example of Christian scholarship in any useful sense of the word "Christian." It succumbs to the age; it does not challenge it. There is not a shred of evidence in this thesis that the author has thought long and hard about what the Bible says about God's activity in the world, or about the pouring out of his Spirit, or about the Bible's story-line, or about the power of the gospel, or a host of other things—though doubtless he has. The book could have been written by a well-informed and sympathetic atheist.

In fact, in a remarkable paper by a young Catholic scholar, Christian historians are gently taken out to the woodshed for precisely that reason: they are guilty of thinking and writing within their disciplines like liberals who leave little place for God acting in the world.[91] I remarked in an earlier chapter that virtually all academic history a century and a half ago was done within the framework of a belief in Providence.[92] There is simply nothing in Hatch's work that points the way out of the modern secularist paradigm.

Noll quotes Machen:

> We may preach with all the fervor of a reformer, and yet succeed only in winning a straggler here and there, if we permit the whole collective thought of the nation or of the world to be controlled by ideas which, by the resistless force of logic, prevent Christianity from being regarded as anything more than a harmless delusion.... What is to-day a matter of academic speculation, begins to-morrow to move armies and pull down empires.[93]

I entirely agree. But I cannot see how scholarly work by evangelicals, even first-class scholarly work, avoids the pitfalls or reverses the trends if it is sold out to the regnant paradigms. Part of what is needed in a renewed evangelical mind is the commitment, knowledge, and learning, to say nothing of the

---

91. Michael J. Baxter, "Let's Do Away with 'Faith' and 'History': A Critique of H. Richard Niebuhr's False Antinomies" (unpublished paper presented at the Wheaton College Philosophy Conference, October 29, 1993), slated for publication in a forthcoming issue of *Modern Theology.*

92. I am indebted to a former student, Jonathan Boyd, for a copy of his unpublished paper, "'Thy Pious Heart Wilt Deeply Feel': Providence and Historical Consciousness in Antebellum American-History Schoolbooks" (1992). Cf. also Jay D. Green, "Church Historiographical Participation in the Early Twentieth Century Revolt Against Formalism: Shirley Jackson Case and Socio-Historicism" (M.A. thesis, Trinity Evangelical Divinity School, 1994).

93. J. Gresham Machen, "Christianity and Culture," *Princeton Theological Review* 11 (1913): 7; cited in Noll, *The Scandal of the Evangelical Mind*, 35.

strength of the Spirit of God, to take on these paradigms and challenge them with a biblical worldview. It is in that area, I fear, that we have a very long way to go.

E. Frustration

The more one studies contemporary evangelicalism, the more one senses the profound frustration that grips many of its leaders. The statistics say we should be powerful and influential, and we are not. The intellectuals think they should be followed, and they are largely ignored. The entrepreneurs and media stars act as if they will bring in revival, and of course they don't. The culture is hell-bent to discard the Judeo-Christian outlook that once predominated, and a lot of conservatives feel cheated. Theologians and historians and pastors alike continuously expand the definition of evangelicalism, but instead of drawing in a wider circle they are gutting what is central. The level of frustration is high.

But not, I fear, the level of brokenness.

F. Concluding Reflections

1. If postmodern thought has tried to gag God, unsuccessfully, by its radical hermeneutics and its innovative epistemology, the church is in danger of gagging God in quite another way. The church in Laodicea, toward the end of the first century, thought of itself as farsighted, respectable, basically well off. From the perspective of the exalted Christ, however, it was blind, naked, bankrupt. The nearby town of Colossae enjoyed water that was fresh and cold, and therefore useful; the nearby town of Hierapolis enjoyed hotsprings where people went to take the cure: its water, too, was useful. But Laodicea's foul water was channeled in through stone pipes, and it was proverbial for its nauseating taste. The church had become much like the water it drank: neither hot and useful, nor cold and useful, but merely nauseating. Jesus is prepared to spue this church out of his mouth (Rev. 3:16). This church makes the exalted Jesus gag.

I cannot escape the dreadful feeling that modern evangelicalism in the West more successfully effects the gagging of God, in this sense, than all the postmodernists together, in the other sense.

2. This calls for repentance. The things from which we must turn are not so much individual sins—greed, pride, sexual promiscuity, or the like, as ugly and as evil as they are—as fundamental heart attitudes that squeeze God and his Word and his glory to the periphery, while we get on with religion and self-fulfillment.

3. At issue is not only what we must turn from, but also what we must turn to:

We will not be able to recover the vision and understanding of God's grandeur until we recover an understanding of ourselves as creatures who have been made to know such grandeur. This must begin with the recovery of the idea that as beings made in God's image, we are fundamentally *moral* beings, not consumers, that the satisfaction of our psychological needs pales in significance when compared with the enduring value of doing what is right. Religious consumers want to have a spirituality for the same reason that they want to drive a stylish and expensive auto. Costly obedience is as foreign to them in matters spiritual as self-denial is in matters material. In a culture filled with such people, restoring weight to God is going to involve much more than simply getting some doctrine straight; it's going to entail a complete reconstruction of the modern self-absorbed pastiche personality.[94]

4. It follows that teachers and preachers in seminaries and churches must be people "for whom the great issue is the knowledge of God,"[95] whatever their area of specialization might be. Preachers and teachers who do not see this point and passionately hold to it are worse than useless: they are dangerous, because they are diverting.

---

94. Wells, *God in the Wasteland*, 115.

95. Peter Jensen, "The Teacher as Theologian in Theological Education," *Reformed Theological Review* 50 (1991): 83.

Chapter 12

ON HERALDING THE GOSPEL IN A PLURALISTIC CULTURE

B efore launching into the substance of this chapter, it may be wise to explain why it is placed here; for clearly I might have put it in part 3, as further reflection on how Christians should respond to our increasingly pluralistic culture. After all, if part 4 is devoted to forms of pluralism *within the camp*, how is discussion of evangelism appropriate here? Placing the material here was a judgment call based on two considerations.

First, placing this chapter on heralding the gospel in part 3 might have given the impression that evangelism and the conversion of men and women is merely a means to greater political success, a shrewd strategy which, if fruitful, ensures our place in the sun. That is such a pragmatic interpretation of evangelism that it must be avoided at all costs. One finds it in some political conservatives who want the Christian religion to be a solid bulwark and an abettor of political conservatism. But God will never be relegated to a useful plank in someone's agenda.

Second, many of the feelings of fragmentation and frustration that occupy contemporary evangelicalism have erupted, as this book has shown, because the culture has changed so quickly, and we feel out of place. *Empirical pluralism* makes our evangelistic task more complicated, in much the same way that a missionary called to evangelize several alien cultures at once would have a more difficult task than one called to evangelize a monolithic culture. In any case, as much of Western culture increasingly distances itself from its Judeo-Christian roots, the task of evangelism takes on the overtones of a missionary enterprise to an alien culture: part of the task is bound up with understanding that culture.[1] *Philosophical pluralism* goes further and challenges our right to evangelize. Older opponents might deny the truth of Christianity; newer opponents accuse Christianity of being ridiculous when it claims to declare the truth. We face new levels of hostility, new levels of biblical illiteracy, new forms of resistance,[2] even while this generation speaks freely and somewhat wantonly of "spirituality." These pressures have contributed to the confusion in contemporary evangelicalism. So if at one level this chapter draws together some of the strands from earlier parts of the book, at another level it directly addresses some of the problems evangelicalism is forced to confront because of its own corruptions, outlined in chapter 11; therefore, I place this material here.

Not long before he died, Max Warren wrote:

> Reacting, and reacting rightly, against the dogmatic triumphalism of much past Christian approach to men of other faiths, it is all too easy to swing to the other extreme and talk happily of different roads to the summit, as if Jesus were in no particular and distinctive sense "the Way, the Truth, and the Life." Of course where this point is reached, the Great Commission is tacitly, if not explicitly, held to be indefinitely in suspense if not quite otiose. This is a view forcefully propounded by some Christians holding professorial Chairs in Britain and across the Atlantic. Are they right? Is courtesy always to preclude contradiction? Is choice now just a matter of taste, no longer a response to an absolute demand? Is the Cross on Calvary really no more than a confusing roundabout sign pointing in every direction, or is it still the place where *all* men are meant to kneel?[3]

It will come as no surprise that I answer Warren's last question with a whole-hearted "Yes!" The assumption, of course, is that human beings are lost without Jesus Christ: I am necessarily assuming the arguments advanced in parts 1 and 2 of this book. As Hunter rather simply puts it:

---

1. The point is now widely recognized, within a number of frameworks. See, for example, Lesslie Newbigin, "Can the West be Converted?" *International Bulletin of Missionary Research* 11 (1987): 2–7; George Hunsberger, "The Newbigin Gauntlet: Developing a Domestic Missiology for North America," *Missiology* 19 (1991): 392–408; Craig van Gelder, "A Great New Fact of Our Day: America as a Mission Field," *Missiology* 19 (1991): 409–18; Harold A. Netland, "Truth, Authority, and Modernity: Shopping for Truth in a Supermarket of Worldviews," in *Faith and Modernity*, ed. Philip Sampson, Vinay Samuel, and Chris Sugden (Oxford: Regnum Books, 1994), 89–115.

2. Cf. Hervé Carrier, *Evangelizing the Culture of Modernity* (Maryknoll: Orbis Books, 1993), 1: "Today, the capillary spread of Gospel values into the social fabric is blocked because of the wide gap existing between the Christian faith and the prevailing ethos of the industrialized world."

3. Max A. C. Warren, *I Believe in the Great Commission* (London: Hodder & Stoughton, 1976), 150–51.

Apostolic congregations[4] know . . . that people who are not following Jesus Christ and are not working out their salvation within the body of Christ are lost, and they cannot find the way to abundant life by themselves. They know this from Scripture, for our Lord revealed that such people are "lost, like sheep without a shepherd." This revelation is confirmed as these churches observe contemporary society. . . . But the congregations also observe that many (declining) churces do not perceive that secular people are lost. Tragically, too many churches view the world through rose colored glasses; they mistake the masks that lost people wear for their real faces. Some churches even brand all people (and life-styles) as okay, and settle in with no mission at all. Apostolic churches are astonished by this myopia in the majority of churches. . . . [5]

By contrast, as Gay rightly comments,

the concern for tolerance, openness, and the willingness to dialogue in religious matters may actually mask despair in our contemporary situation. That the celebration of these virtues often functions only to undermine traditional theological orthodoxy in such a way that appeals may then be made to another kind of orthodoxy that is almost entirely devoid of transcendence— that is, devoid of a God who can speak and act effectively in the world—is a clear indication of this. The openness touted in the various theologies of world religions, it seems, is ultimately openness only to human autonomy. It is no wonder, then, that these theologies give way so quickly to the exigencies and objective autonomy of contemporary public life.[6]

Although in this chapter I am focusing on evangelizing postmodern people, it is important to remember that there are countless cultural variations. European postmodernism is not exactly the same as what one finds in North America,[7] and of course there are many variations within Europe, and within individual countries in Europe. There are important distinctions between Canada and the United States,[8] and many variations within each country.

One example of a particularly interesting variation deserves mention. Those who have read this book right through to this point will doubtless recall the Willow Creek survey mentioned in chapter 11. About twenty years ago,

---

4. By which Hunter refers to congregations that are faithful to the apostolic gospel.

5. George G. Hunter, III, *How to Reach Secular People* (Nashville: Abingdon, 1992), 144–45. Cf. also Ajith Fernando, *The Christian's Attitude Toward World Religions* (Wheaton: Tyndale House, 1987).

6. Craig M. Gay, "Plurality, Ambiguity, and Despair in Contemporary Theology," *Journal of the Evangelical Theological Society* 36 (1993): 224.

7. See, for instance, the helpful essay by W. A. Visser 'T Hooft, "Evangelism Among Europe's Neo-Pagans," *Evangelical Review of Theology* 18 (1994): 335–47.

8. E.g., see Douglas John Hall, *Professing the Faith: Christian Theology in a North American Context* (Minneapolis: Fortress Press, 1993), 108–10.

evidence showed that people in the area did not attend churches because they found the services boring, the music old-fashioned, and so forth. Recently Dr. David Fisher, senior minister of Park Street Church in Boston, arranged for a somewhat similar survey to find out about their 50,000 nearest neighbors. The results were interesting. About 65 percent were single and under the age of thirty. Many of those interviewed, when asked why they did not attend church, thought it surprising that anyone should think they should. Music was not listed as a major factor in drawing people. Why should they attend church to hear contemporary music? The had their own CDs. But 85 percent were at least "somewhat" interested in "spiritual" issues—an astonishing figure in secular Boston, even allowing for the the diversity and ambiguity behind "spiritual." Of the factors that might draw these people to church, the response with the highest percentage (65 percent) had nothing to do with program, entertainment, excitement, music, or the like: these people said they would probably come to church if a friend invited them. Moreover, when Sunday evening services were "slanted" to the people they discovered their neighbors to be, the "twentysomething" Christians in the church, much to the minister's delight, insisted that these be "church" services, not entertainment or amusement. Their big word was "authentic": they wanted their friends to see what *real* Christianity looked like. Dietrich Bonhoeffer's *Cost of Discipleship* is making a comeback.[9] There were negatives, of course—but whether negatives or positives, some of these results were certainly unexpected.[10]

Clearly the results are very different from what Willow Creek discovered twenty-five years ago. These differences may stem from time (two decades is a substantial period: the Willow Creek findings may be out of date), geographical location (New England is not the same as the relatively conservative Midwest), and the peculiar demographics around Park Street Church (such a high percentage of singles under thirty).

But I shall not pursue such nice distinctions here. For my purposes, it is enough to think through what form a faithful and wise articulation of the exclusive gospel of Jesus Christ will take as it confronts postmodern perils. Perhaps I may venture five points.

A. Often It Is Helpful to Critique the Intellectual, Moral, and Existential Bankruptcy of the Age

On the intellectual front, that is a substantial element of what was attempted in the first two parts of this book. The problems of privatization,

9. New York: Macmillan, 1963.
10. Most of this information is from a private letter from Dr. David C. Fisher (April 28, 1994).

relativism, philosophical pluralism, skepticism, postmodernity, and ethical "openness" largely control the mental thought processes of most university students, and of a substantial member of others. That is scarcely surprising: "*the notion that one particular religious figure and one religious perspective can be universally valid, normative, and binding upon all peoples in all cultures . . . is widely rejected today as arrogant and intellectually untenable in our pluralistic world.*"[11] But as I have devoted so much of this book to the intellectual arena, I must turn to other elements of the contemporary moral and spiritual bankruptcy.

In one of his essays, Charles Colson tells of one of his attempts to witness to an acquaintance.[12] Colson's testimony was easily dismissed by appealing to New Age relativism; his appeal to the authority of Scripture and to arguments for its historical validity proved unconvincing; discussion about the afterlife soon became futile. Somewhat frustrated, Colson brought up the Woody Allen film, *Crimes and Misdemeanors*. In this film a doctor hires a killer to murder his mistress. He is not caught, but is haunted by guilt. Unlike the plot in Dostoevsky's *Crime and Punishment*, however, this doctor finally decides that there is no justice in the universe, and therefore no need for him to suffer the pangs of conscience. There is only Darwinian struggle. Ruthlessness wins. When Colson asked, "When we do wrong, is that the only choice? Either live tormented by guilt—or kill our conscience and live like beasts?" the man began to listen. Colson went on to Tolstoy's *War and Peace*, in which Pierre, wrestling with his conscience, cries out, "Why is it that I know what is right, but do what is wrong?" This led in turn to C. S. Lewis, and finally to Romans, and to some introductory reflection on conscience. And from there you are not far from a Christian worldview, and from the gospel itself.

Recognized or not, acknowledged or not, there is a profound and bitter emptiness at the hearts of many men and women in Western culture. I am not therefore suggesting that the gospel be reshaped to become that which meets my emptiness: so crassly put, this would be one more way by which evangelicalism is only a whisker from affirming that God exists in order to meet my needs, as I perceive them. Human emptiness and moral confusion must be traced to its roots *in biblical theology*; only in that framework can the historic gospel truly address the underlying problem. Nevertheless, this is an important way into some people's minds and hearts. Not a few people are hungry to escape their isolation. They would like to experience transcendence; at some deep level they long to know God, even as they flee him, and to experience relationships, with God and with others, that escape the merely

USc⁴

---

11. Netland, "Truth, Authority and Modernity," 94 (emphasis his).

12. Charles Colson, "Reaching the Pagan Mind," *Christianity Today* 36/13 (November 9, 1992): 112.

trivial and transient, even while, quite impossibly, they still want to be at the center of the universe.]

If the gospel is presented, then, as that gracious message which connects fallen human beings with the good and sovereign God who made them, and with other people who have tasted and seen that the Lord is good, some men and women will be open to hear more.[13] In other words, the critique of this age must not be only at the intellectual level, as important as that level is. The bankruptcy of the moral, ethical, relational, and spiritual dimensions must be lovingly exposed again and again.]

B. In Our Evangelism We Must Start Further Back and Nail Down the Turning Points in Redemptive History

Perhaps this point can be established most simply by taking two steps. First, I shall reflect on the example of Paul in Athens; and second, I shall insist on the priority, in the present culture, of preaching biblical (as opposed to systematic) theology.

1. The Example of Paul in Athens (Acts 17:16–31)

Before looking at the text itself, we should remind ourselves that the world confronting the early church was a highly pluralistic world.[14] That is one of the reasons why Paul's Athenian address is so interesting. Although the pluralism he confronted was quite different from anything we face, and although the apostle emerged from a Christian community that was not put into a defensive position trying to preserve cultural elements others were trying to abandon, some of the similarities with our own day are quite striking. Not least is the fact that here we see Paul attempting to evangelize people who were utterly biblically illiterate, and whose worldview was far removed from that of the Judeo-Christian tradition.

At one level, there is great encouragement for us in this fact. We earlier observed that on certain points it was probably harder to make a fair application from the New Testament Scriptures to evangelical Protestantism during the two centuries when Protestantism exercised a gentle hegemony in the land, than it is today. The responses of the New Testament writers to the pluralism of their day can be applied with relative directness to the analogous pluralism of our day.

Thus, against the claims of other intermediaries, Colossians insists not only on the supremacy of Christ, but also on the exclusiveness of his suffi-

---

13. Jay C. Rochelle, "Mystery and Relationship as Keys to the Church's Response to Secularism," *Currents in Theology and Mission* 19 (1992): 267–76.

14. See the discussion and documentation in chap. 6.

CARSON ASSUMES THAT, PEOPLE ARE ILLITERATE TO THE CHRISTIAN MESSAGE!

ciency. While others recognize many "lords," many (pagar
variety of "hopes" (i.e., diverse visions of the *summum bonu₁*
ognize one Lord, one faith, one baptism, one hope, and on
6). While some Greek philosophers opined that there was "one god," this
projected deity was almost always portrayed in pantheistic terms (which is
one of the prime reasons why many Greek writers could alternate between
"god" and "gods" without any apparent difference in meaning). They could
speak of "one god" but could not confess that "God is One." Paul insists that
the one God is the God and Father of our Lord Jesus Christ, the God of creation and of the old covenant, who has supremely disclosed himself in his Son
(Rom. 1; 1 Cor. 8). One cannot read Revelation 2–3 without discerning the
titanic struggle the early church faced from the multifaceted pressures of pluralism. Indeed, it is surely safe to conclude that, by and large, the New
Testament writers did not readily distinguish the pluralism of the day from the
idolatry of the day: the destruction of the one was the destruction of the other.

Doubtless the reasons why we today are becoming more pluralistic (in
the third, philosophical sense I developed in the first chapter) are almost all
bad. Nevertheless, they bring us into a situation where many New Testament
texts address us with more immediate power than at any time during the last
two or three centuries. These passages just cited, and many more, show the
early church not so much opposing the *existence* of pluralism (on some philosophical ground), as defying it, insisting on the uniqueness of Jesus Christ
and the exclusiveness of the saving power of his gospel. But they did so in
such a way that they showed they understood the people they were addressing. We must develop similar firmness, and similar flexibility.

Now we are ready to outline some of the key elements, according to
Luke, of Paul's address in Athens. I shall not attempt a detailed exposition.[15]
I merely draw attention to an apostolic number of points.

(a) Paul's approach, preaching to these people who had never read the
Old Testament and had never heard of Moses, was radically different from his
approach in, say, the synagogue of Pisidian Antioch (Acts 13:13ff.), where the
burden of his preaching is that Jesus really did fulfill the Old Testament
prophecies, rightly understood, and that failure to bow to him would bring
down Old Testament promises of judgment.[16] Clearly, such an approach
would mean nothing to those who had never heard of the Hebrew Bible,
much less read it.

---

15. Among the plethora of relevant books and articles that might be cited, one of the
more interesting is Khiok-Khng Yeo, "A Rhetorical Study of Acts 17.22–31: What Has
Jerusalem To Do with Athens and Beijing?" *Jian Dao* 1 (1994): 75–107.

16. Cf. John R. Davies, "Biblical Precedents for Contextualization," *ATA Journal* 2 (1994):
10–35.

(b) While some might have been mightily impressed by Athenian architecture, sculpture, and learning, Paul "was greatly distressed to see that the city was full of idols" (17:16). In other words, his reactions were based not on aesthetics, but on a Christian analysis of the culture.

(c) When he is finally brought before the Areopagus, he begins with courtesy and sensitivity, coupled with certain restraint: "I see that in every way you are very religious" (17:22). Courtesy, yes; but there is no approval of their religion as an alternative way of salvation. At the same time, Paul chooses forms of expression which, initially at least, link his thought with that of Stoics and Epicureans, already carefully introduced to us (17:18). Stoics believed the human race was indeed one, and made for a special relation with God. And, as C. K. Barrett points out, "Epicureans opposed superstitious popular religion, as Paul does."[17] F. F. Bruce draws similar lines. For example, on 17:25 Bruce comments, "Here may be discerned approximations to the Epicurean doctrine that God needs nothing from human beings and to the Stoic belief that he is the source of all life."[18] Indeed, in defense of the historical reliability of Luke's account, Bruce writes, "If the author of Rom. 1–3 had been invited to address an Athenian audience on the knowledge of God, it is difficult to think that the general purport . . . of his words would have been much different from what Luke reports Paul as saying in vv. 22–31. If the tone of the Areopagita is different from that of Rom. 1–3 (as it is), Paul's ability to adapt his tone and his approach to his audience must not be underestimated."[19] Other scholars have drawn attention to parallels with particular Greek writers, e.g., the Stoic historian Posidonius.[20]

On this basis, James Barr thinks he can find in Paul an example of one who happily appeals to "natural theology" when the occasion warrants.[21] At a certain level, of course, he is right: whether in Acts 17 or Romans 1–3, Paul makes it clear that God has not left himself without witness. But there are limits in how far Paul will go. Unlike Barr, Paul will not use "natural theol-

---

17. C. K. Barrett, "Paul's Speech on the Areopagus," in *New Testament Christianity for Africa and the World*, ed. M. E. Glasswell and E. W. Fasholé-Luke (London: SPCK, 1974), 73.

18. *The Acts of the Apostles: Greek Text with Introduction and Commentary*, rev. ed. (Grand Rapids: Eerdmans, 1990), 382.

19. Ibid., 379.

20. So David L. Balch, "The Areopagus Speech: An Appeal to the Stoic Historian Posidonius Against Later Stoics and the Epicureans," in *Greeks, Romans, and Christians*, Festschrift for Abraham J. Malherbe, ed. David L. Balch, Everett Ferguson, and Wayne Meeks (Minneapolis: Fortress Press, 1990), 52–79. Some of Balch's parallels are unconvincing. But Posidonius "was one of the few philosophers in antiquity to stress that God is 'without form'" (79).

21. James Barr, *Biblical Faith and Natural Theology*, Gifford Lectures for 1991 (Oxford: Clarendon Press, 1993), esp. 27–28.

ogy" *against* biblical revelation. And even in this passage, as we shall see, Paul carefully *distances* himself from some things that Stoics and Epicureans would say, and eventually introduces themes that are essential to the gospel even though Paul knows they will alienate many of his hearers. In short, Paul displays courtesy and sensitivity, but there is restraint in his tactical alignments, lest he jeopardize the gospel.

(d) Paul finds a way into his subject by referring to the inscription "To an Unknown God" (17:23).[22] Probably such altars reflected the fears of animistic strata in pagan culture. There are powers beyond what one can know, and just to be on the safe side, it is important to offer sacrifices to all of them— even to unknown ones. By contrast, Paul insists he is introducing the God who is known, the God who has revealed himself.

(e) It has often been pointed out that there are other elements in the surrounding culture that Paul specifically confronts.[23] Acts 17:18 specifically mentions "Epicurean and Stoic philosophers." In the first century, "philosophy" did not have the fairly esoteric and abstract connotations it has today. It referred to an entire way of life, based on a rigorous and self-consistent intellectual system. The ideal of Epicurean philosophy was an undisturbed life, a life of tranquility, untroubled by undue involvement in human affairs. The gods themselves are composed of atoms so fine they live in calmness in the spaces between the worlds. As the gods are nicely removed from the hurleyburley of life, so human beings should seek the same ideal. But over against this vision, Paul presents a God who is actively involved in this world as its Creator, providential Ruler, Judge, and self-disclosing Savior.

Stoic philosophy thought of god as all-pervasive, more or less in a pantheistic sense, so that the human ideal was to live life in line with what is ultimately real, to conduct life in line with this god/principle of reason, which must rule over emotion and passion. Stoicism was "marked by great moral earnestness and a high sense of duty."[24] Against such a vision, the God Paul presents, far from being pantheistic, is personal, distinct from the creation, our final Judge. Instead of focusing on "universal reason tapped into by human reasoning,"[25] Paul contrasts divine will and sovereignty with human dependence and need.

---

22. Although archaeologists have not uncovered such an inscription in the ruins of ancient Athens, Pausanias, a second-century traveler, reports that in Athens there are "altars of gods named unknown" (*Description of Greece* 1.1.4).

23. E.g., in addition to the major commentaries, John Proctor, "The Gospel from Athens: Paul's Speech Before the Areopagus and the Evangel for Today," *Evangel* 10 (1992): 69–72.

24. F. F. Bruce, *The Acts of the Apostles: The Greek Text with Introduction and Commentary*, 3d ed. (Leicester: IVP/Grand Rapids: Eerdmans, 1990), 377.

25. This felicitous phrase is Proctor's, "The Gospel from Athens," 70.

500 ◆ THE GAGGING OF GOD

(f) Specifically, Paul introduces God as separate from the universe. He is the Creator (he "made the world and everything in it," 17:24), he is sovereign (he "is the Lord of heaven and earth," 17:24), and he is so transcendent that he cannot be domesticated by human forms of worship (he "does not live in temples built by hands," 17:24).

(g) Verse 25 is of enormous importance: God "is not served by human hands, as if he needed anything, because he himself gives all men life and breath and everything else." This passage not only insists that God sustains life and rules providentially, but that he is characterized by aseity. This fine word has largely dropped out of theological discussion, though the truth that God is the God of aseity was once a commonplace. It means that God is so independent that he does not need us. We cannot give him anything he lacks, or wheedle something out of him by cajoling him. He is the God who declares, "If I were hungry I would not tell you, for the world is mine, and all that is in it" (Ps. 50:12).

(h) All of the human race has descended from one man, himself created by God. This means that the one God rules over all, governing all people, their nations and their history ("he determined the times set for them and the exact places where they should live," 17:26).[26] Thus not only is there no room for racism or elitist tribalism, but one of the entailments of monotheism is that if there is one God he must in some sense be God of all, whether acknowledged or not.

(i) God's purpose in his ordering of history is to incite human beings to pursue him (17:27). The assumption, in other words, is that they otherwise would not. This hint at human rebellion is then further teased out and expanded: idolatry is a practice both culpably ignorant and evil, and all must one day answer to this Creator-God who is also Judge (17:29–30). None of this means that God is playing hard to get, or that he has hidden himself somewhere and must be discovered by noble feats of exploration: "he is not far from each one of us" (17:27). Paul even allows that such insight is recognized by some pagan poets (17:28).

(j) History is not going around and around in endless cycles, as many Greeks thought. History is teleological; it is pressing on in one direction, to the day of final judgment: God "has set a day when he will judge the world with justice" (17:31). Not only so, but there are developments *within* history; in modern theological parlance, there are salvation-historical or redemptive-historical developments. History is constrained not only by creation at one end and judgment at the other, but by singularities. In particular, God has

---

26. The Greek is given a slightly different rendering by Balch, "Areopagus Speech."

largely overlooked the pagan nations of the world *until this point*, but "*now* he commands all people everywhere to repent" (17:30).

(k) Although it is none less than God himself who will judge on the last day (17:31a), he will do so through a particular man, a man accredited by the brute historical fact that God raised him from the dead. We need to observe three things. First, only at this point, after he has set out an entire worldview and even something of a philosophy of history, does Paul introduce Jesus. Second, so far as the record goes, Paul refers to Jesus' miraculous resurrection without mentioning either his divine status or his atoning death. Probably he was about to do so; the narrative gives the impression that at this point Paul is cut off before he can complete his address. Third, not only does the picture Paul paints contradict animism, Epicureanism, and Stoicism, but by so boldly introducing physical resurrection ascribed to God himself, Paul is directly taking on one of the commonplaces in a great deal of Greek thought, namely neo-Platonic dualism. If the spiritual is good, the physical world bad, it is inconceivable that God, who is by definition good, would raise someone up to physical life, which is at least relatively bad. That is the very point that causes some to sneer (v. 32). But Paul does not flinch: his insistence on the resurrection of Jesus, as reported here by Luke, is entirely in line with what Paul says in his first letter to the Corinthians: "if Christ has not been raised, our preaching is useless and so is your faith" (1 Cor. 15:14). Paul will never compromise the gospel so as to make it pleasantly compatible with the culture he is evangelizing.

(l) Finally, whereas we can read this record of Paul's address in two or three minutes, doubtless he took an hour or two or more to deliver it. Although we have only the skimpiest record, what we have is crucial as we try to think through what themes need to be articulated and stressed as we preach the gospel to modern pagans.

2. The Primacy of Biblical Theology

At the risk of oversimplification, most evangelistic tools in the Western world are subsets of systematic theology. By this I mean that they tend to ask atemporal questions, and give atemporal answers: What is God like? What is at the heart of human need? What is sin? What is God's provision? How do we receive it? And so forth. This assessment, I think, is almost as true of, say, John Stott's *Basic Christianity* as it is of the Four Spiritual Laws or of the five points of Evangelism Explosion.

There is nothing intrinsically wrong with this pattern, as long as most of the people to whom it is presented have already bought into the Judeo-Christian heritage. A generation ago, the overwhelming majority of Americans enjoyed at least *some* knowledge of the pattern "creation/fall/ten commandments/Christ/judgment." Many had no real idea why Jesus died; virtually all believed that sin is an offense against God, who holds us accountable. But if you present these atemporal outlines of the gospel to those who know nothing about the Bible's plot-line, and who have bought into one form or another of New Age theosophy, how will they hear you? "God loves you and has a wonderful plan for your life": Is this the god of Shirley MacLaine? Of course he/she/it loves me: I'm lovable, aren't I? And this wonderful life: will I be wealthy? happy? Will I have wonderful kids? wonderful sex? a lot of respect? What do I have to do to get this wonderful life?

In short, the good news of Jesus Christ is virtually incoherent unless it is securely set into a biblical worldview. We observed that John Frame has addressed the problem in an *atemporal* framework, the framework of systematic theology.[27] I have no fundamental objection. However, to establish such a framework while simultaneously tracing out the rudiments of the Bible's plot-line strikes me as wiser, more strategic. One is simultaneously setting forth a structure of thought, and a meta-narrative; one is constructing a worldview, and showing how that worldview is grounded in the Bible itself. One is teaching people how to read the Bible. For these reasons, evangelism might wisely become, increasingly, a subset of biblical theology.

As I use the expression, *biblical theology* refers to the theology of the biblical corpora as God progressively discloses himself, climaxing in the coming of his Son Jesus Christ, and consummating in the new heaven and the new earth. In other words, sequence, history, the passage of time—these are foundational to biblical theology, and relatively minor in systematic theology. I am suggesting, then, that a world both biblically illiterate and sold out to philosophical pluralism demands that our proclamation of the gospel be a subset of biblical theology.

This was the lesson learned by a friend of mine who went to India as a missionary three decades ago. He learned to speak Hindi quite fluently, and preached evangelistically in countless villages. In ten years, he saw many professions of faith, but had planted no churches. He could not get around Hinduism's intrinsic syncretism and pluralism. Hindus could easily accept Jesus, adding him to the religious pot. Deeply discouraged, my friend returned home on furlough (as "home assignment" was then called), tried to think things through, and returned again to India. This time he restricted himself to two villages. There he began with the nature of God, the doctrine of creation, the nature of the Fall, and so forth. *Within this framework* he introduced Jesus. During the next four years, he saw relatively few conversions, but he planted two small churches.

---

27. *Apologetics to the Glory of God* (Phillipsburg: Presbyterian and Reformed, 1994).

This, surely, is part of the lesson of Acts 17. Paul felt it necessary to establish an entire framework, a framework very largely at odds with the various outlooks of paganism, if the gospel of Christ was to be understood and accepted on its own terms.[28] If we have trouble coming to terms with this, it may be because "few Americans have been taught to think in terms of worldviews."[29] One begins to see the problem when one talks frankly with the rising generation of postmodern biblical illiterates. A Christian witness at an east coast university recently wrote that in trying to communicate with an undergraduate who had come along to a Christian meeting out of mild curiosity to find out what Christianity is, part of the conversation developed like this:

> I told him Jesus was the solution to his problem. He wondered, "What problem?" I told him Jesus could forgive his sins. He wondered, "Why is that necessary?" I told him that he could escape the fear of death. He told me that he never really thinks about death. He wasn't trying to be difficult. He was one of the most sincere students I've ever met.

In some recent evangelistic series, I have set myself a similar task. The first address may be "The God Who Does Not Wipe Out Rebels": the exposition concerns the doctrines of God, Creation, and the Fall, and leads naturally to the need for a new humanity—with obvious ties to Ephesians, and to Jesus as the new Adam. The second address might be "The God Who Writes

---

28. The suggestion that in Acts 17 Paul erred by appealing to natural theology and then recognized the error of his ways and abandoned such a path is an interpretive mistake that could only be made by those who have never tried preaching to biblical illiterates with a fundamentally alien worldview. A certain plausibility for this reading is sought in 1 Corinthians 1:21ff. (usually dated after the Areopagus address), where Paul determines to reject human wisdom and preach nothing but the cross, and in Acts 17:32–34 where (it is argued) only a few responded to his message. But it is far from clear that Paul would have assessed what he says in Acts 17 as only human wisdom: it is entirely in line with Romans 1, which is on the way toward Romans 3 and 5, just as the Areopagus address is on the way to a fuller exposition of Jesus, before Paul is cut off. Moreover, a careful examination of Luke's handling of the various addresses reported in Acts shows that *he* did not think this one a failure (see Barr, *Biblical Faith and Natural Theology*, 28–32). For instance, Acts 17 does not say that "only a few" believed, but that certain people (τινὲς δὲ) believed, including a member of the Areopagus and a (probably distinguished) woman, along with some others (ἕτεροι). For the rest, some (οἱ μὲν) mocked, and some (οἱ δὲ) declared they wanted to hear Paul again on these matters. Comparison with the language depicting results from others' sermons in Acts betrays no fundamental shift. "Whether Pauline or not, the Areopagus speech can legitimately be considered a typical exemplar of the first Christian sermons to the Gentiles" (Bertil Gärtner, *The Areopagus Speech and Natural Revelation* [Uppsala: C. W. K. Gleerup, 1955], 71).

29. Ronald H. Nash, *Worldviews in Conflict: Choosing Christianity in a World of Ideas* (Grand Rapids: Zondervan, 1992), 9.

His Own Agreements," a treatment of the Abrahamic covenant, with obvious ties to the gospel in Romans 4 and Galatians 3. The third is "The God Who Legislates": Moses, Sinai, and the Ten Commandments are laid down, with ties to the Sermon on the Mount, the nature of sin, the need for forgiveness. In this way I work through large swaths of the Bible's plot-line. I try, with mixed success, to use categories the secular person can understand, but use them as an "in" into the biblical categories. In each sermon, I move to Jesus and the gospel at some point, for many people, after all, do not come to the entire series, but only to one talk.

There are, of course, many possible variations. One preacher-theologian not long ago preached an evangelistic series (a "mission") at Durham University, and in eight messages preached through the first eight chapters of Romans. Obviously one could take years working through those chapters: Lloyd-Jones did. But here, by working through the flow of the argument, students were introduced to God, Creation, the nature of sin and law, the place of the atonement in God's redemptive purposes, the nature of grace and faith, justification, and the gift of the Spirit, and ultimately the hope of a new heaven and a new earth—all of this applied closely and tellingly to students who (it was assumed) started off knowing nothing at all of what the Bible says. I know of one evangelistic tool, "2 Ways to Live," that tries to present Christ in six steps, the six steps offering, in contemporary English, something of the Bible's plot-line as the necessary framework in which to understand the gospel.[30]

What I am arguing is that without this kind of structure the gospel will not be rightly heard. The doctrine of Creation establishes the grounds of our responsibility before God: he made us for himself, and it is the essence of our culpable anarchy that we ignore it. The doctrine of the Fall establishes the nature of our dilemma: by nature and choice we are alienated from God, deceived, justly condemned, without hope in the world, unless God himself delivers us. All of our ills trail from this profound rebellion. Solutions that do not address our alienation from the personal/transcendent God who made us are at best superficial palliatives, at worst deceptive placebos that leave us to die. In this framework, the philosophical pluralist is not on the vanguard of progress, but an idolater.

In a similar way we could work through all the major turning points of redemptive history to establish the framework *which alone makes the good news of Jesus Christ coherent*. Perhaps I should mention in passing that this insistence on establishing a biblical/theological framework does not in itself dic-

---

30. The training booklet is by Phillip Jensen and can be obtained, along with a very helpful teacher's manual, from Anglican Information Office, 1st Floor, St. Andrew's House, Sydney Square, Sydney NSW 2000, Australia.

tate the style of approach, or the point of entry. In a private communication (February 5, 1992), Paul Hiebert reminds me that Wisdom Literature can sometimes be used to facilitate transcultural communication,

> although it has problems since the logic systems in different cultures are not always the same. We tend to operate by abstract analytical thought. Many cultures make use of a more concrete-functional thought system. But wisdom is worldwide and codified in proverbs, riddles and aphorisms, etc. We use these with great impact in Indian villages.[31]

Hiebert goes on, "Another bridge is the facticity of historical events. We can always say, 'In a distant country there was a man named Jesus....'" In other words, the possibilities for beginning cross-cultural communication are legion. But my chief point is that all such "bridges" must sooner or later set the gospel within a particular worldview, or the gospel will not be understood.

This approach to preaching the gospel is, I think, essential when the audience belongs to those most afflicted with biblical illiteracy and philosophical pluralism. But it is scarcely less important, in my view, among the marginally churched (a very large group indeed), and even among the thoroughly churched, for all the trends in our society suggest that this basic biblical framework is being lost. It is easier to maintain it than to retrieve it after we lose it by our neglect.

C. We Must Herald, Again and Again, the Rudiments of the Historic Gospel

This point has two components.

1. The primary content is the historic gospel.

The historic gospel embraces a comprehensive articulation of what God has disclosed of himself in history, climactically in Jesus Christ and his death and resurrection. Doubtless we shall expound, as part of this good news, the inauguration of the kingdom, the gift of the Spirit, the forgiveness of sins, the nature of faith, the nature of eternal life, the fruit of the Spirit, the beauty of genuine, God-centered holiness, the nature and purpose of the church, the prospect of the new heaven and new earth, and much more. But everything will be tied to the center, the historic gospel. That was a major point of chapter 6. While many evangelicals today think of the "gospel" as the "simple

---

31. A modern partial parallel is the preparation one needs to handle a delicate debate on television. It is never enough simply to know the terrain. One needs to reduce some of the principle points to memorable "one-liners" if one is to be heard.

gospel"—something than can be articulated in three, four, five, or six memorable points to be shared during personal evangelism—a study of the "gospel" word-group in the New Testament[32] shows that what is at stake is more commonly what might be called the "comprehensive gospel." It is the good news of God's redemption and the dawning of the eschatological kingdom in the person and work of Christ, with all that means for this life and for the life to come. All of our preaching and teaching must revolve around the great, central truths of the gospel.

There is intellectual content in this heralded gospel, content that must be grasped, proclaimed and taught, grasped afresh, proclaimed afresh, in an ongoing cycle. Doubtless the decaying modern world shaped too much of Christianity into a merely rationalistic mold. Doubtless in many circles defense of truth and articulation of doctrine became an excuse for aridity that gradually sidled into barrenness and embarrassing inauthenticity. One can make a very good case for the view that many of the vibrant movements that sprang up around the fringes and sometimes at the center of evangelicalism during the past decades have in part been a reaction against the modernist impact on confessing evangelicalism. Included here is an emphasis on tongues speaking and modern prophecies, certain styles of strongly emotional corporate worship, inclination to incorporate drama and dance into public services. Whatever we think of these developments, we shall err if we do not see in them, at least in part, a rebuke of the sense of arid unreality that pervades not a few congregations.

Lest all my more enthusiastic friends congratulate themselves and go off feeling justified in all their ways, the question that must now be asked is twofold: (a) At what point has the pendulum swung too far the other way? (b) More strategically, at what point are the enthusiasts unwittingly becoming snookered by postmodernist ideology, exactly as many of their forebears were snookered by modernism? Granted, there is more to authentic Christianity than proofs for the existence of God, or evidences of the resurrection, or left-brain sermons. Is there not also more than personal opinion, feeling good, right-brain exuberance, and endless, contentless subjectivism? As a friend has pointed out, "The most important thing about Joyce Huggett's best-selling book, *Listening to God*,[33] was this: if anyone had written a book thirty years ago with that title, you would have expected it to be about Bible study, not about prayer. ... Many [Christians] now rely far more on inward promptings than on their Bible knowledge to decide what they are going to do in a situation."[34]

---

32. I.e., εὐαγγέλιον, εὐαγγελίζω.

33. London: Hodder & Stoughton, 1986.

34. Roy Clements, "An Overview of Evangelicalism Today," unpublished paper prepared for the UCCF Triennial Consultation (May 6–8, 1994), 6.

My contention, then, is that if we read our own times aright, instead of merely reacting to excesses of yesteryear, then while we must, for example, espouse patterns of corporate worship that engage the entire person and review from time to time all that the New Testament says about joy and love and peace and oppose the *merely* rational and intellectual, we must also insist that biblical Christianity brings with it unavoidable, nonnegotiable, knowable intellectual content. We need a spirituality of the Word;[35] in our evangelism, we must convey content. The kerygma has content; the good news is definable. That was the burden of much of part 2 of this volume.

I have heard the example of Jesus' use of parables cited in order to justify more narrative preaching that provokes, incites reflection, excites, fires the imagination—everything and anything that seems opposed to "cold, doctrinal, rationalistic, preaching." A superficial (though certainly true) response is that if doctrinal preaching is cold and rationalistic, it is simply bad preaching; but properly done, there is nothing intrinsic to doctrinal preaching that necessarily links it to either "cold" or "rationalistic." One might also observe that in Jesus' ministry the parables function in a number of important ways: sometimes to reveal, sometimes to conceal, very often to explode a person's prejudices (think of the Good Samaritan!). But above all, one must recognize that Jesus shared with his hearers a culture steeped in Old Testament thought. Within that shared theological framework, and within the shared cultural framework of first-century second-temple Judaism, parables such as the five wise and foolish virgins or the wheat and tares or the grain of mustard seed are all more or less coherent, as innovative and thought-provoking as they were when first delivered. But if they were retold today to people who had never read the Bible, were either atheistic or pantheistic in outlook, and knew little of first-century Jewish culture, it is far from clear that they would be the most effective ways of conveying what they did to the first readers of the gospels. In other words, it may be entirely appropriate to engage in narrative preaching, to expound the parables, and to tell moving and thought-provoking stories; but in the postmodern environment, such approaches *must* be anchored in objective, propositional, confessional truth—or the entire heritage of biblical Christianity will be sold for a mess of subjectivist pottage.

I am not for a moment denying that there is an affective element to gospel preaching, or that there is no appeal to the will. Far from it: I insist on both. But the affective element must spring from the play of truth on personality; the appeal to the will must be grounded in content. Gospel proclamation is, in this sense, an intellectual exercise; it is a truth-conveying exercise. There is a battle going on for the minds of men and women;[36] well does the apostle

---

35. See the appendix.
36. Cf. Melvin Tinker, "Battle for the Mind," *Churchman* 106 (1992): 34–44.

know that in the Spirit-empowered proclamation of the whole counsel of God, men and women escape conformity to this world and are transformed *by the renewing of their minds* (Rom. 12:2).

American evangelicalism is in desperate need of intellectual and theological input. We have noted that not a little evangelical television is almost empty of content. It is mawkishly sentimental, naively optimistic, frighteningly ignorant, openly manipulative. Let me again insist: I am not arguing for dry intellectualism, for abstract disputation. But entertainment is not enough; emotional appeals based on tear-jerking stories do not change human behavior; subjective experiences cannot substitute for divine revelation; evangelical clichés can never make up for lack of thought. The mentality that thinks in terms of marketing Jesus *inevitably* moves toward progressive distortion of him; the pursuit of the next emotional round of experience easily degenerates into an intoxicating substitute for the spirituality of the Word. There is non-negotiable, biblical, intellectual content to be proclaimed. By all means insist that this content be heralded with conviction and compassion; by all means seek the unction of the Spirit; by all means try to think through how to cast this content in ways that engage the modern secularist. But when all the footnotes are in place, my point remains the same: the historic gospel is unavoidably cast as intellectual content that must be taught and proclaimed.

2. We shall herald this good news; we shall proclaim it.

A fair number of voices in our culture advocate dialogue. If what is meant by "dialogue" is that we need to talk to people to find out what they think, and to treat them courteously and respectfully, there can be no objection. Similarly, there can be no objection to "dialogue" as opposed to "monologue": that is, two or more people can talk together, and such talk may be the vehicle for the proclamation of the gospel.

But many voices advocating dialogue go much farther. In our pluralistic environment, they start to insist that dialogue between, say, a Christian and a Muslim must be so evenhanded, so open-ended, that the Christian, far from entering the discussion with an "arrogant" assumption that Christians have the "right" answer, assumes nothing, and accords opposing opinions the same authority as Christian opinions.

Certainly opposing voices should be accorded the same *courtesy*. But if we insist that they be accorded the same *authority*, we are implicitly adopting philosophical pluralism, at the cost of affirming biblical Christianity. Although various people in the New Testament engage in dialogue (e.g., Paul *reasons* with people, Acts 17:2), they never do so except from a position of equivocal confidence in the truthfulness and exclusive saving power of the gospel message to which they bear witness. Marshall has shown that the forms of dialogue found in the New Testament are communication devices, not instruments whereby people with opposing views come together to discover the truth.[37] In other words, Christians are never less than heraldic; they are proclaimers; they discharge an ambassadorial function; they are preachers.

But there is also a strategic reason why we must never abandon proclamation. Sue Brown, reflecting on years of working with university students around the world, writes:

> . . . if the image has replaced the word, music has replaced the book. Young people watch and listen more than they read (though—gratifyingly—Christian students, certainly in some of the less visual-media oriented societies, still do read). Music appeals primarily to the emotions and does precisely what Routley says, it carries words past the critical faculty into the affections where they may do either good or harm.
>
> Music and the image, then, the two most potent influences on young people today, conspire to bypass the reasoning powers of the mind and to encourage thinking by association rather than by analysis. The relationship between this trend and the emotional orientation of modern young people is too complex a subject to enter into here, but it should give us pause for thought whenever we discern signs of spiritual shallowness (only let us be sure we are judging aright) among student Christians.[38]

What is true among students is scarcely less true in the larger population. This tells us that, if the issues are as they have been painted in this book, it is necessary to insist on proclamation—however informed, well-prepared, designed to address the whole person, genuinely anointed—precisely because a necessary component in conversion and in Christian discipleship is the proper use of the mind. Pastors committed to the ministry of the Word have often seen new converts become interested in reading, sometimes serious reading, for the first time in their lives. God is worth thinking about. God's thoughts, insofar as he has disclosed them, can become our thoughts. Evangelism that does not engage people at that level, whatever other levels are touched, is necessarily betraying something vital. Proclamation is not an optional "extra."

These two elements, then, make up my point: we must herald, again and again, the rudiments of the historic gospel.

---

37. I. Howard Marshall, "Dialogue with Non-Christians in the New Testament," *Evangelical Review of Theology* 16 (1992): 28–47.

38. "Patterns of Worship Among Students Worldwide," in *Worship: Adoration and Action*, ed. D. A. Carson (Grand Rapids: Baker, 1993), 200.

D. While Trying to Think Through What to Say, We Must Think Through How to Live

In one of his essays Clive Calver reminds us of a line from "My Fair Lady": "Words, words, words, I'm so sick of words.... Sing me no song, read me no rhyme, don't waste my time, show me." Calver comments, "I think our world is looking for the evidence of the truth that we claim to have. It is looking for it in the way that we live."[39] If Western culture's renewed interest in "spirituality" is, from a Christian perspective, swamped by uncontrolled sentimentalism and subjectivism, it nevertheless betrays a hunger for authenticity and significance that neither naturalism nor hedonism, let alone postmodernism, can ever provide.

Contextualization is not an exclusively theoretical challenge; it is also immensely practical. We glimpse this point in 1 Corinthians 8–10, where Paul wrestles with the rights and wrongs of Christians eating meat offered to idols. The steps in the argument are too complex to explore here. The least that must be said, however, is that within certain absolute boundaries, Paul is clearly prepared to let Christians indulge in such food under some circumstances, and not under others. It is within this framework that Paul himself confesses that he becomes all things to all people, so that by all means he may save some (9:19–23). There is no hint of rigid inflexibility in the great apostle. His motives are stunning: he wants by all means to win some.

As long as American culture embraced so many Christian values, there were few easily observed cultural distinctives connected with being a Christian. As the culture shucks off this heritage, it is becoming more and more important for Christians to live *in styles that openly conflict with the culture*. Perhaps we will not take a job promotion that would mean more time away from the family; perhaps we will choose a simpler lifestyle in order to give more away to missions and to the poor; perhaps we shall be so committed to elementary Christian discipleship that we shall be largely inured against flattery; perhaps we shall treat old and young, rich and poor, the well-connected and the socially unimportant, with the same degree of dignity and respect—a decidedly Christ-like characteristic; perhaps we shall be known as people who work at their marriages and love their children without trying to live their lives through them; perhaps we shall be known as people who are disciplined in their use of time, in what they watch on TV, in their freedom to make intelligent and moral judgments precisely because they are thoroughly committed to the living God; perhaps we shall be known as people who like to read, think, and talk about God and about right and wrong.

---

39. "Red Herrings and Hot Potatoes: The Real Issues for Evangelicals Today," *Vox Evangelica* 24 (1994): 50.

For those who travel internationally, postcolonial modesty will be not only a strategic necessity, but the entailment of living under the shadow of the cross (see 1 Cor. 4:7). Whether at home or abroad, our love for holiness, justice, and integrity will thrive not only at the personal level, but at every level we can wisely influence.[40] Just because some have reduced the gospel to social justice we should not deny that Christians have any stake or obligation in this arena.

The precise way in which the gospel will be contextualized in our lives will vary, in part, according to the culture in which we live. We must never succumb to the temptation to think that gospel living necessarily means conformity to a batch of conservative societal rules. What is clear, however, is that gospel living must be tied to gospel preaching.

E. A Short List of Practical Points

(1) The primary reason why people in our churches do not invite more of their friends to come to church is that they are embarrassed by what goes on there. If such embarrassment is triggered by anything other than the offense of the cross, it is the pastors' fault.

(2) Many Christians, not least Christian preachers, simply do not know any out-and-out pagans. It is time they did. They should rearrange priorites and befriend some of them. When more and more people think of church as alien, the only way, humanly speaking, that people are going to attend public services and hear the gospel well articulated in the context of a worshiping community is if friends invite them.

(3) Those committed to seeker services ought to ask themselves constantly if commendable zeal for the lost does not sometimes lead them into a lamentable pragmatism that unwittingly displaces worship by aesthetics, transforms biblical understanding of conversion into the shallowest kinds of decisionism with all the real life-transforming content introduced after "conversion" in various small-group therapy sessions, and reduces God to the status of divine genie: he helps me when I need him. Those committed to traditional services may be safe enough in conservative enclaves in the country, but if they exist in a social context where virtually everything they do in corporate meetings is utterly alien to men and women all around them, they must ask what pains they ought to take to explain what they are doing to outsiders, and to forego their own comfort zones for the sake of communicating the gospel.

---

40. Cf. John Stott, *The Contemporary Christian* (Leicester: Inter-Varsity Press, 1992), esp. 339–55.

(4) There are many useful alternatives to the antithesis, seeker service *or* traditional service. Many churches use "guest services" to which believers are especially encouraged to bring unconverted guests. Those services include singing, prayers, preaching—but every element is carefully and wisely explained. The leader does not say, "Turn to hymn number 33." Rather, he or she says, "Christians have always loved to sing praises to the God they have come to know and trust. In this church we sing many such songs, drawn from various periods of the church's history. The one we are going to sing now was written about two centuries ago, by a man whose Christian faith was tested by recurring bouts of mental illness. You will find it as number 33 of the blue book on the rack in front of you. When the musical instruments begin, it is our custom to stand to sing."

Something similar can be done for each aspect of the service, including prayers, liturgical readings, testimonies. Assume visitors have *never* been to *any* church. Those who have will not be offended by such gentle explanations and may be instructed by them; those who have not will be greatly helped. As we have seen, the value in preserving the normal patterns of corporate worship, even while gently explaining them, is that outsiders are introduced to the church as a *worshiping* community and feel the power of corporate reverence.

(5) Develop evangelistic Bible studies for complete outsiders.

(6) Some churches in big cities develop brief and pungent noon-hour services for business people, often combined with an inexpensive lunch.

(7) Many companies allow their employees, during lunch breaks, to form themselves into various groups or clubs or societies for diverse purposes. It is quite possible to start evangelistic studies in such settings, provided there is just one employee in the company with a little courage.

(8) Very frequently I begin an evangelistic series to complete outsiders (university students, perhaps) with something like this: "If you think I have come to defend Christianity, guess again! For some of us, Christianity is so little known and understood that defending it would be like defending the general theory of relativity to a first year arts major. What I shall be doing, rather, is outlining, explaining, and showing the relevance of some of the fundamentals of any kind of Christianity that tries to be faithful to its founding documents, gathered together in a book that we call the Bible. If there is defense, it will be largely implicit. But I hope you will listen carefully as you enter into a world of thought and experience that you may never before have encountered." I find that some such introduction as that changes the focus of expectations. At the end of each talk, people come out talking about the gospel, not about apologetics.

(9) Be bold. That is not an invitation to discourtesy. But boldness, coupled with an unassuming humility that conveys the impression that Christians are

only poor beggars telling others where there is bread, will always elicit better attention than the half-embarrassed, semi-apologetic bearing of the person who is more frightened of people than of the living God.

(10) In my view, it is usually best (though there are exceptional circumstances that overturn this preference) that these evangelistic sermons be expository messages, not topical ones. Of course, unbelievers will not bring Bibles, so it is necessary to instruct people to turn to a certain page number in the book in front of them (assuming there is a pew Bible). Where the address is not in a church, so that Bibles are not available (e.g., at a university mission), put a typed copy of the relevant passage on each seat.[41] This approach is wiser than the purely topical approach with minimal reference to biblical texts because (1) it directs people's attention to the Bible, not to the preacher, and, if done properly, draws them into reading the Bible for themselves, and (2) by directing people to think through texts, the preacher is helping them to think linearly, coherently, through God's gracious self-disclosure in human words.

(11) Remember that men and women are not converted, finally, by your sagacity, oratory, theological brilliance or homiletical skill. God in his mercy may use all these and many more gifts. But only God is able to bring people to himself. That is ample incentive to prayer.

(12) Finally, speaking of prayer, it is vitally important, once again, that we recall how our secular, postmodern society affects those of us who are believers. We may think we are being faithful, when somehow we no longer believe in the God of the Bible—the God who is sovereign, the God who hears and answers prayer, the God who alone can save. Reflecting on Ellul's warnings about the technological society, Volf comments:

> In this situation, it is increasingly difficult for Christians to hold seriously to the belief that God governs history and that the salvation of the world can, let alone must, come from God. And the more God is pushed out of our world—out of the spheres of nature, of society, and of individual human beings—the more difficult it will be to address this loving God in prayer and thanksgiving, and to stand before this holy God in awe and reverence. . . . Technological culture does not deny God (it is not atheistic), but it makes God superfluous (it is a-theistic) and thus cuts off the worship of God at its roots. For adoration of a superfluous God is a religious impossibility. Where technique reigns, talking to God gives way to talking about God (or even to talking about talking about God!), reverence is replaced by manipulation, and joyous celebration of God's acts and God's character

---

41. This does *not* infringe copyright—at least, not for the NIV, which I have normally used. A copy of their policy statement is available from Zondervan Publishing House; I have verified my reading of it by personal correspondence with the publishing house.

degenerates either into self-congratulatory praises of human vain-glory or into oppressive demands for better and greater deeds.[42]

In other words, it is of paramount importance that those of us who are believers live and breathe in the atmosphere of God-centeredness, of gospel-centeredness. This will drive us to our knees in intercession, and incite us again and again to reform our lives, our churches, and, so far as we our able, our world, in line with the Word of God. The alternative is that, whatever genuine insight we pick up about evangelism in the world of pluralism and postmodernism, all we really attempt to change is a few techniques.

F. Final Reflections

A grain of sand in an oyster produces a pearl; in the view of Hulmes, agnosticism can similarly become an "irritant" that generates richer witness.[43] In the same way, the worst features of pluralism may grind us down, or they may become "irritants" which, in the providence of God, are used to recall the church to a renewed emphasis on the gospel within the framework of the Bible's plot-line.

If many remain unconvinced, so be it. The Scots preacher James S. Stewart was not perturbed that some people did not believe in mission. They had no right to believe in mission, he reflected, since they did not believe in Christ.[44] By contrast, the missionary statesman Stephen Neill wrote:

> When a man, by constant contemplation of the Passion and Resurrection of our Lord, finds himself so inflamed with love of God and man that he cannot bear the thought of any man living and dying without the knowledge of God, he may begin to bear the Cross of Christ. If, as he bears it, this longing for the glory of God and for the salvation of all men becomes so great that it fills all his thoughts and desires, then he has that one thing without which no man can truly be a messenger of Christ.[45]

---

42. Miroslav Volf, "Worship as Adoration and Action: Reflections on a Christian Way of Being-in-the-World," *Worship: Adoration and Action*, 205–6.

43. Edward Hulmes, "The Irritant of Agnosticism," *Princeton Seminary Bulletin* 6 (1985): 14–24.

44. I draw this example from Nigel M. de S. Cameron, "Perspectives on Religious Pluralism," *Scottish Bulletin of Evangelical Theology* 10/2 (1992): 79.

45. Stephen Neill, *Out of Bondage* (Edinburgh: Edinburgh House Press, n.d.), 135–36. Cited also in Hulmes, "The Irritant of Agnosticism," 19.

Chapter 13

ON BANISHING THE LAKE OF FIRE

The final judgment is a difficult subject both because of its complexity and because the subject is grisly. But for at least three reasons, we must say something about it in this book.

First, there is widespread perception that the expanding definition of evangelicalism and the fragmentation within the camp is nicely (or painfully) exemplified by the diversity of views on this subject, and in particular by the rising number of self-confessed evangelicals who now publicly espouse some form of annihilationism.

Second, in the handling of some of these theologians (though certainly not all), some form of annihilationism or conditional immortality is linked to their views on the final state of those who have never heard of Christ, to the possibilities of post-death evangelism, and to a number of other matters that obviously tie in to the central concerns of this volume. Strictly speaking, of course, if one holds to universalism—the view that eventually all the offspring of Adam are saved, even if it takes a sojourn in hell to bring them to repentance—then there is no need to appeal to annihilationism, for hell will eventually be emptied of human beings anyway. Those who hold this position do not read the relevant biblical texts as saying that punishment is ended by annihilation, but as saying that the emphasis in Scripture on the love of God surely forces us to conclude that God's love will so triumph in the end that there will be no one left for the fires of hell to consume.[1]

---

1. See, for instance, N. F. S. Ferré, *The Christian Understanding of God* (New York: Harper, 1951), 228–29; William Barclay, *A Spiritual Autobiography* (Grand Rapids: Eerdmans, 1975), 60–61.

Third, in the minds of some evangelicals, recent developments in this doctrinal area signal a clear departure from Scripture, a lessening of biblical authority, perhaps a denial of inerrancy; in the minds of others, the issue is entirely hermeneutical, a matter of interpretation. For the former, pluralism and relativism and postmodernism have softened up the exegetical firmness that once characterized evangelicalism; for the latter, conservatives are ignoring how indebted they are to mere traditionalism, and are proving unwilling to be corrected by more careful exegesis, unwilling to recognize that fresh questions may call forth more light from God's Holy Word. Thus, this doctrinal area becomes a test case for assessing the changing face of evangelicalism, quite apart from its obvious bearing on how we go about evangelism, construction of doctrine, and other similar important matters.

A. Introduction

Because this is only a brief discussion, certain elements of the topic will be skipped over lightly or entirely ignored.

(1) I do not intend to provide complex taxonomies of the various positions.[2] For example, some hold that the unrepentant are instantly annihilated at death. In this way, punishment is unending, but never experienced as conscious suffering. More commonly among evangelicals, it is held that the unrepentant suffer consciously for a while, and are then annihilated. In this view, punishment is unending, but the conscious suffering is temporary. Some speculate that there will be new opportunities to repent during this period of suffering; others deny it. Those who hold to the possibility usually do so by drawing inferences from the love of God. They then divide as to whether this further opportunity to repent will sooner or later be taken by all, thus emptying hell. The more conservative of those who espouse annihilation find such theories not only overly speculative, but impossible to sustain in the light of specific texts of Scripture.

Many "annihilationists" object to the term "annihilation," holding that it puts the emphasis on the wrong place and betrays a platonic worldview. They are annihilationists in the sense that they hold that there is finally a cessation of existence, but they are uncomfortable with the term because it sounds to them as if God is destroying what would otherwise have endured forever—and this they deny. They prefer an expression such as "conditional immortality"—i.e., men and women are not "naturally" or constitutionally immortal, but become immortal under certain conditions. If they fail to meet those

---

2. For some useful distinctions see Kendall S. Harmon, "The Case Against Conditionalism," in *Universalism and the Doctrine of Hell*, ed. Nigel M. de S. Cameron (Carlisle: Paternoster/Grand Rapids: Baker, 1992), 196–99.

conditions, then inevitably their mortality prevails, and they are finally and completely destroyed.[3] For our purposes we shall not usually distinguish between annihilationism and destruction that flows from conditional immortality, for the two positions are alike in that they both deny that hell is a place of everlasting, conscious punishment. They do differ in their anthropology, however, and this affects their approach to the intermediate state. I shall have to say something later about that. Moreover, the focus here will be on the more conservative annihilationists, largely because if their position cannot be sustained, the further extrapolations have little chance of robust defense.

(2) I shall not devote space here to an evaluation of the recent works that treat the earliest or most extended discussions of hell that have come down to us,[4] essays and monographs that examine the place of hell in certain historical epochs,[5] treatments which for different purposes chart the decline in serious mention of hell in sermons and books today,[6] specialist treatments of certain words,[7] or standard treatments of the subject from the past[8] (though

---

3. E.g., D. A. Dean, *Resurrection: His and Ours* (Charlotte: Advent Christian General Conference of America, 1977).

4. E.g., Alan E. Bernstein, *The Formation of Hell: Death and Retribution in the Ancient and Early Christian Worlds* (London: Univ. College London Press, 1993); Martha Himmelfarb, *Tours of Hell: An Apocalyptic Form in Jewish and Christian Literature* (Philadelphia: Fortress Press, 1985).

5. E.g., Frank Burch Brown, "The Beauty of Hell: Anselm on God's Eternal Design," *Journal of Religion* 73 (1993): 329–56; D. P. Walker, *The Decline of Hell: Seventeenth-Century Discussion of Eternal Torment* (Chicago: Univ. of Chicago Press, 1964); Philip C. Almond, *Heaven and Hell in Enlightenment England* (Cambridge: Cambridge Univ. Press, 1994); Jonathan M. Butler, *Softly and Tenderly Jesus Is Calling: Heaven and Hell in American Revivalism, 1870–1920* (Brooklyn: Carlson, 1991); and several of the essays in Cameron, *Universalism and the Doctrine of Hell.*

6. E.g., Martin E. Marty, "Hell Disappeared. No One Noticed. A Civic Argument," *Harvard Theological Review* 78 (1985): 381–98; John Blanchard, *Whatever Happened to Hell?* (Durham: Evangelical Press, 1993); Larry Dixon, "Warning a Wrath-Deserving World: Evangelicals and the Overhaul of Hell," *Emmaus Journal* 21 (1993): 7–21; Alan M. Linfield, "Sheep and Goats: Current Evangelical Thought on the Nature of Hell and the Scope of Salvation," *Vox Evangelica* 24 (1994): 63–75; Howard Davies, "Judgement: The Doctrine Lost to the Modern Pulpit," *Banner of Truth Magazine* 364 (January 1994): 13–18.

7. In addition to the standard lexica and theological dictionaries, I am thinking of recent essays such as Hans Scharen, "Gehenna in the Synoptics," *Bibliotheca Sacra* 149 (1992): 304–15, 454–70.

8. E.g., W. G. T. Shedd, *The Doctrine of Endless Punishment* (Edinburgh: Banner of Truth Trust, 1986 [1855]). It is worth remembering his own historical awareness: "Take the doctrine of eternal perdition, and the antithetic doctrine of eternal slavation, out of the Confessions of Augustine; out of the Sermons of Chrysostom; out of the Imitation of á Kempis; out of Bunyan's Pilgrim's Progress; out of Jeremy Taylor's Holy Living and Dying; out of Baxter's Saints' Everlasting Rest; and what is left?" (vii).

I fear these are largely unread by those who espouse annihilationism). I shall also avoid idiosyncratic interpretations.[9]

(3) I shall not here embark on the larger question of the fate of those who have never heard the gospel. That subject I addressed in part 2, especially chapter 7.

(4) Finally, I shall not address at any length a number of important synthetic questions about how the Bible's teaching on hell, however understood, relates to God's sovereignty, foreknowledge, and omnipotence, and to human responsibility. This is not because the questions are unimportant, but because they will take us farther away from the first-order questions I am primarily addressing in this chapter. Moreover, some of the relevant issues have already been briefly discussed earlier in this book (chaps. 5 and 6) and, from somewhat different perspectives, by Simon Chan[10] and Paul Helm.[11]

B. The Case for Conditional Immortality

Recent writers who have defended conditional immortality do not invariably do so for the same reasons, or with the same degree of certainty.[12] But their principal arguments may be fairly summarized as follows:

---

9. E.g., David Pawson, *The Road to Hell* (London: Hodder & Stoughton, 1992). Pawson accepts that hell involves eternal self-conscious punishment, but seeks to make an "original" contribution by pointing out that most of Jesus' teaching on the subject is addressed to his disciples. From this he infers various elements of a semi-Pelagian soteriology.

10. "The Logic of Hell: A Response to Annihilationism," *Evangelical Review of Theology* 18 (1994): 20–32.

11. *The Last Things: Death, Judgment, Heaven, Hell* (Edinburgh: Banner of Truth Trust, 1989).

12. See, among others, the arguments of John Stott in David L. Edwards and John Stott, *Essentials: A Liberal-Evangelical Dialogue* (London: Hodder & Stoughton, 1988), 312–20; idem, "The Logic of Hell: A Brief Rejoinder," *Evangelical Review of Theology* 18 (1994): 33–34; Philip Edgcumbe Hughes, *The True Image: The Origin and Destiny of Man in Christ* (Grand Rapids: Eerdmans, 1989), esp. 402–7 (reprinted in *Evangel* 10/2 [Summer 1992]: 10–12, from which the page references below are drawn); Clark H. Pinnock, "The Conditional View," in *Four Views on Hell*, ed. William Crockett (Grand Rapids: Zondervan, 1992), 135–66, and his responses to other contributors; idem, "The Destruction of the Finally Impenitent," *Criswell Theological Review* 4 (1990): 243–59; Leroy Froom, *The Conditionalist Faith of Our Fathers* (Washington: Review and Herald, 1965); Edward William Fudge, *The Fire That Consumes: The Biblical Case for Conditional Immortality* (Carlisle: Paternoster, 1994); Jonathan L. Kvanvig, *The Problem of Hell* (Oxford: Oxford Univ. Press, 1994); Stephen T. Davis, "Universalism, Hell, and the Fate of the Ignorant," *Modern Theology* 6 (1990): 173–86; Stephen H. Travis, *Christ and the Judgment of God: Divine Retribution in the New Testament* (London: Marshall, Morgan & Scott, 1986); idem, *Christian Hope and the Future* (Downers Grove: InterVarsity Press, 1980); John W. Wenham, "The Case for Conditional Immortality," in Cameron, *Universalism and the Doctrine of Hell*, 161–91.

(1) A number of biblical passages speak of the *destruction* of the wicked (e.g., Phil. 3:19; 1 Thess. 5:3; 2 Thess. 1:9; 2 Peter 3:7). Fair exegesis of the words involved suggests *total* destruction, i.e., cessation of existence.

(2) Even the imagery of fire suggests that which devours and utterly destroys. In other words, the focus of fire is not the pain that it causes, but the destruction it exacts: the Judge burns up the chaff with unquenchable fire (Matt. 3:12).

(2) The Greek word commonly rendered "forever" (αἰών and cognates) properly means "age." Even if in some contexts this "age" may be endless, why must we assume that this is the case in passages describing hell? Why take the harshest view?

(3) Even in passages where the same word is used to describe both "*eternal* life" and "*eternal* punishment" in parallel (e.g., Matt. 25:46), demanding therefore that the one last as long as the other, the eternality of the punishment need not be construed as consisting in self-conscious punishment. If the wicked suffer conscious pain for a period of time, and then are annihilated without hope of reprieve or restoration, their punishment can still rightly be said to be "eternal."

(4) Surely an eternal hell full of conscious torment is irreconcilable with what the Bible says about the love of God, even about the justice of God. Assuming that we take what the Bible says seriously, surely any exegesis that avoids such blatant and eternal cruelty is to be preferred to the traditional view.

This particular point is held with various degrees of passion. At one end is Pinnock:

> Let me say at the outset that I consider the concept of hell as endless torment in body and mind an outrageous doctrine, a theological and moral enormity, a bad doctrine of the tradition which needs to be changed. How can Christians possibly project a deity of such cruelty and vindictiveness whose ways include inflicting everlasting torture upon his creatures, however sinful they may have been. Surely a God who would do such a thing is more nearly like Satan than like God, at least by any ordinary moral standards, and by the gospel itself.... Does the one who told us to love our enemies intend to wreak vengeance on his own enemies for all eternity? As H. Küng appropriately asks, "What would we think of a human being who satisfied his thirst for revenge so implacably and insatiably?" ... [E]verlasting torment is intolerable from a moral point of view because it makes God into a bloodthirsty monster who maintains an everlasting Auschwitz for victims whom he does not even allow to die.[13]

---

13. Pinnock, "The Destruction of the Finally Impenitent," 246–47, 253. Similarly, Michael Green, *Evangelism Through the Local Church* (Nashville: Nelson, 1992), writes of this "doctrine of such savagery" (73).

By contrast, John Stott, who like Pinnock defends conditional immortality, does so with much more caution:

> I find the concept [of eternal conscious punishment in hell] intolerable and do not understand how people can live with it without either cauterising their feelings or cracking under the strain. But our emotions are a fluctuating, unreliable guide to truth and must not be exalted to the place of supreme authority in determining it. As a committed Evangelical, my question must be—and is—not what does my heart tell me, but what does God's word say?[14]

(5) Along the same lines, one must surely question whether the notion of an eternal hell of conscious torment is *fair*. No matter how grievous the offence, no matter how wretched the sinner—a Hitler, perhaps—is *eternal* hell appropriate? Searing pain that goes on and on, for billions of years, and then more billions of years, and never stops, because all of those billions of years are as a drop in the ocean?

(6) Does not the notion of a continuing hell with conscious suffering inmates jar against the image of the new heaven and the new earth, created to reflect God's glory and extol his perfections? Would not an ongoing hell mar heaven?

C. Biblical and Theological Responses

Without here attempting to list every passage and itemize every metaphor, we should remind ourselves of representative terms and passages. *Sheol* in the Old Testament and *Hades* in the New have roughly the same semantic range and overtones. Although both words can refer in fairly neutral ways to the abode of the dead, or stand in parallel to death itself, in some contexts torment is in view. The rich man, for example, is in torment in Hades when he glimpses the blessedness of Lazarus in heaven (Luke 16:23). Revelation 20:10, 14 link Hades, the lake of fire, Satan, and suffering that goes on day and night forever. The Abyss can be a synonym for Sheol (Pss. 71:20; 107:26; cf. Rom. 10:6–7); in the New Testament it is more commonly linked with Satan or with the demonic. It is a prison for demons (Luke 8:31) from which smoke rises (Rev. 9:2), a place whose ruler is Abaddon or Apollyon (Rev. 9:11), usually identified with Satan (though some dispute the identification). *Gehenna* occurs twelve times in the New Testament, all but one (James 3:6) in the Gospels. The eleven gospel references offer five distinct sayings or pictures, once parallels are taken into account. The word itself is transliterated from a Semitic expression referring to the "Valley of Hinnom," the burning dump outside of Jerusalem that would not only be

---

14. Edwards and Stott, *Essentials*, 314–15.

obnoxious but would be doubly offensive to Jews because of its ability to defile all who entered it. This word then becomes a metaphor for hell, conveying not only notions of suffering, destruction, and judgment (e.g., Matt. 5:22, 29–30; 10:28; 18:9) but also of the archetypal source of evil (hence the Pharisees can be labeled "sons of Gehenna," 23:15, as well as being sentenced there, 23:33). Both body and soul are destroyed in Gehenna (Matt. 10:28 = Luke 12:5).

Of course, one should not restrict oneself to isolated words. The New Testament repeatedly warns of the certainty of final judgment and the danger of final ruin (e.g., Rom. 2:5–9, 11, 16). When the Lord Jesus is finally revealed from heaven "in blazing fire with his powerful angels," he will "punish those who do not know God and do not obey the gospel of our Lord Jesus. They will be punished with everlasting destruction and shut out from the presence of the Lord and from the majesty of his power" (2 Thess. 1:7–9). Hell is described as a place where "their worm does not die, and the fire is not quenched" (Mark 9:48), a place of outer darkness, characterized by "weeping and gnashing of teeth" (Matt. 8:12). God's searing holiness is bound up with this wrath (Rom. 2:5–9; Rev. 14:9–11): God is a "consuming fire" (Heb. 12:29), and one must be careful not to fall into his hands when he acts in judgment (Heb. 10:31). There is no escape from hell: there is a great, fixed chasm (Luke 16:26), the door is shut (Matt. 25:10–12), and the condemned are in "dungeons" and bound by "everlasting chains" (2 Peter 2:4; Jude 6). The lost "suffer the punishment of eternal fire" (Jude 7), and beatings of greater or lesser intensity (Luke 12:47–48). They suffer "everlasting contempt" (Dan. 12:2). One of the most horrific series of scenes comes from Revelation 14, to which I shall, regretfully, return.

The images are diverse. They variously suggest exclusion, actual punishment, destruction, restraint. No one with the least sensitivity finds these passages easy to preach and write about. But they are there in the Bible, and not only will they not go away, but much of the most graphic language about hell comes from the Lord Jesus himself. How shall we understand these texts?

I offer six brief reflections, of varying degrees of significance, and in no particular order.

(1) It is often argued that the meaning of some of the critical Greek words deployed in the relevant passages favors the annihilationist position. Stott, for instance, argues that the verb ἀπόλλυμι ("to destroy") and its cognate noun ἀπώλεια ("destruction") are best understood, in contexts dealing with perdition, to refer to cessation of existence.[15] When the verb "to destroy" is transitive, it means "to kill [someone]," just as Herod wanted to kill the baby

---

15. Ibid., 315.

Jesus (Matt. 2:13). Jesus instructed his followers not to be frightened of those who kill the body but cannot kill the soul. "Rather," he insists, " be afraid of the One who can destroy both soul and body in hell" (Matt. 10:28). Stott comments, "If to kill is to deprive the body of life, hell would seem to be the deprivation of both physical and spiritual life, that is, an extinction of being."[16] The same reasoning applies to the middle, intransitive use of the verb, i.e., "to perish": one can perish physically (e.g., Luke 15:17; 1 Cor. 10:9) or eternally in hell (e.g., John 3:16; Rom. 2:12; 1 Cor. 15:18; 2 Peter 3:9). The same argument applies to the noun, where "destruction" is set over against life (e.g., Matt. 7:13). Similarly, another word for "destruction," ὄλεθρος (1 Thess. 5:3; 2 Thess. 1:9), surely suggests ultimate cessation of existence. In Stott's words, "It would seem strange . . . if people who are said to suffer destruction are in fact not destroyed."[17]

But the argument is too hasty. The ἀπώλεια word-group has a range of meanings, depending on the context. It can refer to the "lost" coin or son of Luke 15, and to the "ruined" wineskin of Matthew 9:17: in neither case is cessation of existence in view. Similarly, the ointment lavishly poured out on Jesus is in the mind of his disciples a "waste" (Matt. 26:8): the same noun is deployed, with no suggestion that the ointment goes out of existence. Moreover, when "life" and "destruction" are contrasted (as in John 3:16, etc.), one might reasonably infer that "destruction" refers to cessation of existence only if "life" means no more than mere existence. But is Christ doing no more than contrasting mere survival and extinction? "Rather, Christ is contrasting two qualitatively different types of existence, one involving a loving communion with God and another lacking it (a state of 'ruin')."[18] Stott's conclusion ("It would seem strange . . . if people who are said to suffer destruction are in fact not destroyed") is memorable, but useless as an argument, because it is merely tautologous: *of course* those who suffer *destruction* are *destroyed*. But it does not follow that those who suffer destruction cease to exist. Stott has assumed his definition of "destruction" in his epigraph.

None of this response so far demonstrates that the words in the New Testament for destruction, found in the context of perdition, necessarily refer to something eternally ongoing. The only point so far is that they do not militate against such a view, and therefore the issue itself must be decided on other grounds.

---

16. Ibid.
17. Ibid., 316.
18. Timothy R. Philips, "Hell: A Christological Reflection," in *Through No Fault of Their Own? The Fate of Those Who Have Never Heard*, ed. William V. Crockett and James G. Sigountos (Grand Rapids: Baker, 1991), 51 n. 8.

Although a few critics have argued that the word often rendered "forever"—viz., αἰών and its cognate adjective αἰώνιος—properly means simply "age," and therefore that "aional" punishment simply does not mean eternal punishment, it is widely recognized that the argument does not work. The "age" in question may be eternal, as it clearly is with respect to the new heaven and the new earth. The parallelism found in some verses such as Matthew 25:46 ("Then [the goats] will go away to *eternal* punishment, but the righteous to *eternal* life") is decisive.[19] Therefore it is far more common to argue that the adjective αἰώνιος in the relevant passages refers to the *result* of the action and not to the action itself. Indeed,

> when the adjective . . . is used in Greek with nouns of *action* it has reference to the *result* of the action, not the process. Thus the phrase "everlasting punishment" is comparable to . . . "everlasting salvation." . . . No one supposes that we are . . . being saved forever. We were . . . saved once and for all by Christ with eternal results.[20]

Thus eternal punishment occurs once and for all, but has "eternal" results.

As common as the argument is, even some annihilationists acknowledge that it is very weak,[21] and several others have roundly challenged it.[22] The critical question is whether the adjective αἰώνιος, even when applied to salvation, refers *only* to the once-for-all work of Christ and its results. Can the redeemed in heaven not say that they are being saved by Christ, but only that they have been saved by Christ? In any case, "salvation" itself has a broad semantic range; it can refer to the ongoing blessedness introduced by the consummation—and if this is the case, one must at least ask if "eternal punishment" likewise refers to ongoing punishment. More importantly, Harris agrees with Sasse, to the effect that αἰώνιος more commonly has temporal/eternal overtones, rather than qualitative force. And even when it has the latter, the temporal sense is rarely forfeited.[23]

Similar results obtain for other disputed words.

---

19. This verse merits closer attention: see below.

20. Basil F. C. Atkinson, *Life and Immortality* (Taunton: Goodman, 1962), 101 (emphasis his). See especially the extended argument in Fudge, *The Fire That Consumes*, 37–50, 194–96.

21. E.g., Stephen H. Travis, *Christian Hope and the Future* (Downers Grove: InterVarsity Press, 1980), 133–36; John W. Wenham, *The Enigma of Evil* (Grand Rapids: Zondervan, 1985), 34–41.

22. E.g., Philips, "Hell: A Christological Reflection," 51–52; Harmon, "The Case Against Conditionalism," 205–6.

23. Murray J. Harris, *Raised Immortal* (Grand Rapids: Eerdmans, 1983), 182–83; cf. H. Sasse, "αἰών," *Theological Dictionary of the New Testament*, vol. 1, ed. Gerhard Kittel, trans. and ed. Geoffrey D. Bromiley (Grand Rapids: Eerdmans, 1964): 198–208.

(2) More important perhaps than the individual words are the graphic images of hell themselves. Fire consumes: "the main function of fire is not to cause pain, but to secure destruction, as all the world's incinerators bear witness."[24] John the Baptist pictures the sovereign Judge "burning up the chaff with unquenchable fire" (Matt. 3:12): the fire may be unquenchable, but the chaff certainly isn't fire resistant. If hell is the place where "their worm does not die, and the fire is not quenched" (Mark 9:48; cf. Isa. 66:24), it is not necessary to conjure up the kind of vengeance depicted by Judith (and later many Christians), who pictures God putting "fire and worms in their flesh" so that "they shall weep and feel their pain for ever" (Judith 16:17). Jesus simply says that the worm will not die and the fire will not be quenched—i.e., their destruction is implacable, "until presumably their work of destruction is done."[25] Even the use of "Gehenna" supports this view: the garbage is finally burned up.

But there are several weaknesses to this argument. Most interpreters recognize that there is a substantial metaphorical element in the Bible's descriptions of hell. This does not mean that hell itself is merely metaphorical: one must not infer from the fact that someone thinks that many of the descriptions of hell are metaphorical and not literal the conclusion that hell itself is not literal. Hell is real; the question is how far the descriptions of it are to be taken literally. Normally, we do not think of unquenchable fire and worms coexisting: the former will devour the latter as easily as they will consume people. It is hard to imagine how a lake of fire coexists with utter darkness. And if one is cast into a lake of fire, what need of chains?

Inevitably, this means that the metaphors need interpreting. Virtually all sides (except those who, like Jehovah's Witnesses, think of instantaneous annihilation at death) acknowledge that the least that is at stake is suffering. I am reluctant to say that *none* of this suffering is physical in some sense, when the Bible speaks of the resurrection of the unjust (e.g., John 5:28–29). But the argument of Stott and others is that the natural inference from the language of fire is that it totally consumes what it burns, that the natural inference from the worms (probably maggots) is that total corruption accompanies their work until there is nothing left to be destroyed. But one must at least ask if there is anything in the text that encourages this reading of the language, or, alternatively, if there are elements that point away from such inferences. For example, if the worms do not die, what keeps them alive once they have devoured all the people? The question is ugly and silly, precisely because it is demanding a concrete and this-worldly answer to the use of lan-

24. John Stott in Edwards and Stott, *Essentials*, 316.
25. Ibid., 317.

guage describing the realities of punishment in a future world still largely inconceivable.

In fact, there are more than a few hints in the text that the annihilationist reading is incorrect. Observe the wording of Jesus' famous words: "And if your eye causes you to sin, pluck it out. It is better for you to enter the kingdom of God with one eye than to have two eyes and be thrown into hell, *where 'their worm does not die, and the fire is not quenched'*" (Mark 9:47–48; emphasis mine). It is not "*the* worm" but "*their* worm," which suggests that it is perpetually bound up with those who are suffering. By itself, fire that is "not quenched" might be taken to mean "unquenchable" in the sense that nothing can stand in its path for as long as it burns, rather than in the sense that it burns forever. But this leads to new difficulties. In a parallel passage, Jesus speaks of those who are thrown into the *eternal* fire (Matt. 18:8).[26] Besides, one is surely entitled to ask why the fires should burn forever and the worms not die if their purpose comes to an end. And if one draws the inferences Stott draws about being totally consumed, must we not also infer that fire consumes everyone at more or less the same rate, and that death (i.e., cessation of existence) would be almost instantaneous? Where then is there place for degrees of punishment before annihilation, as usually accepted by those who espouse annihilationism or conditional immortality? It appears that the interpretation of these passages is going off track precisely because illegitimate and arbitrary inferences are being drawn from the language, against the more natural readings, in order to support a theory that is being imposed on the text.

There are three passages that are peculiarly difficult for annihilationists. These passages do not easily allow for the view that the destruction is total and decisive while the judgment is eternal in the sense that it is irreversible, i.e., that there is no coming back from the cessation of existence.

The first is Revelation 14:10–11: those who worship the beast and his image "will be tormented with burning sulfur in the presence of the holy angels and of the Lamb. And the smoke of their torment rises for ever and ever. There is no rest day or night for those who worship the beast and his image, or for anyone who receives the mark of his name." The Greek expression rendered "for ever and ever" (εἰς τοὺς αἰῶνας or εἰς τοὺς αἰῶνας τῶν αἰώνων) is consistently the most emphatic way of saying "forever" in the New Testament. Annihilationists commonly take one of two steps. (a) Some introduce sequence: those who have the mark of the beast suffer, then they are totally consumed, and then the smoke eternally memorializes their destruction.[27] But why then does John insist that the lost enjoy "no rest day

---

26. Not "the fire of hell," as in the NIV (Greek εἰς τὸ πῦρ τὸ αἰώνιον).

27. E.g., Fudge, *The Fire That Consumes*, 297–98: "Actually torment is meted out according to the mixture of God's cup. *Then*, as the next image points out, it is forever memorialized in the smoke that remains [emphasis mine]."

or night"? It is surely special pleading to argue that "the action described is not a day-time action, nor is it a night-time action. It happens either and both."[28] The truth is that while the New Testament writers use many images to describe the awfulness of hell, which are often summarized as punishment, destruction, and exclusion, writers like Fudge constantly resort to serialization of these elements. As Harmon rightly points out,

> For Fudge, God's final sentence *begins* with banishment, *continues* with a period of conscious suffering, and *ends* with destruction. In fact, not a single New Testament passage teaches exactly this sequence. Instead, some texts speak of personal exclusion, some of punishment, and others of destruction, and these images need to be understood as giving us hints at the same eschatological reality. Fudge not only chronologizes these images, but he also emphasises one to the exclusion of the other two: destruction dominates while punishment and exclusion fall into the background. Indeed, the latter image is hardly discussed.[29]

(b) Other annihilationists compare this passage to Isaiah 34:9–10: "Edom's streams will be turned into pitch, her dust into burning sulfur; her land will become blazing pitch! It will not be quenched night and day; its smoke will rise forever." As Edom was wiped out, and the result is permanent, with the "perpetual smoke" a symbol of irreversible judgment, so the smoke in Revelation 14:11 may simply be an evocative way of saying that the torment of the lost, though itself not endless, is irreversible.[30] But that is surely less than clear. Revelation 14 stipulates that "the smoke *of their torment* rises for ever and ever," of those who enjoy no rest day or night. If there is an allusion to the sufferings of Edom in Isaiah 34, I suspect that Edom has the same sort of typological reference to hell that Sodom and Gomorrah have: "They [Sodom and Gomorrah] serve as an example of those who suffer the punishment of eternal fire" (Jude 7).

The second critical passage is Revelation 20:10–15: "And the devil . . . was thrown into the lake of burning sulfur, where the beast and the false prophet had been thrown. They will be tormented day and night for ever and ever. . . . And I saw the dead, great and small, standing before the throne, and books were opened. Another book was opened, which is the book of life. The dead were judged according to what they had done as recorded in the books. The sea gave up the dead that were in it, and death and Hades gave up the dead that were in them, and each person was judged according to what he had done. Then death and Hades were thrown into the lake of fire. The lake of fire is the

---

28. Ibid., 300.
29. "The Case Against Conditionalism," 213 (emphasis his).
30. So Froom, *The Conditionalist Faith of Our Fathers*, 1:298, 301, 409.

second death. If anyone's name was not found written in the book of life, he was thrown into the lake of fire." Stott points out that verse 10 "refers not only to the devil, but to 'the beast and the false prophet.'"[31] The beast and the false prophet, and for that matter the harlot of Revelation 17–18, "are not individual people but symbols of the world in its varied hostility to God. In the nature of the case they cannot experience pain" (318). For that matter, neither can "death and Hades" which follow the others into the lake of fire. Thus "the most natural way to understand the reality behind the imagery is that ultimately all enmity and resistance to God will be destroyed" (318).

It is disagreeable to differ with John Stott when he interprets Scripture, for ordinarily his exegesis is a model of clarity and sanity and has often been an inspiration for my own work. But I have to say that this really will not do. (a) In my view the beast and the false prophet are best thought of as *recurring* individuals, culminating in supreme manifestations of their type, rather than mere symbols that cannot experience pain. (b) More importantly, Stott does not comment on the devil's pain. Even if Stott were right in his reading of the beast and the false prophet, the devil is cast into the lake of fire with them, and the torment "day and night for ever and ever" is *his* experience. Stott does not side with those who depersonalize the devil. Thus Satan (cf. Rev. 12:9) constitutes at least one sentient being who is clearly pictured as suffering conscious torment forever. We may not feel as much sympathy for him as for fellow human beings, and we may cheerfully insist he is more evil than any human being, but even so, it is hard to see how the arguments deployed against the notion of eternal conscious suffering of sinful human beings would be any less cogent against the devil. Conversely, if this text demonstrates that there cannot be a sound argument in principle against the eternal suffering of a sentient being, it is difficult to see why humans should be a special case.[32] (c) Stott does not mention verse 15: "If *anyone's* name [not just the beast and the false prophet, or even the devil himself] was not found written in the book

---

31. Edwards and Stott, *Essentials*, 318. Other annihilationists follow a similar tack.

32. Incidentally, this sort of passage also stands against the universalism of, among others, Madeleine L'Engle, *The Irrational Season* (New York: Seabury Press, 1977), 97: "I know a number of highly sensitive and intelligent people in my own communion who consider as a heresy my faith that God's loving concern for his creation will outlast all our willfulness and pride. No matter how many eons it takes, he will not rest until all of creation, including Satan, is reconciled to him, until there is no creature who cannot return his look of love with a joyful response of love. . . . I cannot believe that God wants punishment to go on interminably any more than does a loving parent. The entire purpose of loving punishment is to teach, and it lasts only as long as is needed for the lesson. And the lesson is alway love." Regrettably, L'Engle pays little attention to what the Bible actually says, but simply expounds what she can and cannot believe. On the notion of punishment as *exclusively* remedial, see below.

of life, he was thrown into the lake of fire." In this context, why should it be thought that they would be consumed when the same fire does not manage to consume the devil, but only to torment him "day and night for ever and ever"? Again in the next chapter, we are told that the place of the ungodly "will be in the fiery lake of burning sulfur. This is the second death" (Rev. 21:8). Clearly the reference is to the lake of fire at the end of Revelation 20, where the torment never ends. What warrant is there for thinking, then, that in this passage total destruction, thoroughgoing annihilation, is in view?[33]

The third critical passage is Matthew 25:46, at the end of the parable of the sheep and the goats. The latter "will go away to eternal punishment, but the righteous to eternal life." Pinnock comments,

> Jesus does not define the nature of eternal life or eternal death in this text. He just says there will be two destinies and leaves it there. One is free to interpret it to mean either everlasting conscious torment or irreversible destruction. The text allows for both possibilities and only teaches explicitly the finality of the judgment itself, not its nature. Therefore, one's interpretation of this verse in respect to our subject here will depend upon other considerations. In the light of what has been said so far, I think it is better and wiser to read the text as teaching annihilation.[34]

But this is close to wishful thinking. We have seen that annihilationists take one of two approaches to αἰών/αἰώνιος, the "eternal" word-group. Some argue that it refers exclusively to a limited period, an "age," failing to recognize that the "final age" is open-ended. Matthew can use αἰών both in a temporal sense and in an eternal sense, even within one verse (12:32).[35] The adjective αἰώνιος, however, Matthew uses only for what is eternal.[36] Here there can be little doubt, since "eternal life" and "eternal punishment" are in parallel. So most annihilationists argue, like Pinnock, that the punishment is indeed eternal, but that this might mean only that the wicked have been destroyed in the sense of annihilated, and that this annihilation is irreversible. But note: (a) One must take into account verse 41 where the Lord says to those on his left, "Depart from me, you who are cursed, into the eternal fire prepared for the devil and his angels." As Harmon points out, annihilationists again

---

33. Cf. also John Piper, *Let the Nations Be Glad! The Supremacy of God in Missions* (Grand Rapids: Baker, 1993), 125–26.

34. "The Destruction of the Finally Impenitent," 256.

35. See the useful discussion in Scot McKnight, "Eternal Consequences or Eternal Consciousness?" in Crockett and Sigountos, *Through No Fault of Their Own?* 151–57.

36. McKnight rightly points out that it is methodologically unhelpful to find in this passage some notion more typical of *another* author, e.g., "eternal life" understood as "qualitatively new life" in the Fourth Gospel (ibid., 152, n. 14). Cf. also the earlier discussion in this chapter.

introduce temporal serialization: first the fire that annihilates, then the eternal punishment which in fact constitutes the nonreversing of the annihilation.[37] It is more natural to read verses 41 and 46 in parallel. (b) In the light of Revelation 20, where the devil endures the eternal fire forever, it is hard to discern any ground on which to conclude that the punishment of the goats is something qualitatively different. (c) The word "punishment" is graphic, and at least suggests suffering. (d) In the context of first-century Palestinian Judaism, Jesus could not have used such words as these without being understood to be in line with Pharisaic beliefs on the matter, beliefs that also took Gehenna as a model for eternal, conscious punishment. If Jesus had wanted to distance himself from that view, and make his espousal of annihilationism abundantly clear, he certainly forfeited numerous opportunities to do so.

(3) I have tried to discuss these distressing themes and texts coolly, precisely so that I can hear what at many levels I would prefer not to hear. I cannot say I find any of this easy. Even at the brutal level of having relatives and loved ones who have quite openly spurned the gospel, meditation on these texts is painful. Before pressing on with our exploration of these themes, it may be beneficial to reflect on the charges of "savagery" and "cruelty" that are often brought against the traditional interpretation of the relevant passages.

(a) As difficult as this subject is, some annihilationists should temper their language. They speak and write so fluently about the cruelty, savagery, hatefulness, implacable vengefulness, and sadism of the traditional view that they overlook the entailment: if they are wrong, they are using all those words of God, and if they are right they are using all those words of the overwhelming majority of Christian brothers and sisters across the last two millennia, including not a few of the gentlest, tenderest, most compassionate and loving believers one could hope to meet. Mercifully, not all annihilationists speak so intemperately. For example, Hughes cites one of the "purple passages" drawn from Edwards's most famous sermon,[38] but fairly comments, "It is only right to point out ... that the purpose of Edwards in this sermon was compassionately to urge his hearers to flee from the wrath to come and all its terrors by taking refuge in the redeeming grace of the gospel."[39] By contrast, it takes

---

37. "The Case Against Conditionalism," 113–15.

38. Jonathan Edwards, *Sinners in the Hands of an Angry God* (Phillipsburg: Presbyterian and Reformed, repr. 1992).

39. "Conditional Immortality," 11. R. C. Sproul, "The Limits of God's Grace: Jonathan Edwards on Hell," *Tabletalk* 14 (July 1990): 4, comments that if Edwards were "a sadist who believed in hell [he] would probably be more likely to give assurances to people that they were in no danger of hell, so that he could deliciously relish the contemplation of their falling into it." Cited also in Larry Dixon, "Warning a Wrath-Deserving Hell: Evangelicals and the Overhaul of Hell," *Emmaus Journal* 2 (1993): 15.

considerable grace to listen sympathetically to Pinnock's passionate pleas that his view be granted legitimacy, when his own purple prose condemns as sadists devoid of the milk of human kindness all those who disagree with him.

(b) Should it not be pointed out that it is the Lord Jesus, of all persons in the Bible, who consistently and repeatedly uses the most graphic images of hell? And regardless of the duration of conscious suffering, is it not clear that he does so precisely to warn people against hell, and to encourage them to repent and believe? Should we not therefore do the same?

(c) Could not the same thing be said of a number of passages in Revelation? Consider, for instance, the image of Revelation 14:17–20. At the appointed hour the wicked are harvested like bunches of grapes, thrown into "the great winepress of God's wrath" where they are trampled down until the blood that flows from the vat is as high as a horse's bridle for an outrageous distance. So far as graphic pictures go, it is difficult to see how anything that Edwards says is more horrific than that.

(d) The assumption that eternal conscious punishment would be needlessly cruel owes something, I suspect, to a shift in our view of suffering. As Bray puts it, "Here the model has shifted from punishment justly deserved for sins committed to suffering pointlessly prolonged. The suggested remedy for this is therefore not a belated pardon, which would fit the imprisonment model, but euthanasia."[40] One might reasonably wonder why, if people pay for their sins in hell before they are annihilated, they cannot be released into heaven, turning hell into purgatory. Alternatively, if the sins have not yet been paid for, why should they be annihilated? The truth of the matter is that annihilation does not account for what Jesus calls "an eternal sin" (Mark 3:29), i.e., for sin that "will not be forgiven, either in this age or in the age to come" (Matt. 12:32).

The shift in model is surely behind Pinnock's rhetorical question, cited earlier: "Does the one who told us to love our enemies intend to wreck vengeance on his own enemies for all eternity?"[41] But the logic of his question surely demands revision: "Does the one who told us to love our enemies intend to wreck vengeance on his own enemies?" So far as I know, Pinnock would answer that question in the affirmative, though probably he would want to recast the question a little. Justice must prevail; just punishment must be meted out; vengeance in the purest sense belongs to the Lord. What then is different about the question by adding the three final words, "for all eternity"? If justice is still prevailing, if just punishment is still being meted out

---

40. Gerald Bray, "Hell: Eternal Punishment or Total Annihilation?" *Evangel* 10/2 (Summer 1992): 23.

41. "The Destruction of the Finally Impenitent," 247.

(points we shall explore below), then Pinnock's objection falls to the ground. If it was *ever* justly being meted out, then Pinnock should not cast his question as if to imply that *any* display of justice contradicts the command to love one's enemies.

(e) Pinnock forcefully reacts against any "softening" of the doctrine of hell by treating the language metaphorically. He wants the language to be harsh, literal, and unbending precisely because he thinks that only then will the doctrine be seen for the savage thing it is, and this will turn the church toward annihilationism. He fails to see that annihilationism itself might be seen as a "softening" of hell, or that his tentative suggestion of post-death evangelism, based on a doubtful exegesis of 1 Peter 3:19–20,[42] might be taken the same way.

Crockett's response is telling:

> Pinnock rails against the evangelicals (the vast majority, it turns out) who support the metaphorical view. To hold anything other than the traditional view, he says, takes the hell out of hell and amounts to nothing more than an attempt to weasel out of an uncomfortable doctrine. But to say that the metaphorical view takes the hell out of hell is an emotional trick that begs the question, and I think Pinnock knows that. He starts with the assumption that hell must be interpreted as a literal fire and that any change from that takes the hell out of hell. On this reckoning, Jude takes the hell out of hell because in verses 7 and 13 he talks about hell as being both eternal fire and the blackest darkness ... clearly metaphorical expressions. ... Jesus also takes the hell out of hell because he uses opposing images of fire and darkness to describe the final place of retribution. The truth is that these incompatible images were never intended to be literal, but were metaphors to describe the awful place we call hell. You cannot take the hell out of hell if the hell you describe is true to the intentions of the biblical authors. If Pinnock objects to the metaphorical view, he must do so by showing why the metaphors should be understood as literal expressions, not by throwing out clichés for emotive effect.[43]

This is not to deny that some speculations as to what precise reality lies behind the metaphorical language have gone too far. One thinks, for instance, of Lewis's suggestion that just as heaven makes human beings (as we now think of them) *more* than human, so hell, like fire that burns wood into ash that is no longer wood, but only remains, makes a human into something *less*

---

42. *A Wideness in God's Mercy* (Grand Rapids: Zondervan, 1992), 169, 172. Similarly, cf. Stephen T. Davis, "Universalism, Hell, and the Fate of the Ignorant," *Modern Theology* 6 (1990): 183.

43. William V. Crockett, "Response," in *Four Views on Hell*, 172–73.

than human, an "ex-man" or "damned ghost."[44] I suppose this is possible, but it certainly leaves the texts a long way behind. More satisfactory (though I remain uncertain of some of its arguments) is the classic treatment by Robert Anderson,[45] praised by Spurgeon as the best treatment of the subject. But my point is that hell may be very different from the depictions of many medieval imaginations. John Donne is more modern:

> When all is done, the hell of hells, the torment of torments, is the everlasting absence of God, and the everlasting impossibility of returning to his presence.... [T]o fall out of the hands of the living God, is a horror beyond our expression, beyond our imagination.... What Tophet is not Paradise, what Brimstone is not Amber, what gnashing is not a comfort, what gnawing of the worme is not a tickling, what torment is not a marriage bed to this damnation, to be secluded eternally, eternally, eternally from the sight of God?[46]

(f) It is vital that we reflect on how the Bible's teaching about hell is related to its teaching about God. The earlier chapters that began to paint a biblical theology (chaps. 5 and 6) insisted that God is both holy and loving; that he is sovereign and yet personal; that the good news of Jesus Christ cannot properly be understood if one neglects to hold together these polarities. In reading the annihilationist literature, one sometimes gains the impression that all who hold to the traditional view of hell ignore everything else the Bible says. Doubtless some do. But most of us, I think, remember Jesus' tearful words over Jerusalem (Luke 19:41–44) and his compassion for the daughters of Jerusalem (Luke 23:28–31). We remember Paul's heartrending cry for the conversion of his fellow-Jews (Rom. 9:2–3; 10:1), Jeremiah's tears for the slain of his people (Jer. 9:1; cf. 13:17; 14:17), and Jude's frank exhortation to "snatch others from the fire and save them" (Jude 23). Here Stott sounds exactly the right note: "I long that we could in some small way stand in the tearful tradition of Jeremiah, Jesus and Paul. I want to see more tears among us. I think we need to repent of our nonchalance, our hard-heartedness."[47]

(4) That the retributive judgment of hell is fair "rests upon this correspondence between enormity and severity."[48] In the ancient pagan world,

---

44. See, for example, C. S. Lewis, *The Problem of Pain* (New York: Macmillan, 1943), 113–14.

45. *Human Destiny: After Death—What?* (London: Pickering & Inglis, 1913).

46. *Sermons* IV, 86.

47. Edwards and Stott, *Essentials*, 313.

48. Daniel P. Fuller, *The Unity of the Bible: Unfolding God's Plan for Humanity* (Grand Rapids: Zondervan, 1992), 192.

many judges made their decisions while keeping in mind the social status of the person being judged. If this is tied in our minds to the notion that punishment is primarily remedial, we shall begin to think that we might get off before the bar of God's justice provided we can be represented by a first-class English QC. But such an attitude overlooks how central *retributive* punishment is in the Bible. At stake is the issue of justice. If we do not get this matter straight, it will radically affect how we view the cross, and thus the gospel.

The Bible's concern to assure us that the punishment of hell is fair is tied to the rather common biblical insistence that there are degrees of punishment there. That is presupposed, for instance, not only by Jesus' explicit words about some being beaten with more blows and some with fewer blows (Luke 12:47–48), but also by his insistence that God even takes into account how some guilty sinners, like those of Sodom, might have acted under different circumstances (Matt. 11:20–24). They are not thereby excused. What is clear is that for Jesus to talk about the final day being "more bearable" for some than for others, on the basis of how much light each has received (cf. also Rom. 1–2), presupposes not only that justice will be done, but that it will be seen to be done. Similarly, some are treated more severely for consciously trampling under foot the Son of God (Heb. 10:26–29).[49]

What is hard to prove, but seems to me probable, is that one reason why the conscious punishment of hell is ongoing is because sin is ongoing. Even some annihilationists recognize that this is an important consideration. Thus Stott questions whether "'eternal conscious torment' is compatible with the biblical revelation of divine justice, *unless perhaps (as has been argued) the impenitence of the lost also continues throughout eternity.*"[50] There is surely at least one passage that hints at this reality. In the last chapter of the Bible, the interpreting angel says to John, "Do not seal up the words of the prophecy of this book, because the time is near. Let him who does wrong continue to do wrong; let him who is vile continue to be vile; let him who does right continue to do right; and let him who is holy continue to be holy" (Rev. 22:10–11). Of course, the primary emphasis here is on the time from "now" *until* judgment: there is a kind of realized judgment, within time, that sometimes takes place. Nevertheless the parallelism is telling. If the holy and those who do right continue to be holy and to do right, *in anticipation of the perfect holiness and rightness to be lived and practiced throughout all eternity*, should we not also conclude that the vile continue their vileness *in anticipation of the vileness they will live and practice throughout all eternity?* Moreover, does not Revelation 16:21 provide a portrait of those who are being punished and who curse God?

---

49. Cf. Ajith Fernando, *Crucial Questions About Hell* (Eastbourne: Kingsway, 1991), 33–35.
50. Edwards and Stott, *Essentials*, 319 (emphasis mine).

Blocher strongly objects to this view, largely on the ground that the ultimate triumph of Christ, with all enemies destroyed (e.g., 1 Cor. 15), demands the conclusion that sin no longer exists. Hell will be full of remorse, but empty of sin.[51] I find this reasoning unconvincing. The triumph of Christ should be understood in slightly different terms, as we shall see below. Meanwhile, are we to imagine that the lost in hell love God with heart and soul and mind and strength, and their neighbors as themselves? If not, they are breaking the first and second commandments. Are they full of spontaneous worship and praise?

Far better to understand Revelation 22 as I have suggested. But that means that at the end hell's inmates are full of sin. They hate and attract retribution, they still love only themselves and attract retribution, they are neither capable of nor desirous of repenting, and attract retribution. As dark as these reflections are, I suspect they go a long way to providing a rationale for the eternal nature of hell and its torments.[52]

(5) The argument for what is sometimes called "mortalism" is filled with pitfalls. Over against the view that human beings are *intrinsically* immortal (a view that is sometimes charged with being overly dependent on Greek thought), some have argued that human beings this side of the Fall are all mortal, but that the redeemed gain immortality. Thus if the wicked die and cease their existence, whether immediately upon death or after appropriate punishment, strictly speaking they are not being "annihilated" but merely experiencing the inevitable result of their fallenness and sin, apart from redeeming grace. This, it is argued, is a truly Hebraic and biblical view of human beings.

The arguments are complex, and cannot be delved into fully here.[53] But note the following:

(a) Even if there were no sense in which human beings are constitutionally immortal, the annihilationist position would not therefore necessarily be

---

51. Henri Blocher, "Everlasting Punishment and the Problem of Evil," in Cameron, *Universalism and the Doctrine of Hell*, 283–312.

52. At the same time, I would argue that we human beings are poorly placed to assess the enormity of our own sin. One must not firmly conclude (as many annihilationists do) that punishment must be finite because we are finite and our actions are finite. Is the magnitude of our sin established by our own status, or by the degree of offense against the sovereign, transcendent God? Cf. Piper, *Let the Nations Be Glad!* 127: "The essential thing is that degrees of blameworthiness come not from how long you offend dignity, but from how high the dignity is that you offend." The point is well established by Jonathan Edwards, *Works* (Edinburgh: Banner of Truth Trust, repr. 1974), 1:669.

53. See Eryl Davies, *An Angry God? What the Bible Says About Wrath, Final Judgement and Hell* (Bridgend: Evangelical Press of Wales, 1992), chap. 9.

substantiated. For John 5:28–29, as we have seen, speaks of the resurrection of the just and of the unjust. One must wrestle with what purpose the latter serves. Perhaps the resurrection of the unjust is to their *mortal* bodies again (as many annihilationists argue), but the texts do not say so.

(b) The strict dichotomy between Greek thought and Hebrew thought is now rightly dismissed by most scholars as far too rigid. For example, the apostle Paul, when he reflects on his experience of being caught up into the third heaven, is quite unsure whether it was in his body or out of his body (2 Cor. 12:1–10). The least that this uncertainty presupposes is that Paul is not at all uncomfortable with the possibility of existence *apart* from his body.

(c) Doubtless some affirmations of human immortality are misleading, since they tend to give the impression of intrinsic indestructibility that not even God could reverse. It is better to think of the sovereign God, through his triumphant Son, upholding all things by his powerful word. In other words, however "immortal" we are, we live and move and have our being because God sanctions it, not because we have achieved some semi-independent status.

Within some such framework, I perceive no decisive argument against a properly articulated view of human "immortality," and much to commend the idea.

(6) Many annihilationists have argued that the continuing existence of sin and punishment would mar the joy of heaven, or betray an unacceptable cosmological dualism, or signal the sad fact that Christ's triumph is still not complete.

It is far from clear that any of this is convincing. "[W]hile evil *that remains unpunished* does detract from God's glory in the universe, we must also recognize that when God *punishes* evil and *triumphs* over it, the glory of his justice, righteousness and power to triumph over all opposition will be seen (see Rom. 9:17, 22–24). The depth of the riches of God's mercy will also then be revealed."[54] As Packer puts it:

> [I]t is said that the joy of heaven will be marred by knowledge that some continue under merited retribution. But this cannot be said of God, as if the expressing of his holiness in retribution hurts him more than it hurts the offenders; and since in heaven Christians will be like God in character, loving what he loves and taking joy in all his self-manifestation, including his justice, there is no reason to think that their joy will be impaired in this way.[55]

---

54. Wayne Grudem, *Systematic Theology* (Grand Rapids: Zondervan, 1994), 1151.

55. James I. Packer, "The Problem of Eternal Punishment," *Evangel* 10/2 (Summer 1992): 18.

D. Concluding Reflections

Despite the sincerity of their motives, one wonders more than a little to what extent the growing popularity of various forms of annihilationism and conditional immortality are a reflection of this age of pluralism. It is getting harder and harder to be faithful to the "hard" lines of Scripture. And in this way, evangelicalism itself may contribute to the gagging of God by silencing the severity of his warnings and by minimizing the awfulness of the punishment that justly awaits those untouched by his redeeming grace. Newbigin is right: "It is one of the weaknesses of a great deal of contemporary Christianity that we do not speak of the last judgement and of the possibility of being finally lost."[56]

56. Lesslie Newbigin, "Confessing Christ in a Multi-Religion Society," *Scottish Bulletin of Evangelical Theology* 12 (1994): 130–31.

Chapter 14

"THIS IS MY FATHER'S WORLD": CONTEXTUALIZATION AND GLOBALIZATION

T he questions raised in current discussion about contextualization and globalization are so complex that a thorough investigation would require a book at least the size of this one. Fortunately, my aims in this brief chapter are modest. My purpose is twofold: first, to indicate some of the ways in which current debates over contextualization and globalization are intimately tied to the themes of this book and are illumined by placing them in this broader context; and second, to suggest some ways in which post-modernism and pluralism, rightly constrained, can strengthen evangelical mission, theology, and proper contextualization.

A. Definitions and Fundamentals

Frequently in this book I have used the word *culture* without bothering to define it, for the contexts made the meaning clear enough. Now it will be helpful to be a little more precise. Anthropologists used to define culture as "all learned behavior which is socially acquired, that is, the material and non-material traits which are passed on from one generation to another."[1] More recently the emphasis has shifted from learned behavior to the communication and symbolism of all behavior, learned and unlearned: culture is "a *signifying system* through which . . . a social order is communicated, reproduced, experienced, and explored."[2] In other words, each social order communicates

---

1. Eugene A. Nida, *Customs, Culture and Christianity* (London: Tyndale Press, 1954), 28.
2. Raymond Williams, *The Sociology of Culture* (New York: Schocken Books, 1982), 13 (emphasis his).

537

internally and passes on its core to the next generation through language, nonlogical symbols, images, rituals, narratives, and so forth. This leads us to the comprehensive definition proffered by Newbigin:

> By the word *culture* we have to understand the sum total of ways of living developed by a group of human beings and handed on from generation to generation. Central to culture is language. The language of a people provides the means by which they express their way of perceiving things and of coping with them. Around that center one would have to group their visual and musical arts, their technologies, their law, and their social and political organization. And one must also include in culture, and as fundamental to any culture, a set of beliefs, experiences, and practices that seek to grasp and express the ultimate nature of things, that which gives shape and meaning to life, that which claims final loyalty. I am speaking, obviously, about religion.[3]

Lints shrewdly observes:

> It is easy to think of culture in the abstract, as if it were some entity far removed from the concrete life of ordinary people. However, culture is nothing more than the constant and curious conversation that goes on between every one of us and the environment in which we reside—we ourselves being part of that environment.[4]

The neologism *globalization* was first coined in the field of economics, more specifically in currency speculation.[5] The currency market is subject to no national or international political control. With the links provided by modern computers, transactions can be implemented anywhere on the globe, twenty-four hours a day, and affect other areas of the globe. By the sheer power of moving large quantities of currency around the world, jobs can be lost or created, stocks driven up or down, special interests served or despoiled. In other words, there is a moral element in the move toward globalization in the economic arena.

But nowadays globalization refers, rather broadly, to the changes brought about in almost any discipline owing to the fact that the various parts of the world are demonstrably more interdependent than they have ever been, and that it is increasingly difficult to work in any discipline, not least biblical and theological disciplines, without taking into account the global picture. At one time, those interested in theological education preferred the term "interna-

---

3. Lesslie Newbigin, *Foolishness to the Greeks: The Gospel and Western Culture* (Grand Rapids: Eerdmans, 1986), 3.

4. Richard Lints, *The Fabric of Theology: A Prolegomenon to Evangelical Theology* (Grand Rapids: Eerdmans, 1993), 104.

5. Cf. David Jobling, "Globalization in Biblical Studies/Biblical Studies in Globalization," *Biblical Interpretation* 1 (1993): 97.

tionalization." It soon became clear, however, that this latter expression already betrays a certain chauvinism: theological education was once the primary responsibility of Western culture, but now we are prepared to "internationalize" it. To avoid the colonial overtones, "globalization" was adopted as the word best suited to avoid overtones of a now defunct colonialism.[6]

At one level, as some wag has put it, globalization is nothing other than the persistent recognition that "the entire population of the universe, with one trifling exception, is composed of others."[7] This makes it sound as if globalization is nothing more than a kind of dampening of individual hubris, a belated recognition that I am not at the center of the universe after all. In fact, the issue is more complex. The combination of extraordinary worldwide mobility and almost instantaneous communication has shrunk our world, and assured that it is getting harder and harder to live and think and "theologize" entirely within a closed culture. Globalization is not only the recognition that the extraordinary diversity of cultures in the world exists (a commonplace, at least in educated circles, for half a millennium), but that each culture has as much right to speak and be heard as ours does and that this shapes the way we do things. Moreover, in the urgency with which they need to sift out truth from local culture, Christians in the Two-Thirds World are recapitulating early church history; while the church in the West wrestles again with what it means to articulate the gospel in an age of complex, cosmopolitan characteristics.[8]

In particular, the globalization of theology means that when we think and write theologically, we take heavily into account these global realities; so also the globalization of theological education means that we shape our theological education systems (e.g., goals, curricula, faculty hiring, etc.) taking into account these global realities.

Contextualization is a slippery term with diverse connotations, depending very much on who is using it. We saw early in the book that at one level it is nothing more than an extension of the old indigenous principle: it has long been recognized that churches freshly planted become "indigenous," and thus free from the support and control of sending churches and agencies, by rapidly becoming self-supporting, self-governing, and self-propagating. But young churches that are properly indigenous within a culture that is quite different from the culture of the mother church or agency that planted the

---

6. Cf. David S. Schuller, "Globalizing Theological Education: Beginning the Journey," *Theological Education* 30 (1993): Suppl. 1:3.

7. The quotation is attributed to John A. Holmes, about whom I know nothing, and is cited by Jonathan J. Bonk, "Globalization and Mission Education," *Theological Education* 30 (1993): 47.

8. See especially Max L. Stackhouse, *Apologia: Contextualization, Globalization, and Mission in Theological Education* (Grand Rapids: Eerdmans, 1988), esp. 159–61.

work may still be remarkably dependent on the mother church for theological reflection, theological education, theological texts, biblical commentaries, and so forth. In some cases, where the receptor culture is either not literate or barely literate, this may be related in difficult ways to educational challenges. But the same dependency may be no less prevalent when the receptor culture is highly literate. Such dependency may have been fostered in the colonial era, when it was widely assumed that colonial powers knew best. In a time when colonialism is despised and nationalism is a powerful force, it is unsurprising that the old dependencies in the theological arena are being called into question.

At its best, then, contextualization simply takes the indigenous principle one step further: churches should become not only self-supporting, self-governing, and self-propagating, but they should also become, shall we say, self-theologizing—i.e., they should think through their theology in their own context thus *contextualizing* it.

So far, so good. Thoughtful Christians will instantly see the sense in this line of reasoning. Calvin did not simply print Augustine; he did his own theological work. Hodge did not simply reprint Calvin; he wrote his own systematic theology. Cultural changes across time find analogues in cultural changes across space: whether one moves from sixteenth-century Calvin to nineteenth-century Hodge (across time), or from twentieth-century Norway to twentieth-century Zaire (across space), cultural differences demand fresh theological reflection and publication. Moreover, because Christians look forward to the day when the number of the redeemed will be drawn from every nation, tribe, people, and language (Rev. 7:9), we rejoice in the diversity of the multicultural mosaic that makes up the church. Indeed, whatever her failures and sins, the church has more experience, not to mention success, in dealing with multiculturalism than any other institution or tradition in the world.

Nevertheless, contextualization has split into roughly two approaches that are quite distinct.

The first recognizes the once-for-all truthfulness and authority of God's self-disclosure in Scripture, but then also frankly recognizes that all attempts to interpret that Scripture are culture-laden efforts undertaken by sinners (redeemed or otherwise), and therefore subject to more or less distortion. It is not so arrogant as to think that all biblical and theological reflection has been accurately and exhaustively accomplished by one group of Christians (ours!), and therefore that the only task remaining is to translate and promulgate the results for the sake of others. It fully appreciates how contextualization, properly defined, is the logical extension of indigenization.

The second so emphasizes the priority of the context that the text of Scripture is gradually domesticated to serve contemporary agendas.

Beginning from the observation that interpreters cannot help but interpret texts from the context of their own culture, "praxis" becomes the hermeneutical control.

Obviously this debate has clear parallels with contemporary pluralism and postmodernism. The sheer diversity of cultures (empirical pluralism) serves, for many, as an implicit defense of the view that each culture has exactly the same value as any other (philosophical pluralism)—as if there is nothing in any culture of transcendent moral significance, or anything (or anyone) who stands above all cultures. If there is no objective truth that binds all cultures together and evaluates them, then epistemologically, there is only truth for the individual, or for the individual culture, or for the diverse interpreting communities found within each culture (postmodernism). To insist that meaning lies primarily or even exclusively in the interpreter or in the interpretive community is merely to recognize the realities that operate whether we recognize them or not. So it may be a virtue to pick texts apart, not least the Bible, and mine them for what is most useful in our particular culture, thereby offering a critique of everything else in the Bible (deconstruction).

I have devoted enough space to the weaknesses of postmodernism, philosophical pluralism, and deconstruction that I need not review the arguments here. At the same time, I am thoroughly uncomfortable with the cultural imperialism of an earlier generation that could on occasion prove positively barbaric, and was in any case grounded in a form of modernism that has now been eclipsed. The positive contributions of restrained postmodernist insight more than justify the quiet, moderate contextualization outlined above. The brasher, unrestrained form of contextualization is merely another way of deploying Scripture to serve one's own agenda, and finally serves the worst extremes of unbridled postmodernism.

What, then, is the relationship between globalization and contextualization? The short answer is: exceedingly complex. From one vantage point, the two are somewhat at odds. "Contextualization from a world perspective becomes essential because of the inevitability of globalization. Contextualization is finding one's own voice against the backdrop of global media."[9] In other words, the pressures we face from globalization have the odd effect of making people in defined cultures think more clearly about their own contexts as the place where *they* "do theology." On the other hand, the perception that *inevitably* people "do theology" from within a particular culture, and

---

9. Editor's note introducing Robert J. Schreiter, "The ATS Globalization and Theological Education Project: Contextualization from a World Perspective," *Theological Education* 30 (1994): 81.

that there are many, many cultures, contributes to our assessment of globalization.

Theologians with the current "politically correct" agendas are not content to leave things there. They speak and write of the globalization of hermeneutics with little sense of any need to justify any particular hermeneutical procedure (for that would be to criticize someone's culture), provided the resulting interpretations serve one of five constantly recurring topics: liberation theology, feminism, economics of a vaguely leftist sort, religious pluralism, and praxis-driven contextualization. It is not long before one longs for ancient simplifications.

But before we press for a way forward, we need to see these ancient simplifications for what they are. They have to do with the ways in which systematic theology has been crafted in the West during the last few centuries.

Begin with the distinctions between biblical theology and systematic theology. I have recently argued that biblical theology has been defined, implicitly or explicitly, in six different ways.[10] For our purposes, those definitions that incorporate delineation of the historical development and diverse literary genres of the biblical books into the task of forming a biblical theology are of fundamental importance. Biblical theology asks what Galatians or the Pauline corpus says. It asks how truth about God is conveyed in Wisdom Literature, in law, in epistles, in apocalyptic. In short, it is primarily an inductive discipline that tracks the Bible's story-line. By contrast, systematic theology asks and answers atemporal questions: What is God like? What is a human being? What is sin? How may a person be right with God? There are other elements to systematic theology, of course, including the commitment to interact with some of the more important treatments of a given topic throughout the history of the church, and the concern to phrase the resultant theology in ways that address contemporary thought.[11] But it is the atemporal nature of the questions it poses and the answers it provides that is of primary interest to us here.

Biblical theology and systematic theology, as defined here, enjoy some measure of overlap: the systematician may sometimes distinguish the demands of God under the Mosaic covenant, for example, from the demands of God under the new covenant, while the biblical theologian may occasionally venture synthetic comments that bring together bits and pieces inferred

---

10. D. A. Carson, "Current Issues in Biblical Theology: A New Testament Perspective," *Bulletin for Biblical Research* 5 (1995).

11. To sharpen the focus, I leave aside here the "systematic theologies" that are *primarily* sophisticated discussions of positions taken throughout the history of the church, or that are *primarily* philosophical treatises that presuppose a certain amount of Christian tradition but that make no conscious effort to be constrained and delimited by the Scriptures.

from various biblical corpora. But by and large the biblical theologian and the systematician live in different worlds. When the former is invited to paint the big picture, he or she demurs, quietly leaving the field to the systematician. When the latter is challenged at the level of exegesis and biblical theology, he or she is tempted to defer to some favorite biblical scholar as the sufficient authority.

Precisely because systematic theology is so independent of biblical theology, Vanhoozer is only a trifle too harsh when he writes, "One typically begins with a doctrinal confession and then sets off trawling through the Scriptures. One's exegetical 'catch' is then dumped indiscriminately into parentheses irrespective of where the parts were found."[12]

We are ready now, I think, to see how systematic theology, as commonly practiced, is rather inadequate to handle the contemporary challenges from contextualization and globalization. (1) Thinking itself almost immune from the pressures of postmodernism, it is of all the biblical and theological disciplines most apt to be snookered by it. For the topics raised and the categories deployed as one "trawls" through the Scriptures are only sometimes generated by the text. More often they are the atemporal categories of tradition, or the "relevant" categories of praxis. The former do not adequately address the questions postmodernists are asking, let alone the kinds of worldviews presupposed by neighbors who are Shintos, Buddhists, Hindus, New Age pagans, or eclectic animists; the latter read the texts so arbitrarily that the text is often domesticated by the current agenda. *Neither the former nor the latter are very good at being corrected by careful exegesis and biblical theology.* (2) In addition, much Western systematic theology has been written "under the assumption that the world in which Christians live is entirely populated by scientists and atheists," as D'Costa puts it. And he therefore suggests that precisely because globalization has impressed on us just how diverse the world we live in really is, we have come to the end of this kind of systematic theology.[13] That is too hasty a judgment, for the world of scientists and atheists is *one* of the worlds in which we live,[14] but D'Costa is right to point out that it is far from being

---

12. Kevin J. Vanhoozer, "From Canon to Concept: 'Same' and 'Other' in the Relation Between Biblical and Systematic Theology," *Scottish Bulletin of Evangelical Theology* 12 (1994): 104.

13. Gavin D'Costa, "The End of Systematic Theology," *Theology* 45 (1992): 324–34, esp. 324.

14. There is wisdom in the remark of Jonathan Bonk, "Globalization and Mission Education," 49: "'What will I be when I grow up?' a little girl asked her grandfather. 'Simply more of what you are now,' the wise man replied. I must confess to a certain skepticism regarding the notion that in globalization has been discovered a means of transforming moribund Western theology and its concomitant institutions. We in the West need to be aware that much of what we do—no matter what we might call it—is simply more of what we have always done."

the only one. (3) Some cultures find it extremely difficult to think in analytic, abstract categories, but swing naturally to the poetic, the picturesque, the narrative, the evocative. We are thereby reminded that the challenges faced by systematic theology include not only its distance from the biblical text and the dangers arising from the fact that the questions it seeks to answer are sometimes somewhat out of step with the text, but also the fact that the *form* in which it is expressed may not be suitable for every culture.

So what is the way ahead?

B. Pointers

(1) If the first two parts of this book demonstrate anything, it is that human beings can know objective truth—doubtless not exhaustively and absolutely, but truly nonetheless. We can approach the truth "asymptoti-cally." Postmodernism gently applied rightly questions the arrogance of modernism; postmodernism ruthlessly applied nurtures a new hubris and deifies agnosticism.

These lessons from the first half of the book need to be applied here. We need to think through how we will go about the disciplines of biblical and systematic theology. Doubtless postmodernist purists will say that neither biblical theology nor systematic theology can attain objective truth. But Christians will insist that the sovereign/personal God is a talking God; that he has left a record of his words in Scripture; that we can understand those words truly, if not wholly or flawlessly. And in this regard biblical exegesis and biblical theology have an advantage over systematic theology: their agenda is set by the text. For believers who are passionately committed to finding out what the text says, and who are willing to adjust their beliefs and their practices to conform to the text, biblical theology is of first importance. As we spiral in on the text and correct ourselves by listening to the text and to one another's interpretations of the text, we find again and again that for-mer biases and unsubstantiated positions are whittled away and revised and reformed by the Word of God.

This suggests, I think, that systematic theology must increasingly seek to build on biblical theology. Instead of trawling through the Scriptures in order to adduce support for a position (regardless of how faithful the position), sys-tematic theologians must increasingly build outward from the work of bibli-cal theologians—from their inductive syntheses of biblical corpora, including what Vanhoozer calls "genre analysis,"[15] and from their tracing of the Bible's story-line. This does not mean that systematicians must abandon their inter-est in atemporal questions and answers or throw over their commitment to

---

15. "From Canon to Concept," 111–14.

interact with historical theology and to engage the present. It means, rather, that their own worldviews will be so wonderfully steeped in biblical theology that they will be much less likely to put a foot wrong.

(2) One of the distinctions between "trawling through the Bible" and building on the basis provided by biblical theology is this: the structure of systematic thought, however expressed, must reflect the Bible's story-line. Each major strand must be woven into the fabric that finds its climax and ultimate significance in the person and work of Jesus Christ.

The failure to keep this in mind vitiates some otherwise useful theological work. Let us consider some examples of quite varying importance. Someone in the West may ask the question, "What does the Bible say about keeping fit?" The expected answers will be trotted out: our bodies are the temple of the Holy Spirit; bodily exercise may not profit eternally but does profit somewhat in this life; and in any case we are not dualists or gnostics: *all* of life, including physical life, is to be lived under Christ's lordship. And at the consummation we will receive resurrection bodies. None of the answers is false. Our trawling has not been entirely without profit. But all the answers are skewed, in that the Bible does not set out to answer questions about keeping fit. Even at the tangential level it says things that may be relevant to the question *only within the context of larger, bigger questions* that are finally tied to God's plan of redemption and thus to God's priorities, God's purposes for his people.

Consider other questions: What does the Bible say about leadership? What does the Bible say about abortion? What does the Bible say about the poor? What does the Bible say about social justice? What does the Bible say about capital punishment?

How the Bible addresses each of these questions varies enormously. The Bible *narrates* much about many leaders; it *prescribes* a relatively small number of pithy things. Can these things be properly understood apart from the example of Christ? Is the Bible interested in leadership as an end in itself? Is not the emphasis in the New Testament on Christian leadership *in the church*—the only institution that will survive into the new heaven and the new earth, rather than on leadership in some abstract sense? Yet are there not implications for Christian leaders operating in the worlds of business and government? What are they? Are there qualifications mandated of Christian leaders within the church that should *not* be enforced on leaders outside? Why or why not? How can one possibly decide *on the basis of looking at the leadership passages alone*? Is it not the case that responsible interpretive answers can be offered to such questions only by considering the Bible's plot-line, and the priorities and scales of that plot-line?

What about abortion? Here the Bible says very little of a *direct* nature, but lays out a fundamental worldview as to what it means to be human, to be created in the image of God. By contrast, the Bible says an enormous amount about poverty, some of it in terms that denounce oppressors categorically (e.g., Amos, parts of Isaiah), and some of it in terms that recognize the many sources of poverty, including personal indolence and drunkenness (e.g., Proverbs). How is the sheer wealth and variety of material on the subject to be integrated into a holistic view of God and human beings? How is it to be integrated into the Bible's plot-line, the story of God's intervention into the history of a rebellious race, an intervention climaxing in Christ, to call out and form a new humanity? How do justice and justification intersect? When liberation theologians appeal to the Exodus as the archetype of all liberation from slavery and oppression, should one not ask how Exodus functions in the canon? Why have they chosen the Exodus, instead of, say, Jeremiah's insistence to bow to Babylon, the superpower of his day? Is there any criterion for the choice, apart from praxis? As Escobar has shrewdly observed, "Without a story that includes Creation, Covenant, Desert, Promised Land, Exile, the Messiah, the Cross, and the Resurrection, there is no key to understand the Exodus in a way that it becomes a word for the present."[16]

If the Bible says little directly on abortion, and a great deal on poverty, it says scattered things about capital punishment. "Whoever sheds the blood of man, by man shall his blood be shed; for in the image of God has God made man" (Gen. 9:6) seems clear enough. But should one not at least ask what is the relationship between the Noachic covenant, in which this passage is embedded, and the Mosaic covenant, and the new covenant? How are these relationships established?

Now let us take up a question that in most circles in North Atlantic countries would scarcely be a burning issue, but that in many parts of sub-Saharan black Africa is vital and pressing: What does the Bible say about demons, and how are Christians to beat them? In the semipopular Christian literature, patterned after a certain systematic mold, one trawls through Scripture and examines, in the first instance, the exorcisms practiced by Jesus and pulls out texts mentioning "demon" or "demonization" and gradually constructs first a theology, and then pastoral counsel, to help Christians address these matters. But if one places these texts within the Bible's plot-line, and asks fundamental questions about the nature of the conflict in which we are engaged and the nature of the victory that Christ has won, one soon perceives that there are other themes that are being overlooked. How much of the presentation

---

16. Samuel Escobar, "The Search for a Missiological Christology in Latin America," in *Emerging Voices in Global Christian Theology*, ed. William A. Dyrness (Grand Rapids: Zondervan, 1994), 207. I am not certain that Escobar has always applied this important criterion to all of his analyses of the Bible's treatment of the poor.

of demonic activity in the Synoptic Gospels is bound up with the dawning of the kingdom and the coming of the King? How is such activity related to the End? How much of the proper confrontation of the demonic is bound up with gospel solutions—as in Ephesians 6 and Revelation 12? This is not to say that there is no place for explicit exorcism. It is to say, rather, that the framework of the discussion and the priorities that emerge look rather different when the Bible's story-line, climaxing in Christ and his cross-work, resurrection, exaltation and reign, are taken into account.

(3) All of this presupposes that there is a "given," a revelation, a truth-standard, that cannot be ignored. We have returned to the questions of authority and revelation raised in chapter 4. In her penetrating essay, Soskice may occasionally be accused of giving too much away, but she certainly puts her finger on the nub of the problem. The voices of "liberation, black and feminist theology, amongst others," she says, all "emphasise historical and social particularity, and stress their own contexts as the scenes of witness to God's redemptive love—we drink from our own wells, says Gutiérrez, or, we might say 'the truth looks different from here.'"[17] But this drinking from our own wells invites a further question, "the question of 'how it is we can be certain that the truth we are approximating, the water we are drinking, in South America or South Africa or a women-church in Detroit, is the same as that drunk in Rome or Geneva or Canterbury?' How do we preserve the unity of faith from a diversity of perspectives?"[18] More fundamentally, she writes,

> To my mind, if we are to continue within what is recognisably Christian orthodoxy when we embrace a diversity of perspectives, we must cleave to the idea that it is "the truth" that we are approximating, however inadequately, and "the truth" that looks different from here. That is, a concern for "that which is certain in itself but subjectively uncertain to us" will continue to be at the heart of the Christian message. What I have tried to show thus far is that not only is it perfectly acceptable, epistemologically speaking, to seek a unity of truth from a diversity of perspectives, it is often desirable to do so. A complex description is more likely to provide an adequate account of complex subject matter than a simple single view.... In this case, a reversal of Sadolet's dictum would be called for: truth is multi-form, error is one.[19]

Much of this is shrewd, even though some of its formulation begs certain questions. Soskice wants to preserve objective truth: it is impossible to be a Christian in any historic sense without applauding her judgment in this

---

17. Janet Martin Soskice, "The Truth Looks Different from Here, or On Seeking the Unity of Truth from a Diversity of Perspectives," in *Christ and Context*, ed. Hilary Regan and Alan J. Torrance (Edinburgh: T & T Clark, 1993), 51.

18. Ibid.

19. Ibid.

regard. Moreover, by admitting that all human knowing is "approximation," she indicates she has broken free from the worst positivist impulses of modernity. But she goes too far. Apparently building on the absolute dichotomies much loved by postmodernists and deconstructionists ("either we know absolutely and certainly, or all our knowledge is relative"), she assigns no place to an *appropriate* certainty (e.g., Luke 1:4), other than the certainty that the truth must exist out there. There is no hint of asymptotic approaches to truth, of fusion of horizons, of a hermeneutical spiral (see chaps. 2–3), which may yield, if not the certainty enjoyed only by Omniscience, at least true and certain knowledge (however partial and mixed elsewhere with error). One begins to wonder how Soskice knows there is objective truth out there. Worse, one wonders if the diversity of perspectives which she thinks testify to the unity of the one Christian truth can ever be falsified—i.e., are some "perspectives" already guilty of controverting that one truth? How can we know when we are dealing with complementary perspectives on the one truth, and when we are dealing with distortions that steal that truth from us, or mask it with the glare of some other agenda?[20]

Wilson Chow is right: however sensitive we may be to the life situation of the interpreter or of the interpreting community, however important it is to wrestle with the illuminating work of the Holy Spirit, however vital it is that we use our reason as we interpret Scripture, however fundamental it is that we cherish holiness and love of God while reviling sin, the fact of the matter is that the proper source for Christian theology is God's gracious self-disclosure in the Scriptures.[21] Otherwise there is no possibility of God's objective truth standing over against culture, ours or anyone else's, when that

---

20. These questions are constantly overlooked in the literature. For example, Kwame Bediako, in his important book *Theology and Identity: The Impact of Culture Upon Christian Thought in the Second Century and in Modern Africa* (Oxford: Regnum Books, 1992), offers in chapter 10 an unrelenting critique of Byang Kato (especially his book *Theological Pitfalls in Africa* [Kisumu: Evangel Publishing House, 1975], but also his *Theological Trends in Africa Today* [WEF Theological News, Monograph 6; April 1973] and his numerous articles). Kato was a self-confessed "conservative evangelical" who warned against the rise of what he called a "Christo-paganism." Although there are significant theological differences between the two scholars, one comes away with the strong impression that Bediako makes no allowance for the fact that Kato's tragic and premature death by drowning in 1975 meant that he passed from the scene before the onset of postmodernism or the publication of the best confessional work on contextualization could have influenced him, and that meanwhile Bediako leaves himself open on many counts to the suspicion that he has not thought through what epistemological principles will prevent him from slipping into the universalism he clearly wishes to avoid.

21. Wilson W. Chow, "Biblical Foundations for Evangelical Theology in the Third World," in *The Bible and Theology in Asian Contexts: An Evangelical Perspective on Asian Theology*, ed. Bong Rin Ro and Ruth Eshenaur (Taichung: Asia Theological Association, 1984), 79–92.

culture goes astray. Only by returning to the font again and again do we have any hope of cutting away unfortunate cultural accretions to biblical faith in the believing community, of condemning cultural elements that defy the Word of God or are inconsistent with it, of transforming and calling into being cultural values that reflect and are consistent with God's gracious self-disclosure. As Lints puts it, "The object is not to substitute a Marxist or a feminist or a Latin American enculturation of the gospel for a North American capitalist enculturation of the gospel but rather to see the gospel in its critique of North American capitalism *and* Marxism *and* feminism *and* Latin American liberation theology."[22]

(4) All this presupposes that we learn the culture where we live and serve. The better seminaries have long included courses in the missions curriculum to help prospective missionaries "read" the culture they are about to enter. By such means they are assisted in their cross-cultural communication. Nowadays books are being produced to facilitate cross-cultural theological education.[23] "Dialogue," which was once a banner flown by liberals to prove their renunciation of any suggestion that Christianity is superior to other religions, and which was therefore seen by conservatives as a sign of implicit denial of the primary importance of heraldic ministry, is now being used in new and sophisticated ways. It can be a way of getting to know a culture (including its religion), a form of interpersonal communication useful in witness, and so forth.[24]

---

22. *The Fabric of Theology*, 253. This is the perhaps the place to mention in passing that attempts to read the New Testament as a kind of manual of contextualization—the gospel passes from a Jewish context to a hellenistic context, from an Aramaic-speaking world to a Greek-speaking world, and so forth, in order to develop principles for further change and development today—are not only uncontrolled, but even where they bring important insights, they abstract these events from the Bible's story-line. What becomes normative for such theologians is not what the Bible says, but the principles of change one can infer from the changes that take place along the redemptive-historical plane. The best of these studies is probably that of Daniel von Allmen, "The Birth of Theology: Contextualization as the Dynamic Element in the Formation of New Testament Theology," *International Review of Mission* 64 (1975): 37–52. I have responded at some length in "Church and Mission: Reflections on Contextualization and the Third Horizon," in *The Church in the Bible and the World: An International Study*, ed. D. A. Carson (Carlisle: Paternoster, 1987), 213–57, 342–47. Cf. further Warren Chastain, "Contextualization: Some Cautions and Criticism," *Stulos* 2 (1994): 3–8.

23. E.g., William David Taylor, ed., *Internationalizing Missionary Training: A Global Perspective* (Exeter: Paternoster, 1991); Alice Frazer Evans, Robert A. Evans, David A. Roozen, eds., *The Globalization of Theological Education* (Maryknoll: Orbis Books, 1993).

24. Cf. Stephen Healey, "Religious Truth Claims, Violence and the Pluralistic Hypothesis: A Defense of Interreligious Apologetics," *Andover Newton Review* 3 (1992): 17–30; Terry C. Muck, "Evangelicals and Interreligious Dialogue," *Journal of the Evangelical Theological Society* 36 (1993): 517–29.

But such courses are rarely required of students in the pastoral track. The assumption is that these students are returning to their *own* culture, so they do not need such assistance. But the rising empirical pluralism and the pressures from globalization ensure that the assumption is usually misplaced. Apart from isolated pockets, Western culture is changing so quickly that the church now struggles to understand what is going on. Indeed, it is less and less easy to speak of "Western culture" in such a monolithic fashion: there is a plethora of competing cultures in most Western nations, and many pastors will minister to several of them during their ministry. Indeed, in many metropolitan areas, pastors may find themselves ministering to several of them at once.

Through seminars, books, lectures, and finally by curricular changes, we simply must plug this lacuna. Otherwise we shall fall far short of the flexibility displayed by the apostle Paul when he crossed freely from witness in the synagogue to witness in the pagan Empire.

C. Examples

The literature offering examples of contextualization, of various types, is now very extensive.[25] It would be tedious to comment on many, but perhaps a few observations on a handful of them might flesh out some of the principles articulated.

Blomberg has little difficulty showing that passages in James dealing with poverty and the corruption of the wealthy are better handled by Elsa Tamez, a Mexican professor teaching in Costa Rica, and by Pedrito U. Maynard-Reid, a Jamaican pastor, than by any of the standard commentaries on James coming out of the North Atlantic countries.[26] For a long time theologians from the Two-Thirds World spent more time criticizing the West and underlining the importance of contextualized theology, than in preparing any. They were as locked into anti-colonialism as their forebears were locked into colonialism. But this is changing. In India, Sunand Sumithra, a national theologian has attempted what he calls "a doxological approach to systematic

---

25. To cite but a few works: Dean S. Gilliland, ed., *The Word Among Us: Contextualizing Theology for Mission Today* (Dallas: Word Books, 1989); R. S. Sugirtharajah, ed., *Voices from the Margin: Interpreting the Bible in the Third World* (Maryknoll: Orbis Books, 1991); William A. Dyrness, *Learning About Theology from the Third World* (Grand Rapids: Zondervan, 1990); idem, *Invitation to Cross-Cultural Theology: Case Studies in Vernacular Theologies* (Grand Rapids: Zondervan, 1992); Craig Blomberg, "The Globalization of Hermeneutics" (unpublished paper delivered at the annual meeting of the Evangelical Theological Society, November 1994).

26. Elsa Tamez, *The Scandalous Message of James* (New York: Crossroad, 1990); Pedrito U. Maynard-Reid, *Poverty and Wealth in James* (Maryknoll: Orbis Books, 1987). Cf. Blomberg, "The Globalization of Hermeneutics," 5–9.

theology."[27] In Africa, Lamin Sanneh has commented tellingly on how the missionaries' commitment to providing the Bible in the vernacular has given African believers the Scriptures that enable them to challenge what some missionaries have claimed the Bible says.[28] Doubtless these and other works can be criticized on a number of fronts, but the attempts are valuable and reflect efforts to listen to the text of Scripture.

But there are less helpful examples. Ogbonnaya's interpretation of the Trinity owes much more to African polytheism than to the Bible.[29] Hodgson's response to the culture of postmodernity is to succumb to it.[30] The control of the debate exercised by emphasizing praxis surfaces in an astonishing way when Pryor affirms, "For followers of Jesus today, the question is not: what did the first-century Jesus think of men and women in relationship? but: what would a contemporary Jesus think? Would that Jesus presume patriarchy or deny it?"[31]

In short, examples of both appropriate and inappropriate contextualization abound. One of the church's most urgent responsibilities is to distinguish between the two.

D. Concluding Reflections

Richard Bauckham writes:

> Disciplined listening to the text in its original and canonical contexts is one protection against this danger [of misinterpreting Scripture]. Of course, historical exegesis is never *wholly* objective, but the rigorous attempt at historical objectivity can liberate us from all kinds of misuse of the text. . . . Study of the history of interpretation can also be helpful, since historical distance enables us to appreciate what was going on in the church's political use of the Bible in the past more easily than we can in the present.[32]

---

27. Sunand Sumithra, *Holy Father: A Doxological Approach to Systematic Theology* (Bangalore: Theological Book Trust, 1993).

28. Lamin Sanneh, *Encountering the West. Christianity and the Global Cultural Process: The African Dimension* (Maryknoll: Orbis Books, 1993).

29. A. Okechukwu Ogbonnaya, *On Communitarian Divinity: An African Interpretation of the Trinity* (New York: Paragon House, 1994).

30. Peter C. Hodgson, *Winds of the Spirit: A Constructive Theology* (Louisville: Westminster/John Knox, 1994), esp. 53–66.

31. John Pryor, "Jesus and Women—A Second Look at the Issue," *Interchange* 50 (1993): 18. One is reminded of the kind of emphasis on praxis one finds in Thomas Groome. Cf. Miriam L. Charter, "Thomas H. Groome's Shared Praxis Approach to Ministry: Questioning Its Application in the Protestant Evangelical Church," *Trinity Journal* 15 (1994): 89–113.

32. *The Bible in Politics: How to Read the Bible Politically* (Louisville: Westminster/John Knox, 1989), 18.

That last point—the importance of studying the history of interpretation—calls to mind a passage from C. S. Lewis:

> Most of all, perhaps, we need intimate knowledge of the past. Not that the past has any magic about it, but because we cannot study the future, and yet need something to set against the present, to remind us that the basic assumptions have been quite different in different periods and that much which seems certain to the uneducated is merely temporary fashion. A man who has lived in many places is not likely to be deceived by the local errors of his native village: the scholar has lived in many times and is therefore in some degree immune from the great cataract of nonsense that pours from the press and the microphone of his age.[33]

In a similar way, listening to diverse cultures today can be an entirely salutary experience, when it is coupled with a profound desire to understand and obey what God has disclosed of himself in Scripture and supremely in Jesus Christ. Globalization exposes us to a kind of "instant history." Instead of appealing to principles of contextualization to justify the assumption that every interpretation is as good as every other interpretation, we will recognize that not all of God's truth is vouchsafed to one particular interpretive community—and the result will be that we will be eager to learn from one another, to correct and to be corrected by one another, provided only that there is a principled submission to God's gracious self-disclosure in Christ and in the Scriptures. The truth may be one, but it sounds less like a single wavering note than like a symphony.[34]

The result could foster synergy in mission.[35] Far from vainly trying to gag God by relativizing all he has said, an informed grasp of the diversities of culture will sharpen our proclamation.[36] There will also be mutual enrichment in our grasp of the mind of God, and wonderful opportunities to transcend the barriers that bigotry erects. "To be the Church in a pluralistic society

---

33. *The Weight of Glory and Other Addresses*, ed. Walter Hooper (New York: Macmillan, 1980), 28–29.

34. It is in this sense that the thesis of Vern S. Poythress, *Symphonic Theology: The Validity of Multiple Perspectives in Theology* (Grand Rapids: Zondervan, 1987), is to be supported.

35. See William D. Taylor, ed., *Kingdom Partnerships for Synergy in Mission* (Pasadena: William Carey Library, 1994).

36. One thinks, for instance, of the rising number of works like that of Gailyn Van Rheenen, *Communicating Christ in Animistic Contexts* (Grand Rapids: Baker, 1991), or Phil Parshall's *Beyond the Mosque: Christians Within Muslim Community* (Grand Rapids: Baker, 1985). Graduate students with experience in diverse cultures have recently produced for me thoughtful papers on such topics as how to present the superiority of Jesus Christ as priest/king to the people of Central and East Java, or how to teach what the Bible says about the *imago Dei* to Somalis. In every case the effort is to find points of contact and similarity as well as points of divergence.

means that we rise above the nationalism, the ethnicity, the language, the culture which separates and that we deliberately incorporate people of diverse ethnicities into our family and fellowship. Such an action will not destroy us; it will purify and enrich us as a part of God's great family."[37] Perhaps as well we will see more clearly where we have been seduced by our culture, and grow in faithfulness, witness, and transforming power in the conflict that inevitably erupts between social environment and Christ whenever Christians find grace to live faithfully.[38]

---

37. Leslie E. Mark, "The Role of the Church in a Pluralistic Society," *Direction* 12 (April 1983): 13–14.

38. Cf. Sherwood Lingenfelter, *Transforming Culture: A Challenge for Christian Mission* (Grand Rapids: Baker, 1992).

APPENDIX

When Is Spirituality Spiritual?
Reflections on Some
Problems of Definition*

The current interest in "spirituality" is both salutary and frightening.

It is salutary because in its best forms it is infinitely to be preferred over the assumed philosophical materialism that governs many people not only in the West, but in many other parts of the world as well. It is salutary wherever it represents a self-conscious rebellion against the profound sense of unreality that afflicts many churches. We speak of "knowing" and "meeting with" and "worshiping" the living God, but many feel that the corporate exercises are perfunctory and inauthentic, and in their quietest moments wonder what has gone wrong.

It is frightening because "spirituality" has become such an ill-defined, amorphous entity that it covers all kinds of phenomena that an earlier generation of Christians, more given to robust *thought* than is the present generation, would have dismissed as error, or even as "paganism" or "heathenism."[1] Today "spirituality" is an applause-word—i.e., the kind of word that functions in the "spiritual" realm the way "Mom and apple pie" function in the cultural realm: who is bold enough to offer a caution, let alone a critique?

What is quite certain is that the topic currently generates enormous interest.

A. Some Current Definitions, Explicit or Implicit

Despite the contention of Joann Wolski Conn that originally spirituality was "a christian term—from Paul's letters,"[2] it is nothing of the kind. True, "spirit" and "spiritual" are found in the New Testament, but very few writers

---

*A slightly shorter version of this paper was published in the *Journal of the Evangelical Theological Society* 37 (1994): 381–94.

1. Cf. the well-considered warnings against what he calls the "new spirituality"—various forms of New Age-related mysticism—issued by Gordon R. Lewis, "The Church and the New Spirituality," *Journal of the Evangelical Theological Society* 36 (1993): 433–44.

2. Joanne Wolski Conn, "Spirituality," *The New Dictionary of Theology* (Dublin: Gill & Macmillan, 1987), 972.

on spirituality begin with inductive study of such terms in order to establish what "spirituality" means. As a term, "spirituality" emerged from French Catholic thought, though for the last century or so it has been common in Protestantism as well. Earlier writers could speak of "the spiritual life" and mean something rather more narrowly defined than Paul meant by "the spiritual man" in 1 Corinthians 2, but it is this focus on "the spiritual life" that ultimately led to Christian coinage of the term "spirituality."

In fact, in the history of the Christian church until the Reformation, there were many different elements connected with spiritual life, only a few of them achieving prominence at any time or place: sacraments, community, prayer, asceticism, martyrdom, vows of poverty and/or celibacy, images, monasticism, and much more. Increasingly, spiritual life came to be associated with the pursuit of perfection, so far as that is possible this side of the consummating *visio Dei*. Thus it was not for all Christians, but only for those who particularly panted after God. Although spirituality (to use the term anachronistically) embraced all of life, it embraced all of life *only for some believers*. By the beginning of the eighteenth century, Giovanni Scaramelli (1687–1752) of the Society of Jesus, building on long-established traditions, sharply distinguished ascetic and mystical theology as the primary components of the study of spiritual life. The former has to do with the exercises to which all Christians who aspire to perfection will devote themselves, while the latter deals with the extraordinary states of consciousness and their secondary manifestations during times of mystical union with God. Thus "spirituality" became a discipline, "spiritual theology," to be distinguished from dogmatic theology, which tells us what must be believed, and from moral theology, which tells us how we must act. These are the essential distinctions that govern the classic treatment by P. Pourrat.[3]

In his three-volume history, Bouyer sought a more precise definition:

> Christian spirituality (or any other spirituality) is distinguished from dogma by the fact that, instead of studying or describing the objects of belief as it were in the abstract, it studies the reactions which these objects arouse in the religious consciousness. But, rightly, it does not entertain the pseudo-scientific, and in fact wholly extravagant, prejudice that the understanding of the objects polarizing the religious consciousness is essentially foreign to an understanding of this consciousness itself. On the contrary, spirituality studies this consciousness only in its living relationship with these objects, in its real apprehension . . . of what it believes. Dogmatic theology, therefore, must

---

3. *Christian Spirituality*, 4 vols. (Westminster, MD: N.p., 1953–55). Cf. also the important work by Cheslyn Jones, Geoffrey Wainwright, and Edmond Yarnold, *The Study of Spirituality* (Oxford: Oxford Univ. Press, 1986).

always be presupposed as the basis of spiritual theology, even though the
latter concerns itself with the data of the former only under the relationship
that they entertain with the religious consciousness.[4]

That last point, that spiritual theology presupposes dogmatic theology, a
point emphasized by both Pourrat and Bouyer, is denied today by some
authors,[5] who maintain the reverse: that spirituality is what shapes our theology, that we must experience something before we proceed to articulate it in
dogmatic forms. Part of the difference between these two perspectives, one
suspects, stems from the concern of the former to relate dogmatics to experience *in the experience of most individuals*, and the concern of the latter to relate
experience to dogmatics *in the genesis and formation of a movement*.

It is worth pausing to draw attention to several features that have already
come to light:

(1) Catholicism (and Orthodoxy too, for that matter) has invested far
more heavily in "spirituality" studies than has Protestantism, owing in no
small measure to the emphasis (until very recent times) on the pursuit of perfection (sometimes thought of as mystical union) by a subset of Christians, by
"elite" Christians (though of course they would never think of themselves
under such a term), not infrequently monastics. This traditional Catholic
interest is still reflected in details such as the relative amounts of space given
to the subject in recent Catholic and Evangelical dictionaries of theology,[6] or
the number of books congregating around the theme of spirituality published
by Paulist Press as compared to Zondervan or Eerdmans.

(2) At least since the eighteenth century, "spirituality" could refer either
to certain approaches to the knowledge of God (still being defined), or to the
study of such approaches.

(3) The parenthetical remark "or any other spirituality" (in the extended
quote from Bouyer, above) reflects another development that is harder to handle. In its context this refers to spirituality in non-Christian religions: Hindu
spirituality, Islamic spirituality, Buddhist spirituality, animist spirituality, and
so forth. In the context of Bouyer's work—a study of the *history* of Christian
spirituality, based for the most part on textual evidence—non-Christian

---

4. Louis Bouyer et al., *History of Christian Spirituality*, 3 vols. (London: Burns & Oates,
1963–68), 1:viii.

5. E.g., R. N. Flew, *The Idea of Perfection* (Oxford: Oxford Univ. Press, 1934); G.
Wainwright, *Doxology* (London: Epworth Press, 1980).

6. The article by Joann Wolski Conn, already mentioned, takes up 14 pages out of 1106;
the corresponding article by T. R. Albin in *New Dictionary of Theology* (Leicester: Inter-Varsity
Press, 1988) takes up less than 2 pages out of 738. One should also reckon with the substantial number of articles in the Catholic volume on related themes, most of which have no parallel in the IVP volume.

spirituality may be an eminently useful category: it refers to something like the interplay between dogma and religious consciousness in non-Christian religions, based, once again, on textual (or other largely phenomenological) evidence. But is the related dogma true in each instance? Does it matter? Is the "spirituality" related to these mutually exclusive systems of dogma valid or true or useful or helpful when the dogma to which it is tied is *not* true? Are we dealing only with the mind, the stuff of human consciousness? Or if we are insisting that there is a transcendent dimension to spirituality, is that transcendent dimension the same for the Christian who believes the gospel and for the animist who is imploring the spirits for a fat baby? Do we adopt the position of the radical pluralists who assume that virtually every form of spirituality is as valid as any other form, and this in itself becomes a way of authenticating the relative truthfulness of *all* dogma? In that case, of course, one must say something fuzzy, e.g., argue that although these systems of dogma transparently contradict one another, they all point equivalently to some greater system beyond the ken of any one of them. To such questions I shall briefly return.

This side of Vatican II, Catholic emphases on spirituality have been less associated with the pursuit of perfection by the "elite" than with growth in Christian experience by all Catholics. Thus the Dogmatic Constitution on the Church issued a universal call to holiness: "all the faithful of whatever rank .... are called to the fullness of the Christian life and to the perfection of charity" (L.G.40). The Constitution on the Sacred Liturgy asserts that the primary goal of the entire Vatican II council is to intensify Christian spirituality, "the daily growth of Catholics in Christian living" (S.C.1). This is given as one of the reasons for making the liturgy, and especially the mass, more accessible (S.C.2). At the same time, it can scarcely be denied that post-Vatican II Catholicism has fostered a diversity of views on spirituality, many of which are less and less eucharistically centered. Now a great deal of attention is focused on feminist spirituality, the spirituality of a life of poverty or of social transformation, and so forth. A great deal of contemporary publication in the area of spirituality explores what are judged to be complementary dimensions: the philosophical, the psychological, the theological, the mystical, the social, and so forth. It is becoming exceedingly difficult to exclude absolutely anything from the purview of spirituality, provided that there is some sort of experiential component in the mix. In this environment the pursuit of such "spirituality" is far from being a merely Catholic interest.[7] In this light, one of the most recent definitions of spirituality to appear in a Catholic

---

7. See, for instance, G. S. Wakefield, ed., *The Westminster Dictionary of Christian Spirituality* (Philadelphia: Westminster, 1983).

publication is entirely coherent, even if so all-embracing as to be rather daunting:

> The term spirituality refers to both a lived experience and an academic discipline. For Christians, it means one's entire life as understood, felt, imagined, and decided upon in relationship to God, in Christ Jesus, empowered by the Spirit. It also indicates the interdisciplinary study of this religious experience, including the attempt to promote its mature development.[8]

During the last century or so, "spirituality" has become part of the regular vocabulary of Protestants. Until the last few decades, when liberal Protestantism's conception of spirituality has gradually expanded to roughly the same dimensions as that within post-Vatican II Catholicism, Protestantism's interest in spirituality has largely been that associated with godliness and the devotional life in traditional evangelicalism. Although "spirituality" was not a term in vogue among the English Puritans, for instance, it is hard not to appreciate their emphases on conformity to Christ, personal moral examination, confession of sin, meditation on the Word, full-hearted use of "the means of grace." William Law's *Serious Call to a Devout and Holy Life* (1728) is, within this tradition, a classic in spirituality. Much more recently, and from a slightly different doctrinal structure within the heritage of evangelicalism, Richard Foster and Richard Lovelace have issued somewhat similar calls.[9] Building on the Puritans, not a few of Packer's books are essentially works designed, at least in part, to nurture the spiritual life.[10]

This is the matrix, then, out of which so many books and articles on spirituality (whatever that word means!) are now being produced. I have barely begun to mention the resources available. For example, there is a substantial literature on Orthodox spirituality. Perhaps one of the most accessible entry points into this heritage is a little book by an anonymous monk of the Eastern church.[11] A very remarkable book explores the patterns of life of several Catholic and Orthodox believers who are prepared to be "fools for Christ's sake."[12] The medieval emphasis linking voluntary poverty and perfection still

---

8. Conn, "Spirituality," 972.

9. Richard J. Foster, *The Celebration of Discipline*, 2d ed. (San Francisco: Harper & Row, 1978); Richard Lovelace, *Dynamics of Spiritual Life* (Downers Grove: InterVarsity Press, 1979); idem, *Revival as a Way of Life* (Downers Grove: InterVarsity Press, 1985).

10. E.g., J. I. Packer, *Knowing God* (London: Hodder & Stoughton, 1973); idem, *A Quest for Godliness: The Puritan Vision of the Christian Life* (Wheaton: Crossway Books, 1990).

11. Anonymous, *Orthodox Spirituality: An Outline of the Orthodox Ascetical and Mystical Tradition*, 2d ed. (London: SPCK, 1978).

12. John Saward, *Perfect Fools: Folly for Christ's Sake in Catholic and Orthodox Spirituality* (Oxford: Oxford Univ. Press, 1980).

finds its advocates.[13] The great boom in feminist spirituality is now calling forth, from within the presuppositions of that heritage, reflections on male spirituality.[14] For readers interested in the understanding of spirituality outside Christianity, perhaps one should start with Jewish spirituality.[15] The rage of the age is pluralism, or perhaps syncretism. Thus one recent book attempts to tie spirituality to Western depth psychology, eastern meditation, Christian thought, and the author's own experience.[16] It takes a sociologist to advise us that baby boomers are attempting to define spirituality in a new way.[17] Another writer insists that the change from a typographic culture to an electronic culture "is altering our sense of ourselves and our definition of religious experience and spirituality."[18] (I am getting nervous as I pound this out on my computer.)

Some of the problems are terminological. For instance, while evangelicals write not only technical commentaries on biblical books but also "devotional" commentaries, Catholics write not only technical commentaries but "spiritual" commentaries.[19] Recently a Protestant has adopted a somewhat similar tack: Barton's book on the Gospels is not interested in the "devotional" approach, but on exploring the Gospels to find out what they can tell us of "the sense of the divine presence and living in the light of that presence."[20] He locates a great deal of the "spirituality" of the Gospels—that is, the sense of the divine presence illustrated in or advocated by the Gospels—in the spirituality of Jesus, i.e., in Jesus' own experience of the divine presence. There is much more of Jesus as example or prototype here than of Jesus as Savior or Lord. The two themes do not have to be antithetical, but one of them is hardly heard in this book.

---

13. E.g., Michael D. Guinan, *Gospel Poverty: Witness to the Risen Christ. A Study in Biblical Spirituality* (New York: Paulist Press, 1981).

14. E.g., Philip Culbertson, *New Adam: The Future of Male Spirituality* (Minneapolis: Fortress Press, 1992).

15. Cf. Arthur Green, ed., *Jewish Spirituality From the Bible Through the Middle Ages* (New York: Crossroad, 1985); idem, ed., *Jewish Spirituality From the Sixteenth-Century Revival to the Present* (New York: Crossroad, 1988).

16. Donald Evans, *Spirituality and Human Nature* (Albany: State Univ. of New York Press, 1993).

17. Wade Clark Roof, *A Generation of Seekers: The Spiritual Journeys of the Baby Boom Generation* (San Francisco: HarperCollins, 1993).

18. Richard Thieme, "Computer Applications for Spirituality: The Transformation of Religious Experience," *Anglican Theological Review* 75 (1993): 345–58.

19. E.g., Leonard Doohan, *Luke: The Perennial Spirituality* (Santa Fe: Bear & Co., 1982)— to cite but one example from scores of entries. See in particular the Michael Glazier series on different biblical books "for spiritual reading."

20. Stephen C. Barton, *The Spirituality of the Gospels* (London: SPCK, 1992).

The discipline of the historical study of spirituality also continues apace, usually from a vantage point of strong advocacy. As compared with the earlier histories of Pourrat and Bouyer, these works tend to reflect much broader definitions (explicit or implicit) of spirituality, typical of the last three decades that have suffered from the driving impact of philosophical pluralism.[21] Thus in a book on Asian Christian spirituality, the opening address by Samuel Rayan, a Jesuit theologian from India, proposes this definition for spirituality: "To be spiritual is to be ever more open and response-able to reality."[22] Another recent history of spirituality constantly stresses the importance of feminist spirituality and rejoices that Christian spirituality is plural (Orthodox, Catholic, Reformed, whatever) and must become more culturally diverse, even while warning that "in this movement outwards, it is not helpful to be rootless or to wander aimlessly from one spiritual culture to another in search for somewhere to be at home. To enter fruitfully into the unfamiliar one needs a real sense of where one belongs."[23] A recent book on Reformed spirituality includes a breadth of perspectives that many believers in the Reformed tradition would find hard to recognize.[24] Even some recent important works on theology have been heavily influenced by contemporary trends in spirituality.[25] Evangelicals have plunged into this discussion.[26] One recent evangelical writer, after arguing that evangelicals who are ignorant of their own rich heritage of spirituality (he was thinking not least of the Puritans) are in danger of constantly borrowing the forms of other heritages,[27]

---

21. On which see D. A. Carson, "Christian Witness in an Age of Pluralism," in *God and Culture*, ed. D. A. Carson and John D. Woodbridge (Grand Rapids: Eerdmans, 1993), 31–66.

22. Virginia Fabella, Peter K. H. Lee, and David Kwang-Sun Suh, eds., *Asian Christian Spirituality: Reclaiming Traditions* (Maryknoll: Orbis Books, 1992), 22.

23. Philip Sheldrake, *Spirituality and History: Questions of Interpretation and Method* (New York: Crossroad, 1991), esp. 210.

24. Howard L. Rice, *Reformed Spirituality: An Introduction for Believers* (Louisville: Westminster/John Knox, 1991).

25. E.g., Jürgen Moltmann, *The Spirit of Life: A Universal Affirmation* (London: SCM, 1992). Part 1 deals with "Experiences of the Spirit," including a section on the spirituality of Jesus. When Moltmann outlines a "theology of mystical experience," mystical means "the intensity of the experience of God in faith." One reviewer, though deeply appreciative, comments, "The whole is passionate and impressionistic, authentic as a piece of literary art, and curiously unsatisfactory as a rational account of anything in particular" (George Newlands, *Expository Times* 104 [1993]: 148). Of course, some might judge this characteristic to be an advantage.

26. E.g., J. I. Packer and L. Wilkinson, eds., *Alive to God: Studies in Spirituality*, Festschrift for James Houston (Downers Grove: InterVarsity Press, 1992).

27. Alister E. McGrath, *Evangelical Spirituality: Past Glories, Present Hopes, Future Possibilities* (London: St Antholin's Lectureship Charity Trustees, 1993); idem, "Borrowed Spiritualities," *Christianity Today* 37/13 (November 8, 1993): 20–21.

rather strangely insists that the modern pace of life makes it "quite unrealistic" to present Christians with the demand to read the Bible and pray daily.[28] One wonders exactly what one is to learn from the historical highpoints of evangelical spirituality, which were very much rooted in the "spirituality of the Word."

My concern, then, in this survey of spirituality, is to bring to light the implicit and explicit definitions that the literature casts up. Although my survey has been neither deep nor broad, perhaps it has cast up enough evidence for some useful reflection on the problems of definition. In what follows in this next section I wish to articulate a number of inferences from the literature cited about the way "spirituality" as a term is used.

B. Reflections on the Current Use of "Spirituality"

(1) Spirituality is a theological construct. There is no way of getting *direct* access to what is good or bad about spirituality, or about any particular study of spirituality, by appealing to biblical texts that discuss spirituality, because so far as the *term* is concerned, none do.

Moreover, it is not a theological construct whose constituent components are widely agreed. For example, the doctrine of the Trinity is also a theological construct. It may be believed or denied, articulated in a number of ways, set into the fabric of Christian theology and life in quite different arrays; but the substance of the doctrine, not least the array of its basic constituent theological parts, is not under dispute among informed confessional thinkers,[29] however warm and complex the dispute may be when it comes to precise and refined definition and defense of the details. To put the matter another way, however disputed the doctrine of the Trinity may be, all parties know what the dispute is about. By contrast, spirituality is a *person-variable* synthetic theological construct: one must always inquire as to what components enter into the particular construct advocated or assumed by a particular writer, and what components are being left out. Only rarely are such matters made explicit; therefore, readers are constantly trying to infer what theological underpinnings are presupposed.

(2) Because mutually contradictory theologies may undergird these person-variable definitions of spirituality, the degree of real commonality among those working on the topic may be minimal. For example, The Annand

---

28. McGrath, *Evangelical Spirituality*, 13.

29. I add "informed" because I wish to rule out massively *mis*informed caricatures of the doctrine of the Trinity, such as the one held by a fair bit of street-level Islam, viz., that the doctrine teaches that God is made up of three persons, Father, Mary, and Jesus—the first impregnating the second to produce the third.

Center for Spiritual Growth at the Berkeley Divinity School at Yale, according to its brochure, has on its board strong syncretists, liberal Protestants, Catholics, and a Hindu Spiritual Master in the Vedic tradition;[30] its teachers include local Episcopalian charismatics. The fact remains that the different understandings of spirituality represented by different world religions needs careful delineation.[31] The sheer diversity of the implicit theological structures means that the meaning of "spirituality" degenerates into something amorphous like "an experience of the numinous," in which everyone loads "numinous" with that which is right in his or her own eyes. It is presupposed that such experiences of the numinous are a good thing, whatever the numinous consists in. Suddenly spirituality becomes something of a Trojan Horse that introduces the most radical religious pluralism into what is nominally a Christian enterprise.

From a Christian perspective, worship is not only a verb, as Robert Webber likes to remind us,[32] but a transitive verb, and the most important thing about this transitive verb is its direct object. We worship *God*, the God and Father of our Lord Jesus Christ, and all other worship is in some measure idolatrous, however much the gifts of common grace have preserved within such alien worship some insight into spiritual realities. To put the matter another way, not every experience of the numinous, whether understood psychologically and/or as some engagement with the spiritual world, can be properly considered a "spiritual" experience in any New Testament sense. In short, *not all spirituality is spiritual*.

(3) Spirituality may devolve into a technique. By the application of certain disciplines—study, fasting, prayer, self-denial, whatever—one seeks a more intimate experience of the numinous, however the numinous be understood.[33]

The two questions that must then be asked are these: *First*, to what extent are such techniques value-neutral? *Second*, to what extent are they transportable? These are not easy questions about which to give generalizing

---

30. Viz., Pundat Ravi Shankar—though I am told he is no longer on the board. I am grateful to the Reverend J. Ashley Null for bringing this particular instance to my attention.

31. For an attempt to sort out Hindu, Buddhist, and Muslim understandings of spirituality, see the relevant chapters of D. A. Carson, ed., *Teach Us to Pray: Prayer in the Bible and the World* (Exeter: Paternoster, 1990).

32. Robert E. Webber, *Worship Is a Verb* (Waco: Word Books, 1987).

33. Thus in a recent book by Janet O. Hagberg and Robert A. Guelich, *The Critical Journey: Stages in the Life of Faith* (Dallas: Word Books, 1989), the authors manage to talk about "spirituality" without wrestling with sin, guilt, forgiveness, or the unique place of Jesus Christ. Their text focuses on personal experience, self-analysis, gifts, self-acceptance, and the like.

answers, though it is fairly easy to think up examples that illustrate quite different problems. Consider four examples.

(a) Part of spirituality (in this sense of technique and discipline) for the educated Hindu will be the careful reading of the *Vedas* and other Hindu scriptures. How well can that be transported to, say, evangelical Christianity? Is not the actual reading of sacred texts, or texts perceived to be sacred, value-neutral?

As a Christian, I would respond by saying that at one level the Hindu example can be transported to Christianity fairly well. Of course, what is read is different: our Scriptures are not their scriptures. Nevertheless, we would surely want to tie Christian spirituality to the thoughtful reading of the Bible. So I suppose it could be said that this practice, this technique, is transportable. But what, exactly, is being transported? If it is something like "the reading of texts perceived to be sacred," then although the practice is transportable, it is *not* value-neutral. For there are many texts that are perceived to be sacred that are not, from my perspective, anything of the kind—including the *Book of Mormon* and the *Bhagavad Gita*. I deny, therefore, that the reading of texts perceived to be sacred is inherently a good thing; I deny that the act is value-neutral. It is merely the mechanical art of *reading* that is value-neutral—which is surely not saying very much.

(b) Suppose, then, I turn to the breathing and concentration exercises connected with *yoga*. How well can they be transported to Christianity? And are they value-neutral?

At one level, surely the breathing exercises are intrinsically value-neutral: one learns a slightly different set in preparation for natural childbirth. But the association of certain breathing exercises with concentration on a black dot on an expanse of white, coupled with the chanting of mantras in order to achieve a state of dissociation associated with achieving a higher state of "spirituality," is something else. How much of that is transportable to Christianity? Not very much; certainly not the chanting of mantras, still less the kind of meditation that is characterized by concentration on a spot on a blank expanse. I suppose certain breathing and relaxation exercises that help some uptight people to relax are unobjectionable; and if the purpose of such relaxation were to enable the person to concentrate in meditation and prayer on the Bible, I suppose this could be labeled part of a technique for growing in Christian spirituality. But it is getting pretty far removed: it is more like a technique in preparation for the discipline that could then genuinely be labeled Christian, rather than an exercise in "spirituality" *per se*.

(c) Consider the Lord's Supper, holy communion. Is participation by a genuine Christian always a good thing? Surely if any spiritual discipline is not value-neutral, this is it, isn't it? But is it transportable?

Once again, the answers are not as simple as one might like. Surely nothing of significance here is transportable. True, some other religions have rituals of eating, but all of the associations connected with the Lord's Supper are quite radically unlike the eating rituals of other religions. The naked act of eating may be value-neutral, but the Lord's Supper is not a naked act of eating.

Nor is participation, even by genuine believers, always a good thing. For many of the problems in the Corinthian church Paul has a sort of "Yes, but" answer: "*Yes*, it is good for a man not to touch a woman, *but* since there is so much immorality, each man should have his own wife" (cf. 1 Cor. 7:1–2); "*Yes*, an idol is nothing at all in this world, *but* not everyone knows this" (cf. 1 Cor. 8:4, 7); and so on. But with respect to the Lord's Supper, Paul writes, "In the following directives I have no praise for you, for your meetings do more harm than good" (1 Cor. 11:17). This is not, it transpires, because the celebration of the Lord's Supper becomes an intrinsically evil act, but because relationships within the congregation are selfish and thoughtless, and the sin is both unconfessed and unrecognized. So here we have a spiritual discipline that is not value-neutral (it is surely intrinsically good), not transportable, but can become thoroughly bad, not on intrinsic grounds but because of sins in the congregation.

(d) What about various vows of self-denial practiced by medieval monastics? Can they be transported? Are they value-free, so that they can be detached from medieval Catholicism?

Certainly our generation could do with some self-discipline. We remember, for example, Paul's determination in 1 Corinthians 9:24–27, and we are ashamed of our sloth and indolence. But vows of chastity are not something that a married believer should undertake, unless it is in agreement with one's spouse, for a strictly limited period, and in order to set aside time for prayer (1 Cor. 7:5). A vow of chastity undertaken by a celibate person might be a good thing, but not if it is merely a frustrating attempt to suppress lust (1 Cor. 7:9). Vows of poverty or relative poverty might be entirely salutary in this hedonistic and profligate age, but they might also prompt pride or foster merit theology. What about vows of silence? Some quiet in our noisy, self-expressive age would surely be a good thing. But how easily can, say, the Trappist vows of silence undertaken by Thomas Merton be disassociated from his deepening devotion to Mary as the Mother of God? How about self-flagellation? Can it have any place whatsoever in a system of thought that has truly grasped the freedom of the grace of God provided in the death and resurrection of his Son Jesus Christ? How intrinsically is it tied to medieval notions of elitist perfectionism not open to ordinary Christians?

In short, one cannot assume approaches to spirituality that are little more than discussions of technique, as if there were no hidden shoals to avoid.

C. Some Priorities for Christians

Since I write out of evangelical convictions, the following brief points frankly reflect those commitments, though of course I cannot here defend them. Moreover, the few points I make here are rather more in the nature of priming the pump than of majesterial articulation: almost every item could do with a lengthy chapter.

My fear is that many charismatics and, increasingly, many noncharismatic evangelicals, having emerged from the shadows of a fairly narrow, parochial heritage into the broader streams of church history, are in danger of over-compensating and taking on board almost anything, provided it falls under the rubric "spirituality" (applause!). Yet at the same time, there is much to learn about spiritual life, as about theology, from many of those with whom we disagree. If spirituality, with all its intellectual fuzziness, is not to become the new *summum bonum* by which all things are to be tested, but must itself be brought to the test of Holy Scripture, what priorities can help us preserve a healthy perspective without retreating into entrenched traditionalism?

(1) Spirituality must be thought of *in connection with the gospel.* There may be some heuristic and historical value in conceiving of spirituality in purely neutral terms ("the experience of the numinous, and the study of such experience," or the like), but from a confessional, Christian perspective it is worse than useless: it is dangerous. To put matters bluntly, if the gospel is true, what will be the value, fifty billion years from now, of spending time in this life meditating on a black spot on a white expanse while chanting mantras?[34] Questions as to the nature of spirituality, the purpose of the putative experience of the transcendent, the nature of the God who is the ultimate source of the experience, the locus of the revelation he has given of himself, and the techniques and forms by which we may ostensibly know him better, must be brought to the test of the gospel. For it is the gospel that is the power of God unto salvation; it is by faith in God's Son that we know the Father; it is by the cross and resurrection that we who were alienated from God have been reconciled to our Maker, Judge, and Redeemer.

(2) Christian reflection on spirituality must work outward from the center. During the past twenty years or so there has been a quite frightening tendency to assume the center without really being able to articulate much about it, and then to gravitate to the periphery. Indeed, the tendency has been to focus on some element on the periphery that then attracts our passion, inter-

---

34. I am sure my friends who are devoted to syncretism and philosophical pluralism will be suitably aghast at this point and dismiss my stance as ignorant hubris. In current literature, however, there is more hubris (not to mention cultural bias) attached to the absolute proposition that no religion *can* take precedence over another in its claims to truth.

est, time. It is not that Christians should avoid thinking through the changing agendas on the periphery: we must. But if all our time and passion are devoted to abortion, styles of worship, women's ordination, church government, counseling techniques, the latest sociology report, or the best advertised marriage seminar, largely detached from the core of biblical theology, then sooner or later the periphery is in danger of displacing the core—at least in our affections and energy, and perhaps in our theology (or that of our children).

So it is with spirituality. If spirituality becomes an end in itself, detached from the core, and largely without biblical or theological norms to define it and anchor it in the objective gospel, then pursuit of spirituality, however nebulously defined, will degenerate into nothing more than the pursuit of certain kinds of experience.[35] I must reiterate that I am not for that reason writing off all pursuit of all forms of spirituality: I shall say more about that in my next point. But *spirituality must be thought about and sought after out of the matrix of core biblical theology.*[36]

(3) At the same time we should be rightly suspicious of forms of theology that place all the emphasis on coherent systems of thought that demand faith, allegiance, and obedience, but do not engage the affections, let alone foster an active sense of the presence of God. If the kingdom of God has to do with "righteousness, peace and joy in the Holy Spirit" (Rom. 14:17), we must not reduce it to righteousness and systems of thought. The Spirit whom Jesus bequeathed to his followers is the Spirit announced as part of the newness of the new covenant (Ezek. 36/John 3; Joel 2/Acts 2): not only does he convict the world (John 16), he lives in believers (Rom. 8:9), leading them (v. 14) and testifying with their spirit that they are God's children (v. 16).

This is not at all to suggest that the experience of the presence of the transcendent/personal God of the Bible should ever be considered as something entirely apart from holy living, self-discipline, love for others, solemn and enthusiastic praise, hatred of sin, conformity to Christ, ongoing confession and repentance, growth in understanding God's Word, and more. It is to say that there is a certain kind of evangelicalism that tries to think of these *as discrete factors divorced from any experience of the Spirit.* The Spirit becomes

---

35. It is at this juncture that I sometimes have misgivings about some of the priorities of Henri J. M. Nouwen—from whom, nevertheless, there is much to be learned. See, for example, his *Life of the Beloved: Spiritual Living in a Secular World* (New York: Crossroad, 1993). His popularity *across almost all confessional lines* is, I think, possible precisely because his attractive emphasis on spirituality is not very well anchored in the gospel.

36. Cf. Gordon R. Lewis, "God's Word: Key to Authentic Spirituality," in *A Call to Christian Character*, ed. Bruce Shelley (Grand Rapids: Zondervan, 1970), 105–20; Alister E. McGrath, *Spirituality in an Age of Change: Rediscovering the Spirit of the Reformers* (Grand Rapids: Zondervan, 1994).

a credal item, no more. Sometimes this stance is simply an overreaction to the obvious excesses of the charismatic movement. But whatever its cause, it stands against both Scripture and the entire heritage of the best of Christianity, where men and women, by God's grace, *know God*. True, that knowledge of God, mediated by the Spirit, is concomitant with the things I have just listed, and more besides; but it is *real knowledge of the living God*, not a mere mental image (like a mental image of, say, Peter Pan) that serves no real purpose other than to order the system of thought we call theology.

Certainly in times of revival (I use the term in its historic sense, not in one or more of its modern, degenerate senses), but at other times as well, Christians have known the presence of God so powerfully that they walk before him with a holy reverence and a genuine, persistent acknowledgement of his majesty and grace that is life-transforming. If the knowledge of the true God and of his Son Jesus Christ whom he has sent *means* eternal life (John 17:3), we must examine very carefully what the knowledge of God really is, and embrace it wholly. If such life-transforming knowledge of God lies at the focus of what is meant by "spirituality," which then stands over against a merely traditional adherence to a creed, no matter how orthodox that creed, then let us stress spirituality.

(4) Nevertheless, what God uses to foster this kind of gospel spirituality must be carefully delineated. Only God himself gives life; it is God who discloses himself, not only in the great acts of redemptive history, but by his Spirit to "natural" men and women (1 Cor. 2:14) who do not have the Spirit of God and cannot understand the things of God. He "reveals" himself to Christians who mature and take on a biblical view of things (Phil. 3:15). But normally God uses means. What are they?

It is precisely at this point that evangelicals need to reclaim their heritage. People speak of the spirituality of sacraments, or the spirituality of poverty, or the spirituality of silence. It is true that God may become very real to his people in the context of poverty; it is true that the corporate celebration of the Lord's Supper may be a time of self-examination, confession, forgiveness, joy in the Holy Spirit. There are many means of grace. But perhaps the most important means of grace—certainly the means of grace almost entirely unmentioned in current publication on spirituality—is the Word of God.

On the night he was betrayed, Jesus prayed, "Sanctify them by the truth; your word is truth" (John 17:17)—and there will never be much sanctification apart from the Word of Truth. It is the entrance of God's Word that brings light; it is constant meditation on God's law that distinguishes the wise from the unwise, the just from the unjust (Ps. 1). I do not deny that certain kinds of Bible study can be singularly arid, skeptical, merely formal, just as certain approaches to the Lord's Supper may do more harm than good (1 Cor. 11:17ff.). But the heavy stress in Scripture on understanding, absorbing, meditating upon, proclaiming, memorizing ("hiding it in one's heart"), reading, and hearing the Word of God is so striking that it will be ignored at our peril. That is why the best of the evangelical heritage has always emphasized what might be called "the spirituality of the Word."

It is within this framework that other "techniques," rightly deployed, may be of some value. If self-denial is merely an attempt to commend ourselves to God, or a way of feeling good about oneself (which feeling we then mistake for being spiritual), it is positively dangerous. But if self-denial is part of our response of gratitude and faith to the God who has manifested the greatest self-denial of all in the death of his Son, and if it thus aids our concentration on his Word, our obedience of it, and our delight in it, then it is surely a good thing that will foster spiritual growth. One may evaluate most of the proffered "techniques" with the same Word-centered perspective: journaling, quiet days, accountability/prayer groups, and so forth.

(5) Finally, such Word-centered reflection will bring us back to the fact that spirituality, as we have seen, is a theological construct. We will be forced to revise our construct in terms of what we find in the Scriptures. If spirituality is related to the knowledge of God by his Spirit, then the experience of genuine spirituality must be tied to what it means to have the Spirit. In one sense, then, all those who by God's grace exercise saving faith in Christ Jesus have the Spirit (Rom. 8:9) and are "spiritual" (1 Cor. 2:14–15). But then we are to "live by the Spirit" (Gal. 5:16), and that means self-consciously putting to death the "acts of sinful nature" and producing the "fruit of the Spirit": there is a profoundly moral and ethical dimension to spirituality. The Spirit is also the one who enables and empowers believers to testify about Jesus (John 15:26–27; Acts 4:8; etc.): there is a kerygmatic dimension to spirituality. The Spirit is the ἀρραβών, the downpayment and guarantee of the promised inheritance: there is an eschatological dimension to spirituality, as the bride, the church, joins the Spirit in crying, "Come, Lord Jesus!" (Rev. 22). And so we could go on, adding dimensions to any construct of spirituality controlled by the Word of God, correcting ourselves and our experience by Scripture, so that we may enjoy the fullness of the heritage that is ours in Christ Jesus, while remaining entirely unwilling to be seduced by every passing fad. Only then shall we approximate an all-of-life approach to spirituality—every aspect of human existence, personal and corporate, brought under the discipline of the Word of God, brought under the *consciousness* that we live in the presence of God, by his grace and for his glory. We shall cry to God that all our expressions of spirituality may be truly spiritual.

Selected Bibliography

(NB: With but a few exceptions, this bibliography contains only works cited in this book. Where an essay in a volume of essays is listed under its author's name, the book itself may have a separate listing if there are other essays in the collection that are worth reading in connection with this subject, whether or not they have been cited in this work.)

Abraham, William J. *The Logic of Evangelism*. Grand Rapids: Eerdmans, 1989.
_____. "A Theology of Evangelism: The Heart of the Matter." *Interpretation* 48 (1994): 117–30.
Achtemeier, Paul J. *The Inspiration of Scripture: Problems and Proposals*. Philadelphia: Westminster, 1980.
Adams, William C., et al. *The Williamsburg Charter Survey on Religion and Public Life*. Washington: Williamsburg Charter Foundation, 1988.
Adler, Mortimer J., and Charles Van Doren. *How to Read a Book*. New York: Simon & Schuster, 1972 [1940].
Albertz, Rainer. *Religionsgeschichte Israels in alttestamentlicher Zeit*. Grundrisse zum Alten Testament. Göttingen: Vandenhoeck & Ruprecht, 1992.
Aldwinckle, Russell F. *Jesus—A Savior or the Savior? Religious Pluralism in Christian Perspective*. Macon: Mercer University Press, 1982.
_____. *More Than a Man: A Study in Christology*. Grand Rapids: Eerdmans, 1976.
Allen, Diogenes. "The End of the Modern World." *Christian Scholars Review* 22 (1993): 339–47.
Allison, C. FitzSimons. *The Cruelty of Heresy: An Affirmation of Christian Orthodoxy*. London: SPCK, 1994.
Allison, Kirk. "Blind-Sight? The Controversy Concerning the Early Belgian Writings of Paul de Man." 1988.
Almond, Brenda. "New Occasions Teach New Duties? 3. Seven Moral Myths." *Expository Times* 105 (1994): 164–67.
Almond, Philip C. *Heaven and Hell in Enlightenment England*. Cambridge: Cambridge University Press, 1994.
Andersen, Francis J. "Yahweh, the Kind and Sensitive God." In *God Who Is Rich in Mercy*. Festschrift for D. Broughton Knox. Edited by Peter T. O'Brien and David G. Peterson, 41–88. Homebush West: Anzea, 1986.
Anderson, Gerald H., and Thomas F. Stransky. *Third World Theologies*. Mission Trends, vol. 3. New York/Grand Rapids: Paulist/Eerdmans, 1976.
_____, eds. *Christ's Lordship and Religious Pluralism*. Maryknoll: Orbis Books, 1981.
_____, eds. *Faith Meets Faith*. Mission Trends, vol. 5. Grand Rapids: Eerdmans, 1981.
Anderson, Leith. *A Church for the 21st Century*. Minneapolis: Bethany House, 1992.
_____. *Dying for Change: An Arresting Look at the New Realities Confronting Churches and Para-church Ministries*. Minneapolis: Bethany House, 1990.

Anderson, Norman. *Christianity and World Religions: The Challenge of Pluralism*. Downers Grove: InterVarsity Press, 1984.

Anderson, Robert. *Human Destiny: After Death—What?* London: Pickering & Inglis, 1913.

Anthony, Dick, and Thomas Robbins. "Culture Crisis and Contemporary Religion." In *In Gods We Trust: New Patterns of Religious Pluralism in America*. Edited by Thomas Robbins and Dick Anthony, 9–31. New Brunswick: Transaction Books, 1981.

Aquinas, Saint Thomas. *Summa Contra Gentiles*. Translated and edited by Anton C. Pegis. Notre Dame: University of Notre Dame Press, 1975.

Arendt, Hannah. *The Origins of Totalitarianism*. 2d ed. Cleveland: World Publishing Company, Meridian, 1958.

Ariaraja, S. Wesley. *The Bible and People of Other Faiths*. Maryknoll: Orbis Books, 1989.

————. *The Bible and People of Other Faiths*. Geneva: World Council of Churches, 1989.

Arnold, Clinton E. *Ephesians: Power and Magic—the Concept of Power in Ephesians in Light of Its Historical Setting*. SNTSMS, vol. 63. Cambridge: Cambridge University Press, 1989.

Arnold, Matthew. "Literature and Science." In *Prose of the Victorian Period*. Edited by William E. Buckler, 486–501. Boston: Houghton Mifflin, 1958.

Atallah, Ramez. "The Objective Witness to Conscience: An Egyptian Parallel to Romans 2:15." *Evangelical Review of Theology* 18 (1994): 204–13.

Austin, J. L. *How To Do Things with Words*. Cambridge: Harvard University Press, 1975.

Bahnsen, Greg L. *No Other Standard: Theonomy and Its Critics*. Tyler: Institute for Christian Economics, 1991.

Balch, David L. "The Areopagus Speech: An Appeal to the Stoic Historian Posidonius Against Later Stoics and the Epicureans." In *Greeks, Romans, and Christians*. Festschrift for Abraham J. Malherbe. Edited by David L. Balch, Everett Ferguson, and Wayne A. Meeks, 52–79. Minneapolis: Fortress Press, 1990.

Ball, William Bentley, ed. *In Search of National Morality: A Manifesto for Evangelicals and Catholics*. Grand Rapids/San Francisco: Baker/Ignatius Press, 1992.

Balmer, Randall. *Mine Eyes Have Seen the Glory: A Journey Into the Evangelical Subculture in America*. New York: Oxford University Press, 1989.

Barbour, Ian G. *Religion in an Age of Science: The Gifford Lectures*. San Francisco: HarperCollins, 1990.

Barbour, R. S., ed. *The Kingdom of God and Human Society*. Edinburgh: T & T Clark, 1993.

Barclay, William. *A Spiritual Autobiography*. Grand Rapids: Eerdmans, 1975.

Barker, Margaret. *The Great Angel: A Study of Israel's Second God*. London/Louisville: SPCK/Westminster John Knox, 1992.

Barker, William S., and W. Robert Godfrey, eds. *Theonomy: A Reformed Critique*. Grand Rapids: Zondervan, 1990.

Barna, George. *Church Marketing: Breaking Ground for the Harvest*. Ventura: Regal, 1992.

————. *The Invisible Generation: Baby Busters*. Glendale: Barna Research Group, 1992.

————. *What Americans Believe: An Annual Survey of Values and Religious Views in the United States*. Ventura: Regal Books, 1991.

Barnes, Michael. *Religions in Conversation: Christian Identity and Christian Pluralism*. London: SPCK, 1989.

Barnett, Paul. *The Two Faces of Jesus*. Sydney/London/ Toronto: Hodder & Stoughton, 1990.

Barnhart, Joe Edward, and Mary Ann Barnhart. *The New Birth: A Naturalistic View of Religious Conversion*. Macon: Mercer University Press, 1981.

Barr, James. *Biblical Faith and Natural Theology*. Gifford Lectures (1991). Oxford: Clarendon Press, 1993.

Barrett, C. K. "Paul's Speech on the Areopagus." In *New Testament Christianity for Africa and the World*. Edited by M. E. Glasswell and E. W. Fasholé-Luke, 69–75. London: SPCK, 1974.

Barron, Bruce. *Heaven on Earth? The Social and Political Agendas of Dominion Theology*. Grand Rapids: Zondervan, 1992.

Barth, Karl. *The Göttingen Dogmatics: Instruction in Christian Religion*. Edited by Hannelotte Reiffen. Translated by Geoffrey W. Bromiley, vol. 1. Grand Rapids: Eerdmans, 1991.

Barton, John. *People of the Book? The Authority of the Bible in Christianity*. London: SPCK, 1988.

_____. *What Is the Bible?* London: SPCK, 1991.

Bastide, Roger. *Applied Anthropology*. Translated by Alice L. Morton. New York: Harper Torchbooks, 1973.

Bauckham, Richard. *The Bible in Politics: How to Read the Bible Politically*. Louisville: Westminster/John Knox, 1989.

Bauckham, Richard J. "Universalism: A Historical Survey." *Themelios* 4, no. 2 (1979): 48–54.

Bauer, Walter. *Orthodoxy and Heresy in Earliest Christianity*. Translated by Philadelphia Seminar on Christian Origins. Appendices by Georg Strecker. Edited by Robert A. Kraft and Gerhard Krodel. Philadelphia: Fortress Press, 1971.

Bauman, Michael. "Jesus, Anarchy and Marx: The Theological and Political Contours of Ellulism." *Journal of the Evangelical Theological Society* 35 (1992): 199–216.

Baxter, Michael J. *Let's Do Away with "Faith" and "History": A Critique of H. Richard Niebuhr's False Antinomies*. Wheaton College Philosophy Conference, 1993.

Bayfield, Tony. "Mission—A Jewish Perspective." *Theology* 96 (1993): 180–90.

Bayle, Martha. *Hole in the Soul: The Loss of Beauty and Meaning in American Popular Music*. New York: The Free Press, 1994.

Bayly, Joseph. *Out of My Mind*. Wheaton: Tyndale House, 1970.

Bebbington, D. W. *Evangelicalism in Modern Britain: A History from the 1780s to the 1980s*. London/Grand Rapids: Unwin Hyman/Baker, 1988/1992.

Bebbington, David. *Patterns in History: A Christian Perspective on Historical Thought*. 2d ed. Grand Rapids: Baker, 1990 [1979].

Beck, Norman A. *Mature Christianity in the 21st Century: The Recognition and Repudiation of the Anti-Jewish Polemic of the New Testament*. 2d ed. New York: Crossroad, 1994 [1985].

Becker, Ernest. *The Denial of Death*. New York: The Free Press, 1977.

Bediako, Kwame. "Cry Jesus! Christian Theology and Presence in Modern Africa." *Vox Evangelica* 23 (1993): 7–25.

_____. *Theology and Identity: The Impact of Culture Upon Christian Thought in the Second Century and Modern Africa*. Regnum Books / Lynx Communications, 1992.

Beker, J. Christiaan. *The Triumph of God: The Essence of Paul's Thought*. Translated by Loren T. Stuckenbruck. Minneapolis: Fortress Press, 1990.

Bellah, Robert N. *Beyond Belief: Essays on Religion in a Post-Traditionalist World*. Berkeley: University of California Press, 1970 [1967].

Bellah, Robert N., Richard Madsen, William M. Sullivan, Ann Swidler, and Steven M. Tipton. *The Good Society*. New York: Vintage Press, 1992.

_____. *Habits of the Heart: Individualism and Commitment in American Life*. New York: Harper & Row, Perennial Library, 1985.

Bennett, James T., and Thomas J. DiLorenzo. *Destroying Democracy: How Government Funds Partisan Politics*. Washington, D.C.: Cato Institute, 1985.

Berger, Peter. *The Sacred Canopy: Elements of a Sociological Theory of Religion*. Garden City: Doubleday, 1967.

Berger, Peter L. "Different Gospels: The Social Sources of Apostasy." In *American Apostasy: The Triumph of "Other" Gospels*. Edited by Richard John Neuhaus, 1–14. Grand Rapids: Eerdmans, 1989.

————. *A Rumor of Angels: Modern Society and the Rediscovery of the Supernatural*. Garden City: Anchor, 1970 [1969].

Berger, Peter L., and Thomas Luckmann. *The Social Construction of Reality: A Treatise in the Sociology of Knowledge*. Garden City: Doubleday, Anchor, 1967.

Bergman, Jerry. "Censorship in Secular Science: The Mims Case." *Perspectives on Science and Faith* 45, no. 1 (1993): 37–45.

Berkouwer, G. C. *The Return of Christ*. Grand Rapids: Eerdmans, 1972.

Bernhardt, Reinhold. *Christianity Without Absolutes*. London: SCM Press, 1994.

Bernstein, Alan E. *The Formation of Hell: Death and Retribution in the Ancient and Early Christian Worlds*. London: University College London Press, 1993.

Bernstein, Richard J. *Beyond Objectivism and Relativism: Science, Hermeneutics, and Praxis*. Philadelphia: University of Pennsylvania Press, 1983.

Berry, Philippa, and Andrew Wernick, eds. *Shadow of Spirit: Postmodernism and Religion*. London: Routledge, 1993.

Best, Ernest. *Interpreting Christ*. Edinburgh: T & T Clark, 1993.

Bishop, Steve. "Green Theology and Deep Ecology: New Age or New Creation?" *Themelios* 16, no. 3 (1991): 8–14.

————. "Science and Faith: Boa Constrictors and Warthogs?" *Themelios* 19, no. 1 (1993): 4–9.

Blackstone, William T. *The Problem of Religious Knowledge*. Englewood Cliffs: Prentice-Hall, 1963.

Blanchard, John. *Whatever Happened to Hell?* Durham: Evangelical Press, 1993.

Bleicher, Joseph. *The Hermeneutic Imagination: Outline of a Positive Critique of Scientism and Sociology*. London: Routledge & Kegan Paul, 1982.

Bloch-Smith, Elizabeth. "The Cult of the Dead in Judah: Interpreting the Material Remains." *Journal of Biblical Literature* 111 (1992): 213–24.

Blocher, Henri. "Everlasting Punishment and the Problem of Evil." In *Universalism and the Doctrine of Hell*. Edited by Nigel M. de S. Cameron, 283–312. Carlisle: Paternoster Press, 1992.

————. "The Scope of Redemption and Modern Theology." *Scottish Bulletin of Evangelical Theology* 9 (1991): 80–103.

Bloesch, Donald G. "'All Israel Will Be Saved': Supersessionism and the Biblical Witness." *Interpretation* 43 (1989): 130–42.

Blomberg, Craig. *The Historical Reliability of the Gospels*. Leicester: Inter-Varsity Press, 1987.

Bloom, Allan. *The Closing of the American Mind: How Higher Education Has Failed Democracy and Impoverished the Souls of Today's Students*. New York: Simon & Schuster, 1988.

Bock, Darrell L. "Athenians Who Have Never Heard." In *Through No Fault of Their Own?* Edited by William V. Crockett and James G. Sigountos, 117–24. Grand Rapids: Baker, 1991.

Bockmuehl, Klaus. *The Unreal God of Modern Theology: Bultmann, Barth and the Theology of Atheism: A Call to Recovering the Truth of God's Reality*. Translated by G. Bromiley. Colorado Springs: Helmers and Howard, 1988.

Bockmuehl, Markus. "Public Ethics in a Pluralistic Society? Lessons from the Early Church." *Crux* 28, no. 3 (1992): 2–9.

Bockmuehl, Markus N. A. *This Jesus: Martyr, Lord, Messiah*. Edinburgh: T & T Clark, 1994.

Boer, Harry R. *Pentecost and Missions*. Grand Rapids: Eerdmans, 1961.

Bolt, John. "Some Reflections on Church and World, Worship and Evangelism." *Calvin Theological Journal* 27 (1992): 96–101.

Bonhoeffer, Dietrich. *The Cost of Discipleship*. Rev. ed. New York: Macmillan, 1963.

Bonk, Jonathan J. "Globalization and Mission Education." *Theological Education* 30 (1993): 47–94.

Boone, Kathleen C. *The Bible Tells Them So: The Discourse of Protestant Fundamentalism*. Albany: State University of New York Press, 1989.

Booth, Wayne C. *Critical Understanding: The Powers and Limits of Pluralism*. Chicago: University of Chicago Press, 1979.

Boring, E. Eugene. "The Language of Universal Salvation in Paul." *Journal of Biblical Literature* 105 (1986): 269–92.

Bosch, David J. *Transforming Mission—Paradigm Shifts in Theology of Mission*. Maryknoll: Orbis Books, 1991.

Boyd, Jonathan A. T. "'Thy Pious Heart Wilt Deeply Feel': Providence and Historical Consciousness in Antebellum American-History Schoolbooks." Baltimore: The Johns Hopkins University, 1992.

Braaten, Carl E. *No Other Gospel! Christianity Among the World's Religions*. Minneapolis: Fortress Press, 1992.

_____. "The Uniqueness and Universality of Jesus Christ." In Mission Trends, vol. 5: *Faith Meets Faith*. Edited by Gerald H. Anderson and Thomas F. Stransky, 69–8919. Grand Rapids: Eerdmans, 1981.

Bradford, M. E. *Founding Fathers: Brief Lives of the Framers of the the United States Constitution*. 2d ed. Lawrence: University Press of Kansas, 1994 [1981].

Bradley, James E., and Richard A. Muller, eds. *Church, Word, and Spirit: Historical and Theological Essays*. Festschrift for Geoffrey W. Bromiley. Grand Rapids: Eerdmans, 1987.

Brattston, David. "Hades, Hell and Purgatory in Ante-Nicene Christianity." *Churchman* 108 (1994): 69–79.

Bray, Gerald. "Hell: Eternal Punishment or Total Annihilation?" *Evangel* 10 (1992): 19–24.

Bray, Gerald L. *Creeds, Councils and Christ*. Downers Grove: InterVarsity Press, 1984.

Braybrooke, Marcus. *Time to Meet: Towards a Deeper Relationship Between Jews and Christians*. London: SCM Press, 1990.

Brearley, Margaret. "Matthew Fox and the Cosmic Christ." *Anvil* 9 (1992): 39–54.

Brennan, John Patrick. *Christian Mission in a Pluralistic World*. Slough, England/Wilton, CT: St. Paul Publications/Morehouse Publishing, 1990.

Briner, Bob. *Roaring Lambs: A Gentle Plan To Radically Change Our World*. Grand Rapids: Zondervan, 1993.

Bromiley, Geoffrey W. "Eschatology: The Meaning of the End." In *God and Culture*. Festschrift for Carl F. H. Henry. Edited by D. A. Carson and John D. Woodbridge, 67–84. Grand Rapids: Eerdmans, 1993.

Bronowski, J. *Science and Human Values*. Rev. ed. New York: Harper Torchbooks/Perennial Library, 1972.

Brown, Colin. *Christianity and Western Thought: A History of Philosophers, Ideas and Movements*. Vol. 1. *From the Ancient World to the Age of Enlightenment*. Downers Grove: InterVarsity Press, 1990.

Brown, Frank Burch. "The Beauty of Hell: Anselm on God's Eternal Design." *The Journal of Religion* 73 (1993): 329–56.

Brown, Harold O. J. "Darwin on Display." *The Religion and Society Report* 8 (December 1991): 1–4.

————. "Our Chosen Tyranny, or The Illusions of Democracy." *The Religion & Society Report* 11 (July 1994): 4–6.

Brown, J. Dickson. "Barton, Brooks, and Childs: A Comparison of the New Criticism and Canonical Criticism." *Journal of the Evangelical Theological Society* 36 (1993): 481–89.

Brown, Sue. "Patterns of Worship Among Students Worldwide." In *Worship: Adoration and Action.* Edited by D. A. Carson, 189–200. Grand Rapids: Baker, 1993.

Browning, Don, ed. *Habermas, Modernity, and Public Theology.* New York: Crossroad, 1992.

Bruce, F. F. *The Acts of the Apostles: Greek Text with Introduction and Commentary.* 3d ed. Grand Rapids: Eerdmans 1990.

————. *The New Testament Documents—Are They Reliable?* 5th ed. Grand Rapids: Eerdmans, 1982.

Brueggemann, Walter. *The Bible and Post-Modern Imagination: Texts Under Negotiation.* London: SCM Press, 1993.

————. "A Gospel Language of Pain and Possibility." *Horizons in Biblical Theology* 13 (1991): 95–133.

————. "The Prophetic Word and History." *Interpretation* 48 (1994): 239–51.

————. *Texts Under Negotiation: The Bible and Postmodern Imagination.* Minneapolis: Fortress Press, 1993.

Brümmer, Vincent. *The Model of Love: A Study in Philosophical Theology.* Cambridge: Cambridge University Press, 1993.

Brunner, Emil. *Eternal Hope.* Edinburgh: Lutterworth Press, 1954.

————. *The Mediator: A Study of the Central Doctrine of the Christian Faith.* Translated by Olive Wyon. Philadelphia: Westminster Press, 1947.

Buckley, William F., Jr. *God and Man at Yale: The Superstitions of "Academic Freedom."* Washington: Regnery Gateway, 1986 [1951].

Bultmann, Rudolf. *Jesus and the Word.* Translated by Louise Pettibone Smith and Erminie Huntress Lantero. New York: Scribner's, 1958.

————. *Jesus Christ and Mythology.* New York: Scribner's, 1958.

Burbidge, Geoffrey. "Why Only One Big Bang?" *Scientific American* 226, no. 2 (1992): 120.

Burkhardt, Helmut. "Jesus und die Götter—Synkretismus Einst und Jetzt." *European Journal of Theology* 2 (1993): 31–38.

Burnside, Jonathan, and Nicola Baker, eds. *Relational Justice: Repairing the Breach.* Winchester: Waterside Press, 1994.

Burtt, Edwin Arthur. *The Metaphysical Foundations of Modern Physical Science.* Garden City: Doubleday, Doubleday Anchor, 1954 [1952].

Bury, J. B. *The Idea of Progress: An Inquiry Into Its Origin and Growth.* With an introduction by Charles A. Berad. New York: Dover Publications, Inc., 1955.

Butler, Jon. *Awash in a Sea of Faith: Christianizing the American People.* Cambridge: Harvard University Press, 1990.

Butler, Jonathan M. *Softly and Tenderly Jesus Is Calling: Heaven and Hell in American Revivalism, 1870–1920.* Brooklyn: Carlson, 1991.

Butterfield, H. *The Origins of Modern Science 1300–1800.* New York: Macmillan, 1960.

Calver, Clive. "Red Herrings and Hot Potatoes: The Real Issues for Evangelicals Today." *Vox Evangelica* 24 (1994): 42–54.

Cameron, Nigel M. de S. "Bioethics and the Challenge of the Post-Consensus Society." *Ethics and Medicine* 11, no. 1 (1995): 1–7.

————. "Perspectives on Religious Pluralism." *Scottish Bulletin of Evangelical Theology* 10, no. 2 (1992): 79.

_____. "Universalism and the Logic of Revelation." *Evangelical Review of Theology* 11 (1987): 321–35.

Campbell, William S. *Paul's Gospel in an Intercultural Context*. Frankfurt-am-Main: Peter Lang, 1991.

Canavan, Francis, S.J. "Pluralism and the Limits of Neutrality." In *Whose Values? The Battle for Morality in Pluralistic America*. Edited by Carl Horn, 153–65. Ann Arbor: Servant Books, 1985.

Capps, Walter H. *The New Religious Right: Piety, Patriotism, and Politics*. Columbia: University of South Carolina Press, 1990.

Capra, Fritjof. *The Tao of Physics*. London: Flamingo, 1986.

_____. *The Turning Point*. London: Flamingo, 1985.

Carey, John. *The Intellectuals and the Masses: Pride and Prejudice Among the Literary Intelligentsia, 1880–1939*. New York: St. Martin's Press, 1993.

Carr, David. "The Politics of Textual Subversion: A Diachronic Perspective on the Garden of Eden Story." *Journal of Biblical Literature* 112 (1993): 577–95.

Carrier, Hervé, S.J. *Evangelizing the Culture of Modernity*. Maryknoll: Orbis Books, 1993.

Carroll, M. Daniel. "Context, Bible and Ethics: A Latin American Perspective." *Themelios* 19, no. 3 (1994): 9–15.

Carroll, Robert P. *Wolf in the Sheepfold: The Bible as a Problem for Christianity*. London: SPCK, 1991.

Carson, D. A. "Christian Witness in an Age of Pluralism." In *God and Culture*. Festschrift for Carl F. H. Henry. Edited by D. A. Carson and John D. Woodbridge, 31–66. Grand Rapids: Eerdmans, 1993.

_____. "Church and Mission: Reflections on Contextualization and the Third Horizon." In *The Church in the Bible and the World*. Edited by D. A. Carson, 213–57, 342–47. Exeter: Paternoster, 1987.

_____. "Current Issues in Biblical Research: A New Testament Perspective." *Bulletin for Biblical Research* 5 (1995).

_____. *Divine Sovereignty and Human Responsibility: Biblical Themes in Tension*. Grand Rapids: Baker, 1994 [1981].

_____. "Evangelicals, Ecumenism and the Church." In *Evangelical Affirmations*. Edited by Kenneth S. Kantzer and Carl F. H. Henry, 347–85. Grand Rapids: Zondervan, 1990.

_____. *Matthew*. In *The Expositor's Bible Commentary*, vol. 8. Grand Rapids: Zondervan, 1984.

_____. *How Long, O Lord? Reflections on Suffering and Evil*. Grand Rapids: Baker, 1990.

_____. "Matthew 11:19 / Luke 7:35: A Test Case for the Bearing of Q Christology on the Synoptic Problem." In *Jesus of Nazareth: Lord and Christ. Essays on the Historical Jesus and New Testament Christology*. Festschrift for I. Howard Marshall. Edited by Joel B. Green and Max Turner, 128–46. Grand Rapids/Carlisle: Eerdmans/Paternoster, 1994.

_____. "Unity and Diversity in the New Testament: The Possibility of Systematic Theology." In *Scripture and Truth*. Edited by D. A. Carson and John D. Woodbridge, 65–95. Grand Rapids: Zondervan, 1983.

_____. "When Is Spirituality Spiritual?" *Journal of the Evangelical Theological Society* 37 (1994): 381–94.

Carson, D. A., Douglas J. Moo, and Leon Morris. *An Introduction to the New Testament*. Grand Rapids: Zondervan, 1992.

Carson, D. A., R. T. France, J. A. Motyer, and G. J. Wenham, consulting editors. *New Bible Commentary: 21st Century Edition*. Leicester/Downers Grove: InterVarsity Press, 1994.

Carson, D. A., and John D. Woodbridge, eds. *God and Culture: Essays in Honor of Carl F. H. Henry*. Festschrift for Carl F. H. Henry. Grand Rapids: Eerdmans, 1993.

_____, eds. *Hermeneutics, Authority, and Canon*. Grand Rapids: Zondervan, 1986.

_____, eds. *Scripture and Truth*. Grand Rapids: Zondervan, 1983.

Carter, Stephen L. *The Culture of Disbelief: How American Law and Politics Trivialize Religious Devotion*. New York: Basic Books, 1993.

Casey, P. Maurice. *From Jewish Prophet to Gentile God: The Origins and Developments of New Testament Christology*. The Edward Cadbury Lectures at the University of Birmingham, 1985–86. Cambridge/Louisville: James Clarke & Co./Westminster/John Knox, 1991.

Catherwood, Sir Fred. "The Christian and Politics." In *God and Culture*. Festschrift for Carl F. H. Henry. Edited by D. A. Carson and John D. Woodbridge, 195–214. Grand Rapids: Eerdmans, 1993.

Chan, Simon. "Asian Pentecostalism, Social Concern and the Ethics of Conformism." *Transformation* 11 (1994): 29–33.

_____. "The Logic of Hell: A Response to Annihilationism." *Evangelical Review of Theology* 18 (1994): 20–32.

Chancellor, James D. "Christ and Religious Pluralism." *Review and Expositor* 91 (1994): 535–47.

Chandler, Russell. *Racing Toward 2001: The Forces Shaping America's Religious Future*. Grand Rapids: Zondervan, 1992.

_____. *Understanding the New Age*. Dallas: Word, 1988.

Chang, Lit-sen. *Zen-Existentialism: The Spiritual Decline of the West*. Phillipsburg: Presbyterian and Reformed Publishing Co., 1969.

Chapman, Colin. *The Christian Message in a Multi-Faith Society*. Oxford: Latimer House, 1992.

Charlesworth, James H. "Is the New Testament Anti-Semitic or Anti-Jewish?" *Explorations* 7, no. 2 (1993): 2–3.

_____. *Jews and Christians: Exploring the Past, Present, and Future*. New York: Crossroad, 1990.

Charnock, Stephen. *The Existence and Attributes of God*. Grand Rapids: Sovereign Grace Publishers, 1971.

Charter, Miriam. "Thomas H. Groome's Shared Praxis Approach to Ministry: Questioning Its Application in the Protestant Evangelical Church." *Trinity Journal* 15 (1994): 89–113.

Chastain, Warren. "Contextualization: Some Cautions and Criticisms." *Stulos Theological Journal* 2 (1994): 3–8.

Chesterton, G. K. *The Penguin Complete Father Brown*. Harmondsworth: Penguin Books, 1981.

Chillingworth, William. *The Religion of Protestants: A Safe Way to Salvation*. Oxford: Liechfield, 1638.

Chilton, Bruce. "The Kingdom of God in Recent Discussion." In *Studying the Historical Jesus: Evaluations of the State of Current Research*. Edited by Bruce Chilton and Craig A. Evans, 255–80. Leiden: E. J. Brill, 1994.

Chodes, John. "Mutiny in Paradise." *Chronicles* (February 1988): 10–13.

Chow, Wilson W. "Biblical Foundations for Evangelical Theology in the Third World." In *The Bible and Theology in Asian Contexts*. Edited by Bong Rin Ro and Ruth Eshenaur, 79–92. Taichung: Asia Theological Association, 1984.

Clark, David K. "Narrative Theology and Apologetics." *Journal of the Evangelical Theological Society* 36 (1993): 499–515.

Clark, Gordon H. *Historiography Secular and Religious.* Nutley: The Craig Press, 1971.

Clarke, Andrew D., and Bruce W. Winter, eds. *One God One Lord in a World of Religious Pluralism.* Cambridge: Tyndale House, 1991.

Clemens, David M. "The Law of Sin and Death: Ecclesiastes and Genesis 1–3." *Themelios* 19, no. 3 (1994): 5–8.

Clements, Roy. "An Overview of Evangelicalism Today." Unpublished paper for UCCF Triennial Consultation, 1994.

Clooney, Francis X. "Christianity and World Religions: Religion, Reason, and Pluralism." *Religious Studies Review* 15 (1989): 197–203.

Clouser, Roy A. *The Myth of Religious Neutrality: An Essay on the Hidden Role of Religious Belief in Theories.* Notre Dame: University of Notre Dame Press, 1991.

Clowney, Edmund P. "Living Art: Christian Experience and the Arts." In *God and Culture.* Festschrift for Carl F. H. Henry. Edited by D. A. Carson and John D. Woodbridge, 235–53. Grand Rapids: Eerdmans, 1993.

_____. *The Politics of the Kingdom.* Mars Hill Monographs. Powhatan: Berea Publications, n.d.

_____. *Preaching and Biblical Theology.* Grand Rapids: Eerdmans, 1961.

Cobb, John B., Jr. *A Christian Natural Theology: Based on the Thought of Alfred North Whitehead.* Philadelphia: Westminster, 1965.

Coleridge, Mark. "Life in the Crypt or Why Bother with Biblical Studies?" *Biblical Interpretation* 2 (1994): 139–51.

Colson, Charles. *Against the Night: Living in the New Dark Ages.* In collaboration with Ellen Santilli Vaughn. Ann Arbor: Servant, 1989.

_____. "Reaching the Pagan Mind." *Christianity Today* 36 (November 9, 1992): 112.

Colson, Chuck. "Making the World Safe for Religion." *Christianity Today* 37 (November 8, 1993): 31–33.

Conn, Harvie M. "The Secularization Myth." *Evangelical Review of Theology* 12 (1988): 78–92.

Conyers, A. J. *The Eclipse of Heaven: Rediscovering the Hope of a World Beyond.* Downers Grove: InterVarsity Press, 1992.

Cook, Robert. "Postmodernism, Pluralism and John Hick." *Themelios* 19, no. 1 (1993): 10–12.

Cooper, John W. "Reformed Apologetics and the Challenge of Post-Modern Relativism." *Calvin Theological Journal* 28 (1993): 108–20.

Cotterell, Peter. *Mission and Meaninglessness: The Good News in a World of Suffering and Disorder.* London: SPCK, 1990.

Coward, Harold. *Pluralism: Challenge to World Religions.* Maryknoll: Orbis Books, 1985.

Cox, Harvey. *Many Mansions: A Christian's Encounter with Other Faiths.* Boston: Beacon Press, 1988.

_____. *The Secular City: Secularization and Urbanization in Theological Perspective.* New York: Macmillan, 1965.

Cox, Stephen. "Theory, Experience and 'The American Religion.'" *Journal of the Evangelical Theological Society* 36 (1993): 363–73.

Cragg, Kenneth. *The Christ and the Faiths: Theology in Cross Reference.* Philadelphia: Westminster Press, 1986.

Craig, W. L., and Q. Smith. *Theism, Atheism and Big Bang Cosmology.* Oxford: Clarendon Press, 1993.

Cresswell, Roger, and Peter Hobson. "The Concept of Tolerance and Its Role in a Pluralist Society, with Particular Reference to Religious Education." *Journal of Christian Education* 98 (1990): 23–30.

Crockett, William, ed. *Four Views on Hell*. Grand Rapids: Zondervan, 1992.

Crockett, William V., and James G. Sigountos, eds. *Through No Fault of Their Own? The Fate of Those Who Have Never Heard*. Grand Rapids: Baker, 1991.

Crosman, Robert. "Is There Such a Thing as Misreading?" In *Criticism and Critical Theory*, 1–12. London: Edward Arnold, 1984.

Crossan, John Dominic. *The Historical Jesus: The Life of a Mediterranean Jewish Peasant*. San Francisco: Harper San Francisco, 1991.

Culbertson, Philip L. "The Seventy Faces of the One God: The Theology of Religious Pluralism." In *Introduction to Jewish-Christian Relations*. Edited by Michael Shermis and Arthur E. Zannoni, 145–73. New York: Paulist Press, 1991.

Culler, Jonathon. *On Deconstruction: Theory and Criticism After Structuralism*. Ithaca: Cornell University Press, 1983.

Culley, Robert C., and Robert B. Robinson, eds. *Semeia* 62 (1993). *Textual Determinacy: Part One*.

Culpepper, R. Alan. *Anatomy of the Fourth Gospel: A Study in Literary Design*. Philadelphia: Fortress, 1983.

Cupitt, Don. *Only Human*. London: SCM Press, 1985.

————. *The Sea of Faith*. London: BBC Publications, 1984.

————. *The Time Being*. London: SCM, 1992.

D'Costa, Gavin. *Christian Uniqueness Reconsidered: The Myth of a Pluralistic Theology of Religion*. Maryknoll: Orbis Books, 1990.

————. "The End of Systematic Theology." *Theology* 95 (1992): 324–34.

————. *John Hick's Theology of Religions: A Critical Evaluation*. Lanham: University Press of America, 1987.

————. "The New Missionary: John Hick and Religious Plurality." *International Bulletin of Missionary Research* 15 (April 1991): 66–69.

————. *Theology and Religious Pluralism*. Oxford: Basil Blackwell, 1986.

Dale, R. W. *Fellowship with Christ, and Other Discourses Delivered on Special Occasions*. London: Hodder and Stoughton, 1900.

Daniélou, Jean. *The History of Early Christian Doctrine Before the Council of Nicaea*. Edited and translated, postscript by John Austin Baker. Vol. 2. *Gospel Message and Hellenistic Culture*. London: Darton, Longman and Todd, 1973.

Davidson, Donald. "On the Very Idea of a Conceptual Scheme." In *Post-Analytic Philosophy*. Edited by John Rajchman and Cornel West, 129–44. New York: Columbia University Press, 1985.

Davies, Eryl. "1993." *Foundations* 24 (1990): 16–21.

————. *An Angry God? What the Bible Says About Wrath, Final Judgement and Hell*. Bridgend: Evangelical Press of Wales, 1992.

Davies, Howard. "Judgment: The Doctrine Lost to the Modern Pulpit." *Banner of Truth Magazine* 364 (January 1994): 13–18.

Davies, John R. "Biblical Precedents for Contextualization." *ATA Journal* 2 (1994): 10–35.

Davies, W. D. "Reflections on Thirty Years of Biblical Study." *Scottish Journal of Theology* 39 (1986): 43–64.

Davis, Stephen. *Logic and the Nature of God*. Grand Rapids: Eerdmans, 1983.

Davis, Stephen T. "Universalism, Hell, and the Fate of the Ignorant." *Modern Theology* 6 (1990): 173–86.

Dawkins, Richard. *The Blind Watchmaker*. London/New York: Longman/W. W. Norton, 1986.

Dawson, Christopher. *Religion and the Rise of Western Culture*. Garden City: Doubleday, Image, 1958.

Dayton, Donald W., and Robert K. Johnston, eds. *The Variety of American Evangelicalism*. Nashville: University of Tennessee, 1991.

de Jouvenel, Bertrand. *Du Pouvoir, Histoire Naturelle de Sa Croissance*. Geneva: Editions Du Cheval Ailé, 1945.

_____. *The Ethics of Redistribution*. Cambridge: Cambridge University Press, 1951.

_____. *Sovereignty: An Inquiry Into the Political Good*. Chicago: University of Chicago Press, 1957 [1955].

Dean, D. A. *Resurrection: His and Ours*. Charlotte: Advent Christian General Conference of America, 1977.

Degler, Carl N. *In Search of Human Nature: The Decline and Revival of Darwinism in American Social Thought*. Oxford: Oxford University Press, 1991.

Dembski, Bill. "Truth with a Capital 'T'." *Transactions* 2 (February 1994): 2–3.

Dembski, William A. *The Incompleteness of Scientific Naturalism and Its Implications for a Scientifically Defensible Account of Intelligent Design in Nature*. Richardson: Foundation for Thought and Ethics, 1992.

Denton, Michael. *Evolution: A Theory in Crisis*. Bethesda: Adler & Adler, Publishers, 1986.

Derrida, Jacques. "Différance." In *Margins of Philosophy*. Translated by Alan Bass, 1–27. Chicago: University of Chicago Press, 1982.

_____. *Of Grammatology*. Translated by Gayatri Chakravorty Spivak. Baltimore: Johns Hopkins University Press, 1976 [1974].

_____. "Passions: 'An Oblique Offering.'" In *Derrida: A Critical Reader*. Edited by David Wood, 5–35. Oxford: Basil Blackwell, 1992.

_____. *Positions*. Translated by Alan Bass. Chicago: University of Chicago Press, 1981.

_____. "Structure, Sign, and Play in the Discourse of the Human Sciences." In *The Structuralist Controversy*. Edited by Richard Macksey and Eugenio Donato, 247–65. Baltimore: Johns Hopkins University Press, 1970.

_____. *The Truth in Painting*. Translated by Geoff Bennington and Ian McLeod. Chicago: University of Chicago Press, 1987.

_____. *Writing and Difference*. Edited by Alan Bass. Chicago: University of Chicago Press, 1978.

Descartes, René. *Discourse on Method*. Great Books of the Western World, vol. 31. Chicago: Encyclopaedia Britannica, 1952.

Descombes, Vincent. *Objects of All Sorts: A Philosophical Grammar*. Translated by Lorna Scott-Fox and Jeremy Harding. Baltimore: The Johns Hopkins University Press, 1986 [1983].

Desjardins, Michel. "Bauer and Beyond: On Recent Scholarly Discussions of Αιρεσις in the Early Christian Era." *The Second Century* 8 (1991): 65–82.

Dewey, John. *A Common Faith*. New Haven: Yale University Press, 1934.

_____. *The Quest for Certainty: A Study of the Relation of Knowledge and Action*. New York: Capricorn Books, 1929.

Dick, Judith. "The Morals Maze: Religious and Moral Education in the Public School System." *Direction* 12 (1983): 34–39.

Dixon, Larry. "Warning a Wrath-Deserving World: Evangelicals and the Overhaul of Hell." *Emmaus Journal* 2, no. 1 (1993): 7–21.

Dockery, David S., ed. *Southern Baptists and American Evangelicals: The Conversation Continues*. Nashville: Broadman & Holman, 1993.

Donohue, William A. *Twilight of Liberty: The Legacy of the ACLU*. New Brunswick: Transaction Publishers, 1994.

Donovan, Peter. "The Intolerance of Religious Pluralism." *Religious Studies* 29 (1993): 217–29.

Dooyeweerd, Herman. *Roots of Western Culture: Pagan, Secular, and Christian Options*. Translated by John Kraay. Toronto: Wedge Publishing Foundation, 1979.

————. *In the Twilight of Western Thought: Studies in the Pretended Autonomy of Philosophical Thought*. University Series, Philosophical Studies. Nutley: Craig Press, 1968.

Douglas, J. D., ed. *Let the Earth Hear His Voice: International Congress on World Evangelization, Lausanne, Switzerland*. Minneapolis: World Wide Publications, 1975.

Douglas, Mary, and Steven M. Tipton, eds. *Religion and America: Spirituality in a Secular Age*. Boston: Beacon Press, 1983.

Dragga, Sam. "Genesis 2–3: A Story of Liberation." *Journal for the Study of the Old Testament* 55 (1992): 3–13.

Driver, S. R. *An Introduction to the Old Testament*. 8th ed. Edinburgh: T & T Clark, 1909.

Driver, Tom F. "The Case for Pluralism." In *The Myth of Christian Uniqueness: Toward a Pluralistic Theology of Religions*. Edited by John Hick and Paul F. Knitter, 203–18. Maryknoll: Orbis Books, 1987.

Duesenberg, Richard W. "Economic Liberties and the Law." *Imprimis* 23, no. 4 (1994): 1–4.

Dulles, Avery. *The Assurance of Things Hoped For: A Theology of Christian Faith*. Oxford: Oxford University Press, 1994.

Dunn, James D. G. *Christology in the Making: A New Testament Inquiry Into the Origins of the Doctrine of the Incarnation*. Philadelphia: Westminster Press, 1980.

————. *The Partings of the Ways Between Christianity and Judaism and Their Significance for the Character of Christianity*. London: SCM, 1991.

Dyrness, William A. *Emerging Voices in Global Christian Theology*. Grand Rapids: Zondervan, 1994.

————. *How Does America Hear the Gospel?* Grand Rapids: Eerdmans, 1989.

————. *Invitation to Cross-Cultural Theology: Case Studies in Vernacular Theologies*. Grand Rapids: Zondervan, 1992.

————. *Learning About Theology from the Third World*. Grand Rapids: Zondervan, 1990.

Eastland, Terry, ed. *Religious Liberty in the Supreme Court: The Cases That Define the Debate Over Church and State*. Grand Rapids: Eerdmans, 1995.

Ebeling, Gerhard. *Word and Faith*. Philadelphia: Fortress Press, 1963.

Eco, Umberto. *The Limits of Interpretation*. Advances in Semiotics. Bloomington: Indiana University Press, 1994.

Eddy, Paul R. "Paul Knitter's Theology of Religions: A Survey and Evangelical Response." *Evangelical Quarterly* 39 (1993): 225–45.

Eden, Martyn, and David Wells, eds. *The Gospel in the Modern World*. Festschrift for John Stott. Leicester: Inter-Varsity Press, 1991.

Edwards, Bruce L. *The Suicide of Liberal Education: Deconstruction in Academia*. The Heritage Lectures, vol. 277. Washington, D.C.: The Heritage Foundation, 1990.

Edwards, Bruce L., and Branson L. Woodard, Jr. "Wise as Serpents, Harmless as Doves: Christians and Contemporary Critical Theory." *Christianity and Literature* 39 (1990): 303–15.

Edwards, David L., and John R. W. Stott. *Essentials: A Liberal-Evangelical Dialogue*. London: Hodder & Stoughton, 1988.

Edwards, David Lawrence. *The Real Jesus: How Much Can We Believe?* London: Fount, HarperCollins Publishers, 1992.

Edwards, Jonathan. *Sinners in the Hands of an Angry God.* Phillipsburg: Presbyterian and Reformed, 1992 [1741].

_____. *Works.* Edinburgh: Banner of Truth Trust, 1974.

Eidsmoe, John. *Christianity and the Constitution: The Faith of Our Founding Fathers.* Grand Rapids: Baker, 1987.

Eisenberg, Anne. "Metaphor in the Language of Science." *Scientific American* 266 (May 1992): 144.

Ellis, John M. *Against Deconstruction.* Princeton: Princeton University Press, 1989.

Ellul, Jacques. *The Meaning of the City.* With an introduction by John Wilkinson. Translated by Dennis Pardee. Grand Rapids: Eerdmans, 1970.

_____. *The Technological Bluff.* Translated by Geoffrey Bromiley. Grand Rapids: Journal of the Evangelical Theological Society, 1990.

_____. *The Technological Society.* Translated by John Wilkinson. With an introduction by Robert K. Merton. New York: Random House, Vintage, 1967.

_____. *The Technological System.* Translated by Joachim Neugroschel. New York: Continuum, 1980.

_____. *The Theological Foundation of Law.* Translated by Marguerite Wieser. New York: Seabury Press, 1969.

_____. *What I Believe.* Translated by Geoffrey W. Bromiley. Grand Rapids: Eerdmans, 1989.

Engelhardt, H. Tristram, Jr. *Bioethics and Secular Humanism: The Search for a Common Morality.* London/Philadelphia: SCM/Trinity Press International, 1991.

Erickson, Millard J. *Evangelical Interpretation: Perspectives on Hermeneutical Issues.* Grand Rapids: Baker, 1993.

_____. *The Word Became Flesh: A Contemporary Incarnational Christology.* Grand Rapids: Baker, 1991.

Escobar, Samuel. "The Search for a Missiological Christology in Latin America." In *Emerging Voices in Global Christian Theology.* Edited by William A. Dyrness, 199–227. Grand Rapids: Zondervan, 1994.

Estep, William R. *Revolution Within the Revolution: The First Amendment in Historical Context, 1612–1789.* Grand Rapids: Eerdmans, 1990.

Evans, Alice Frazer, Robert A. Evans, and David A. Roozen, eds. *The Globalization of Theological Education.* Maryknoll: Orbis Books, 1993.

Evans, C. Stephen. "Evidentialist and Non-Evidentialist Accounts of Historical Religious Knowledge." *Philosophy of Religion* 35 (1994): 153–82.

Exum, J. Cheryl. *Fragmented Women: Feminist (Sub)versions of Biblical Narratives.* Valley Forge: Trinity Press International, 1993.

Exum, J. Cheryl, and David J. A. Clines, eds. *The New Literary Criticism and the Hebrew Bible.* Valley Forge/Sheffield: Trinity Press International/Sheffield Academic Press, 1993.

Fackre, Gabriel. *Ecumenical Faith in Evangelical Perspective.* Grand Rapids: Eerdmans, 1993.

_____. "Eschatology and Systematics." *Ex Auditu* 6 (1990): 101–17.

_____. "I Believe in the Resurrection of the Body." *Interpretation* 46 (1992): 42–52.

Falconer, Ronald. *Message, Media, Mission.* The Baird Lectures 1975. Edinburgh: The Saint Andrew Press, 1977.

Farley, Edward, and Peter C. Hodgson. "Scripture and Tradition." In *Christian Theology: An Introduction to Its Traditions and Tasks.* Edited by Peter C. Hodgson and Robert H. King. 2d ed., 61–87. Philadelphia: Fortress Press, 1985.

Fea, John. "Understanding the Changing Facade of Twentieth-Century American Protestant Fundamentalism: Toward a Historical Definition." *Trinity Journal* 15 (1994): 181–99.

Feder, Don. *A Jewish Conservative Looks at Pagan America.* Lafayette: Huntington House Publishers, 1993.

Feinberg, John S. "Process Theology." *Evangelical Review of Theology* 14 (1990): 291–334.

Feinberg, Paul D. "The Meaning of Inerrancy." In *Inerrancy.* Edited by Norman L. Geisler, 267–304. Grand Rapids: Zondervan, 1979.

Fernando, Ajith. *The Christian's Attitude Toward World Religions.* Wheaton: Tyndale House, 1987.

_____. *Crucial Questions About Hell.* Eastbourne: Kingsway Publications, 1991.

Ferré, Frederick. *Language, Logic and God.* New York: Harper & Row, 1969.

Ferré, N. F. S. *The Christian Understanding of God.* New York: Harper, 1951.

Feyerabend, Paul. *Against Method.* London: New Left Books, 1975.

Finger, Thomas. "Modernity, Postmodernity—What in the World Are They?" *Transformation* 10 (October/December 1993): 20–26.

Finke, Roger, and Rodney Stark. *The Churching of America, 1776–1990: Winners and Losers in Our Religious Economy.* New Brunswick: Rutgers University Press, 1992.

Fish, Stanley. *Is There a Text in This Class?* Boston: Harvard University Press, 1980.

Ford, David F. "Religions in Transformation: An Intellectual Challenge. Lecture Delivered at the Alumni Weekend, September 1992." *Cambridge* 32 (Summer 1993): 87–96.

Fortin-Melkevik, Anne. "Le Statut de la Religion dans la Modernité Selon David Tracy et Jürgen Habermas." *Studies in Religion/Sciences Religieuses* 22 (1993): 417–36.

Foster, Richard J. "The Good Life." *Christianity Today* 31 (December 11, 1987): 20–23.

Fowles, John. *The Magus.* 2d ed. London: Jonathan Cape, Ltd., 1977.

Fox, Matthew. *The Coming of the Cosmic Christ: The Healing of Mother Earth and the Birth of Global Renaissance.* San Francisco: Harper & Row, 1988.

Frame, John M. *Apologetics to the Glory of God.* Phillipsburg: Presbyterian and Reformed Publishing, 1994.

_____. *The Doctrine of the Knowledge of God: A Theology of Lordship.* Phillipsburg: Presbyterian and Reformed Publishing, 1987.

France, R. T. "The Church and the Kingdom of God: Some Hermeneutical Issues." In *Biblical Interpretation and the Church.* Edited by D. A. Carson, 30–44. Exeter: Paternoster Press, 1984.

_____. *The Evidence for Jesus.* London: Hodder & Stoughton, 1985.

France, R. T., and A. E. McGrath, eds. *Evangelical Anglicans: Their Role and Influence in the Church Today.* London: SPCK, 1993.

France, R. T., David Wenham et al. *Gospel Perspectives.* Sheffield: JSOT Press, 1980–86.

Freedman, David Noel. *The Unity of the Hebrew Bible.* Distinguished Senior Faculty Lecture Series. Ann Arbor: University of Michigan Press, 1991.

Freeman, Douglas. *Margaret Mead and Samoa: The Making and Unmaking of an Anthropological Myth.* Cambridge: Harvard University Press, 1983.

Froom, Leroy. *The Conditionalist Faith of Our Fathers.* Washington: Review and Herald, 1965.

Frye, Northrop. *The Educated Imagination.* Bloomington: Indiana University Press, 1964.

_____. *The Great Code: The Bible and Literature.* San Diego: Harcourt Brace Jovanovich, Harvest/HBJ, 1983.

Fudge, Edward William. *The Fire That Consumes: The Biblical Case for Conditional Immortality*. Carlisle: Paternoster Press, 1994.

Fuller, Daniel P. *The Unity of the Bible: Unfolding God's Plan for Humanity*. Grand Rapids: Zondervan, 1992.

Funk, Robert W. *Jesus as Precursor*. Semeia Supplements, vol. 2. Philadelphia/Missoula: Fortress Press/Scholars Press, 1975.

_____. *Language, Hermeneutic, and Word of God: The Problem of Language in the New Testament and Contemporary Theology*. New York: Harper & Row, 1966.

Gadamer, Hans-Georg. *Truth and Method*. Translated and revised by Joel Weinsheimer and Donald G. Marshall. 2d ed. New York: Crossroad, 1991.

Gaede, S. D. *When Tolerance Is No Virtue: Political Correctness, Multiculturalism and the Future of Truth and Justice*. Downers Grove: InterVarsity Press, 1994.

Gaiser, Frederick J. "The Emergence of Self in the Old Testament: A Study in Biblical Wellness." *Horizons in Biblical Theology* 1992 (14): 1–29.

Gale, Richard M. *On the Nature and Existence of God*. Cambridge: Cambridge University Press, 1992.

Gallup, George, Jr., and Sarah Jones. *100 Questions and Answers: Religion in America*. Princeton: Princeton Religion Research Center, 1989.

Gallup, George, Jr., and Jim Catelli. *The People's Religion: American Faith in the 90s*. New York: Macmillan, 1989.

Gärtner, Bertil. *The Areopagus Speech and Natural Revelation*. Uppsala: C. W. K. Gleerup, 1955.

Gay, Craig M. "Plurality, Ambiguity, and Despair in Contemporary Theology." *Journal of the Evangelical Theological Society* 36 (1993): 209–27.

_____. *With Liberty and Justice for Whom? The Recent Evangelical Debate Over Capitalism*. Grand Rapids, Eerdmans, 1991.

Gay, Peter. *The Enlightenment: An Interpretation: The Rise of Modern Paganism*. New York: Random House, Vintage, 1968.

Geisler, Norman L. "The New Age Movement." *Bibliotheca Sacra* 144 (1987): 79–104.

Gellner, Ernest. *Postmodernism, Reason, and Religion*. London/New York: Routledge, 1992.

Gentry, Kenneth L. Jr., *God's Law in the Modern World: The Continuing Relevance of Old Testament Law*. Phillipsburg: Presbyterian and Reformed Publishing, 1993.

George, Thomas D. "John R. W. Stott and C. René Padilla Critiqued: A Response to Their Views on Evangelism / Social Responsibility." *Crux* 28, no. 3 (1992): 34–41.

Gerhart, Mary. "Generic Competence in Biblical Hermeneutics." *Semeia* 43 (1988): 29–44.

Gilkey, Langdon. *Through the Tempest: Theological Voyages in a Pluralistic Culture*. Selected and edited by Jeff B. Pool. Minneapolis: Fortress Press, 1991.

Gill, David W. J. "Behind the Classical Façade: Local Religions of the Roman Empire." In *One God One Lord in a World of Religious Pluralism*. Edited by Andrew D. Clarke and Bruce W. Winter, 72–87. Cambridge: Tyndale House, 1991.

Gill, Robin. *The Myth of the Empty Church*. London: SPCK, 1993.

Gilliland, Dean S., ed. *The Word Among Us: Contextualizing Theology for Mission Today*. Dallas: Word, 1989.

Gillis, Chester. *Pluralism: A New Paradigm for Theology*. Grand Rapids: Eerdmans, 1993.

Gnanakan, Ken. *Kingdom Concerns: A Theology of Mission Today*. Leicester: Inter-Varsity Press, 1993.

_____. *The Pluralistic Predicament*. Theological Issues Series. Bangalore: Theological Book Trust, 1992.

Goldingay, John E., and Christopher J. H. Wright. "'Yahweh Our God Yahweh One': The Old Testament and Religious Pluralism." In *One God One Lord in a World of Religious Pluralism*. Edited by Andrew D. Clarke and Bruce W. Winter, 34–52. Cambridge: Tyndale House, 1991.

Goldman, Ari L. *The Search for God at Harvard*. New York: Times Books, 1991.

Golka, Friedemann W. *The Leopard's Spots: Biblical and African Wisdom in Proverbs*. Edinburgh: T & T Clark, 1993.

Gordon, T. David. "Critique of Theonomy: A Taxonomy." *Westminster Theological Journal* 56 (1994): 23–43.

Goulder, Michael, ed. *Incarnation and Myth: The Debate Continued*. Grand Rapids: Eerdmans, 1979.

Graham, Terry. "The Dual Aspect of Hermeneutics." *Studies in Religion/Sciences Religieuses* 22 (1993): 105–16.

Grant, George, and Mark A. Horne. *Legislating Immorality: The Homosexual Movement Comes Out of the Closet*. Chicago/Franklin: Moody Press/Legacy Communications, 1993.

Gray, Paul. "The Assault on Freud." *Time* 142 (November 29, 1993): 47–59.

Green, Jay D. *Church Historiographical Participation in the Early Twentieth Century Revolt Against Formalism: Shirley Jackson Case and Socio-Historicism*. M.A. thesis, Trinity Evangelical Divinity School, 1994.

Green, Joel B., and Max Turner, eds. *Jesus of Nazareth: Lord and Christ. Essays on the Historical Jesus and New Testament Christology*. Festschrift for I. Howard Marshall. Grand Rapids: Eerdmans, 1994.

Green, Michael. *Evangelism Through the Local Church*. London: Hodder & Stoughton, 1990.

_____, ed. *The Truth of God Incarnate*. Grand Rapids: Eerdmans, 1977.

Gregorios, Paulos Mar. *A Light Too Bright: The Enlightenment Today. An Assessment of the Values of the European Enlightenment and a Search for New Foundations*. Albany: State University of New York Press, 1992.

Grenz, Stanley J. *Revisioning Evangelical Theology: A Fresh Agenda for the 21st Century*. Downers Grove: InterVarsity Press, 1993.

_____. *Theology for the Community of God*. Nashville: Broadman & Holman, 1994.

Grenz, Stanley J., and Roger E. Olson. *20th-Century Theology: God & the World in a Transitional Age*. Downers Grove: InterVarsity Press, 1992.

Grey, Sherman W. *The Least of My Brothers, Matthew 25:31–46: A History of Interpretation*. SBLDS, vol. 114. Atlanta: Scholars Press, 1989.

Griffin, David Ray. "Postmodern Theology and A/theology: A Response to Mark C. Taylor." In *Varieties of Postmodern Theology*. Collaborators David Ray Griffin, William A. Beardslee, and Joe Holland, 29–61. Albany: State University of New York, 1989.

Griffin, David Ray, William A. Beardslee, and Joe Holland. *Varieties of Postmodern Theology*. Albany: State University of New York, 1989.

Griffiths, Paul, and Delmas Lewis. "On Grading Religions, Seeking Truth, and Being Nice to People—A Reply to Professor Hick." *Religious Studies* 19 (1983): 75–80.

Grigg, Russel. "Could Monkeys Type the 23rd Psalm?" *Interchange* 50 (1993): 25–31.

Grothe, Jonathan F. "Confessing Christ in a Pluralistic Age." *Concordia Journal* 16 (1990): 217–30.

Grounds, Vernon C. "The Final State of the Wicked." *Journal of the Evangelical Theological Society* 24 (1981): 211–20.

Grudem, Wayne. *Systematic Theology: An Introduction to Biblical Doctrine*. Grand Rapids: Zondervan, 1994.

Gruenler, Royce Gordon. *The Inexhaustible God: Biblical Faith and the Challenge of Process Theism*. Grand Rapids: Baker, 1983.

Guarino, Thomas. "Contemporary Theology and Scientific Rationality." *Studies in Religion/Sciences Religieuses* 22 (1993): 311–22.

Guinness, Os. *The American Hour: A Time of Reckoning and the Once and Future Role of Faith*. New York: The Free Press, 1992.

_____. "America's Last Men and Their Magnificent Talking Cure." In *No God But God: Breaking with the Idols of Our Age*. Edited by Os Guinness and John Seel, 111–19. Chicago: Moody Press, 1992.

_____. *Dining with the Devil: The Megachurch Movement Flirts with Modernity*. Grand Rapids: Baker, 1993.

_____. *The Dust of Death: A Critique of the Establishment and the Counter Culture and a Proposal for a Third Way*. Downers Grove: InterVarsity Press, 1973.

_____. *Fit Bodies, Fat Minds: Why Evangelicals Don't Think and What To Do About It*. Grand Rapids: Baker, 1994.

_____. *The Gravedigger File: Secret Papers on the Subversion of the Modern Church*. London: Hodder & Stoughton, 1983.

_____. "Tribespeople, Idiots or Citizens? Evangelicals, Religious Liberty and a Public Philosophy for the Public Square." In *Evangelical Affirmations*. Edited by Kenneth S. Kantzer and Carl F. H. Henry, 457–97. Grand Rapids: Zondervan, 1990.

_____. *In Two Minds: The Dilemma of Doubt and How to Resolve It*. Downers Grove: InterVarsity Press, 1977.

_____, ed. *The Williamsburg Charter Survey on Religion and Public Life*. Washington: The Williamsburg Charter Foundation, 1988.

Guinness, Os, and John Seel, eds. *No God But God: Breaking with the Idols of Our Age*. Chicago: Moody Press, 1992.

Guinness, Os, et al. *Transformation* 10, no. 4 (1993). *The Bible, Truth and Modernity*.

Gunn, David M., and Danna Nolan Fewell. *Narrative in the Hebrew Bible*. Oxford: Clarendon Press, 1993.

Gunton, Colin. *The One, the Three, and the Many*. Cambridge: Cambridge University Press, 1993.

_____. "Universal and Particular in Atonement Theology." *Religious Studies* 28 (1992): 453–66.

Gunton, Colin E. *The Promise of Trinitarian Theology*. Edinburgh: T & T Clark, 1991.

Guthrie, Donald. *New Testament Introduction*. 4th ed. Downers Grove: InterVarsity Press, 1990.

Gutting, Gary, ed. *Paradigms and Revolutions: Applications and Appraisals of Thomas Kuhn's Philosophy of Science*. Notre Dame: University of Notre Dame Press, 1980.

Hafemann, Scott J. "The Glory and Veil of Moses in 2 Cor 3:7–14: An Example of Paul's Contextual Exegesis of the OT—a Proposal." *Horizons in Biblical Theology* 14 (1992): 31–49.

_____. *Suffering and Ministry in the Spirit: Paul's Defense of His Ministry in II Corinthians 2:14–3:3*. Grand Rapids: Eerdmans, 1990.

Hagberg, Janet O., and Robert A. Guelich. *The Critical Journey: Stages in the Life of Faith*. Dallas: Word, 1989.

Hagner, Donald A. *The Jewish Reclamation of Jesus: An Analysis and Critique of Modern Jewish Study of Jesus*. Grand Rapids: Zondervan, 1984.

Hahn, Eberhard. "Die Einzigartigkeit Jesu Christi: Eine evangelikale Position." *European Journal of Theology* 3 (1994): 137–44.

Hahn, Lewis Edwin, and Paul Arthur Schilpp, eds. *The Philosophy of W. V. Quine*. LaSalle: Open Court, 1986.

Hall, Douglas John. *Professing the Faith: Christian Theology in a North American Context*. Minneapolis: Fortress Press, 1993.

Hall, Sidney G., III. *Christian Anti-Semitism and Paul's Theology*. Minneapolis: Fortress Press, 1993.

Halverson, Richard C. *We the People*. Ventura: Regal, 1987.

Hamerton-Kelly, Robert. "Sacred Violence and Sinful Desire: Paul's Interpretation of Adam's Sin in the Letter to the Romans." In *The Conversation Continues: Studies in Paul & John*. Festschrift for J. Louis Martyn. Edited by Robert T. Fortna and Beverly R. Gaventa, 35–54. Nashville: Abingdon, 1990.

Hammond, Phillip E. *Religion and Personal Autonomy: The Third Disestablishment in America*. Columbia: University of South Carolina Press, 1992.

Hanegraaff, Hank. *Christianity in Crisis*. Eugene: Harvest House, 1993.

Hanks, Joyce M. "The Politics of God and the Politics of Ellul." *Journal of the Evangelical Theological Society* 35 (1992): 217–30.

Hanson, Norwood. *Patterns of Discovery*. Cambridge: Cambridge University Press, 1958.

Harakas, Stanley S. "Educating for Moral Values in a Pluralistic Society." *Greek Orthodox Review* 29 (1984): 393–99.

Harmon, Kendall S. "The Case Against Conditionalism: A Response to Edward William Fudge." In *Universalism and the Doctrine of Hell*. Edited by Nigel M. de S. Cameron, 193–224. Carlisle: Paternoster Press, 1992.

Harnack, Adolf von. *What is Christianity?* With an introduction by Rudolf Bultman. Translated by Thomas Bailey Sauders. New York: Harper & Row, Harper Torchbooks/Cloister Library, 1957.

Harpur, Tom. *Life After Death*. Buffalo: McClelland & Stewart, 1991.

Harrington, Daniel J. "The Reception of Walter Baueer's *Orthodoxy and Heresy in Earliest Christianity* During the Last Decade." *Harvard Theological Review* 77 (1980): 289–99.

Harris, Murray J. *Jesus as God: The New Testament Use of Theos in Reference to Jesus*. Grand Rapids: Baker, 1992.

————. "The Translation of *Elohim* in Psalm 45:7–8." *Tyndale Bulletin* 35 (1984): 65–89.

Harrop, Jonathan D. "The Limits of Sociology in the Work of David Martin. Towards a Critique of David Martin's Sociology of Religion Centred on His Essay: 'Can The Church Survive.'" *Religion* 17 (1987): 173–92.

Hart, D. G. "Presbyterians and Fundamentalism." *Westminster Theological Journal* 55 (1993): 331–42.

————, ed. *Reckoning With the Past*. Grand Rapids: Baker, 1995.

Hartshorne, Charles. *A Natural Theology for Our Time*. LaSalle, Ill.: Open Court, 1967.

Harvey, David. *The Condition of Postmodernity: An Enquiry Into the Origins of Cultural Change*. Cambridge, MA/Oxford: Blackwell, 1990.

Hatch, Nathan O. *The Democratization of American Christianity*. New Haven: Yale University Press, 1989.

Hauerwas, Stanley. *Unleashing the Scripture: Freeing the Bible from Captivity to America*. Nashville: Abingdon Press, 1993.

Hauerwas, Stanley, and William H. Willimon. *Resident Aliens*. Nashville: Abingdon Press, 1989.

Hawking, Stephen W. *A Brief History of Time: From the Big Bang to Black Holes*. New York: Bantam, 1988.

Hawthorn, Jeremy, ed. *Criticism and Critical Theory*. London: Edward Arnold, 1984.

Hawtrey, Kim. "Economic Justice: A Twin Axiom Framework." *The Reformed Theological Review* 50 (1991): 98–105.

Hayek, Friedrich A. *The Constitution of Liberty*. South Bend: Gateway, 1960.

_____. *Law, Legislation and Liberty*. London: Routledge & Kegan Paul, 1982.

Haynes, Stephen R. *Prospects for Post-Holocaust Theology*. Atlanta: Scholars Press, 1991.

Haynes, Stephen R., and Steven L. McKenzie, eds. *To Each Its Own Meaning: An Introduction to Biblical Criticisms and Their Application*. Louisville: Westminster/John Knox, 1993.

Hays, Richard B. "The Church as a Scripture-Shaped Community: The Problem of Method in New Testament Ethics." *Interpretation* 44 (1990): 42–55.

Healey, Stephen. "Religious Truth Claims, Violence and the Pluralistic Hypothesis: A Defense of Interreligious Apologetics." *Andover Newton Review* 3, no. 1 (1992): 17–30.

Hebblethwaite, Brian. *The Incarnation: Collected Essays in Christology*. Cambridge: Cambridge University Press, 1987.

_____. *The Ocean of Truth: A Defence of Objective Theism*. Cambridge: Cambridge University Press, 1988.

Hedlung, Roger E. *The Mission of the Church in the World: A Biblical Theology*. Grand Rapids: Baker, 1991 [1985].

Heidegger, Martin. *Being and Time*. Translated by John Macquarrie and Edward Robinson. New York: Harper & Row, 1962.

Heim, Mark. "Thinking About Theocentric Christology." *Journal of Ecumenical Studies* 24 (1987): 1–16.

Heim, S. Mark. *Is Christ the Only Way? Christian Faith in a Pluralistic World*. Valley Forge: Judson Press, 1985.

Heimerdinger, Jean-Marc. "The God of Abraham." *Vox Evangelica* 22 (1992): 41–55.

Helm, Paul. *Eternal God: A Study of God Without Time*. Oxford: Oxford University Press, Clarendon, 1988.

_____. *The Last Things: Death, Judgment, Heaven, Hell*. Edinburgh: Banner of Truth Trust, 1989.

_____, ed. *Divine Commands and Morality*. Oxford Readings in Philosophy. Oxford: Oxford University Press, 1981.

_____, ed. *Objective Knowledge: A Christian Perspective*. Leicester: Inter-Varsity Press, 1987.

Hemer, Colin J. *The Letters to the Seven Churches of Asia in Their Local Settings*. JSNTSS, vol. 11. Sheffield: JSOT Press, 1986.

Henry, Carl F. H. *The Christian Mindset in a Secular Society*. Portland: Multnomah Press, 1985.

_____. *Evangelicals in Search of Identity*. Waco: Word Books, 1976.

_____. *God, Revelation and Authority*. Waco: Word Books, 1976–83.

_____. "Reflections on Postmodernity." 1994.

Hess, Richard S. "Yahweh and His Asherah? Epigraphic Evidence for Religious Pluralism in Old Testament Times." In *One God One Lord in a World of Religious Pluralism*. Edited by Andrew D. Clarke and Bruce W. Winter, 5–33. Cambridge: Tyndale House, 1991.

Hick, John. *Disputed Questions in Theology and the Philosophy of Religion*. London: Macmillan, 1993.

_____. *Evil and the God of Love*. London/ New York: Macmillan/Harper & Row, 1966.

_____. *God and the Universe of Faiths*. London: Fount, 1977.

_____. "An Inspiration Christology for a Religiously Plural World." In *Encountering Jesus*. Edited by Stephen T. Davis, 5–38. Atlanta: John Knox Press, 1988.

_____. *An Interpretation of Religion: Human Responses to the Transcendent*. The Gifford Lectures. London: Macmillan Press, 1989.

_____. "Jesus and the World Religions." In *The Myth of God Incarnate*. Edited by John Hick, 167–85. London: SCM Press, 1977.

_____. *The Metaphor of God Incarnate: Christology in a Pluralistic Age*. Louisville: Westminster/John Knox, 1993.

_____. "The Non-Absoluteness of Christianity." In *The Myth of Christian Uniqueness: Toward a Pluralistic Theology of Religions*. Edited by John Hick and Paul F. Knitter, 16–36. Maryknoll: Orbis Books, 1987.

_____. *Problems of Religious Pluralism*. New York: St. Martin's Press, 1985.

_____, ed. *The Myth of God Incarnate*. London: SCM Press, 1977.

Hick, John, and Paul F. Knitter, eds. *The Myth of Christian Uniqueness: Toward a Pluralistic Theology of Religions*. Faith Meets Faith Series, vol. 2. Maryknoll: Orbis Books, 1987.

Hill, Brian V. "Educational Responses to Modern Pluralism." *Evangelical Review of Theology* 16 (1992): 82–96.

Hille, Rolf. *Das Ringen um den sëkularen Menschen: Karl Heims Auseinandersetzung mit der idealistischen Philosophie und den pantheistischen Religionen*. Giessen: Brunnen Verlag, 1990.

Himmelfarb, Gertrude. *On Looking Into the Abyss: Untimely Thoughts on Culture and Society*. New York: Alfred A. Knopf, 1994.

Himmelfarb, Martha. *Tours of Hell: An Apocalyptic Form in Jewish and Christian Literature*. Philadelphia: Fortress Press, 1985.

Hirsch, E. D., Jr. *Cultural Literacy: What Every American Needs to Know*. Boston: Houghton Mifflin, 1987.

_____. "Transhistorical Intentions and the Persistence of Allegory." *New Literary History* 25 (1994): 549–67.

Hodgson, Peter C. *Winds of the Spirit: A Constructive Christian Theology*. Louisville: Westminster/John Knox, 1994.

Hoekstra, Harvey T. *Evangelism in Eclipse: World Mission and the World Council of Churches*. Exeter: Paternoster, 1979.

Hofstadter, Richard. *Social Darwinism in American Thought*. Rev. ed. Boston: Beacon Press, 1955.

Hoge, Dean R., Benton Johnson, and Donald A. Luidens. *Vanishing Boundaries: The Religion of Mainline Protestant Baby Boomers*. Louisville: Westminster/John Knox, 1994.

Hoitenga, Dewey. *Faith and Reason from Plato to Plantinga*. Albany: State University of New York Press, 1991.

Holder, Rodney. *Nothing But Atoms and Molecules?* Tunbridge Wells: Monarch, 1993.

Holloway, David. "What is an Anglican Evangelical?" In *Restoring the Vision: Anglical Evangelicals Speak Out*. Edited by Melvin Tinker, 15–37. Eastbourne: MARC, 1990.

Holmquist, David. "Will There Be Baseball in Heaven?" *Christianity Today* (January 10, 1994): 29–33.

Hooykaas, R. J. *Religion and the Rise of Modern Science*. Edinburgh: Scottish Academic Press, 1972.

Hopper, David H. *Technology, Theology, and the Idea of Progress*. Louisville: Westminster/John Knox, 191.

Horn, Carl. "'World Views' and Public Policy." In *Whose Values? The Battle for Morality in Pluralistic America*. Edited by Carl Horn, 167–86. Ann Arbor: Servant Books, 1985.

_____, ed. *Whose Values? The Battle for Morality in Pluralistic America*. Ann Arbor: Servant Books, 1985.

Horton, Michael S. *Beyond the Culture Wars*. Chicago: Moody Press, 1994.

_____. "Corinthian Distractions." *Modern Reformation* (March/April 1993): 22–24.

_____. *Made in America: The Shaping of Modern American Evangelicalism*. Grand Rapids: Baker, 1991.

Howard, Philip K. *The Death of Common Sense: How Law is Suffocating America*. New York: Random House, 1994.

Howard, Thomas. *Chance or the Dance? A Critique of Modern Secularism*. Wheaton: Harold Shaw Publishers, 1969.

Howe, Neil, and William Strauss. "The New Generation Gap." *The Atlantic Monthly* (December 1992): 67–89.

Howell, Don N., Jr. "God-Christ Interchange in Paul: Impressive Testimony to the Deity of Jesus." *Journal of the Evangelical Theological Society* 36 (1993): 467–79.

Hughes, Philip Edgcumbe. *The True Image: The Origin and Destiny of Man in Christ*. Grand Rapids/Leicester: Eerdmans/Inter-Varsity Press, 1989.

Hughes, Philip Edgcumbe. "Conditional Immortality." *Evangel* 10, no. 2 (1992): 10–12.

Hughes, Robert. *Culture of Complaint: The Fraying of America*. New York: Oxford University Press, 1993.

Hull, Bill. *Can We Save the Evangelical Church? The Lion Has Roared*. Grand Rapids: Fleming H. Revell, 1993.

Hulmes, Edward. "The Irritant of Agnosticism." *Princeton Seminary Bulletin* 6 (1985): 14–24.

Hultberg, Alan. "William Chillingworth on Certainty." Deerfield, 1993.

Hultgren, Arland J. *The Rise of Normative Christianity*. Minneapolis: Fortress Press, 1994.

Hunsberger, George. "The Newbigin Gauntlet: Developing a Domestic Missiology for North America." *Missiology* 19 (1991): 392–408.

Hunsberger, George R. "Is There Biblical Warrant for Evangelism?" *Interpretation* 48 (1994): 131–44.

Hunter, George G., III. *How to Reach Secular People*. Nashville: Abingdon Press, 1992.

Hunter, James Davison. *Before the Shooting Begins: Searching for Democracy in America's Culture War*. New York: The Free Press, 1994.

_____. *Culture Wars: The Struggle to Define America*. New York: Basic Books, 1992.

_____. *Evangelicalism: The Coming Generation*. Chicago: University of Chicago Press, 1987.

Hunter, James Davison, and Os Guinness, eds. *Articles of Faith, Articles of Peace: The Religious Liberty Clauses and the American Public Philosophy*. Washington: The Brookings Institute, 1990.

Hurtado, Larry W. *One God, One Lord: Early Christian Devotion and Ancient Jewish Monotheism*. London/Philadelphia: SCM Press/Fortress Press, 1988.

Huyssen, Andreas. *After the Great Divide: Modernism, Mass Culture, Postmodernism*. Bloomington: Indiana University Press, 1986.

Illich, Ivan. *Disabling Professions*. London: Marion Boyars, 1977.

Jaki, Stanley L. *The Road of Science and the Ways to God*. Chicago: University of Chicago Press, 1978.

_____. "The Universe in the Bible and in Modern Science." *Ex Auditu* 3 (1988): 137–47.

James, Robison B., and David S. Dockery. *Beyond the Impasse? Scripture, Interpretation, and Theology in Baptist Life*. Nashville: Broadman Press, 1992.

Jasper, David, ed. *Postmodernism, Literature and the Future of Theology*. London: Macmillan, 1993.

Jeanrond, Werner G. *Text and Interpretation as Categories of Theological Thinking*. Translated by Thomas J. Wilson. New York: Crossroad, 1988 [1986].

————. *Theological Hermeneutics: Development and Significance*. New York: Crossroad, 1991.

————. "Theology in the Context of Pluralism and Postmodernity: David Tracy's Theological Method." In *Postmodernism, Literature and the Future of Theology*. Edited by David Jasper, 143–63. New York: St. Martin's Press, 1993.

Jeanrond, Werner G., and Jennifer L. Rike, eds. *Radical Pluralism and Truth: David Tracy and the Hermeneutics of Religion*. New York: Crossroad, 1991.

Jeeves, Malcolm A. *The Scientific Enterprise and the Christian Faith*. London: The Tyndale Press, 1969.

Jenkins, David E. *Still Living with Questions*. London: SCM Press, 1990.

Jensen, Peter. "The Teacher as Theologian in Theological Education." *The Reformed Theological Review* 50 (1991): 81–90.

Jewett, Paul K. *God, Creation, and Revelation: A Neo-Evangelical Theology*. Grand Rapids: Eerdmans, 1991.

Jewett, Robert. *Paul: The Apostle to America*. Louisville: Westminster/John Knox, 1994.

Ji, Won Jon. "Witnessing to Christ in a Pluralistic Age: Theological Principle and Practice." *Concordia Journal* 16 (1990): 231–44.

Jobling, David. "Globalization in Biblical Studies / Biblical Studies in Globalization." *Biblical Interpretation* 1 (1993): 96–110.

Johnson, Paul. *Intellectuals*. New York: Harper & Row, 1988.

Johnson, Phillip E. *Darwin on Trial*. Washington: Regnery Gateway, 1991.

————. *Evolution as Dogma: The Establishment of Naturalism*. Dallas: Haughton Publishing Company, 1990.

————. "The Modernist Impasse in Law." In *God and Culture*. Festschrift for Carl F. H. Henry. Edited by D. A. Carson and John D. Woodbridge, 180–94. Grand Rapids: Eerdmans, 1993.

————. "The Religion of the Blind Watchmaker." *Perspectives on Science and Faith* 45 (1993): 46–48.

————. "Shouting 'Heresy' in the Temple of Darwin." *Christianity Today* 38 (October 24, 1994): 22–26.

————. "Unbelievers Unwelcome in Science Lab." *Los Angeles Times* (November 3, 1990), Section B, 7.

Johnston, Robert K., ed. *The Use of the Bible in Theology: Evangelical Options*. Atlanta: John Knox Press, n.d.

Jones, A. H. M. *Were Ancient Heresies Disguised Social Movements?* Facet Books Historical Series. Philadelphia: Fortress Press, 1966.

Jones, Hywel. "No Other Name." *Foundations* 24 (1990): 23–31.

Jones, Peter. *The Gnostic Empire Strikes Back: An Old Heresy for the New Age*. Phillipsburg: Presbyterian and Reformed Publishing, 1992.

Juhl, P. D. "Playing with Texts: Can Deconstruction Account for Critical Practice?" In *Criticism and Critical Theory*. Edited by Jeremy Hawthorn, 59–71. Stratford-Upon-Avon Studies. London: Edward Arnold, 1984.

Kaiser, Christopher. *Creation and the History of Science*. Grand Rapids: Eerdmans, 1991.

Kaiser, Walter C., Jr. "'Pluralism' as a Criterion for Excellence in Faculty Development." *Theological Education* 28 (1991): 58–62.

Kane, J. Herbert. *Understanding Christian Missions*. 4th ed. Grand Rapids: Baker, 1988.

Kant, Immanuel. "Prolegomena to Every Future Metaphysics That May Be Presented as a Science." In *The Philosophy of Kant*. Edited by Carl J. Friedrich, 40–115. New York: Modern Library, 1949.

_____. "What is Enlightenment?" In *The Philosophy of Kant*. Edited by Carl J. Friedrich, 132–39. New York: Modern Library, 1949.

Kato, Byang. *Theological Pitfalls in Africa*. Kisumu: Evangel Publishing House, 1975.

Kaufman, Gordon D. *An Essay on Theological Method*. American Academy of Religion Studies in Religion, vol. 11. Missoula: Scholars Press for the American Academy of Religion, 1975.

_____. "Religious Diversity, Historical Consciousness, and Christian Theology." In *The Myth of Christian Uniqueness: Toward a Pluralistic Theology of Religions*. Edited by John Hick and Paul F. Knitter. Maryknoll: Orbis Books, 1987.

Keegan, John. *A History of Warfare*. New York: Alfred A. Knopf, 1993.

Keen, Ralph. "The Limits of Power and Obedience in the Later Calvin." *Calvin Theological Journal* 27 (1992): 252–76.

Keith, Graham. "Issues in Religious Toleration from the Reformation to the Present Day." *Evangelical Quarterly* 66 (1994): 307–29.

_____. "Justin Martyr and Religious Exclusivism." *Tyndale Bulletin* 43 (1992): 57–80.

Kekes, John. *The Morality of Pluralism*. Princeton: Princeton University Press, 1993.

Kelly, Douglas F. *The Emergence of Liberty in the Modern World: The Influence of Calvin on Five Governments from the 16th Through 18th Centuries*. Phillipsburg: Presbyterian and Reformed Publishing, 1992.

Kelsey, David H. *Between Athens and Berlin: The Theological Education Debate*. Grand Rapids: Eerdmans, 1993.

_____. *To Understand God Truly: What's Theological About a Theological School*. Louisville: Westminster/John Knox, 1992.

Kepel, Gilles. *The Revenge of God: The Resurgence of Islam, Christianity and Judaism in the Modern World*. Translated by Alan Braley. University Park: The Pennsylvania State University Press, 1994.

Kettler, Christian D. *The Vicarious Humanity of Christ and the Reality of Salvation*. London/New York: University Press of America, 1991.

Kidner, Derek. *The Christian and the Arts*. London: Inter-Varsity Fellowship, 1959.

Kierkegaard, Søren. *The Present Age*. New York: Harper & Row, 1962.

Kilner, John F. *Life on the Line: Ethics, Aging, Ending Patients' Lives and Allocating Vital Resources*. Grand Rapids: Eerdmans, 1992.

Kilpatrick, William K. *Why Johnny Can't Tell Right from Wrong: Moral Illiteracy and the Case for Character Education*. New York: Simon & Schuster, 1992.

Kinsley, Michael. "Judges, Democracy and Natural Law." *Time* 138 (August 12, 1991): 68.

Kirk, Russell. *America's British Culture*. New Brunswick: Transaction Publishers, 1993.

Kitagawa, Joseph Mitsuo. *The Christian Tradition: Beyond Its European Captivity*. Philadelphia: Trinity Press International, 1992.

Klaaren, Eugene M. *Religious Origins of Modern Science: Belief in Creation in Seventeenth-Century Thought*. Grand Rapids: Eerdmans, 1977.

Knitter, Paul. *No Other Name? A Critical Survey of Christian Attitudes Toward the World Religions*. Maryknoll: Orbis Books, 1985.

Knitter, Paul F. "Theocentric Theology: Defended and Transcended." *Journal of Ecumenical Studies* 24 (1987): 41–52.

_____. "Toward a Liberation Theology of Religions." In *The Myth of Christian Uniquess: Toward a Pluralistic Theology of Religions*. Edited by John Hick and Paul F. Knitter, 178–200. Maryknoll: Orbis Books, 1987.

Koester, Helmut. "The Divine Human Being." *Harvard Theological Review* 78 (1986): 243–52.

————. "Gnomai Diaphorai: The Origin and Nature of Diversification in the History of Early Christianity." In *Trajectories Through Early Christianity*. Edited by James M. Robinson and Helmut Koester, 114–57. Philadelphia: Fortress Press, 1971.

Koivisto, Rex A. *One Lord, One Faith: A Theology for Cross-Denominational Renewal*. Wheaton: Victor Press, 1993.

Kraemer, Hendrik. *The Christian Message in a Non-Christian World*. With a foreword by Archbishop of Canterbury. Grand Rapids: Kregel Publications, 1956 [1938].

Kraft, Charles. *Christianity in Culture: A Study in Dynamic Biblical Theologizing in Cross-Cultural Perspective*. Maryknoll: Orbis Books, 1980.

Kreeft, Peter. *Back to Virtue*. San Francisco: Ignatius Press, 1992.

Krieger, David J. *The New Universalism: Foundations for a Global Theology*. Maryknoll: Orbis Books, 1991.

Kroeker, P. Travis. "The Ironic Cage of Positivism and the Nature of Philosophical Theology." *Studies in Religion/Sciences Religieuses* 22 (1993): 93–103.

————. "Reply to Donald Wiebe." *Studies in Religion/Sciences Religieuses* 23 (1994): 81–82.

Kuehnelt-Leddihn, Erik von. *Liberty or Equality: The Challenge of Our Time*. With a foreword by Russell Kirk. Front Royal: Christendom Press, 1993 [1952].

Kuhn, Thomas S. *The Structure of Scientific Revolutions*. 2d ed. Chicago: University of Chicago Press, 1970 [1962].

Kuitert, H. M. *I Have My Doubts: How To Become a Christian Without Being A Fundamentalist*. Translated by John Bowden. London/Philadelphia: SCM/TPI, 1993.

Küng, Hans. *On Being a Christian*. Translated by Edward Quinn. Garden City: Doubleday, 1976.

————. "To What Can We Still Cling?" In *Humanizing America's Iconic Book*. Edited by G. M. Tucker and D. A. Knight, 39–56. Chico: Scholars Press, 1988.

Küng, Hans, and Jürgen Moltmann. *Christianity Among World Religions*. Edinburgh: T & T Clark, 1986.

Küng, Hans, et al. *A Global Ethic: The Declaration of the Parliament of the World's Religions*. London: SCM Press, 1993.

————. *Christianity and the World Religions: Paths to Dialogue with Islam, Hinduism and Buddhism*. Garden City: Doubleday, 1986.

Kvanvig, Jonathan L. *The Problem of Hell*. Oxford: Oxford University Press, 1994.

L'Engle, Madeleine. *The Irrational Season*. New York: Seabury Press, 1977.

LaFargue, Michael. "Are Texts Determinate? Derrida, Barth, and the Role of the Biblical Scholar." *Harvard Theological Review* 81 (1988): 341–57.

Lakatos, Imre. "Falsification and the Methodology of Scientific Research Programmes." In *Criticism and the Growth of Knowledge*. Edited by Imre Lakatos and Alan Musgrave, 91–196. Cambridge: Cambridge University Press, 1970.

Lalonde, Marc P. "From Postmodernity to Postorthodoxy, or Charles Davis and the Contemporary Context of Christian Theology." *Studies in Religion/Sciences Religieuses* 22 (1993): 437–49.

Larkin, William J., Jr. *Culture and Biblical Hermeneutics: Interpreting and Applying the Authoritative Word in a Relativistic Age*. Grand Rapids: Baker, 1988.

————. "Culture, Scripture's Meaning, and Biblical Authority: Critical Hermeneutics for the 90's." *Bulletin for Biblical Research* 2 (1992): 171–78.

Larmer, Robert A. "Goodness and God's Will." *Journal of the Evangelical Theological Society* 35 (1992): 193.

Larsen, Daniel P. *Justice Hugo L. Black and the "Wall" of Separation: Reasons Behind the Everson V. Board of Education Decision*. M.A. thesis, Trinity Evangelical Divinity School, 1984.

Lasch, Christopher. *The Culture of Narcissism: American Life in an Age of Diminishing Expectations*. New York: Warner, 1979.

_____. *The True and Only Heaven: Progress and Its Critics*. New York: W. W. Norton & Company, 1991.

Laudan, Larry. *Science and Relativism: Some Key Controversies in the Philosophy of Science*. Chicago: University of Chicago Press, 1990.

Lavine, T. Z. *From Socrates to Sartre: The Philosophic Quest*. Toronto: Bantam Books, 1984.

Le Brun, Jacques. "Autorité doctrinale, définition et censure dans le Catholicism moderne: notes critiques." *Revue de L'Histoire Des Religions* 211 (1994): 335–43.

Lee, James Michael. "The Blessings of Religious Pluralism." In *Religious Pluralism and Religious Education*. Edited by Norma H. Thompson, 57–124. Birmingham: Religious Education Press, 1988.

Leff, Arthur Allen. "Unspeakable Ethics, Unnatural Law." *Duke Law Journal* 6 (1979): 1229–49.

Lemonick, Michael D. "Secrets of the Maya." *Time* 142 (August 9, 1993).

Levenson, Jon D. "Exodus and Liberation." *Horizons in Biblical Theology* 13 (1991): 134–74.

Levinskaya, Irina A. "Syncretism—the Term and Phenomenon." *Tyndale Bulletin* 44 (1993): 117–28;

Lewis, C. S. *God in the Dock: Essays on Theology and Ethics*. Edited by Walter Hooper. Grand Rapids: Eerdmans, 1970.

_____. *The Problem of Pain*. New York: Macmillan, 1943.

_____. *The Weight of Glory and Other Addresses*. Edited by Walter Hooper. New York: Macmillan, 1980.

Lewis, Gordon R. "God's Word: Key to Authentic Spirituality." In *A Call to Christian Character*. Edited by Bruce Shelley, 105–20. Grand Rapids: Zondervan, 1970.

Lewis, James R., and J. Gordon Melton, eds. *Perspectives on the New Age*. Albany: State University of New York, 1992.

Lewis, Peter. *The Glory of Christ*. London: Hodder & Stoughton, 1992.

Lindbeck, George A. "The Church's Mission to a Postmodern Culture." In *Postmodern Theology: Christian Faith in a Pluralist World*. Edited by Frederic B. Burnham, 37–55. San Francisco: Harper & Row, 1989.

_____. *The Nature of Doctrine: Religion and Theology in a Post-Liberal Age*. Philadelphia: Westminster, 1984.

Linfield, Alan M. "Sheep and Goats: Current Evangelical Thought on the Nature of Hell and the Scope of Salvation." *Vox Evangelica* 24 (1994): 63–75.

Lingenfelter, Sherwood G. *Transforming Culture: A Challenge for Christian Mission*. Grand Rapids: Baker, 1992.

Lints, Richard. *The Fabric of Theology: A Prolegomenon to Evangelical Theology*. Grand Rapids: Eerdmans, 1993.

Lloyd-Jones, D. M. "Biblical Intolerance." *Banner of Truth* 371–372 (August-September 1994): 54–56.

_____. *Knowing the Times: Addresses Delivered on Various Occasions 1942–1977*. Edinburgh: Banner of Truth Trust, 1989.

_____. *Preaching and Preachers*. London: Hodder & Stoughton, 1971.

Locke, John. *Two Treatises of Government*. Rev. ed. Revised and introduced by Peter Laslett. New York: New American Library, Mentor, 1963.

Lockerbie, D. Bruce. *The Cosmic Center*. Portland: Multnomah Press, 1986.

Lohfink, Norbert. *The Covenant Never Revoked: Biblical Reflections on Christian-Jewish Dialogue*. Translated by John J. Scullion, S.J. New York: Paulist Press, 1991.

Lonergan, Bernard J. F. *Method in Theology*. The Seabury Library of Contemporary Theology. New York: Crossroad, 1979.

Long, Thomas G. *Preaching and the Literary Forms of the Bible*. Philadelphia: Fortress, 1989.

Long, V. Philips. *The Art of Biblical History*. Foundations of Contemporary Interpretation, vol. 5. Grand Rapids: Zondervan, 1994.

Longenecker, Richard N. *The Christology of Early Jewish Christianity*. London: SCM Press, 1970.

————. "The 'Faith of Abraham' Theme in Paul, James and Hebrews: A Study in the Circumstantial Nature of New Testament Teaching." *Journal of the Evangelical Theological Society* 20 (1977): 203–12.

Lorenzen, Thorwald. "Baptists and the Challenge of Religious Pluralism." *Review and Expositor* 89 (1992): 49–69.

Lotz, David W., Donald W. Shriver, Jr., and John F. Wilson, eds. *Altered Landscapes: Christianity in America, 1935–1985*. Festschrift for Robert T. Handy. Grand Rapids: Eerdmans, 1989.

Louth, Andrew. *Discerning the Mystery: An Essay on the Nature of Theology*. Oxford: Clarendon, 1983.

Lowe, Malcolm, ed. *Immanuel* 24–25 (1990). *The New Testament and Christian-Jewish Dialogue*. Festschrift for David Flusser.

————. *Immanuel* 22–23 (1989). *People, Land and State of Israel: Jewish and Christian Perspectives*.

Lucas, Ernest C. "God, CUTs and Gurus: The New Physics and New Age Ideology." *Themelios* 16, no. 3 (1991): 4–7.

Lundin, Roger. *The Culture of Interpretation: Christian Faith and the Postmodern World*. Grand Rapids: Eerdmans, 1993.

Lundin, Roger, Anthony C. Thiselton, and Clarence Walhout. *The Responsibility of Hermeneutics*. Grand Rapids: Eerdmans, 1985.

Lyotard, Jean-François. *The Postmodern Condition: A Report on Knowledge*. Translated by Geoff Benningtron and Frian Massumi. Theory and History of Literature, vol. 10. Minneapolis: University of Minnesota Press, 1984.

Mabee, Charles. *Reading Sacred Texts Through American Eyes: Biblical Interpretation as Cultural Critique*. Macon: Mercer University Press, 1991.

McCartney, Dan, and Charles Clayton. *Let the Reader Understand: A Guide to Interpreting and Applying the Bible*. Wheaton: Bridgepoint, 1994.

McCartney, Dan G. "*Ecce Homo*: The Coming of the Kingdom as the Restoration of Human Vicegerency." *Westminster Theological Journal* 56 (1994): 1–21.

MacCormac, Earl R. *Metaphor and Myth in Science and Religion*. Durham: Duke University Press, 1976.

McDermott, Gerald. *One Holy and Happy Society: The Public Theology of Jonathan Edwards*. University Park: The Pennsylvania State University Press, 1992.

McGinley, Phyllis. *Times Three*. New York: Viking, 1961.

McGrath, Alister. "The Challenge of Pluralism for the Contemporary Christian Church." *Journal of the Evangelical Theological Society* 35 (1992): 361–73.

McGrath, Alister E. *Bridge-Building: Effective Christian Apologetics*. Leicester: Inter-Varsity Press, 1992.

————. "The Christian Church's Response to Pluralism." *Journal of the Evangelical Theological Society* 35 (1992): 487–501.

————. "The European Roots of Evangelicalism." *Anvil* 9 (1992): 239–48.

_____. *The Genesis of Doctrine: A Study in the Foundations of Doctrinal Criticism.* The Bampton Lectures. Oxford: Blackwell, 1990.

_____. *Intellectuals Don't Need God & Other Myths: Building Bridges to Faith Through Apologetics.* Grand Rapids: Zondervan, 1993.

_____. "Pluralism and the Decade of Evangelism." *Anvil* 9 (1992): 101–14.

McGrath, Joanna, and Alister McGrath. *The Dilemma of Self-esteem: The Cross and Christian Confidence.* Wheaton/Cambridge: Crossway Books, 1992.

Machen, J. Gresham. "Christianity and Culture." *Princeton Theological Review* 11 (1913): 1–15.

_____. *Christianity and Liberalism.* Grand Rapids: Eerdmans, 1923.

_____. *The Origin of Paul's Religion.* Grand Rapids: Eerdmans, 1947 [1925].

_____. *What Is Faith?* Grand Rapids: Eerdmans, 1946.

McIntosh, John. "Biblical Exclusivism: Towards a Reformed Approach to the Uniqueness of Christ." *Pressure Points* (1993): 14–23.

McKenzie, Richard B. *What Went Right in the 1980s.* San Francisco: Pacific Research Institute for Public Policy, 1994.

McKenzie, S. L., and S. R. Haynes. *To Each Its Own Meaning: An Introduction to Biblical Criticisms and Their Application.* Louisville: Westminster/John Knox, 1993.

McKnight, Edgar V. *The Postmodern Use of the Bible: The Emergence of Reader-Oriented Criticism.* Nashville: Abingdon Press, 1988.

McKnight, Scot. "Eternal Consequences or Eternal Consciousness?" In *Through No Fault of Their Own? The Fate of Those Who Have Never Heard.* Edited by William V. Crockett and James G. Sigountos, 147–57. Grand Rapids: Baker, 1991.

_____. *A Light Among the Gentiles: Jewish Mission in the Second Temple Period.* Minneapolis: Fortress, 1991.

Macksey, Richard, and Eugenio Donado, eds. *The Structuralist Controversy: The Languages of Criticism and the Sciences of Man.* Baltimore: The Johns Hopkins University Press, 1970.

Maier, Gerhard. *Biblische Hermeneutik.* Wuppertal: R. Brockhaus Verlag, 1990.

Malina, Bruce. "Is There a Circum-Mediterranean Person? Looking for Stereotypes." *Biblical Theology Bulletin* 22 (1992): 66–87.

Malina, Bruce J., and Richard L. Rohrbauch. *Social-Science Commentary on the Synoptic Gospels.* Minneapolis: Fortress Press, 1992.

Mannoia, V. James. "The Perils of Professionalism." *Faculty Dialogue* 13 (1990): 7–20.

Marchant, George. "Christian Gospel and European Culture." *Anvil* 9 (1992): 197–209.

Mark, Leslie E. "The Role of the Church in a Pluralistic Society." *Direction* 12 (1983): 7–14.

Markham, Ian S. *Plurality and Christian Ethics.* Cambridge: Cambridge University Press, 1994.

Marsden, G. M., and B. J. Longfield, eds. *The Secularization of the Academy.* Oxford: Oxford University Press, 1992.

Marsden, George M. *Evangelicalism and Modern America.* Grand Rapids: Eerdmans, 1984.

_____. "Evangelicalism in the Sociological Laboratory." *Reformed Journal* 34 (June 1984): 20–24.

_____. *The Soul of the American University: From Protestant Establishment to Established Nonbelief.* New York/Oxford: Oxford University Press, 1994.

Marshall, I. Howard. "Are Evangelicals Fundamentalists?" *Vox Evangelica* 22 (1992): 7–24.

_____. "Dialogue with Non-Christians in the New Testament." *Evangelical Review of Theology* 16 (1992): 28–47.

_____. *I Believe in the Historical Jesus.* Grand Rapids: Eerdmans, 1979.

_____. *The Origins of New Testament Christology*. Downers Grove: InterVarsity Press, 1976.

_____. "Orthodoxy and Heresy in Earlier Christianity." *Themelios* 2, no. 1 (1976): 5–14.

Marshall, Molly Truman. *No Salvation Outside the Church? A Critical Inquiry*. NABPR Dissertation Series, vol. 9. Lewiston: Edwin Mellen, 1993.

Martin, David. *A General Theory of Secularization*. New York: Harper & Row, 1978.

Martinson, Paul V. "Dynamic Pluralism." *Dialog* 28, no. 1 (1989): 6–11.

Marty, Martin. "The Clergy." In *The Professions in American History*. Edited by Nathan O. Hatch, 73–91. Notre Dame: University of Notre Dame Press, 1988.

Marty, Martin E. "American Religious History in the Eighties: A Decade of Achievement." *Church History* 62 (1993): 335–77.

_____. "Hell Disappeared. No One Noticed. A Civic Argument." *Harvard Theological Review* 78 (1985): 381–98.

_____. "Tensions Within Contemporary Evangelicalism: A Critical Appraisal." In *The Evangelicals: What They Believe, Who They Are, Where They Are Changing*. Edited by David F. Wells and John D. Woodbridge, 170–88. Nashville: Abingdon Press, 1975.

Marty, Martin E., and R. Scott Appleby. *Fundamentalisms and the State*. The Fundamentalism Project, vol. 3. Chicago: The University of Chicago Press, 1993.

_____, eds. *Fundamentalisms and the State: Remaking Polities, Economies, and Militance*. The Fundamentalism Project, vol. 5. Chicago: University of Chicago Press, 1993.

Mascall, E. L. *Christian Theology and Natural Science: Some Questions in Their Relations*. London: Longmans, Green and Co., 1956.

Masson, Jeffrey Moussaieff. *The Assault on Truth: Freud's Suppression of the Seduction Theory*. Harmondsworth, Middlesex, England: Penguin, 1985.

Maudlin, Michael G., and Edward Gilbreath. "Selling Out the House of God?" *Christianity Today* 38 (July 18, 1994): 20–23.

Maynard-Reid, Pedrito U. *Poverty and Wealth in James*. Maryknoll: Orbis Books, 1987.

Mays, James L. "What Is a Human Being? Reflections on Psalm 8." *Theology Today* 50 (1994): 511–20.

Mead, Margaret. *Coming of Age in Samoa: A Psychological Study of Primitive Youth for Western Civilization*. New York: William Morrow and Company, 1967 [1928].

Medved, Michael. *Hollywood Vs. America*. New York: HarperCollins, 1992.

Menninger, Karl. *Whatever Became of Sin?* New York: Hawthorn, 1975.

Messer, Donald E. *A Conspiracy of Goodness: Contemporary Images of Christian Mission*. Nashville: Abingdon Press, 1992.

Metzger, Bruce M. *The Canon of the New Testament: Its Origin, Development, and Significance*. Oxford: Clarendon Press, 1987.

Meyer, Ben F. *The Aims of Jesus*. London: SCM Press, 1979.

_____. *Christus Faber: The Master Builder and the House of God*. Princeton Theological Monograph Series, vol. 29. Allison Park: Pickwick Press, 1992.

_____. "The Primacy of Consent and the Uses of Suspicion." *Ex Auditu* 2 (1986): 7–18.

Meyer, Kenneth M. "The M. J. Murdock Charitable Trust Review of Graduate Theological Education in the Pacific Northwest." *Faculty Dialogue* 21 (1994): 175–83.

Miller, Ed. L. "'The True Light Which Illumines Every Person.'" In *Good News in History*. Festschrift for Bo Reicke. Edited by Ed. L. Miller, 63–82. Atlanta: Scholars Press, 1993.

Miller, William Lee. *The First Liberty: Religion and the American Republic*. New York: Paragon House Publishers, 1985.

Mills, Jonathan. "Plato's 'Formalismgate': A Dialogue on the Cover-up of the American Judiciary's Theological Rationales for 'Strict Separationism.'" *Crux* 28, no. 3 (1992): 27–33.

Mitchell, Basil. *Law, Morality, and Religion in a Secular Society*. London: Oxford University Press, 1967.

Moberly, R. W. L. *The Old Testament of the Old Testament*. Overtures to biblical theology. Minneapolis: Fortress Press, 1992.

Moltmann, Jürgen. "Christianity in the Third Millennium." *Theology Today* 51 (1994): 75–89.

Moore, Stephen D. *Literary Criticism and the Gospels: The Theoretical Challenge*. New Haven: Yale University Press, 1989.

_____. *Mark and Luke in Poststructuralist Perspectives: Jesus Begins to Write*. New Haven: Yale University Press, 1992.

_____. *Poststructuralism and the New Testament: Derrida and Foucault at the Foot of the Cross*. Minneapolis: Fortress Press, 1994.

Moore, W. Ernest. "'Outside' and 'Inside': Paul and Mark." *The Expository Times* 103 (1992): 331–36.

Moran, Gabriel. *Uniqueness: Problem or Paradox in Jewish and Christian Traditions*. Maryknoll: Orbis Books, 1992.

Moreland, J. P. *Christianity and the Nature of Science*. Grand Rapids: Baker, 1989.

_____, ed. *The Creation Hypothesis: Scientific Evidence for an Intelligent Designer*. Downers Grove: InterVarsity Press, 1994.

Morey, Robert A. *Battle of the Gods: The Gathering Storm in Modern Evangelicalism*. Southbridge: Crown Publications, 1989.

Morgan, Robert, and John Barton. *Biblical Interpretation*. Oxford: Oxford University Press, 1988.

Moriarty, Michael G. *The New Charismatics: A Concerned Voice Responds to Dangerous New Trends*. Grand Rapids: Zondervan, 1992.

Moritz, Thorsten. "'Summing-up All Things': Religious Pluralism and Universalim in Ephesians." In *One God One Lord in a World of Religious Pluralism*. Edited by Andrew D. Clarke and Bruce W. Winter, 88–111. Cambridge: Tyndale House, 1991.

Morris, Thomas V. "Our Idea of God: An Introduction to Philosophical Theology." In *Contours of Christian Philosophy*. Edited by C. Stephen Evans. Downers Grove: InterVarsity Press, 1991.

_____. *The Logic of God Incarnate*. Ithaca: Cornell University Press, 1986.

Morrow, Lance. "Evil." *Time* 137, no. 23 (1991): 48–53.

Mott, Stephen Charles. *Biblical Ethics and Social Change*. New York: Oxford University Press, 1982.

_____. *A Christian Perspective on Political Thought*. Oxford: Oxford University Press, 1993.

Moule, C. F. D. *The Origin of Christology*. Cambridge: Cambridge University Press, 1977.

Mouw, Richard J. *Consulting the Faithful: What Christian Intellectuals Can Learn from Popular Religion*. Grand Rapids: Eerdmans, 1994.

Mouw, Richard J., and Sander Griffioen. *Pluralisms and Horizons: An Essay in Christian Public Philosophy*. Grand Rapids: Eerdmans, 1993.

Mowrer, O. Hobart. *The Crisis in Psychiatry and Religion*. Princeton: D. Van Nostrand, 1961.

Muck, Terry C. "Evangelicals and Interreligious Dialogue." *Journal of the Evangelical Theological Society* 36 (1993): 517–29.

Muller, Richard A. *God, Creation, and Providence in the Thought of Jacob Arminius: Sources and Directions of Scholastic Protestantism in the Era of Early Orthodoxy*. Grand Rapids: Baker, 1991.

Munck, Johannes. *Paul and the Salvation of Mankind*. Translated by Frank Clarke. Richmond: John Knox Press, 1959.

Murphy, Nancey. "Phillip Johnson on Trial: A Critique of His Critique of Darwin." *Perspectives on Science and Faith* 45, no. 1 (1993): 26–36.

_____. *Theology in the Age of Scientific Reasoning.* Ithaca: Cornell University Press, 1990.

Murray, Charles. *In Pursuit of Happiness and Good Government.* New York: Simon & Schuster, 1988.

Murray, Iain. "The Scots at Westminster Assembly: With Special Reference to the Dispute on Church Government and Its Aftermath." *Banner of Truth* 371–372 (1994): 6–40.

Murray, Iain H. *Revival and Revivalism: The Making and Marring of American Evangelicalism 1750–1858.* Edinburgh: Banner of Truth Trust, 1994.

_____. "Who Is a Christian." *Evangelicals Now* 4 (April 1989): 7.

Myers, Ken. *Christianity, Culture, and Common Grace.* Mars Hill Monographs. Powhatan: Berea Publications, 1994.

Myers, Kenneth A. *All God's Children and Blue Suede Shoes: Christians and Popular Culture.* Westchester: Crossway, 1989.

Nash, Ronald. *The Concept of God: An Exploration of Contemporary Difficulties with the Attributes of God.* Grand Rapids: Zondervan, 1983.

Nash, Ronald H. *Is Jesus the Only Savior?* Grand Rapids: Zondervan, 1994.

_____. *Social Justice and the Christian Church.* Milford: Mott Media, 1983.

_____. *The Word of God and the Mind of Man: The Crisis of Revealed Truth in Contemporary Theology.* Grand Rapids: Zondervan, 1982.

_____. *Worldviews in Conflict: Choosing Christianity in a World of Ideas.* Grand Rapids: Zondervan, 1992.

Nazir-Ali, Michael. *From Everywhere to Everywhere: A World View of Christian Mission.* London: William Collins Sons & Co., 1991.

Neill, Stephen. *Christian Faith and Other Faiths.* Downers Grove: InterVarsity Press, 1984.

_____. *Out of Bondage.* Edinburgh: Edinburgh House, n.d.

Nelson, Robert H. *Reaching for Heaven on Earth: The Theological Meaning of Economics.* Lanham: Rowman and Littlefield Publishers, 1991.

Netland, Harold A. "Apologetics, Worldviews, and the Problem of Neutral Criteria." *Trinity Journal* 12 (1991): 39–58.

_____. *Dissonant Voices: Religious Pluralism and the Question of Truth.* Grand Rapids: Eerdmans, 1991.

_____. "Truth, Authority, and Modernity: Shopping for Truth in a Supermarket of Worldviews." Consultation on Modernity, Uppsala, Sweden, June 10–15. In *Faith and Modernity.* Edited by Philip Sampson, Vinay Samuel, and Chris Sugden, 89–115. Oxford: Regnum Books, 1994.

Neufeldt, Ronald W. "The Study of Other Religons: Its Necessity and Problems." *Direction* 12 (1983): 28–33.

Neuhaus, Richard John. *America Against Itself: Moral Vision and the Public Order.* Notre Dame: University of Notre Dame Press, 1992.

_____. *The Naked Public Square: Religion and Democracy in America.* Grand Rapids: Eerdmans, 1984.

_____, ed. *American Apostasy: The Triumph of "Other" Gospels.* Encounter Series, vol. 10. Grand Rapids: Eerdmans, 1989.

_____, ed. *The Structure of Freedom: Correlations, Causes, and Cautions.* Encounter Series, vol. 14. Grand Rapids: Eerdmans, 1991.

Neuhaus, Richard John, and Michael Cromartie, eds. *Piety and Politics: Evangelicals and Fundamentalists Confront the World.* Washington: Ethics and Public Policy Center, 1987.

Neusner, Jacob. "The Jewish-Christian Argument in the First Century: Different People Talking About Different Things to Different People." In *The Law in the Bible and Its Environment*. Edited by Timo Veijola, 173–87. Helsinki/Göttingen: The Finnish Exegetical Society/Vandenhoeck & Ruprecht, 1990.

_____. *Jews and Christians: The Myth of a Common Tradition*. Philadelphia: Trinity Press International, 1991.

_____. *Telling Tales: Making Sense of Christian and Judaic Nonsense: The Urgency and Basis for Judeo-Christian Dialogue*. Louisville: Westminster/John Knox, 1993.

Neveu, Bruno. *L'erreur et son juge. Remarques sur les censures doctrinales á l'époque moderne*. Naples: Biblipolis, 1993.

Newbigin, Lesslie. "Can the West Be Converted?" *International Bulletin of Missionary Research* 11 (1987): 2–7.

_____. "Certain Faith: What Kind of Certainty?" *Tyndale Bulletin* 44 (1993): 339–50.

_____. "Confessing Christ in a Multi-Religion Society." *Scottish Bulletin of Evangelical Theology* 12 (1994): 125–36.

_____. *Foolishness to the Greeks: The Gospel and Western Culture*. London: SPCK, 1986.

_____. *The Gospel in a Pluralist Society*. Grand Rapids: Eerdmans, 1989.

_____. *Honest Religion for Secular Man*. Philadelphia: Westminster Press, 1966.

_____. *Truth to Tell: The Gospel as Public Truth*. Grand Rapids: Eerdmans, 1991.

Newsome, David. *The Parting of Friends: The Wilberforces and Henry Manning*. Grand Rapids: Eerdmans, 1993 [1966].

Neyrey, Jerome H. "Acts 17, Epicureans, and Theodicy: A Study in Stereotypes." In *Greek, Romans, and Christians*. Festschrift for Abraham J. Malherbe. Edited by David L. Balch, Everett Ferguson, and Wayne A. Meeks, 118–34. Minneapolis: Fortress Press, 1990.

Nichols, Bruce J. "The Witnessing Church in Dialogue." *Evangelical Review of Theology* 16 (1992): 48–65.

Nicole, Roger R., and J. Ramsey Michaels, eds. *Inerrancy and Common Sense*. Grand Rapids: Baker, 1980.

Nida, Eugene A. *Customs, Culture and Christianity*. London: Tyndale Press, 1954.

Niebuhr, H. Richard. *Christ and Culture*. New York: Harper & Row, Harper Torchbooks/Cloister Library, 1956.

_____. *Radical Monotheism and Western Culture*. New York: Harper & Row, Harper Torchbooks, 1970.

Nielsen, Niels C., Jr. *Fundamentalism, Mythos, and World Religions*. Albany: State University of New York Press, 1993.

Nietzsche, Friedrich. *A Nietzsche Reader*. Harmondsworth: Penguin Books, 1977.

Nisly, Paul. "A Word of Hope." *Faculty Dialogue* 17 (1992): 113–17.

Noll, Mark. "Traditional Christianity and the Possibility of Historical Knowledge." *Christian Scholar's Review* 19 (1990): 388–406.

Noll, Mark, Cornelius Plantinga, Jr., and David Wells. "Evangelical Theology Today." *Theology Today* 51 (1995): 495–507.

Noll, Mark A. *A History of Christianity in the United States and Canada*. Grand Rapids: Eerdmans, 1992.

_____. *The Scandal of the Evangelical Mind*. Grand Rapids: Eerdmans, 1994.

Noll, Mark A., David W. Bebbington, and George A. Rawlyk, eds. *Evangelicalism: Comparative Studies of Popular Protestantism in North America, the British Isles, and Beyond, 1700–1990*. New York: Oxford University Press, 1994.

Norman, Edward. *Entering the Darkness: Christianity and Its Modern Substitutes*. London: SPCK, 1991.

North, Gary. *Dominion and Common Grace: The Biblical Basis of Progress*. Tyler: Institute for Christian Economics, 1987.

_____. *Political Polytheism: The Myth of Pluralism*. Tyler: Institute for Christian Economics, 1989.

_____, ed. *Theonomy: An Informed Response*. Tyler: Institute for Christian Economics, 1991.

North, Gary, and Gary DeMar. *Christian Reconstruction: What It Is, What It Isn't*. Tyler: Institute for Christian Economics, 1991.

Novak, David. *Jewish-Christian Dialogue: A Jewish Justification*. New York: Oxford University Press, 1989.

Novick, Peter. *That Noble Dream: The "Objectivity Question" and the American Historical Profession*. Cambridge: Cambridge University Press, 1988.

Nyquist, John. *The Use of the New Testament as Illustrated in Missiological Themes Within Selected Documents of the Second Vatican Council*. Ed.D. Diss., TEDS, 1991.

O'Brien, Peter T. "Divine Analysis and Comprehensive Solution: Some Priorities from Ephesians 2." *Reformed Theological Review* (1995): (forthcoming).

_____. *The Epistle to the Philippians: A Commentary on the Greek Text*. NIGTC. Grand Rapids: Eerdmans, 1991.

_____. "Paul's Missionary Calling Within the Purposes of God." In *In the Fullness of Time*. Festschrift for Donald Robinson. Edited by David Peterson and John Pryor, 131–48. Homebush West: Anzea, 1992.

O'Rourke, P. J. *Give War a Chance: Eyewitness Accounts of Mankind's Struggles Against Tyranny, Injustice and Alcohol-Free Beer*. New York: The Atlantic Monthly Press, 1992.

Odell-Scott, David W. *A Post-Patriarchal Christology*. American Academy of Religion Academy Series, vol. 78. Atlanta: Scholars Press, 1991.

Oden, Thomas C. *After Modernity . . . What? Agenda for Theology*. Grand Rapids: Zondervan, 1990.

_____. *Two Worlds: Notes on the Death of Modernity in America and Russia*. Downers Grove: InterVarsity Press, 1992.

Offner, Kevin. "American Evangelicalism: Adrift with Amnesia." *Regeneration Quarterly* 1, no. 1 (1995): 6–9.

Ogbonnaya, A. Okechukwu. *On Communitarian Divinity: An African Interpretation of the Trinity*. New York: Paragon House, 1994.

Ogden, Schubert M. *Is There Only One True Religion or Are There Many?* Dallas: Southern Methodist University Press, 1992.

_____. *The Reality of God and Other Essays*. New York: Harper & Row, 1966.

Olasky, Marvin. *The Tragedy of American Compassion*. Wheaton: Crossway Books, 1992.

Olasky, Marvin, Herbert Schlossberg, Pierre Berthoud, and Clark H. Pinnock. *Freedom, Justice, and Hope: Toward a Strategy for the Poor and the Oppressed*. Westchester: Crossway Books, 1988.

Olneck, Michael R. "Is Pluralism Possible in American Public Education?" In *The Challenge of Pluralism: Edcuation, Politics, and Values*. Edited by F. Clark Power and Daniel K. Lapsley, 251–71. Notre Dame: University of Notre Dame Press, 1992.

Oosthuizen, George C. "Southern African Independent Churches Respond to Demonic Powers." *Evangelical Review of Theology* 16 (1992): 414–34.

Opitz, Edmund A. *Religion: Foundation of the Free Society*. Irvington-on-Hudson: The Foundation for Economic Education, Inc., 1994.

Orenstein, Alex. *Willard Van Orman Quine*. Boston: Twayne Publishers, 1977.

Ortberg, John. "Happy Meal Spirituality: Why My Kids Are Convinced They Have a McDonald's-shaped Vacuum in Their Little Souls." *Christianity Today* 37 (May 17, 1993): 38–40.

Osborne, Grant R. *The Hermeneutical Spiral: A Comprehensive Introduction to Biblical Interpretation.* Downers Grove: InterVarsity Press, 1992.

Oswalt, John N. "Golden Calves and the 'Bull of Jacob': The Impact on Israel of Its Religious Environment." In *Israel's Apostasy and Restoration.* Festschrift for Roland K. Harrison. Edited by Avraham Gileadi, 9–18. Grand Rapids: Baker, 1988.

Otto, Randall E. "God and History in Jürgen Moltmann." *Journal of the Evangelical Theological Society* 35 (1992): 375–88.

Otto, Rudolf. *The Idea of the Holy: An Inquiry Into the Non-rational Factor in the Idea of the Divine and Its Relation to the Rational.* Translation and preface by John W. Harvey. London: Oxford University Press, 1958 [1923].

Oyelade, E. O. "Islamic Theocracy and Religious Pluralism in Africa." *Asia Journal of Theology* 7, no. 1 (1993): 149–60.

Packer, J. I. *God's Words.* Downers Grove: InterVarsity Press, 1981.

_____. *A Quest for Godliness: The Puritan Vision of the Christian Life.* Wheaton: Crossway Books, 1990.

_____. "Theism for Our Time." In *God Who Is Rich in Mercy.* Festschrift for D. Broughton Knox. Edited by Peter T. O'Brien and David G. Peterson, 1–23. Homebush West: Anzea, 1986.

_____. "The Problem of Eternal Punishment." *Evangel* 10 (1992): 13–19.

Palmer, Gordon R. "No More Than a Spoonful of Sugar? Evangelicals and Social Involvement." *Scottish Bulletin of Evangelical Theology* 12 (1994): 80–95.

Palmer, Richard E. *Hermeneutics: Interpretation Theory in Schleiermacher, Dilthey, Heidegger, and Gadamer.* Northwestern University Studies in Phenomenology and Existential Philosophy. Evanston: Northwestern University Press, 1969.

Panikkar, R. *The Intrareligious Dialogue.* New York: Paulist Press, 1978.

_____. "The Meaning of Christ's Name." In *Service and Salvation.* Edited by Joseph Pathrapankal, 235–63. Bangalore: C.M.I., 1973.

_____. *The Unknown Christ of Hinduism: Towards an Ecumenical Christophany.* Maryknoll: Orbis Books, 1981.

Pannenberg, Wolfhart. *Human Nature, Election and History.* Philadelphia: Westminster Press, 1977.

_____. *Systematic Theology,* vol. 1. Translated by Geoffrey W. Bromiley. Grand Rapids: Eerdmans, 1991.

Park, Chris C. *Caring for Creation: A Christian Way Forward.* London: Marshall Pickering, 1992.

Parshall, Phil. *Beyond the Mosque: Christians Within Muslim Community.* Grand Rapids: Baker, 1985.

Pawson, David. *The Road to Hell.* London: Hodder & Stoughton, 1992.

Peacock, Roy E. *A Brief History of Eternity.* Wheaton: Crossway, 1990.

Peacocke, Arthur. *Theology for a Scientific Age: Being and Becoming—Natural and Divine.* Oxford: Basil Blackwell, 1990.

Pearce, Joseph Chilton. *Evolution's End: Claiming the Potential of Our Intelligence.* San Francisco: HarperCollins, 1992.

Pelikan, Jaroslav. *Christian Doctrine and Modern Culture (since 1700).* The Christian Tradition: A History of the Development of Doctrine, vol. 5. Chicago: University of Chicago Press, 1989.

_____. *The Finality of Jesus Christ in an Age of Universal History: A Dilemma of the Third Century*. Ecumenical Studies in History, vol. 3. London/Richmond: Lutterworth/John Knox Press, 1965/1966.

_____. *Jesus Through the Centuries: His Place in the History of Culture*. New Haven: Yale University Press, 1985.

Perkins, Pheme. "Theological Implications for New Testament Pluralism." *Catholic Biblical Quarterly* 50 (1988): 5–23.

Perrin, Norman. *Jesus and the Language of the Kingdom*. Philadelphia: Westminster Press, 1976.

Peters, Ted. "The Lutheran Distinctiveness in Mission to a Pluralistic World." *Dialog* 22 (1983): 18–29.

Pettit, Philip. *The Concept of Structuralism: A Critical Analysis*. Berkeley: University of California Press, 1977.

Philips, Timothy R. "Hell: A Christological Reflection." In *Through No Fault of Their Own?* edited by William V. Crockett and James G. Sigountos, 47–59. Grand Rapids: Baker, 1991.

Phillips, D. Z. *Faith and Philosophical Enquiry*. New York: Schocken Books, 1970.

Phillips, W. Gary. "Evangelicals and Pluralism: Current Options." *Evangelical Quarterly* 64 (1992): 229–44.

Pinnock, Clark. "Acts 4:12—No Other Name Under Heaven." In *Through No Fault of Their Own?* Edited by William V. Crockett and James G. Sigountos, 107–15. Grand Rapids: Baker, 1991.

_____. "The Conditional View." In *Four Views on Hell*. Edited by William Crockett, 135–66. Grand Rapids: Zondervan, 1992.

_____. "Toward an Evangelical Theology of Religions." *Journal of the Evangelical Theological Society* 33 (1990): 359–68.

_____. *Tracking the Maze: Finding Our Way Through Modern Theology from an Evangelical Perspective*. San Francisco: HarperCollins, 1990.

Pinnock, Clark, Richard Rice, John Sanders, William Hasker, and David Basinger. *The Openness of God: A Biblical Challenge to the Traditional Understanding of God*. Downers Grove: InterVarsity Press, 1994.

Pinnock, Clark H. "The Destruction of the Finally Impenitent." *Criswell Theological Review* 4 (1990): 243–359.

_____. "The Finality of Jesus Christ in a World of Religions." In *Christian Faith and Practice in the Modern World: Theology from an Evangelical Point of View*. Edited by Mark A. Noll, and David F. Wells, 152–68. Grand Rapids: Eerdmans, 1988.

_____. "The Role of the Spirit in Interpretation." *Journal of the Evangelical Theological Society* 36 (1993): 491–97.

_____. *A Wideness in God's Mercy: The Finality of Jesus Christ in a World of Religions*. Grand Rapids: Zondervan, 1992.

_____, ed. *A Case for Arminianism: The Grace of God, the Will of Man*. Grand Rapids: Zondervan, 1989.

Piper, John. *Let the Nations Be Glad! The Supremacy of God in Missions*. Grand Rapids: Baker, 1993.

_____. *The Pleasures of God: Meditations on God's Delight in Being God*. Portland: Multnomah, 1991.

Piryns, Ernest D. "Current Roman Catholic Views of Other Religions." *Missionalia* 13 (1985): 55–62.

Placher, William C. "Revealed to Reason: Theology as 'Normal Science.'" *Christian Century* (February 1, 1992): 192–95.

_____. *Unapologetic Theology: A Christian Voice in a Pluralistic Conversation.* Louisville: Westminster/John Knox, 1989.

_____. "Why Bother with Theology?" *Christian Century* (February 2–9, 1994): 104–8.

Plantinga, Alvin. *God and Other Minds: A Study of the Rational Justification of Belief in God.* Edited by Max Black. Contemporary Philosophy. Ithaca: Cornell University Press, 1967.

_____. "Pluralism: A Defense of Religious Exclusivism." 1992.

_____. "Reason and Belief in God." In *Faith and Rationality: Reason and Belief in God.* Edited by Alvin Plantinga and Nicholas Wolterstorff, 16–93. Notre Dame: University of Notre Dame Press, 1983.

Pointer, Richard W. *Protestant Pluralism and the New York Experience: A Study of Eighteenth-Century Diversity.* Bloomington: Indiana University Press, 1988.

Poland, Lynn M. *Literary Criticism and Biblical Hermeneutics: A Critique of Formalist Approaches.* AARAS, vol. 48. Chico: Scholars Press, 1985.

Polanyi, Michael. *Knowing and Being.* Chicago: University of Chicago Press, 1969.

_____. *Personal Knowledge: Towards a Post-Critical Philosophy.* New York: Harper & Row, Harper Torchbooks/Academy Library, 1962.

Polkinghorne, John. *Reason and Reality: The Relationship Between Science and Theology.* London: SPCK, 1991.

Pope John Paul II. *Veritatis Splendor: Encyclical Letter Addressed by the Supreme Pontiff Pope John Paul II to All the Bishops of the Catholic Church Regarding Certain Fundamental Questions of the Church's Moral Teaching.* London: Catholic Truth Society, 1993.

Popper, Karl R. *The Logic of Scientific Discovery.* New York: Harper & Row, Harper Torchbooks, 1968.

_____. *The Poverty of Historicism.* New York: Harper & Row, Harper Torchbooks, 1964.

Postman, Neil. *Amusing Ourselves to Death: Public Discourse in the Age of Show Business.* New York: Penguin Books, 1985.

Power, F. Clark, and Daniel K. Lapsley, eds. *The Challenge of Pluralism: Education, Politics and Values.* Notre Dame: University of Notre Dame Press, 1992.

Poythress, Vern Sheridan. *Symphonic Theology: The Validity of Multiple Perspectives in Theology.* Grand Rapids: Zondervan, 1987.

Prestige, G. L. *God in Patristic Thought.* London: SPCK, 1952.

Priest, Robert J. "Cultural Anthropology, Sin, and the Missionary." In *God and Culture.* Festschrift for Carl F. H. Henry. Edited by D. A. Carson and John D. Woodbridge, 85–105. Grand Rapids: Eerdmans, 1993.

Proctor, John. "The Gospel from Athens: Paul's Speech Before the Areopagus and the Evangel for Today." *Evangel* 10 (1992): 69–72.

Pryor, John. "Jesus and Women—a Second Look at the Issue." *Interchange* 50 (1993): 7–18.

Punt, Neal. *Unconditional Good News.* Grand Rapids: Eerdmans, 1980.

Quine, W. V. *Ontological Relativity and Other Essays.* New York: Columbia University Press, 1969.

_____. *Word and Object.* Cambridge: Cambridge University Press, 1960.

Race, Alan. *Christians and Religious Pluralism: Patterns in the Christian Theology of Religions.* Maryknoll: Orbis Books, 1985.

Rahner, Karl. *Theological Investigations.* New York: Seabury, 1961–92.

Rainbow, Paul. "Jewish Monotheism as the Matrix for New Testament Christology: A Review Article." *Novum Testamentum* 33 (1991): 78–91.

_____. *Monotheism and Christianity in 1 Corinthians 8:4–6.* D.Phil. dissertation, Oxford University, 1987.

Read, Leonard E. "I, Pencil." *Imprimus* 21, no. 6 (1992): 1–3.

Regan, Hilary D., and Alan J. Torrance, eds. *Christ and Context: The Confrontation Between Gospel and Culture.* Edinburgh: T & T Clark, 1993.

Reicke, Bo. "Positive and Negative Aspects of the World in the New Testament." *Westminster Theological Journal* 49 (1987): 351–69.

Reid, Gavin. *The Gagging of God: The Failure of the Church to Communicate in the Television Age.* London: Hodder and Stoughton, 1969.

Reist, Benjamin A. *Processive Revelation.* Louisville: Westminster/John Knox, 1992.

Reumann, John. *Variety and Unity in New Testament Thought.* Oxford Bible Series. Oxford: Oxford University Press, 1991.

Richard, Ramesh. *The Population of Heaven.* Chicago: Moody Press, 1994.

Richmond, Kent D. "Preaching in the Context of Pluralism." *Quarterly Review* 3 (Summer 1983): 43–50.

Ricoeur, Paul. *Essays on Biblical Interpretation.* Introduction by Lewis S. Mudge. Philadelphia: Fortress, 1980.

_____. *Hermeneutics and the Human Sciences.* Edited and translated by John B. Thompson. Cambridge: Cambridge University Press, 1981.

_____. *Interpretation Theory: Discourse and the Surplus of Meaning.* Fort Worth: Texas Christian University Press, 1978.

Rissi, M. *The Future of the World.* London: SCM Press, 1972.

Rivers, A. J. "Blasphemy Law in the Secular State." *Cambridge Papers* 1 (December 1992).

Ro, Bong Rin, and Ruth Eshenaur, eds. *The Bible and Theology in Asian Contexts.* Taichung: Asia Theological Association, 1984.

Robbins, Thomas, and Dick Anthony, eds. *In Gods We Trust: New Patterns of Religious Pluralism in America.* New Brunswick: Transaction Books, 1981.

Roberts, Maurice. "Our Good Opinion of Ourselves." *Banner of Truth* 353 (May 1993): 1–4.

Roberts, Robert C. "Psychobabble." *Christianity Today* 38 (May 16, 1994): 18–24.

_____. *Taking the Word to Heart: Self and Other in an Age of Therapies.* Grand Rapids: Eerdmans, 1993.

Roberts, Vaughan. "Reframing the UCCF Doctrinal Basis." *Theology* 95 (1992): 432–46.

Robertson, Pat. *The Turning Tide: The Fall of Liberalism and the Rise of Common Sense.* Dallas: Word Publishing, 1993.

Robinson, H. Wheeler. *Corporate Personality in Ancient Israel.* Philadelphia: Fortress Press, 1964 [1935].

Robinson, Haddon W. "Call Us Irresponsible." *Christianity Today* 38 (April 4, 1994): 15.

Robinson, J. A. T. *In the End God.* 2d ed. London: Collins, 1968.

_____. "Universalism—Is It Heretical?" *Scottish Journal of Theology* 2 (1949): 139–55.

_____. *Honest to God.* London: SCM Press, 1963.

Robinson, Thomas A. *The Bauer Thesis Examined: The Geography of Heresy in the Early Christian Church.* Lewiston: Edwin Mellen Press, 1988.

Roche, George. *The Fall of the Ivory Tower: Government Funding, Corruption, and the Bankrupting of American Higher Education.* Washington, D.C.: Regnery Publishing, Inc., 1994.

_____. *A World Without Heroes: The Modern Tragedy.* Hillsdale: Hillsdale College Press, 1987.

Rochelle, Jay C. "Mystery and Relationship as Keys to the Church's Response to Secularism." *Currents in Theology and Mission* 19 (1992): 267–76.

Rogers, Jack B., and Donald K. McKim. *The Authority and Interpretation of the Bible: An Historical Approach*. San Francisco: Harper & Row, 1979.

Rohrbaugh, Richard L. "'Social Location of Thought' as a Heuristic Construct in New Testament Study." *Journal for the Study of the New Testament* 30 (1987): 103–19.

Roof, Wade Clark. *A Generation of Seekers: The Spiritual Journeys of the Baby Boom Generation*. San Francisco: Harper San Francisco, 1993.

Rookmaker, H. R. *Modern Art and the Death of a Culture*. London: Inter-Varsity Press, 1970.

Rorty, Richard. *Consequences of Pragmatism: Essays 1972–1980*. Minneapolis: University of Minnesota Press, 1982.

_____. "Nineteenth-Century Idealism and Twentieth-Century Textualism." In *Consequences of Pragmatism*. Minneapolis: University of Minnesota Press, 1982.

_____. *Philosophy and the Mirror of Nature*. Princeton: Princeton University Press, 1979.

Rosenzweig, Franz. *Star of Redemption*. New York: Holt, Rinehart and Winston, 1970.

Rosner, Brian S. "'Stronger Than He'? The Strength of 1 Corinthians 10:22b." *Tyndale Bulletin* 43 (1992): 171–79.

Rossano, Pietro. "Christ's Lordship and Religious Pluralism." In Mission Trends, vol. 5: *Faith Meets Faith*. Edited by Gerald Anderson and Thomas Stransky, 20–35. Grand Rapids: Eerdmans, 1981.

Rowdon, H. H., ed. *Christ the Lord*. Festschrift for Donald Guthrie. Leicester: Inter-Varsity Press, 1982.

Rowland, Christopher, and Mark Corner. *Liberating Exegesis: The Challenge of Liberation Theology to Biblical Studies*. Louisville: Westminster/John Knox, 1989.

Rudin, A. James, and Marvin R. Wilson, eds. *A Time to Speak: The Evangelical-Jewish Encounter*. Grand Rapids: Eerdmans, 1987.

Ruether, Rosemary Radford. "Feminism and Jewish-Christian Dialogue." In *The Myth of Christian Uniqueness*. Edited by John Hick and Paul Knitter, 137–48. Maryknoll: Orbis Books, 1987.

Runia, Klaas. "The Challenge of the Modern World to the Church." *Evangelical Review of Theology* 18 (1994): 301–21.

Ruse, Michael. "A Few Last Words—Until the Next Time." *Zygon* 29 (1994): 75–79.

Rushdoony, Rousas J. *The Institutes of Biblical Law*. Nutley: Craig Press, 1973.

Rusher, William A. *The Coming Battle for the Media: Curbing the Power of the Media Elite*. New York: William Morrow and Company, 1988.

Ryken, Leland. "Literature in Christian Perspective." In *God and Culture*. Festschrift for Carl F. H. Henry. Edited by D. A. Carson and John D. Woodbridge, 215–34. Grand Rapids: Eerdmans, 1993.

Samartha, S. J. *One Christ—Many Religions: Toward a Revised Christology*. Bangalore: SATHRI and Wordmakers, 1992.

Sampson, Philip. "The Rise of Postmodernity." In *Faith and Modernity*. Edited by Philip Sampson, Vinay Samuel, and Chris Sugden, 29–57. Oxford: Regnum Books, 1994.

Sampson, Philip, Vinay Samuel, and Chris Sugden, eds. *Faith and Modernity*. Oxford: Regnum Books, 1994.

Samuel, David. "The Place of Private Judgment." *Churchman* 108 (1994): 6–21.

Samuel, Vinay, and Christ Sugden, eds. *A.D. 2000 and Beyond: A Mission Agenda*. Festschrift for John R. W. Stott. Oxford: Regnum Books, 1991.

Sanders, John. *No Other Name: An Investigation Into the Destiny of the Unevangelized*. Grand Rapids: Eerdmans, 1992.

Sanders, John E. "Is Belief in Christ Necessary for Salvation?" *Evangelical Quarterly* 60 (1988): 241–59.

Sandmel, Samuel. *We Jews and Jesus*. London/New York: Oxford University Press, 1965.

Sanneh, Lamin. "Christian Missions and the Western Guilt Complex." *Christian Century* (April 8, 1987): 330–30.

_____. *Encountering the West. Christianity and the Global Cultural Process: The African Dimension*. Maryknoll/London: Orbis Books/Marshall Pickering, 1993.

Schaeffer, Francis A. *How Should We Then Live? The Rise and Decline of Western Thought and Culture*. Old Tappan: Fleming H. Revell, 1976.

Schall, James V. *Another Sort of Learning: Selected Contrary Essays on How Finally to Acquire an Education While Still in College or Anywhere Else: Containing Some Belated Advice About How to Employ Your Leisure Time When Ultimate Questions Remain Perplexing in Spite of Your Highest Earned Academic Degree, Together with Sundry Book Lists Nowhere Else in Captivity to Be Found*. San Francisco: Ignatius, 1988.

Scharen, Hans. "Gehenna in the Synoptics." *Bibliotheca Sacra* 149 (1992): 304–15, 454–70.

Schleiermacher, Friedrich. *Hermeneutics: The Handwritten Manuscripts*. Edited by Heins Kimmerle. Translated by James Duke and Jack Forstman. American Academy of Religion Texts and Translation Series, vol. 1. Missoula: Scholars Press, 1977.

Schlette, H. R. *Towards a Theology of Religions*. London: Burns and Oates, 1963.

Schlossberg, Herbert. *Idols for Destruction: Christian Faith and Its Confrontation with American Society*. Wheaton: Crossway, 1990 [1983].

Schlossberg, Herbert, and Marvin Olasky. *Turning Point: A Christian Worldview Declaration*. Wheaton: Crossway Books, 1987.

Schluter, M., and R. Clements. *Reactivating the Extended Family: From Biblical Norms to Public Policy in Britain*. Cambridge: Jubilee Centre Publications, 1986.

Schluter, Michael, and David Lee. *The R Factor*. London: Hodder & Stoughton, 1993.

Schneiders, Sandra M. *The Revelatory Text: Interpreting the New Testament as Sacred Scripture*. San Francisco/London: HarperCollins, 1991.

Scholes, Robert. *Textual Power: Literary Theory and the Teaching of English*. New Haven: Yale University Press, 1985.

Schouls, A. *The Imposition of Method*. Oxford: Oxford University Press, 1980.

Schreiter, Robert J. "The ATS Globalization and Theological Education Project: Contextualization from a World Perspective." *Theological Education* 30 (1994): 81–88.

Schuller, David S. "Globalizing Theological Education: Beginning the Journey." *Theological Education* 30 (1993): Supplement 1, 3–14.

Schultze, Quentin J. *Televangelism and American Culture: The Business of Popular Religion*. Grand Rapids: Baker, 1991.

Schwäbel, Christoph, and Colin E. Gunton, eds. *Persons, Divine and Human: King's College Essays in Theological Anthropology*. Edinburgh: T & T Clark, 1992.

Scott, Waldron. "'No Other Name'—An Evangelical Conviction (plus Rejoinders and a Surrejoinder)." In *Christ's Lordship and Religious Pluralism*. Edited by Gerald H. Anderson and Thomas F. Stransky, 58–95. Maryknoll: Orbis Books, 1981.

Scroggs, Robin. *The Text and the Times*. Minneapolis: Fortress Press, 1993.

Sedgwick, Colin J. "Where Liberal Theology Falls Short: A Response to the Revd Martin Camroux." *Expository Times* 104 (1992): 3–6.

Seeley, David. *Deconstructing the New Testament*. Biblical Interpretation Series, vol. 5. Leiden: E. J. Brill, 1994.

Segal, Alan F. *Two Powers in Heaven: Early Rabbinic Reports About Christianity and Gnosticism*. Leiden: E. J. Brill, 1977.

Senior, John. *The Death of a Christian Culture*. Harrison: RC Books, 1994.

Shedd, W. G. T. *The Doctrine of Endless Punishment*. Edinburgh: Banner of Truth Trust, 1986 [1855].

Sheehan, Robert. "Creeds, Confessions and Criticisms." *Banner of Truth Trust* 367 (April 1994): 20–25.

Shelley, Bruce L. *The Gospel and the American Dream*. Portland: Multnomah, 1989.

Shermis, Michael, and Arthur E. Zannoni, eds. *Introduction to Jewish-Christian Relations*. New York: Paulist Press, 1991.

Shuger, Debora Kuller. *The Renaissance Bible: Scholarship, Sacrifice, and Subjectivity*. Berkeley: University of California Press, 1994.

Shuster, Marguerite, and Richard Muller, eds. *Perspectives on Christology*. Festschrift for Paul K. Jewett. Grand Rapids: Zondervan, 1991.

Siker, Jeffrey S. *Disinheriting the Jews: Abraham in Early Christian Controversy*. Louisville: Westminster/John Knox, 1991.

Silva, Moisés. "Systematic Theology and the Apostle to the Gentiles." *Trinity Journal* 15 (1994): 3–26.

Silverman, Hugh J., and Don Ihde, eds. *Hermeneutics & Deconstruction*. Selected Studies in Phenomenology and Existential Philosophy, vol. 10. Albany: State University of New York Press, 1985.

Simon, Marcel. *Versus Israel: A Study of the Relations Between Christians and Jews in the Roman Empire (135–425)*. Translated by H. McKeating. The Littman Library of Jewish Civilization. Oxford: Oxford University Press, 1986.

Singer, C. Gregg. *From Rationalism to Irrationality: The Decline of the Western Mind from the Renaissance to the Present*. Phillipsburg: Presbyterian and Reformed Publishing Co., 1979.

Smith, David. "The Image of Humanity in Contemporary Culture." *Scottish Bulletin of Evangelical Theology* 10 (1992): 113–23.

Smith, David W. "In Praise of Ambiguity: A Response to Jonathan Harrop's Critique of the Sociology of David Martin." *Religion* 18 (1988): 81–85.

Smith, Ian. "God and Economics." In *God and Culture*. Festschrift for Carl F. H. Henry. Edited by D. A. Carson and John D. Woodbridge, 162–79. Grand Rapids: Eerdmans, 1993.

Smith, Mark S. *The Early History of God: Yahweh and the Other Deities in Ancient Israel*. San Francisco: Harper & Row, 1990.

Smith, Norman Kemp. *New Studies in the Philosophy of Descartes: Descartes as Pioneer*. London: Macmillan, 1952.

Smith, Samuel. "Words of Hope: A Postmodern Faith." *Faculty Dialogue* 20 (1993–94): 131–45.

Smith, Wilfred Cantwell. "An Attempt at Summation." In *Christ's Lordship and Religious Pluralism*. Edited by Gerald H. Anderson and Thomas F. Stransky, 196–203. Maryknoll: Orbis Books, 1981.

_____. *Belief and History*. Charlottesville: University of Virginia Press, 1977.

_____. "Idolatry in Comparative Perspective." In *The Myth of Christian Uniqueness: Toward a Pluralistic Theology of Religions*. Edited by John Hick and Paul F. Knitter, 53–68. Maryknoll: Orbis Books, 1987.

_____. *The Meaning and End of Religion*. New York: Harper & Row, 1962.

_____. *Religious Diversity*. Edited by Willard G. Oxtoby. New York: Crossroads, 1982.

_____. *Towards a World Theology: Faith and the Comparative History of Religion*. Philadelphia: Westminster, 1989.

_____. *What Is Scripture? A Comparative Approach*. Minneapolis: Fortress Press, 1993.

Smith-Christopher, Daniel L. "Gandhi on Daniel 6: Some Thoughts on a 'Cultural Exegesis' of the Bible." *Biblical Interpretation* 1 (1993): 321–38.

Snook, Lee E. *The Anonymous Christ: Jesus as Savior in Modern Theology*. Minneapolis: Augsburg, 1986.

Sommers, Christina Hoff. "Teaching the Virtues." *Imprimus* 20 (Nov. 1991): 1–5.

Soneson, Jerome Paul. *Pragmatism and Pluralism: John Dewey's Significance for Theology*. Harvard Dissertations in Religion, vol. 30. Minneapolis: Fortress Press, 1992.

Sontag, Frederick. "The Metaphysics of Biblical Studies." *Journal of the Evangelical Theological Society* 35 (1992): 189–92.

Soskice, Janet Martin. "The Truth Looks Different from Here, or On Seeking the Unity of Truth from a Diversity of Perspectives." In *Christ and Context*. Edited by Hilary Regan and Alan J. Torrance, 42–59. Edinburgh: T & T Clark, 1993.

Sowell, Thomas. *A Conflict of Visions: Ideological Origins of Political Struggles*. New York: William Morrow and Company, 1987.

_____. *Inside American Education: The Decline, the Deception, the Dogmas*. New York: The Free Press (Macmillan), 1993.

_____. *Is Reality Optional? and Other Essays*. Stanford: Hoover Institution Press, 1993.

Sparks, John A. *Reader on Economics and Religion*. Grove City: Public Policy Education Fund, 1994.

Speer, James A. "'Dynamic Field Theologizing': An Agenda for Theological Education." *Trinity World Forum* 19 (Winter 1994): 1–4.

Spencer, Stephen R. "Is Natural Theology Biblical?" *Grace Theological Journal* 9 (1988): 59–72.

Spinoza, Benedict de. *A Theological-Political Treatise and a Political Treatise*. Translated and introduced by R. H. M. Elwes. New York: Dover, 1951.

Sproul, R. C. "The Limits of God's Grace: Jonathan Edwards on Hell." *Tabletalk* 14 (July 1990): 4–5.

Sprung, Mervyn. *After Truth: Explorations in Life Sense*. Albany: State University of New York Press, 1994.

Stackhouse, Max L. *Apologia: Contextualization, Globalization, and Mission in Theological Education*. Grand Rapids: Eerdmans, 1988.

Stafford, Tim. "The Next Sexual Revolution." *Christianity Today* 36, no. 3 (1992): 28–29.

Starkey, Peggy. "Biblical Faith and the Challenge of Religious Pluralism." *International Review of Mission* 71 (1982): 66–77.

Steiner, George. *Language and Silence: Essays 1958–1966*. London: Faber & Faber, 1967.

_____. *Real Presences*. Chicago: University of Chicago Press, 1989.

Sternberg, Meir. *The Poetics of Biblical Narrative: Ideological Literature and the Drama of Reading*. Indiana Literary Biblical Series. Bloomington: Indiana University Press, 1985.

Stibbe, Mark, ed. *The Gospel of John as Literature*. Leiden: E. J. Brill, 1993.

Stiver, Dan R. "Much Ado About Athens and Jerusalem: The Implications of Postmodernism for Faith." *Review and Expositor* 91 (1994): 83–102.

_____. "The Uneasy Alliance Between Evangelicalism and Postmodernism: A Reply to Anthony Thiselton." In *The Challenge of Postmodernism: An Evangelical Engagement*. Edited by David S. Dockery. Nashville: Broadman Press, 1995.

Stivers, Richard. *The Culture of Cynicism*. Oxford: Blackwell, 1994.

Stott, John. *Issues Facing Christians Today: A Major Appraisal of Contemporary Social and Moral Questions*. London: Marshall, Morgan & Scott, 1984.

_____. "The Logic of Hell: A Brief Rejoinder." *Evangelical Review of Theology* 18 (1994): 33–34.

Stout, Harry S. *The Divine Dramatist: George Whitefield and the Rise of Modern Evangelicalism.* Grand Rapids: Eerdmans, 1992.

Stout, Jeffrey. *Ethics After Babel: The Languages of Morals and Their Discontents.* Boston: Beacon Press, 1988.

Strelan, John G. "The Age of Pluralism." *Concordia Journal* 16 (1990): 202–16.

Strickland, Wayne G. *The Law, the Gospel, and the Modern Christian: Five Views.* Grand Rapids: Zondervan, 1993.

Stromberg, Peter B. *Language and Self-Transformation: A Study of the Christian Conversion Narrative.* Cambridge: Cambridge University Press, 1993.

Sturch, Richard. *The Word and the Christ: An Essay in Analytic Christology.* Oxford: Clarendon Press, 1991.

Sugirtharajah, R. S., ed. *Voices from the Margin: Interpreting the Bible in the Third World.* Maryknoll: Orbis Books, 1991.

Sumithra, Sunand. "Conversion: To Cosmic Christ?" *Evangelical Review of Theology* 16 (1992): 385–97.

_____. *Holy Father: A Doxological Approach to Systematic Theology.* Bangalore: Theological Book Trust, 1993.

Sunstein, Cass R. *Democracy and the Limits of Free Speech.* New York: The Free Press, 1993.

Suppe, Frederick, ed. *The Structure of Scientific Theories.* 2d ed. Urbana: University of Illinois Press, 1977.

Sweeney, Douglas A. "The Essential Evangelicalism Dialectic: The Historiography of the Early Neo-Evangelical Movement and the Observer-Participant Dilemma." *Church History* 60 (1991): 70–84.

Sweet, Leonard I. "The Modernization of Protestant Religion in America." In *Altered Landscapes: Christianity in America, 1935–1985.* Edited by David W. Lotz, Donald W. Shriver, Jr., and John F. Wilson, 19–41. Grand Rapids: Eerdmans, 1989.

Swidler, Leonard. *After the Absolute: The Dialogical Future of Religious Reflection.* Minneapolis: Fortress, 1990.

_____, ed. *Toward a Universal Theology of Religion.* Faith Meets Faith Series, vol. 1. Maryknoll: Orbis Books, 1987.

Sykes, S. W., and J. P. Clayton, eds. *Christ, Faith, and History.* Cambridge Studies in Christology. Cambridge: Cambridge University Press, 1978 [1972].

Sykes, Stephen. *The Identity of Christianity: Theologians and the Essence of Christianity from Schleiermacher to Barth.* Philadelphia: Fortress Press, 1984.

_____. *The Integrity of Anglicanism.* New York: Seabury, 1978.

Taber, Charles R. *The World Is Too Much with Us: "Culture" in Modern Protestant Missions.* The modern mission era, 1792–1992: an appraisal. Macon: Mercer University Press, 1991.

Tambiah, Stanley Jeyaraja. *Magic, Science, Religion, and the Scope of Rationality.* Cambridge: Cambridge University Press, 1990.

Tamez, Elsa. *The Scandalous Message of James.* New York: Crossroad, 1990.

Taylor, Daniel. *The Myth of Certainty: Trusting God, Asking Questions, Taking Risks.* Grand Rapids: Zondervan, 1992.

Taylor, Howard. "Watchmakers Are Not Blind." *Evangel* 10, no. 1 (1992): 26–29.

Taylor, Mark C. *Deconstructing Theology.* AAR Studies in Religion, vol. 28. New York: Crossroad, 1982.

_____. *Erring.* Chicago: University of Chicago Press, 1984.

Taylor, William D., ed. *Kingdom Partnerships for Synergy in Missions*. Pasadena: William Carey Library, 1994.

_____, ed. *Internationalizing Missionary Training: A Global Perspective*. WEF Volume. Exeter: Paternoster Press, 1992.

Thaxton, Charles B. "A Dialogue with 'Prof' on Christianity and Science." In *God and Culture*. Festschrift for Carl F. H. Henry. Edited by D. A. Carson and John D. Woodbridge, 275–300. Grand Rapids: Eerdmans, 1993.

Thielicke, Helmut. *African Diary: My Search for Understanding*. Waco, Tex.: Word, 1974.

_____. *The Freedom of the Christian Man: A Christian Confrontation with the Secular Gods*. Translated by John Doberstein. Thielicke Library. Grand Rapids: Baker, 1963.

Thiemann, Ronald F. *Constructing a Public Theology: The Church in a Pluralistic Culture*. Louisville: Westminster/John Knox, 1991.

Thiselton, Anthony C. *New Horizons in Hermeneutics*. London: HarperCollins, 1992.

_____. *The Two Horizons: The New Testament Hermeneutics and Philosophical Description with Special Reference to Heidegger, Bultman, Gadamer, and Wittgenstein*. With a foreword by J. B. Torrance. Grand Rapids: Eerdmans, 1980.

Thomas, Brook. *The New History and Other Old-Fashioned Topics*. Princeton: Princeton University Press, 1991.

Thomas, Cal. *The Death of Ethics in America*. Waco, Tex.: Word Books, 1988.

_____. *The Things That Matter Most*. New York: HarperCollins, 1994.

Thomas, M. Am. *Risking Christ for Christ's Sake: Towards an Ecumenical Theology of Pluralism*. Geneva: World Council of Churches, 1987.

Thompson, Norma H., ed. *Religious Pluralism and Religious Education*. Birmingham: Religious Education Press, 1988.

Thorson, Walter R. "Scientific Objectivity and the Listening Attitude." In *Objective Knowledge: A Christian Perspective*. Edited by Paul Helm, 59–83. Leicester: Inter-Varsity Press, 1994.

Tinker, Melvin. "Battle for the Mind." *Churchman* 106 (1992): 34–44.

_____. "Content, Context and Culture: Proclaiming the Gospel Today." In *Restoring the Vision*. Edited by Melvin Tinker, 59–82. 1990.

_____. *Restoring the Vision: Anglican Evangelicals Speak Out*. Eastbourne: MARC, 1990.

Tomasino, Anthony J. "History Repeats Itself: The 'Fall' and Noah's Drunkenness." *Vetus Testamentum* 42 (1992): 128–30.

Tong, Joseph. "On the Finality of Christ." *Bandung Theological Seminary* 1, no. 1 (1993): 3–16.

Torrance, Thomas F. "The Atonement. The Singularity and the Finality of the Cross: The Atonement and the Moral Order." In *Universalism and the Doctrine of Hell*. Edited by Nigel M. de S. Cameron, 225–56. Carlisle: Paternoster Press, 1992.

Torrey, E. Fuller. *Freudian Fraud: The Malignant Effect of Freud's Theory on American Thought and Culture*. New York: HarperCollins Publishers, 1992.

Toulmin, Stephen. *Cosmopolis: The Hidden Agenda of Modernity*. New York: Free Press, 1990.

Toynbee, Arnold J. *A Study of History*. Oxford: Oxford University Press, 1972.

Tracy, David. *The Analogical Imagination: Christian Theology and the Culture of Pluralism*. New York: Crossroads, 1981.

_____. *Blessed Rage of Order: The New Pluralism in Theology*. New York: Seabury Press, Crossroads, 1975.

_____. "Christianity in the Wider Context: Demands and Transformations." In *Worldviews and Warrants: Plurality and Authority in Theology*. Edited by William Schweiker and M. Anderson, 1–15. New York: University Press of America, 1987.

_____. *Plurality and Ambiguity*. New York: Harper & Row, 1987.

_____. "The Questions of Pluralism: The Context of the United States." *Mid-Stream: An Ecumenical Journal* 22 (1987): 273–85.

_____. "Theology and the Many Faces of Postmodernity." *Theology Today* 51 (1994): 104–14.

Travis, Stephen H. *Christ and the Judgment of God: Divine Retribution in the New Testament*. London: MMS, 1986.

_____. *Christian Hope and the Future*. Downers Grove: InterVarsity Press, 1980.

Tribe, Laurence H. *Abortion: The Clash of Absolutes*. New York: Norton, 1990.

Trigg, Roger. *Reality at Risk: A Defence of Realism in Philosophy and the Sciences*. Sussex: Harvester Press, 1980.

_____. "Religion and the Threat of Relativism." *Religious Studies* 19 (1983): 297–310.

Trocmé, E. "Un Christianisme Sans Jésus-Christ?" *New Testament Studies* 38 (1992): 321–36.

Turner, H. E. W. *The Pattern of New Testament Truth: A Study in the Relations Between Orthodoxy and Heresy in the Early Church*. Bampton Lectures. London: A. R. Mowbray & Co., 1954.

Turner, Max. "'Empowerment for Mission'? The Pneumatology of Luke-Acts: An Appreciation and Critique of James B. Shelton's *Mighty in Word and Deed*." *Vox Evangelica* 24 (1994): 103–22.

_____. "The Spirit of Prophecy and the Power of Authoritative Preaching in Luke-Acts: A Question of Origins." *New Testament Studies* 38 (1992): 66–88.

Uenuma, Masao. "A Christian View of Prayer and Spirituality in Buddhist Thought." In *Teach Us to Pray: Prayer in the Bible and the World*. Edited by D. A. Carson, 192–204. Exeter: Paternoster Press, 1990.

van den Toren, Benno. "A New Direction in Christian Apologetics: An Exploration with Reference to Postmodernism." *European Journal of Theology* 2 (1993): 49–64.

van Gelder, Craig. "A Great New Fact of Our Day: America as a Mission Field." *Missiology* 19 (1991): 409–18.

van Huyssteen, J. Wentzel. "Is the Postmodernist Always a Postfoundationalist?" *Theology Today* 50 (1993): 373–86.

Van Rheenen, Gailyn. *Communicating Christ in Animistic Contexts*. Grand Rapids: Baker, 1991.

Van Til, L. John. *Liberty of Conscience: The History of a Puritan Idea*. Phillipsburg: Presbyterian and Reformed Publishing, 1972.

Vanhoozer, Kevin J. *Biblical Narrative in the Philosophy of Paul Ricoeur: A Study in Hermeneutics and Theology*. Cambridge: Cambridge University Press, 1990.

_____. "From Canon to Concept: 'Same' and 'Other' in the Relation Between Biblical and Systematic Theology." *Scottish Bulletin of Evangelical Theology* 12 (1994): 96–124.

_____. "A Lamp in the Labyrinth: The Hermeneutics of 'Aesthetic' Theology." *Trinity Journal* 8 (1987): 25–56.

_____. "The Semantics of Biblical Literature." In *Hermeneutics, Authority, and Canon*. Edited by D. A. Carson and John D. Woodbridge, 53–104. Grand Rapids: Zondervan, 1986.

_____. "The World Well Staged? Theology, Culture, and Hermeneutics." In *God and Culture*. Festschrift for Carl F. H. Henry. Edited by D. A. Carson and John D. Woodbridge, 1–30. Grand Rapids: Eerdmans, 1993.

Veith, Gene Edward, Jr. *Postmodern Times: A Christian Guide to Contemporary Thought and Culture*. Wheaton: Crossway Books, 1994.

Verhey, Allen, and Stephen Lammers, eds. *Theological Voices in Medical Ethics*. Grand Rapids: Eerdmans, 1993.

Vibert, Simon. "TV Advertising—Shaping or Reflecting Society?" *Evangel* 10 (1992): 11–15.

_____. "The Word in an Audio-visual Age: Can We Still Preach the Gospel?" *Churchman* 106 (1992): 147–48.

Vickers, Douglas. *Christian Truth in Critical Times*. Philadelphia: Skilton House Publishers, 1989.

Visser 'T Hooft, W. A. "Evangelism Among Europe's Neo-Pagans." *Evangelical Review of Theology* 18 (1994): 335–47.

Vitz, Paul. *Censorship: Evidence of Bias in Our Children's Textbooks*. Ann Arbor: Servant Books, 1986.

Vitz, Paul C. "Leaving Psychology Behind." In *No God But God: Breaking with the Idols of Our Age*. Edited by Os Guinness and John Seel, 95–110. Chicago: Moody Press, 1992.

_____. *Psychology as Religion: The Cult of Self-worship*. 2d ed. Grand Rapids: Eerdmans, 1994 [1977].

Voegelin, Eric. *The New Science of Politics: An Introduction*. Charles R. Walgreen Foundation Lectures. Chicago: University of Chicago Press, 1952.

Volf, Miroslav. "Worship as Adoration and Action: Reflections on a Christian Way of Being-in-the-World." In *Worship: Adoration and Action*. Edited by D. A. Carson, 203–11. Grand Rapids: Baker, 1993.

von Balthasar, Hans Urs. *Truth Is Symphonic: Aspects of Christian Pluralism*. Translated by Graham Harrison. San Francisco: Ignatius Press, 1987.

Vroom, Hendrik M. *Religions and the Truth: Philosophical Reflections and Perspectives*. Grand Rapids: Eerdmans, 1989.

Wakefield, Dan. "New Age, New Opportunities." *Theology Today* 51 (1994): 142–47.

Wakefield, Gordon. "God and Some English Poets: 7. W. H. Auden." *Expository Times* 105 (1994): 265–69.

Walden, Wayne. *God's Government: In Defense of Political Abstinence*. Plymouth: Living Books, 1989.

Walker, Andrew. *Enemy Territory*. 2d ed. Bristol: Bristol House, 1990.

_____. "We Believe." *Christianity Today* 35 (April 29, 1991): 25–27.

_____, ed. *Betraying the Gospel*. Bristol: Bristol House, 1988.

Walker, D. P. *The Decline of Hell: Seventeenth-Century Discussion of Eternal Torment*. Chicago: University of Chicago Press, 1964.

Wallace, Howard N. *The Eden Narrative*. Harvard Semitic Monographs, vol. 32. Atlanta: Scholars Press, 1985.

Walls, Jerry L. "What Is Theological Pluralism?" *Quarterly Review* 5 (1986): 44–62.

Walter, J. A. *A Long Way from Home: A Sociological Exploration of Contemporary Idolatry*. Exeter: Paternoster, 1979.

Ward, Keith. *A Vision to Pursue: Beyond the Crisis in Christianity*. London: SCM, 1991.

Warkentin, Marvin L. "Church Discipline in a Pluralistic Society." *Direction* 12 (1983): 15–27.

Warren, Max. *I Believe in the Great Commission*. Grand Rapids: Eerdmans, 1976.

Watson, David Lowes. *God Does Not Foreclose: The Universal Promise of Salvation*. Nashville: Abingdon, 1990.

Watson, Francis, ed. *The Open Text: New Directions for Biblical Studies?* London: SCM Press, 1993.

Watts, A. *The Way of Zen*. London: Penguin, 1990.

Weathers, Robert A. "Leland Ryken's Literary Approach to Biblical Interpretation: An Evangelical Model." *Journal of the Evangelical Theological Society* 37 (1994): 115–24.

Webber, Robert E. *The Church in the World: Opposition, Tension, or Transformation?* Grand Rapids: Zondervan, 1986.

Webster, Douglas D. *Selling Jesus: What's Wrong with Marketing the Church*. Downers Grove: InterVarsity Press, 1992.

Weinfeld, Moshe. "The Charge of Hypocrisy in Matthew 23 and in Jewish Sources." *Immanuel* 24/25 (1990): 52–58.

Weir, J. Emmette. "'With the Eyes of Marx.'" *Expository Times* 105 (1994): 205.

Wells, David. "On Being Evangelical: Some Theological Differences and Similarities." In *Evangelicalism: Comparative Studies of Popular Protestantism in North America, the British Isles, and Beyond, 1700–1990*. Edited by Mark A. Noll, David W. Bebbington, and George A. Rawlyk, 389–410. New York: Oxford University Press, 1994.

Wells, David F. "The D-Min-ization of the Ministry." In *No God But God: Breaking with the Idols of Our Age*. Edited by Os Guinness and John Seel, 175–88. Chicago: Moody Press, 1992.

————. *God in the Wasteland: The Reality of Truth in a World of Fading Dreams*. Grand Rapids: Eerdmans, 1994.

————. "'No Offense: I Am an Evangelical': A Search for Self-Definition." In *A Time to Speak: The Evangelical-Jewish Encounter*. Edited by A. James Rudin and Marvin R. Wilson, 20–40. Grand Rapids: Eerdmans, 1987.

————. *No Place for Truth*, or *Whatever Happened to Evangelical Theology?* Grand Rapids: Eerdmans, 1993.

Wengst, Klaus. *Pax Romana and the Peace of Jesus Christ*. London: SCM, 1987.

Wenham, John W. *The Enigma of Evil: Can We Believe in the Goodness of God?* Grand Rapids: Academic Books, 1985.

Whaling, Frank. *Christian Theology and World Religions: A Global Approach*. Basingstoke: Marshall Pickering, 1986.

White, James Emery. *What Is Truth: A Comparative Study of the Positions of Cornelius Van Til, Francis Schaeffer, Carl F. H. Henry, Donald Bloesch, Millard Erickson*. Nashville: Broadman and Holman Publishers, 1994.

White, Vernon. *Atonement and Incarnation: An Essay in Universalism and Particularity*. Cambridge: Cambridge University Press, 1991.

Whitehead, Alfred North. *Process and Reality: An Essay in Cosmology*. Corrected ed. Edited by David Ray Griffin and Donald W. Sherburne. New York: Free Press, 1979.

Whitehead, Barbara Dafoe. "Dan Quayle Was Right." *The Atlantic Monthly* (April 1993): 1–21.

Whitehead, John W. *The Rights of Religious Persons in Public Education*. Wheaton: Crossway, 1991.

Wiebe, Donald. "Argument or Authority in the Academy? On Kroeker on *The Irony of Theology*." *Studies in Religion/Sciences Religieuses* 23 (1994): 67–79.

————. *The Irony of Theology and the Nature of Religious Thought*. Montreal and Kingston: McGill/Queen's University Press, 1991.

Wiles, Maurice. *Christian Theology and Inter-religious Dialogue*. London/Philadelphia: SCM Press/Trinity Press International, 1992.

————. *God's Action in the World*. The Bampton Lectures for 1986. London: SCM, 1986.

Wilkes, Paul. "The Hands That Would Shape Our Souls." *The Atlantic Monthly* (December 1990): 59–88.

Wilkinson, Loren. "Gaia Spirituality: A Christian Critique." *Themelios* 18, no. 3 (1993): 4–8.

————. "The Uneasy Conscience of the Human Race: Rediscovering Creation in the 'Environmental' Movement." In *God and Culture*. Festschrift for Carl F. H. Henry. Edited by D. A. Carson and John D. Woodbridge, 301–20. Grand Rapids: Eerdmans, 1993.

Williams, John. "The Gospel as Public Truth: A Critical Appreciation of the Theological Programme of Lesslie Newbigin." *Anvil* 10 (1993): 11–24.

Williams, Raymond. *The Sociology of Culture*. New York: Schocken Books, 1982.

Williams, Stephen. "Revelation and Reconciliation: A Tale of Two Concepts." *European Journal of Theology* 3, no. 1 (1994): 35–42.

Wills, Garry. *Lincoln at Gettysburg: The Words That Remade America*. New York: Simon & Schuster, 1992.

————. *Under God: Religion and American Politics*. New York: Simon & Schuster, 1990.

Wilson, Marvin R. *Our Father Abraham: Jewish Roots of the Christian Faith*. Grand Rapids: Eerdmans, 1989.

Wimberly, Edward P. *Using Scripture in Pastoral Counseling*. Nashville: Abingdon, 1994.

Winter, Bruce. "Theological and Ethical Response to Religious Pluralism—1 Corinthians 8–10." *Tyndale Bulletin* 41 (1990): 209–26.

Winter, Bruce W. "In Public and in Private: Early Christian Interactions with Religious Pluralism." In *One God One Lord in a World of Religious Pluralism*. Edited by Andrew D. Clarke, and Bruce W. Winter, 112–34. Cambridge: Tyndale House, 1991.

Witherington, Ben, III. *Paul's Narrative Thought World: The Tapestry of Tragedy and Triumph*. Louisville: Westminster/John Knox, 1994.

Wittgenstein, Ludwig. *Philosophical Investigations*. Translated by G. E. M. Anscombe. New York: Macmillan, 1958.

Wolterstorff, Nicholas. *Reason Within the Bounds of Religion*. Grand Rapids: Eerdmans, 1976.

Wood, David, ed. *Derrida: A Critical Reader*. Cambridge, MA/Oxford: Blackwell, 1992.

Wood, Ralph C. "What Ever Happened to Baptist Calvinism? A Response to Molly Marshall and Clark Pinnock on the Nature of Salvation in Jesus Christ and in the World's Religions." *Review and Expositor* 91 (1994): 593–608.

Woodbridge, John D. *Biblical Authority: A Critique of the Rogers/McKim Proposal*. Grand Rapids: Zondervan, 1982.

————. "Culture War Casualties." *Christianity Today* 39 (March 6, 1995): 20–26.

Wright, Chris. "Deuteronomic Depression." *Themelios* 19, no. 2 (1994): 3.

————. "Ethical Decisions in the Old Testament." *European Journal of Theology* 1 (1992): 128–40.

————. "P for Pentateuch, Patriarchs and Pagans." *Themelios* 1993 (2 1993): 3–4.

————. "The Uniqueness of Christ: An Old Testament Perspective." In *A.D. 2000 and Beyond: A Mission Agenda*. Festschrift for John R. W. Stott. Edited by Vinay Samuel and Chris Sugden, 112–24. Oxford: Regnum Books, 1991.

Wright, Christopher J. H. *An Eye for an Eye: The Place of Old Testament Ethics Today*. Downers Grove: InterVarsity Press, 1983.

Wright, Iain. "History, Hermeneutics, Deconstruction." In *Criticism and Critical Theory*. Edited by Jeremy Hawthorn, 83–96. Stratford-Upon-Avon Studies. London: Edward Arnold, 1984.

Wright, N. T. "Taking the Text with Her Pleasure: A Post-Post-Modernist Response to J. Dominic Crossan *The Historical Jesus: The Life of a Mediterranean Jewish Peasant* (T & T Clark, Harper San Francisco 1991) (With Apologies to A. A. Milne, St Paul and James Joyce)." *Theology* 96 (1993): 303–10.

_____. *Who Was Jesus?* London: SPCK, 1992.

_____. γενόμενος and the Meaning of Philippians 2:5–11." *Journal of Theological Studies* 37 (1986): 321–53.

Wuthnow, Robert. *Acts of Compassion: Caring for Others and Helping Ourselves*. Princeton: Princeton University Press, 1991.

_____. *The Restructuring of American Religion: Society and Faith Since World War II*. Princeton: Princeton University Press, 1988.

_____. *The Struggle for America's Soul: Evangelicals, Liberals, and Secularism*. Grand Rapids: Eerdmans, 1989.

_____, ed. *"I Come Away Stronger": How Small Groups Are Shaping American Religion*. Grand Rapids: Eerdmans, 1994.

Yankelovich, Daniel. *New Rules: Searching for Self-Fulfillment in a World Turned Upside Down*. New York: Random House, 1981.

Yeo, Khiok-Khng. "A Rhetorical Study of Acts 17.22–31: What Has Jerusalem to Do with Athens and Beijing?" *Jian Dao* 1 (1994): 75–107.

Ziesler, John. "Historical Criticism and a Rational Faith." *Expository Times* 105 (1994): 270–74.

Zoll, Donald Atwell. *Twentieth Century Political Philosophy*. Englewood Cliffs: Prentice-Hall, 1974.

Scripture and Ancient Text Index

Index to Modern Authors

W

Wakefield, G. S., 558
Walden, Wayne, 407
Walker, Andrew, 361
Walker, D. P., 517
Wallace, Howard N., 213
Walls, Jerry L., 54
Walter, J. A., 41
Ward, Keith, 319
Warfield, Benjamin B., 152
Warkentin, Marvin L., 366
Warren, Max, 94–95
Warren, Max A. C., 492
Watson, David Lowes, 282
Watson, Francis, 29, 85
Weathers, Robert A., 189
Webber, Robert E., 563
Webster, Douglas, 480
Weil, Simone, 476
Weinfeld, Moshe, 337
Wells, David F., 38, 208, 335, 451–52, 463, 471–72, 480–81, 489

Wengst, Klaus, 406
Wenham, David, 323
Wenham, G. J., 151
Wenham, John W., 518, 523
Wernick, Andrew, 29
Westcott, B. F., 450–51
White, Vernon, 327–28
Whitehead, Alfred North, 225
Whitehead, Barbara DaFoe, 427
Whitehead, John W., 427
Wiebe, Donald, 86
Wiles, Maurice, 329
Wilkinson, Loren, 212, 330, 561
Williams, Raymond, 537
Williams, Stephen, 184, 332, 425
Williamson, H. G. M., 256
Willimon, William H., 478
Wills, Garry, 378, 386
Wilson, A. N., 317
Wilson, Marvin R., 335
Wimberly, Edward P., 467

Winter, Bruce W., 270, 273
Witherington, Ben, III, 269
Wittgenstein, Ludwig, 69
Wolterstorff, Nicholas, 95
Wood, Ralph C., 280
Woodard, Branson L., Jr., 132
Woodbridge, John D., 153, 160, 203, 383
Wright, Christopher J. H., 220, 243–44, 249, 251–52, 298
Wright, Iain, 111, 136
Wright, N. T., 105, 115–116, 317, 324, 344
Wuthnow, Robert, 15–16, 49, 467

Y

Yankelovich, Daniel, 48
Yeo, Khiok-Khng, 497

Z

Zannoni, Arthur E., 333
Ziesler, John, 317

Subject Index

A

Abortion, biblical plot-line and, 545
Abraham
   call of, 243–45
   syncretism in account of Melchizedek and, 249–50
   Two-Covenant Theory and, 342
Agnosticism, postmodernism and, 544
Anglican evangelicals, 459–60
Annihilationism, evangelicalism and, 515–17
Anti-semitism, 335, 337, 343–44
Aquinas, Thomas, hermeneutic of, 65–66
Argument from design, 197–98
Artemis, early Christians and, 271
Atheism, systematic theology and, 543–44
Atonement, 264, 327–28
Attributes of God, 223–39, 286
Audience, gospel message and, 471–72
Augustine, hermeneutic of, 65
Authorial intent
   inspiration of Scripture and, 152–53
   text and, 103–4
   United States Constitution and, 386–87

B

Baby Busters, pluralism and, 45–46
Belief, 173–74, 308–10
Bible. See also Scripture and Biblical text
   European Protestantism and, 373
   evangelicals and, 445–49
   guidance and, 506
   Holy Spirit's role in understanding of, 266–68
   religious pluralism and, 151–63
   Renaissance and, 373
   Western culture and, 373
Bible reading, biblical mind and, 484
Bible studies, evangelism and, 512
Biblical authority, 473, 480–88, 516
Biblical christianity, 360
Biblical illiteracy, 37, 42–44, 483–85, 502
Biblical inerrancy, 153–54, 165–66, 516
Biblical interpretation
   absolute dichotomies and, 547–48
   anachronism and, 356–57
   biblical criticism and, 156–58
   high view of Scripture and, 212–13
   history of, 156–57
   Holocaust and, 336–38
   individual's role in, 168
   objective truth and, 548–49
   persuasion and, 166
   Pharisaic hypocrisy and, 337
   pluralism and, 177–80
   scholarship and authority in, 373

Biblical narratives, interpretation of, 545
Biblical plot-line
   biblical theology and, 542, 544
   evangelism and, 502–5, 514
   fundamental issue of, 343
   gospel message and, 471
   interpretation and, 545–46
   love of God in, 239
   New Testament and, 253–78
   pluralism and, 514
   systematic theology and, 545–47
Biblical story-line. See Biblical plot-line
Biblical text. See also Bible and Scripture
   authority and, 194
   referent of, 172
   systematic theology and, 544
Biblical theology
   biblical illiteracy and, 502
   biblical plot-line and, 542, 544
   definition of, 502
   evangelism and, 501–5, 503–5
   genre and, 544
   human emptiness and, 495–96
   moral confusion and, 495–96
   objective truth and, 544
   philosophical pluralism and, 502
   postmodernism and, 544
   spirituality and, 566–67
   systematic theology and, 542–43
   worldview and, 545
Biblical worldview. See also Worldview
   gospel and, 502
   secular paradigms and, 487–88
Big bang theory, 199–200
Bioethics, pluralism's influence on, 404

C

Caesar worship, early Christians and, 271
Canon, 131–32, 326
Capital punishment, biblical plot-line and understanding of, 546
Catholics, spirituality and, 557
Chalcedon, orthodoxy related to, 361
Change, evangelicalism and, 473 ff.
Cherished pluralism, 18–19
Choice, evangelism and, 480
Christian doctrine
   absoluteness of, 322–23
   faith and, 353
   orthodoxy, heresy and, 366
   philosophical pluralism and, 31
Christian lifestyle, evangelism and, 514
Christian missions
Globalization and, 552–53

R

Racism, gospel and, 500
Radical hermeneutics. *See also* Hermeneutics
Christianity and, 36–37
definition of, 20
postmodernism and, 77
Radical pluralism. *See also* Pluralism
biblical plot-line and, 313–14
Radical religious pluralism
postmodernism and, 26
requirements of faith and love and, 28
Radical religious pluralism. *See* Radical pluralism *and* Pluralism
Rationality, 183
Reality
Christians, pluralists and, 277–78
evangelical imagination and, 169
human consciousness and, 67
understanding of, 89
Reason
biblical interpretation and, 173
faith and, 63, 65
modernity and, 58–59
Rebirthing, 467–69
Reconciliation in Christ, 276–77
Redemptive history, 243–45
Reductionism *See also* Secular reductionism
Christian revelation and, 328
exclusivism and, 287
inclusivism and, 287
love of God and, 286
postmodernism and, 133
theology and, 118–19
Relativism, 23, 33, 107–8, 176
Relevance
change and, 480
choice and, 480
gospel and, 470–80
long-term effects of, 479–80
Religion
distinctives of, 357
human meaning and purpose and, 28
philosophical pluralism and, 391
revelation and, 348
separation of church and state and, 379–80
Religion in America, disestablishment of, 49–50
Religion in education, 390, 393–94
Religious devotion, 23
Religious diversity, 14, 379
Religious freedom
final authority and, 378
pluralism's impact on, 378–82
tolerance and, 33
Religious institutions, secularization and, 37–38
Religious pluralism
Bible and, 151–63
biblical themes and plot-line and, 238
Christ as representative in, 149–50
Christianity and, 278
early Christians and, 271–73
exclusivism and, 254–55
faith and love requirements and, 145–46

God's Spirit and, 148
New Testament and, 253
objective truth and, 350
orthodoxy and, 354
philosophical pluralism and, 26–32
reality centeredness and, 146–47
theocentrism and, 146–47
tolerance and, 32–35
truth and freedom and, 148
truth claims of, 150
Religious rites and syncretism, 250–51
Religious superiority, philosophical pluralism and, 19
Religious thought, stages of, 319
Repentance, secularism and, 488
Revelation
gospel truth and, 182–89
interpretation and, 351–52
non-Christian experience of, 180
religious pluralism and, 348
Revival, 18th century era of, 483–86
Right and wrong, pagan recognition of, 311
Rights, tolerance and, 423
Roman Catholics, coalition of evangelicals and, 418

S

Salvation
inclusivism and, 296–97, 304, 307–8
love of God and, 240, 289
pagans and, 311–12
Scholarship
biblical authority and, 373
evangelicals and, 486–88
preaching and, 485
secular reductionism and, 486–88
Science
God in relation to, 200–1
modernist and postmodernist views, 86–91
philosophical pluralism and, 22
subject matter in study of, 118
systematic theology and, 543–44
Scientific models, theologians' use of, 116–20
Scientific research, repeatability of, 119
Scripture. *See also* Bible *and* Biblical text
authority of, 131–32, 480–88, 540
authorship of, 151–53
church discipline and, 366
contextualization and, 540–41
contradictions in, 324–25
cultural context and, 540–41
deconstruction of, 324–25
early Christian convictions and, 159–60
evangelicals and, 448–49
history and, 172
infallibility of, 163
inspiration of, 152 n. 39, 152–53, 160–61
knowledge of God and, 188–89
nature of, 161–62
orthodox view of, 158, 361–62
perspective of, 154
pluralistic approach to, 155–56
postmodernism and, 541
purpose of, 167